ECONOMIC GEOGRAPHY
John W. Alexander
© Prentice-Hall, Inc. 1963

ECONOMIC GEOGRAPHY

ECONOMIC GEOGRAPHY

JOHN W. ALEXANDER UNIVERSITY OF
WISCONSIN PRENTICE-HALL, INC.
ENGLEWOOD CLIFFS, NEW JERSEY

Dedicated to Clarence F. Jones and the late Vernor C. Finch

Economic geographers and friends to whom the author is deeply indebted

CARTOGRAPHY BY RANDALL SALE

University of Wisconsin

Current printing (last digit):
15   14   13   12   11   10   9

Designed by Walter Behnke

22514–C

PREFACE

In writing this text, I have adopted a deliberate strategy. Geography, like most disciplines, is going through a transition period in which increasing attention is being given to quantification and the use of statistical methods of analysis. The reaction of geographers has been varied. Consequently, it seemed to me that there was a need for a "bridge" textbook, one to span the gap between the traditional and new approaches to geography. Accordingly, the early portion—in fact, most—of this text conforms to traditional geographic methods. The chapters have been deliberately structured around three basic geographic questions that apply to all economic activities, the questions of location, characteristics, and relationships. After this method is introduced, attention is directed to individual types of endeavor, moving through the sequence of primary, secondary, and tertiary economic activities. The later chapters weave in, very gradually at first, some of the "new geography," until finally, in Part Nine, statistical methodology is the main subject matter. By being introduced slowly and gradually to statistical concepts, even the student with little mathematical background may find it easy to glide into an understanding of these ideas. In a phrase, I have adopted the strategy of the soft sell. I trust that my educational engineering is sound, and that this bridge proves to be useful and sturdy.

Many scholars and friends have had a role, either direct or indirect, in the making of this book. First, I owe a general debt to teachers who have stimulated my interest and understanding of the field: to Harland James, high school teacher in Urbana, Illinois; to W. O. Blanchard, my undergraduate mentor at the University of Illinois; and to Vernor C. Finch, Glenn Trewartha, and Richard Hartshorne, under whom I took graduate work at the University of Wisconsin. I must acknowledge, too, Clarence F. Jones, of Northwestern University, whose concept of economic geography has strongly influenced my thinking.

Second, my thanks to colleagues. Any strong points in this textbook are attributable, at least in part, to my fellow geographers at the University of Wisconsin. I am grateful to: Arthur Robinson, for interesting me in statistical techniques; Andrew Clark, for showing me the value of historical geography (See Chapter 15); Henry Sterling, for information (and a photograph) on primitive cultivation; Kirk

Stone, for information (and photographs) on Scandinavia; Clarence Olmstead, for reading a portion of the manuscript and teaching me a lot on the geography of agriculture; John Hidore, for permission to use two maps in Chapter 31; and Edwin Hammond, Fred Simoons, Robert Finley, and Karl Butzer, for stimulating my thinking in many ways. I shall happily share with them credit for any strengths in this textbook; but, needless to say, the reverse does not hold—I cannot share with them blame for any flaws.

I owe a great debt to Randall Sale who designed and directed the production of most of the maps, which were drawn in the University of Wisconsin Cartographic Laboratory, principally by Miss Mei-Ling Hsu, Rodney Helgeland, and George McCleary. Special thanks, too, to Robert Taaffe of Indiana University, who made numerous constructive comments on the Soviet Union section of Chapter 25.

There is insufficient space here to express appreciation individually to fellow economic geographers at other institutions upon whose ideas, maps, and photographs I have drawn in the pages to follow. Due credit is given them with quotations and illustrations. Several of my graduate students have helped by constructing maps, contributing ideas, and commenting on the manuscript, particularly Tom McKnight, William Wallace, George Stevens, Kenneth Martin, Roy Officer, Richard Hough, James Lindberg, and George McCleary. The United States Census authorities graciously made available numerous maps. Most of the burden of typing the manuscript and the mass of correspondence pertaining to this book has been cheerfully and neatly executed by Mary Jane Johnson and Judy Christenson. My wife, Betty, has graciously and patiently endured those exigencies of life associated with a husband's ups and downs in trying to haul a book over the long road from preliminary planning to final publication. And I gratefully acknowledge the patience, criticism, and suggestions of my editor, Ronald Nelson.

Finally, a request: I desire the suggestions of any reader for improving this book—suggestions for clarifying ideas, organization, and presentation, suggestions for giving maps, photographs, and other illustrations a stronger role. I would appreciate, too, having my attention called to any errors of fact alert readers might detect.

John W. Alexander

CONTENTS

PART ONE

INTRODUCTION

Economic geography: What is it? Many people have at least a vague idea of the meaning of the term *economic*. They know that it pertains to farming and fishing, incomes and expenses, transportation and taxes, and a good deal else that is somehow related to money. And most people likewise have some notion of what geography means. But here opinions vary sharply. Some think it merely involves the memorization of place names, whereas others regard it as a twin sister of geology. Clearly, then, because of this prevalent vagueness and confusion, before we can pin down the concept of *economic geography* we should find out what each of the component words means.

This will be precisely our first task in Chapter 1. Then, after fixing our definitions, we can go on to a consideration of the distinctive method of economic geography. As we shall see, it involves three basic questions, which deal with the locations, characteristics, and relationships of economic activities.

We shall first apply this geographic method of analysis in Chapter 2 to population—for people are the fundamental subject matter of the economic geographer. Then we shall use the method to approach the principal economic activities in which the people of the world are engaged.

We shall give attention first to subsistence economic activities (Part Two) and then to commercial activities (Parts Three to Eight), treating of the latter in the following sequence: commercial gathering, commercial agriculture (or bioculture), mining, manufacturing, transportation, and services (or tertiary activity). Finally, in Part Nine (Chapters 31-33) we shall take up measurements and geographic theory as applied to economic endeavors.

Early chapters are structured explicitly around the three basic questions in order that the reader may become familiar with the *method* of geographic analysis as well as with content material. In these early chapters, geographical relationships are usually approached in terms of the pairs of physical and cultural phenomena or of intraregional and extraregional phenomena, the reason being that information now available in the geographic literature makes these approaches more feasible for these topics.

Later chapters will be different in that usage of the three basic questions will be more implicit than explicit (for by this time they will have become second-nature to the reader). Another difference is that later chapters will weave in certain aspects of correlation analysis. This topic is reserved for later stages of the book because it is new, more difficult to grasp, and has been used mostly by researchers in producing information which deals with topics covered in Parts Six, Seven, and Eight.

The names of many nations and other places will be mentioned in the chapters to follow. Therefore, every reader should own an atlas—an indispensable tool in mastering the material of geography as well as for comprehending world affairs. Among the best atlases for economic geography are *The Oxford Economic Atlas of the World*, the *Prentice-Hall World Atlas*, Humlum's *Atlas of Economic Geography*, the *Atlas of Economic Development* published by the University of Chicago Press, and *Goode's World Atlas*. In addition, it would often be helpful to procure blank maps at a bookstore to make notations about places and areas discussed in the text.

*Primary production. The Fraser open-pit mine near Chisholm, Minnesota,
covers 120 acres, is ¾ mile long, ¼ mile wide and 300 feet deep. In its 30 years,
the mine has yielded about 27,000,000 tons of ore. Electric shovels
load ore into railway cars which are hauled by diesel engines to the surface.
(Courtesy Oliver Iron Mining Division, U. S. Steel Corp.)*

ONE

The Meaning of Economic

The word *economic* pertains to all the activities that men engage in the world over in the production, exchange, and consumption of items of value. Anything man will pay money for, or will barter, or will work to produce is an economic item.

PRODUCTION

In the *production* of economic items, men busy themselves in a wide range of pursuits that can be classified primary, secondary, and tertiary (see Table 1-1, page 6). *Primary production* includes the age-old activities involved in withdrawing objects of value from nature's storehouse and in collaborating with nature to increase the generation and proliferation of items that are available in their "wild" state. For example, in agriculture, man harvests crops from the soil; in mining, he harvests ores from the earth's crust; in fishing, he harvests animals from the rivers, lakes, and oceans; in forestry, he harvests trees from the wooded areas of the earth.

In *secondary production* man increases the value (that is, the utility) of an already existing item by changing its *form*. Such activity is called manufacturing. The miller, for instance, changes grains of wheat into a more usable product, flour. Steelmakers turn iron ore into a more durable metal in blast furnaces and steel mills.

In *tertiary production* man does not harvest substances from nature, nor does he upgrade

Table 1-1 Classification of Economic Activities

A. Production

1. Primary
   Harvesting commodities from nature (agriculture, forestry, fishing, mining)
2. Secondary
   Increasing the value of commodities by changing their form (manufacturing)
3. Tertiary
   Performing services (repair, banking, teaching, entertainment, etc.)

B. Exchange

1. Location
   a. Increasing the value of commodities by changing their location (freight transportation)
   b. Satisfying the needs of people by changing their location (passenger transportation)
2. Ownership
   Increasing the value of commodities by changing their ownership (wholesale and retail trade)

C. Consumption

Use of commodities and services by human beings to satisfy their desires.

their worth by changing their form. Rather, he renders *services* that are of value to his fellow men. Repair men hammer the dents out of automobile fenders. Teachers impart knowledge and try to stimulate thought. Government employees enforce laws, collect taxes, and maintain highways. Other services are rendered by musicians, lawyers, doctors, real estate men, bankers, and housekeepers.

EXCHANGE

The *exchange* of items of value (whether the result of primary, secondary, or tertiary production) may be accomplished through *freight transportation,* which increases the value of commodities by changing their *location.* Iron ore, for example, is worth more in Chicago than in Hibbing; wheat is more valuable in Buffalo than in Saskatchewan. Changing the location of people themselves, through *passenger transportation,* is another activity which man rates highly. Still another way to increase the value of a commodity is by change of *ownership.* This is the purpose of wholesale trade and retail trade. A radio

Secondary production. Kawasaki industrial area between Tokyo and Yokohama on the western side of Tokyo Bay. A steel mill (Nippon Kokan) is in the foreground; behind it is a chemical factory (Showa Denko). Nearly all the land in this view is artificial fill. (Courtesy John H. Thompson, The Geographical Review, *and Sangyo Keizai newspaper.)*

Tertiary production. In the center of such metropolitan areas as London, retail trade, wholesale trade, banking, government administration and many other tertiary services become concentrated. (Courtesy British Information Services.)

is worth more to a distributor than to its manufacturer, and its value continues to increase as it passes from distributor to retailer and from retailer to ultimate consumer.

CONSUMPTION

The final stage in the *economic* sequence is the *consumption* of goods and services. Some forms of consumption destroy goods quickly—eating food or burning coal, for instance. Other forms use up a commodity slowly, bringing about its gradual depreciation—wearing a suit of clothes or driving a car. Still other forms of consumption do not destroy the commodity at all—gazing at the Alps or skiing down the snowy slopes. Occasionally, indeed, consumption may actually increase the worth of an object—as in enjoying an antique table or a Rembrandt painting.

Now, all these economic activities are studied by economists, historians, and several other social scientists, as well as by geographers. Just how does geography differ from these other disciplines in the study of economic activity? A partial answer can be found in the meaning of *geography* itself.

The Meaning of Geography

First of all, there are three widely held false notions of geography that should be dispensed with in order to clear the air for a definition of what geography really is.

A good many people seem to think that geography is simply a matter of *place names;* to them, a geographer is a person who knows the location of county seats, state capitals, rivers, and seas. When a contestant on a quiz program announces that he is an "expert" on geography, he is invariably asked a series of questions that involve nothing but place names.

Other people have the idea that geography is the study of the *natural environment.* To them, the geography of Illinois would deal only with climate, topography, drainage, natural vegetation, soil, and minerals. In this view geography is nothing more than a medley of excerpts from geology, meteorology, and biology. Indeed, some people may think that geography and geology are inseparable. They cannot understand why a geographer should be interested primarily in such things as the manufacture of flour or the circulation of newspapers. The trouble with this concept is that it omits man and all his doings. A geographer who sets about to interview factory managers in a city-wide study is likely to encounter surprise. If he were an economist or a historian, they would not be astonished, for they expect economists and historians to study manufacturing. But when he identifies himself as a geographer, they ask, "What is the connection between geography and manufacturing?"

Still a third group believes that geography is the study of the *influence of the natural environment on man's activities. Environmentalism* is the term applied to this still widely held concept. At one time, indeed, it was the prevailing notion among many American geographers themselves. But many of thèm have now concluded that it covers only *part* of geography and that by itself it may lead to false conclusions. Admittedly, natural environments set certain limits on what man can do; but, as we shall learn, two regions with similar environments may have dissimilar economies because their cultures are different.

These three concepts of geography are deeply ingrained in the minds of many people. Perhaps the reader will have to make an effort to shake off these old and unacceptable notions in favor of the new and expanded concept of geography about to be presented.

The word geography comes from two Greek roots, *geo,* which means earth, and *graphos,* which means description. The meaning would seem to be simple and clear. But many scholarly disciplines "describe the earth," for instance, geology, pedology, botany, zoology, and meteorology. Surely geography cannot claim to be the sum total of all earth sciences. In fact, the hallmark of geography is not so much *what* it studies as *how* it studies. Geography is unique because of the perspective from which its practitioners study the earth.

ANALOGY WITH HISTORY

In many respects, geography is similar to history. There would be no history if human events were invariable from day to day; it is because of variation through time that the discipline of history is possible. Because of *temporal* variations, the historian can identify *periods,* such as the Elizabethan Period, the Middle Ages, the Atomic Era. A scholar primarily interested in military developments can break down the record into successive ages of armed conflict and strategy. If his main concern is with the manner in which people express themselves, he can identify various cultural periods, such as the Renaissance or the Victorian. Regardless of the historian's predilection, then, the fundamental fact that phenomena differ from one time to another enables him to distinguish chronological periods.

But this is only the beginning. The historian's main objective is to understand *relationships* between events. He wants to know how an incident in 1914 is related to other events that took place in that year, in subsequent years, and in earlier years.

The geographer is concerned with variation *from place to place,* rather than from time to time. And he is bent on understanding relationships among places. There would be no geography if physical and human phenomena were distributed uniformly over the face of the earth. But rainfall, elevation, temperature, population, farming, mining, and manufacturing do vary markedly from one location to another. Any phenomena that differ from place to place are termed *spatial variables* and qualify as the *elements of geography.*

DEFINITION OF GEOGRAPHY

It is at present impossible to formulate a definition of geography that is both complete and simple—and that all geographers will accept. Nevertheless, beginning students are entitled to some declaration of position on the field. To that end, the following definition is proposed: *Geography is the study of spatial variation on the earth's surface.* "Earth's surface" is construed rather broadly here to refer to the milieu in which human life exists—the lower portion of the *atmosphere*, which man breathes, the outer part of the *lithosphere*, upon which he walks and from which he extracts minerals, and the *hydrosphere*, through which he sails and from which he withdraws fish and other aquatic substances.

Spatial variation, like temporal variation, has profound significance for human life and underlies many of the problems facing nations, states, cities, farms, factories, families, and individuals. The historian, we saw, deals in temporal variables, discerns distinct periods, and seeks to discover temporal relationships. In like manner, the geographer deals in spatial variables, identifies regions or areas, and searches for relationships among variables of location, or place. Thus, a more complete definition of geography would be: the discipline that *analyzes spatial variation in terms of areas (regions) and relationships among spatial variables.* Other definitions embodying the same concept are: *the study of places,* and *the analysis of areal (regional) variation.*

Unfortunately, the word geography itself does not connote accurately any of these concepts. Perhaps a better name for the discipline just described might be *spatial science* or *areal science* or *regional science.* Still, despite its limitations, geography remains the common term, so we shall retain it here.

The Method of Economic Geography

Now, we are in a position to answer our original question: What is economic geography? By blending our definitions of the two constituent terms we can derive this statement: *Economic geography is the study of areal variation on the earth's surface in man's activities related to producing, exchanging, and consuming wealth.*

In pursuit of that goal the economic geographer asks three basic questions. As we present these questions in the following paragraphs, consider how they compare with the basic questions asked by economists, historians, and other scholars.

QUESTION 1:

Where Is the Economic Activity Located?

The fundamental geographic fact is *location.* If someone wants to investigate corn farming, he begins by asking: Where is corn being farmed? The best way to find out is to inspect a map, because maps provide the clearest and quickest answers to the question "where?" Perhaps an agricultural economist or a corn specialist has already produced a "corn map," such as Figure 1-1, which shows the location of corn production in the United States. If no such map exists, the geographer will have to construct one for himself. In any case, maps are his basic tools and are essential to his ultimate understanding of areal relationships.

The idea of *pattern,* or *distribution,* may facilitate our grasp of the concept of location.

Figure 1-1 (*From U. S. Bureau of the Census.*)

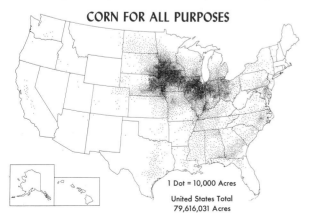

CORN FOR ALL PURPOSES

1 Dot = 10,000 Acres

United States Total
79,616,031 Acres

A pattern for us is the arrangement of an element over the face of the earth. The world pattern of population (shown on the front end-paper), for example, reveals some densely populated areas in China and India, some spots of less extreme density in the United States and U.S.S.R., and some sparsely settled stretches in northern Africa and inner Australia. (Since we shall use "distribution" as a synonym for "pattern," we could also say the population map shows the distribution of people over the earth.) In a way, maps are pictures of locational patterns that enable a geographer to begin delimiting the areas in which he is interested.

And this brings us to another term whose definition we need to settle. _An area is any portion of the earth's surface that is homogeneous in terms of any selected geographic element or group of elements._ An area, in short, is a distinctive portion of the earth's surface. In this book, we shall also employ the terms _region, belt, zone, land,_ and _realm_ to identify such portions of the earth.

QUESTION 2:

What Are the Characteristics of the Economic Activity?

After the geographer has pinpointed all the places where corn is grown, he will want to investigate other matters. What are the characteristics of corn farming that distinguish the regions devoted to it? How many acres do the farms occupy? What kinds of buildings are on them? What kinds of animals? How much corn is grown? What other crops are grown? In what respects are these regions different from dairy belts, from wheat-raising regions, from cotton-growing areas? Careful observation of the various aspects of corn farming will enable him to distinguish the American Corn Belt both from regions of contrasting activities (such as cotton belts and lumbering regions) and from other regions of corn production (for example, the corn areas in Iowa are similar in many respects to those in Argentina, but in some ways they are different). Clearly, the geographer must first decide what the significant characteristics of corn-farming regions are. Then, in terms of these characteristics, he finally decides where on his map to draw the boundaries of those distinctive regions.

Thus, question number two deals with _description_ and number one with _location._ But these two questions are not enough. A person can know the location of every place on earth without knowing much geography. And he can go on to familiarize himself with the characteristics of all these places and still not understand areal variation. He must go beyond these matters and search out the significance of the location and characteristics of the regions under study. Only then does he raise the question of analysis, which is the mark of mature scholarship. To this end, then, the economic geographer asks a third basic question.

QUESTION 3:

To What Other Phenomena Is the Economic Activity Related?

There are four ways to investigate relationships: (1) One useful approach is through an analysis of _cause_ and _effect._ (2) Some geographic studies, however, concentrate fruitfully on relationships with _physical_ and _cultural_ phenomena. (3) An alternative approach is to consider relationships _within_ a region and those _between regions._ (4) Finally, some geographers prefer to study relationships in terms of _correlations._ Let us look at each of these four analytical approaches more closely.

Cause and Effect   An understanding of _causal relationships_ enables us to answer such questions as these: Why is the Corn Belt located where it is? And why has the Corn Belt developed its distinguishing characteristics?

An understanding of _consequential relationships_ enables us to answer such questions as these: What has been the impact of corn farming upon soil erosion? What roles does corn farming play in the economic life of Iowa and of other Corn Belt states?

There are some geographers who believe these questions to be the most important parts of analysis. Accordingly, they contend that there should be four basic questions in economic geography. With the Corn Belt as an example, these would be: (1) Where is the Corn Belt? (2) What is it like? (3) Why is it there? (4) What are the consequences of its being where it is and as it is?

Physical and Cultural Relationships

Physical phenomena constitute the *natural environment*—the stage on which man plays out his drama. That environment is the sum total of the physical elements (moisture, heat, soil, terrain, and so on) that exist in a region apart from man and his works. In a sense, the physical environment consists of everything that was present before man appeared on the scene. Thus, analyzing the geography of corn production, we should understand the relationship between the rate of plant growth on the one hand and the inches of summer rainfall and the number of consecutive frost-free days on the other.

But a word of caution is not amiss here. The physical environment *does not determine* what man will produce or consume in a given region of the world, though, to be sure, it does have an enormous effect. For one thing, it may *prevent* man from carrying on certain economic activities. Coal cannot be mined in regions that lack coal deposits. Sometimes, too, the physical environment *promotes* certain endeavors. Although oranges can be grown anywhere on earth if men want to go to the expense of constructing adequate buildings, transporting soil, and providing moisture, heat, and light in handicapped regions, certain areas of the world naturally have a physical environment that is particularly well suited to orange cultivation. Thus, the environment may prevent some endeavors and promote others, but it never *determines* that man will support himself in a particular manner in a particular place. Still, an economic geographer must always recognize that a significant relationship may exist between a region's economic activities and its physical environment.

To the economic geographer, *culture* means the sum total of human achievements: knowledge, attitudes, arts, tools, social institutions, political organizations, religious convictions, systems for controlling capital investments, patterns of marketing, and habits of consumption. Cultural attributes differ from place to place as surely as do physical ones, and economic activity is strongly related to both.

Here is an example that illustrates the importance of culture in the economic life of a region. Most of northern Africa has a physical environment so dry that there is insufficient moisture for abundant vegetation. Yet there is some plant life, enough to support sheep and goats. The prevailing economy is nomadic herding, which yields scarcely any surplus of wool, skins, or meat to ship from this region to the huge nearby European market. Now, ten thousand miles to the southeast, in Australia, there is a physical environment highly similar to that of northern Africa. Little rain falls and vegetation is scanty. Yet in this region the prevailing economy is commercial grazing—quite different from the nomadic herding of North Africa—which yields a surplus of wool, skins, and meat. The reason for the contrast between the economic activities of these two arid regions lies mainly in the differences between African and Australian cultures, a factor which will be discussed more fully in Chapters 3 and 7.

There are some geographers who believe it unrealistic to distinguish between physical and cultural features. They contend that cultivated soil, for example, is a cultural, not a physical phenomenon because it bears man's imprint. Similarly, the climate over cities is a cultural phenomenon because so much of its dust, gas, and heat content has come from the city. They argue that many of the features we term "physical" actually have been produced by nature and man together. "Both nature and man are intrinsic to the particular character of the areas, and indeed in such intimate union that they cannot be separated from each other." * This school of thought

* Richard Hartshorne, *Perspective on the Nature of Geography*, Association of American Geographers Monograph, Rand McNally, (Chicago: 1959), p. 51. This quotation is from Alfred Hettner's "Das Wesen und die Methoden der Geographie," *Geographische Zeitschrift*, (1905), p. 554.

contends that if we are going to study relationships with physical features and those with cultural features, it would be just as logical to analyze relationships with animate and inanimate phenomena, with visible and invisible features, or with the material and nonmaterial.

However, some topics lend themselves to analysis in terms of relationships with physical and cultural features. Accordingly, some chapters in this book are built along this approach. Other topics however, are suited better to analysis from one of the other viewpoints, as will be seen in subsequent chapters.

Internal and External Relationships
Another fruitful way to analyze relationships between spatial variables is to consider those that involve features *within* a region and those that link the region *to other* regions. For example, to understand the geography of the American Corn Belt we must know how corn farming is related to such local phenomena as length of the frost-free season, temperature of summer nights, degree of mechanization, and transportation costs within the corn-growing area. Such associations within a region are termed *internal relationships*.

But to understand the geography of Corn Belt farming as it occurs in Iowa and Illinois we also need to know that there are millions of people in Indiana, Michigan, Ohio, Pennsylvania, and New York who do not live on farms and who therefore depend on others for the food they eat. Moreover, these people have developed dietary habits in which meat plays a large role. Not only do they want meat, but they can also afford to buy it, for they have great purchasing power. Much of their meat comes from animals fattened in the Corn Belt. In short, demand for meat in one region is related to specialized agriculture in another. Such associations between different regions are termed *external relationships*.

To illustrate the power of such relationships, we can turn again to the two arid regions specializing in animal production, northern Africa and Australia. Neither con-

tains many customers for animal products. But western Europe has millions of people who want animal products and can afford to pay for them. We might suppose that dry Africa, thousands of miles closer to Europe than dry Australia, would dominate the European market. Yet the trade between Africa and Europe is far less developed than that between Australia and Europe. The external relationships of these two dry regions with the European market are markedly different. Consequently, thousands of tons of wool, skins, and meat move annually from Australia along the longest sea lanes on earth, past the very doors of Africa, to European customers.

Analysis of Correlation   These first three approaches to the question of relationship have been used for some time and are rather well known. More recent and less familiar is a fourth approach, *analysis of correlation*.

Correlation analysis employs statistical techniques to measure the variance or covariance of geographic elements. If two variables reach their peak value in region A and their lowest value in region Z, and if they become progressively lower from regions B and C down through regions X and Y, they covary to a high degree. That is, they have a *high positive correlation* in their geographic distribution, or a *high geographic correlation*. To illustrate, let's examine the correlations in Table 1-2 between six variables (in the columns) as they vary spatially through the four states of Ohio, Indiana, Iowa, and North Dakota. There seems to be a correlation between number of people, population density per square mile, employment, and median personal income. Since each of these elements attains its highest value in the same place (Ohio) and its lowest value in the same place (North Dakota) and has similar intermediate values in Indiana and Iowa, we can say that they covary *positively* through this quartet of states. Conversely, there is a *negative* (or *inverse*) correlation between these four variables and a fifth: percentage of the population engaged in agriculture. That is, as population, density, employment, and income go *up* (in

Table 1-2 *Selected Spatial Variables for Selected States*

State	Number of People (000)	Population per Square Mile	Number Employed (000)	Median Personal Income	Population Percentage Employed in Agriculture	Median Age
Ohio	9,706	237	3,702	$3,363	3	31.2
Indiana	4,662	128	1,790	$3,197	4	30.4
Iowa	2,757	49	1,200	$3,068	11	31.0
North Dakota	632	9	230	$2,933	15	27.1

the states under consideration), the percentage employed in agriculture goes *down*. The correlation with a sixth variable, median age, is weakly positive with the first four variables.

The need for scholarly investigation along the lines of this fourth approach has been expressed as follows:

It seems clear that geographic investigation is concerned with discovering and describing areal variations in the occurrence of phenomena on the earth's surface, and also with the search for other areally associated factors that may help to explain the observed distributions. In all such cases, questions are bound to arise as to the degree of association that exists between two (or more) phenomena. Areal association is indicated when a variation from place to place in the occurrence of one variable is accompanied by a similar place-to-place variation in the occurrence of another.

In geographic research, areal associations in the occurrence of related phenomena (such as wheat yields and rainfall) have often been discovered by comparing maps of the distributions of those phenomena; and the resulting generalizations have usually taken a form such as, "In this region, there is a tendency for wheat yields to decrease as rainfall decreases." Vague generalizations such as these leave much to be desired, but they have been extremely useful in teaching and explaining areal variations in land-use patterns. Many associations, however, are not so clearly discernible as the wheat-rainfall association to which we have just referred. In those situations in which associations are less clearly defined, it has often been difficult to secure agreement even among competent professional geographers as to the degree, or even the existence, of such associations. Under these circumstances, it is impossible to escape the conclusion that these types of generalizations would have more value if they could be quantified. If some objective, quantified measure of association could be applied that would make such expressions as "slight tendency" or "strong tendency" more precise, it appears that the advancement of geographic analysis would be expedited materially.*

* Harold H. McCarty, John C. Hook, and Duane S. Knos, *The Measurement of Association in Industrial Geography* (Iowa City: State University of Iowa, 1956), p. 20.

Within the ranks of professional geographers a new school of thought is arising which holds (a) that correlation analysis should constitute the heart of the geographic method and (b) that the term *relationship* should be reserved only for covariation (in this connection, no two variables can be said to be *positively* related unless both are high in the same regions; conversely, a negative relationship exists when one variable is high in regions where the other variable is low), and (c) that the term *association* should be used only for geographic elements that vary similarly from place to place.

At this point a statement is in order concerning *correlation* and *cause and effect:* High correlation between two variables does not prove cause and effect. Indeed it is possible for the two variables to have absolutely no functional relationship; both might be unrelated results of a third variable as yet unobserved. The author recognizes that the whole notion of *cause and effect*, except in a highly restricted and technical sense, has been so thoroughly attacked by philosophers that some people think it a useless concept. The author frankly declares, however, that he belongs to a different school of thought, which holds that railway lines, for example, are where they are and their traffic is as it is *because* of definite forces which have influenced their location and the characteristics of their traffic. Although complete scientific proof cannot be given that markets influence the location of roads, or that topography influences the position of railways, it seems reasonable to believe that a *probabilistic* relationship exists between them. Where it appears *probable* that railways have been influenced by factor X, we would use the term *causal relationship* on the assumption that X has had at least some effect in causing railways to be *where* they are and *as* they are. Conversely, where it appears *probable* that railways have exerted an influence on variable Z, we would use the term *effect relationship,* assuming that railways have played some part in the location and character of Z. In brief, the term *cause,* as used in this book, applies to factors which *probably* have had an *influence on* the topic being studied; the term *effect* applies herein to elements which *probably* have been *influenced by* the topic analyzed.

Of the four approaches to Question 3 (on relationships) in this book we proceed from the premise that the relationships derived by the fourth approach (covariation) are *corelationships,* or *correlations,* whereas those appropriate to the first three approaches (cause-effect, physical-cultural, internal-external) are *functional* relationships. Synonyms for *functional relationships* are *connections* and *linkages.* For example, Minnesota and Pennsylvania are functionally related, or connected, or linked together, by the flow of iron ore from northern Minnesota mines to Pittsburgh steel mills. Again, there is functional relationship, or connection, or linkage, between Israel, southern Africa, and the United States by means of diamond traffic. Rough diamonds are mined in Africa, shipped to Israel for cutting and polishing, and then sent to customers in the United States.

THE VALUE OF GEOGRAPHIC ANALYSIS

The geographic method of analysis enables us to understand more fully the world in which we live. In satisfying the innate curiosity of the human intellect, geography contributes knowledge in a distinctive dimension. Beyond that, there are practical applications: Federal officials can deal better with the governments of other nations if they are informed about geography; state government officials will have a sounder base for making decisions regarding state policies if they understand the geography of their state; city officials and city planners can plan more wisely for future developments if they are familiar with geographic principles; industrialists, wholesalers, retailers, and other businessmen can find geographic analysis helpful in making decisions regarding location of factories, warehouses, stores, and advertising efforts. Every person, whether businessman, housewife, or student, will find that the ability to apply the geographic method of analysis to the events of everyday life will add a new dimension of interest and satisfaction to his intellectual experiences.

Suggested Readings

Ackerman, Edward A., *Geography as a Fundamental Research Discipline,* Chicago, 1958, 37 pp.

———, "Regional Research—Emerging Concepts and Techniques in the Field of Geography," *Economic Geography,* 1953, pp. 189-197.

Ballabon, Maurice B., "Putting the 'Economic' into Economic Geography," *Economic Geography,* 1957, pp. 217-223.

Balzak, S. S., Yasyutin, V. F., and Feigin, Y. G., *Economic Geography of the U.S.S.R.* American edition edited by Chauncy D. Harris, translated by Robert M. Hankin and Olga A. Titelbaum, New York, 1949, 620 pp.

Berg, L. S., *Natural Regions of the U.S.S.R.* Edited by John A. Morrison and C. C. Nikiforoff, translated from the Russian by Olga Adler Titelbaum, New York, 1950, 435 pp.

Berry, Brian J. L., "Further Comments Concerning 'Geographic' and 'Economic' Economic Geography," *The Professional Geographer,* January, 1959, pp. 11-13.

Blaut, J. M., "The Language of Maps," *The Professional Geographer,* January, 1954, pp. 9-12.

Curry, Leslie, "Climate and Economic Life: A New Approach," *Geographical Review,* 1952, pp. 367-383.

Ginsburg, Norton and Berry, Brian J. L., *Atlas of Economic Development,* Chicago, 1961.

Ginsburg, Norton, editor, *Essays on Geography and Economic Development,* Chicago, 1960.

Ginsburg, Norton, "Natural Resources and Economic Development," *Annals of the Association of American Geographers,* 1957, pp. 196-212.

Gregor, Howard F., "German vs. American Economic Geography," *The Professional Geographer,* January, 1957, pp. 12-13.

Hartshorne, Richard, "What Is Meant by Geography as the Study of Areal Differentiation?" *Perspective on the Nature of Geography,* Chicago, 1959, pp. 12-21.

———, "Must We Distinguish Between Human and Natural Factors?", *ibid.,* pp. 48-64.

———, "Does Geography Seek to Formulate Scientific Laws or to Describe Individual Cases?", *ibid.,* pp. 146-172.

Isard, Walter, *et al., Methods of Regional Science: An Introduction to Regional Science*, New York, 1960, 784 pp.

James, Preston E., "The Hard Core of Geography," *New Viewpoints in Geography*, Preston E. James, ed., 29th Yearbook of the National Council for the Social Studies, Washington, 1959.

———, "The Region as a Concept," *Geographical Review*, 1962, pp. 127-129.

———, "Toward a Further Understanding of the Regional Concept," *Annals of the Association of American Geographers*, 1952, pp. 195-222.

Jones, Emrys, "Cause and Effect in Human Geography," *Annals of the Association of American Geographers*, 1956, pp. 369-377.

Klimm, Lester E., "Mere Description," *Economic Geography*, 1959, p. 1.

Lukermann, Fred, "Toward a More Geographic Economic Geography," *The Professional Geographer*, July 1958, pp. 2-11.

———, "The Concept of Location in Classical Geography," *Annals of the Association of American Geographers*, 1961, pp. 194-210.

McCarty, H. H., Review of *Atlas of Economic Development*, edited by Norton Ginsburg, *Economic Geography*, 1962, pp. 184-185.

———, "Toward a More General Economic Geography," *Economic Geography*, 1959, pp. 283-289.

McNee, Robert B., "The Changing Relationships of Economics and Economic Geography," *Economic Geography*, 1959, pp. 189-198.

Sauer, Carl O., "The Education of a Geographer," *Annals of the Association of American Geographers*, 1956, pp. 287-299.

Saushkin, Julian G., "Economic Geography in the U.S.S.R.," *Economic Geography*, 1962, pp. 28-37.

Schnore, Leo F., "Geography and Human Ecology," *Economic Geography*, 1961, pp. 207-217.

Smith, Wilfred, *An Economic Geography of Great Britain*, New York, 1949, 747 pp.

Thomas, William L., editor, *Man's Role in Changing the Face of the Earth*, Chicago, 1956, 1193 pp.

Thompson, John H., Sufrin, Sidney C., Gould, Peter R., and Buck, Marion A., "Toward a Geography of Economic Health," *Annals of the Association of American Geographers*, 1962, pp. 1-20.

Ullman, Edward, "Amenities as a Factor in Regional Growth," *Geographical Review*, 1954, pp. 119-132.

van Cleef, Eugene, "Must Geographers Apologize?", *Annals of the Association of American Geographers*, 1955, pp. 105-108.

Van Valkenburg, S., "The World Land Use Survey," *Economic Geography*, 1950, pp. 1-5.

Warntz, William, "Contributions Toward a Macroeconomic Geography: A Review," *Geographical Review*, 1957, pp. 420-424.

———, "Progress in Economic Geography," *New Viewpoints in Geography*, James, Preston E., ed., 29th Yearbook of the National Council for the Social Studies, Washington, D. C., 1959.

Webb, Martyn J., "Economic Geography: A Framework for a Disciplinary Definition," *Economic Geography*, 1961, pp. 254-257.

Yi-faai, Laai; Michael, Franz; and Sherman, John; "The Use of Maps in Social Research: A Case Study in South China," *Geographical Review*, 1962, pp. 92-111.

Zimmerman, Erich W., *World Resources and Industries*, New York, 1951, 832 pp.

*The ocean front of Hong Kong is typical of many urban centers
of eastern Asia where thousands of people reside in boats and depend largely
on fishing for food. (Photo by United Nations.)*

TWO

To the economic geographer the most important single topic is *people*—the producers, the exchangers, and the consumers of every item and service of economic value. Therefore, we must first have a clear picture of the distribution of the world's population before we can develop an understanding of the geography of agriculture, forestry, manufacturing, railroading, or any other economic activity.

How many people are involved in the world's economic life? Most of us have only a foggy notion of the number of human beings who are living today. If you were to stand on a street corner and put this question to passersby, only about one in ten could give you an answer that was even approximately correct. Are there a hundred million people, a billion, ten billion, a hundred billion? Try this question on your friends and notice the range of answers.

At present, the total population of the earth is approximately three billion. But what does a figure of this magnitude really mean? Take the number of years that have elapsed since Christ was born (approximately 1965 years) and multiply it by the number of days per year. The product—717,225—is not even close to the number of world inhabitants today. Now multiply that figure by 24, to get the number of hours in 1965 years—17,213,-400. But this is merely the approximate present population of New York State. Now multiply this by 60 to give the number of minutes—1,032,804,000. But this is less than the number of people in the two nations of China and

India. We would still have to multiply the number of *minutes* since Christ was born by 3 to equal the number of human beings on earth today.

The Distribution of Population

As geographers we want to know how these three billion are distributed around the globe. So the first thing we must do is consult a map (see the front endpaper). Three-fourths of the earth's surface is covered by water where naturally few people live. Thus, the three billion people live on the quarter of the earth composed of land and its adjacent water fringes.

As we analyze the map of population, we discover several important facts. First, most of the people are packed into a tiny part of the earth's land area—about 90 per cent of them on 10 per cent of the land. The other 90 per cent of the land supports only about 10 per cent of the people. Clearly, population is very unequally distributed over the face of the earth.

Table 2-1   Population and Area for Selected Nations

Place	Population in Millions	Land Area in Millions of Square Kilometers *	Persons per Square Kilometer *	Arable Acres per Person
WORLD	2,907	135.1	22	1.3
Asia				
Afghanistan	13	.6	20	0.4
Burma	20	.6	30	1.1
China	669	9.5	70	0.3
Taiwan	10	.03	285	0.2
India	438	3.2	123	0.9
Indonesia	90	1.4	61	0.5
Iran	20	1.6	12	1.9
Israel	2	0.02	100	0.5
Japan	93	0.3	251	0.1
Korea	32	0.2	145	0.3
Pakistan	93	0.9	92	0.7
Philippines	27	0.3	82	0.6
Saudi Arabia	6	1.6	4	0.07
Thailand	25	0.5	43	0.9
Turkey	27	0.7	35	2.3
Viet-Nam	29	0.3	89	0.4
Europe				
Austria	7	0.08	84	0.6
Belgium	9	0.03	298	0.2
Czechoslovakia	13	0.12	106	1.0
Denmark	4	0.04	106	1.5
Finland	4	0.33	13	1.5
France	45	0.55	82	1.2
Germany (E)	16	0.10	151	0.7
Germany (W)	52	0.24	213	0.4
Hungary	9	0.09	107	1.4
Italy	49	0.30	163	0.8
Netherlands	11	0.03	350	0.2
Norway	3	0.32	11	0.5
Poland	29	0.31	94	1.4
Romania	18	0.23	77	1.3
Spain	29	0.50	59	1.7
Sweden	7	0.44	17	1.2
Switzerland	5	0.04	127	0.2
United Kingdom	52	0.24	214	0.3
Yugoslavia	17	0.25	72	1.1

People—The Producers and Consumers

The map further reveals that this unequally distributed population is concentrated in four major regions—eastern Asia, southern Asia, western Europe, and eastern Anglo-America (that is, southeastern Canada and the eastern United States). The map also reveals several large regions of population void, and several transitional areas that lie between the two extremes of population centers and sparsely inhabited wildernesses.

THE FOUR MAJOR REGIONS
OF POPULATION MASSES

The greatest heavily populated region of the world lies in eastern Asia, embracing China,

Japan, Korea, the Philippines, and Vietnam. Probably 30 per cent of all the people of the world live in this area. China alone has a population of nearly 700,000,000—almost one of every four people living in the world today. Japan has 93,000,000. (Table 2-1 lists the population of the leading countries of the world.) In eastern China along the coast there is an area that extends north to south for nearly 1000 miles; in it, on the map, the dots are crammed as densely as in the most heavily populated portion of the United States. A similar belt runs east to west through China along the Yangtze Valley. The Yangtze Valley and the North China Plain (which includes

Table **2-1** *Population and Area for Selected Nations* (cont.)

Place	Population in Millions	Land Area in Millions of Square Kilometers *	Persons per Square Kilometer *	Arable Acres per Person
Africa				
Algeria	10	2.3	5	1.7
Congo	13	2.3	6	9.6
Egypt	26	1.0	26	0.2
Ethiopia	21	1.1	18	1.4
Kenya	6	0.5	11	0.6
Nigeria	33	0.8	38	1.6
Rhodesia and Nyasaland	8	1.2	6	2.0
Sudan	11	2.5	5	2.0
Tanganyika	9	0.9	10	3.2
Uganda	6	0.2	27	1.2
Union of South Africa	16	1.2	12	1.5
North America				
Canada	17	9.9	2	6.1
Cuba	6	0.1	58	0.8
Mexico	34	1.9	17	1.5
United States	179	9.3	19	2.8
South America				
Argentina	20	2.7	7	3.8
Brazil	64	8.5	8	0.8
Chile	7	0.7	10	2.0
Colombia	13	1.1	12	0.5
Peru	10	1.2	8	0.4
Venezuela	6	0.9	7	1.1
U.S.S.R.	210	22.4	9	2.7
Oceania				
Australia	10	7.7	1	5.9
New Zealand	2	0.2	9	0.5
New Guinea	1	0.2	6	—

Sources: United Nations *Demographic Yearbook 1960*, Table 1 and *Food and Agriculture Organization Yearbook, 1960*, Table 1.

* A kilometer is 3281 feet (approximately ⅝ of a mile). A square kilometer covers 39% of a square mile. The world population density of 22 people per square kilometer can also be expressed as 57 per square mile.

the delta of the Hwang Ho) are two of the largest areas of extremely dense settlement on the face of the earth. To appreciate the magnitude of congestion, imagine an area as thickly settled as northeastern Illinois that extends all the way from Canada to the Gulf of Mexico and spreads from the Mississippi River to the Atlantic Ocean.

The second region, southern Asia, consists essentially of India (438,000,000 inhabitants), Ceylon (10,000,000), portions of Pakistan (93,000,000), and coastal areas in Burma (20,000,000), Thailand (25,000,000) and Cambodia (4,000,000). We might also include Malaya (7,000,000) and Indonesia (90,000,000) as outlying fringes of this general region. India contains the Ganges Valley, the most intensely congested long valley in the world. If transposed to the United States, this Ganges belt would extend from New York City almost to Salt Lake City. In southeast Asia, population clusters occur at the deltas of the Irrawaddy, Menam, and Mekong rivers. The number of people in these countries is astonishing compared with the 179,-000,000 in the United States in 1960. In total, this second region has 700,000,000 people, nearly 25 per cent of the world's inhabitants.

Thus, over half the earth's people are jammed into the comparatively small space of eastern and southern Asia. This is one of the most significant facts in economic geography; its importance cannot be overemphasized, for it is fundamental to an understanding of many of the economic, social, and political problems that confront mankind in the twentieth century.

The third major region of habitation is Europe. One-quarter of the world's population is located within a wedge-shaped zone that is broad to the west along the Atlantic Coast (from Gibraltar to Scotland) and tapers as it runs eastward more than 3000 miles into central Russia. Nearly 700,000,000 people live in this area, which contains most of the Soviet Union (210,000,000), Western Germany (52,000,000), Great Britain (52,-000,000), Italy (49,000,000), France (45,-000,000), Spain (29,000,000), Poland (29,-000,000), and Eastern Germany (16,000,000).

(For comparison, remember that Canada has 17,000,000 people and New York State 17,-000,000.) Visualize this third region transposed to the United States: It would reach from the Atlantic seaboard clear across the continent and into the Pacific Ocean.

Compared with these three gigantic areas, the fourth seems small, in population and limited in extent. Roughly 8 per cent of the world's people are situated in eastern Anglo-America, along the southern border of Canada and in the northeastern quadrant of the United States, from the Mississippi River to the Atlantic Coast. According to the 1960 Census, there were about 179,000,000 people in the United States. The population is growing so fast, however, that the figure now is closer to 190,000,000. Still, since most present statistics are based on the official census figure, we shall adhere to it for most purposes.

THE EIGHT MAJOR VOIDS

At the other extreme from these thickly peopled zones are vast stretches of land where hardly anyone lives. By far the most extensive is the African-Asian void, which runs almost 10,000 miles from the Atlantic shores of northern Africa eastward through the Sahara Desert, Arabia, and Afghanistan, deep into the heart of Asia. Mongolia marks its eastern extremity. Interrupted by only a few populous ribbons (such as the Nile Valley) and scattered oases (such as in Turkestan and western Sinkiang), this tremendous void extends over 20 per cent of the earth's land. And only a narrow, but conspicuous, band of settlement across southern Siberia separates it from another void that stretches 6000 miles across northern Eurasia from the Atlantic cliffs of Norway to the Pacific coast of Kamchatka.

Then there is northern North America, most of which is very sparsely settled, which, in fact, is virtually empty (except for military outposts) of permanent occupants all the way across northern Alaska, Canada, and Greenland. A southward prong extends, with only a few small anomalies, through the western United States deep into Mexico.

About equal in size to the North American void is Antarctica's 5,000,000 square miles

People—The Producers and Consumers

Many vast land areas of the earth are uninhabited, like this stretch of Australia's Northern Territory. Across this desert Stuart Highway (near Tennant Creek) runs for nine hundred miles, between Alice Springs at the south to Darwin at the north. (Courtesy Australian News and Information Bureau.)

(for comparison, the land area figure for the United States is 3,000,000). A fifth population void (about the same size as the United States) shows up in the Amazon Basin, which makes up a major segment of South America. A comparable expanse is that part of Oceania which comprises Australia and New Guinea. Other areas where few people have chosen to live are southwest Africa and the southern tip of South America.

Altogether, these eight sparsely settled sections constitute about 75 per cent of the earth's land area.

TRANSITIONAL REGIONS

Between the two extremes are several transitional areas, some of which are beginning to stand out as conspicuous, if minor, clusters of people—for example, the Nile Valley and the Near East (particularly Israel, Lebanon, Turkey, and the northern portions of Iraq and Iran). In addition, there are the oases of Russian Turkestan and Sinkiang, which have already been mentioned. And deep in the heart of Africa is a surprising population cluster—in Ruanda-Urundi. Nigeria and the southeastern coast of the Union of South Africa are also noteworthy. A counterpart to these areas appears at Africa's other margin, along the coasts of Morocco, Algeria, and Tunis.

South America's population pattern resembles beads on a string. The continent is encircled with appreciable concentrations on the coasts of Brazil and Argentina and on the peripheries of Venezuela, Colombia, and Chile. In Middle America, we find a concentration in southern Mexico, along with a few small aggregates elsewhere.

People—The Producers and Consumers

Another way of approaching the question of where mankind is located is to strike off ratios between numbers of people and amounts of land. The most familiar ratio, of course, is population per square mile. Such a statement expresses a relationship known as "density of population" or as "the man/land ratio." The distribution shown in Figure 2-1 is based on this relationship. Compare Figure 2-1 with the front endpaper: Is the dot map or the density map the more effective in presenting a regional view? Or does each have advantages and disadvantages?

Table 2-1 presents information on density of population by means of two measurements: number of persons per square kilometer, and number of arable acres per person. Both measurements vary markedly from nation to nation. When we use the persons per square kilometer ratio, we discover a sharp contrast between Australia and the Netherlands. In between these two extremes, there are many shadings. But notice that the *average for the world as a whole* is 22 persons per square kilometer (57 per square mile). (These ratios are based on *land* areas; they do not include the surface areas of oceans or inland seas.) The average for the United States is almost the same as the world average. It is scarcely surprising, though, to find that the average number of persons per square kilometer in the other three dense regions is markedly higher than in the U.S. and in the sparsely settled areas.

But what do these bald figures really tell us? Are the citizens of Australia scattered evenly all over the landscape? For so large and varied a country as the United States, how meaningful is it to say that there are 22 persons per square kilometer? The point of course is that land is not all of equal value. Some

Figure 2-1 (*From U. S. Bureau of the Census.*)

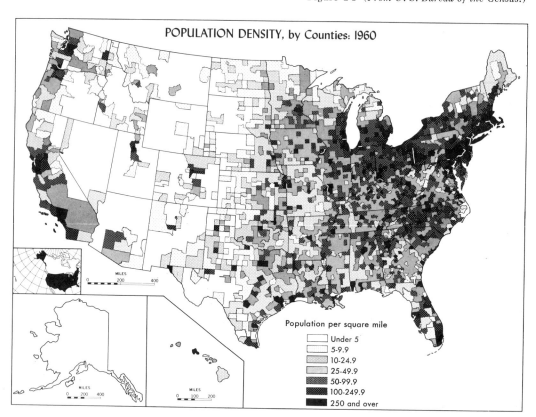

POPULATION DENSITY, by Counties: 1960

Population per square mile

- Under 5
- 5-9.9
- 10-24.9
- 25-49.9
- 50-99.9
- 100-249.9
- 250 and over

People—The Producers and Consumers

acres produce an abundance of the items that man cherishes. Others are unproductive—at least of what twentieth-century man desires and of what his present knowledge enables him to produce. So a more meaningful way of stating land-per-person ratios is to specify the number of *arable* acres per person, arable land being land that can be cultivated to produce useful crops. When we modify our ratios in this way, we discover substantial changes. As Table 2-1 shows, although Arabia has a vast amount of open land, very little of it is arable—in fact, there is less than one-tenth of an acre of arable land per person. At the other extreme is the Congo, where there are over 9.6 acres per inhabitant. For the world as a whole, the figure is 1.3, and the average for the United States is about twice the world average. Notice how little arable land there is per person in such countries as Japan, Belgium, the Netherlands, China, the United Kingdom, and Germany.

Although these ratios appear in the table simply as statistics, they tell a vivid story about the economic problems of nations. For impersonal statistics often stand for empty stomachs and low standards of living. Indeed, two of the most significant maps for the understanding of world problems are the front and back endpapers of this book—the first showing the location of people and the second the location of diet-deficit areas. Study these two maps carefully, compare them, and keep them in mind as we come to the economic activities by which the people in the nations of the world are trying to support themselves. (Anyone interested in population problems can find considerable information in the United Nations' *Demographic Yearbook*. The United Nations has published several other studies of population that you may find in your college library. For the first time in history, we have in these sources something resembling world census materials.)

The observations we have made on the basis of the ratios listed in Table 2-1 lead to some provocative questions. Why are so many people located in the densely settled regions? Why are so few people located in the sparsely settled regions? Can the sparsely populated regions be used to support more people? These are major questions challenging mankind today, questions on which there is wide difference of opinion. Topics presented in this book will shed at least some light on them.

This picture of the present-day population of the world becomes more meaningful when we compare it with scenes in years gone by. For in geography, as in many other disciplines, it is impossible to understand the present without some knowledge of the past. So let us familiarize ourselves with the principal changes that have taken place in the total number of people and in their location.

The Past

CHANGES IN NUMBER OF PEOPLE

Only recently has the earth teemed with nearly three billion people; for centuries only a few million people lived at any one time. We do not know for sure how many people there were at any given moment in the past, but the most reasonable estimate is that during the centuries before Christ there were never more than 200 or 300 million people. In fact, when Christ was born the population of the whole world was probably about 250 million, considerably less than the present-day population of India alone. A thousand years later the world figure was still less than 500 million; by the year 1650, it had apparently passed the half-billion mark. By 1800, it stood at one billion, and by 1900 it had reached about 1.5 billion. Then, in the few decades since 1900, the population of the world seems suddenly to have exploded. In just five decades the number of people shot up by over 1.5 billion.

How can we account for this rapid growth in just a few decades when for so many centuries the number of inhabitants changed so little? Here is one general explanation— not completely satisfactory, but nevertheless suggestive. Theoretically an increase in the number of people can result from either an increase in the number of births (while the death rate holds steady), from a decrease in the number of deaths (while the birth rate holds steady), or from both. Regardless of how high the birth rate is, if the death rate is equally high the population will not increase. Again, no matter how low the death rate is, if the birth rate is similarly low the total population will not increase. Now, birth rates have scarcely changed over the centuries. The population explosion of recent times, then, seems to have resulted directly from a sharp reduction in death rates.

Before about 1650, the total population remained low because the death rate was kept high by starvation, disease, and war. Then man learned some new lessons. He discovered ways of improving his agriculture and increasing his food supply; he learned to irrigate arid lands, drain wet lands, and develop hardier strains of seeds. Man also discovered better methods of transportation. Surfaced roads, railroads, power-driven vehicles, larger ships: These and other inventions made it possible to distribute the new supplies of food to deficient areas. So starvation became less menacing and death rates began to fall.

Man also learned to combat diseases. He discovered germs and the manner in which they live and reproduce. He devised new methods for destroying their habitats, remedial measures that we call sanitation. By pushing forward the science of medicine, he learned how to prevent disease and to cure people who had been infected.

All these advances in science served to reduce the high death toll that had been levied by starvation and disease since the dawn of history. Although birth rates remained about the same, fewer newborn babies died, and those who lived began to live longer. All these discoveries have sharply reduced the death rate and so have enabled the population of the world to multiply at a dramatic pace. Unquestionably science has added years to our lives. (A relevant issue is whether science has added "life to our years.")

CHANGES IN LOCATION OF PEOPLE

The regions that are most densely settled today have not always been in the top positions. At one time the most populous area was located in southwestern Asia, in the valley of the Tigris and Euphrates rivers. A few centuries later, three new spots had appeared on the map: southeastern Asia (especially India and China), northern Africa, and southern Europe. By 1700 west-central Europe had become a conspicuous region, but North and South America were still very sparsely settled. Only recently have people streamed across the oceans from regions of high densities to occupy the American voids.

The front endpaper in the book, then, is simply a single picture in a long series. If we were to run through the series chronologically, we would have a motion picture of the continuous changes in the population regions of the world, a complex pattern of population shifts from place to place and from time to time.

Prospects for the Future

What about the future? How many people will the earth have to support? Will the number of people continue to multiply at the present rate, with the curve shown in Figure 2-2 shooting steadily upward?

If so, a host of troublesome new questions will arise. Will there be enough food? What is the maximum number of people the earth can feed? Will enough fuel be available for heat and power and enough fiber for clothing? Or will the rate of growth slow down so that

the curve, though continuing upward, will rise more gradually? Is there any evidence that the graph will level off, with the population stabilized at one figure? Is there any likelihood that the curve will reverse itself some time in the future to indicate a shrinkage of the world's population? If so, at how many billions and in what period might that occur?

Since even well-informed authorities disagree on the answers to these questions, the reader need not hesitate to make a start at

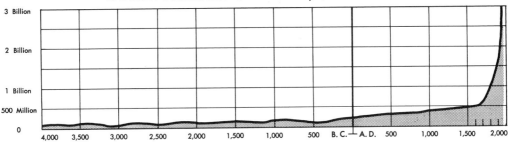

WORLD: NUMBERS OF PEOPLE, 4,000 B. C. TO 1960 A. D.

Figure 2-2

forming his own opinion. And there are a number of other questions to ponder as well. What about the school of thought that regards the spread of population over the face of the earth as analogous to the spread of cancer in the human body? In cancerous growth, the normal body cells begin to multiply at an excessive rate, and, for some reason that we still do not understand, accumulate in abnormal concentrations. According to this analogy, although the rapid increase in population may not be undesirable in itself, the danger is that billions of people swarming over the globe may eventually exhaust and vitiate the host on which they live, the earth itself. There is just so much energy available to man for use in producing the food, fuel, clothing, shelter, and tools he needs, and all that is at his disposal either arrives from the sun moment by moment or is already stored up in the substances of the earth—in the form of coal, petroleum, or nuclear fuel. How many billions of people—and at what standard of living—can be supported by the energy resources of the earth? Can the resources of other celestial bodies be tapped? Clearly, these questions are crucial to anybody who is interested in the future economic activities of the earth's people.

Trends in location are also worth pondering. Where will the populous regions be two centuries from now? Will man infiltrate today's vacant stretches as he makes further discoveries in science and further changes in his economic and social organization? Or have human beings reached a climax at which we have finally worked out the locational

pattern that most perfectly fits our needs—the pattern that makes it possible for us to be supported at the highest possible level by the earth's resources? Or will the locational pattern of resources continue to interact with changes in culture to produce some new regional pattern of population?

At the present level of economic and cultural development, certain regions are better equipped than others to support people. Throughout most of man's history, people have had to live rather close to their food supply. And even today most food does not have to be transported very far to get it from the place it is produced to the place it is consumed. But the relatively recent revolutions in transportation and economic productivity may one day make it possible for great numbers of men to live in regions far removed from their food-producing regions.

We have already seen evidence of this tendency in the shift of population in the United States. A great wave of people has moved to the West Coast, where life is easier, where winters are less severe, where many of the amenities of life are ready at hand. And yet the West Coast cannot provide all the varieties of food, in the quantities demanded, for this new population. The region does provide the means, however, by which people can produce items and services of value to exchange with food-producers in other regions. Inhabitants of the Pacific Coast now generate a surplus of airplanes, motion pictures, timber, fruit, and vegetables. But this blossoming of a new population region never could have occurred had it not been for the efficient transportation system that enables the surplus of the West to be exchanged for food from other regions. As transportation becomes more and more efficient, people everywhere can, if they wish, settle in regions ever farther and farther removed from the areas in which their food is grown.

For the present, at least, most of our food still comes from the soil. The plants we eat subsist on soil nutrients, moisture, sunshine, and the atmosphere. The animals we consume also subsist on the same botanical base. The fundamental truth is that, at our present level of knowledge, some regions are distinctly handicapped in their ability to produce the kind of food we can and want to eat. Some regions are too cold, some are too hot, or too dry, or too wet, or too rough, and some have very poor soil. And the location of these physical factors is not very likely to change.

Consequently, if the regions of population shift, the change will come about through the cultural efforts of man—in devising new techniques that will make it possible to irrigate deserts and drain swamps. Man has had some success in terracing hilly regions and in trans-

forming rough lands into productive areas. Can he devise techniques for improving soils that are now too poor to produce crops? If so, the sparsely settled regions that now appear on the world population map may, in the future, rank among the chief population centers on earth.

An even more striking shift in the location of people would probably occur if we could devise some means of producing food from sources other than soil. If, for example, we could produce an adequate supply of nutrients in chemical laboratories, the people of the world would suddenly be freed from their attachment to the soil. The criteria by which human beings evaluate places for living would change, and with improving means of transportation they could—and many perhaps would—eventually move into areas that are now completely devoid of human life.

The reader should think about these problems for himself. Nobody has a ready-made set of answers that can be set forth in a neat list, so he should try to look into the future and predict the regional patterns that the world's population is likely to follow.

Suggested Readings

Bennett, M. K., *The World's Food: A Study of the Interrelations of World Populations, National Diets and Food Potentials*, New York, 1954, 282 pp.

Bogue, Donald J., "The Geography of Recent Population Trends in the United States," *Annals of the Association of American Geographers*, 1954, pp. 124-134.

Burgdörfer, Friedrich, editor, *World Atlas of Population: Distribution of the Population of the World about the Year 1950*, Hamburg, 1954, 26 pp.

de Castro, Josué, *The Geography of Hunger*, Boston, 1952, 337 pp.

Chandrasekhar, S., *Hungry People and Empty Lands: An Essay on Population Problems and International Tensions*, London, 1954, 306 pp.

Cressey, George B., *Land of the 500 Million*, New York, 1955, 387 pp.

Klimm, Lester E., "The Empty Areas of the Northeastern United States," *Geographical Review*, 1954, pp. 325-345.

Lowenthal, David and Comitas, Lambros, "Emigration and Depopulation: Some Neglected Aspects of Population Geography," *Geographical Review*, 1962, pp. 195-210.

May, Jacques M., "The Mapping of Human Starvation," *Geographical Review*, 1953, pp. 253-255 and pp. 403-404.

Proudfoot, Malcolm, J., *European Refugees: 1939-1952, A Study in Forced Population Movement*, Evanston, 1956, 542 pp.

Roof, Michael K., and Leedy, Frederick A., "Population Redistribution in the Soviet Union, 1939-1956," *Geographical Review*, 1959, pp. 208-221.

Russell, E. John, *World Population and World Food Supplies*, London, 1954, 516 pp.

Trewartha, Glenn T., "A Case for Population Geography," *Annals of the Association of American Geographers*, 1953, pp. 71-97.

United Nations, *Demographic Yearbook*, New York.

United Nations, Food and Agriculture Organization, *Yearbook of Food and Agricultural Statistics: Part I, Production, Part II, Trade*, New York.

Velikonja, Joseph, "Postwar Population Movements in Europe," *Annals of the Association of American Geographers*, 1958, pp. 458-472.

Woytinsky, W. S., and Woytinsky, E. S., *World Population and Production*, New York, 1953, 1268 pp.

———, and ———, *World Commerce and Production*, New York, 1953.

Zobler, Leonard, "A New Areal Measure of Food Production Efficiency," *Geographical Review*, 1961, pp. 549-69.

PART TWO

SUBSISTENCE ECONOMIC ACTIVITIES

All the world's three billion people are supported by economic activity of one sort or another. Given such a bewildering amount of activity, how can we detect the patterns by which it is organized from place to place? In a sense, doing so is precisely the task of economic geography.

In terms of numbers of workers, the world's leading economic activity is agriculture, for about 75 per cent of the producers on earth are agriculturalists. Manufacturing engages about 10 per cent of the world's labor force. Trade, transportation, and services account for 12 per cent. The remaining 3 per cent busy themselves in mining, fishing, and forestry.

In this book we shall apply the geographic method of analysis to, and organize our discussion around, *production* rather than *consumption*. We do so for two reasons. First, spatial variation is more pronounced for the former than the latter. Coffee-drinkers are more ubiquitous than coffee-growers; paper is consumed in almost every inhabited area of the world, but paper is manufactured in only a few spots; and although the consumption of cotton is well-nigh universal, cotton growing and cotton-textile production are carried on only in certain specific regions that can be clearly delimited. Second, there is much less information, scientifically analyzed, about consumption compared to the information dealing with production.

For our purposes, we can divide production efforts into two great categories— *subsistence* and *commercial*. In *subsistence* endeavors, each producer lives directly on what he produces. He bends all his efforts to meeting the immediate needs of himself and family and so has little left over for bartering or selling. He and the members of his family must provide the food they eat, the clothes they wear, the fuel that warms them, the dwelling that shelters them, the implements they use, and any items of culture they enjoy.

In *commercial* economies, by contrast, each producer generates a surplus of something that he can exchange for surpluses of other things others produce. Little of his effort goes into directly providing the food, clothing, fuel, and shelter his family needs.

The basic distinction between subsistence and commercial economies lies, then, in the source of satisfaction of economic needs. Obviously, there are variations in the degrees of either subsistence or commercial economies. Businessmen who live in city apartment houses are entirely dependent on other producers for every one of their economic needs. Primitive tropical tribesmen who avoid contact with outsiders provide themselves with everything they consume. But in between these two extremes are countless shadings—areas in which the economy is partly subsistence and partly commercial.

We shall confine our discussion to regions that are clearly either subsistence or commercial—or at least we shall confine our chapter headings to such activities. For now, in Part Two, we shall deal primarily with subsistence economies. Chapter 3 treats of primitive subsistence economies, while Chapter 4 deals with a more advanced activity—intensive subsistence cultivation.

*An Auca Indian village in Ecuador. The Aucas
are primitive gatherers who subsist simply on what they can pluck from jungle
and stream. (Courtesy Dan Derr-Maf; Magnum Photos.)*

THREE

On the subsistence level, man's economic efforts fall into two main categories: primitive and intensive (or advanced). Chapter 3 deals with endeavors in the first category: primitive gathering, primitive herding, and primitive cultivation. We shall investigate each according to our method of identifying locations, characteristics, and relationships.

Primitive Gathering

Primitive gathering, the lowest order of economic activity, is fading rapidly from the face of the earth, and is currently practised by only a few thousand people. Nevertheless, it still warrants a brief treatment in any survey of economic endeavors.

WHERE IS PRIMITIVE GATHERING LOCATED?

Primitive gathering persists in isolated pockets within two major realms: the very high and the very low latitudes (Figure 3-1, page 32). The high-latitude zone includes portions of northern Canada, northern Eurasia, and southern Chile. The low-latitude area consists of the territories of some Indian tribes dispersed through the Amazon Basin (Brazil, Peru, Ecuador, and Venezuela) along with a few stretches within tropical Africa, the northern fringe of Australia, the interior of New Guinea and Borneo, and even the interior of southeastern Asia (Burma, Thailand, and China).

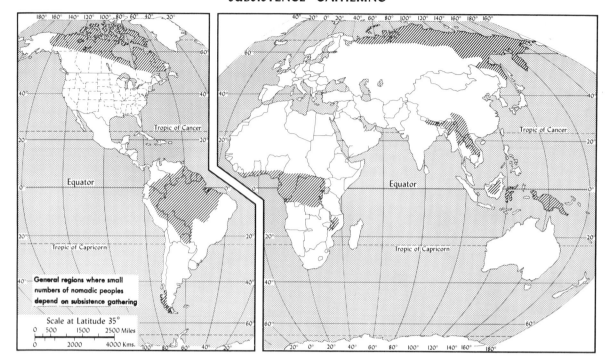

Figure 3-1

WHAT ARE THE CHARACTERISTICS OF PRIMITIVE GATHERING?

Primitive gathering is the oldest economy known, for it was by collecting items from nature's bounty that early man supported himself. Even today, in regions of primitive gathering, man collects fruits, nuts, and wood from trees, and gathers berries, roots, leaves, and fibers from shrubs and smaller plants. He hunts wild animals, preys upon wild birds, and snares fish. From all kinds of wild life, plant and animal, on land, in the air, and in the waters, he extracts enough to satisfy his needs for nourishment, shelter, warmth, clothing, and tools. He plants few seeds and spends little time cultivating the soil. He exerts no effort to breed, feed, or protect animals, nor does he try to control or improve their habitat. Of all economic endeavors, gathering requires the least amount of capital investment. Yields per acre and yields per man are so low that surpluses are virtually nonexistent.

Primitive gathering in the high latitudes is based almost entirely on animal life, especially caribou and musk ox from the land, seal, walrus, and salmon from the seas, birds from the air, and eggs snatched from nests. Typical of the peoples of this realm are the North American Eskimos, who have developed hunting into a fine art: They have become skillful in fashioning kayaks from skins and harpoons from bones and they display remarkable ingenuity in adapting animal products to satisfy all their physical needs. Farther south, in a few parts of Canada, occasional Indian tribes remain essentially at the gathering stage. These Indians are landsmen, whose main targets are deer; they themselves are sometimes called "people of the deer." The Yukaghirs of Siberia and the Yahgans of southern Chile are other high-latitude peoples who still subsist mainly on harvests of wild animals.

Primitive gatherers in the tropics utilize plant life as well as animal life; they collect fruits, roots, leaves, and wood. Fish also constitute an important part of their diet, especially on tropical islands of the Pacific. Typical primitive gatherers in the tropics are the Auca Indians of Ecuador, the bushmen of northern Australia, and the pygmies of the Congo. A fascinating description of one such group appears in the passage entitled "The Aucas" in Elizabeth Elliott's *Through Gates of Splendor.**

TO WHAT OTHER PHENOMENA IS PRIMITIVE GATHERING RELATED?

For this economic type we shall consider the third question of the geographic method in terms of physical and cultural relationships.

Physical Phenomena The physical environments in which primitive gatherers are located seem foreboding in many ways. In the *tropics*, the atmosphere is hot and humid, and vegetation grows profusely. This is the land of the *rainforest* where great trees tower into the sky, often with crowns spreading out 60 or 70 feet. The dense canopy shuts out the sunlight and cloaks the ground in semi-darkness. Since there is little in the way of browse, or ground-covering plants, this is a rather poor habitat for wildlife. Only on the fringes of the rainforest, where trees are shorter, smaller, and farther apart, and in the adjacent savannas (regions of tall, coarse grass) is there abundant animal life. The heavy precipitation of the rainforest, however, creates numerous rivers that are endowed with nutrients—a good habitat for fish.

In some other low-latitude regions of subsistence gathering the environment is exceedingly dry. For example, in central Australia the Bindibu tribe has lived for 10,000 years in a desert, surviving on drought-resistant plants and on animals dependent on the same type of vegetation.

In the *high latitudes*, primitive gathering is carried on in a physical environment of low average temperatures and short growing seasons. The barren land supports a meager growth termed *tundra* (mosses, lichens, and shrubs), which makes poor food for humans.

* (New York, 1957), pp. 96-120.

But tundra provides an adequate diet for caribou, musk ox, and deer, and these animals in turn furnish food to the human beings who range over these uninviting expanses in search of animal prey.

Cultural Phenomena Subsistence-economy cultures are backward. The people still live in the Stone Age, much like their ancestors of a hundred centuries ago. Indeed, some of them are not even that far advanced; the Charante and Camayura tribes in the wilds of Mato Grosso, western Brazil, do not yet have stone points for their arrows, according to Edward M. Weyer of the Museum of Anthropology at the University of California in Berkeley. Primitive gatherers lack written languages. Their health is generally poor; life expectancy is short. The Eskimos are probably the most advanced of all the gatherers, yet even they never domesticated a herd until they were taught to do so by Laplanders from Scandinavia.

Clearly, by our standards, their way of life has little to recommend it. Yet primitive gatherers can be credited with maintaining a fine balance between the supply and the harvest of animal resources, in sharp contrast to the performance of some members of more "advanced" economies who have seriously damaged such resources and have actually extinguished certain types of animals. Of course, we might argue that the poor health of these primitive peoples prevented them from becoming numerous enough to threaten their food supply. But when we realize that these peoples waste scarcely any part of the animals they capture—using skins for shelter, tendons for cord, bones for tools—we must recognize their conservation of natural resources. Primitive gatherers seem never to have destroyed their economic base by over-harvesting the food supply except where techniques or tools—such as firearms—were introduced from other cultures.

Gathering economies are associated with tribal societies in which individuals or single families rarely function as independent units, for the jobs of tracking down wild animals with primitive weapons and protecting the families against enemies are conducted more efficiently in groups.

The man-to-land ratio is extremely low in regions of subsistence gathering—in fact, there are only about two persons per square mile. But this figure in itself is almost meaningless, for a traveler can pass for miles through these regions without meeting a single person. Then he comes upon a small cluster or tribe before traveling on across more empty miles. Plainly that portion of the earth's surface on which primitive gathering appears supports a very small fraction of the earth's three billion inhabitants. (This raises an interesting question about the best way of indicating population on a map: Would it be more realistic to portray these regions, not by working out over-all averages of the total number of people divided by the total area, but rather by identifying areas that are altogether unpopulated and those that have some population?)

With no surplus production, there is little need for transportation or trading centers. Cities are absent in primitive-gathering regions, except as enclaves of other economic activities such as mining. Economic relationships with other regions are virtually nonexistent.

THE FUTURE

Occasionally, explorers discover a new tribe of primitive gatherers unknown to civilization. In 1956, Brazilian surveyors stumbled on to just such a tribe, the Xetas, in the rugged, jungle-tangled, almost inaccessible Serra dos Dourados mountains in the western part of Paraná, one of Brazil's southern states. How many more such tribes await discovery is open to speculation. In any case, the extent of gathering as an activity is decreasing as more and more tribes, in contact with outside cultures, begin to upgrade their means of livelihood.

Thus, primitive gathering, which once was widespread, once the prevailing economy of the inhabitants of Europe, Asia, Africa, North America, South America, and Australia, has steadily retreated in the face of advanced economies and now holds out only in isolated pockets.

It is indeed puzzling why these ancient peoples—the Eskimo, the Auca, the Xeta, and others of their type—have taken no step "upward" on the ladder of economic production, whereas other cultures of much later vintage have scurried up that ladder. The term "upward" is used advisedly, though, for some observers think that the Aucas and Eskimos will continue to inhabit the earth long after "civilized" man and his "higher" economies have disappeared, and that the economic activity of subsistence gathering will, at some future date, blanket all the populated portions of the earth as it once did, at the dawn of history.

Primitive Herding

Primitive herding is a step above primitive gathering in that men who live by it make at least some investment to enhance natural production. The product is animal, and the investment is labor—not just the labor required to extract from the natural supply, but the labor necessary to *increase* that supply.

The domestication of animals marks the step upward from animal gathering to primitive herding. Once this step has been taken, man begins to play a significant role in producing his commodities—that is, in bringing them to maturity—as well as in harvesting them. No longer is he merely a parasite living off the earth's bounty, for now he is making an investment of his own.

LOCATION

By the mid-twentieth century, man had occupied the earth in such a way that one vast area of primitive herding (see Figure 3-2) extended across northern Africa, all the way from the Atlantic shores eastward through Arabia, then deep into the heart of Asia, almost to the Pacific—a longitudinal extent of over 8000 miles. This is one-third the circumference of the earth! Latitudinally, the region extends from 5° south latitude (on the

Primitive Subsistence Activities

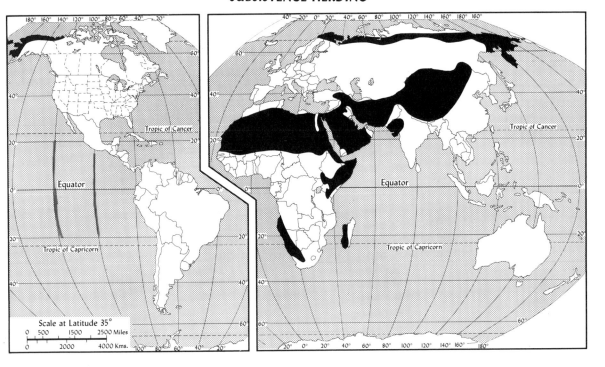

Figure 3-2

primitive herding *

east coast of Africa) to 50° north latitude (in inner Asia)—a range of over 3500 miles. This is the largest single economic region on earth.

A lesser region of primitive herding runs across northern Eurasia, reaching over into Alaska. In the Southern Hemisphere, too, there are small areas in Southwest Africa and Madagascar. Primitive herding is absent from Australia, South America, and most of North America.

A word of caution: The existence of the foregoing pattern does not mean that there are *no other types* of economic activity in the regions identified as primitive (or nomadic) herding, rather than primitive herding is the *predominant* form of employment activity there.

CHARACTERISTICS

The economic needs of the primitive herders are met by animals that feed on wild plants rather than on cultivated crops. The animals supply food (milk, cheese, and meat), materials for clothing (fibers and skins), shelter (skins), fuel (refuse), and tools (bones). The animals that have proved most satisfactory in these roles are sheep, goats, cattle, camels, yak, and deer. Horses are used in some areas, but they perform the special function of transporting the herdsmen as they tend their herds.

Primitive herding is a migratory undertaking, and these people are typically nomads. (Indeed, some scholars prefer *nomadic herding* over *primitive herding* as a label for this endeavor.) Their migrations are both horizontal (often hundreds of miles) and vertical (often thousands of feet.)

INTERNAL RELATIONSHIPS

We shall consider primitive herding in relation to several other phenomena, first, those *within* its regions and then those in *other* regions.

Regions of primitive herding invariably have rigorous physical environments, in terms of aridity and vegetation, and rather backward cultures; each of these topics merits comment in some detail.

Primitive Subsistence Activities

Aridity Most of these lands have a dry climate. In a dry climate annual precipitation is *less than* the annual evaporation, no matter how many inches of rain (or snow) fall. A place that gets 8 inches of rain has a *humid* climate if its annual evaporation is only 7 inches; a place with 16 inches of precipitation has a *dry* climate if its annual evaporation exceeds 16 inches. Thirst—and the search for water—are critical facts of life in these regions.

Vegetation Plant life reflects the amount of available moisture. In general, the earth's wetter lands tend to have forests, the drier lands grass. This generalization applies, of course, to *natural* vegetation undisturbed by human activity. The relationship between vegetation and amount of available moisture is suggested by Figure 3-3, in which the solid line represents variation in amount of moisture available and the sketches represent types of natural vegetation.

Most primitive herding occurs in the regions of shrubs, bunch grass, and short grass. Goats, which can endure considerable aridity, constitute the herds in the driest regions; sheep and camels predominate in regions with somewhat heavier rainfall. The moister fringes of these vast dry realms can support herds of cattle.

Not only the type but also the amount of natural vegetation is conditioned by the precipitation. The vegetative cover in these areas is extremely sparse, which means that the amount of food available for fodder is severely restricted. So the search for forage is never-ending. The herdsmen leave their animals in one place as long as possible until forage gives out; then they move on to some other place where a meager supply of water and grass suffices briefly—until the next move.

The unending migration of subsistence herdsmen and animals is, as was mentioned, both lateral and vertical. They must move hundreds of miles across the earth both because supplies at any given time in any one place are limited and because the rains come at different times in different areas. And since highlands tend to be wetter than lowlands, the nomadic herdsmen often move *up* to higher altitudes to find grass for their herds. Again, there are seasonal variations in the forage supply, the determining factor usually being

Figure 3-3

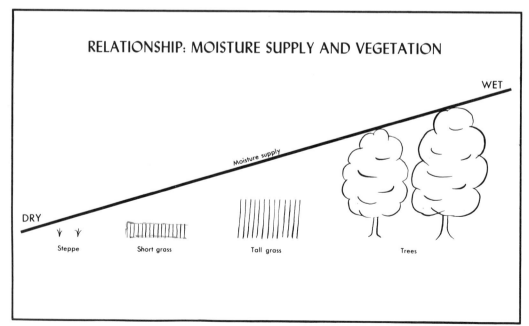

RELATIONSHIP: MOISTURE SUPPLY AND VEGETATION

WET

Moisture supply

DRY

Steppe   Short grass   Tall grass   Trees

temperature rather than precipitation. Herdsmen tend to winter in the lowlands and migrate upward to mountain pastures during the summer. As autumn approaches and the frosts begin, they drive their herds back to the lowlands.

Here is a vivid description of the arid setting and nomadic herding as carried on in Saudi Arabia.

On either side the land rolled away tan and light gold beneath the burning sun of May, with little more than thistles and stubbly grass rising seared above the sand. Over the land herds of camels wandered, sometimes in long single lines, with their awkward necks thrust ungainly forward and their bodies almost the color of the sand. Always the landscape was the same, beneath a sky milky with haze at the horizon, ranging to deeper blue at the zenith, and white puffballs of cloud drifting high. Once, far to the east, a range of sandy hills, carved in the most delicate pastel shades all based on brown, rose out of the sand. Flocks of black goats moved over the tan of the earth, and here and there a Bedouin's black goat hair tent was staked out upon a slope. This was nomad country, and the Bedouins filed past on their way to a new location.*

One might wonder why nomadic herdsmen do not set their sights on green pastures in humid regions, head straight for them, and stay there. Would not this move unshackle them forever from the need to roam? It would. But there seems to be a geographic law at work that subsistence herding quickly fades as a way of life in humid regions. Newly arrived nomads soon settle down, and economic metamorphosis sets in. Usually the change is from subsistence herding to subsistence cropping, or to commercial livestocking. Underlying this metamorphosis are various cultural forces, which will be considered in later chapters.

The physical environment is different in the primitive herding region of northern Eurasia. Precipitation is low but evaporation is lower resulting in humid climates. However, temperatures drop so low that cold climates prevail and the natural vegetation is tundra; there are no trees, just a few shrubs,

* Harry B. Ellis, in "Desert Road to Arabia," *The Christian Science Monitor*, August 13, 1955.

and only a little grass. Forage is scanty, like steppe and desert, but here the major handicap is cold, not aridity. Plants that withstand the climate of the tundra are no more palatable to man than are the shrubs of the deserts or the grass of the steppes. But certain animals—in this case, caribou and deer—can exist even on this meager vegetation, and in some parts of the tundra (for example, the Lapland area of Europe) man has learned the art of domesticating them. Where he has not, the economy persists at the level of primitive gathering.

Because of limited forage, the herds migrate —toward the pole in summer when the tundra plants germinate and mature, toward the equator in winter when the intense cold drives the plants into dormancy.

But the physical environment is only part of the story. There are other areas of the world that have an environment as meager in forage as that of North Africa and Central Asia, yet have little subsistence herding. Australia, southern South America, and western North America are conspicuous examples. If the natural environment were the determining factor on the economic activities of men, these places would also be regions of subsistence herding. Clearly, we cannot understand the geography of herding without investigating the *cultural* phenomena with which it is associated.

Antiquity of Cultures Without exception, subsistence herding occurs in areas of surviving ancient cultures. At some time in the distant past, an alert gatherer first conceived the idea of protecting wild animals (from predators) and helping them in their search for food and water. This introduction of domestication, one of the major cultural developments in man's history—a significant economic step forward—occurred long ago in southwestern Asia and northeastern Africa.

By contrast, dry regions that have been settled by peoples with more recently developed cultures are not areas of subsistence herding. Australia, South America, and North America were settled by peoples of European culture, which is of much more recent vintage

Nomad herdsmen of northern Africa assemble for a Morocco sheep festival. (*Courtesy U. S. Department of Agriculture*, Foreign Agriculture, *and the New York* Times.)

than that of the nomadic herders. And, as far as we know, the first European immigrants did not find nomadic herdsmen when they arrived in Australia and the Americas. They found gatherers. The conclusion seems to be that during the long period when man subsisted in the gathering stage he migrated from the starting point in southwestern Asia to each of several continents. Later, at that same starting point, he developed the idea of domesticating animals. Here we encounter an interesting question, whose answer is still obscure: Why did not this new idea of domesticating animals radiate outward to all the continents? Apparently it penetrated only into Asia, Africa, and Europe.

Low Man/Land Ratio

The relationship of numbers of people to land area is marked by a low ratio in regions of subsistence herding. Some of the great voids on the population map coincide with these areas. But this correlation is not reversible, for there are many population voids that do *not* have nomadic herding.

It is a basic principle that subsistence herding simply cannot sustain great numbers of people. This generalization leads to another, which will unfold fully later: The earth can support fewer people by means of animal food than it can by means of plant food. Acre for acre, a larger number of vegetarians than meat-eaters live on the land. This recalls one of the questions raised in Chapter 2: How many people can the earth feed? For one answer, it can feed about twice as many people if man is content with a vegetarian diet than if he insists on eating meat.

Tribal Settlements

There are no isolated herdsmen. The people cluster in clans or tribes, and their settlements are temporary in location. The flexibility demanded by a migratory economy of this sort has led to the development of a peculiar type of dwelling —usually the tent—which is easy to fold up

Primitive Subsistence Activities

and carry along. Some nomads live in huts that can be disassembled and loaded on the backs of camels, or else stored in tree tops when the dry season keeps the herders on the move day after day.

To be sure, the herding regions on the map do contain a few cities and towns, but these rest on some other economic base, such as mining, or else they are centers on trade routes that cut across the herding regions.

Tribal Spirit   Another cultural phenomenon is an intense *esprit de corps*—the fierce loyalty to the tribe. Some of these people are friendly to outsiders, but many of them are hostile—tough people, lean people, always hungry, always on the move, always searching for water and forage—as were their forefathers, who lived for millenia on these same barren plains and slopes. Success in their unceasing search for water and grass and their mutual protection depends on membership in a loyal, tightly knit group.

Political Boundaries   In recent years, the political boundaries that thread through these vast regions have involved the nomadic herders in some troublesome problems; even though, in some instances, the very existence of such man-defined boundaries was unknown to the herdsmen. In inner Asia, for example, tribes wander back and forth across the frontiers of Siberia, China, Afghanistan, and Iran, without thinking about leaving one "country" and entering another. The movement of Laplanders between Russia and Finland caused disputes between these governments. To which of these two nations do the nomads owe citizenship? Or are they men without a country?

EXTERNAL RELATIONSHIPS

Normally, there is little contact between the people in regions of primitive herding and those in other places. Since the herdsmen have no surplus to export, outsiders have no incentive to ship commodities to them. Moreover, some of the nomads feel a genuine aversion toward the rest of the world. Proud

of their ancient traditions and imbued with a fiery tribal spirit, they disdain other cultures. Nevertheless, they have experienced some contacts with the outside world. In some instances the herdsmen moved outward, and in other instances the outsiders penetrated nomadic herding regions.

Outward Movements of Subsistence Herders   Occasionally, during periods of starvation induced by unusually severe droughts, herdsmen have struck fiercely into neighboring areas. From the African Sahara they have raided southward into zones of primitive subsistence farming, and northward into more advanced agricultural regions. As far back as 1000 B.C., farmers along the Mediterranean coast of Asia were being attacked by nomadic tribes from the east. One such assault was described as follows:

> And so it was, when Israel had sown, that the Midianites came up, and the Amalekites came up, and the children of the east, even they came up and encamped against them and destroyed the crops in their fields as far as Gaza. They came up with their animals and their tents . . . and lay along the valley like grasshoppers for multitude, for they and their camels were without number, as the sand by the seaside for multitude. (*Judges* 6:2 and 7:12)

Similar outbursts marked the history of the European frontier. In the 5th century A.D., the Huns (nomads from eastern Asia) swept westward across Europe almost to the Atlantic. In 1242, Mongol nomads poured into the West again, annihilating every army that dared stand against them. And in 1529, the Turks, nomads from southwestern Asia, besieged the walls of Vienna. Often these invaders settled down in the regions they had penetrated, losing their identity in the indigenous population. The Huns, for example, never returned to Asia; they simply "disappeared" in the melting pot of Europe.

But not all out-movements of nomadic herdsmen are belligerent. Take, for example, the following relationship of Laplanders and Eskimo. For ages, the economy of the Eskimo in northwestern Alaska was based on *subsistence* hunting and fishing. Then, in the

1880's, the federal government of the United States arranged for the shipment into Alaska of a small herd of caribou from Lapland (the nomadic herding region of northern Europe). A few Lapps were persuaded to visit Alaska to teach the art of their husbandry to the Eskimo. The successful transplanting of this economic activity transformed the northwestern edge of North America from a primitive gathering area into a region of nomadic herding.

And on the margins of other nomadic herding areas there frequently occurs a process which might be termed "cultural osmosis" whereby some nomads quietly shed their herding habits, settle down at the edge of advanced agricultural areas (to be discussed in later chapters), and adopt agricultural techniques from their more progressive neighbors. Such migration is occurring in western Asia and in northern Africa, especially along the margins of the Nile Valley.

Inward Movements of Outsiders and Their Cultures
External relationships are discernible also in terms of movements of people and ideas from other regions into the herding realm. Since antiquity, trade routes have cut across the realms of nomadic herding from China to Europe, from India to Europe, from Central Africa to Northern Africa. The merchants traveling over these routes were simply passing *through* these regions; they had no interest in going *to* them, since the herdsmen had little to sell and little with which to buy. Countless times the nomads ambushed the traders, whom they regarded as interlopers at best and as competitors for precious water at worst, because the typical trade route was strung out from oasis to oasis across the desert.

Now not only transient traders but also settlers are moving into many of the nomadic herding regions from territories with higher economies. And they bring with them modern scientific methods: irrigation, drought-resistant strains of crops, healthier animals, and improved methods of handling them. In Africa, advanced agriculture is pushing its way south from the Mediterranean into Morocco,

Algeria, and Libya. In Central Asia the Chinese peasants have been pushing ever northward and westward, staking out farms on the shrinking margins of nomad country.

Settling the Nomads
Many nations containing nomad country have decided that the wanderers must be settled. The most vigorous programs are being undertaken by the Soviet Union and Iran. The Iranian government, for example, launched a program in the 1930's to induce Iran's 500 nomadic tribes (2,000,000 tribesmen) to stay put in permanent settlements. At first, these proud, independent people resisted stubbornly—almost violently. But the government helped them dig wells and construct irrigation systems and, in lean years, it augmented their food supply. The nomads' children are being educated in government schools, so the new generation may be willing to concede that permanent occupancy of the land is more desirable than following the flocks. Some Iranians even think that nomadism will vanish from their country within the next two generations.*

THE FUTURE

On maps of the world's economic regions, the areas of nomadic herding will probably shrink as nomads are assimilated along the margins. And even within their domain, some herdsmen are beginning to settle down themselves, often assisted or even coerced by national governments. In such places, an economic and social revolution is currently underway.

*Two interesting case studies of this phenomenon are Mohamed Awad's "The Assimilation of Nomads in Egypt," *Geographical Review* (1954), pp. 240-252, and Anthony D. Marshall's "Somalia: A. United Nations Experiment," *Focus* (April 1956), pp. 1-6. Both are excellent analyses of the developments, problems, and prospects of improving the economic life of primitive herdsmen. These articles go into such matters as the strategems employed by the governments of Egypt and the United Nations in Somalia to induce the migrants to settle down, the relative successes of these stratagems, the consequences of outside influence on the nomads, and the resulting impact on the rest of the nation in which they live.

Primitive Cultivation

From primitive gathering, some peoples have taken a step "upward" on the economic ladder by learning the art of domesticating plants, and their economy has moved into primitive cultivation. This activity encompasses large portions of the earth's surface and brings us for the first time to an economic endeavor that involves large numbers of people.

LOCATION

There are three broad regions of primitive cultivation (termed *rudimental cultivation* by some scholars) portrayed on Figure 3-4. The largest is in Central Africa; it straddles the Equator and abuts on the realm of nomadic herding. On the west, it fronts the Atlantic Ocean almost continuously for nearly 3000 miles. Eastward it reaches the Indian Ocean, though the frontage is less than on the Atlantic coast. A portion of Madagascar lies in this zone.

A second major region appears in the Western Hemisphere, embracing most of the Amazon Basin, all the way from the Atlantic coast to the Andes Mountains and from Bolivia to Venezuela. It leaps the Andes in Ecuador and Colombia to reach the Pacific coast and runs northward through Central America to southern Mexico. A good part of the West Indies is included.

The third major region lies in southeastern Asia and the adjacent off-shore islands, from Sumatra eastward through Borneo, New Guinea, New Hebrides, and numerous tropical islands of the Pacific. On the mainland of Asia, primitive cultivation tends to be absent along the coast and to be confined to the interior of Burma, Thailand, Cambodia, and adjacent portions of India and China.

Once again, of course, all other economic activities are not necessarily absent from the regions of primitive cultivation, for here and there are pockets of less advanced primitive gathering or of more advanced commercial gathering, mining, and so on. Nevertheless, the *prevailing* endeavor is primitive cultivation.

Figure 3-4

PRIMITIVE SUBSISTENCE FARMING

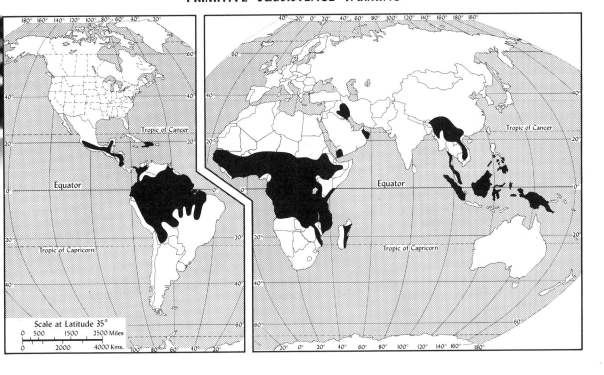

Scale at Latitude 35°
0   500   1500   2500 Miles
0   2000   4000 Kms.

This is a crop-based economy, the leading crops being corn (maize), millet, rice, manioc (the source of tapioca), yams, and sugar. The diet is heavy in carbohydrates, although some protein is provided by peanuts and beans. Tomatoes, cucumbers, and bananas are common adjuncts. There is some regional variation in the leading grain: maize in the Western Hemisphere, millet in Africa, and rice in the Far East.

For these farmers, fire plays a unique role in the clearing of land. Most of the trees and underbrush they hack out by means of primitive knives and then burn the cuttings, though sometimes they dispense with the cutting and let fire alone do the job of clearing. Accordingly, this primitive technique is often called _slash-and-burn_ farming. Methods of preparing the soil for planting are equally primitive. These people simply scratch the surface of the soil with sticks or crude hoes. Plows are almost unknown.

The farmers have scarcely any knowledge of soil science, and they return few nutrients to the soil by means of fertilizers. Erosion is severe, particularly on the slopes, since they usually leave crops untended until harvest time, and the harvest consists of plants that have managed to compete successfully with the weeds. Animals play only a minor role in these economies—all food produced is required to feed the people—but there are a few poultry and swine, which subsist on waste or what they can scavenge. Farm units are small and consist of a few tiny fields, often isolated from one another by patches of forest or brush. The aggregate of all these clearings makes up only a small proportion of the total area— mere droplets of cultivation sprinkled lightly on a sea of wild vegetation.

Three general subtypes of primitive cultivation are distinguishable in terms of permanence of settlement: shifting, semi-shifting, and sedentary. In _shifting_ cultivation, which is the most common type, the farmers abandon both their fields and their dwelling sites every three or four years and move on to fresh territories. In the _semi-shifting_ type, the farm dwellings remain fixed but the farmers change their fields throughout the environs, actually abandoning the fields, turning them back to wild vegetation after a few years of cropping. So at any given moment most of the area encompassing a settlement is in the wild—either having been cast away or waiting its turn for clearance. The most advanced variety is the _sedentary_ type in which the farmers shift neither their fields nor their dwellings but maintain the same dwellings and the same fields year after year. These farmers evidence a rudimentary soil science; they clear the soil, plant their seeds carefully, and husband and harvest the crops with some diligence so they need not move.

"Slash-and-burn" subsistence-cultivation plot recently cleared from the tropical rainforest (background). Standing and fallen tree trunks, partly burned, litter the clearing in which the main crops are yuca (manioc) and maize. Plantain (green cooking banana) trees are visible to the left of the house. The dwelling, one-and-a-half stories tall, is built of poles with mud stucco over part of the walls. Sheet metal roofing was supplied by the government. This picture was taken in 1957 in Venezuela, northeast of El Vigia and the Chama River at an altitude of about 300 feet. (Courtesy Henry Sterling; see Problemas Economicos y Sociales de los Andes Venezolanos, by him and others, Consejo de Bienestar Rural (Caracas), Vol. I, 1955, pp. 160-165.)

But in all three types, agricultural methods are primitive at best. No other form of cultivation has such low yields per acre and man.

Temperature Primitive cultivation generally occurs in areas that lack a cold season. Only in very high altitudes and on the poleward margins of the tropics is there threat of frost. On a map of climate (in any atlas) notice that there is a moderately strong correlation between the tropics and primitive cultivation.

Precipitation These regions are wet. No zone of primitive subsistence farming receives less than 20 inches of rainfall a year, most areas have over 60 inches, and some parts (the Amazon Basin, Indonesia, and a part of Central Africa) are drenched with 80 or more inches. A warm, moist environment explains, in part, why animals play such a small role in this economy. Meat spoils rapidly and must be eaten within a few hours of slaughter. Hence, small animals such as poultry are the most numerous.

Vegetation The regions of this endeavor tend to have one of the following types of flora—*tropical rainforest, lighter tropical forests, scrub and thorn forests,* or *savannas*—which reflect variation in precipitation from the wetter to the drier areas respectively (as a map of vegetation in any atlas demonstrates). Thus the first problem that confronts a primitive farmer is how to clear land that is either forested or overgrown with savanna. Handicapped by his primitive tools, he often finds it easier to fell a few large trees from a forested acre than to clear the same amount of savanna land of thousands of grass stalks, some of which are ten feet tall and exceedingly coarse. Ages ago, the people in these regions discovered that fire was a useful ally in clearing land of wild vegetation, and for years fire has supplemented hand-cutting operations. But the use of fire boomerangs by damaging the soil, as we shall now see.

Soil Most forest soils are deficient in plant nutrients. At least two factors are re-

sponsible for this condition: slow accumulation of *organic matter* and *leaching*. Organic matter (which consists of the remains of dead plants and animals—such as roots and earthworms) is an important source of nutrients to living plants. But trees do not return much organic matter to the soil. And although savannas tend to have somewhat better soils than rainforests, even they are less fertile than mid-latitude grasslands. Man compounds the problem by his use of fire, for organic matter is combustible and burns like peat. Thus, the fire that clears the surface simultaneously destroys a part of the soil's precious organic matter.

Leaching is the process by which ground water filtering downward robs the soil of nutrients. In order to be assimilated by plant roots, soil nutrients must be soluble—the very attribute that makes them so vulnerable to leaching. Steadily percolating downward, water robs the nutrients from the soil and carries them beneath the reach of the roots of crop plants. Rapid depletion of nutrients in naturally infertile soil is the basic reason why primitive farmers shift their cultivation. In many places they can grow satisfactory crops for only three or four consecutive years. Then they abandon the fields and wild vegetation quickly takes over. If the need for land is great enough, they may clear the plots again for the next cycle of cultivation in a few decades. Usually, though, 40 or 50 years must elapse before the soil has recovered.

Landforms Topography is related to several different aspects of primitive cultivation. For content of organic matter the best tropical soils are in the valleys, having been deposited there by surface run-off from adjacent slopes. But lowland farming frequently has two enormous handicaps: poor drainage and disease.

Lowlands in the humid tropics tend to be very wet. Swamps are numerous. Crops are in danger of drowning. Therefore, the farmers often choose hillside plots. But the hills have a severe disadvantage too, since exposing the raw soil of a rainforest slope to the heavy rainfall of the tropics results in erosion.

Lowlands are warmer than highlands, and in the tropics they furnish an ideal breeding ground for insects and other pests that not only are bothersome in themselves but also carry disease. Malaria, for instance, is prevalent throughout tropical lowlands. Sometimes a lowland village becomes so infested with insects and rats that it must be abandoned and burned to the ground.

Man/Land Ratio   Primitive cultivation supports more people than primitive gathering or primitive herding. Even so, the density scarcely exceeds two persons per square mile in South America, Borneo, and New Guinea, and 25 per square mile in Africa. But the ratio does vary considerably within each area, being most obviously correlated with altitude and type of cultivation. Thus, low population density tends to occur in lowlands, high density in highlands: note the contrast, for example, between the vast population void of the Amazon Lowland and the greater settlement of the Andes. In Equatorial Africa ratios exceeding 100 people per square mile coincide with the highlands of Ruanda-Urundi, Uganda, Ethiopia, and western Kenya. That most of South America's zone of primitive cultivation is lowland while most of Africa's is upland helps to explain, partially, why the population of equatorial Africa exceeds that of equatorial America (see front endpaper).

Man/land ratios also vary with type of cultivation. Where methods have been devised for better treatment of the soil and better techniques of cultivation, yields have increased to sustain a higher man/land ratio. The sedentary variety supports higher densities than does the semi-shifting type, which in turn supports more people per square mile than does the shifting kind. (This is not to say that all dense populations in the tropics correlate with sedentary primitive cultivation. As we shall see later, plantations, mines, and other complex economic activities support large numbers of people in the tropics.)

An Old Culture   Long ago primitive cultivators took a single step upward from primitive gathering and have remained at that level ever since. The farming techniques they use today have prevailed for thousands of years. Their living standards are low, and, for all the "time" they have had, most of them have not developed a written language. Again we encounter the puzzle of why these peoples have remained at this level. Why, after graduating from primitive gathering to primitive cultivation, did they not continue to advance up the economic ladder?

RELATIONSHIPS TO OTHER AREAS

Primitive cultivators, in contrast to primitive herders, initiate few contacts with peoples of other areas. More numerous are the contacts initiated by representatives of other regions: nomads, traders, plantation operators, immigrants, and political authorities.

Nomads   For centuries, primitive farms on the drier margins of the tropics have been subjected to sporadic depredations of hungry nomadic herdsmen, goaded by excessive droughts into adjoining areas where food was being produced by primitive cultivators.

Trade   Although subsistence farmers rarely have a surplus crop of their own cultivation, they can gather small amounts of nuts, gums, wax, spices, ivory, dyes, cinchona (for quinine), and rubber. If the farmers are located in villages that are accessible to the outside world (along navigable rivers), they can bolster their economy by selling these gathered items to traders. Where this occurs, the farmers need not keep shifting around because their economy no longer depends entirely on what is produced by cultivated patches of land. For this reason, the sedentary type of primitive farming frequently occurs along rivers while the *shifting* type occupies the interfluves (land between streams).

Plantations   In certain equatorial areas (to be studied in Chapter 12) promoters from Europe and Anglo-America have developed plantations, with large labor forces of native workers, that specialize in sugar cane, pineapples, rubber, or other plants native to the tropics. When prices are high for a plantation's crop, the demand usually exceeds the supply, and the primitive cultivators in the immediate vicinity often respond by growing a little of the crop. But the quality is inferior to that from plantations and is never in demand during periods of low prices and low demand. Since these primitive farmers adopt some of the superior plantation-type methods of tending crops, primitive cultivation near plantations is often *sedentary*.

Immigration   For several decades there has been a gradually increasing rate of migration from regions of intense population pressure in the mid-latitudes to the sparsely populated tropics. Thousands of Japanese are now in Brazil. There are a million Indians in tropical Africa. Thousands of Europeans have immigrated into Kenya, Ghana, and other present and former European colonies in Africa. But these immigrants were not lured by prospects for primitive cultivation, but by rich opportunities in plantations, commercial livestocking, mining, and trading.

Political Control   These immigrants made capital investments in docks, roads, warehouses, marketing facilities, and agricultural equipment. And since these investments had to be protected, the outsiders took steps to insure political stability. Before long, nations in distant regions, especially Europe, had established control over most of the primitive-cultivation realm. Spanish, Portuguese, French, Dutch, Italian, German, and British colonies soon covered the tropics from the Americas through Africa and the Far East. The U. S. controlled the Philippines.

This political penetration, following in the wake of the original economic penetration, has had severe repercussions. The markets of the outside world have benefited economically, of course, from the relationship. And the regions of primitive cultivation have derived such benefits as hospitals, schools, and roads. But the indigenous peoples bristle under outside political control, as was illustrated in the trouble the British settlers of Kenya had with the Mau Mau movement among the Kikuyu tribe, who are primitive cultivators.

After World War II, many of the foreign powers began to ease the political reins and to return control to the nationals, but some have been forcibly ejected through revolution. In 1946 the United States granted independence to the Philippines; French Indo-China has been replaced by Vietnam, Cambodia, and Laos. Malaya and Indonesia have been granted independence from Britain and the Netherlands. On the African scene, a remarkable number of nations have become independent, such as Ghana, Ivory Coast, Guinea, Nigeria, Cameroon, Gabon, and the two Congos.

The realm of primitive cultivation appears destined to shrink in the future, both as the indigenous peoples abandon it for more complex activities and as immigrants bring more advanced techniques into the tropics.

Suggested Readings

Awad, Mohamed, "The Assimilation of Nomads in Egypt," *Geographical Review*, 1954, pp. 240-252.

Brooke, Clarke, "The Rural Village in the Ethiopian Highlands," *Geographical Review*, 1959, pp. 58-75.

Clarke, John I., "Studies of Semi-Nomadism in North Africa," *Economic Geography*, 1959, pp. 95-108.

————, "Summer Nomadism in Tunisia," *Economic Geography*, 1955, pp. 157-167.

Davis, Charles M., "Fire as a Land-Use Tool in Northeastern Australia," *Geographical Review*, 1959, pp. 552-560.

Elbo, J. G., "Lapp Reindeer Movements Across the Frontiers of Northern Scandinavia," *The Polar Record*, 1952, pp. 348-358.

Fisk, Brad, "Dujaila: Iraq's Pilot Project for Land Settlement," *Economic Geography*, 1952, pp. 343-354.

Jones, Wellington D., and Whittlesey, Derwent, "Nomadic Pastoral Regions," *Economic Geography*, 1932, pp. 378-385.

Pelzer, Karl J., "The Shifting Cultivator," *Pioneer Settlement in the Asiatic Tropics*, New York, 1945, pp. 16-34.

————, "The Sedentary Cultivator," *ibid.*, pp. 43-78.

Platt, Robert S., "Six Farms in the Central Andes," *Geographical Review*, 1932, pp. 245-259.

Sterling, Henry S., *et al.*, *Problemas Economicas y Sociales de los Andes Venezolanos*, Consejo de Bienestar Rural, Caracas, Vol. I, 1955, pp. 160-165.

Whittlesey, Derwent, "Fixation of Shifting Cultivation," *Economic Geography*, 1937, pp. 139-154.

————, "Shifting Cultivation," *Economic Geography*, 1937, pp. 35-52.

In Indonesia, terraced paddy fields for rice creep down to valley bottoms and stretch over the interfluves. Trees occupy the steepest slopes. (Courtesy Embassy of Indonesia.)

FOUR

Of the world's three billion people, nearly one-third support themselves by intensive subsistence farming. From the standpoint of sheer numbers of people involved, this is the most important economic activity on earth.

The General Pattern

LOCATION

The principal region of intensive subsistence farming is the Far East, the bulk of it in China and India; Japan and Korea mark the eastern frontier of the realm. From Manchuria in the north, it stretches southward to blanket all of eastern China. At the widest point, it spreads from the East China Sea to the frontier of Tibet. Further south it thins rapidly to a narrow band that runs along the coast of Vietnam. Westward it covers most of Cambodia and Thailand, much of Burma, almost all of India, eastern Pakistan, and a good part of western Pakistan. Adjacent island territories that are included in this region are Taiwan, the northern parts of the Philippines, part of Sumatra, and Java. What we have then is a broad zone that covers 40 degrees of latitude and 80 degrees of longitude. It covers about twice as much land as the United States. Notice that this vast expanse of intensive subsistence farming is nearly cleft in two by a wedge of primitive subsistence farming that runs 1500 miles from inland Burma through Laos almost to the Vietnam coast.

Outside of the Far East the only intensive subsistence farming of any consequence shows up in the valleys of the Tigris and Euphrates rivers and of the Nile. It is absent from Europe, North America, South America, nearly all of Africa, western Asia, northern Asia, and Australia.

Intensive subsistence farming can be distinguished from other economic activities on several counts: crops grown, cropping methods, farm layout, the role of animals, and the role of fishing.

Heavy Emphasis on Crops Crops are substantially more important than animals in this farming economy. Of the various crops grown, grains are by far the most numerous. Of the grains, rice is the most widespread. Rice predominates in most of Japan, Korea, southern China, the coastal fringes of Vietnam and Burma, eastern India and a narrow belt along the western coast of India. The deltas of the Mekong, Menam, Irrawaddy, and Ganges rivers are particularly productive rice-growing lands. At least two reasons account for the widespread popularity of rice. First, it produces more food per acre than any other grain. For example, the world average yield per acre is 1600 pounds for rice, 1470 pounds for corn, and 1030 pounds for wheat. Second, because of its tightly fitting husk, the rice kernel keeps well in humid climates.

There are two kinds of rice—wet and dry. The more important by far is the *wet* (or *lowland* or *paddy*) type. This requires tremendous amounts of moisture, which often is provided through the careful irrigation of rice fields, which are known as *paddies.* Yields of wet rice are high, sometimes soaring to 3000 pounds per acre per year. *Dry* (or *upland*) rice will thrive on less water and can be grown in highland plots that would be difficult to irrigate. But upland rice yields considerably less per acre than does paddy rice.

Other grains predominate in areas unfit for rice culture. Wheat, barley, sorghum, and millet carry the dietary burden in northern China, Hokkaido, western India (except the coast), Pakistan, the Tigris and Euphrates valleys, and the Nile Valley. But rice and other grains are not the only food crops. Most farmers augment their cereal supply with beans, peas,

Figure 4-1

INTENSIVE SUBSISTENCE FARMING

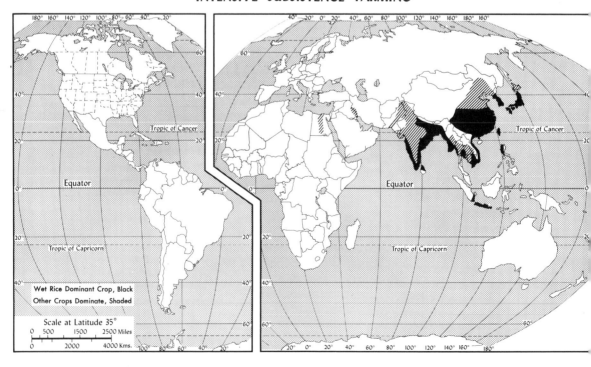

corn, peanuts, yams, sugar cane, melons, and a wide variety of vegetables and fruit. In addition to food crops, considerable cotton is grown, since cotton garments comprise most of the clothing of Asia's millions.

Cropping Methods Whatever the crop, the yields reflect a tremendous investment of human effort. Draft animals are used in some places, but farm machines are virtually unknown. Agricultural implements in fact are rather crude, for this is another realm of hoe culture.

Although their tools are primitive, these farmers display a remarkable understanding of the soil. Ages ago these Oriental farmers had devised ingenious schemes for conserving this precious resource. By terracing rough land, transporting baskets of eroded soil back to its starting place, draining swampy areas, irrigating subhumid land, and fertilizing every patch of ground that might conceivably be coaxed into productivity, these peasants transformed their treatment of the soil into a fine art. This is an endeavor that requires vast expenditures of muscle and sweat, and these are probably the hardest-working farmers on earth. Still, cropping methods differ considerably within this realm, being most intensive in Japan, moderately so in China, and only slightly so in India.

Two unusual methods are *interculture* and *multiple-cropping*. Interculture is the practice whereby two different crops grow together in the same field. Their plantings are timed so that as one crop matures the other is getting started. Multiple cropping is the technique of growing two successive crops on the same land per year; the first is harvested before the second is sown. Sometimes, if climate permits, rice is followed by rice; otherwise rice is grown in the summer and another grain in the winter. Where the environment is unusually favorable, three crops of rice can be harvested annually from one plot of ground.

With so many millions of farmers applying such intensive methods, rice has become the world's leading cereal (see Table 4-1). Although rice is cultivated to some extent in

Szechuan Province, southwest China. Reaping of rape seeds going on alongside transplanting of early rice. (*Eastfoto.*)

many other parts of the earth, the Far East generates nine-tenths of the total and stands unrivaled as the rice bowl of the world.

Nevertheless, in spite of such intensive cropping methods, the result is not an abundant

Table **4-1** *World Production of Leading Grains*

Grain	Total Metric Tons	Average Yield in Pounds per Acre
Rice	199,100,000	1,600
Corn	157,800,000	1,470
Wheat	157,500,000	1,030
Millets, Sorghums	72,300,000	590
Barley	69,100,000	1,110
Oats	53,800,000	1,240
Rye	19,900,000	1,220

Source: Computed from data in United Nations, *Yearbook of Food and Agricultural Statistics.*

surplus. The yields *per farmer* are low, just enough to meet his family's needs without much of a remainder for sale. Where yields *per acre* are high (as in Japan) the farms are small; where somewhat larger farms occur (as in India) the yields *per acre* are low. In either case, this intensive farming, generally, is a *subsistence* economic activity.

Farm Layout   Farms are small. In a few places they cover little more than an acre. In the lowlands of Japan the average farm is about three acres, China's farms are somewhat larger, and a few in India are as big as ten acres. In general, however, the rice farms of the Far East are the smallest farms on earth.

Still, although the individual farms are small, in the aggregate they cover an enormously high percentage of the usable land. In few other regions has the terrain been so completely modified by man's agricultural activities as in the Orient. Indeed, the natural flora was stripped away hundreds of years ago by the unceasing efforts of these vigorous farmers. Yet not *all* the land in these countries is blanketed by farms. In fact, only 12 per cent of Japan's land is arable, only 15 per cent of China's, and 45 per cent of India's. The point here is that where the environment is favorable, man has pressed into cultivation every square inch of land he could.

Tiny as these farms are, they are usually chopped up into several smaller plots separated from one another by intervening plots belonging to other farms. Rarely does a farm consist of contiguous fields. Notice in Figure 4-2 that the property of Farmer C is made up of 13 plots in seven different locations separated from one another by distances of from 1000 to 2000 feet. And farmer E has 19 plots clustered in eight separate groups. Such land pattern adds immeasurably to the already staggering burden of these farmers, for they must trudge many miles each year just to reach their fields. A major reason behind such fragmentation is the inheritance system by which a man's land is subdivided among his children who marry and acquire other land that may be widely separated from the first parcels.

Role of Animals   Animals have a subordinate role in this economy because less human food can be produced per acre if crops are fed to livestock than if the food is consumed directly by people. Plots of ground that are totally unfit for cropping may be left in pasture, but rarely is arable land devoted to the support of animals. Still,

Figure 4-2 (*After Clarence F. Jones and Gordon Darkenwald (from John L. Buck)*, Economic Geography, *p. 223, Macmillan, 1954.*)

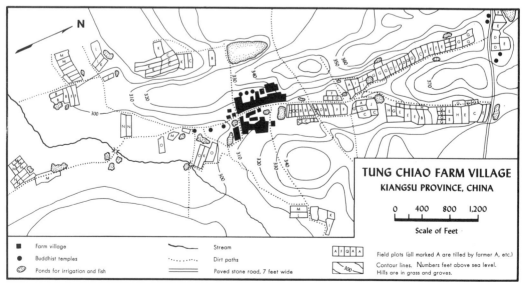

Intensive Subsistence Farming

certain domestic animals are maintained. Draft animals, particularly cattle, are fairly common. In hot and humid zones the water buffalo performs most of the heavy work. And in the hillier and cooler places, a few mules or asses are kept to help with the daily round of farming. Fortunately, draft animals can subsist on the by-products of food crops: straw, bran, and bean meal.

Certain other animals (swine, poultry, and goats) play an entirely different role. These are all small creatures that occupy little space and do not compete with crops for use of the land, for they do not require feeding but thrive as scavengers. The goat is an especially avid scavenger although chickens and swine produce a greater amount of human food from the waste and garbage they consume. Indeed, the hog has been dubbed by J. Russell Smith the world's best "animated, productive, and edible garbage can."

The function of these animals is twofold: to provide fertilizer for the soil and to provide what little meat and milk these people consume. Swine produce most of the fertilizer, although the excrement of poultry, goats, and cattle is also carefully collected. Understandably, meat is only a negligible component of the diet of these farmers, but they occasionally vary their fare by goat milk or by meat dishes of poultry, pork, or goat.

In China, Japan, or India nearly every farm has chickens and, in the lowlands, ducks and geese. Farms too small to afford cattle or an ox usually have at least some poultry and one hog. China alone has 87,000,000 hogs, one-fourth of the world total! (This seems to be a tremendous pork supply, but remember that China has 700,000,000 people.) India and Pakistan have 70,000,000 goats—21 per cent of the world total.

Role of Fishing   Since the land does not provide enough food for its millions of people, and since the crops it does yield are heavy with carbohydrates, many of these peoples resort to fishing both to augment the quantity of food and to increase the protein supply. Two practices are followed: *fish farming* and *fish gathering.*

Fish farming is characteristic in humid places with cool winters but warm summers; the paddies are planted to rice in one season and stocked with carp in the other. Like pigs in a pen, these carp are fed exclusively on garbage; they even rival pigs in their ability to convert waste into human food. Carp also perform the function of fertilizing paddy soil. In addition to these seasonal fish farms, swamps and ponds unfit for cropping are diked off to serve as permanent pens for carp. In inland China carp has for generations been the leading fish.

In the early 1950's the Thailand Ministry of Agriculture, in conjunction with the United States Mutual Security Agency and the United Nation's Food and Agriculture Organization, launched an experiment with *tilapia,* a fish that is native to Africa. The tilapia multiplies with incredible rapidity. In just one year, a single pair will produce progeny numbering 10,000. And it takes only four months for a fingerling to attain a weight of eight ounces, which makes a good meal. Moreover, at that age tilapia begin to reproduce and they continue to hatch 500 young fish every three months. These remarkably productive fish are no trouble to keep and they live well in either brackish water or fresh water, in tanks, ditches, canals, swamps, or rice paddies. They thrive on garbage and whatever small aquatic plants and animals they can find. The Thai government launched a campaign in 1953 to describe the merits of fish to its people. Illustrated pamphlets were distributed showing how to cultivate the fish; specimens were taken on tour; radio talks advertised the venture. King Phumiphot Aduldet stocked the fish in palace pools, and the Minister of Agriculture set up a big tank teeming with tilapia for free distribution to anyone willing to raise them. Tens of thousands of householders now have "pens" of tilapia, which are adding, at almost no cost, valuable protein to the Thai diet.

Fish gathering is practiced elsewhere, along rivers and the seacoast, where people augment their diet by gathering fish from the natural habitat. Some persons, in fact, have abandoned farming and gone into full-time fishing. Along the coasts of China and Japan the population pressure has become so intense that many people have literally been forced off the land and now reside on their boats. When these subsistence fishermen do come in to shore, they tie up their boats in tightly packed masses like cars in a New York City parking lot.

In order to understand why intensive subsistence farming occurs where it does, we must inquire into its geographic relationships. Let us begin with the *internal* ones.

INTERNAL RELATIONSHIPS

Temperature If this realm straddled the Equator, temperature would be rather uniform throughout it. But it does not straddle the Equator—it runs from 10° north latitude to 50° north latitude. This means that the southern areas of intensive subsistence agriculture are located in the tropics, where temperatures are always high—even in the coldest month the average temperature here is nearly 70°, frosts are unknown in the lowlands, and the growing season is uninterrupted from one end of the year to the other.

But the northern areas of this zone experience appreciably lower temperatures. In parts of Hokkaido, for example, the average temperature of the *warmest* month is only 63°, and during three months of the year the average is below freezing: February averages 22°. Hokkaido's temperatures are rather mild, being ameliorated by the encircling sea. On the mainland of Asia, though, the range is more extreme; Mukden, for example, in Manchuria averages a high of 77° in July but is exposed to five months of subfreezing temperatures: January's average is only 8° above zero.

Clearly, then, there is little homogeneity of temperature in the realm of intensive subsistence farming. And this pronounced spatial variation in temperature helps explain some of the agricultural characteristics that we have just observed. For instance, anywhere from four to six months are required to plant, cultivate, and harvest a single rice crop, and during this growing period an average temperature of 70° must prevail. Therefore, rice cannot be grown successfully in the northern parts of this region. The line that separates the territory which is warm enough for rice from that which is too cold for rice runs between Hokkaido and Honshu, bisects Korea, and splits China just north of the Yangtze Valley.

Because of regional variation in temperature, it is possible to distinguish three cropping zones. (1) A warm zone in the tropics permits rice to grow in both summer and winter, so at least two crops of rice can be grown every year on a parcel of land. The first is set out in the spring and harvested in July; after that harvest, the second, which is started beforehand in seedbeds, is transplanted to the main plots and is harvested in November. A few particularly favorable tropical sites can even generate *three* crops of rice every year from each field. (2) In somewhat cooler zones rice grows well only in the summer; however, winters are still mild enough to permit multiple cropping. Fields that grow rice in the summer are subsequently sown to wheat, millet, barley, beans, or some other hardy plant. Multiple cropping in both these zones helps explain why small farms can support entire families in the Far East. (3) The coolest areas prohibit rice even in summer and even the hardier crops in winter.

Moisture Supply Precipitation varies greatly within the area of intensive subsistence farming. Extremely heavy annual rainfall (over 80 inches) distinguishes southwestern India, the lower Ganges and Brahmaputra valleys, southern Burma, northern Luzon, and a portion of southern China. Yet some parts of this realm are very dry: The extreme northern areas of China receive less than 20 inches of rain, and the Hwang Ho Basin and western India less than 40.

These spatial variations in precipitation have great significance for the locational pattern of cropping practices, just as temperature variations do. Three zones can be observed on this basis, too. (1) The wettest zone, which gets over 80 inches, is devoted to *wet* rice. High yields of wet rice are maintained by intensive conservation of water, the farmers keeping their fields inundated for two or

Intensive Subsistence Farming

three months. Paddies are enclosed by dikes so that during the period of·maturation the rice plants can be engulfed with half a foot of water. To prevent stagnation, the water is kept moving slowly. (2) A drier zone, which receives between 50 and 80 inches, contains the lands given over to dry rice. Dry rice does not need to be inundated and can be sown like wheat. But it needs more rainfall than wheat. Since its yields per acre are lower than those of wet rice, it occupies a minority of the land. Indeed, in most countries of the Far East, wet rice occupies at least ten times as much acreage as does dry rice. (3) The driest zone of intensive subsistence farming receives less than 50 inches of annual rain, a figure of significance on two counts. For it is the *bottom* limit for rice culture and the *top* limit for wheat culture. Excessive moisture causes the wheat plant to produce straw instead of grain, and what grain there is shrivels before harvest and molds quickly thereafter. Moreover, in a humid climate the wheat plant is highly vulnerable to *wheat rust* and other fungus diseases. In this dry zone, barley and millet supplement wheat as the predominant grains.

Seasonal Precipitation   In the Far East, regardless of the annual amount of moisture in any one place, the striking fact is that most of it falls in the *summer* months. This is of particular significance for northern India and China for it means that the wettest season *coincides with* the hottest season, a coincidence that favors seed germination and plant growth; conversely, the dry season in northern India and China comes in winter, when the temperatures are too low for good plant growth. In-

deed, winters in northern China are too cold for any crops even if moisture were available In Table 4-2 we see an indication of the pronounced seasonal variation of rainfall at selected Far Eastern places. Compare these with the much more uniform rainfall distributions in selected American stations.

The explanation for the dry winters and wet summers of the Far East lies in the *monsoon wind system*. It tends to work this way: In winter the interior of Asia becomes very cold; high air pressures develop over the land, much higher than those over the warmer Pacific Ocean to the east and Indian Ocean to the south. Accordingly, winter winds blow *out* from the land mass. They contain very little moisture since they travel over no expanses of water before they reach the zone of intensive subsistence farming. But in summer the pressures and winds are reversed. Then the interior of Asia heats up, so that a vast area of low pressure develops, much lower than the pressures over the oceans. Therefore, summer winds blow *in* toward central Asia and are laden with moisture sucked up in their long glide over thousands of miles of ocean.

From year to year, the precipitation is comparatively reliable, with relatively slight variations from year to year. Occasionally, however, the summer monsoon fails to bring the usual heavy rains, and then the results are catastrophic. In some districts famine has devastated a third of the population in a single year.

Landforms   Intensive subsistence farmers prefer lowlands, but where population densities are high the lowlands simply cannot

Table 4-2   *Average Inches of Monthly Precipitation*

Place	J	F	M	A	M	J	J	A	S	O	N	D	Yearly Total
Calcutta, India	0.4	1.1	1.4	2.0	5.0	11.2	12.1	11.5	9.0	4.3	0.5	0.2	58.8
Rangoon, Burma	0.2	0.2	0.3	1.4	12.1	18.4	21.5	19.7	15.4	7.3	2.8	0.3	99.6
Wuhan, China	2.1	1.1	2.8	4.8	5.0	7.0	8.6	4.6	2.2	3.9	1.1	0.6	43.8
Mukden, Manchuria	0.2	0.3	0.8	1.1	2.2	3.4	6.3	6.1	3.3	1.6	1.0	0.2	26.5
Boston, Mass.	3.7	3.5	4.1	3.8	3.7	3.1	3.5	4.2	3.4	3.7	4.2	3.8	44.6
Chicago, Illinois	2.1	2.1	2.6	2.9	3.6	3.3	3.4	3.0	3.1	2.6	2.4	2.1	33.2
Mobile, Alabama	4.7	5.2	6.4	4.9	4.4	5.4	7.0	7.1	5.3	3.5	3.7	4.9	62.5

support the human load. Then the farms creep up the hillsides, in some places to as high as 2000 feet above sea level. There are certain identifiable relationships between landforms on the one hand and the types of crops grown and cropping methods employed on the other. Since wet rice must be inundated during a good part of the growing season, it must be cultivated on *flat land*. Valley bottoms provide the ideal topography for this crop, especially in areas where temperature and rainfall are high. Wet rice predominates even in valleys where the precipitation is too low, so long as irrigation is feasible. A common method is to impound water from the surrounding hills and to lead it down gradually under the in-

fluence of gravity to the rice paddies on the valley floor. When even this supply is inadequate, additional water can be pumped up from valley streams to the nearby paddies.

But the amount of flat land in this part of the world is quite limited. In fact, the only extensive areas of flat land are the deltas of the Ganges-Brahmaputra, Irrawaddy, Mekong, Yangtze, and Yellow rivers. The only flat plain that does not front on the sea is a small area 500 miles up the Yangtze Valley, though a few other areas, not quite as flat as the deltas, occur inland along several major rivers. Unfortunately, most of the land that is warm enough and wet enough for rice growing is in hill country. So the industrious

In the mountain province of Ifugao in northern Luzon (the Philippines), slopes that originally lay at angles as steep as 30 per cent are terraced for rice paddies. The most extensive area of terracing is in Banaue, Ifugao, where such converted slopes cover 100 square miles. Their retaining walls, placed end to end, would extend 14,000 miles. Construction on this project began as early as 2000 BC; today new terraces are continually added and old ones repaired. Work on these terraces has two important phases: First, the construction of the walls, by carving the mountain sides and building stone walls, piece by piece, with bare hands and primitive implements; second, the channeling and control of the flow of water, by diverting and regulating mountain streams higher up on the slopes. (Courtesy Philippine Travel Information Office.)

farmers of those hilly regions have revised the topography by constructing terraces—steps of flat paddies that march up and down the hillsides. Where the natural slopes are gentle only low dikes are needed to create broad paddy flats. But steeper slopes require higher dikes. In some places—northern Luzon, for example—the farmers have terraced slopes with nearly a 30 per cent incline (that is, 30 feet of vertical drop with every 100 feet of horizontal distance). There, the hillsides are tiered like bleacher seats and the height of the dikes measures a third of the width of the paddies themselves.

A prodigious amount of labor is required to remodel such natural landforms. First, the farmer must clear the land of all natural vegetation, then construct the dike and level off the paddy. At many points he has to tap streams that flow down the hillsides to lead off water to each tier of paddies. The dikes must be strong enough to withstand the gentle underground seeping of this water. Think of the catastrophe that would result if the higher dikes were to give way during a heavy downpour. The suddenly released mass of water would cascade down the hillside with accelerating momentum, completely demolishing the lower terraces. But the farmer's job is not done when he has completed the construction of his carefully engineered terraces, for the maintenance of the dikes requires constant attention.

Land that is too rough to terrace is devoted to dry rice if temperature and precipitation are favorable. Otherwise the rough land may be in wheat, millet, vegetables or other crops. Where land is too rough to crop it is left in pasture or woodland.

Soils   The soils of the Far East are moderately well endowed in soluble plant nutrients. They are richer than the leached soils of the tropics, but poorer than the grassland soils of the mid-latitudes. Erosion of hill slopes invariably carries off soluble materials and small particles of soil. Hard as these farmers try, it is impossible for them to prevent erosion completely. The materials picked up by the moving water are carried

along to the lowlands, where as the velocity of the water slackens, they are deposited on the valley floor as alluvium.

Rice plants will tolerate a variety of soils, but they prefer about two or three feet of alluvium deposited on a clay subsoil. This combination is propitious because alluvium usually is friable and permits the rootlets to penetrate and spread, while the impervious clay checks the downward movement of water. If the underlying soil were indefinitely pervious, of course, it would be almost impossible to keep the paddies flooded during the growing season. Such soil conditions help to explain the limited role of draft animals in this economy, for only the water buffalo can work belly-deep in the muddy alluvium of a rice paddy under a hot and humid sky.

Yet many parts of the world have an environment comparable to that just sketched out for the Far East, but they are not regions of intensive subsistence farming. We can understand the presence of this economic activity only as we look also at the cultural phenomena with which it is associated. Within the region of intensive subsistence farming the cultural environment is marked by a staggering man/land ratio, by cultural antiquity, by a distinctive understanding of soil, an unusual religious concept, a village pattern of settlement, and limited transportation.

Man/Land Ratios   In no other rural region on earth is the population density as great as here. On the alluvial soils of the lower Ganges Valley, for example, the density ranges between 1000 and 2250 per square mile, or from two to four people *per acre!* The pressure of such population is a major reason for the heavy emphasis on rice-growing and the intensive cropping of the soil. But population density varies from place to place within the Far East. For India as a whole there is 0.9 acre of arable land per person, for China the figure is 0.3 acre, and for Japan 0.1. The yields of rice per acre correlate inversely with these ratios: 3500 pounds in Japan, 2200 in China, 1000 in India.

With population so delicately balanced against food production, it is no wonder that famines have been so severe in this region—indeed, the worst in the world. The *minimum* daily food requirement for health is 2100 calories per person, yet the total quantity of food available in India, for instance, allows for only 1900 calories per person per day. In a sense, India is caught up in a perpetual famine. Were the population burden less severe, the lower yields resulting from an unusually dry year, or an unusually cool summer, or a season of violent floods, would be less catastrophic. But the trouble is that the number of people is so large that even the best harvests cannot feed everybody. Consequently, millions of these people never go to bed with a full stomach—even in good years. And the margin of production is so narrow, the line between life and death so thin, that in poor years millions starve to death. In this vein of thought, consider the world map of diet deficit on the back endpaper of this book.

Thus, for all their tremendous investment of labor, the people of this realm have insufficient food to nourish themselves. With little surplus production of any kind, a subsistence economy is all they can manage. If they had some other economic base from which to operate—mining, for example, or manufacturing, or even a surplus of forest products or fish—they could barter some of their output in exchange for more food, thereby reducing the pressure on their own land. Precisely such an attempt to broaden the economic base is behind the strategy of all political powers in these regions today, especially in Japan, India and China. Industrialization has already come (principally to Japan, and to a degree to China and India); nevertheless, all three still have a tremendous reliance on agriculture as their major economic activity.

The problem would be serious enough if the population figures remained constant. But they do not. The greatest *increments* in the world's population are occurring in the very regions that already bear the heaviest population burden. Since 1940 China's population has increased by an astonishing 200,000,000. And the increase is continuing unabated. India is now adding 50,000,000 to her population every decade. The *rate* of increase in India is not particularly high in itself—only 1.0 per cent a year. But with such tremendous numbers involved, even small percentage gains produce a dramatic increase in the demand for food supplies.

Cultural Antiquity Regions of intensive subsistence farming are among the oldest inhabited areas on earth. This type of agriculture has prevailed here for at least 4000 years, and over the centuries the peoples have developed advanced cultures. They had developed written languages and formal literatures when Europe and the Americas were still in a state of semi-barbarism, and philosophers in China and India were searching for the principles of religious and intellectual wisdom before Greece had stepped forth as a major power. It seems paradoxical, then, that such an ancient culture—so advanced in many respects and with such an "early start" on the rest of humanity—has not produced a more "advanced" economy as well. We wonder at an agricultural system that, after so many centuries, is still shackled by the same primitive implements that it used ages ago. After so long a time, why have these farmers failed to devise a "better" system? Is it that they have been too lacking in natural resources to produce metal hoes instead of sticks, metal blades instead of crude wooden plows? Is it that education has been traditionally reserved for the few? Until recently, 80 per cent of the people of India and China were illiterate. In any case, social science has yet to answer completely *why* the cultures of the Far East have remained at their economic levels.

Soil Science On one front, at least, these farmers, especially in Japan and China, have made noticeable advancements. Early in history they developed a remarkable understanding of soil science, an awareness of the simple fact that plants rob the soil of its nutrients and that man can help restore those nutrients to the soil. And so they recognized

Intensive Subsistence Farming

what is now known as *the manure cycle,* in which waste products from plants, animals, and human beings are ultimately returned to the soil.

The waste products are fed back in the form of *green manure* (plant tissues), *animal manure* (urine contains greater amounts of soluble potash, phosphorus, and nitrogen, and is preferred to feces, which contain largely insoluble matter), and *night soil* (human excreta).

The manure of draft animals is commonly reserved for the rice seed-bed.... Japanese farmers have discovered that the presence of fish in flooded rice paddies acts as a fertilizer and increases rice yields as much as 10 to 20 per cent. The use of night soil in China, Japan, and Korea has been so emphasized that the importance of animal manure has been overshadowed. Shen, for instance, estimates that night soil represents only one-fifth of the manure produced in China. Trewartha indicates that night soil comprises only one-third of the manure used in Japan. Throughout China large numbers of swine are kept as scavengers and manure-producers.... Farm manure provides only one-fourth of the fertilizer required on Japanese farms, and much of the so-called manure is actually compost, green manure crops, seaweed, ashes, and other farm refuse; fertilizers are in such short supply that even silkworm excrement is used.*

The art of fertilizing is more highly developed in Japan than in China, where in turn it is more advanced than in India.

Theology   Religious concepts have economic significance in explaining the role of animals in specific areas of intensive subsistence farming. In Japan and China, where relatively few people practice religions that forbid the consumption of meat,. the meat of scavengers is a welcome addition to the diet, even though the land shortage is too acute to permit livestocking. In India, however, the leading religions forbid the consumption of some or all meat. Approximately 85 per cent of India's people are Hindus. Although adherents of some of the numerous branches of that faith can eat no meat whatsoever, nearly all Hindus are permitted to eat fish

* Eugene Mather and John Fraser Hart, "The Geography of Manure," *Land Economics* (February 1956), page 35.

and goat; only a fourth of them, however, may partake of beef, and then only provided it meets certain rituals of slaughter. Moreover, since many Hindus consider animals to be the embodiment of former human souls, they are reluctant to kill animals or even to disturb them when they molest the crops. Hence, this amazing paradox in India: 200,-000,000 cattle and millions of hungry people. A tremendous meat supply goes untouched— left to die of old age. India and Pakistan also have millions of Moslems to whom pork is forbidden though goat is permitted. It is not surprising that these two countries have a fourth of the world's goats.

Village Pattern of Settlement   Intensive subsistence farming is associated with a system of *farm villages* whereby the rural millions occupy the land by grouping themselves in agglomerations of residences rather than dispersing in individual farm dwellings over the countryside. Some of these clusters contain only 250 people, but others contain 10,000. These farm villages are *not* primarily commercial centers; they are dormitory settlements from which the land workers commute every morning to their respective fields.

If we could fly over these settled areas, we would be impressed with a multitude of small villages dotting the landscape, surprisingly close to one another. Picture an intensively cultivated plain on which the average farm consists of two acres. Assume that the average family has five members, and that everyone lives in villages of no more than 1000 inhabitants. How far apart would the villages be? Let's work it out this way: With an average of two acres per farm, there would be 320 farms on *one* square mile. If each farm supported five people, one square mile would support 1600 people! And if all these people were clustered in villages of 1000 each, these settlements would be sprinkled over the plain at intervals of *less than* one linear mile!

This pattern of settlement is a cultural phenomenon generally unknown today in the United States. Figure 4-3 shows a portion of the North China Plain, 45 miles by 60 miles.

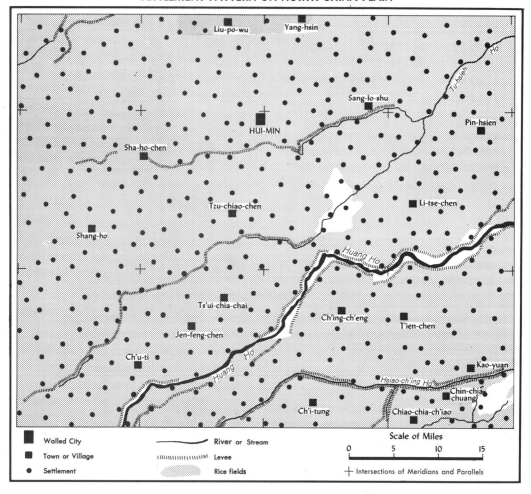

Figure 4-3

In this area there are nearly 400 farm villages and settlements. Contrast this with the pattern prevailing in agricultural regions of the United States, where the individual farmstead (that is, the buildings occupied by one farmer and his immediate family) is the distinctive form of land occupancy, where, in fact, farm villages are virtually nonexistent.

The Oriental farm-village system is fostered by two conditions—one economic and one sociological. The *economic factor* is the ever-present threat of hunger which helps weld each family into a cohesive production unit. In a subsistence economy where each family's daily ration must be wrested directly from the land the family works, mutual dependence among family members is bound to develop in order to get all the work accomplished.

The *sociological factor* is family loyalty. The philosophy of life of these peoples puts strong emphasis on reverence for deceased family members and on responsibility for the living. When children marry, the bride becomes a member of the groom's family and often moves into that family's abode. As son after son marries, the population of a household expands to the point where more houses are needed. Such a process, in time, transforms what was originally a one-family residence into a one-family village.

One of the most startling sociological revolutions in all human history has been launched

Intensive Subsistence Farming

by the Chinese Communists. Their aim is to destroy the family loyalty of the peasants, and replace it with loyalty to the state. They have retained the village pattern, but each village is no longer a family of workers who choose to abide there but a collection of laborers who have been assigned to it.

Transportation Intensive subsistence farming is generally associated with poorly developed transportation. This realm, for all its millions of people, has comparatively few railroads and surfaced roads. Footpaths and dirt roads predominate. The rivers serve as important thoroughfares, and the open sea is a "main street" over which much of the traffic moves. It may seem surprising that a region which supports such a mass of humanity should have so few transportation facilities. We might expect some sort of positive correlation between population density and transportation media. But this correlation does not always exist, as we shall see in subsequent chapters on transportation. In the region that we are exploring here, the basic reason for the lack of a highly developed system of transportation is that the economy is still in the subsistence stage. Little surplus for outbound shipments means little buying power for inbound purchases. Furthermore, since these farmers have little money with which to pay for commercial transportation, they travel by foot, by animal, or by boat. Even so, they take trips only rarely, for they can spare little time from their constant round of farming activities. Millions of them are born, grow up, marry, raise a family, and die without ever leaving their villages and fields. In short, since there is very little movement of freight, and even less movement of pas-

The countryside of rural Japan is dotted with numerous small agricultural villages (such as the ones in the upper left and far right background of this picture) surrounded by small, intensively cultivated plots of land. (Monkmeyer Press Photo Service.)

sengers, there has been no pressing need to develop elaborate transportation systems.

There are two notable exceptions to this generalization. The southeastern Asiatic peninsula (consisting of Burma, Thailand, Cambodia and Laos) *does* generate a small surplus of rice. Japan, China, and India have great deficiencies of rice. (One explanation for the contrast between these rice-surplus and rice-deficiency countries lies in the following ratios of number of arable acres per person: Japan 0.1, China 0.3, India 0.9; Burma 1.1, Cambodia 1.7, Laos 1.7.) These countries with rice surpluses, however, are short of textiles, of which Japan has a large, and India a small, surplus. Transportation has been set up to link these rice-surplus and rice-deficit areas.

The second exception is the island of Honshu where railway transportation is highly developed. The island is laced with a network of trackage over which electric trains run at high speeds and short intervals with probably the world's best record for punctuality. The explanation for the transport development is not to be found in the type of agricultural development in the rural countryside but in the high development of manufacturing and commerce in her cities. Japan is an anomaly in the world's economic geography in this contrast between an agriculture which is largely subsistence and an urban complex of manufacturing and trade which are considerably advanced. A basic reason for this is found in her relationships with other regions.

EXTERNAL RELATIONSHIPS

We can consider the relationships between the region of intensive subsistence farming and other geographic areas under three headings: international trade, political maneuvering, and migrations.

International Trade   The international trade of the Far East is small. China, with almost a quarter of the world's people, exports commodities worth little more than those of Switzerland, a nation with 5,000,000 people. India contributes little more than *half* as much export traffic as Belgium. Here is one of the most significant aspects of the world's

economic geography at the midpoint of the twentieth century: The world's two most populous countries generate only a small volume of international trade because they are essentially subsistence-farming regions.

Japan is an exception in this region, however, for she carries on a large amount of trade, the largest in Asia. For countless generations the Japanese subsisted on a rice-based economy similar to that of other parts of Asia. Then, a century ago, they launched into new activities that eventually brought them into the mainstream of world trade. Although they had no surplus of food to sell, they did produce a surplus of tea and silk. And with these commodities as a starter, they purchased modern machinery abroad and began to manufacture textiles—mainly from raw cotton imported from other areas. In one century they have advanced to the stage at which their subsistence agricultural economy has been overlaid by an industrial economy. Whereas 73 per cent of China's labor force and 71 per cent of India's is still in agriculture, Japan's proportion is down to 47 per cent. (Compare these figures with highly industrialized western nations; Germany 23 per cent, United States 12 per cent, United Kingdom 6 per cent). Present governments in China and India are endeavoring to duplicate Japan's achievement.

Political Maneuvering   At the moment, the most significant relationship between this realm and the rest of the world lies, perhaps, in the area of political ideologies. Since almost half of the world's inhabitants live here, many of the more advanced countries of the world are vitally concerned with the attitudes and ideas (political, religious, and economic) that these people will embrace as they move away from subsistence farming. We cannot escape the conclusion that the choices these people make will have a profound effect on every other part of the world. Consequently, the Western powers and the Soviet Union have engaged in a bitter struggle in their attempts to win over the minds of these Far Eastern peoples. No scholar of international relations and political ideologies can ignore the

Intensive Subsistence Farming

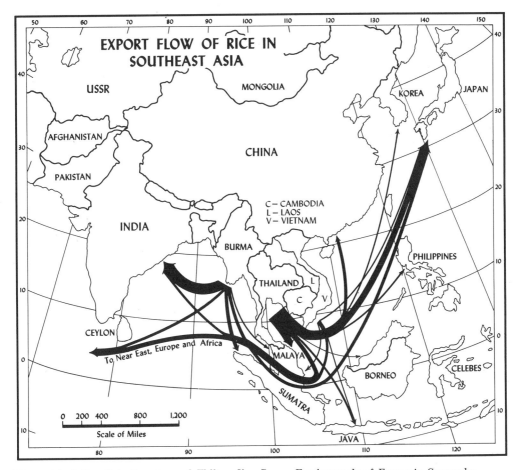

Figure 4-4 (*After Nels Bengston and William Van Royen*, Fundamentals of Economic Geography, *4th.* © *1956, Prentice-Hall.*)

dependence of most of the people of China and India and many other Far Eastern countries on intensive subsistence farming or the hunger that dogs them year after year in spite of their best efforts.

Population Migrations   One of the five major migrations of human beings in world history * has flowed out from China and India. Millions of Chinese and Indians have migrated from these hunger-ridden lands; they and their progeny now number over 13,000,000 and reside in many other parts of the world. Most of the migrants have headed toward the less densely settled countries of southeast Asia. Several hundred thousand others moved to Africa's eastern and southern territories and to the Americas.

India: A Case Study

We shall conclude this chapter with a closer look at India, a nation whose problems are intimately related to intensive subsistence farming, a country that is typical of the economic realm we have been discussing.

India has a population of 438,000,000—

* The other four major migrations in world history were (1) the 15,000,000 Negroes who were hauled from Africa to slave markets in the Americas; (2) a smaller number of Europeans who traveled southeast- ward to Africa, Australia and New Zealand; (3) approximately 18,000,000 Europeans who went to Latin America; and (4) 25,000,000 Europeans who migrated to the United States and Canada.

greater than that of the United States and the Soviet Union combined. Her population density is six times the world average. With an annual birth rate of 30 per 1,000 against a death rate of 20 per 1,000 her population is increasing at a rate of 1.0 per cent a year. Better medical facilities and the use of modern drugs have reduced the threat of epidemics and have effectively lowered the death rate. The birth rate, however, has remained fairly constant. Between 1940 and 1956 India added 71,000,000 people to her population total. Were this an industrial nation, such an increment might have been absorbed by manufacturing, commerce, and other urban economic activities. But India is still an agrarian country and this astonishing population increase has simply brought additional people onto the arable land which already was overcrowded. A third of India's people are now jammed onto 6 per cent of the land—the best land. Although 71 per cent of India's people are farmers, only 45 per cent of her land is suited for even marginal farming, and most of this would support less than 50 persons per square mile. Today, as we have seen, there is only 0.9 acre of cultivated land per person; 50 years ago there were 1.5 such acres. These two ratios provide dramatic evidence of the problem that is now facing this nation. In 1901, the area that is now known as India had a population of 235,000,000, of whom over three-fifths (146,-000,000) were farmers. The proportion has only increased to about seven-tenths. But today, India has 438,000,000 people, of whom almost 300,000,000 are living directly off the land! In short, here is a country where the pressure on the land, intense enough to begin with has steadily mounted as the number of farmers has increased, not only absolutely (by an astounding 150,000,000) but also proportionately to the national total. As India's population has skyrocketed over the years, her farmers have fallen deeper and deeper into debt, and there has been a tremendous increase in the number of landless farm laborers. In 1900, there were only 20,000,000; now there are 76,000,000!

Since this dramatic rise in population has not been accompanied by any substantial increase in the total amount of cultivated land, or in crop yield per acre, the food shortage has grown more acute every year. The quantity of food produced per capita each year slumped from 600 pounds in 1901 to 450 pounds in 1951. The threat of famine hovers constantly over large portions of the land, and most Indians struggle along on starvation rations. As we saw, the average diet provides only 1900 calories per day per person—200 calories below the *minimum* health requirement! And this is substandard in quality as well as in quantity, for, as we have seen, there is a dearth of meat and protein.

Professor George Kuriyan,* head of the Geography Department at the University of Madras, has studied this grave problem and outlined four possible solutions which are summarized below:

1. Concentrate on the growing of food crops that will yield more per acre than cereals do. Ten tons of cassava (tapioca) can be obtained from lands that now produce less than one ton of rice. At present India's consumption of cereals exceeds her production by 4,000,000 tons, a deficit that would necessitate an additional 10,000,000 acres planted in cereals to overcome. But if only 1,000,000 of the presently cultivated acres were switched from rice to cassava, the deficit would disappear. The main problem here, however, is that Indians have a strong preference for rice over tapioca. Probably nowhere in the world is a dietary habit more strongly entrenched than is rice-eating in the Far East.

2. Increase the amount of land under cultivation. In almost every part of India, the number of acres being cultivated today is the same as it was at the turn of the century, and in some places it has actually declined due to erosion. The trouble is that much of the land is either too dry, too wet, too infertile, or too rough, and the expense of correcting these deficiencies is too great for the Indian farmers to shoulder. Strong leadership and

* George Kuriyan, "India's Population Problem," *Focus*, American Geographical Society (October, 1954), pp. 1-6.

Intensive Subsistence Farming

an adequate supply of capital are needed to bring about the construction of facilities for irrigating, draining, terracing, and fertilizing the land.

3. Increase the yield per acre of crops already under cultivation. For a nation that has advanced above the level of primitive agriculture, yields *per acre* are notoriously low in India. Table 4-3 lists some statistics for India and other countries of the world for four major food crops and also for cotton, the leading fiber used in clothing.

Some people might suggest that the farms be mechanized. But mechanization brings about a higher yield *per worker*, not a higher yield *per acre*. Mechanization is a fine solution in regions where the supply of labor is limited and the amount of land is great. But the situation is just the reverse in India, which has a painfully limited supply of land, but an unlimited number of unoccupied workers. The main effect of mechanization would be to throw millions of farm laborers out of work.

Table **4-3** *Yields in Pounds per Acre in Selected Nations*

Country	Rice	Country	Wheat	Country	Corn	Country	Cane Sugar	Country	Cotton
Italy	4000	Germany	2400	U.S.A.	2100	Java	113	Egypt	495
Japan	3500	Egypt	1800	Egypt	1800	Egypt	70	U.S.A.	290
Egypt	3400	Japan	1500	Italy	1600	Japan	48	China	160
China	2200	Italy	1400	Germany	1550	U.S.A.	43	Java	115
U.S.A.	2200	U.S.A.	900	China	1200	India	35	Japan	105
Java	1400	China	900	Japan	1100			Italy	100
India	1100	India	550	Java	750			India	95
				India	600				

Notice that China and Japan are far more successful than India in enhancing crop yields through intensive cultivation. Indeed, India's yields per acre are even below those in many countries that practice "extensive" farming methods. One way of increasing these yields would be through better application of animal manure. And India has almost 200,000,000 cattle—nearly 170 per square mile. But the trouble here is that Indian peasants burn cow dung as a fuel, and if they were to divert it to use as fertilizer, some alternative source of cheap fuel would have to be devised. Large-scale use of artifical fertilizers is clearly out of the question, for the subsistence farmer has little money with which to buy them.

4. Increase the efficiency of the farms. In India they are fragmented into small, widely scattered plots burdened with impossible debts. Kuriyan suggests a scheme whereby each village would operate one cooperative farm consisting of all the cultivated parcels now being worked by individual peasants. This, of course, would require that the present owners pool their holdings.

Having studied all these possible courses of action, the Indian government at present is concentrating on an attempt to unlock more acres for cultivation by means of irrigation. Several multipurpose projects have been undertaken that will provide water for farming and electricity for industrial use. Some of these have already been completed and have added 16,000,000 new acres of farmland.

With assistance from the United States government, the Ford and Rockefeller Foundations, the International Monetary Fund, and the World Bank, the Indian government is also launching a campaign to educate its people in modern agricultural techniques and to upgrade the over-all economy of the country. India has 500,000 farm villages in which there are only 300,000 schools; four-fifths of the people are illiterate. The World Health Organization and the United Nations International Children's Emergency Fund are conducting programs to fight tuberculosis, malaria, and other diseases that have plagued the country for centuries. And, in an attempt to solve the acute population problem, Kuriyan points out, the government is "conducting experiments to find suitable methods for the introduction of birth control and planned parenthood. It seems abundantly clear that unless there is a planned policy in this respect, the population will continue to increase too fast."

This has been a long chapter. But in it we have been exploring an economic activity that supports *almost half of the people of the world*. For most of the world's people are still farmers, and most of those farmers are still operating at the intensive subsistence level.

Suggested Readings

Ahmad, Nafis, "The Pattern of Rural Settlement in East Pakistan," *Geographical Review*, 1956, pp. 388-398.

Anderson, Elna, "Millet Provides Food for Millions," *Foreign Agriculture*, 1948, pp. 235-239.

Burt, Arthur L., *et al.*, "Santo Domingo de los Colorados—A New Pioneer Zone in Ecuador," *Economic Geography*, 1960, pp. 221-231.

de Castro, Josué, *The Geography of Hunger*, Boston, 1952, 337 pp.

Clyde, William, "The Rice Problem in Eastern Asia," *Geographical Magazine*, 1951, pp. 11-21.

Dobby, E. H. G., "The North Kedah Plain—A Study in the Environment of Pioneering for Rice Cultivation," *Economic Geography*, 1951, pp. 287-320.

Engebretson, T. O., "Agriculture and Land Tenure in India," *Foreign Agriculture*, 1951, pp. 262-267.

Eyre, John D., "Japanese Inter-Prefectural Rice Movements," *Economic Geography*, 1962, pp. 78-86.

——, "Water Controls in a Japanese Irrigation System," *Geographical Review*, 1955, pp. 197-216.

Farmer, B. H., *Pioneer Peasant Colonization in Ceylon: A Study in Asian Agrarian Problems*, London, 1957, 387 pp.

Firth, Raymond, "The Peasantry of Southeast Asia," *International Affairs*, 1950, pp. 503-514.

Gamble, Sidney D., "Four Hundred Chinese Farms," *Far Eastern Quarterly*, 1945, pp. 341-366.

Grist, D. H., *Rice*, London, 1953, 331 pp.

Hall, Robert B., Jr., "Hand-Tractors in Japanese Paddy Fields," *Economic Geography*, 1958, pp. 312-320.

Jen, Mei-Ngo, "Agricultural Landscape of Southeastern Asia,"

Economic Geography, 1948, pp. 157-169.

Ladejinsky, W. I., "Japan's Land Reform," *Foreign Agriculture*, 1951, pp. 187-190.

Lebon, J. H. G., "The New Irrigation Era in Iraq," *Economic Geography*, 1955, pp. 47-59.

Patel, Ahmed Mohammed and Shamsi, Farid-Uddin, "Dansmari Village: A Study in Land Use," *The Oriental Geographer*, July, 1961, pp. 121-136.

Phillips, Ralph W., "Livestock in the Lives of the Chinese," *Scientific Monthly*, 1945, pp. 269-285.

Russell, Sir John, "Food Production Problems in India," *International Affairs*, 1952, pp. 15-28.

Thirumalai, S., *Post-War Agricultural Problems and Policies in India*, New York, 1954, 280 pp.

Trewartha, Glenn T., "Land Reform and Land Reclamation in Japan," *Geographical Review*, 1950. pp. 376-396.

PART THREE

There are several distinguishing characteristics by which we can recognize a region of commercial economic activity: surpluses, specialization, transportation and trade, and services.

Where commercial economy prevails each individual produces a *surplus* of something above the needs of himself and of his dependents. In a subsistence economy, where each family performs the roles of farmer, fisherman, hunter, miner, and manufacturer, there is likely to be no surplus—or a very small one at best. But when a family's breadwinner concentrates on one of these roles and becomes a full-time farmer or fisherman or miner or manufacturer, the usual result is an immediate surplus—more of some commodity than the family can consume.

A region of commercial economy is also characterized by a division of labor whereby everyone *specializes* in turning out goods for which he is best suited. As the economy of a region tends more and more toward commercialism, producers intensify their specialization and produce larger quantities of fewer items. Thus, there is specialization in *agriculture* when farmers stop trying to grow a little bit each of several crops in favor of concentrating on the most salable items, becoming wheat farmers, vegetable farmers, fruit growers, and dairymen. Frequently there is comparable specialization in the other forms of primary production: *fishing, forestry,* and *mining.* Specialization appears also in secondary production, or *manufacturing,* as some manufacturers narrow their lines: Tool makers, say, concentrate on hand tools or on power tools, or on metal-working machines. The result is greatly increased surpluses.

But the existence of a surplus in a region usually means that there is a deficiency in that region of something else, because energies are being directed toward the surplus commodities. The inevitable result is an exchange of commodities: The surpluses go out and the goods that are in short supply come in. This exchange requires and gives rise to *transportation and trade.*

With a still further intensification of commercialism, an entirely new type of production arises—commercial *services.* Now we find specialists who concentrate not on producing or handling goods but on meeting personal needs. Physicians, teachers, entertainers, clergymen, government officials, stenographers, lawyers, repairmen, household help: All exemplify the service type.

In light of the foregoing ideas, we can make the following generalizations about the stages through which any region's economy will progress. As yet, we have insufficient evidence to prove these generalizations—they are still only hypotheses—but they provide matter for stimulating speculation.

1. The lower the level of commercial development in a region, the higher the proportion of its people who are engaged in *agriculture, fishing,* and *forestry.*

2. As the degree of commercialism in a region begins to increase, the proportion of people engaged in those three activities tends to shrink, the proportion engaged in *trade and transportation* to rise.

3. As a region continues to advance up the ladder of commercialism, it reaches a third stage, at which *manufacturing* is the most rapidly expanding endeavor. Indeed, manufacturing may eventually claim more workers than any other activity.

4. With further commercial development, the most rapid rate of growth obtains in *services,* which ultimately take over as the leading endeavor in the region's economy.

As you read through the following chapters, and as you become more alert to the economic life of the world you will find considerable evidence in support of these hypotheses.

From now on, our attention will be focused on regions where the economy is geared to commercial endeavors. First, we shall turn to the harvesting of biotic and mineral resources: In Part Three we shall deal with commercial gathering of plants and animals, in Part Four with commercial agriculture, and in Part Five with mining. Then, Part Six is devoted to activities in which the form of products is altered (manufacturing), Part Seven to activities in which the location and ownership of economic items are changed (transportation and trade), and Part Eight to *services.* The accompanying diagram on page 68 suggests the framework in which we shall be considering these topics.

Gathering, in our usage, refers to the harvesting of natural, uncultivated resources whether for subsistence or commercial objectives. From wild plants, from wild animals, or from the earth's crust, man extracts the commodities he needs. Nature produces the entire supply; man's only role is to collect it.

Commercial gathering is the term used if the primary objective of collecting is sale. In certain regions the product is animal life, as we shall see in Chapter 5, in others, it is plant life, as we shall see in Chapter 6.

MAJOR CATEGORIES OF ECONOMIC ACTIVITIES

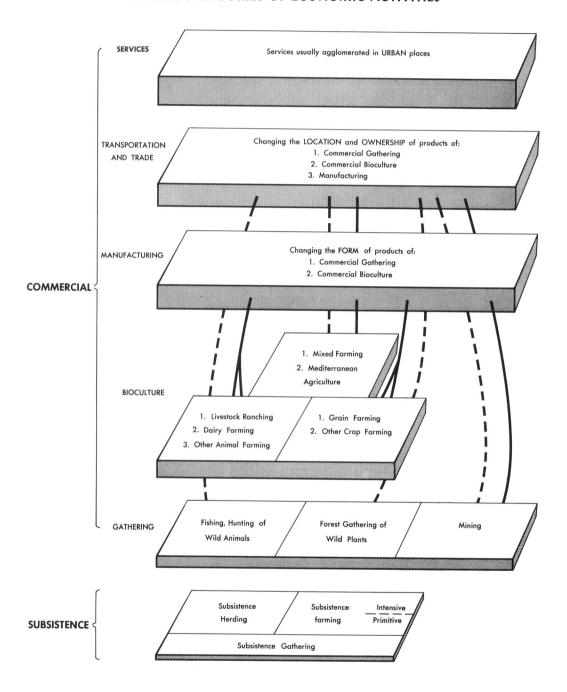

COMMERCIAL GATHERING OF WILD ANIMALS

*Japanese fishermen hauling in a catch. Numerous small boats
such as these operate from large fishing ships, returning to them with each boatload
of fish. (Courtesy Information Office, Consulate General of Japan.)*

FIVE

Men gather substantial surpluses of animal products from both land and water by hunting and fishing. The latter is by far the more important, so the bulk of this chapter will be devoted to it.

Commercial Hunting

Commercial hunting is rapidly fading away, generally giving way to ranching and animal farming. A good illustration of this change is what happened in the Great Plains of North America over the last few centuries. Until the arrival of white men, the Indians carried on a subsistence economy based on the hunting of buffalo, which supplied them with meat, skins, and bones for tools. Then, with the white man's demand for buffalo robes and the introduction of firearms, hunters went swarming over the Plains, ruthlessly slaughtering the great herds, and subsistence hunting gave way to commercial hunting. Today only a few buffalo are left—in reservations, parks, and zoos. The Great Plains still support millions of animals—but now they are sheep, cattle, and horses raised on commercial ranches and farms.

The smaller animals of North America, such as the fox, and raccoon, were at first hunted on the subsistence level. This activity too has been replaced by commercial hunting. Even so, comparatively few men earn their living by commercial gathering of these animals.

Historically, commercial hunting played an important role in launching the economic development of many regions, for instance, the interior of North America. Two centuries before the signing of the Declaration of Independence, French, British, and Spanish fur trappers were working through the St. Lawrence Valley, the Mississippi Valley, and the Great Lakes area. Because furs were extremely valuable and relatively small in bulk, they could be profitably transported even from sparsely settled hunting grounds far from populous centers. By establishing isolated fur-trading posts, these trappers and hunters took the first step toward developing a commercial economy. Many such posts later became sizeable cities (for example, Detroit and Green Bay). Even today, fur-trading posts persist in northern Canada and Alaska, where trapping remains as the sole economic base of many small communities. Trapping lines radiate from these communities much as fishing fleets radiate from coastal villages. Elsewhere in Anglo-America, the only notable remaining hunting region is the lower Mississippi Valley, where muskrat harvests bring in an appreciable amount of money to trappers.

The progress of commercial economy has been similar in the far reaches of the Soviet Union, where fur trappers have led the way for settlers from the Urals to the Pacific. Even today, fur-trading posts are scattered throughout eastern Siberia, northern Manchuria, and Mongolia; the U.S.S.R. is now the world's leading source of wild fur.

Commercial hunting probably will remain a prominent endeavor in many areas unsuitable for agriculture. But as soon as land is cleared of trees for farms, or as soon as grasslands are occupied by ranches, commercial hunting quickly fades in importance.

Commercial Fishing

LOCATION

Now that we have swung over to commercial economies, we have access to more complete data than those available for subsistence economies. So we can now construct meaningful maps: Figure 5-1, page 72, for instance, shows which countries front on waters that abound in large-scale fishing activity. (For convenience we shall apply the term "fishing" to the harvest of all water creatures, whether fish, mollusks, or mammals.) And we can compile meaningful tables: Table 5-1 shows which countries lead in fishing activity. Japan and China are conspicuously in the forefront, ranking far ahead of the United

Table **5-1** *Fish Catches by Areas and Leading Nations, in Thousands of Metric Tons*

Area	Amount	Area	Amount	Area	Amount
WORLD	37,730	*Europe*	7,890	*North America*	4,050
Asia	16,060	Norway	1,598	United States	2,796
Japan	6,192	Spain	935	Canada	928
China	5,020	United Kingdom	923	Mexico	190
India	1,159	Germany, West	674		
Indonesia	753	France	596	*South America*	4,320
Philippines	476	Iceland	592	Peru	3,531
Korea	342	Denmark	581	Chile	339
Pakistan	304	Portugal	475	Brazil	243
Taiwan	259	Netherlands	314	Argentina	100
Thailand	220	Sweden	254		
Malaya	167	Italy	212	*Africa*	2,230
		Poland	183	Union of South Africa	579
				South West Africa	319
		Soviet Union	3,050	Angola	252
				Morocco	154
				Congo	153
				Australia	62

Source: United Nations, Food and Agriculture Organization, *Yearbook of Fishery Statistics*, 1960, Table A-4.

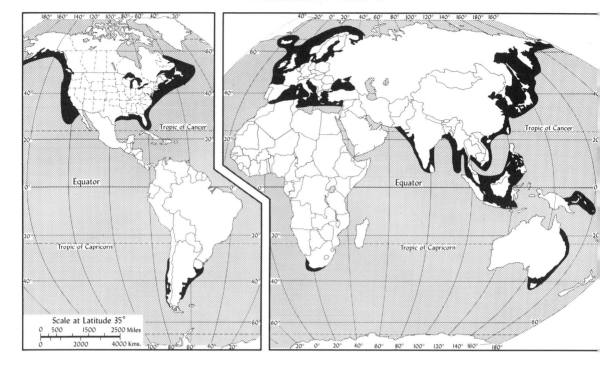

Figure 5-1

States and the Soviet Union. Notice that nearly all the leading nations are situated in the middle latitudes of the Northern Hemisphere. We shall see why below.

Fishermen from these nations range near and far in search of fish. Four-fifths of their catch comes from the ocean, one-fifth from rivers and inland seas.

Ocean Fishing Ocean fishing is a prominent economic activity in four regions. (1) The foremost area is in the northwestern Pacific, extending from Kamchatka to India, enveloping Japan, and following the China coast. (2) Almost as important is the northeastern Atlantic Ocean and adjacent waters of the Arctic Ocean. An arm reaches northward around Norway to the Barents Sea and the shores of the Soviet Union. Southward it envelops the British Isles and touches Spain. Westward it encircles Iceland. (3) Considerably less important is a fishing zone in the northwestern Atlantic running from Labrador

and Newfoundland, down along the coasts of Nova Scotia and the United States, to the Gulf of Mexico. (4) Another region, in the northeast Pacific, swings in an arc from Alaska to California. Over 3,000,000 fishermen derive their livelihood from these four principal regions.

Other fishing areas of less importance occupy the Mediterranean Sea, the waters between Asia and Australia, and the coastal shallows of open sea bordering most other land masses.

For the United States, the principal fishing areas and the leading states are given in Table 5-2. Our leading fish, by weight, is menhaden—responsible for over 40 per cent of all fishing tonnage. But by value, shrimp, tuna, and salmon are the principal products (Table 5-3).

Inland Fishing Commercial fishing is also carried on in inland waters throughout the world, particularly in the Great Lakes and Mississippi River, and in the inland seas of southeastern Europe (especially the Black and the Caspian) and their tributary rivers (the Danube, Don, Dnieper, Dniester and Volga).

Table 5-2 *United States Fisheries*

Place	Value of Catch in Millions of Dollars	Quantity of Catch in Millions of Pounds
United States Total	$346.0	5,121
LEADING AREAS, 1959		
Atlantic	146.3	2,752
New England	66.2	933
Middle Atlantic	22.8	760
Chesapeake Bay	38.4	589
South Atlantic	18.9	469
Pacific	104.2	1,055
Gulf	77.6	1,155
Mississippi River System	7.6	77
Great Lakes	7.1	65
Hawaii	3.2	16
LEADING STATES, 1959		
California	47.4	524
Massachusetts	40.8	537
Alaska	28.7	323
Texas	26.2	211
Louisiana	25.8	556
Virginia	25.7	526
Florida	23.2	212
Washington	21.5	155

Source: United States Department of Interior, Fish and Wildlife Service, *Fishery Statistics of the United States*, 1959, Statistical Digest No. 51, pp. 12-25.

Table 5-3 *Leading Species of Fish in United States*

Species	Value, 1959, Millions of Dollars	Quantity, 1959, Millions of Pounds	Record Year	Record Quantity, Millions of Pounds
Shrimp	58.1	240	1954	268
Tuna	37.4	285	1950	391
Salmon	35.7	201	1936	790
Oysters	29.4	64	1908	152
Menhaden	26.2	2,202	1959	2,202
Crabs	14.8	174	1959	174
Lobsters	14.4	29	1889	30
Flounders	12.6	121	1948	138
Scallops	11.8	24	1959	24
Clams	11.5	44	1959	44
Haddock	10.9	112	1929	293

Source: United States Department of Interior, Fish and Wildlife Service, *Fishery Statistics of the United States*, 1959, Statistical Digest No. 51, pp. 12-25.

CHARACTERISTICS OF THE FISHING INDUSTRY

Although approximately 3,000,000 men make their living at it, fishing does not rank high in world economy, though it contributes a good deal in a few countries. Thus, Japan has the largest number of fishermen, but Iceland has the highest proportion of labor force, 20 per cent, engaged at least part-time in fishing. Neither is the *quantity* of fish caught so very large—the world's total of 37,000,000 tons is scarcely half the weight of milk produced on United States farms—and by *value*, the world's total fish catch is not much greater than that of eggs produced in the United States. Yet in Iceland and parts of Japan, China, and Indonesia fish is a major component in the diet.

Since fish migrate through their extensive feeding areas and, in the course of a year, may traverse thousands of miles, commercial fishing is mainly a seasonal endeavor. Where market prices are high enough, fishermen may find it profitable to pursue their prey over these vast distances. Otherwise, though, they wait until the schools return to waters closer to home. Depending on local condition and circumstance, some crews put out from port each morning and return in the evening of the same day, while others spend weeks or months at sea.

Equipment Most commercial fishing these days is a corporate affair; the lone commercial fisherman is rare. Fishing fleets are highly modernized. They even employ electronic sounding devices (adapted from naval sounding equipment used to track submarines in World War II) that reveal the direction, distance, rate of movement, and size of great schools of fish. Occasionally experts can even identify types of fish from electronic reports. The fleets also are streamlined in numerous other ways.

Commercial fishermen use craft that vary all the way from primitive boats run by manpower and sail to modern machine-driven vessels. Steam was first used in fishing vessels during the 1880's, and gasoline and diesel internal combustion engines appeared 50 years later. Today, steam and diesel ships make up most of the world's commercial fishing fleets, although sailing vessels persist in all regions. The Norwegian fleet is the most modern in the world; of its 25,000 vessels, 20,000 are powered either by steam or gasoline. The other European fleets are also highly modernized, though not to so high a degree. The Japanese and Russian fleets still consist largely of sailing vessels, although mechanical power is rapidly coming into use.

Over the years a variety of ingenious nets has been devised for different depths, types of ocean bottom, and types of fish. Bulk catches are snared in *purse nets*, which are looped around whole schools of fish and then drawn in, like a cowboy's lasso around a steer. Another technique is to float a *trawl line*, several hundred feet long, from which hang hundreds of vertical lines carrying hooks. *Trawl nets*, or *drags*, are cone-shaped nets towed behind powered vessels called *trawlers*. Some fish, however, such as tuna, are caught by rod, line, and hook; other sea creatures such as lobsters, are trapped in crates.

Some modern fishing boats are fitted with refrigeration equipment to preserve the catch until it is brought in to port. The most complex of these are the Japanese *floating canneries* and the European whaling ships. Some years ago, Japanese fishermen began to roam so far to the east in search of salmon (almost to the shores of North America) that the cost of transporting and preserving their catch over the 5000-mile voyage home proved excessive. Moreover, the time required for the return trip was wasted. To combat both problems, the Japanese designed special ships fitted out with canning equipment so that the fishermen could spend the return trip in preparing the fish for market.

Modern whaling ships are also equipped to serve as floating factories. The largest fishing vessels ever built (some of them weigh 20,000 tons), they are specially designed so that whales can be towed aboard across the stern and then cut up on deck. The ship itself is a combination slaughter house, packing plant, and refrigerator. Every bit of the whale is put to some use, and no scrap is thrown overboard.

Species   Of the thousands of species of animals that dwell in the waters of the world, only a few are significant to man—few overall, and very few in any one region. Consider this breakdown. Off northwest Europe lie the world's best cod-fishing grounds; the catch there is augmented by masses of herring and haddock. In the Mediterranean, the most valuable economic items are sardine, eel, and sprat. Off Greece, the commercial fishermen concentrate mainly on sponges, in the Black Sea, Caspian Sea, and tributary rivers, on sturgeon. Off eastern Asia, the main commercial creatures are cod, herring, salmon, and crab. From the northwest Atlantic the biggest catches are haddock, rosefish, flounder, and cod. Menhaden and shrimp constitute the major catches in the Gulf of Mexico, except for sponges in the waters right off Florida. In the northeast Pacific, we find the world's leading salmon and halibut grounds, along with a good supply of sardines. And from California to the Equator, the waters are rich in tuna. No more than four types are important in any one region, and there is a great deal of duplication among regions.

The distribution of sea creatures in the main fishing regions follows a latitudinal pattern. In the northern waters, for example, we find abundant supplies of cod, herring, mackerel, haddock, sole, and pilchards, all of which are scarce or absent in the waters to the south. And in the lower latitudes we find menhaden and sponges, which are relatively thinly represented in the higher latitudes. Originally whale, at least, swam in all the seas, but they have been virtually exterminated except in the Antarctic Ocean and adjacent waters of the Pacific and Atlantic.

Transplantings   Occasionally man has succeeded in transplanting sea life from one region to another. For one notable instance, a successful oyster industry in Puget Sound and the mouth of the Columbia River in the northwestern United States has been built up with oysters introduced from Japan.

PHYSICAL RELATIONSHIPS

In nature, all these regions are typified by shallow, cool, mixed waters, by nearness to continental runoff, indented shorelines, and forests, and by periodic exposure to storms, fog, and icebergs.

Shallow Waters The profile of the ocean bottom consists of three recognizable sections: (1) The part that drops gently away from dry land is known as the *continental shelf*. The width of shelf varies considerably. Off the western United States, for instance, the shelf is very narrow, rarely reaching out as far as 20 miles. Off our Atlantic Coast, however, it is much wider,

extending as far as 150 miles from shore. (2) The shelf ends in a precipitous stretch called the *continental slope;* the average depth at which the one gives way to the other is 450 feet, although off some coasts it occurs as deep as 1200 feet. (3) The slope plunges sharply to an average depth of 12,000 feet before leveling off in the third section, the *abyss*. Scarcely any commercial fishing is carried on in the waters of the abyss or the continental slopes, for reasons to be seen in a moment. Instead, the fishermen draw most of their catch from the relatively shallow waters of the continental shelves.

Sealife is concentrated over the continental shelves because that is where the most abundant food supply is. This is so because of the *biotic pyramid* which prevails in the ocean just as it does on land. Since animals cannot manufacture their own food, they must consume either plants or other animals that sub-

Shallow waters encircling the Lofoten Islands off the coast of Norway constitute one of the world's foremost fishing areas. The cod season there takes place during the spawning season (February-April). Over 4000 Norwegian boats and 25,000 fishermen participate. (Courtesy Norwegian Information Service.)

sist on plants. Thus, plants provide the foundation of the biotic pyramid. In the ocean, tiny plants, such as the *diatoms,* drift through the surface waters like fine dust; indeed, a cupful of water may contain millions of these minute organisms. These sea vegetables extract nutrients in the form of dissolved minerals and organic matter from the sea water and, in the presence of sunlight, convert them into substances that can be assimilated by animals. Those that feed directly off the diatoms and other unicellular flora are minute animals such as protozoa, crustacea (for example, small crabs and barnacles) sea worms, and tiny fish. In turn, larger carnivores feast off the grazers.

Neither the microscopic plants nor the microscopic animals can propel themselves through the water. Since they move only when they are borne along by currents and other water movements, they are known collectively as *plankton,* derived from a Greek word meaning "wandering." *Phytoplankton* are the plants, *zooplankton* the animals.

Plankton supply the complete diet of many fish, such as herring, menhaden, and mackerel. Carnivores—like bluefish, tuna, shark and some of the large jellyfish—in turn prey on the plankton-eaters. Not all the large sea animals live off smaller fish, however; certain whales, for example, live entirely on plankton.

Each type of fish tends to concentrate in the waters where its favorite food is most abundant. That is why we find some species in warm waters, others in cold; some in clear waters, others in turbid; some in waters rich in phosphates, others in waters rich in silicates.

There is one condition, however, that seems to be essential to almost every kind of fish, and that is *shallow water.* One reason is that the penetration of sunlight, which is required by all plants for photosynthesis, diminishes as the depth of the water increases. In fact, below 600 feet so little sunlight penetrates that few plants can live. In most waters, the limit is 200 feet. But sunlight alone is not enough to insure abundant plant and animal life. After all, the surface water in the middle of the oceans receives as much sunlight as

does the water over the continental shelves, and yet the mid-ocean waters are normally poorer in plankton. Apparently, something more than sunlight is needed.

A second reason is access to plant nutrients (such as the remains of dead sea life) which tend to drift downward and accumulate on the ocean floor. In the abyss such nutrients are beyond the reach of sunlight. But on the shelf they collect in shallows where plants can utilize them in photosynthesis.

Thus, the most propitious environment for sea vegetables is in shallow waters, and these prevail either just offshore or else farther from the continents above elevated portions of the shelves known as *banks.*

Most offshore (or coastal) shallows are in the Northern Hemisphere. (Off the coast of Africa in the Southern Hemisphere there is virtually no continental shelf, and the ledges around South America and Australia are very narrow.) The shallows encircling Iceland, the Faeroe Islands, the Lofoten Islands, and other margins of northwestern Europe provide that region with 300,000 square miles of excellent fishing grounds. Off the coasts of eastern Asia we find approximately 100,000 square miles of shallow water. There is about an equal extent off the coast along the northwestern Atlantic.

As for the banks, some are enormous. The Dogger Bank in the North Sea (Figure 5-2), for instance, covers nearly 20,000 square miles, and over this whole extent the depth of the water ranges from only 40 to 100 feet.* In the western Atlantic several banks are dispersed along a zone 1100 miles long and from 50 to 250 miles wide that runs from Newfoundland to Massachusetts (Figure 5-3). In this part of the world the largest bank is Grand Bank, which covers 37,000 square miles, much of it lying less than 300 feet beneath the surface. Georges Bank, which covers 8500 square miles, is at no point more

---

* Apparently this great bank once protruded as an Island. North Sea fishermen trawling over the Dogger Bank have dragged up pieces of trees, animal bones, and flint heads used by hunters in tracking game. It appears that the Dogger Bank once supported an economy in which man preyed on land animals as he now preys there on the fish of the sea.

Commercial Gathering of Wild Animals

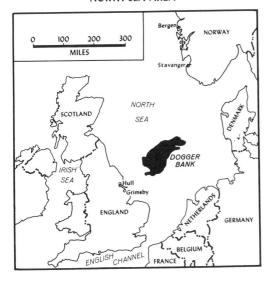

Figure 5-2

brought in by river waters. Through erosion the land loses such resources to the rivers, but those losses provide nourishment for the plants and creatures of the sea. Obviously these dissolved nutrients are most abundant in water that is adjacent to the land from which the dissolved substances have been carried.

Mixed Waters   Food for sea plants at the base of the biotic pyramid is most abundant in *mixed* waters. The reason is that mineral and organic matter in the sea—which consists of material eroded from the continents, and the shells, skeletons, and other remains of sea organisms—drifts slowly toward the bottom. But, since most of the plant and animal life that needs these nutrients is restricted, by the plants' need for sunlight, to water near the surface, they could better survive if this organic and mineral matter were somehow churned upward once again. This mixing action takes place in the following three ways.

1. Convectional mixing: In the higher latitudes the winter is severe enough to lower the temperature of surface water almost to the freezing point. As water becomes cooler,

than 100 feet below the surface, and in a few places it lies under only 20 feet of water.

Continental Run-Off   Much of the dissolved minerals and organic matter (nutrients for the one-celled plants) in the ocean is

Figure 5-3   (*After Clarence Jones and Gordon Darkenwald*, Economic Geography, *Macmillan, 1954.*)

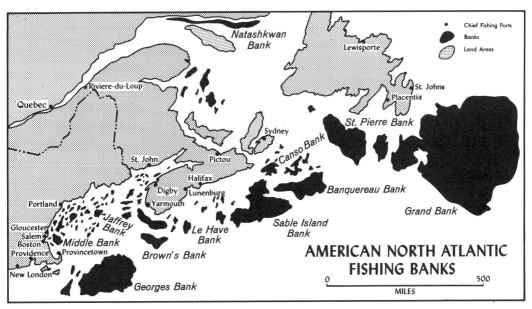

its density *increases* (reaching its greatest density at 39° Fahrenheit) and it "sinks," thereby churning up water from the depths. But this process does not go on indefinitely, for when water is cooled below that critical temperature (39° F. for fresh water, somewhat lower for salt water, depending on salinity) its density *decreases*. As the water approaches the freezing point and gets lighter, it floats upward to the surface. With the approach of springtime, the temperature of surface water rises; if the winter temperatures have been below the critical point, the warming water sinks once more, again churning up water from below. This vertical movement of water under the influence of temperature changes is known as convectional mixing.

2. Conflict of currents: Where a cold-water current encounters a warm-water one, the warm usually glides over the cool, driving it downward to churn up the mineral-laden water at the lower depths. Fortunately for commercial fishermen, the areas in which cool and warm currents meet are located along the coastlines in latitudes from 40° to 70°; it so happens that these are the very areas in which convectional mixing is also most effective. The most significant interactions are those between the Labrador Current and the Gulf Stream in the northwest Atlantic and between the Kamchatka Current and the Japanese Current in the northwest Pacific.

3. Upwelling: Another phenomenon that helps replenish the surface layers with nutrients from the ocean basement is known as *upwelling*. This action develops when surface currents swing away from the land masses, leaving a "vacuum" which is filled by water rushing in from the depths. The most vigorous upwellings are caused by the California Current, the Humboldt Current, and the Benguela Current, which benefit the coastal fisheries of, respectively, California, Peru and Chile, and South Africa.

Cool Waters   Average sea temperatures vary from a high of 96° in the Persian Gulf to 28° in polar waters. Sea creatures are much more abundant in polar seas than the Persian Gulf. As a rule, cool waters yield far more commercial fish than do warm waters. Why is this so? In the first place, fish from warm-water habitats have a high oil content which makes them unpalatable to most people. In the second place, warm waters contain less plant food because of the presence of water-borne denitrifying bacteria that destroy organic material.

A characteristic of cool-water fish which makes them susceptible to large-scale fishing is that they tend to cluster together and move about in *schools*. Why the fish of the mid-latitudes exhibit this tendency more than the fish of the tropics is a question that awaits an answer from ichthyologists. The significance of this *schooling* tendency for us is that fishermen can specialize in one kind of fish—cod, for example. The point is, their production costs are lower than when they have to handle different types of equipment for different kinds of fish, and they also save on marketing costs by selling boat loads of one fish rather than small amounts of several species.

Indented Shorelines   An area characterized by the foregoing physical characteristics, *plus* an irregular, indented shoreline, would provide an ideal natural setting for commercial fishing. The reason is simple: The abundance of good harbors along an indented shoreline makes it easy to develop the port facilities that are essential for commercial fishing.

Forests   By coincidence, the best ocean fishing grounds adjoin land that is to a large extent well forested. The forests, of course, historically facilitated the construction of ships. Even with the advent of steel for ship construction, though, wood is still needed for dories and other small boats, for fuel to smoke fish, and for the making of barrels, boxes, and crates for marketing the catch.

Physical Disadvantages   All the physical conditions we have considered so far expedite commercial harvests of fish. But the environment in fishing regions is not completely favorable to this business. There are three definite physical handicaps: storms, fogs, and icebergs.

According to meteorologists, cyclonic storm tracks that cross North America converge over the Atlantic where cool and warm air masses converge. Thus, the fishing regions of the northwest Atlantic (off New England and Newfoundland) are plagued by rough seas and stormy weather associated with cyclonic storms. The same conditions exist in the northwest Pacific fishing grounds, where the storms converge in their movement from eastern Asia.

Over oceans, cyclonic storms usually suck in warm moist air from their sides toward the equator; and when a mass of warm moist sea air glides over a cool ocean current, condensation occurs, and countless droplets of water fill the atmosphere. Consequently, the foggiest seas coincide with the major fishing regions.

In the northwest Atlantic the southward-moving Labrador Current often carries great masses of ice that have broken away from the glacier fronts of Greenland. Spring thaws unlock these monsters and send tremendous blocks of ice slipping into the sea to drift southward across the shipping lanes and into the fishing grounds. The worst months for icebergs are April through July.

MARKET FACTORS

The commercial harvesting of fish is closely related to several aspects of cultural environment, especially market factors, international relations, and problems resulting from man's activities.

The demand for fish depends on such factors as population density, dietary habits, the inability of agriculture to provide adequate diets, market price of fish, and use of fish by-products in industry. Meeting the demand involves some unusual marketing procedures.

Population Density   If you compare the front endpaper (map of world population) and Figure 5-1, you will see that three of the four principal regions of commercial

fishing are located near dense populations. Of the world's four most heavily populated areas, only India is not adjacent to a major commercial fishing realm; conversely, of the four major fishing regions, only the northeast Pacific does not border a major population region.

Dietary Habits   In some areas strong cultural forces foster the consumption of fish. One of these forces derives from religious practices. In southern Europe, for example, the population is predominantly Catholic. Here the people eat no meat on Fridays and on many other holy days. But they do eat fish. And there are enough of them to constitute an enormous market for fish not only from the Mediterranean and mid-Atlantic, but also from the North Sea and the Norwegian coastal waters. Similarly, in the Far East, most adherents of Hinduism and Islam are prohibited from eating the meat of at least some, if not all, land animals; but most of them can eat fish. Fish is a big item in the diet of millions of Indians, Pakistani, and Burmese.

Limited Agriculture   A scarcity of arable land is a strong factor in driving men to the sea in search of a livelihood. Notice the low proportion of arable acres per person in the following countries, all of which have large relative numbers of fishermen: Norway 0.5, Iceland 0.02, the United Kingdom 0.3, and Japan 0.1. It is scarcely surprising, then, that the Japanese consume more fish than the people of any other country—60 pounds per capita every year—and that the Scandinavians rank second. Alaska, British Columbia, Maine, Nova Scotia, Newfoundland, and Scotland are other areas where fishermen have been encouraged by an environment which is rather inhospitable for agriculture.

In some places, men work one season as farmers and another season as fishermen. Norway, for instance, has 115,000 fishermen. of whom 80,000 go to sea in February for the cod runs, return to their farms in the summer, and then go to sea for herring runs in October and November. Similarly in Iceland, where virtually all her 15,000 fishermen are bi-occupational—working part-time in the fishing fleets and part-time in filet-freezing plants and other occupations.

Meat Prices   One basic reason behind the demand for fish is cheapness. Fish cost less than many other kinds of meat, not only in port cities but also in cities far from the sea.

Illustrative of such differences are these retail prices which prevail in a grocery chain in the Midwest. Examples of fish prices per pound: eel 39¢, perch 49¢, sardines 49¢, halibut 49¢, swordfish 49¢, haddock 55¢, scallops 59¢, shrimp $1.19. Some examples of meat prices per pound: ground beef 39¢, pork butt 59¢, spare ribs 59¢, pork loin roast 69¢, lamb leg 75¢, chuck roast 79¢, rump roast 79¢, standing rib 85¢, sliced ham 89¢, pork chops center cut 99¢, veal sirloin 99¢, round steak 99¢, Swiss steak 99¢, sirloin steak $1.09, porterhouse steak $1.35.

Other Uses for Fish   Although the main use for fish has always been as human food, increasing quantities are going into the manufacture of soil fertilizers and animal feed. Today, in fact, the most important species in United States fishing, by quantity, is the oily, unpalatable menhaden (Table 5-2). The carcasses of all these fish are ground up for use as oil, animal feed, and fertilizer.

Manufacturing and Marketing   Fishing regions and market regions are linked by highly organized processing and transportation systems. Historically, most of the fish shipped to consumers were salted or dried, though ice-packed fish in barrels were sent inland from New England as far as central Pennsylvania in the nineteenth and early twentieth centuries. Then, with the development of canning processes in the late nineteenth century, salting and drying began to give way to canning. Next came refrigeration, and now freezing. All these techniques permit fish to be sold and eaten thousands of miles from port. Today, for example, carloads of iced and frozen fish from the Pacific Northwest are hooked on to passengers trains and rushed to cities in the eastern United States. Occasionally these cars make up entire fish-trains that take priority over other trains on the track.

Fishing Ports   The processing and marketing functions have long been concentrated in fishing ports. Countless small villages in which fishing is the principal economic activity dot the coasts of Norway, Iceland, Newfoundland, Nova Scotia, Maine, British Columbia, Alaska, eastern U.S.S.R., and Japan. Frequently such settlements are extremely small—only a few people whose life centers around a cannery and its fishing fleet. On the rugged Pacific coasts of North America, completely isolated out in the wilderness, sit several canneries that are built on the flat land near the mouth of a salmon stream. Surrounded by steep forested slopes, their only avenue of transportation with the outside world is the sea. Some of these Pacific Coast settlements are merely semipermanent villages inhabited by migrants who come in only for the fishing and canning season. Those that are permanent experience a sizable influx of workers during fishing season. For example, the salmon canners in Alaska annually import hundreds of seasonal laborers from other states and Canada. Just recently they have begun using Eskimos, flying them in from dozens of villages in central and northern Alaska.

Where fishing villages are somewhat larger they function not only as home bases for fishing boats, for personnel, and for canning, but also as manufacturing centers of boats and equipment, and even as headquarters for fishing companies.

With increasing mechanization of techniques and complexity of manufacturing and marketing, the small fishing villages are beginning to disappear. More and more their functions are becoming concentrated in cities, notably Gloucester, Boston, Baltimore, and Los Angeles. Although fishing is a small component in the economy of such cities (for example, only 15 per cent of Gloucester's labor force is in the fishing business), these places now dominate the fishing industry. Particu-

Fishing villages line the coasts of Japan's major islands. Some homes are on the lowlands, just inside the high-tide mark (left margin of picture), others are on the cliffs. The narrow beaches abound in boats, nets, and facilities for handling and drying fish. Where so much acreage is inhospitable to farming, the people, not surprisingly, turn to the sea. Indeed, most citizens of such villages are part-time farmers and part-time fishermen. Although Japan has hundreds of fishing villages, the bulk of her commercial catch is harvested by crews on engine-driven vessels and is marketed through a few major cities, notably Tokyo. (Courtesy Information Office, Consulate General of Japan.)

larly noteworthy fishing settlements in other countries are Grimsby and Hull in England (the world's two leading fishing ports) and Bergen and Stavanger in Norway (Fig. 5-2).

COMMERCIAL FISHING
AND INTERNATIONAL RELATIONS

International Trade   The world's leading fishing nations (Japan, China, the United States, and the U.S.S.R.) consume most of what they catch. Consequently, the surpluses for international trade come from elsewhere —principally Norway, Canada, and Iceland. Western Europe and the United States are the main importers (Table 5-4).

Table 5-4   *International Trade in Fish and Fish Products*

Leading Exporters	Weight in Thousands of Metric Tons
Norway	332.0
Canada	229.1
Iceland	154.4
Denmark	152.0
Netherlands	149.0
Leading Importers	
United States	486.0
United Kingdom	197
France	114
Italy	109.4
Germany	103 *
Belgium	81.1

Source: United Nations *Yearbook of International Trade Statistics*, 1959, pages on each nation's exports and imports.

* 1957; later data not given.

Fish products constitute a considerable portion of sales abroad for a few countries, notably Iceland whose economy is based to an astounding degree on this one type of commodity. By percentage of value of fish in all exports for each nation, the chief fish-exporting countries are Iceland 79 per cent, Norway 16, Panama 12, Japan 4, and Denmark 3.

International Agreements   Fishermen from England, France, the Netherlands, Germany, Denmark, and Norway have mingled for centuries on the waters of the North Sea. And for over 400 years European fishermen have pushed across the Atlantic to the Grand Bank and the other fishing grounds off North America. Japanese craft range 5000 miles across the Pacific, and tuna boats from California strike west to Hawaii and along the cool California Current southward to Panama.

Inevitably, these wide-ranging activities have led to negotiations among the governments concerned. On the one hand, some treaties have been designed to conserve the valuable resources of the sea. In 1930, for example, the United States and Canada signed a treaty to limit the size of halibut catches. And back in 1911 the United States, Canada, Russia, and Japan agreed to control the killing of seals in the Pribilof Island area. From a population of 10,000,000, the herd had been reduced to 12,000, but since the signing of this treaty, the herd has built itself up to 3,000,000. In response to the virtual extermination of whales from the oceans of the world except in the southernmost Pacific and the Antarctic, in 1935 an international agreement was worked out prohibiting the catch of calves and females with calves; subsequently a limit was set on the number of adult whales that can be caught. In the North Sea Conventions of 1936, 1943, and 1946, several European nations collaborated in establishing net regulations and size limitations for fish.

On the other hand, the purpose of certain government actions seems to have been to limit the freedom of fishermen from other nations. Nowhere has this been more apparent than in the Pacific. Before World War II, Japanese fishermen cruised at will over the whole Pacific. Then in 1952 Korea established the "Rhee Line" barring Japanese vessels from the western Sea of Japan, an area rich in sardines, mackerel, and flatfish. And just to the southwest, the Chinese Communists ruled that the Japanese could not approach closer than 100 miles to the China coast, thus blocking them from the best trawling grounds in the East China Sea. Next, the United States established a 420,000-square-mile nuclear testing area in the tuna and bonito grounds of the mid-Pacific.

The plight of Japanese fishermen was further intensified in 1953 when the United

Commercial Gathering of Wild Animals

States and Canada signed an agreement barring them from the northeast Pacific where they had previously fished for salmon and halibut. Finally, in 1956, immediately after the Japanese broke off treaty talks with the U.S.S.R., the Russians retaliated by closing the Sea of Okhotsk, the western Bering Sea, and part of the northwest Pacific to Japanese fishermen. For decades, the Japanese had been coming to this area to harvest the tremendous runs of salmon.

PROBLEMS FACING COMMERCIAL FISHING

Aside from international restrictions and bad weather, the successful harvesting of fish is adversely affected by ocean shipping, overfishing, pollution, and the encouragement of predators.

Ocean Shipping Lanes   Unfortunately, some of the world's most-traveled shipping routes cut across fishing grounds. The most direct route between New York and the ports of western Europe, for example, passes through Georges Bank and the Grand Bank. In daytime during clear weather, there is no particular problem, but at night and on foggy days (remember that this is one of the world's foggiest zones), there is a constant danger of collision between freighters and fishing boats. Less dangerous but more frequent is damage to nets and trawl lines. The same perils exist on the busy lanes of the North Sea.

Overfishing   Not very many years ago, men regarded the supply of sea animals as inexhaustible, and they pulled in all kinds in unlimited amounts. But then something happened: Fishermen began to bring smaller and smaller catches back to port. It now appears that some species of sea life do not multiply indefinitely regardless of how favorable the habitat. We now realize that some animals were snatched up faster than they reproduced themselves. The examples of halibut, salmon, and seal illustrate this problem.

The *halibut* lies lazily on its side on the floor of the continental shelf, feeding on the nutrients that drift down from the surface and on the organisms that live on the floor. Thou-

sands of halibut congregate in relatively immobile schools. Back in the late 1800's, fishermen hauled in tremendous catches of halibut from fishing grounds off the American shores. But when they returned to the same grounds, they had very poor luck. Concluding that the school had moved on, the fishermen moved along to a new spot and once again they came up with huge catches. Once more, however, on their return, they found that the fish had vanished. Almost too late, around 1920, the fishermen realized that the schools of halibut were not moving from place to place at all; instead, one school after another was being exterminated. The fishing fleets were simply scraping the bottom clean. As a result, today catches of halibut in American waters are controlled by American (United States-Canada) agreements.

Salmon are intensely mobile, migrating hundreds of miles. Yet they have a peculiar homing instinct which man has capitalized on. After being spawned upstream in fresh water, the salmon go out to the open sea where they spend most of their lives. Then, usually five years later, they come back to do their own spawning in the very stream from which they came. (It is said that one loyal salmon came home to the University of Washington Fisheries School up a pipe!) These regular, predictable runs make it easy for fishermen to draw in tremendous catches in a few days' time. But the effects of the severe overfishing of a stream in any one year do not show up generally until five years later—when the inbound spawners would be markedly fewer than normal. As a result of excessive catches in spawning rivers, salmon are nearly extinct in New England where they were once numerous. The salmon runs have also declined sharply in the rivers of northern California, Oregon, and Washington. The Columbia River catch, once worth $10,000,000 now fails to reach even $1,000,000. At the turn of the century the Sacramento River supplied salmon meat for hundreds of thousands of cases; since 1920 it has supplied none. By tonnage, the United States harvest of salmon is now scarcely a quarter of what it was in our record year—1936 (see Table 5-2).

Fur seals of the northern Pacific were also once seriously decimated. They are especially vulnerable because once a year they are impelled to go "home" to the Pribilof Islands west of Alaska, where they are, in effect, sitting ducks. From an original population of 10,-000,000 the herd was nearly exterminated by 1911. As we have seen, though, through international agreement the herds have been protected and enabled to expand.

Over and over again, hampered by inadequate knowledge of the living habits of sea animals but armed with powerful ships and modern equipment, men have proceeded to devastate some of the world's best resources of sea life. The pattern has become painfully familiar: tremendous harvests followed by declining supplies and by the subsequent shifts of the fishermen to more distant seas. As yet, the commercial fisherman has failed to maintain the conserving balance between supply and demand that the subsistence fisherman achieved ages ago. A belated awareness of the problem has developed, though, and stringent laws have been passed to protect some species—for instance, controlling the type of nets and other devices used in catching salmon, controlling the quantity of halibut and salmon that will be accepted at commercial ports, and controlling the number of seals that can be slain.

Overfishing is a menace, and yet it is evidently not the only problem. When a single mackerel or sole spawns from 100,000 to 1,000,000 eggs a year, and a cod or haddock produces 5,000,000 eggs, it would seem that enough would mature to replenish the adult population if fishermen were the only enemy. Clearly, other factors are in the equation. One of these is pollution.

Pollution   In countless fresh water streams and in the ocean margins at the mouths of many rivers, the habitat of sea life has been damaged by excessive mud from eroded land, and by slime and poison chemicals from city wastes. Such noxious substances destroy fish eggs and increase the death rate of small fry. Pollution has severely damaged mackerel, cod, sole, and haddock

grounds fringing large urban areas; it has virtually ruined the waters off our northern Atlantic coast where shad fishing has nearly disappeared and oyster harvests have plummeted to only a third of those in 1900.

Predators   Further, man has ruined some fisheries by unwittingly unleashing predators that destroy commercial fish. As far as we know, this disruption is more serious in inland waters than in oceans. What has happened to commercial fishing in Wisconsin will serve as a good example of the problem. Table 5-5 presents the story. Notice that although the tonnage of the yield from Lake Michigan is steadily *increasing*, the value of the catch has been *decreasing*—and this in a period of inflation! What is the explanation? First of all, the two fish—trout and whitefish —that for years brought the highest prices and provided Lake Michigan fishermen with their greatest revenue are vanishing. Trout are already extinct, and the whitefish are rapidly becoming so. These valuable fish have been victims, not of overfishing, but of the ravages of a predator—the sea lamprey. The lamprey is a water worm that measures up to two feet in length, and looks somewhat like a garden hose with a suction-cup at one end. The lamprey fastens this mouth, which is lined with dozens of needle-sharp teeth, to the side

Table **5-5**   *Returns of Wisconsin's Commercial Fishing in Lake Michigan*

Year	Thou- sands of Pounds of Fish	Value of Catch in Thou- sands of Dollars	Thou- sands of Pounds of Trout	Thou- sands of Pounds of White- fish
1940	10,933	$ 843	2,478	196
1944	10,713	$2,359	2,851 *	343
1947	12,657	$2,111	1,177	1,806 **
1948	12,579	$1,686	540	984
1952	14,932	$1,687	0.5	289
1956	15,055	$1,633	0.0	18
1958	14,837	$1,795	0.0	9
1959	12,426	$1,281	0.0	19
1960	14,836	$1,414	0.0	67

Source: Wisconsin Conservation Department, *Great Lakes Commercial Fishing Statistical Report*, 1960.

* Peak year for trout.
** Peak year for whitefish.

Commercial Gathering of Wild Animals

of a fish and then lives as a parasite by sucking the lifeblood from its host. Eventually the host dies and the lamprey moves on to another fish. The average lamprey destroys 20 pounds of fish during its four years of mature existence.

Apparently there has always been a population of lampreys in the St. Lawrence River and Lake Ontario, but Niagara Falls formerly barred them from entering the other Great Lakes. Then, in 1829, the Welland Canal was constructed to make it possible for ships to bypass Niagara. The new canal also provided a convenient bypass for the lampreys into Lake Erie. For reasons that are still obscure, the lampreys have never been much of a problem in the shallow water of Lake Erie; apparently they reserved their attack for the fish of the deeper waters of Lakes Huron, Michigan, and Superior.

In the 1930's, trout catches in Huron dwindled sharply and fishermen noticed that, of the fish they were drawing in, an increasing number bore circular scars on their sides. In 1948, Lake Huron's trout industry collapsed.

The first lamprey was discovered in Lake Michigan in 1936. From that time on, the number of scarred fish steadily increased, and the trout harvest began to slip. From a peak year in 1944 (Table 5-5) the catch rapidly declined until 1952 when it amounted to less than 1000 pounds, and by 1955 there was no catch at all—Lake Michigan's trout were extinct.

Now that the best fish of the Great Lakes had been destroyed, the fishermen turned to the next best—the whitefish. But so did the lampreys. In 1947, the peak year for whitefish, the catch amounted to 1,806,000 pounds (Table 5-5). Then the lampreys, deprived of their trout diet, closed in. Nine years later the whitefish catch was only 18,295 pounds, even though the fishermen had constantly been improving their techniques and equipment.

But this it not the end of the story. As a result of these shifts in the natural life of the lakes, a small species of lake chub, unmarketable except as animal feed, has increased in number by 300 per cent, and is particularly abundant in Lake Michigan. Formerly, this small chub provided the lake trout with their main source of food. But now that the trout have been exterminated by the lampreys, the chub population has increased spectacularly. Unfortunately, these fish are a nuisance to the fisherman, for their gills become ensnared in the nets and they have to be removed by hand—a time-consuming task. And when they are marketed as animal feed they bring only 2½ to 3 cents per pound.

There is a larger species of chub, however, which in smoked form has proved palatable. So commercial fishermen have now turned to this chub and to perch as their major sources of revenue. But once again they are bedeviled by the lampreys, which, now that the whitefish are disappearing, are feasting not on the small species of chub but the larger ones! So the harassed fishermen of Lake Michigan are now shifting to lake smelt, a fish that ranks even lower on the income ladder.

For several years, researchers have been searching for means to combat the lamprey nuisance. One method which held some promise was that of establishing electrical weirs at the mouths of spawning streams—the idea being to generate a mild electric shock to the lamprey, discouraging it from entering the stream to spawn. Thousands of lampreys have been killed at the weirs since their inception in 1955. But this method is slow and very expensive, and probably could never eliminate the lamprey population. Recently a chemical has been discovered which kills lamprey larvae but causes no injury whatsoever to other forms of life in the stream or to animals which drink its water. Results have been astonishingly successful—100 per cent kill in streams where the method has been tried.

One encouraging indicator of the success of these measures is the definite signs of recovery in the whitefish harvest by Wisconsin fishermen from Lake Michigan. As Table 5-5 shows, the take had skidded steadily downward to a nadir in 1958, but since then there has been a conspicuous reversal. It looks as if the battle tide against the lamprey is turning.

Indeed, authorities are so encouraged that they are beginning a program to restock Lake Michigan with trout from fish hatcheries.

THE FUTURE

At present men annually pull in 37,000,000 tons of fish and other animals from the oceans. This may seem an appreciable amount, yet one square mile of plankton-rich sea water produces 4000 tons of vegetable matter— about six times the yield from a comparable area of good Kansas wheat land. The question is whether plankton can ever be used as food for man, and if so, whether it can be extracted economically. If scientists ever produce affirmative answers to these questions the day may come when *aquaculture* supersedes commercial fishing in the water world as surely as agriculture superseded commercial hunting on the continents.

Suggested Readings

Allen, Edward W., "Fishery Geography of the North Pacific Ocean," *Geographical Review*, 1953, pp. 558-563.

Bowen, Richard Le Baron, Jr., "Marine Industries of Eastern Arabia," *Geographical Review*, 1951, pp. 384-400.

Hewes, Gordon, W., "The Fisheries of Northwestern North America," *Economic Geography*, 1952, pp. 66-73.

Katkoff, V., "The Flounder Industry of the Soviet Far East," *Economic Geography*, 1952, pp. 171-180.

Marts, M. E., and Sewell, W. R. D., "The Conflicts Between Fish and Power Resources in the Pacific," *Annals of the Association of American Geographers*, 1960, pp. 42-50.

Mathieson, R. S., "The Japanese Salmon Fisheries: A Geographic Appraisal," *Economic Geography*, 1958, pp. 352-361.

Morgan, Robert, *World Sea Fisheries*, New York and London, 1955, 307 pp.

Padgett, Herbert R., "Sea Industries: A Neglected Field of Geography," *The Professional Geographer*, November, 1961, pp. 26-28.

Sonnenfeld, J., "An Arctic Reindeer Industry: Growth and Decline," *Geographical Review*, 1959, pp. 76-94.

———, "Changes in an Eskimo Hunting Technology, an Introduction to Implement Geography," *Annals of the Association of American Geographers*, 1960, pp. 172-186.

Stanton, William J., "The Purpose and Source of Seasonal Migration to Alaska," *Economic Geography*, 1955, pp. 138-148.

United Nations, Food and Agriculture Organization, *Yearbook of Fishery Statistics*.

United States Department of the Interior, Fish and Wildlife Service, *Commercial Fisheries Review* (monthly). Contains reports on fishing developments in the United States and in numerous foreign countries.

In the forested areas of Siberia, logs clog the rivers during the logging season. These are being floated down the Mana River to chemical and woodworking plants in Krasnoyarsk. (Sovfoto.)

SIX

Chapter 3 included some comments about the gathering of forest products for subsistence purposes. The present chapter deals with economic activities in which man gathers trees and tree products for commercial exchange.

LOCATION

Men gather surplus products from natural stands of trees chiefly in two huge belts, as shown on Figure 6-1. The first virtually encircles the globe in the mid-latitudes of the Northern Hemisphere, southern Alaska, Canada, and contiguous parts of the United States, picks up again in a swath through central Europe, and stretches across Scandinavia and the northern Soviet Union and covers most of Japan. This region is one of the most extensive and comprehensive in all economic geography.

The second forest-gathering realm is found around the tropics, widely through South and Central America, in a long strip in western and central Africa, and again in Southeast Asia.

Apart from these two general regions commercial forest gathering is of significance only in small zones in southern Chile, in southeastern Australia, in New Zealand, and in some of the countries flanking the Mediterranean Sea.

CHARACTERISTICS

Forest gathering consists of two general types of activity: *lumbering*, in which the trees themselves are harvested, and *collecting*,

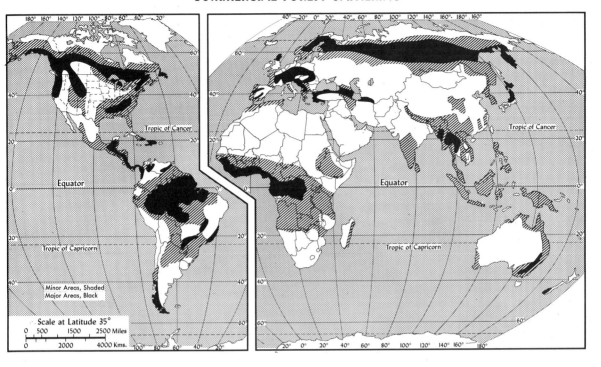

Figure 6-1

in which only tree products (that is, nuts, leaves, sap, fruits, and so on) are taken, leaving the trees intact. When we compare the mid-latitude region with the tropical region, we find contrasts in the relative extents of collecting and lumbering and in the particular commodities gathered.

Gathering in the Tropics
Forest gathering generates much less wealth in the tropics than in the mid-latitudes. In the tropics, collecting—principally of sap, nuts, leaves, and bark—is far more important than is lumbering.

The sap of many different types of trees is collected to be used in manufacturing a diversity of products—from rubber and chewing gum to wiring insulation and golf balls.

Nuts are collected for a variety of purposes. The oil used in the manufacture of soap, margarine, candles, and glycerine is extracted from various tropical nuts. The coconut is the biggest prize because copra (white meat) is over half oil. Most commercial copra comes from forest gatherers in the Philippines, Indonesia, and Malaya. Another oil-yielding nut comes from the oil palm tree, which is common in Nigeria, the Congo, and Indonesia. But oil is not the only use for nuts. Nuts from *cacao* trees and *castanheiro* trees are food items. *Ivory nuts*, which are white and very hard, are useful in making buttons and knife handles. Silky fibers from seeds of the *kapok* tree are made into mattress filler and life-jackets. *Coir*, the fiber from coconut husks, is used in cordage and door mats.

Forest gatherers also pick a wide array of leaves for a variety of purposes. For instance, fibers from the leaves of a tree native to the Philippines are peculiarly resistant to salt water; known as *abaca* (or *Manila hemp*, because most of it is marketed through Manila), the fiber is indispensable in the making of ropes, twine, and cordage. Leaves of the *coca* bush contain the drug cocaine.

As for bark, quinine is manufactured from the covering of the *cinchona* tree, and the aromatic bark of the cinnamon tree, which grows in Ceylon, Malaya, and Indochina, is used as a spice.

Thus, forest gathering in the tropics yields a great diversity of commodities from a wide assortment of plants. Some of these commodities, such as bananas, have become so highly valued that today they are produced primarily on carefully managed *tree farms* rather than in wild forests.

Tropical *lumbering* is less varied than collecting, but it yields an important group of commercial products. The most valuable are certain timbers, tanning chemicals, and drugs.

The principal timber is mahogany, which comes primarily from tropical America, including Haiti and the Dominican Republic, though some comes from the Guinea coast of Africa. Other important woods are cedar, teak, and ebony. Cedar, a soft, fragrant wood, is shipped mainly from Mexico, Central America, and Brazil. Teak is a strong, hard wood that contains an unusually high amount of oil which acts as a natural preservative in both fresh and salt water. The wood also resists both rot and white ants, and does not burn easily. Accordingly, teak is highly valued in the construction of wooden boats and as pilings for wharves and piers. Teak trees are rarely found outside Burma, Thailand, Laos, Cambodia, Vietnam, and Java. One of the earliest woods to be gathered commercially in the tropics was ebony, a hard, jet-black, fine-grained wood from Central Africa, Madagascar, and southeast Asia. Ebony has for a long time been used in making chests, figurines, and handles.

Until the late nineteenth century, most commercial tannin (for tanning leather) was extracted from the oak, chestnut, and hemlock trees of the mid-latitudes. Then it was discovered that the quebracho tree of South America was rich in tannin, and it soon became the single most important natural source of tannin. Northern Argentina yields the greatest supplies, although the output of southern Brazil is also important.

Gathering in the Mid-Latitudes   In the mid-latitudes, collecting is much less important than lumbering. At one time large quantities of commercial tannin were extracted from the bark of chestnut, oak, and hemlock trees in the United States and Europe, but as we just saw, the quebracho tree proved a better source. Certain wood products are still economically valuable, however, notably cork and naval stores. Cork comes primarily from oak trees in Portugal (half the world total) and along the northwestern fringe of Africa. Turpentine, tar, and pitch (collectively termed naval stores because of their wide use in caulking wooden ships) are derived from the sap of yellow pine trees. When this resinous fluid is heated, the turpentine is driven off and collected for use in paints and varnishes; the distillate, called rosin, is employed in the manufacture of soap and a wide array of chemicals. Most of the world's commercial supply of naval stores comes from the southeastern United States (South Carolina, Georgia, Florida, and Alabama) and from southwestern France.

Lumbering in the mid-latitude region provides roughly 80 per cent of the world's wood (Table 6-1); Figure 6-1, which shows the world pattern of forest gathering, provides an illustration of the regional concentration. Within the United States the leading states by volume of wood harvest are Oregon and Washington; but by general area, the South outproduces the Pacific Coast states and now accounts for half the wood cut from the nation's forests.

For the world as a whole, almost as much wood is cut for fuel as for boards, pulp, veneer and other industrial purposes. But the proportion between fuelwood and industrial wood varies sharply from place to place. Within the tropics the chief use is as fuelwood—84 per cent in Brazil, 93 per cent in Indonesia, 75 per cent in India, and nearly 100 per cent in Tanganyika, Uganda, and other tropical nations. Throughout the continent of South America, 84 per cent of the wood cut is for fuel; in Africa that figure is 94 per cent. By contrast the harvest in mid-latitude forests is mainly for industrial use, although fuelwood does attain a rather high percentage in France (59 per cent), Yugoslavia (55), Rumania (47), Japan (39), and the U.S.S.R. (33).

Table 6-1 *World Harvest of Wood by Leading Countries (Millions of Cubic Meters)*

Area	Total	Industrial Wood	Fuel Wood
WORLD	1690	1017	673
North America	408	359	49
United States	311	269	42
Canada	96	90	6
U.S.S.R.	369	261	108
Europe	308	209	99
Sweden	46	41	5
Finland	42	29	13
France	41	21	20
Germany, West	25	22	3
Italy	17	4	13
Rumania	17	10	7
Poland	16	14	2
Yugoslavia	16	8	8
Asia	270	126	144
Indonesia	76	5	71
Japan	69	52	17
China	58	39	19
India	15	4	11
South America	154	23	131
Brazil	102	12	90
Colombia	12	3	9
Argentina	11	2	9
Africa	130	18	112
Tanganyika	21	—	21
Sudan	13	—	13
Uganda	10	—	10
Australia	15	10	5

Source: United Nations, Food and Agriculture Organization, *Yearbook of Forest Product Statistics*, 1961, Table 1.

The woods of the mid-latitudes serve such a wide array of uses that it is impossible to associate any one item with a few distinctive purposes. In general, these woods have great strength and are very easy to work. Consequently, they can be adapted to such widely diversified uses as building materials, shingles, implements, wagons, railroad ties, mine props, and furniture. The softwoods (especially poplar and pine) are well suited for conversion into paper pulp; fir and pine are best for structural timbers, studs, and joists; and the hardwoods are most suitable for furniture, wagons, sleds, and tools.

PHYSICAL RELATIONSHIPS

Of the several aspects of the natural environment that have an influence on forest gathering, we shall first consider the forest resource itself and then look at other physical elements such as climate, soils, and drainage.

The Forest Resource   Originally, one-fourth of the earth's land was blanketed with trees, but man has removed nearly half of the tree cover. Today, only about 15 per cent of the land is forested. (The world regions of this forest resource, by types of trees, are shown in almost any atlas.)

The forest resource of the tropics is considerably different from that of the mid-latitudes. In the heart of the tropics lies the *rainforest*, the most luxuriant and variegated community of plants on the face of the earth. The features of the rainforest that are most directly related to forest gathering are profusion of species, "confusion of stands," size of trees, and hardness of woods.

The remarkable profusion of species means a profusion of products. The reasons for the abundance of plant types are not entirely clear, but it appears that the warm humid tropical environment permits rapid maturation and frequent mutations resulting in numerous different species.

The "confusion of stands" in the rainforest means that any given acre of timber land is usually heterogeneous, frequently containing from 15 to 30 different species! Why the stands of timber are mixed rather than uniform is obscure, but the economic consequence is clear: Confusion of stands increases the cost of gathering the forest products. (The cost of logging mahogany, for example, would be lower if pure stands of mahogany existed.)

The large size of tropical trees is an advantage that, to some extent, counteracts the lack of pure unmixed stands. Many soar 150 to 180 feet into the air. As a consequence, the volume of timber that can be harvested from an acre is great. The large size of its trees is one reason why Brazil ranks so high among the nations in quantity of wood logged.

Most tropical woods are hard and very heavy—indeed, some are too heavy to float. In fact, since almost all these woods are too hard to work easily, many tropical countries with a surplus of *trees* have to import *lumber* from the mid-latitudes for building materials and other purposes. One exception is balsa, a tropical wood that is very light; many natives of the tropics have been using balsa logs for centuries in the construction of rafts.

In addition to the rainforest itself, there are in the tropics zones of *light tropical forest*, which consists of shorter trees with thinner trunks. Here the trees grow farther apart and stand over a dense undergrowth of shrubs and grass. All told, the tropical forests constitute nearly half of the world's woodland.

By contrast, the forest resource of the *mid-latitudes* is characterized by fewer species, purer stands, and a mixture of softwoods and hardwoods. The original settlers of the New World often established their villages near pure stands of timber, and today the countryside is still dotted with communities bearing such names as Maplewood, Oak Ridge, Elm Grove, and Pine Village. The purity of stand has important economic consequences, for when foresters work a given stand of timber

in the mid-latitudes they can concentrate on gathering one kind of wood. Being able to harvest whole groves rather than isolated trees means, in effect, that they can employ mass-production techniques, with all the resulting savings of time and expense.

The forest resource of the mid-latitudes is distributed according to the regional patterns of hardwoods and softwoods. The hardwood belt is located along the side toward the Equator of the mid-latitude forest region. This belt is typified by oak, chestnut, hickory, maple, birch, and beech. We find only a few softwoods in this region. Originally, hardwoods were distributed over the eastern United States and over Europe from the Baltic to the Mediterranean, with the belt narrowing into western Siberia. Most of China and Korea, too, were once forested with hardwoods; parts of Japan and Manchuria still are. In the Southern Hemisphere this northern hardwood belt has only limited counterparts:

Figure 6-2 (*From U.S. Department of Agriculture.*)

DISTRIBUTION OF FOREST LAND IN THE UNITED STATES

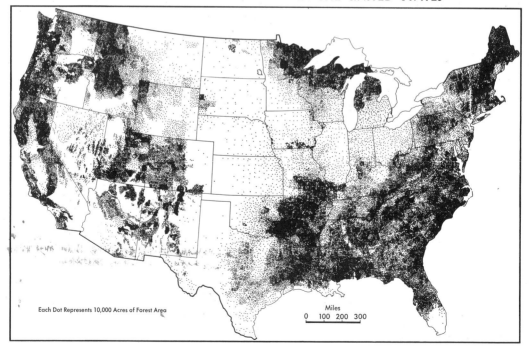

Each Dot Represents 10,000 Acres of Forest Area

Miles
0 100 200 300

Commercial Forest Gathering

the narrow coastal fringes of Chile, southern and eastern Australia, New Zealand, and the tip of Africa.

The softwood belt is much vaster and occupies the poleward flanks of the mid-latitude forests. In Eurasia it forms the world's single largest forest zone, stretching 7000 miles from Scandinavia to eastern Siberia, where it fans out broadly to nearly 2000 miles. It stretches on across North America from Alaska to Labrador; on the west it reaches southward along the Pacific Coast, extending even into Mexico. On the east there is a detached segment in the southeastern United States. The most common trees in this softwood belt are pine, spruce, fir, and larch.

Mixed forests, consisting of both hardwoods and softwoods, are typical of a transition strip that runs along between the hardwood and softwood belts.

The trees in the mid-latitudes are generally smaller than those in the tropics. Yet there is one notable exception to this general rule: The earth's tallest trees grow in the fir and pine forest of northern California, where giant redwood sequoias attain heights of 300 feet and diameters of 20 feet. Douglas fir trees in this region grow 250 feet tall and have trunks that measure 6 feet across.

Although accurate data are not available for the volume of timber now standing in the world's forests, such measurements have been compiled for the United States by the Forest Service. These indicate that three states dominate our volume of standing timber: Oregon, California, and Washington, which contain, respectively, 21 per cent, 18 per cent, and 15 per cent of the nation's total resource—54 per cent altogether. These figures largely represent virgin stands that await the first stroke of axe and saw.

Climate There is a close correlation between moisture supply and forests. Except where average temperatures are too low or drainage too poor, most of the wet regions of the world were tree-covered. It is difficult to generalize on the number of inches of precipitation required for satisfactory tree

growth. Forests in the tropics are associated with 60 or more inches of rain a year, while in Canada and Siberia, forests exist in areas that receive only 10 inches. In part this discrepancy can be explained by this condition: In regions of high average temperatures, the rate of evaporation is also high, consequently more precipitation is required to support trees. In any case, trees require more water than grass and shrubs, because trees have larger transpiring surfaces than other plants have.

Trees also require temperatures favorable to the annual formation of new shoots that need time to mature sufficiently to survive the dormant season. The average temperature during the warmest month must be at least 50°. Since summers become progressively cooler and shorter toward the poles (or upward in highlands) the forests consist of fewer and shorter and smaller trees along the poleward margins of the great softwood belt across Eurasia and North America as well as along the lofty highlands to the south. At high latitudes as well as high altitudes trees cannot survive at all and give way to *tundra* —a stunted growth of shrubs and lichens.

Thus, a warm, moist climate tends to favor maximum forest growth. This explains why, in the United States, the greatest volume of new wood growth is not in the Northwest but in the Southeast where the forests are *adding* a volume of almost seven billion cubic feet of lumber each year, nearly half of the nation's total increment in wood volume in commercial forests.

That the most luxuriant forests develop in warm, humid regions serves, as we have seen, as both a blessing and a curse to the gatherers in the tropical rainforests. On the one hand the volume of tree growth is large, but on the other hand there is a profusion of species in confused stands. Furthermore, since physical activity is burdensome in a hot, humid climate, a forester in the tropics is likely to produce less than a forester in the mid-latitudes. To complicate matters, the muddy ground in many tropical areas makes it difficult to transport products after they have been gathered. And the *lianas* and other climb-

The Lågen River at Lillehammer, Norway. Logs are cut in the mountain forests in the background, stamped with the owners' marks, and floated down river to these pens where they are sorted out by owner. (Courtesy of Kirk Stone.)

ing plants—giant vines which thread their way like huge cables running from tree to tree—fostered by such climates are no help. For vines impede the movement of the lumbermen through the forest, and after a tree trunk has been severed, the tree itself sometimes remains standing, held upright by these vines.

Soils   But warm weather and plenty of rain are not enough, for water that evaporates or runs off the surface is of no use to plants. The soil around the tree roots must be able to retain enough of the precipitation to remain moist throughout the year, since trees are *perennials*, not annuals. Therefore, to overcome short periods of drought, roots of trees drive much deeper than do those of the grasses, which are *annual* plants. This is why green trees may be surrounded by parched grass in an area suffering from a short dry spell. If the dry season lasts too long, however, the trees will die. Thus, not only must the annual supply of moisture be adequate in itself, but the subsoils of the region must also be able to retain it throughout the year.

Apparent exceptions to this rule are the pine forests in the southern United States (from Virginia to Texas) and in southern France. In these places the soils are sandy and the rain sinks rapidly into the ground. But pine trees are able to thrive on sandy soils by driving their roots extremely deep into the subsoil supply of water.

Streams and Rivers   Water courses are essential to forest gathering. In both the tropics and the mid-latitudes, they provide the main arteries of transportation for the products that are lumbered or collected from the forests. In the higher mid-latitudes, where the streams are frozen during the winter months, forest harvesting follows a regular seasonal pattern. In the colder stretches of North America and Eurasia, the foresters spend the long winters transporting logs by sled over the snow-covered countryside to the banks of the frozen streams. By early springtime, the river banks are lined with great piles of logs—the fruits of the winter harvest. When the return of warm weather breaks up the river ice, the streams once again become thoroughfares down which the logs are floated to sawmills and river ports.

The orientation of rivers in a forest region is critical. Where the streams flow in the general direction of the final market, as in Sweden, Finland, and southern Canada, production and marketing costs are relatively low. But where they flow in the opposite direction, as in northern Russia and on the West Coast of the United States, the trip to market must be roundabout and correspondingly more expensive. Where the rivers flow into the sea, however, the cheapest form of transport on earth (ocean transport) becomes available for the remainder of the journey.

Where the general trend of flow is poleward, seasonal flooding imposes a severe handicap on foresters. The rivers of the northern U.S.S.R., for example—the Dvina, Vashka, and Pechora in European Russia, and the Ob, Yenisei, and Lena in Siberia—all flow toward the north. During the winter, all these rivers are frozen over. Then, with approaching springtime, the southern portions naturally begin to thaw first, while the downstream portions to the north are still ice-blocked. The thaw water rushes downstream and floods out over the river banks of the still frozen stretches. Orderly log drives become extremely difficult to conduct, and even the logs piled up along the banks are sometimes floated away by the flooding water.

Topography Irregular terrain favors the growth of forests by discouraging competing types of land use. This was true "in nature" as well as after man's appearance on the scene. In drier climates like that of southern California, for example, the warmer lowlands produced a natural growth of grass and shrubs, while the cooler, moister mountains developed a coverage of trees. The same relationship has persisted in forested regions

Figure 6-3 (*By B. F. Dietrich, Courtesy* Economic Geography.)

DISTRIBUTION OF THE FORESTS OF EUROPE

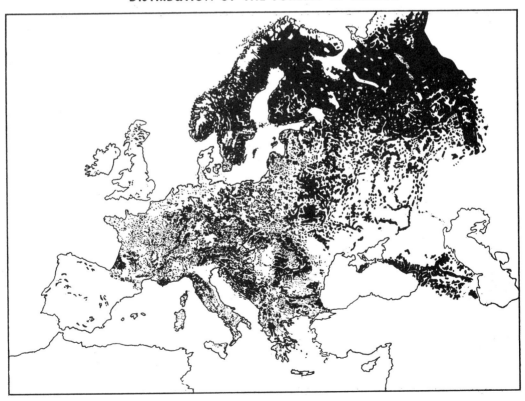

Water buffaloes are used in parts of Burma to haul teak logs. (Courtesy United States Department of Agriculture, Foreign Agriculture.)

where man has cleared the low, level lands for farms, leaving the rougher land in trees.

Thus, we can say that if moisture, temperature, and subsoil conditions are satisfactory, forests tend to be associated with high lands in regions of irregular topography. In North America, the three southerly prongs of the mid-latitude softwood belt correspond to three mountain ranges—the Appalachian, the Rocky, and the Cascade-Sierra Nevada.

Unfortunately, however, rough terrain handicaps workmen. The steep slopes impede the transportation of equipment into the forest, the actual harvesting of timber and other products, and the transportation of products out of the forest. It so happens that some of the best forests in the mid-latitudes—in parts of Scandinavia and western Canada and the United States—are associated with just this sort of topography. Precipitous waterfalls and treacherous rapids make log drives difficult and, on some rivers, quite impossible. The locational pattern of forests in Europe (Figure 6-3, page 95) gives evidence of many of the relationships cited so far with topography, climate and soils.

Role of Animals The fauna within forest regions both help and, more often, hinder forest gathering. In Burma and Thailand, for example, elephants are indispensable in moving teak logs to river banks where they can be floated downstream. But in the African forest the tsetse fly, a small, blood-sucking, disease-carrying fly that attacks cattle and horses, prohibits the use of animal power. Here large numbers of human beings are obliged to tug the felled trees out of the forests to the river banks. In Venezuela and adjacent parts of the Amazon Basin, a carnivorous fish known as the *piranha* poses a moderate threat to logging operations. Frequenting shallow waters at the river's edge, they attack immediately any unfortunate animal or human being that happens to fall in.

In the softwood forests of the mid-latitudes deer, hare and other browsing animals destroy tremendous numbers of seedlings and young trees. Yet the foresters encounter a firm obstacle in a sentimental public that favors laws designed to protect the deer herds from hunters.

Commercial Forest Gathering

The activity of forest gathering depends on several human factors, especially demand, international trade, transportation, forest settlements, manufacturing, agriculture, government policies, and problems of forest gathering.

Demand Wood is chiefly used for fuel. Worldwide, by percentages, consumption by uses lines up as follows: fuel 42 per cent, building material 40, paper 8, railroad ties, mine props, and other uses 10. In the United States the percentage breakdown is quite different: fuel 16 per cent, lumber 52, pulpwood 22, plywood 4, and other uses 6.

The main markets for forest products are in the middle latitudes of the Northern Hemisphere—notably in the U.S.S.R., Europe, and Anglo-America (see Table 6-1). Nearness to these three market regions is one factor helping to explain why lumbering is more extensive and more lucrative in mid-latitude forests than in tropical forests.

Notice how the relationship to markets influences forest gathering in the tropics. There is little demand within this region either because there are few people (as in Amazonia, much of tropical Africa, and New Guinea) or because the economy is not very industrialized. Moreover, tropical forests are remote from customers. To be sure, this distance can be overcome, but transport costs are excessive in proportion to the price wood will bring. Still, light-weight products collected from tropical forests such as rubber and copra can be transported easily and they fetch a price that compensates for transport costs. Thus, the market handicap compounds the physical difficulties already noted. The combination explains why the world's most luxuriant and most rapidly regenerating forests are not the principal areas of forest gathering.

One measurement of the demand for wood is per capita consumption (Table 6-2). The world average is 770 cubic meters per thousand people. The rates in North America and the U.S.S.R. are far above this average, South America's exceeds it, Europe's equals it, but in Africa and Asia the ratios are far below it. By recalling the distinction made earlier between fuel and industrial uses (Table 6-1) we can deduce which countries in Table 6-2 fall in the fuel and industrial categories.

Table **6-2** *World per Capita Consumption of Wood (Cubic Meters per 1000 Persons per Year)*

Region	Amount
WORLD	770
North America	1980
Canada	2525
Guatemala	2100
Haiti	2030
United States	1930
U.S.S.R.	1790
South America	1160
Bolivia	2310
Brazil	1580
Paraguay	905
Surinam	900
Europe	755
Finland	4435
Sweden	2305
Norway	1650
France	965
Denmark	935
Switzerland	890
Czechoslovakia	870
Africa	530
Central Af. Rep.	2785
Bechuanaland	2470
Tanganyika	2330
Gabon	2000
Cameroun	1570
Uganda	1350
Ghana	1335
Sudan	1210
Asia	260
Malaya	1200
Indonesia	840
Nepal	810
Japan	750
Australia	1750
New Zealand	2000

Source: United Nations, Food and Agriculture Organization, *Yearbook of Forest Product Statistics*, 1961, Table 43.

One particular source of demand—house construction— shows an interesting relationship with forest gathering. Within forested regions houses are, naturally enough, likely to be built of logs or boards. In Brazil and Colombia, for instance, many houses are of solid mahogany! Frame houses typify central Europe, eastern Anglo-America, the American Pacific coast, and Japan. But in southern Europe and China—where the forests have long since been cut—houses are of stone or brick or a mixture of earth substances plastered onto a framework of wood. Reeds from marshes or river banks often serve as base for the plaster. But since even in these generally denuded regions the *mountains* are usually forested, wood houses are common in highlands, such as the Swiss Alps, the southern Urals, and the Himalayas. Latitude has a comparable effect in Russia where log cabins and frame houses distinguish the north, sod houses characterize the grassland middle zone (though they are being replaced by wooden structures as the economy improves), and stone houses typify the steppe-desert region in the far south.

One final observation on the location of demand and location of forests: The world's four chief clusters of population (see Chapter 2) are all in regions that were naturally forested. What accounts for this relationship between large populations and forest lands? Can it be that trees provided for more of man's needs (fuel, clothing, tools, housing) than did grasses and therefore attracted man in the early stages of his economic development? Then, as he developed into an agriculturalist, did he find it easier to farm forest land than grass land? This may seem inconceivable at first, but in the early days of farming—until very recently, in fact—only wooden plows were available, and they simply could not break up the matted sod of grasslands. Clearing land of trees took lots of work, but once cleared, such soil could be easily worked.

International Trade

The geographic separation of regions of demand and supply gives rise to a lively international trade in forest products. Most of the trade is southward—from Canada to the United States and from Sweden and Finland to Britain and Germany (Table 6-3). We can account for

Table 6-3 *International Trade in Wood* *(in Millions of United States Dollars)*

Region	Exports	Region	Imports
WORLD	6216	WORLD	6826
Europe	3045	*Europe*	3643
Sweden	858	United	
Finland	742	Kingdom	1278
Austria	233	Germany,	
France	196	West	669
Norway	185	Italy	326
		Netherlands	291
		France	259
		Belgium	177
North America	2201	*North America*	1731
Canada	1593	United	
United		States	1565
States	608	Canada	165
U.S.S.R.	252	*U.S.S.R.*	69
Asia	412	*Asia*	558
Japan	165	Japan	207
Philippines	106	India	48
South America	69	*South America*	182
Brazil	47	Argentina	77
Chile	5	Brazil	33
Africa	164	*Africa*	295
Ghana	45	Union of	
Ivory Coast	26	So. Af.	83
Nigeria	23	Egypt	50
Australia	15	*Australia*	55

Source: United Nations, Food and Agriculture Organization *Yearbook of Forest Products Statistics*, 1961, Tables 39 and 40.

the high rank of some nations in both exports and imports by the fact that a country can grow a surplus of one type of wood yet be short of another.

By importance of wood in a nation's export business, British Honduras far exceeds any other nation (Table 6-4), for her main export is mahogany.

Table 6-4 *Ratio of Wood and Pulp Exports to Total Exports by Nations*

Nation	Percentage
British Honduras	63
Sweden	31
Finland	30
Austria	24
Canada	18
Yugoslavia	18
Norway	13
Nicaragua	10

Commercial Forest Gathering

In Sweden, flumes, sometimes constructed parallel to roads, convey logs downslope from timber areas. (Courtesy of Kirk Stone.)

Transportation For moving wood from forest to mill, men have threaded railroads and roads into forest regions to augment streams. But since truck and rail transportation are more expensive than the waterways, they have generally been constructed in only the accessible fringes of forest regions. In Scandinavia, flumes have been constructed (sometimes parallel to roads) for floating logs down to sawmills.

Vast stretches of mature trees in remote locations (for instance, central Canada, Alaska, Siberia, and also in the tropics) remain untouched except where river or ocean transport is possible. Thus, regions of forests and forest gathering are not coextensive.

Where railroads are used, often narrow-gauge tracks are laid down in the woods. As cutting moves from one location to another, the tracks are relocated. Such use of the railroad has usually been restricted to regions where waterways are inadequate for log drives. Railways are being superseded by trucks in this function, however, especially in the United States and Canada. Some of these trucks have detachable wheel mounts that are affixed to the rear ends of logs too large to load on a truck —occasionally, a loaded truck is 50 feet long. Since such trucking is usually developed in forested regions with rough topography (where rivers are tortuous) the routes are necessarily circuitous with many tight curves. A frequent sight on forest highways is a queue of autos trailing after a log truck snaking its way down the hillside.

For moving lumber from mill to market, man again augments waterways with railroad and truck transportation. In Eurasia, forest products are frequent commodities in the freight traffic of the Trans-Siberian railway and the railroads crossing the Arctic Circle to Vorkuta (just west of Ural Hills), to Arkhangelsk, and also to Murmansk. The same is true for the northernmost railroads in North America, those serving Fairbanks (Alaska), Churchill (Manitoba), and the several ports in Newfoundland. Within the United States the Milwaukee Road, the Great Northern, and the Northern Pacific railroads (all of which connect western lumber regions with eastern markets) report that lumber and other forest products generate 14, 14, and 25 per cent respectively of total freight revenue compared to 7 per cent for United States railroads as a whole.

Nevertheless, tremendous tonnages still move to market by waterway from northern to central Europe, from Canada to the United States, and from northern Russia and Siberia to central Russia. For instance, huge rafts of logs and ships loaded with lumber move by sea along the Arctic coast of Siberia, through the Barents Sea, and along the Atlantic Shores of Norway. Other water "highways" for lumber are the gulfs of Bothnia and Finland, the Baltic and North seas in Europe, the Great Lakes in Anglo-America, the Pacific shores of Alaska, Canada and the United States, and the Pacific shores of U.S.S.R. and Japan. Considerable interoceanic traffic in lumber moves from Washington, Oregon, and California via the Panama Canal to New York and other eastern ports.

Forest Settlements   Transportation routes converge on forest settlements, which thus serve as ganglia in the forest economy. Upon these points the logs and collected items come together from the forest; from these points they move on to markets. Countless such settlements are sprinkled throughout the world's forests. And there are numerous types of them. At one extreme are the temporary *lumber camps,* semipermanent settlements that serve the simplest functions: residence for workers and assembly point of outbound freight. Little sorting and no processing take place. Such settlements may be on banks of rivers where log drives begin, or at the junctions of minor roads or small railroads. Somewhat larger forest settlements may support the additional functions of sawmilling or manufacturing veneer or pulp. Still larger forest settlements may contain businesses supplying saws, ropes, and other equipment used in forest gathering. The largest ones contain headquarters of forestry firms and the financial institutions serving them.

At this point we should have a world map of forest settlements. But so far as the author knows, no such map exists. Before one can be made, somebody must devise a system for classifying *forest settlements.* Is it possible to distinguish *forest hamlets, forest villages, forest towns, forest cities?* If so, by what criteria? If not, what categories *can* be delimited? And when this is done, where does each type occur? Such a study would be a real contribution to economic geography.

Manufacturing   Lumbering invariably leads to manufacturing. Forest settlements, except for the very smallest, usually have at least a saw mill. Some places have a group of factories such as veneer mills, planing mills, or sash and door factories. In Finland and Sweden, many a stream flowing into the Gulf of Bothnia has one or more of these factories at its mouth.

In Europe, too, wood carving is a distinctive industry that occupies many farmers during the winters; their wooden carvings, dolls, and toys are exported in large numbers to America.

But the future will see wood used less and less as lumber or fuel and more and more as a raw material from which scientists will manufacture paper, rayon, and alcohol, among other things. Necessity has already proved what can be done with wood. For instance, during World War II the Germans manufactured cattle feed from pulp, lubricating oil from stumps, and synthetic rubber tires from cellulose. Wood has so many useful by-products that it is a universal raw material. More and more the forester will play the role of provider of raw materials for factories. The remarkable aspect of this function is that forests, if properly treated, are a *renewable* resource in contrast to minerals which, once mined, do not replenish themselves.

Agriculture   In Norway we have found farmer-fishermen; we find farmer-forestrymen in Sweden, Finland, the northern U.S.S.R., and a few in Canada (and at an early date, in the United States)—men who till crops in the summer and cut down trees in the winter. This practice is restricted essentially to regions where the winters are too cold for agriculture.

Agricultural principles are being increasingly applied to trees themselves as the years go by. Cleared land planted in trees (in particular, rubber, cacao, banana, orange, apple, peach, pine, fir, and spruce) which are then protected and harvested is a farm as truly as if it were planted in corn. *Tree farming is a type of agriculture regardless of whether the tree crop takes a century to mature* (for instance, fir, pine) *or just a few years* (apples, rubber).

Governmental Policies   Forest gathering is influenced by governmental policies in many ways, three of which are reforestation, government ownership of forest land, and the taxing of private forests.

China, India, and Japan illustrate contrasts in governmental attitude toward reforestation. Each exhausted its virgin timber long ago. The Chinese and Indian governments did little about it. So today they are forest-poor lands starved for firewood (the people must burn manure in many places) and lumber (they have little wood for implements and even coffins). The Japanese government, on the other hand, was one of the first to urge its people to plant trees on a large scale. Today growth

exceeds cut. Indeed, 60 per cent of the land is now forested—an astonishing percentage for a nation so densely populated. In no country outside the tropics (except Finland) is so high a proportion of the land in trees.

Some nations believe that trees are a resource that should be owned by the public for both best usage and conservation. In France, 37 per cent of the forests are now government-owned and-operated. In Finland the government owns 60 per cent. Canada's forests, which were not exposed to commercial exploitation until comparatively recently, are still largely (90 per cent) owned by the government. Where public domain was sold to private holders, some governments have repurchased land to re-establish forests. The United States federal government now owns 21 per cent of our forest land; state and local governments own an additional 6 per cent.

Government taxing policies influence forest practices on private land. Where such land is taxed at the same rate as crop land, the owners are discouraged from conserving trees. After all, it takes from 75 to 100 years to

A sawmill and wallboard factory at Skinnskatteberg 90 miles northwest of Stockholm, a typical destination for timber after it has been moved by river, flume, truck, railroad, or even huge coastal raft. (Courtesy of Kirk Stone.)

produce a tree crop in the mid-latitudes. Few men would spend $1000 in replanting trees on a piece of land knowing that neither they nor their son, perhaps even grandson, would realize any direct return on it—all the while paying regular taxes on it. Taxation policy is of significance in this instance not to good crop land but to marginal land—territory that might or might not yield an agricultural crop within a year. If regular taxes prevail, the owner will be tempted to plant an annual crop (say, wheat) that will yield an imminent return. But if lower taxes are assessed on wood land, he may decide to leave marginal land in trees or even reforest it.

PROBLEMS OF FOREST GATHERING

Numerous problems stem from carelessness in forest gathering. The most important are cut-over, erosion, and floods. After describing them, we shall consider remedial measures.

Cut-over   This term applies to places where virgin forests have been removed without replenishing themselves. Two agents have usually been responsible. One is the farmer who wants land for tillage and considers trees as nuisances—something to be destroyed. This attitude motivated much of the land-clearing in the central United States. The other agent is the lumberman to whom trees are items of value. Together they have nearly deforested the populous areas of the world. China has suffered the most. Endowed ages ago with extensive and excellent forests, China now has trees on less than 10 per cent of its area, mostly in the remote and very hilly west and south. The forests of central Europe, particularly Germany, France, and Britain, suffered the same fate. The woods of New England, the southeastern United States, and the Great Lakes states were devastated as if by an invading army. Rarely in the history of man has a resource been so ravaged as were mid-latitude forests. As yet, the rainforest bears few such scars.

Erosion   Tree roots and the litter of leaves anchor soil in place. On flat or gently sloping land, trees can be removed and soil cultivated without danger of severe erosion. But moderate slopes must be protected at least with grass (such as pasture) which has roots deep enough to hold soil in place. But even grass roots are unable to bind soil to steep slopes. These must be left in trees, else through erosion the soil is speedily carried away. Conservationists estimate that a fourth of the original soil in the Mississippi Basin has been swept into the Gulf of Mexico. A good deal of this soil was originally firmly anchored by trees.

Floods   The litter of leaves and the tree roots also act like a sponge to retard the rate of run-off, whether of water from heavy rain or melting snow. When forests are removed the water rushes unchecked into the rivers. By carelessly removing trees, man has cursed himself with floods. To be sure, floods occurred in primeval forests occasionally, but man's modification of the landscape has increased both the frequency and severity of floods.

Remedial Measures   Man is learning his lesson and is beginning to practice conservation of forest resources. Conservation is a broad term that means, not preservation, but *wise use*. Two broad practices apply: reforestation and sustained-yield forestry.

These conservation measures are being practiced to an increasing degree by owners of forest land whether they are farmers on small woodlots, industrial companies (such as lumber and pulp manufacturers), or governments (national, state, county, or municipal). The conservation movement originated in regions of dense population and advanced technologies where the forest resource quickly gave out and where the exposed land was poor for farming. These conditions were met best in Germany, Sweden, and Japan, and they are where the movement started.

Reforestation is necessary in cut-over lands, which are handicapped for more productive uses, that is, if the terrain is too rough, the climate too severe, or the soil too poor for agriculture. Thousands of sandy acres in midwestern and in southeastern states are being reforested by high school conservation classes, by sporting clubs, by paper companies, and by government agencies. One of the first such ventures in reclaiming sandy soil occurred in "The Landes," a sandy region of southwestern France where an army of sand dunes was advancing eastward from the Atlantic, swallowing farms and villages. Shortly after 1800 the French launched a successful experiment to anchor these dunes with pine trees. Today the pine forest of southern France protects farms and settlements, and also supports a respectable business in naval stores.

The notion and practices of reforestation are spreading rapidly in the northern United States and northern Europe where land, once cleared for farming, is now being replanted in trees. Agriculture turned out to be a poor venture here for two reasons: Winters are too severe for most cropping, and soils that develop under softwood trees are poor for most crops. Much of the soil here is *podzol*. Now, some farmers are selling their farms to lumber companies, the government, or other agencies who then bear the costs of transforming the land from farm back to forest.

Even on acreage that is technically forested, tree-planting programs are often urged by forest specialists for the simple reason that natural regeneration of understocked land is simply too slow. Right now, less than half the forest land in the United States is well stocked and almost 10 per cent is nonstocked according to United States Forest Service reports. Replantings now cover 5,000,000 acres, but 52,000,000 acres still need replanting if they are to become productive within a reasonable time. Almost 85 per cent of these acres are in the eastern half of the nation.

Sustained-yield forestry involves three ideas.

1. The rate of cut must not exceed the rate of growth. This balance has already been achieved in Japan, Germany, and Sweden. The United States just recently has achieved this objective—not in every part of the nation yet, but for the country as a whole. Our annual increment in volume of standing timber

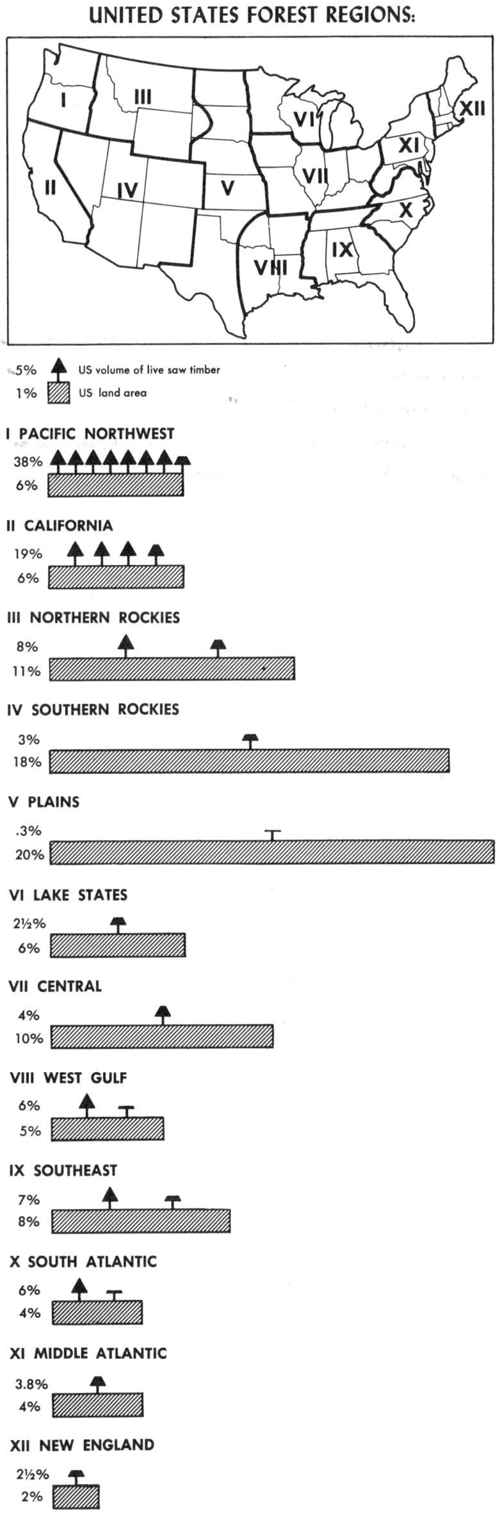

UNITED STATES FOREST REGIONS:

.5% — US volume of live saw timber
1% — US land area

I PACIFIC NORTHWEST
38%
6%

II CALIFORNIA
19%
6%

III NORTHERN ROCKIES
8%
11%

IV SOUTHERN ROCKIES
3%
18%

V PLAINS
.3%
20%

VI LAKE STATES
2½%
6%

VII CENTRAL
4%
10%

VIII WEST GULF
6%
5%

IX SOUTHEAST
7%
8%

X SOUTH ATLANTIC
6%
4%

XI MIDDLE ATLANTIC
3.8%
4%

XII NEW ENGLAND
2½%
2%

Figure 6-4

is 14.2 billion cubic feet; the annual cut is 12.3 billion—a ratio of 114:110. But in the West—where our best-quality wood occurs—cutting greatly exceeds growth. The reverse is true in the South and especially the Northeast where growth is now more than twice the rate of cut. This net gain in the East, however, is mostly from seedling and pulpwood trees while the net loss in the West is of sawtimber.

2. Cuttings must be small enough in extent so that surrounding trees may easily reseed the cut-over segment.

3. Trees must be protected from three major enemies: insects, diseases, and fire. In the United States, for example, these three destructive agents destroy more than one billion cubic feet of wood each year. An additional 2.5 billion cubic feet of potential growth never materializes at all because of these same agents. Diseases such as heart rot, leaf mold, blister rust, oak wilt, and root diseases wreak more havoc than all other offenders combined. Regionally, disease is more devastating in the Northeast and West than in the South. Fire not only destroys growth but also makes surviving trees vulnerable to disease and insects. Fire does more damage in the West and South than in the Northeast where more progress has been made in fire protection. Each year over 125,000 fires strike our forests; 95 per cent of them are started by man, some deliberately. Insects such as bark beetles, borers, weevils, moths, spittlebugs and aphids do most of their damage in the West and least in the North.

The key to the successful application of conservation policies rests in the hands of 3,400,000 farmers and 1,100,000 other owners of private forests who, together, hold the deeds to 73 per cent of our nation's commercial forest acreage. The problem at this point is that the interests of most of these owners is *not primarily* in growing timber.

Will reforestation and sustained-yield forestry be able to save our forests from extinction? The trouble is that our population and anticipated demand are increasing more rapidly than forest growth. The United States Forest Service predicts that *if* our per capita consumption of wood continues at the same level, and *if* our population increases at the predicted rate (to 215,000,000 in 1975 and 275,000,000 in the year 2000), and *if* present forest conditions are maintained, the result will be a 14 per cent deficit in wood by 1975 and a 76 per cent deficit in 2000. Clearly, the United States will become increasingly dependent on foreign forests. Although we are not facing an immediate timber famine, shortages will be severe by 2000 unless forestry programs are substantially intensified in all forest regions. And this acceleration will have to come soon.

Suggested Readings

Coppock, J. T., "A Decade of Post-War Forestry in Great Britain," *Economic Geography*, 1960, pp. 127-138.

Hance, William A., and Van Dongen, Irene S., "Gabon and Its Main Gateways: Libreville and Port Gentil," *Tijdschrift voor Economische en Sociale Geografie*, November, 1961, pp. 286-295.

Hardwick, Walter G., "Log Towing Rates in Coastal British Columbia," *The Professional Geographer*, September, 1961, pp. 1-5.

Parsons, James J., "The Cork Oak Forests and the Evolution of the Cork Industry in Southern Spain and Portugal," *Economic Geography*, 1962, pp. 195-214.

Paterson, Sten Sture, *The Forest Area of the World and Its Potential Productivity*, Göteborg, 216 pp.

Stokes, George A., "Lumbering and Western Louisiana Cultural Landscapes," *Annals of the Association of American Geographers*, 1957, pp. 250-266.

United Nations, Food and Agriculture Organization, *Yearbook of Forest Product Statistics*.

Whaley, W. G., "Rubber, Heritage of the American Tropics," *The Scientific Monthly*, January, 1946, pp. 21-31.

PART FOUR

COMMERCIAL BIOCULTURE

Besides merely extracting (or gathering) commodities from nature, man also manipulates the natural creation of plants and animals he values. These activities will be the subject matter of Part Four. We shall use the term *bioculture* in this book to apply to all such collaborations between man and nature. Thus, bioculture includes all endeavors traditionally known as agriculture and animal husbandry plus others, such as fish farming and fur farming, in which plants or animals are raised for sale.

Activities whereby income is derived mainly from the sales of tended animals or their products will be considered first, in Chapters 7, 8, and 9. Chapter 7 deals with livestock ranching (or commercial grazing), in which domesticated animals are supported largely by natural forage and raised primarily for the sale of meat, wool, and hides. Chapter 8 covers dairying, in which domesticated animals are supported mainly by cultivated crops and raised primarily for milk production. Chapter 9 takes up "mixed" farming, where the emphasis is on production of both animals and crops.

The next two chapters are devoted to types of bioculture in which farmers specialize primarily in the production of commercial crops. Chapter 10 is on the "Mediterranean" type, which is distinguished by a wide variety of crops, while Chapter 11 deals with one of the most highly specialized of all agricultural endeavors: grain farming.

The last two chapters of Part Four will deal with a diversity of biocultural endeavors—Chapter 12 with miscellaneous cropping ventures and Chapter 13 with miscellaneous types specializing in producing animals. The end of Chapter 13 provides a summary of general facts and patterns about bioculture as a whole.

Throughout the chapters on bioculture it will help to refer frequently to five source materials:

1. The most important is the United State *Census of Agriculture*. For decades the United States government has published a periodic agricultural census that contains a wealth of data. For no other economic activity does the federal government compile and make available to the public so vast a body of information.

2. The government recently published the *National Atlas of the United States*, which contains numerous maps and generous analytical comments.

3. The United Nations' Food and Agriculture Organization *Yearbook* contains a wealth of data on biocultural endeavor in member countries of the UN.

4. William Van Royen's *Atlas of the World's Agricultural Resources* contains many maps, and the accompanying text treats of agriculture from the world point of view.

5. *The Shorter Oxford Economic Atlas of the World* provides excellent colored maps of production and excellent data on international trade of biocultural products.

Buildings of the ranchstead on Kings Ranch near Laramie, Wyoming. (United States Department of Agriculture Photograph.)

SEVEN

The World Pattern

LOCATION

The characteristic economy in several parts of the world is the tending of animals for sale (see Figure 7-1, page 110). In North America, the region extends from Canada to central Mexico and blankets a third of the United States. South America has two zones. The larger runs 4000 miles northward from Tierra del Fuego through Argentina and Brazil to the Atlantic; with only three interruptions it covers the southeastern third of the continent and actually penetrates through Chile to the Pacific Coast. A smaller counterpart occupies the coast and interior lowland of Venezuela. Livestock ranching is found all over that portion of Africa which is south of central Angola and Rhodesia except for coastal areas. It prevails over a great portion of Australia and New Zealand—no other land masses have so high a percentage of space devoted to this economy. As in southern Africa, long stretches of the Australian coast are taken by other biocultural types. Livestock ranching is absent in Eurasia save for an area northeast of the Caspian Sea where this activity has recently replaced nomadic herding.

CHARACTERISTICS

The bioculture of these ranching regions is strong on animal husbandry, with comparatively little crop cultivation. Although almost any animal could be grazed commercially,

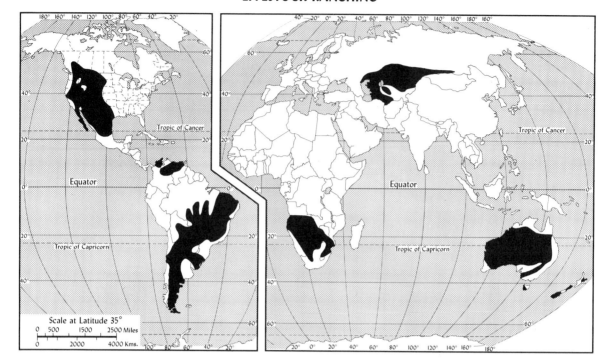

Figure 7-1

only certain ones are deemed really worth-while, namely sheep, cattle, and goats. This is not to say that most of the world's number of these animals is in these regions but rather that these animals typify the bioculture here (for the distribution of sheep, see Figure 7-2).

The items of revenue are mainly wool and hides. Some meat is sold, but there is an increasing tendency to sell live meat animals to farmers in other regions that are better endowed to fatten them.

Scientific methods are applied in the care of both animals and their habitats. With the animals, for instance, breeding practices are scrupulous in order to upgrade strains. Herds are carefully protected not only from marauders but from parasites and diseases; on the most advanced ranches the animals are run through chemical baths and sometimes are inoculated against disease. Natural supplies of water are augmented by wells, which are often powered by windmills and pumps. Although the feed supply is largely natural forage, it is often augmented by alfalfa, grains, or other crops.

The habitat is tended in order to realize its "carrying capacity" to the full. Carrying capacity refers to the number of animals a given amount of land can support with its natural vegetation. The variation is great. Over the desert area of the southwestern United States 100 acres are required to supply forage necessary for just one steer. In the steppes and mountain meadows the carrying capacity varies from 25 to 75 acres per steer. On the eastern margins of the Great Plains the capacity improves to 10 to 25 acres per steer. These figures can also be phrased in terms of "animal units" whereby, for measuring carrying capacity, one steer is equated with one horse or five sheep. If an area has a carrying capacity of 10, a rancher could count on successfully raising 10 steer or 10 horses or 50 sheep or any combination thereof so long as the 10-unit figure were not exceeded.·

A key role in controlling carrying capacity is played by the fence, a simple structure with

SHEEP

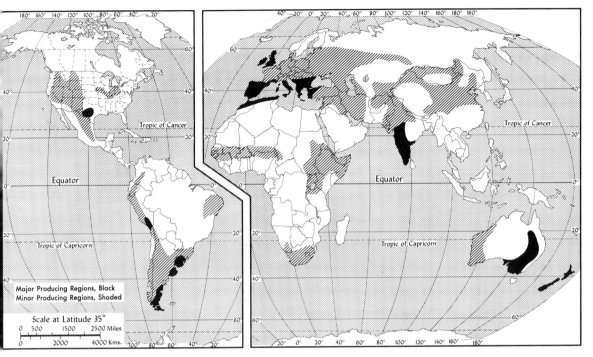

Figure 7-2 *Distribution of sheep does not coincide with pattern on Figure 7-1 because sheep are raised as a sideline in many areas where livestock ranching is not the predominant activity.*

a profound agricultural impact.* ~~Essentially a fence protects a piece of range land by preventing interlopers from bringing the number of grazers above carrying capacity and so exhausting the forage.~~ Further, the fence prevents the herd from wandering and interbreeding with poorer strains of animals; it also protects against marauders.

In contrast to nomadic herding, livestock ranching restricts the animals to parcels of land owned or leased by herdsmen or ranching organizations. The "operating units" consist not only of the natural pasture land but also the ranch house and often acreage given over to supplementary feed crops. Livestock ranching has the largest operating units of any type of bioculture. In the United States they frequently exceed 1000 acres. Most ranches in Wyoming, Nevada, Arizona, New Mexico, and

* An interesting analysis of the significance of the fence to agricultural economy is "The American Fence" by Fraser Hart and Eugene Mather in *Landscape*, Vol. 6, No. 3, 1957, pages 4-9.

Texas are over 2500 acres in size. One ranch in southern Texas encompasses 865,000 acres —over 1000 square miles. But the world's largest ranches are found in Australia where several spread over 5000 square miles; one Australian ranch even covers an astonishing 12,000 square miles!

PHYSICAL RELATIONSHIPS

In many respects, livestock ranching is involved with the same kinds of forces as is nomadic herding, particularly the physical environment; on the other hand, some relationships are quite different, notably those with cultural phenomena, which we shall consider a little later.

Precipitation ~~Most commercial grazing occurs in dry lands.~~ Dry climates prevail in five of the largest ranching areas—those of North America, southern South America, South Africa, Australia, and the U.S.S.R.

A cattle drive in Argentina across the vast treeless pampas. (Courtesy International Packers Limited.)

Anomalies are New Zealand and portions of South America where climates are humid. Rainfall varies from less than 10 inches in the five dry regions to as high as 60 inches in the wet ones. Precipitation is significant in its effect both on natural vegetation (as we shall see in a moment) and on alternate possibilities of bioculture. Generally it is held that 20 inches of annual rainfall marks the limit for unirrigated farming in the mid-latitudes. Beyond that line, the drier regions are too risky for cropping and generally are devoted to animal culture. Most of the plants that can survive in dry lands are not valuable enough to cultivate. But animals can live off such scattered vegetation. This is the basic reason why animal husbandry rather than cropping is the prevailing form of bioculture on dry land which is not irrigated.

Natural Vegetation   For the above reason, livestock ranching occurs in regions of grasslands and desert shrub. But the correla-

tion between ranching and these vegetation types is not complete since nomadic herders also occupy vast stretches of such environments. Conversely, there is some livestock ranching in forest zones—in coniferous forest in portions of North America and in "light" tropical forests in parts of South America and southern Africa. But in these anomalous regions, individual trees are far enough apart so a grass cover can develop.

The type of grass varies regionally. In the low latitudes are the tropical grasslands, generally termed savannas—such as the *llanos* of Venezuela, the *campos* of Brazil, and the *Gran Chaco* of Argentina-Paraguay-Bolivia. Generally, these tropical grasses are tall, coarse, and fibrous, so not very edible, and their carrying capacity is low. Yet some tropical grasses, which are softer and more palatable, can support animals fairly well and would provide rather good range land if their spreading could be encouraged. In a few places, strains of lusher African grasses have been sown in forest clearings in the tropics and, in some instances, seem to be taking hold satisfactorily enough to provide pasturage.

The mid-latitudes have the best grasslands: prairies and steppes. Prairies, however, rarely sustain a ranching economy for very long. Why? Because the rainfall in these regions, though inadequate for trees, does support tall lush grass, and tall grasses are particularly edible and lucrative crops—such grasses as wheat, corn, and oats, for instance, once grew wild but today are domesticated and often hybridized. Consequently, prairies have yielded to the plow and the cultivator, and the rancher has been replaced by the farmer. Not so in the steppes. With decreasing rainfall the carrying capacity decreases—but so do the opportunities for cultivation. Thus, in the mid-latitudes the principal domain of livestock ranching is the steppe. Marginal grass-lands are also used, such as the desert fringes adjoining steppes and grassland patches on the edges of forests that adjoin steppes.

Landforms and Elevations   Sheep and cattle are only slightly deterred by rough land, and goats are famous for their ability to scale steep slopes. There is little direct correlation, then, between ranching regions and landforms: Ranching occurs on plains, hills, plateaus, and mountains, in lowlands and in highlands. If mountains are high enough, they pass the *tree line*, above which grasses are unrivaled. If the country at these altitudes is not too rough, excellent mountain pastures prevail.

Temperature   In the mid-latitudes, variations in temperature are associated with a distinctive practice, called *transhumance*, in which herdsmen move their herds to different

Fall roundup in the dry, sparsely vegetated Copper Basin, near Mackay, Idaho. Twenty outfits had stock in the 2000 head of cattle in this roundup. (Courtesy Standard Oil Company of New Jersey.)

altitudes at different seasons. This system prevails in regions where the climate has one severe season, say, a very cold winter. The usual practice is to graze the herd on lowland forage in the winter when the mountain pastures are inaccessible and then in summer to move the herd to the slopes. This permits the lowland grasses to be replenished. Transhumance is not customary in mild climates where the highland meadows can feed a herd year around. In such places the lowlands can be given over to more remunerative forms of bioculture, and ranching is largely confined to the highlands. This is the case in southern California.

In the tropics, the combination of heat and humidity handicaps commercial grazing (particularly in Venezuela, Brazil, Paraguay, Bolivia, and northern Argentina); furthermore, animal diseases flourish in that climate, as do flies, ticks and other pests. Native animals that have developed a resistance to these environmental handicaps do not, unfortunately, produce the kind of wool, hide, and meat that man esteems. The best fleeces and skins are those of animals in the mid-latitudes.

CULTURAL RELATIONSHIPS

Population Density   Livestock ranching, not surprisingly in view of its physical requirements, is associated with low population density. The regions of commercial grazing generally have densities of less than 25 people per square mile and often less than 2 per square mile. To be sure there are enclaves of denser settlement, but these are based on some other type of economic activity, usually mining.

Settlements   Livestock ranching regions contain two types of settlement: *dispersed* and *agglomerated*. The dispersed settlements consist of *ranchsteads* (the dwellings of ranching families plus associated buildings), each of which is located on its own ranch. This arrangement contrasts with the settlement patterns in the other economic regions we have studied—those of subsistence farming, of commercial fishing, and of commercial foresting (and also, as we shall see, of commercial

mining)—where homes tend to be clustered together.

Agglomerated settlements in ranching areas are mainly service centers (see Chapter 29). A service center is a dual-purpose settlement found only in regions of commercial economies. One function is to assemble the surplus production from its environs (in this case, wool, hides, and so on from the ranches) for forwarding to major markets. The other function is to supply the producers in its surroundings (in this case the ranchers) with everything they do not provide for themselves. Such services are *tertiary* endeavors (see Chapter 1). In ranch country, there may be a little manufacturing, but typically these settlements are service centers rather than manufacturing centers.

What kind of work do people do in these ranching towns? *Employment structure*, which provides for any given political unit a breakdown by percentages of the employment in each economic activity, would be useful to apply here. Unfortunately, nobody has ever made a study of employment structures of ranching settlements to discover what a "typi-cal" ranching center is like. But the United States Census does publish detailed figures on employment in every city in the country over 2500 population. With them we can see what groups of jobs exist in any one place. Table 7-1 shows the employment structure for Torrington, a livestock ranching service center in eastern Wyoming. Perhaps somebody someday will investigate the employment structures of all ranching settlements to discover what the group as a whole is like and how they vary among themselves—not only for Torrington and other towns in the United States but also for ranching centers abroad, such as Torreón (Mexico), Ciudad Bolivar (Venezuela), Correntina (Brazil), San José (Bolivia), Puerto Casado (Paraguay), Kuruman (South Africa), and Cloncurry (Australia).

Where rangeland covers mineral deposits, settlements may take on the additional functions of mining centers. For example, Lead, South Dakota, only 15 miles from the Wyoming border, is a community of 6500 people with 60 per cent of its workers engaged in

Activity	Percentage of Total Employment in Each Economic Activity
Primaries	5
Agriculture	4
Mining	1
Secondaries	17
Construction	9
Manufacturing	8
Tertiaries	78
Trade	30
Professional services	14
Personal services	8
Public administration	8
Transportation and utilities	8
Finance	5
Business services and repair	5

Source: United States Census of Population, 1950, Vol. II, Characteristics of the Population, Table 39.

mining and only a small percentage related to ranching.

The size of a ranching center depends on the amount of service demanded by its hinterland. In many small settlements the assembly function is performed by marketing agencies to which the ranchers bring their wool, hides, or livestock. In truckloads or rail carloads these are then forwarded to larger collecting centers where trainloads are formed. Obviously, the small centers greatly outnumber the larger ones. Depending on the general density of ranches (which in turn depends on the carrying capacity of the land and the standard of living of the ranchers), the small centers may be from 20 to 50 miles apart. Any traveler in the American West, for example, knows how few and far between the towns are. Larger settlements are even farther apart. In the Great Plains of the Dakotas, Nebraska, Wyoming, and Montana, it is often 100 miles between settlements that have even 2500 people. In Nevada the distance reaches 300 miles.

The combined population in such settlements makes up a rather low percentage of the region's total inhabitants, the proportion of rural to urban populace being high. According to the United States Census (in which a settlement must have 2500 inhabitants to be considered "urban"), the urban population in dozens of counties in the livestock ranching region is zero.

In brief, the settlements of commercial ranching regions are small in size, few in number, far apart, and account for only a small proportion of the region's total population.

Age—A New Economy   Livestock ranching is a newcomer on the world map. Whereas nomadic herding has been practiced for millennia, commercial grazing is little more than 200 years old. Not until the period 1750-1800 did world markets generate enough demand for wool, hides, and meat to support a commercial animal economy based on natural vegetation in the dry lands.

Western Culture   The physical environment of nomadic herding is essentially the same as that of livestock ranching. But the cultures are dissimilar. At one time nomadic herding was common to most dry lands with scanty vegetation.

But immigrants to the present regions of livestock ranching were mainly European farmers accustomed to tilling the soil. They found that the dry lands in the new continents would not permit satisfactory farming. Consequently they resorted to raising animals. Although they adopted the nomadic herders' means of existence, they shunned the nomads' way of living, retaining instead their European traditions such as fixed houses and private ownership of the grazing lands. Furthermore—and most importantly—Europeans had different notions of how animals should be tended in a dry habitat. Only they developed the ideas for advanced scientific animal culture mentioned earlier. Europeans also developed breeds of animals that produce particularly prized kinds of fleece (such as Merino sheep) or of hides and of flesh (such as Angus and Hereford cattle).

Recently scientists have tried to cross certain breeds to develop a strain endowed with the resistance of tropical animals to disease and insects yet with the qualities of meat and hides attributed to mid-latitude animals. They have made some progress. Such strains as the Brahmin cattle, probably the most successful of this type, may herald a new day for commercial grazing in tropical grasslands. As more scientific methods are adopted to overcome environmental handicaps in Venezuela, Brazil, Paraguay, and other tropical grazing regions, it seems likely that their inherent environmental advantages can be capitalized on, thereby increasing their role in livestock production.

Markets   Ranchers do not use up much of their own product. In no other economic activity are producing regions so remote from customers. Livestock ranchers in the major world regions depend for their livelihood on two markets: western Europe and eastern Anglo-America. In the early days of commercial grazing the demand was for hides, wool, tallow, and only slightly meat—and even that in dried form. Before the days of refrigeration, fresh meat simply could not stand the long trip from the western United States to the Atlantic Seaboard, from Buenos Aires to Berlin, from Capetown to London, from Freemantle to Liverpool. The population explosion and the increased purchasing power attributable to the Industrial Revolution of these two market areas triggered the development of commercial animal economies. Before these two world markets experienced the Industrial Revolution, their own economies were largely on the same subsistence level as the distant regions that subsequently yielded up surplus animal products.

Source of Personnel and Capital   It takes both money and people with ideas to build a commercial venture. Livestock ranching requires capital investments for fences, herds, lands, and hired hands. Europe and eastern Anglo-America served not only as the destination for products of ranching regions but also as the point of origin for much of the investment capital and personnel that established grazing enterprises in South America, western North America, South Africa, and Australia. Until rather recently, ranching

areas themselves could not raise enough capital to finance ranching ventures.

Transportation   Commercial grazing areas are so far from their markets that cheap transportation is essential to their existence. Fortunately for the most distant ones (Australia, southern Africa, and South America), cheap ocean transportation is possible. Railroads converge from the grazing country on a few port cities such as Buenos Aires, Montevideo, Salvador (Brazil), Lobito (Angola), Capetown (South Africa), and Freemantle (Australia). In the early days of commercial grazing in the United States, Southern Californians shipped hides and tallow clear around Cape Horn to New York and the East Coast. Galveston and New Orleans dockworkers still load ships with wool and hides, but by and large the American grazing region is dependent on rail and truck movements rather than waterways. Notice that on the world map of railways (in almost any economic atlas) a network of railways spreads over the regions of commercial grazing; however, the density of railroads is not as high as in more heavily populated and highly developed areas. Figure 7-3 illustrates, for a portion of the American grazing region, the flow of cattle via railroad from a grazing state. Notice that the dividing line between predominantly eastbound and westbound traffic runs through western Colorado.

International Trade   Most surplus wool, skins, and meat must be transported across international boundaries to reach their markets. In some countries they attain rather high percentages of total exports:

New Zealand	70%
Uruguay	70%
Australia	59%
Argentina	28%
South Africa	25%
Paraguay	20%

These six countries all have mid-latitude grasslands except for Paraguay, and from each of them wool exports bring much more revenue than do hides and skins, again except for Paraguay where hide exports exceed wool.

Livestock Ranching

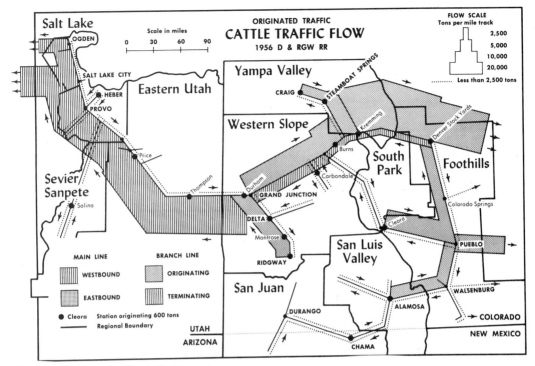

Figure 7-3 (*Courtesy Frank H. Thomas.*)

There is a paradox involving regions of nomadic herding and those of livestock ranching. Since the foremost market for wool and hides is western Europe, it would seem that the nearest dry regions of steppe vegetation would serve that market. Northern Africa and the Middle East satisfy these environmental requirements and lie from 500 to 3000 miles from Europe. Moreover, the Mediterranean Sea links them to Europe. But environmental factors are not enough. Here is a vivid instance of the effect of cultural forces— Australians have bridged the 10,000 miles from their continent to England with wool and hide shipments while in northern Africa, though it is much nearer to England, the people have plodded along with nomadic herding.

Manufacturing   Valuable as wool, hides, and tallow are, their values are increased when their form is changed. Essentially the sequence of movement is from ranch to settlement to port—all on the way to the factory. In the days before commercial grazing, leather

and textiles were largely manufactured by consumers at home or by local specialists. But with the dawn of livestock ranching woolen mills, leather factories, and meat packing factories mushroomed. (The development of these industries will be analyzed in later chapters on manufacturing.)

Farming   In two quite different ways, livestock ranchers find themselves involved with farmers. In some areas they ship their cattle to farmers in humid regions for fattening before final sale. This relationship holds particularly in North America where the ranchers of various western states collaborate with Corn Belt farmers.

On the other hand, as population has increased, the demand for food has risen, and new farms have been staked out, often on the humid margins of range country; the tillers of the soil have steadily invaded grazing land. Friction between farmer and rancher has flamed out many times in open feuds.

Now, it is a basic principle of bioculture that any given amount of land can sustain

Shearing time in Australia starts in July or August. In this scene a stockman is bringing sheep to the ranchyard for shearing in the woolshed (background) at a ranch near Boonoke in Riverina, New South Wales; 70,000 sheep were shorn here in six weeks by 40 shearers plus an equal number of shed-hands (pickers-up, sweepers, rollers, and pressers.) (Courtesy of Australian News and Information Bureau.)

more human beings if it is used for grains and vegetables eaten directly rather than for raising animals for meat. The diet may be better and more enjoyable in the latter instance, but fewer individuals can be supported. Is it not likely, then, that as population mounts, farmers will continue to make inroads on ranching land, even resorting to irrigation, if necessary?

Without irrigation, indeed, cultivating these dry lands is extremely risky. Once the sod is broken by the plow, the soil is no longer anchored by grass roots, and upon drying out, the soil particles become vulnerable to wind erosion. *Dust bowls* (areas where wind erosion strews dust around like sand dunes) are the inevitable result unless there is enough rainfall to enable a grass cover to take root immediately. But annual rainfall in the borderlands between humid climates and dry climates is a rather unreliable affair. The critical boundary sweeps back and forth across a climatic no-man's land several hundred miles wide. For example, during one five-year period on the United States Great Plains the boundary between the *dry* and the *humid* climates oscillated from western Iowa to central Montana (see Figure 7-4). Tilling the soil is clearly a risky business in this transitional area. In United States economic history repeated waves of farmers have invaded this zone—their hopes aroused by a series of a

Figure 7-4 (*After Henry Kendall, in Glenn T. Trewartha's* An Introduction to Climate, *McGraw-Hill, 1954.*)

BOUNDARY OF HUMID CLIMATES

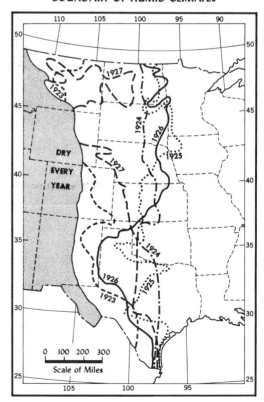

few unusually wet years—only to be driven to bankruptcy during subsequent drought years. Left behind have been two monuments to man's ignorance of nature's ground rules: abandoned farmsteads and ruined land.

An interesting example of how both the characteristics and the relationships of a ranching region can change with the passage of time is illustrated by what has happened in the United States.

Livestock Ranching in the United States

As Figure 7-1 shows, livestock ranching is the predominant economic activity in over a third of the United States, a greater area than that of any other type of bioculture. It extends from Canada to Mexico and from an eastern border which runs through the Dakotas and western Texas almost to the Pacific Ocean. Twelve states are either totally or partially included in this region.

Clarence F. Jones, applying historical geography to commercial grazing, points out that 1880 separates two distinct periods: the *open-range* period and the *organized-ranch* period.

During the *open-range* period, which prevailed from the mid-1700's, commercial grazing characterized the western half of the country. Hides, wool, and tallow were far more important commodities than meat, which was either marketed in dried form or left to rot on the carcass after the hide was removed. The animals on which this economy was based were introduced from abroad. Many of the cattle had been brought in by the Spaniards by way of Mexico. There were no operating units such as those that now exist. Animals were semiwild and were left to graze on the open range, little of which was owned by the men who owned the animals. At that time the federal government still held most of it in the public domain. Harvest season was round-up time, and the herdsmen and their cowboys roamed hundreds of miles corralling the wandering animals. Branding was an essential practice in these days for only by the brand symbol burned into the hide of an animal could a grazer claim possession of it.

Figure 7-5 (*From The Association of American Railroads.*)

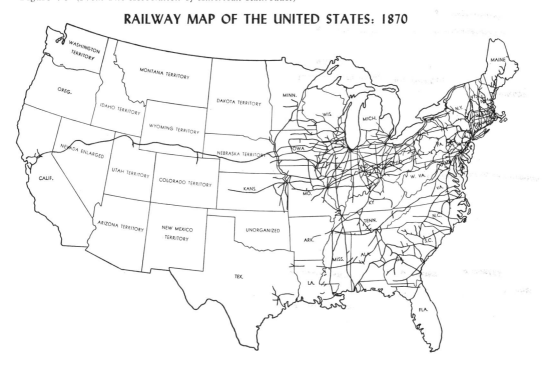

RAILWAY MAP OF THE UNITED STATES: 1870

During the open-range period, transportation was slow. Railroads had made only a few penetrations of range country (Figure 7-5), so most of the animals were driven long distances to the nearest railway station. In the earliest days they were driven all the way from Texas, Oklahoma, Colorado, and other grazing states to the northeastern market states.

These were the days of unbridled independence, of rudimentary law enforcement. Each cowman and sheepman was a law unto himself. Western novels, movies and television shows still embody the spirit of that age, or at least a reasonable facsimile thereof. These were also the days when there were no limits to the number of herdsmen, or to the number of animals, or to the extent of their wanderings. Such uncontrolled grazing exceeded the carrying capacity of the land. It overloaded the pastures and ruined thousands of acres of western dry lands, exposing them to wind erosion. It is doubtful that anywhere else on earth so much semiarid country has ever been destroyed in so short a time by wind erosion as the American steppes. They were laid bare both by overgrazing and by the cultivating of land that never should have felt the plowman's blade.

The *organized-ranch* period began around 1880. Well-planned commercial grazing now emerged. Several characteristics differentiate this phase from the preceding one. Meat was now the main cash item, wool and hides secondary. Since the emphasis turned to beef, cattle became the most numerous animals, especially the white-faced, reddish-brown Herefords and the black Angus (Figure 7-6), followed by sheep (Figure 7-7), and goats. Cattle received priority in the less dry regions, sheep and goats got what was left. The main sheep region today is in west central Texas although numerous smaller zones are conspicuous in Colorado, Utah, Wyoming, and other ranching states.

The chief new feature was the organized ranch. Tremendous pieces of land were purchased by private operators who fenced them in and built ranchsteads. They put in windmills, which became conspicuous features of

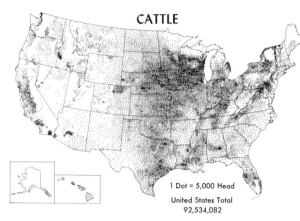

CATTLE

1 Dot = 5,000 Head
United States Total
92,534,082

Figure 7-6 (*From U. S. Bureau of the Census.*)

the landscape, to power pumps in the wells drilled to augment the natural water supply. Similarly they supplemented the natural forage supply by growing crops which tided the animals through the winter in regions where natural grasses were dormant.

The railway network expanded, threading its strands into the grazing regions (Figure 7-8). Irrigation was developed (often from government irrigation projects) to expedite the growth of supplementary feed. The government restricted grazing on public lands—forests as well as grasslands—renting out the privilege each year to ranchers in accordance with the capacity of the range. In 1934 the government's policy was formalized in the Taylor Grazing Act, which divided the public

Figure 7-7 (*From U. S. Bureau of the Census.*)

SHEEP

1 Dot = 10,000 Head

United States Total
33,944,513

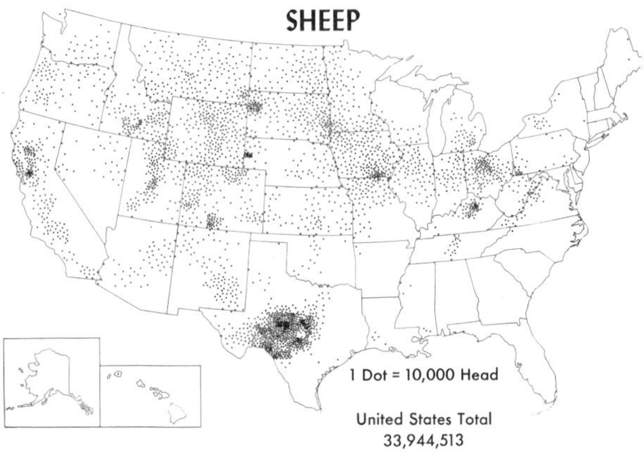

Figure 7-8 (*From The Association of American Railroads.*)

domain into numerous *grazing districts* in which privileges could be leased, established rules and regulations for grazing, and provided for the hiring of personnel to supervise these rules. Over 100,000,000 acres are now in these grazing districts.

Another development in the organized-ranch period was a closer collaboration between ranchers in the West and farmers in the Midwest and East. It came about this way. Animals lose weight in transit from range to market. Moreover, the short grass of ranch country is insufficient for producing cattle as fat as can be produced in the Corn Belt. In the days when the main cash product was hides, this was no handicap. But when meat became the premium product, the animals either had to be shipped to a humid region for fattening, or fattening feeds had to be imported to the dry lands—or grown locally under irrigation. Since the final markets were mostly in the East it made sense to ship the lean steers eastward, first for fattening and then for slaughtering. At the turn of the century farmers as far east as New York

were getting animals through the Buffalo stockyards for fattening on their farms. Today this is a thriving business throughout the humid Midwest along the routes from ranch to market.

With the swing to meat, ranching became more sensitive to economic booms and depressions of the general economy, since there is a close relationship between beef consumption and general prosperity. Only the most prosperous peoples consume much beef, and their demand plunges sharply with depressions.

As late as 1900 the United States was the world's leading exporter of fresh beef and a major exporter of wool. Europe was the principal customer. Europe still is but the United States has reversed position to become an importer of wool, hides, skins, and meat. This reversal resulted from several forces: The American market has expanded so much that there is no longer a surplus for export; other forms of agriculture invaded ranch territory; and vigorous competition from more recently developed ranches in the Southern Hemisphere captured the European market.

Livestock Ranching

Baker, Oliver E., "Agricultural Regions of North America," *Economic Geography*, 1931, pp. 109-153, and 1932, pp. 325-378.

Calef, Wesley, *Private Grazing and Public Lands: Studies of the Local Management of the Taylor Grazing Act*, Chicago, 1960, 292 pp.

————, "Problems of Grazing Administration in the Basins of Southern Wyoming," *Economic Geography*, 1952, pp. 122-127.

————, "The Winter of 1948-49 in the Great Plains," *Annals of the Association of American Geographers*, 1950, pp. 267-292.

Clark, Richard T., *Production Factors in Range Cattle under Northern Great Plains Conditions*, U. S. Government Printing Office, 1958.

Dana, Samuel Trask, *Forest and Range Policy: Its Development in the United States*, New York, 1956, 455 pp.

James, Preston E., "The Process of Pastoral and Agricultural Settlement on the Argentine Humid Pampas," *Geographical Review*, 1950, pp. 121-137.

Mather, Eugene, "The Production and Marketing of Wyoming Beef Cattle," *Economic Geography*, 1950, pp. 81-93.

Nythus, Paul O., "Argentine Pastures and the Cattle Grazing Industry," *Foreign Agriculture*, 1940, pp. 3-30.

Shantz, H. L., "Agricultural Regions of Africa," *Economic Geography*, 1940, pp. 1-47, 122-63, 341-389.

Sprague, Howard B., editor, *Grasslands*, Washington, 1959, 406 pp.

Weir, Thomas R., "The Winter Feeding Period in the Southern Interior Plateau of British Columbia," *Annals of the Association of American Geographers*, 1954, pp. 194-204.

COMMERCIAL DAIRY FARMING

*Dairy cattle in Holland graze atop the dike of the New Waterway,
a man-made channel that brings ocean vessels 18 miles
from the North Sea to Rotterdam. To the left, on polder, a farmstead
and highway lie several feet below sea level.
(Courtesy Standard Oil Company of New Jersey, The Lamp.)*

EIGHT

For hundreds of years men in certain parts of the world have consumed animal milk, principally from cows although the milk of goat, sheep, buffalo and reindeer is used in some places. On the other hand, some peoples —as in portions of Africa—consider animal milk to be excrement and so refuse to partake of it. But among people whose cultural traditions are favorable, milk has long been a staple food. Through most of human history, milk has been produced on a subsistence level. What little was sold commercially came from general farmers. Only within the past 100 years has there been much specialization by farmers in milk production. Today, however, there are thousands of farmers who gear their enterprise to production of this salable fluid. From many dairy farms, though, milk is not the only commodity sold; income is augmented by sale of eggs, poultry and other items.

LOCATION

There are three main regions where commercial farms derive their main income from the sale of milk (Figure 8-1). The largest is in western Europe, a belt extending 2000 miles from the Atlantic Coast almost to Moscow. The second dairy region, that of Anglo-America, is likewise a belt, this one beginning at the Atlantic Coast and running almost 2000 miles inland to the Prairie Provinces of Canada. Dairying is the prevailing type of bioculture in eastern Pennsylvania, New York, every New England state, the St. Lawrence Valley of Canada, the Ontario pen-

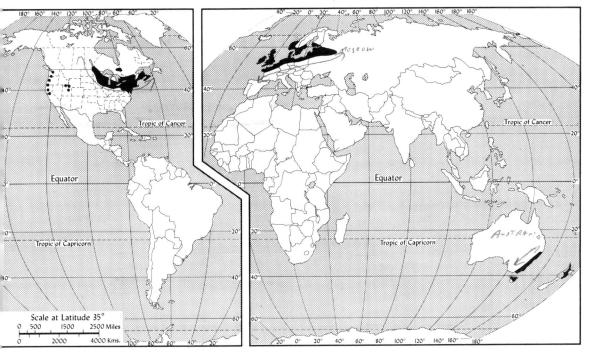

Figure 8-1

insula, and the states of Michigan and Wisconsin. For all its fame for wheat, Minnesota is largely a dairy state. The third region, again a belt, is halfway around the world—in Australia, Tasmania, and New Zealand.

Two other types of dairy areas appear by the hundreds as small pockets, but they are too widely dispersed and too small to show up on a world map. In one type, dairy farms hover around cities outside the main dairy belts in Europe and Anglo-America, and around cities in Latin America and South Africa; each zone radiates outward from a city for only a few miles, displacing the prevailing type of bioculture, whatever it might be, in the general region. In the second type, minute areas are tucked away in valleys (some irrigated) of the western United States; they dot the Pacific coast from San Diego, California, to Vancouver, British Columbia (the general distribution is shown by dots in Figure 8-1.)

From the standpoint of world milk production, the leading countries are listed in Table 8-1. The U.S.S.R., United States, France, and India are the leaders in that order. However, when weight of milk per milking cow is the criterion, then the foremost countries are Israel, the Netherlands, Denmark, and Belgium (Table 8-1).

CHARACTERISTICS OF THE UNITED STATES DAIRY BELT

Although the principal type of bioculture in all these regions is milk production, there are regional differences that warrant separate consideration. We shall look at the United States dairy belt first.

Number and Size of Farms In the United States there are approximately 500,000 dairy farms, roughly one of every nine farms in the nation. The average size is around 190 acres; however, the range in size is considerable since many are less than 100 acres and many exceed 200. Generally, the shorter the distance to a major city and the better the land, the smaller the dairy farm tends to be. Altogether, the dairy farms of the nation occupy almost 100,000,000 acres of land.

Table 8-1 Milk Production for Selected Countries

Area	Annual Production 1,000 Metric Tons	Kilograms of Milk per Milking Cow
Europe		
France	20,600	2,255
Germany, West	18,760	3,300
Poland	12,318	2,040
United Kingdom	11,092	2,830
Italy	7,823	1,560
Netherlands	6,411	4,150
Germany, East	6,003	2,680
Denmark	5,426	3,740
Czechoslovakia	4,021	1,820
Sweden	3,860	2,830
Belgium	3,747	3,710
Finland	3,323	2,870
Spain	3,166	1,650
Switzerland	2,996	3,240
Austria	2,859	2,430
Rumania	2,203	820
Hungary	1,989	2,230
Norway	1,766	2,630
Bulgaria	1,030	1,290
U.S.S.R.	61,742	1,820
North America		
United States	56,425	2,920
Canada	8,260	2,490
Mexico	2,935	—
South America		
Argentina	4,481	—
Brazil	4,407	—
Chile	753	700
Peru	400	560
Venezuela	377	—
Asia		
India	19,718	220
Pakistan	6,340	420
Turkey	4,416	402
Japan	1,715	3,640
Iran	1,178	—
Iraq	774	—
Syria	430	—
Israel	411	4,380
Burma	258	760
Africa		
Union of South Africa	2,279	—
Sudan	1,434	—
Egypt	1,093	680
Morocco	468	350
Algeria	337	—
Uganda	234	280
Oceania		
Australia	6,421	1,930
New Zealand	5,402	2,780

Source: United Nations, Food and Agriculture Organization, *Production Yearbook, 1960*, Tables 83 and 84.

Cows The number of cows per farm varies. A one-man farm may have only 10 or 12; a farm with hired labor may have 100; the average is around 20. Breeds have been developed through the years to produce particular types of milk. The Holstein, a large cow, yields the most milk, but the yield is low in butterfat. The Jersey, a small animal, yields the least amount but the richest in butterfat. Between these extreme types are the Guernsey, Brown Swiss, Ayrshire, and other breeds. A dairy cow does not begin to give milk until two years of age; the milking lifetime lasts about eight years, but may reach 15. Their lives contrast with those of beef cattle, which mature quickly and make the trip to market at the age of two.

All the best breeds of dairy cattle, whether in the Netherlands, Denmark, or England, whether in Maine, Wisconsin, or Oregon, whether in Australia or New Zealand were developed in Europe—Guernseys and Jerseys from the Channel Islands, Ayrshires from Scotland, Holstein-Frisian from the coastal lowlands of Netherlands and Germany, the Brown Swiss from Switzerland.

Milk Sales Unquestionably, by revenue the main commodity on these farms is derived from milk cows; other supplementary income is received from the sale of calves, eggs, poultry, and swine. But more than half the income of most dairy farmers derives from the sale of milk. It is sold either as fluid *market milk* or as *manufactural milk*, the latter being purchased by creameries, dairies, and other factories that turn it into cheese, butter, powdered milk, condensed milk, or ice cream mix. All told, the nation's milk cows produce over 90 billion pounds of milk a year, valued at approximately $4 billion.

On Figure 8-2, which shows United States areas by value of whole milk sold, it is clear that the main dairy belt is split into an eastern portion (especially New York State and eastern Pennsylvania) and a western one (mainly Wisconsin and fringes of Illinois and Minnesota). The western valleys, particularly the Puget Sound, Snake, San Joaquin, and those

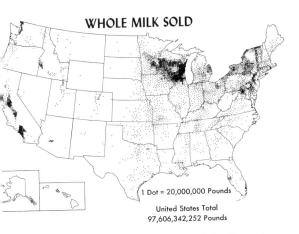

WHOLE MILK SOLD

1 Dot = 20,000,000 Pounds

United States Total
97,606,342,252 Pounds

Figure 8-2 *(From U. S. Bureau of the Census.)*

in the Los Angeles area all stand out conspicuously too.

Wisconsin is unquestionably the leading milk producing state—its dairymen sell 14 billion pounds of milk annually, which is 17 per cent of the national total. Other leaders are New York with 8 billion pounds, California with 6 billion, and Pennsylvania with 5 billion pounds. The single leading county, however, is California's Los Angeles County followed by Wisconsin's Dane County.

Other Animals Milk revenues are augmented by the sale of calves, old dairy cows, poultry, eggs, and swine. There is always a surplus of calves because the breeding of the cows, to keep the milk flowing, automatically

Figure 8-3 *(From U. S. Bureau of the Census.)*

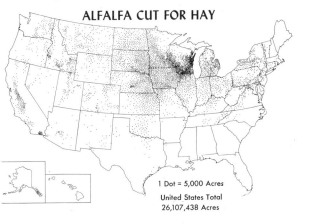

ALFALFA CUT FOR HAY

1 Dot = 5,000 Acres

United States Total
26,107,438 Acres

means more calves than are required to maintain the size of the herd. Veal thus originates largely in the dairy belt. There is some sale, too, of old beef, though it never brings a high price because the beef market is met primarily by Hereford, Angus and other cattle bred specifically for that purpose in other regions (see Chapter 7). Poultry and eggs bring supplementary income; the fowl are fed largely on skim milk, a by-product from the sale of cream, or whey, a by-product from the manufacture of cheese. Swine likewise enable the dairy farmer to convert otherwise waste material (whey or skim milk) into a salable product. (Of course some grains and other solid foods must be grown to supplement the diet of the poultry and swine.)

Land Use The typical American dairy farmer allocates his 190 acres as follows: He puts 80 acres in crops (40 in hay, 15 in corn, 13 in oats, and 12 in minor crops such as potatoes or wheat). About 45 acres are in pasture, which supports the cattle in spring, summer, and fall. Approximately 10 acres comprise the farmstead, feed lot (for poultry, swine, and calves), and vegetable patches or fruit orchards. A surprising amount of acreage (55) is in swamp or woodland, the latter being usually either too rough or stony for cropping and grazing.

Crops The main purpose of growing crops is to feed the animals during the winter, when pastures are dormant. The three most common crops are hay, corn, and oats, as we saw in the acreage allocation above. Yet many dairy areas are deficient in hay—for the distribution of alfalfa, see Figure 8-3—and must bring it in from adjoining regions. For example, Los Angeles County produces more milk than any other American county, but the dry land there grows little natural forage. Some hay is irrigated, but more is trucked in from the San Joaquin Valley; copra feed comes from the Philippines. Dairymen in Wisconsin and Michigan have to buy corn, oats, and hay from farmers of richer croplands to the south. When occasional droughts hit the dairy region, hay is trucked into Wisconsin from as far south as Tennessee. Corn grown on dairy farms is usually cut green, chopped, and stored in silos for winter feeding.

Recent research over a four-year period at a United States Agricultural Experiment Station at Marshfield, Wisconsin, indicates a correlation between yield of milk and type of crops fed to cows. When land is devoted to pasture, and cows are sustained by grazing it, the average yield is 4436 pounds of milk per acre. When the land is devoted to hay and grain—which are then harvested and fed to the cows in feedlots—the average yield is 5796 pounds of milk per acre. The advantages of the latter system (keeping cows in a feedlot and feeding them from the silo and hay mow all year long) is that the farmer can let his hay and grain mature completely in the field and then harvest them at the best stage of growth. Not all farmers, of course, face this option since much dairy land is not physically suited to growing grain (as we shall see later). But the research just cited suggests that on those farms where more grain and hay can be produced than are now being grown, it might be possible to increase milk output by revising cropping and feeding methods.

Large Amounts of Capital Invested   In few types of bioculture is so much money invested per farm. Large amounts of capital are required for buildings, machinery, and stock, although the land itself is not as expensive as in some other regions. The average dairy cow is worth around $300, so an average-size herd is worth the price of a college education.

A small fleet of machinery—tractor, plow, drill, cultivator, mowing machine, harvester, silo-filler—is required for the crops. Then there are milking machines and milk-handling equipment, which must comply with sanitary regulations imposed by the government. Finally, a truck is usually essential.

But the largest investment is in buildings. A large barn is needed to house the herd during the daily milking routine and to store the winter supply of hay. In addition a silo is required to preserve *ensilage*—crops which are cut green and kept green for winter feeding (such as corn and sometimes alfalfa). A single silo may cost as much as $5000, particularly a steel one lined with glass. Most states require still another building for handling milk—the *milk house*—to comply with sanitary regulations. The aggregate costs of herd, machinery, and buildings call for tremendous volumes in capital, often $50,000 or more.

Labor Demands   No other type of bioculture requires the day-after-day, week-after-week, year-after-year, unrelentingly faithful attention of dairy farming. The dairy cow is a valuable possession and must be treated almost as thoughtfully and carefully as a human being. Carelessness can ruin a herd in a matter of days—a herd that has taken years of meticulous attention to build up. It takes scrupulous planning also to maintain an even flow of milk from the herd. Since it takes nine months for a cow to freshen (that is, to calve, and so to begin producing milk again), a farmer must arrange the breeding and freshening periods so that he is always milking essentially the same number of cows. In the average herd, only 80 per cent of the cows yield milk at any given time. The others either are too young or are between freshening periods.

The milking itself is a twice-daily routine. This is the requirement that ties the dairyman as close to his farm as a Chinese peasant. But caring for the cows is not the only work. A farmer with, say, 24 cows is likely also to have 40 hogs and 150 chickens to feed. In the summer there is corn to be cultivated, oats to be sprayed for weeds, and hay to be cut. Anyone who knows a dairy farmer personally can appreciate the tremendous number of things to be done—and the significance of what they call "bent-back work."

It all adds up to the heaviest year-around work load of any kind of bioculture outside the Far East. Many dairy farmers never take a vacation. Some Wisconsin dairymen have

Commercial Dairy Farming

never been outside the state. The author knows one dairy farmer in New York who, in 22 years, has been away from his herd only *one* day—to attend a county fair. He even spent his honeymoon on his farm!

Little Tenancy Such a stringent demand for work discourages owners from renting their farms because the supply of dependable tenants for this type of farm is very small. For the United States as a whole, one-fourth of the farms are tenant-operated, but in the dairy states (see Figure 8-4), the figures are all lower, as the following selections reveal:

Percentages of Farms Operated by Tenants

Minnesota	20
Wisconsin	14
Michigan	7
New York	5
Connecticut	5
Massachusetts	3
New Hampshire	3
Maine	2

Changing Characteristics Currently the trend is toward more mechanization, larger herds, and larger farms. The number of farms is accordingly diminishing. In 1950, for instance, the nation had over 600,000 dairy farms, averaging 160 acres; now there are around 500,000 farms, averaging 190 acres. The number of dairy cattle is about the same, but the average number of milk cows per farm has increased from 16 to 20 and the yield per cow (because of improved feeding methods) has increased: from an average of 4000 pounds per year in 1950 to around 6000 pounds in 1960.

FOREIGN DAIRY REGIONS

Essentially the same characteristics apply to dairying in other countries; however, a few exceptions deserve comment.

Canada Canada is essentially a manufactural milk region. Although Montreal, Toronto, Quebec, Hamilton, and other cities form a market for fluid milk, most of the farmers of the Ontario Peninsula and Maritime Provinces send butter, cheese, and condensed milk to Britain. Comparatively little

Figure 8-4 (*From U. S. Bureau of the Census.*)

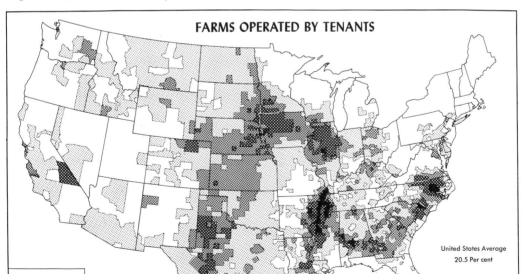

goes to the United States because of import restrictions designed to protect the United States dairymen. Typical Canadian dairy farms have more acreage in hay, less in corn and oats than do the warmer farms to the south.

Europe

Dairying is more intense in western Europe than in America because the man/land ratio is higher. Farms therefore are smaller, around 40 acres. In Denmark, in fact, half the farms have fewer than 15 acres; one-fourth of them are less than two acres in size! Obviously such small farms are not based on natural forage; the farm is not a producer of feed for cows but serves only as a place of residence. The farmers import feed, usually as a more concentrated food than hay. Corn from Argentina and cotton seed meal from the United States are common. Farmers who do grow feed devote little land to pasture, most to crops. In the Netherlands, considerable salt hay is grown, it being one of the few crops that thrive on the polder lands—former sea bottom reclaimed from the ocean. Root crops such as potatoes, beets, turnips and rutabagas are the leading feed items because the very cool European summers discourage corn and oats. Considerable crop land is heavily fertilized.

Expanding urbanization is extending the fluid milk zones contiguous to cities outward into former cheese and butter districts. Thus, the city markets of France, Belgium, Germany, and southeastern Britain absorb most of the milk produced locally. Outside sources are being turned to. Thus, milk is now being brought from eastern Ireland to London. Manufactured milk for much of England now comes from western Ireland, Scotland, Scandinavia, Finland, Denmark, Switzerland, and the hills of central France.

In the mountainous sections of Switzerland and Scandinavia, transhumance is a distinctive practice; in summer the animals graze mountain pastures (termed *alps*). Dairymen migrate with the herds and manufacture cheese on the spot. But in the winter the dairymen, bringing the cheese made in summer, the herd, and

even some surplus hay, move down to the valleys where summer-grown root crops can carry the herd through the winter.

Most of these manufactural milk areas are renowned for certain products. The Danes specialize in butter, for which they are world-famous. The Dutch specialize in cheese. Many cheeses bear the name of the area in which they originated: Edam is a town north of Amsterdam; Gouda is north of Rotterdam; Muenster and Limburger are cheeses of the German area. Every village in these localities has a cheese factory. Italians, too, are great cheese eaters, and the Po Valley is their leading dairy area. Because of Italy's dry, warm, sunny climate many meadows are diked and irrigated. Denmark is, relatively, the continent's leading dairy exporter in that 28 per cent of her sales abroad are dairy products.

Within the European dairy realm, there is spatial variation in the style of dairy barns. Near the seacoasts, winters are mild and there is comparatively little need for sturdy winter shelter for the herd; but inland the barns are larger and sounder in order to provide more protection for the herd against the cold.

In the U.S.S.R., dairying has become the leading activity in a major region developed in the late 1920's in two former Baltic states (that is, Estonia and Latvia). On stony and rough pastures this dairy zone has spread eastward to Leningrad and Moscow.

New Zealand and Southeastern Australia

The lands Down Under are ideal for dairying. Grass grows in profusion nearly all year round. So there is little need for growing supplementary feed or for protective storage buildings. The Taranaki area on the North Island of New Zealand has one of the densest concentrations of dairy cows in the world. Dairymen there have developed highly efficient methods of pasture management, which have attracted study by visiting American and British agriculturalists. New Zealand dairymen are probably the most efficient producers of milk in the world, and can, even with the 10,000 miles of ocean to cross, put cheese and butter on the European market. Were it not

The Waikato dairyland of North Island, New Zealand. The mild climate and year-round open pasture spare dairymen the need to construct large barns and silos for storing hay, grain, and ensilage for winter feeding. (Courtesy New Zealand Embassy.)

for import restrictions in the United States, New Zealanders would probably compete successfully on that market too. Dairy products account for almost 30 per cent of New Zealand's exports—the highest ratio in the world.

CULTURAL RELATIONSHIPS

Western Culture Dairying is closely related to the western world. In many other cultures milk is either taboo or too expensive. Many Africans, as was mentioned earlier, consider milk to be animal excrement. In most of Asia the obstacle is insufficient cash. The people like milk well enough (Middle Easterners, for instance, typify the perfect land as one flowing with milk and honey), but just a little is produced, mostly on a subsistence level. Only in Europe and Anglo-America are there large numbers of milk-drinkers with the ability to pay for this food which is rather expensive (compared to rice, for example). Much of the expense is attributable to storage and preservation since fresh milk sours quickly.

Urbanism Within the western world there is a close relationship between dairying and urbanism. The concentration of cities in eastern Anglo-America and western Europe is the basic reason for their having the world's

two main dairy regions. But wherever there is an Occidental city—whether in Middle America, or South America, or South Africa, or Australia—there is likely to be at least a small ring of dairy farming around it. The city may be so small that the surrounding farmers produce only a sideline of milk, but most settlements of 2500 inhabitants or more are likely to have a few full-time dairy farmers close by.

From this point on in this discussion of relationships, we will deal principally with the North American dairy belt, simply because of expediency.

The specific type of dairy farming in a dairy regions depends to a large degree on the distance to urban markets. Invariably the farms nearest the city sell *fluid milk* to the urban dairies. Today, such milk must meet rigid sanitary standards and is termed *Grade A* milk. Other grades of milk (Grade B and Grade C) come from farms that do not measure up to certain sanitation codes, and this milk is sold only for manufactured purposes. Grade A milk commands the highest price, so most farmers prefer to sell milk this way. But fresh milk is costly to transport since it is both bulky (so not worth much relative to weight) and perishable. Thus, there is a critical distance outward from every city beyond

Commercial Dairy Farming

which it is uneconomical to transport fresh milk. Obviously, the absolute mileage of this distance depends on the size of the city, the rate of milk consumption, the price of milk in that city, the transport costs to it, and the production costs to the farmer. The 150,000 residents of Madison, Wisconsin, for example, reach eight miles into the hinterland for fluid milk. Chicagoans penetrate 150 miles into Wisconsin, and New York's metropolitan area draws milk from 300 miles away—almost to the Canadian border.

Milk Sheds   A milk shed is the area from which a city receives its market, or fluid, milk and is a tangible expression of the relationship between city and farm. Where many large cities are near together as on the Atlantic seaboard, the areas coalesce into one tremendous milk shed.

Every day without fail tank trucks, often bearing the name of city dairies, but sometimes operated by milk marketing associations, wear a steady path up and down the rural roads of milk sheds collecting fresh milk. Before the automobile era, the marketing associations were poorly developed and the milk was either hauled in by the farmers themselves or shipped in on milk trains. Today the milk trains have faded from the picture except for long hauls to the very large cities, such as New York. Even Chicago gets almost all its milk by truck.

Manufactural Milk Areas   But urban centers consume milk in other forms, such as cheese, butter, powdered milk, condensed milk, and ice cream. Only in smaller cities are these products manufactured locally. For large cities it is cheaper to pay transport charges on dairy products made in the manufactural milk areas. The reason is that fresh milk is bulky and perishable, whereas the derivatives are both less bulky and less perishable. Thus, these zones within dairy regions: Milk sheds are adjacent to cities, while the manufactural milk areas are farther out.

Within manufactural milk regions there is a further tendency toward regional specializa-tion in cheese and butter. Cheese regions generally are closer than butter areas to markets. The leading cheese states with their percentages of the national total are Wisconsin (43) and New York (8). But the leading butter states are, by percentage shares of total national value, Minnesota (23), Wisconsin (21) and Iowa (13). Two basic forces seem to be at work in determining the two different regional patterns: transportation and the cultural background of producers.

Transportation   It takes 10 pounds of milk to make a pound of cheese, but a pound of butter requires 20 pounds of milk. Thus, butter is the more economical form. This is one reason buttermakers can survive farther from markets. The law at work is that if a raw material is turned into a product higher in value per unit of weight, it will bear greater transport costs to market. Thus, the over-all pattern within a dairy region bears this out: The greater the distance between production and consumption, the more concentrated the dairy product in value per weight. Prices reflect this principle, too. Butter is more expensive than cheese and cheese than milk. In Madison, Wisconsin, for example the retail prices by the pound of these items are: butter 63 cents, cheese 45 cents, and homogenized milk 12 cents (in half-gallon cartons). Other manufactured dairy products likewise lend themselves to long hauls because they are not so bulky or so perishable as fresh milk.

The transportation networks in dairy regions (particularly the fluid milk sheds) comprise the best systems of rural roads in the world— they are well kept because milk must be delivered quickly. Therefore, rural roads must be closely spaced, well surfaced, and open all year round. Road construction happens to be expedited in the dairy regions of the United States and Europe because the glaciers deposited large quantities of sand and gravel over the land. Roads are poorer in buttermaking areas because the making of butter does not require fresh milk; the milk (or cream—if separated by the farmer) is picked up only twice or thrice a week.

Commercial Dairy Farming

Rural roads in milkshed regions must be well surfaced so that in any season the pick-up truck can reach every dairy farm every day. Here the truck of a milk producers association turns in to a southern Wisconsin farm. (Courtesy Madison Milk Producers Association.)

Cultural Background of Producers But the areal concentration of cheese and butter regions is more complex than transportation alone suggests. Otherwise rather sharp concentric boundaries would separate cheese and butter regions. Cultural background is equally important, particularly in influencing the location of cheese-making areas.

When milk is curdled it separates into a liquid *whey* and a solid *curd*. The whey is waste but the curd can be pressed to form cheese. A wide variety of cheeses can be made, the particular type depending on two things: how the curd is treated, and what *molds* (or bacteria) are cultivated in the curd. The complex techniques involved in cheese-making constitute quite a study in themselves. But the significant fact here is that different groups have developed different traditions and aptitudes for cheese-making. The art is handed down from fathers to sons. In time, areas build up a reputation for a particular type of cheese—which in itself has value for ad-

vertising. This is a major factor explaining the regional concentration of cheese-making in such areas as "the heart of Swissconsin," and other cheese regions in New York, Pennsylvania, Michigan, Utah, and Oregon and, of course, in Europe.

Recent Developments Fluid milk sheds have flooded out into regions of manufactural milk. This expansion is related to the rapid growth of urban population. Once-famous cheese districts in central, northern, and western New York, for instance, have been engulfed by the great milk sheds of the Atlantic Seaboard. Former cheese areas in southeastern Wisconsin have disappeared with the advancing front of the Chicago and Milwaukee milk sheds.

Another development has been the appearance of condenseries and powdering plants. Techniques have been devised for concentrating and preserving the attributes of fluid milk in liquid and in powdered form. But these factories require fresh milk, a great deal of equipment, and, to operate efficiently, they must process large quantities of milk (in contrast to creameries and cheese factories that can be very small operations). Therefore, condenseries and powdering plants tend to locate where large amounts of milk are yielded in a small area.

Recently the trend has been toward multiple-purpose plants, often operated by cooperative organizations, that are equipped to manufacture everything from cheese and butter to ice cream mix depending on demand.

PHYSICAL CONDITIONS

The dairylands around cities are not perfectly circular, of course. For example, Chicago's milk shed extends northward for 150 miles, but southward it fades away in less than 40 miles. A principle seems to be at work that dairymen use the poorer land while more remunerative forms of farming get the better land. This generalization needs qualification, however. Let us examine the individual components of the physical environment.

Precipitation Dairying is associated with humid regions. Beef cattle and animals grown for hides and fleece may wander for miles in search of forage in dry lands, but good milk is not produced that way. The better pastures for dairying require 30 or more inches of annual rainfall, the critical amount increasing with temperature. Dairying in drier regions must depend on irrigated pastures (as in the valleys in Wyoming, Idaho, Utah, and California) or on forage imported from grass-producing areas.

Temperatures A critical average daily temperature of 43° F. delimits the *growing season* for most forage grasses. This is an important factor. Regions that have an almost year-long pasture season offer a tremendous advantage, for a farmer can save on the costs of producing supplementary feed crops, on expenditures for machinery to handle those crops, and on investments for buildings to protect not only the supplemental feed but also the herd. Severe winters are the curse of many

American dairy farmers and are responsible for much of his bent-back work.

Dairying is associated with cool summers, too. For one thing, the best dairy cows so far developed are cool-summer animals. They simply do not yield much good milk in hot weather. What is even more important, in the regions with warm summers farmers can grow crops such as corn, which is more remunerative than raising cows, at least in the American Corn Belt.

Soils Forage grasses such as alfalfa, timothy, and clover tolerate poorer soils than corn and wheat do. The original natural vegetation in the world's great dairy regions was forest. The soils that through eons of time developed under those forests are grayish-brown in color and rather low in organic material. Termed *podzolic soils,* they are less fertile than those developed under prairies and steppe grasses. When men cleared off the trees in what are now the main dairy regions they soon discovered that the most prized crops—wheat and corn—fared poorly. But hay did well. Theoretically, perhaps, they could have switched to a hay diet, but they chose not to—an important geographic factor often ignored because it is so obvious. But dairy cattle convert that hay into a substance men do like—at least in Europe and America. Dairy farming is therefore an efficient use of rather poor soils. This explains in part the strange configuration of the American Dairy Belt in the portion which lies south and west of Lake Michigan. The belt's southern boundary swings northward to be displaced by the Corn Belt (which offers a more remunerative type of farming) in the good prairie soils of Chicago's Illinois hinterland.

In most of the American and European dairy belts, the soils are rendered even harder to work by boulders, stones, and gravel from glacial deposits. Though handicaps to plowing and cultivation, these substances scarcely inhibit the growth of pasture grasses. And the stones can be used to make good fences.

Topography Dairying is closely associated with rough topography. Farm ma-

A dairy farmstead in the gently rolling farm land of southern Wisconsin. The large barn contains milking facilities on the ground floor and a hayloft above. To the right are two silos for storing ensilage. At the far right is a building for young stock. To the left of the main barn is a low chicken coop and a machinery barn. In the left foreground is the pig house. Small feeding racks (for corn, hay, and grain) are in the center foreground. (Courtesy of Fritz Albert, University of Wisconsin, Department of Agricultural Journalism.)

chinery can negotiate flat land devoted to crops, but rough land is better traversed by animals. Furthermore, pasture grasses do better on slopes than do corn and other tilled crops. If the land is very rough, woodlots replace pastures on dairy farms. Again the glaciers played a part, by dumping their sand, gravel, and boulders in irregular moraines which blanket much of the dairy belt with ridges and swamps, swells and swales.

Summarizing these several influences on the location of dairying, we may say that the main American and European dairy belts are essentially coextensive with the main belt of urban settlement. But within those great urban realms the dairy region is bounded on the *north* by severe winters (hence, too short a growing season for grasses) and soils too poor for pastures; on the *south* by high summer temperatures (warm enough for corn and

other crops) and by better soils (good enough for more remunerative crops); and on the *west* (in America) by aridity (land too dry for the lush grasses required by dairy cattle).

THE PACIFIC NORTHWEST AND THE SOUTHEAST UNITED STATES

A fortunate combination of precipitation and temperature spells out peculiar advantages for dairymen in opposite corners of the United States—the Northwest, which already has pockets of dairying in dozens of valleys, and the Southeast, where dairying has only recently been established on a large scale. In both these regions winters are mild; average January temperatures are 39° in Nashville, Tennessee, and 36° in Seattle, Washington. Both regions are humid: The Pacific Northwest highlands receive over 60 inches of rain a year; the lowlands get only 25 to 40 inches;

but so much of it is drizzle and so many days are rainy (150 or more a year) that evaporation is low and pastures are lush. The Southeastern United States receives over 40 inches a year.

For all their advantages, though, neither region has many large urban markets. The dairymen of the Pacific Northwest, however, have developed cheese, butter, and condensing industries that sell to distant markets.

The American Southeast, for all its cities, has few large ones and has never generated a great demand for milk. Nor did its farmers choose to concentrate on manufactural milk as did those in the Pacific Northwest. Still, the economic revolution now underway in the South (see later chapters on manufacturing) is bringing with it an expansion of dairying. Perhaps in a few years the South too may be a major dairy region.

Suggested Readings

Durand, Loyal, Jr., "The American Dairy Regions," *Journal of Geography*, 1949, pp. 1-20.

———, "The Lower Peninsula of Michigan and the Western Michigan Dairy Region: A Segment of the American Dairy Region," *Economic Geography*, 1951, pp. 163-183.

———, "Recent Market Orientations of the American Dairy Regions," *Economic Geography*, 1947, pp. 32-40.

Lambert, Audrey M., "Farm Consolidation and Improvement in the Netherlands: An Example from the Land van Maas en Waal," *Economic Geography*, 1961, pp. 115-123.

Mighell, Ronald L., and Black, John D., *Interregional Competition in Agriculture with Special Reference to Dairy Farming in the Lake States and New England*, Cambridge, Massachusetts, 1951, 320 pp.

Simpson, E. S., "Milk Production in England and Wales: A Study in the Influence of Collective Marketing," *Geographical Review*, 1959, pp. 95-111.

A mixed farm south of Naperville, Illinois.
The feedlot—the heart of a mixed farm specializing in fattening cattle—
is at the left of the farmstead cluster of buildings.
The surrounding fields are in corn. (Courtesy International Harvester Company.)

NINE

In commercial mixed farming, a farmer combines the cultivation of crops and the husbanding of animals *and* gets income from both. Mixed farming can, therefore, conveniently serve as a transition between the animal-raising economies just studied (ranching and dairying) and the crop-raising ones to be taken up in subsequent chapters.

LOCATION

The two most extensive regions of mixed farming are in Eurasia and the United States (see Figure 9-1). This activity takes up more land than any other type of bioculture in Europe and is prevalent eastward in an ever narrowing belt that stretches from the Atlantic to the Pacific, with only one interruption in eastern Siberia. At its thickest point, between the Ukraine and central Finland, it is over 800 miles wide.

Mixed farming is the second most extensive type of agriculture in the United States, after ranching, and covers a large part of the eastern half of the country. It is the prevailing form of farming through Ohio, Indiana, Illinois, Iowa, and Nebraska on the north, and Virginia, Tennessee, Georgia, Oklahoma, and much of Texas on the south. Small areas of this type in the Pacific Northwest are intermixed with dairy farming.

Outside these two principal regions, the distribution is spotty: central Mexico, southern South America, southern Africa. Elsewhere there are occasional patches of mixed farming in the vicinity of Occidental cities; but, as is true for dairy farming, they cover areas too small to constitute important world regions.

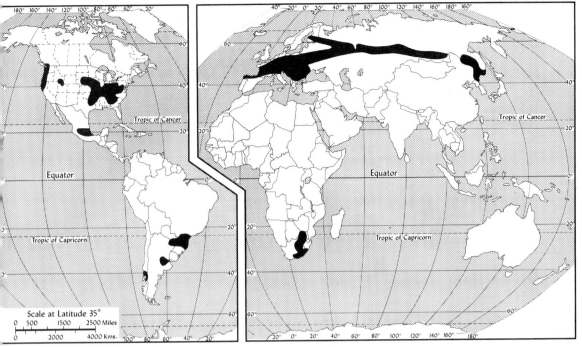

Figure 9-1

CHARACTERISTICS

Both Crops and Animals On each mixed farm, crops are grown for sale and as feed for animals which are also sold. Only two other types of bioculture have significant places for both crops and animals: the Mediterranean type, in which some farms specialize in crops while other farms raise animals (see Chapter 10), and dairy farming, in which an animal product rather than the animals themselves are sold (see diagram, Figure 13-7, p. 210).

Role of Crops Crops, then, play a triple role, being grown for animal feed, for cash sale, and for use by the farm family. The relative importance of each role varies from place to place within the mixed-farming regions. In some places, particularly Iowa and northwestern Illinois, almost all the crops are grown for animal feed. But in northeastern Illinois, in Indiana, and in Ohio, a considerable portion of the crops is sold. In many of the mixed farms of Mexico and eastern Eu-

rope a large share of the crops is consumed by the farm family.

1. Feed crops: The most prevalent feed crop in the United States is corn. Compare the pattern of mixed farming on Figure 9-1 with that of corn, Figure 9-2. *The Corn Belt* is 900 miles long, running from central Ohio westward through Indiana, Illinois, and Iowa, where it fans out into Minnesota, South Dakota, and Nebraska. In the nation as a whole, corn occupies 23 per cent of all harvested cropland, but in the Corn Belt states the percentages are much higher: 34 in Ohio, 42 in Indiana, 44 in Illinois, 46 in Iowa, and 35 in Nebraska. In the Southeast, the figures are even higher (Alabama 48 per cent, Georgia 45, Kentucky 43, Delaware 41). There, though, the yields per acre are low (see Figure 9-2).

Wherever possible, farmers prefer to grow corn because of both its effectiveness in fattening animals and its large yields per acre. In the United States, for example, the average number of harvested bushels per acre is as

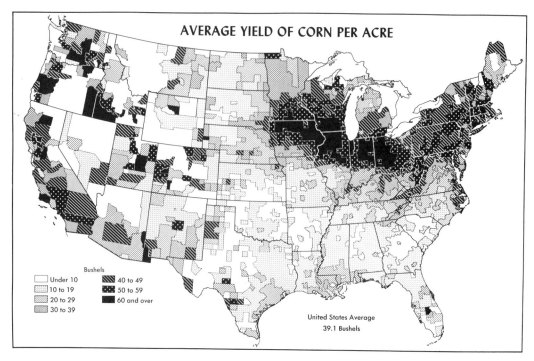

AVERAGE YIELD OF CORN PER ACRE

Bushels

Under 10 | 40 to 49
10 to 19 | 50 to 59
20 to 29 | 60 and over
30 to 39

United States Average
39.1 Bushels

Figure 9-2 (*From U. S. Bureau of the Census.*)

follows: corn 39, oats 35, barley 28, soybeans 19, wheat 17, and rye 10. Moreover, virtually the whole of the corn plant makes edible ensilage.

Secondary feed crops in the United States are hay and oats. Notice how the region of mixed farming correlates rather closely with the location of oats and hay on Figures 9-3 and 9-4.

In Europe, corn is a major feed crop only in the Danube Basin. Over most of Europe hay takes the place of corn; potatoes, turnips,

sugar beets and oats are also important as animal feed.

2. Cash Crops: Wheat is the main cash crop in mixed-farming regions of both the United States and Europe (see Figure 11-2). In the United States, corn and oats are secondary. In recent years soybeans have come into prominence in the central United States (Figure 9-5).

3. Subsistence Crops: These include wheat and a wide array of field crops such as potatoes, cabbage, beans, peas, turnips, beets.

Figure 9-3 (*From U. S. Bureau of the Census.*)   **Figure 9-4** (*From U. S. Bureau of the Census.*)

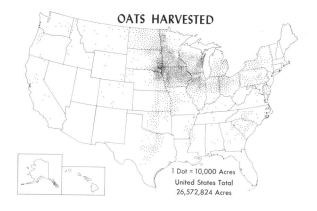

OATS HARVESTED

1 Dot = 10,000 Acres
United States Total
26,572,824 Acres

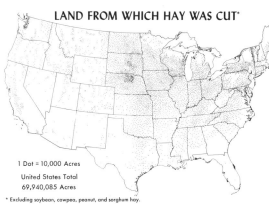

LAND FROM WHICH HAY WAS CUT*

1 Dot = 10,000 Acres
United States Total
69,940,085 Acres

* Excluding soybean, cowpea, peanut, and sorghum hay.

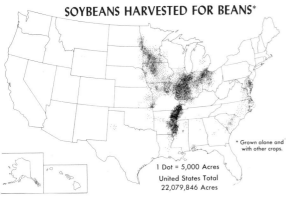

SOYBEANS HARVESTED FOR BEANS*

* Grown alone and with other crops.

1 Dot = 5,000 Acres
United States Total
22,079,846 Acres

Figure 9-5 (*From U. S. Bureau of the Census.*)

Crop Rotation   One of the most distinctive characteristics of mixed farming is the practice of crop rotation whereby each field is devoted to a succession of different uses. There is a dual purpose here: restoring soil nutrients and combatting erosion. Since each plant removes different nutrients in different proportions, soil must be rich indeed to support the same crop year after year. Crops differ too in protecting soil against erosion. On both counts, corn is hard on soil.

Rotation often follows a four-part sequence: (1) A cultivated crop—often corn, although in central Europe it may be potatoes, turnips, or sugar beets—that is the main feed for animals. (2) Hay, particularly alfalfa, timothy, and clover (clover is a legume that is particularly desirable because its roots put nitrogen back *into* the soil); in recent years an Oriental grass, Lespedeza, has been successfully introduced into southern United States as hay. (3) Pasture. (4) A small grain (most often wheat) that is usually grown for cash sale; in Europe, rye replaces wheat where soils are poor and winters cold. Notice that three of the four components in the rotation system are animal feeds. Crop rotation is used in other types of bioculture also, but it is most widely practiced in mixed farming.

Percentage of Land in Crops   The emphasis on crops means that only a small portion of animal feed is natural vegetation. Indeed, a very high percentage of each farm's acreage is cropped. Throughout much of Nebraska, Iowa, and Illinois the figure is 80 per cent (Figure 9-6). The national average is 40.

Figure 9-6 (*From U. S. Bureau of the Census.*)

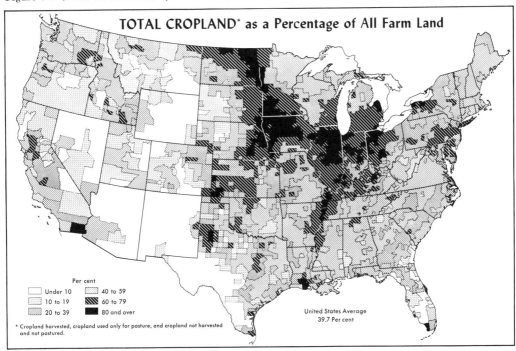

TOTAL CROPLAND* as a Percentage of All Farm Land

Per cent
Under 10
10 to 19
20 to 39
40 to 59
60 to 79
80 and over

United States Average
39.7 Per cent

* Cropland harvested, cropland used only for pasture, and cropland not harvested and not pastured.

Role of Animals The sale of animals brings in most of the revenue of mixed farms. On many farms, in fact, all the income is realized from marketed animals; but on some farms crops are more lucrative.

Hogs, beef cattle, sheep, and poultry are raised in the greatest numbers on mixed farms. Although skins, hides, wool, and eggs are useful by-products, the main product is meat. Many animals could be raised for this purpose, but in mixed-farming regions, the customers prefer beef, bacon, and ham. Notice on the world maps of swine and cattle (Figures 9-7 and 9-8) the concentrations in the mixed-farming regions. These two maps, however, include animals on subsistence as well as commercial farms. Closer parallels would be observable between a map of mixed farming and maps of hogs *sold* and cattle *sold*. Such maps are presently possible to construct for the United States but not for the world.

1. Hogs sold: There is a very close correlation between the locational pattern of hogs sold (Figure 9-9) and the mixed-farming region from eastern Nebraska to Ohio. Few other areas in the United States have many swine at all. The hog population numbers 60,000,000, almost 80 per cent of which are in the twelve north-central states. Each farm in the mixed-farming region has an average of 60 hogs.

2. Cattle sold: A different pattern appears on the map of cattle sold (Figure 9-10). Regions are more widely spread and less conspicuous because farms selling cattle are virtually ubiquitous in the United States. We could define the picture more carefully if three other maps were available: (a) old milk cows sold to slaughter houses, (b) mature beef cattle sold to slaughter houses, and (c) young beef cattle sold to farms for additional fattening. Were such maps available, the mixed-farming regions would stand out conspicuously on the second, livestock ranching regions would dominate the third, and the first would be dominated by the dairy belt.

The cattle in the United States number 95,000,000, of which 20,000,000 are milk cows, most of which are in the dairy regions. The remaining 75,000,000 are being raised primarily for meat. Of this group, 45 per cent are on farms in the mixed-farming regions and 35 per cent are on livestock ranches. The

Figure 9-7

SWINE

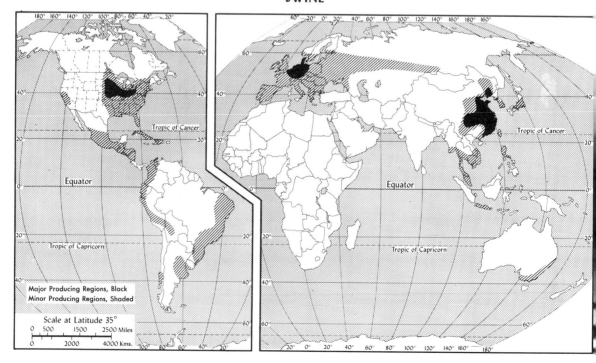

Major Producing Regions, Black
Minor Producing Regions, Shaded

Scale at Latitude 35°
0   500   1500   2500 Miles
0   2000   4000 Kms.

CATTLE

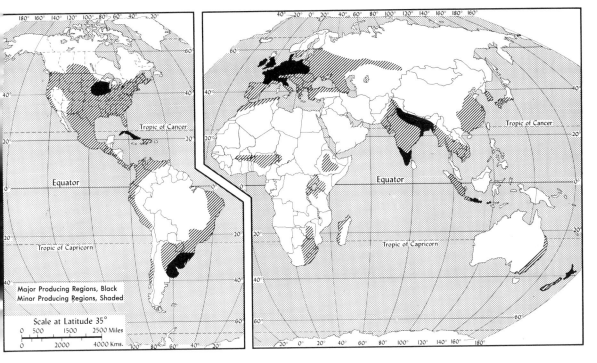

Figure 9-8

average mixed farm in the United States has 40 head of beef cattle accompanying its 60 hogs.

Mixed farms in Europe tend to have fewer cattle and fewer hogs than do American farms mainly because farms are smaller there—there being more farmers per square mile of land.

Size of Farm To shelter all these animals and grow their feed requires an average of 150 acres per farm in the United States. The range is from 120 to 200 acres. Note that these operating units are about the same size as dairy farms but markedly smaller than livestock ranches. The farms in Europe are about half the size of those in the United States, those in South America and South Africa almost as large.

In the United States Corn Belt each farm has a farmstead, covering perhaps ten acres, which consists of the farm dwelling, a barn

Figure 9-9 (*From U. S. Bureau of the Census.*)

HOGS AND PIGS SOLD ALIVE

1 Dot = 10,000 Head
United States Total
57,418,588

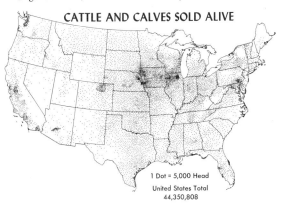

Figure 9-10 (*From U. S. Bureau of the Census.*)

CATTLE AND CALVES SOLD ALIVE

1 Dot = 5,000 Head
United States Total
44,350,808

for sheltering animals and storing grain for winter feeding, a silo for storing corn cut green, a corn bin for storing ripened corn, a shed or two for machinery, and a feed lot for swine, cattle, and chickens. It is the feed lot in which most of the fattening is done—on crops harvested from the field—although sometimes the fields are "hogged off" or "cattled down" by letting the animals roam the fields to forage for themselves.

Farming Methods In Europe mixed farming is less mechanized than in the New World where farmers use a wide assortment of machines to plow, disc, harrow, and cultivate the soil as well as to plant and harvest the crops. It would be instructive to have a world map of agriculture plotted by degrees of mechanization. None is available. But for the United States, at least, a map has been prepared by the Census Bureau that does show by percentages how many farms have tractors (Figure 9-11). Notice that throughout most of the Corn Belt (which is the heart of the mixed-farming region) over 80 per cent of the farms have these machines. As Figure

9-11 indicates, though, in addition to the Corn Belt, farms in other areas, such as the dairy belt and the ranching region, are also highly mechanized.

Use of Manure No other type of commercial farmer makes such intensive use of manure over as broad a region as do the men in mixed farming (Figure 9-12). (Dairymen use almost as much manure but cover a smaller portion of the earth. Intensive farmers of the Orient use tremendous quantities of manure also, but they are not engaged in commercial ventures primarily.) The purpose in using manure is to return nutrients to the soil. In Europe, in fact, many cash-crop farmers maintain a few livestock primarily to ensure a steady supply of barnyard manure.

In a fascinating analysis of the role of manure in bioculture, Eugene Mather and John Fraser Hart write:

The European attitude is best summarized by the statement that "farmyard manure . . . has formed the basis of arable farming throughout the ages. In spite of the great development of fertilizers during the last ninety years, farmyard manure is still the standby of

Figure 9-11 (*From U. S. Bureau of the Census.*)

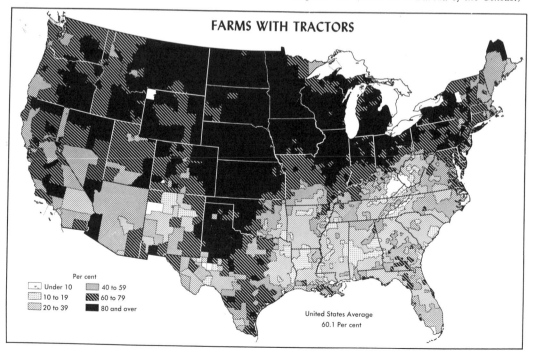

FARMS WITH TRACTORS

Per cent
Under 10
10 to 19
20 to 39
40 to 59
60 to 79
80 and over

United States Average
60.1 Per cent

Mixed Farming

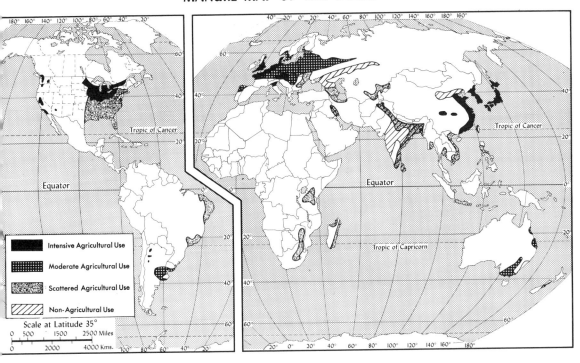

Figure 9-12 (*Courtesy Eugene Mather and John Fraser Hart, and* Land Economics.)

arable farmers; it has been supplemented—not supplanted—by chemical fertilizers." (H. V. Garner, *Manures and Fertilizers*, Great Britain: Ministry of Agriculture and Fisheries Bulletin No. 36, London, 1952, p. 1). Conversely in newer societies, manure is not given the esteem accorded it in older and more stable agricultural communities. The hazards of continuous cropping with little manure are now beginning to be recognized in newly settled lands, however, and Americans can no longer continue to ignore the importance of manure in the agricultural economy....

Manure is obtained from a greater variety of animals, and in greater quantities, in the Corn Belt than in any other part of the western hemisphere. Cattle, hogs, poultry, and sheep all produce significant amounts of manure here, but the most distinctive manurial aspect of the Corn Belt is associated with the feed lot. Most feed lots exist for the fattening of cattle and hogs. The rich grain and protein supplements fed to the cattle produce rich manure. Grain which passes through the cattle undigested is greedily sought by hogs which consume considerable quantities of feces as they root after the grain. Two to four shoats commonly follow each steer.*

*Eugene Mather and John Fraser Hart, "The Geography of Manure," *Land Economics*, February, 1956, pp. 25-38.

Degree of Commercialism The degree of commercialism varies considerably. In west-central Europe, the northern United States, and Argentina, mixed farming is highly commercialized, each farmer and his family consuming only a small fraction of their output. At the other extreme are farmers in the American Appalachian highlands, in eastern Europe (particularly Poland, eastern Austria, Hungary, Yugoslavia, Rumania, and Bulgaria), and in the Soviet Union who have only a comparatively small surplus for sale. Yet change is rapid now behind the Iron Curtain as mixed farmers are advancing from the subsistence stage (where they had been for generations) and are now in the commercial stage, prodded upward by the planned economy of the Soviet system. Just as they converted lands from subsistence herding to commercial grazing, the Soviets have upgraded mixed farming. Southern Brazil and eastern Paraguay are the only other major areas where mixed farmers are still on the subsistence level.

Mixed Farming

Value of Sales   Revenues from cash sales also vary considerably. Very low in the subsistence areas, they rise to respectable heights in the highly commercialized zones. Indeed, farmers there can be among the most prosperous of all farmers. In Figure 9-13, which shows the value of farm products sold *per acre* of all land in farms in the United States, the Corn Belt stands out conspicuously. For the nation as a whole, the average is $27 per acre; through much of the Corn Belt it is over $60 per acre and in a few counties there it exceeds $100 per acre.

Capital Invested per Acre   Finally, the value of operating units is low in the subsistence portions and high in the commercial areas. Figure 9-14 shows that some of the most valuable farms in the nation (in terms of value of land and buildings *per acre*) are in the mixed-farming region. Notice particularly the Corn Belt—the largest single region of highly valued farms (per acre) in the country. The phrase *per acre* is emphasized because some of the huge ranches and wheat farms in the West are, farm for farm, as

valuable as those in the Corn Belt, but some of them are ten times as large.

PHYSICAL PHENOMENA

Where mixed farming predominates, the environment is propitious for the raising of animals for meat. The advantages lie in soil, precipitation, growing season, and topography.

Soils   The soils in mixed-farming regions are intermediate in quality; they are not so rich in plant nutrients as the grassland soils, but they are richer than the leached soils of the forested tropics. Mixed farming is associated with two kinds of soil. Western Europe and the eastern United States have *podzolic* soils, which developed mostly in broadleaf forests. Such soils tend to be more fertile and less acidic than those associated with needle-leaf forests. The west-central United States and eastern Europe have *chernozem* soils, which developed under grasses and are superior to podzolic soils. If fertility of soil were the controlling factor in the location of mixed farming, the less remunerative, subsistence zones would coincide with the poorer

Figure 9-13 (*From U. S. Bureau of the Census.*)

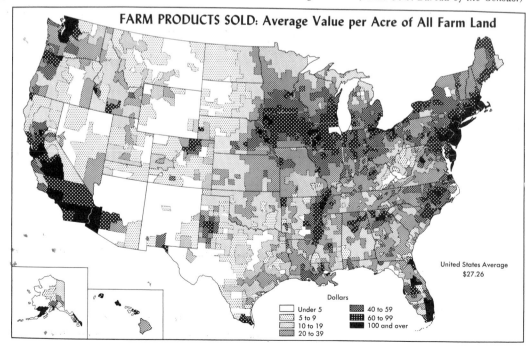

FARM PRODUCTS SOLD: Average Value per Acre of All Farm Land

United States Average
$27.26

Dollars

Under 5	40 to 59
5 to 9	60 to 99
10 to 19	100 and over
20 to 39	

Mixed Farming

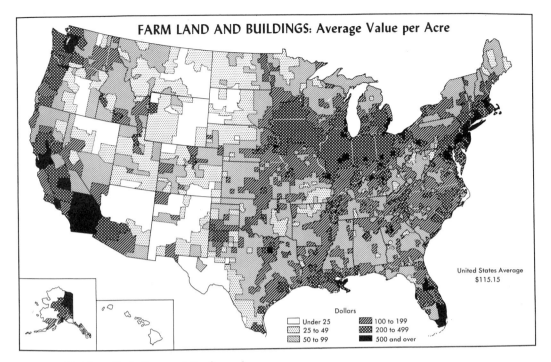

FARM LAND AND BUILDINGS: Average Value per Acre

United States Average
$115.15

Dollars
☐ Under 25
▨ 25 to 49
▨ 50 to 99
▨ 100 to 199
▨ 200 to 499
■ 500 and over

Figure 9-14 (*From U. S. Bureau of the Census.*)

soils of eastern United States and western Europe, while the more prosperous commercialized zones would be on the better soils of western United States (say, Iowa) and eastern Europe (Hungary, Rumania, and Russia). Although this correlation tends to hold in the United States, the opposite is true in Eurasia. One reason for this somewhat strange situation involves available moisture supply, for eastern Europe is drier than western Europe.

Available Moisture   Good soil alone is not enough for prosperous farming since plants need water as well as nutrients. Moreover, the nutrients are actually unavailable if there is insufficient moisture in the soil to dissolve them. Annual rainfall in mixed-farming regions varies from 20 to 60 inches. Most of it falls during the warmer months when growing plants need it, and it falls in *convectional* showers (a considerable volume of rain that falls from a minimum amount of cloud cover). No other type of weather favors growing plants with so much sunshine *and* so much moisture throughout the growing season.

Temperature   There is a rather close locational correlation between mixed farming and intermediate temperatures.

On the basis of *winter* temperatures, climatologists recognize two climatic types: mesothermal and microthermal. Where the average temperature of the coldest month stays above freezing, the climate is called *mesothermal*, the winters *cool*. If the average is below freezing, the climate is *microthermal* and the winters are *cold*.

On the basis of *summer* temperatures, climatologists recognize three types of climate. If the average temperature of the warmest month exceeds 72°, the climate is described as *warm summer*, if the average is between 50° and 72°, *cool summer*, if under 50°, *subarctic*.

Thus, the largest regions of mixed farming occur where the climates are either (a) *cool winter—cool summer* as in most of western Europe and in the Pacific Northwest, or (b) *cool winter—warm summer* as in the southeastern United States (this type of climate occurs in only a small part of southeastern Europe), or (c) *cold winter—warm summer* as in the east-central United States (this

In many German communities the beef cattle of all farmers are fed together on the slopes; in the evening they are returned to their respective owners. (Courtesy German Information Center.)

climate in Europe is restricted to the lower Danube Valley), or (d) *cold winter—cool summer*, as in the Soviet Union. Smaller regions of mixed farming in the Southern Hemisphere all have one of the above climates.

The growing season varies from 120 days on the poleward and interior margins of the Soviet mixed-farming region to 220 days on the southern margin of the United States region. Any period within this range permits the growth of crops which make good animal feed. Even so, corn, the best grain for fattening animals, requires not only a long growing season (140 days) but also warm summers. It thrives best where summer nights as well as summer days are warm. This condition prevails in the mixed-farming region of Anglo-America but not in Europe. Here, then, is a basic reason why livestock are fattened on corn in the United States but on potatoes, sugar beets, and turnips in France, Germany and Poland.

Topography Beef cattle on livestock ranches can roam hills and mountains in search of food. But in mixed-farming areas feed is brought to them, and that feed is best produced on relatively flat land. This holds whether the farmer works largely by hand or by machinery. The regions of mixed farming occur largely in plains—eastern Nebraska, Iowa, and Illinois in Anglo-America and France, Germany, Poland, and vast stretches of European Russia. Only small pockets occur in the hills of the eastern United States, central France, and southwestern Germany (see the photo above).

CULTURAL FEATURES

A physical environment with the attributes just discussed does not inevitably lead to mixed farming. North China has somewhat the same general association of temperatures, precipitation, topography, and soil as do the mixed-farming regions of Europe and Anglo-America. But the millions of farmers in North China busy themselves with subsistence crop-growing. Then, too, for thousands of years the physical features of Europe and Anglo-America were virtually what they are today,

Mixed Farming

but only recently have the inhabitants practiced mixed farming. Obviously it depends on certain cultural phenomena as well as certain physical factors.

Dense Populations Nearly all the mixed-farming regions on Figure 9-1 are associated with dense populations, notably in western Europe. Through Germany and southern Poland, the man/land ratio exceeds 250 per square mile. A slightly lower density prevails over most of the remaining European mixed-farming territory, continuing eastward as far as Moscow, beyond which the population gradually thins out. A somewhat different situation obtains in the Western Hemisphere and in southern Africa where mixed farming coincides with densities of 25 to 125 per square mile; nevertheless, even here, mixed farming is associated with the areas of each continent where the population is relatively dense.

But dense population is not the only cultural force that applies, else China and India would be strong in mixed farming. Is there something relevant in the way the people are distributed?

Urbanization Mixed-farming regions also turn out to have a heavy concentration of people in *cities.* Of the nearly 100 cities with one million or more people, forty are located either within mixed-farming zones or on their poleward margins where they merge with dairy areas. Yet on this basis, the Far East, again, should have a mixed-farming economy because it can boast 25 cities with a million or more inhabitants. We must look at still other phenomena.

Diet Here is an important factor that we must not overlook just because it seems so obvious: Mixed farming is associated with meat diets. Millions of the earth's peoples—many in the Far East—are vegetarians, many for religious convictions; if their cultures took over in western Europe and Anglo-America, the realm of mixed farming would be drastically reduced.

Purchasing Power The large numbers of meat-eating urbanites have a large purchasing power. And it is purchasing power, as we have already seen, that stimulated the development of livestock ranching and com-

A farmstead (*with homestead and barn under one roof*) *in the mixed-farming region of Switzerland.* (*Courtesy United States Department of Agriculture,* Foreign Agriculture.)

mercial dairying. Notice the data in Table 9-1 dealing with diet components (note especially animal protein supply) for several selected countries. These figures relate closely not only to such productive activities as mixed farming, ranching, and dairying, but also to customers' eating habits and buying power.

Table **9-1** *Food Supply per Capita for Selected Countries*

Area	Total Calories per Day	Total Protein, Grams per Day	Animal Protein, Grams per Day
Europe			
Denmark	3340	94	59
United Kingdom	3290	87	52
Switzerland	2980	85	51
Norway	2980	82	49
Netherlands	2970	80	45
Yugoslavia	2970	96	26
Austria	2950	87	46
France	2940	98	52
Belgium	2930	87	47
Sweden	2920	82	52
Greece	2900	93	27
Germany	2890	78	46
Italy	2710	79	27
Portugal	2350	68	25
North America			
Canada	3150	96	64
United States	3130	93	66
Mexico	2490	69	16
Asia			
Taiwan	2310	57	15
Japan	2210	68	18
Philippines	2010	50	14
India	1900	52	6
Pakistan	1940	45	7
Near East			
Turkey	2830	90	14
Israel	2780	85	33
Syria	2290	73	12
Africa			
Egypt	2570	75	13
Union of South Africa	2580	73	30
South America			
Argentina	3040	95	52
Chile	2570	77	27
Uruguay	2960	96	62
Brazil	2520	62	18
Venezuela	2300	64	27
Ecuador	2230	56	18
Peru	1980	53	13
Oceania			
New Zealand	3430	105	72
Australia	3210	92	60

Source: United Nations, Food and Agriculture Organization, *Production Yearbook*, 1960, Table 95.

Transportation   No other type of farming (except dairying) has stimulated the spread of as wide a network of good transport facilities as mixed farming has (see Figure 26-1 and the world map of railroads and roads in any economic atlas). Being highly productive, mixed farming generated much of the tax money with which good roads were built, and the roads in turn facilitated the shipments of farm products to markets.

Prices and Transportation Costs   A bushel of corn commands a lower price on the market than does a bushel of wheat, mainly because the customers of the mixed-farming regions prefer wheat bread and wheat cereal to corn bread and corn cereal for their own diets. Even though wheat will bring a higher price than corn, transport charges by the carload are exactly the same on the two grains. Obviously, the ratio of transport costs to value of product is *higher* for corn and *lower* for wheat—a strong factor discouraging trade in corn and encouraging trade in wheat.

But the farmer has the option of converting corn (or potatoes, or hay or whatever) into meat, which *will* bring him a high price. To be sure, freight rates are higher on meat than on corn, but the value of meat is so much higher than that of corn that the ratio of transport costs to value of the product is lower. Moreover, the farmer has fewer tons of product on which to pay transport costs if he feeds his corn to animals. Six pounds of corn make one pound of pork. Beef is an even more concentrated product—it takes ten pounds of corn plus ten pounds of hay to make a pound of beef—and beef gets a still higher price.

Because of these variations in prices and transport costs, the farmers in mixed-farming regions enjoy a certain flexibility of production. When prices on meat are low, they can devote their fields to growing crops for sale; when meat prices are high they can concentrate on livestock sales.

Contract Farming   A recent experiment within the United States mixed-farming region is *contract farming*. Under this system the individual farmer surrenders his independence

Mixed Farming

as a producer for the general market in favor of signing a contract with a commercial meat-packing company. He accepts the company's decisions on exactly how much of what kinds of meat he will produce; the firm in turn covenants to pay him within the limits of a certain price range. Frequently, the packers also have contracts with distributors and chain stores that sell the meat products. If contract farming succeeds, mixed farmers in the United States will be spared some of the uncertainty of planning each year's activity. Instead of guessing what the market will be, they will have a firm commitment around which to budget their time, effort, and investment.

Settlements   Trade and service centers are spaced about 12 miles apart in the American mixed-farming region. They are closer in Europe where farms are smaller, rural roads poorer, and transportation less mechanized.

The employment structure in such a settlement is geared to service the needs of surrounding farmers (see, for example, Bloomfield, Iowa, in Table 9-2). Yet, since some of the larger settlements have meat-packing plants, in those places manufacturing accounts for a larger number of jobs (for instance, Waterloo, Iowa, in Table 9-2).

Table **9-2**   *Employment Structures of Two Settlements in a Mixed-Farming Region*

	Bloomfield, Iowa	Waterloo, Iowa
Population	2,688	84,000
Total Employment	1,000	36,000
Percentage of employment:		
Primary activities	4	1
Secondary activities	18	47
Manufacturing	9	42
Construction	9	5
Tertiary activities	78	52
Trade	33	22
Transportation	8	5
Business services	6	5
Personal services	24	17
Public administration	7	3

Source: United States *Census of Population* 1950, Vol. II, Characteristics of the Population, Tables 35 and 43.

Source Regions for Feeder Animals

A certain distinctive regional specialization has become important to mixed farmers in the United States. Western ranchers breed cattle and sheep, raising them to semimaturity (approximately one year of age) and then ship them for final fattening to the more humid regions where lusher grasses and grains grow (see Chapter 7). Many of the beef cattle in Iowa, Illinois, Indiana, and Ohio were born in Montana, Wyoming, and other western range states. One of the most specialized *feeder cattle* areas is DeKalb County (40 miles west of Chicago) which stands out conspicuously on Figure 9-10.

This feeder-cattle industry has been encouraged by the *feeder-in-transit* freight rates charged by railroads. Normally, transport charges increase with distance at a diminishing rate. Accordingly, it would cost less to pay one freight rate on 100 tons of cattle moving straight through from the ranges of Wyoming to the slaughter houses of Chicago than to pay freight on two shorter hauls: from Wyoming to DeKalb and then, a few months later, from DeKalb to Chicago. But the railroads have granted a privilege under which feeder cattle can be shipped from Wyoming to Chicago under one rate even though they are permitted to stop in transit for fattening. Since the animals weigh more for the last leg of the journey, the rates are adjusted accordingly.

Men in the feeder business deal mostly with cattle. Hogs are bred and raised (as well as fattened) more satisfactorily right where the crops are. If Americans had as strong a taste for lamb and mutton as for veal and beef, there might be a greater feeder business in sheep.

Meat-Packing Areas   In recent years, many meat-packing factories have left New York, Cincinnati, and Chicago for new locations in smaller cities within the mixed-farming regions. The reasons for this shift are rather complex, as we shall see in the chapters on manufacturing; but whatever they are, a movement is clearly underway.

International Trade   Although Europe and Anglo-America have the most highly de-

Fattening hogs in the feed lot of a Corn Belt farm in Mason County, Illinois. (United States Department of Agriculture Photograph.)

veloped regions of mixed farming, the demand for meat still exceeds the domestic supply. Meat therefore is imported from areas of mixed farming (as well as of livestock ranching) on other continents. The leading meat-importing countries are the United Kingdom, the United States, Italy, and West Germany. The leading exporters are New Zealand, Denmark, Argentina, Australia, and Uruguay. For some of these countries, the value of meat exports makes up a large share of the total sales abroad: Denmark 28 per cent, New Zealand 23, Argentina 19, Uruguay 16, and Australia 9.

Suggested Readings

Black, John D., *The Rural Economy of New England—A Regional Study*, Cambridge, 1950, 796 pp.

Bunting, E. S., "Maize, the Highest Yielding Cereal," *World Crops*, 1950, pp. 5-9.

Butt, Louise, "Belgian Agriculture," *Foreign Agriculture*, 1947, pp. 90-98.

Gibson, Lyle E., "Characteristics of a Regional Margin of the Corn and Dairy Belts," *Annals of the Association of American Geographers*, 1948, pp. 244-270.

Henderson, David A., "Corn Belt Cattle Feeding in Eastern Colorado's Irrigated Valleys," *Economic Geography*, 1954, pp. 364-372.

Jaatinen, S., and Mead, W. R., "The Intensification of Finnish Farming," *Economic Geography*, 1957, pp. 31-40.

Kisselbach, T. A., "A Half Century of Corn Research," *American Scientist*, 1951, pp. 629-655.

Klatt, Warner, "Food and Farming in Germany," *International Affairs*, 1950, pp. 45-58.

Mead, W. R., "The Cold Farm in Finland: Resettlement of Finland's Displaced Farmers," *Geographical Review*, 1951, pp. 529-543.

Mehr, Stanley, "The Farmer and His Land in Communist Czechoslovakia," *Foreign Agriculture*, 1950, pp. 156-160.

Shaw, Earl B., "Swine Production in the Corn Belt of the United States," *Economic Geography*, 1936, pp. 359-372.

Stevenson, Frederick J., "The Potato—A Leading World Food Crop," *Foreign Agriculture*, 1948, pp. 211-216.

Weaver, J. C., Hoag, L. P., and Fenton, B. L., "Livestock Units and Combination Regions in the Middle West," *Economic Geography*, 1956, pp. 237-259.

Grape harvest in Médoc (Château Lafite) in the Bordeaux region in southern France. (Photo Féher—Courtesy France Actuelle.)

TEN

The term *Mediterranean agriculture* applies to a particular mixture of diverse biocultural activities (both animal husbandry and crop farming) that has developed in five major world regions. The largest of these nearly encircles the Mediterranean Sea—and it is from there that the type derives its name, not only because it is the most extensive of the five but also because it was the first. Of the economic activities discussed in this book this is the only one for which the name derives from a *type area,* rather than from characteristics of the economy itself.

LOCATION

The Mediterranean Basin, where this agriculture prevails, is situated amid three continents (see Figure 10-1). The type zone includes a narrow coastal belt 1000 miles long across North Africa from Tunisia to the Atlantic coast, stretches across southern Europe, and bends around southwest Asia (from Turkey, a prong extends eastward through the valleys of Georgia and Azerbaidzhan to northern Iran). Between Israel and Tunisia, however, nomadic herding predominates, except for intensive cultivation in the Nile Valley and the Cirenaica section of Libya.

Elsewhere, this biocultural type prevails in a small part of southwestern Arizona and almost half of California, particularly the Great Valley and the coast south of San Francisco; in central Chile; at the southwestern tip of Africa; and in two detached areas in Australia.

Thus, Mediterranean agriculture occurs on

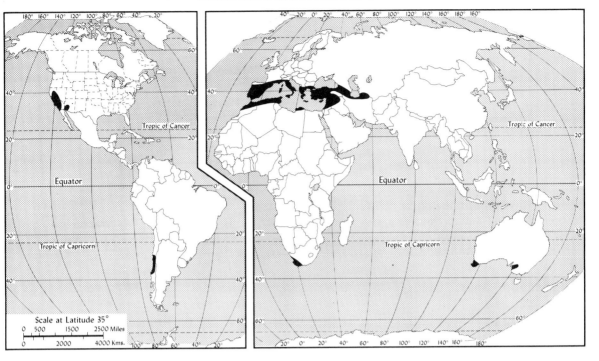

Figure 10-1

every inhabited continent, in both the Northern and Southern Hemispheres, and in the mid-latitudes, roughly between 30 and 45 degrees.

In applying the geographic method of analysis, at this point we would normally turn to the characteristics of the economic activity under study. But, for the sake of variety, and also for a better understanding of the characteristics to be mentioned later, let us instead take up relationships with the physical environment first.

PHYSICAL RELATIONSHIPS

The natural setting that lends itself to Mediterranean agriculture is distinguished by erratic rainfall, mild temperatures, irregular topography, and nearness to large bodies of water.

Amounts of Precipitation   The climate in these regions is subhumid, which means that there is just enough rainfall to keep the climate from being classed as dry. The formula for deciding whether a climate is dry

or humid is rather complex, but for our purposes, we only need to know that Mediterranean-type rainfall varies from 10 inches to 40 inches annually. Annual average precipitation in inches at representative cities are: Los Angeles 15, Rome 33, Jerusalem 25, Adelaide, Australia, 21, and Capetown, South Africa, 25.

Unpredictable Precipitation   These averages do not tell us much about any one year, though, for precipitation is fickle. Some years are very dry, others are quite humid. It is an axiom of physical geography that the lower the annual precipitation the greater its annual variation. Table 10-1, page 156, illustrates this principle with data for three cities. Notice that the *higher* the rainfall average, the *lower* the percentage range between driest and wettest years. Sharp fluctuations can occur between consecutive years. In Los Angeles, for instance, 33 inches fell in 1941 but only 11 inches came in 1942; a scant 8 inches came in 1951, but they were followed by 26 inches in 1952.

Table 10-1 *Annual Precipitation Data for Selected Cities*

City	Annual Average in Inches	Inches in Wettest Year	Inches in Driest Year	Range in Inches	Range as a Percentage of Annual Average
Los Angeles	15″	38″ (1884)	5″ (1899)	33	220%
Chicago	32″	46″ (1954)	22″ (1956)	24	75%
New York City	42″	59″ (1889)	33″ (1935)	26	60%

Source: Personal communications from United States Weather Bureau offices.

Monthly Distribution of Precipitation
In most climatic regions that have pronounced wet and dry seasons the former is in summer, the latter in winter. The reasons for these conditions are complex, involving some of the basic principles of physical geography, but the chief factor is that cold air holds less water vapor than warm air does. In a phrase, summer air in most regions is a richer mixture for forming rain.

Not so in Mediterranean regions. Winters there are markedly wetter than summers which are often exceedingly dry. Climatologists and geographers recognize a specific *Mediterranean Climate* (sometimes termed *Humid Sub-Tropical Dry Summer*), the most distinguishing feature of which is the dry summer-wet winter sequence. Compare the monthly precipitation figures at the weather stations listed in Table 10-2.

Mediterranean climates are invariably bounded on the *equatorial* side by steppes and deserts; the air masses that hover over these dry realms most of the year drift toward the *poles* in the summer. As a result, actual desert conditions prevail in some Mediterranean areas in the summer. For the whole six-month period from May through October, Los Angeles receives less than one inch.

Natural Vegetation The flora of Mediterranean regions is a mixture of trees, shrubs, and grass. The trees, comparatively short and rather widely spaced, form a distinctive type known as *Mediterranean Scrub Forest*. Some of them are deciduous and drop their leaves in summer; they stand dormant in the hot season, thus preventing the loss of too much water in transpiration through leaf surfaces. Other trees are evergreen and endure summer aridity through such adaptations as thick oily leaves and husky bark which reduce evaporation. Examples of Mediterranean trees are the cork oak, the olive, and the fig.

More numerous than the trees are the shrubs and bushes that make up the brush known as *chaparral*. Finally, there are vast areas of grass, lush in winter and dormant in summer. The relative location of trees, shrubs, and grasses within Mediterranean areas is a highly complex association (treated by physical geographers), determined by the landforms, by the variation in precipitation between lowlands and highlands, and by soil types.

Table 10-2 *Monthly Precipitation at Selected Weather Stations*

Place	J	F	M	A	M	J	J	A	S	O	N	D
Mediterranean Regions												
Jerusalem, Israel	6.2	4.6	3.5	1.5	0.3	*	*	*	*	0.4	2.5	5.7
Rome, Italy	3.2	2.7	2.9	2.6	2.2	1.6	0.7	1.0	2.5	5.0	4.4	3.9
Los Angeles, California	3.1	3.0	2.6	1.0	0.3	*	*	*	0.1	0.5	1.1	2.7
Other Regions												
Chicago, Illinois	2.1	2.1	2.6	2.9	3.6	3.3	3.4	3.0	3.1	2.6	2.4	2.1
Berlin, Germany	1.7	1.4	1.6	1.5	1.9	2.3	3.0	2.3	1.7	1.7	1.7	1.9
Foochow, China	3.1	2.5	4.8	5.3	4.6	6.0	4.3	8.7	3.0	1.3	0.8	1.3

* Less than 0.1

Temperature Temperatures are mild for most of the year. Summers are warm, with averages for the warmest month ranging from 71° in Los Angeles up to 80° in Athens, Greece, and down to 67° in Santiago, Chile. More significant, though, are the mild winters. Representative averages for the coldest months are 54° in Los Angeles, 48° in Athens, and 46° in Santiago. The growing season in these regions is almost continuous, so most farming is geared to that expectation. Summer and winter therefore are matters of dryness and wetness rather than of heat and cold. This generalization applies to the lowlands. Frosts do occur there occasionally, but they are frequent and severe in the highlands.

Thus, heat and maximum precipitation come at different seasons, which is a handicap to many plants.

Relation to Water Bodies Mediterranean regions are rarely very far inland. Usually they front on the sea itself, although a few zones extend inland quite a way from the Mediterranean, Black, and Caspian seas. Nearness to large bodies of water is one reason why Mediterranean winters are comparatively mild, especially where the prevailing winds come from the sea. (The oceans remain warmer than the land masses do in winter.)

Landforms Nearly all Mediterranean regions are mixtures of lowlands and highlands, of flat lands and rough lands, both hilly and mountainous. Mountains often mark the poleward border of Mediterranean regions, and therefore provide effective barriers against invasions of cold air. Such air moving southward in Europe encounters the Pyrenees, Alps, and Dinaric Alps. In California and Chile the mountains lie to the east, protecting the Mediterranean regions from colder air blowing westward in winter from the continental interiors. These mountains, by the way, are one reason why California's lowlands, although farther north than Florida's, never have such severe winter temperatures. Florida's lowlands have no mountain bulwarks against outbursts of cold continental air.

Relation to Prevailing Winds In the mid-latitudes on the western portions of continents the prevailing winds are westerly. This fact, coupled with the nature of landforms, the nature of cyclonic storm tracks, and the tendency of land masses to heat and to cool at different rates from those of oceans, explains why the Mediterranean region of California has no counterpart in the same latitude on the east coast of the United States, and why the Mediterranean realm of Europe-Asia-Africa is not repeated in China.

CHARACTERISTICS

In the physical environment just described, a distinctive type of agriculture becomes possible. Mediterranean agriculture is distinguished by an unusual combination of crops and livestock, an association which has prevailed for centuries in the land surrounding the Mediterranean Sea and which has tended to be recurrent in the other four realms of Mediterranean bioculture. The combination involves particular sets of winter crops, of summer crops, and of animals.

Winter Grains Winter crops, whether grains or vegetables, are sown or planted in the fall and nourished by winter rainfall; they ripen in the spring and are harvested in early summer.

The grains usually grown are wheat and barley, the two cereals that survive best on limited amounts of moisture through cool growing seasons. Corn and oats, for instance, require more rainfall and warmer periods of maturation. Moreover, wheat and barley do not require land as flat as does corn, which must be cultivated—a technique that combats weeds but simultaneously lays bare the soil, making sloping land subject to increased erosion. Accordingly, wheat and barley often occupy the sloping land on the fringes of valleys in Mediterranean regions. Wheat is the preferred cereal and bread grain; Italians eat a lot of it as spaghetti. Barley is the poor man's cereal.

Because of the limited moisture, grain yields per acre in Mediterranean regions are low. It takes several acres to produce the cereal crop for even one family, and each worker tends a considerable amount of land.

Dry farming is a grain-growing technique that is frequently resorted to in the drier portions of all Mediterranean regions, wherever the rainfall of a single year is inadequate for a grain crop although the total precipitation in consecutive years is sufficient. The objective in dry farming is to tend the soil in such a manner that it absorbs and retains the greatest amount of water possible. Fields are cropped only once every two years (occasionally once every three years during unusually dry periods) and they lie fallow the other year in order to store up moisture. The soil is tended as carefully during the fallow year as during the cropped year, but the treatment is different. In the former, fields are plowed and harrowed at intervals of approximately three months. During the autumn they are cultivated in order to open the ground for the autumn rainfall. But since rainfall hardens bare soil, increasing the run-off and reducing the intake, the land is plowed and harrowed again in winter. Once more in spring it is cultivated to promote absorption of rainwater. The last plowing and harrowing in the fallow year come in summer, the aim being to break up the soil capillaries through which moisture moves toward the surface where it evaporates. Obviously, in a dry season the rate of upward capillary action exceeds that of downward seepage, so there is a net loss of moisture during these months; however, enough is retained to be useful the following year. Dry farming is practiced on the highlands and upper slopes of valleys where it is too costly to irrigate.

Winter Vegetables   The winter crop in valleys is usually vegetables. The alluvial soils of the valleys are usually better than those of the slopes and so are devoted to crops that yield more food per acre than do wheat and barley. Nearly every vegetable will grow: beans, peas, carrots, onions, radishes, tomatoes, lettuce, cabbage. Planted in the fall, some of these mature so rapidly that two or even three crops can be harvested before the summer drought. Yields per acre of vegetables

are high; therefore, valley farms are likely to be smaller in size than those on the slopes. Surplus vegetables can be dried during the summer.

Summer Crops   Summer crops mature during the summer and are harvested in the autumn. They must be hardy plants capable of enduring a long dry period. Several plants can endure this ordeal, however, by having (a) long tap roots that penetrate soil moisture far below the surface, (b) extensive root systems that reach far out horizontally, and (c) little foliage, which reduces evaporation. Certain trees and vines meet these specifications although most grasses and vegetables do not. Typical summer crops are olives, figs, and grapes. For centuries they have been basic to the Mediterranean diet.

Ninety per cent of all olive acreage, indeed is in the Mediterranean Basin (Figure 10-2). Olive trees are planted 30 feet apart. Closer spacing would be all right in winter but would overtax the soil's supply of moisture in the summer. *Interculture* enables the farmers to reap a dividend from this open space between olive trees during the winter; then, they plant vegetables or winter grains between the trees.

In contrast to the olive tree, the *fig* tree yields two crops of figs a year, one in early summer and one in autumn. Again the trees must be far enough apart so that the land in summer is not overtaxed. Winter interculture also prevails on fig plots.

Most of the world's *grapes* are grown in Mediterranean-type regions (Figure 10-3). Vineyards are rarely interplanted with winter crops, though, for grapes do not tolerate competition. Grapes can be processed into a diversity of foods, and some Mediterranean areas are famous for their grape products: wine from Algeria and Portugal, fruit grapes from the Malaga district in southern Spain, raisins from Greece.

All told, winter crops and summer crops together use up less than one-fifth of the land in regions of Mediterranean agriculture. What cropland there is tends to be on the valley bottoms and lower slopes. Most of the land,

OLIVES

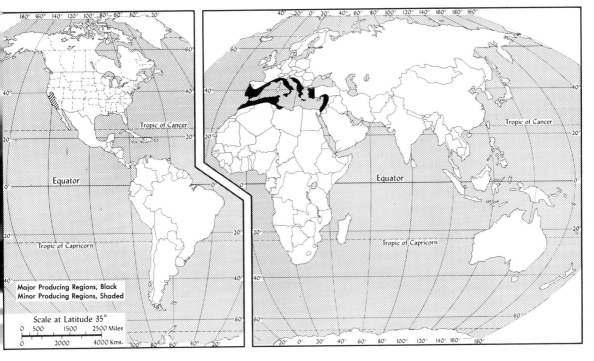

Figure 10-2

Figure 10-3

GRAPES

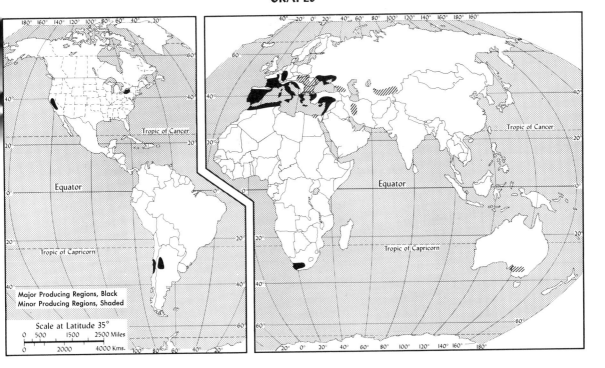

though, is either too dry or too rough for growing anything. There is some tendency toward zonation: Valley bottoms often are devoted to vegetables and intercultured olive and fig groves; the lower slopes have cereals; the steeper slopes, if cropped at all, are in vineyards, or olive or fig groves. Interculture is avoided, however, because of the risk of erosion.

Livestock Agriculture   The role of livestock tending in Mediterranean bioculture varies from farm to farm. At one extreme are farms where the emphasis is almost entirely on crops, and the function of the few animals, if any, is to meet the needs of farm operator and family. At the other extreme are operating units where animals constitute a major source of revenue—but never the only source, else they would be classified as commercial grazing or dairying.

There are two types of livestock husbandry in Mediterranean regions: livestock "grazing" and livestock "farming."

Livestock grazing is based on natural vegetation. Goats and sheep make up most of the herds because they can subsist on the meagre vegetation of these subhumid lands where the carrying capacity varies from 15 acres to 80 acres per animal. As Figure 7-2 shows, considerable numbers of sheep are in areas of Mediterranean agriculture. The main handicap is the dry summer. But since there is usually a little more rainfall in the highlands than in the lowlands as well as less evaporation because of lower temperatures, mountain ranges can often be grazed all year long. Where the economy is mainly on the subsistence level, the people get milk, meat, wool, and skins from the herds. Where commercialism prevails, the main product is wool. Turkey, for example, is famous for Angora wool.

Most grazers do some farming, too, of course, otherwise these grazing areas should be included in the nomadic herding regions (to which they are adjacent in Africa and the Middle East) or to the livestock ranching areas (to which they are adjacent in the United States).

Livestock farming is based on tended vegetation such as alfalfa, clover, pastures of sown

A pastoral scene in Galilee. Grazing is an important component of Mediterranean agriculture. (Courtesy Israel Office of Information.)

grasses, or other forage crops. Swine, beef cattle, and dairy cattle are the main animals on livestock farms, which are located in valleys, often near large cities. Sometimes the crops for these animals are irrigated. Swine, though, succeed particularly well in certain parts of the Mediterranean Basin where they graze on acorns in oak forests.

Other Characteristics   The degree of *commercialism* varies markedly within and among Mediterranean regions. In parts of the Mediterranean Basin (notably southern Italy, central Spain, and the interiors of Greece, Turkey, and Syria) the economy is still largely subsistence—as it has been for thousands of years. But in northern Italy, southern France, coastal Spain, and coastal Algeria there is a good deal of surplus production. In the five other Mediterranean regions, the farming is on the whole rather highly commercialized.

There is no typical *size* of operating unit in Mediterranean agriculture. The largest number of valley vegetable farms is small, sometimes as small as 10 acres. Those depending on grapes, olives, figs, or grains are larger. And those located far from the valley bottoms take up hundreds of acres, most of which are range land.

The characteristics so far mentioned have prevailed for a long time. In the last few decades some new attributes have developed in response to the influence of certain cultural phenomena.

CULTURAL RELATIONSHIPS

Age of Culture and Agricultural Methods
The cultures in the Mediterranean Basin are ancient; in the other regions newer cultures prevail. Areas with recent cultures practice the commercial phase of Mediterranean agriculture while many areas of the old cultures are still in the subsistence stage.

In many of the older areas, methods are crude. Farmers still sow wheat and harvest it by hand in many parts of Spain, Italy, Greece, and Algeria. They use wooden hoes, wooden harvesting equipment, and primitive carts for transporting produce from the fields. But in

Australia, South Africa, Chile, and California, more modern equipment and considerable machinery are employed.

Man/Land Ratio   A moderately high population density is sustained by this economic activity. Rarely is the density less than 25 per square mile, and in many places (Italy, and the coastal zones of Spain, Greece, Turkey, Syria, Lebanon, and Israel) it approaches 200 per square mile.

Settlements   Settlements vary widely. In the Mediterranean Basin most farmers reside in farm villages in buildings made of stone. Timber is scarce in these lands. But in areas of newer cultures most farmers reside on their own land in farmsteads made of wood, some of which is brought in from afar. Few settlements function as trade centers where the subsistence phase prevails. But in California, Chile, and Australia most settlements are service centers, where exactly the same functions are performed as in their counterparts in regions of other commercial activities.

Contacts with Other Regions   Although Mediterranean farming is associated with a very old culture, it did not develop many contacts with distant market regions until recently. In response to these contacts, Mediterranean agriculture has gone through several changes. Let us look at them chronologically. It will be convenient to delimit three time periods with the years 1300 and 1880 as our pegs. Admittedly, no one year clearly marks the boundary between two stages, but it can serve as a rough identification of the point of transition.

1. The period before 1300: Throughout most of history, Mediterranean agriculture has been a subsistence activity. It was, though, one of the first phases of bioculture to emerge from subsistence gathering. Then for centuries the world's major biocultural regions were given over to either subsistence herding, subsistence farming, or to Mediterranean agriculture, which was a blend of both. During this period Mediterranean agriculture was confined

to the Mediterranean Basin and its practitioners made comparatively few sales to customers in other regions.

There was some surplus production in this period, but it went to citizens in Athens, Rome, Alexandria, Carthage and other cities within the Mediterranean Basin rather than to other regions. But people from other regions approached the Mediterranean farmers—particularly the nomadic herdsmen who made annual attacks on the fields and settlements of Mediterranean fringes.

2. The period between 1300 and 1880: The cultural revolution in the western world that ended the Middle Ages and brought the Italian Renaissance, also saw the flowering of commercialism. Agricultural surpluses that for centuries had gone only a few miles from farms to nearby cities now began to move hundreds and thousands of miles to other realms. The contributions of Mediterranean agriculture to this trade were surpluses of her three main commodity groups: (1) easily preserved summer crops (olives, olive oil, figs, wine, raisins), (2) animal products (wool, hides, skins),* and (3) winter crops—mostly grains (more wheat than barley because wheat makes better bread and finer cereal), but also some dried winter vegetables. In every instance, the exported products were relatively imperishable and valuable in proportion to weight so that they were worth the cost of transport. The principal market in this period was western Europe although eastern Anglo-America was beginning to come into prominence.

3. The period after 1880: Most regions of Mediterranean agriculture went through a mild revolution near the end of the nineteenth century in response to four major developments incipient in other regions: (1) the Industrial Revolution in northwestern Europe and America where puchasing power skyrocketed, (2) rapidly increasing population (in Europe and America) which multiplied the number of consumers of Mediterranean products, (3) the transportation revolution, whereby railroads, steamships, and later trucks sharply reduced the time required to move commodities between regions, and (4) the invention of refrigeration.

As a result of these developments, several changes occurred in the geography of Mediterranean agriculture in several categories: location, amount of exports, types of exports, addition of new crops, labor supply, size of farms, and regional specialization.

New Locations Settlers from western Europe developed new regions of Mediterranean agriculture. They recognized the Mediterranean climate and Mediterranean vegetation when they encountered it in California, Chile, South Africa, and Australia, and they also were sensitive to the demand in Europe for the products of Mediterranean agriculture.

A Modest Increase in Traditional Items Summer crops become items of commerce in increasing amounts. Today 90 per cent of all olive oil comes from the Mediterranean Basin (mainly Spain, Italy, Greece, and Tunisia). Wine is now a money-maker, with Algeria alone accounting for half of all wine exports; the beverage is Algeria's leading export—43 per cent of foreign sales. More dried fruits (such as figs and raisins) are also shipped out than before.

Some of the new regions began exporting these items, too. California and Australia now rival Greece and Turkey in exporting raisins. Exports of wool did not keep pace with the increased shipments of crops, however, for livestock ranchers captured the wool market. Wheat shipments also declined because commercial grain regions (Chapter 11) were beginning to specialize and to capture the wheat markets.

Tremendous Increase in New Exports For centuries, the Mediterranean farmer grew winter vegetables, but he had little incentive to produce a surplus of something that would spoil enroute to market. But the trans-

---

* Richard Dana's *Two Years Before the Mast* is a fascinating description of life on a ship which operated in the movement of hides from a region of Mediterranean agriculture in southern California clear around South America's Cape Horn to the markets of New England.

Mediterranean Agriculture

A lemon grove in Ventura County, California. The trees in the foreground are three years old; commercial production usually begins when trees are five. Average size for California lemon groves is 15 acres. Dry hilltops are in the background; foreground plots are irrigated. (Sunkist Photo.)

port revolution and the development of refrigeration enabled him to deliver these perishables in good condition to distant regions. The status of winter vegetables changed immediately: They became major items of export.

In response to this development, summer cropping practices also quickly changed. For centuries, the main drawback of summer was lack of water, a handicap that could be remedied only by irrigation. But irrigation was costly and there was little incentive to incur this expense in the early days. But with a boom in the vegetable market, prices rose high enough to warrant the investment of labor and capital in constructing dams and conduits for irrigation systems. If winter rainfall and snowfall in the high mountains are impounded, gravity will bring water to the valley bottoms. Such water is reasonably inexpensive. By this method, the irrigated valleys of California receive water from the Coast Ranges and the Sierra Nevada Mountains; in addition, Los Angeles and the Imperial Valley of California are supplied by water from the Colorado River.

Introduction of Fruits from Elsewhere
The Mediterranean regions had always been warm enough for many tropical plants. Now, with irrigation, their soils could be made wet enough. Moreover, most Mediterranean farmers were considerably closer than their tropical competitors to the main markets. Several tropical fruits were transplanted successfully to irrigated fields in Mediterranean realms, but the most striking success was with citrus fruits. Oranges and lemons have joined vegetables as the most distinctive exports of the Mediterranean Basin today (see Figure 10-4, page 164).

Irrigation likewise permitted the successful introduction to Mediterranean cropping systems of peaches, walnuts, almonds, apricots, and other humid-area fruits from the mid-latitudes.

This revolution in emphasis on fruits and vegetables in the commercial regions of Medi-

CITRUS FRUIT

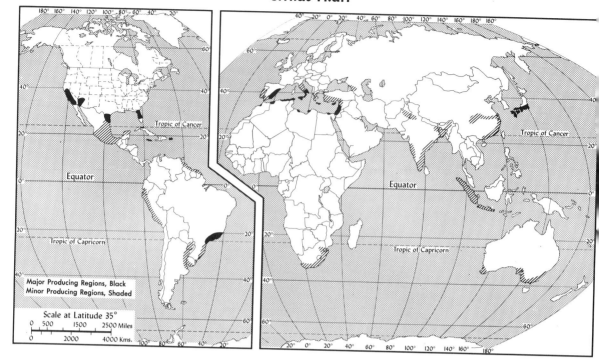

Major Producing Regions, Black
Minor Producing Regions, Shaded

Scale at Latitude 35°
0   500   1500   2500 Miles
0   2000   4000 Kms.

Figure 10-4

terranean agriculture is reflected in the export structure of these areas. The value of fruit and vegetable exports as a percentage of total exports is: Israel 43, Spain 40, Lebanon 30, Greece 23, Italy 16, Turkey 14, and Algeria 10.

Relationships to Labor Supply   Raising fruits and vegetables requires tremendous amounts of hand labor. Some of the work can be mechanized (preparing soil, for instance, or harvesting such crops as onions), but a vast amount of hand labor is still needed to set out plants, extract weeds, and harvest fruit. The Mediterranean Basin has always been one of the world's more densely settled areas. So the abundant labor supply there has been rather cheap. As yet, commercial Mediterranean agriculture elsewhere has not been able to pay very high farm wages either. This has been a problem in California and Arizona where the demand for labor has been met by immigrants from foreign countries, particularly Japan and Mexico. But some of the Mexican labor does not immigrate; retaining

their Mexican citizenship they cross the border seasonally to work on United States farms.

Farm Size   Many small farms were one result of all these developments. The high cost of irrigation meant that an irrigated acre might better be devoted to fruit and vegetables than to grains, for they would bring a higher return on investments. Not only did they command higher prices; but two or three crops of vegetables could be harvested in a single year. As a result, the individual farmer in Mediterranean valleys began applying more intensive methods of farming to smaller parcels of land. But in some instances, rather large farms (sometimes called "ranches") have been organized with a sizable force of hired hands and machinery operating scores of acres.

Regional Specialization   There is an increasing tendency for neighboring farmers in the United States portion of this realm to specialize in the same crops. By doing so, they benefit as a group from certain aspects of large-scale operation. Instead of small shipments of lettuce, full truck loads or full carloads can be assembled. Transport agencies generally quote lower rates on carload shipments than on smaller ones. Where the shipments are large enough, entire trainloads of vegetables and fruit can be sped along to market.

Concomitant with such regional specialization has been the growth in *marketing associations* by which fruit growers and vegetable growers pool their resources to expedite the collecting, grading, sorting, and selling of their produce. These associations operate efficiently in shrinking the interval between the times of harvest and of delivery. The Salinas Valley of California is one of the many areas that have specialized in a single crop for the foregoing reasons. The crop is lettuce, and the valley claims to be "The Salad Bowl of the Nation."

But such specialization is not typical for the Mediterranean Basin, where most of the farmers engaged in this type of bioculture reside. Their endeavors continue to be a mixed type of farming, with both crops and animals present on each farm, and a diversity of crops (winter and summer, grains and vegetables and fruit) being grown.

In its truest form, Mediterranean bioculture is the most "mixed" of all types of farming—mixed in two respects. First of all, most farms as individual operating units are a mixture of productive efforts. Secondly, when farms do specialize (in citrus, or grapes, or avocados, or any other crop) a diverse mixture of such specialized operating units occurs in Mediterranean realms.

Suggested Readings

Ackerman, Edward A., "The Influences of Climate on the Cultivation of Citrus Fruits," *Geographical Review*, 1938, pp. 289-302.

Bonnet, D., "The Olive Industry of France and French North Africa," *World Crops*, 1950, pp. 205-208.

Colby, Charles C., "The California Raisin Industry: A Study in Geographic Interpretation," *Annals of the Association of American Geographers*, 1924, pp. 40-108.

Dobby, E. H. G., "Economic Geography of the Port Wine Region," *Economic Geography*, 1936, pp. 311-323.

Gregor, Howard F., "Agricultural Shifts in the Ventura Lowland of California," *Economic Geography*, 1953, pp. 340-361.

————, "The Plantation in California," *The Professional Geographer*, March 1962, pp. 1-4.

Griffin, Paul F., and Chatham, Ronald L., "Population: A Challenge to California's Changing Citrus Industry," *Economic Geography*, 1958, pp. 272-276.

Isaac, Erich, "The Citron in the Mediterranean: A Study in Religious Influences," *Economic Geography*, 1959, pp. 71-78.

Medici, Giuseppe, *Land Property and Land Tenure in Italy*, Bologna, 1952, 246 pp.

Thompson, Kenneth, "Location and Relocation of a Tree Crop—English Walnuts in California," *Economic Geography*, 1961, pp. 133-151.

One of the enormous terminal grain elevators of a farmers' cooperative commission company in Kansas. This elevator receives grain, mostly wheat and milo, from 165 county cooperative elevators in southwestern Kansas.
Its capacity is 18,000,000 bushels; its length exceeds half a mile. The railroad cars are full of wheat (each carrying 1600-2000 bushels) waiting to be unloaded.
(Courtesy Kansas Industrial Development Commission.)

ELEVEN

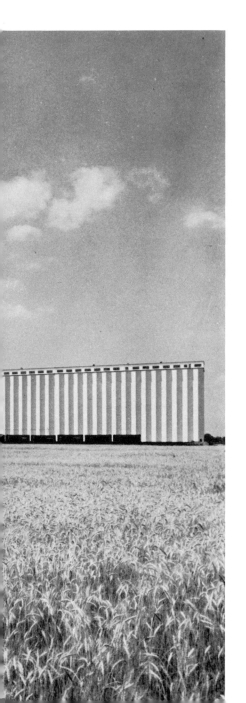

Human beings need starch, gluten, and oils for proper physical health; and many kinds of grasses store up these nutrients in their seeds. It is biologically possible for man to eat the seeds of a wide array of plants, but in the dietary tastes he has developed, he gives first preference to rice, wheat, and corn, with barley, millet, oats, and rye as second choices. These crops can be grown rather widely over

Table 11-1 *World Production of Leading Crops*

Crop	Production in Millions of Metric Tons	Area Cultivated in Millions of Hectares *	Yield in 100 Kilograms per Hectare
Potatoes	276.0	24.8	111.3
Rice, paddy †	258.5	117.4	22.0
Wheat	249.9	204.7	12.2
Maize	219.6	105.7	20.8
Sweet Potatoes and Yams	119.0	14.4	82.6
Barley	84.4	60.7	13.9
Millet and Sorghums	68.1	93.6	7.3
Oats	58.5	46.0	12.7
Sugar	57.7	—	—
Rye	38.6	30.9	12.5

Source: United Nations, Food and Agriculture Organization, *Production Yearbook 1960*, Table 10-B.

* United Nations data are published in terms of the metric system, in which the basic unit of area is the *are:* 100 square meters. A *hectare* is 100 *ares* or 10,000 square meters, the equivalent of 2.471 acres. Similarly, a kilogram is 1000 grams, the equivalent of 2.2 pounds.

† No data for upland rice.

the earth; however, in only a comparatively small number of regions do men specialize in producing surpluses of these grains for sale. Although more rice is produced than any other grain, most of it is grown on subsistence farms. Commercial grain farmers concentrate prima-

COMMERCIAL GRAIN FARMING

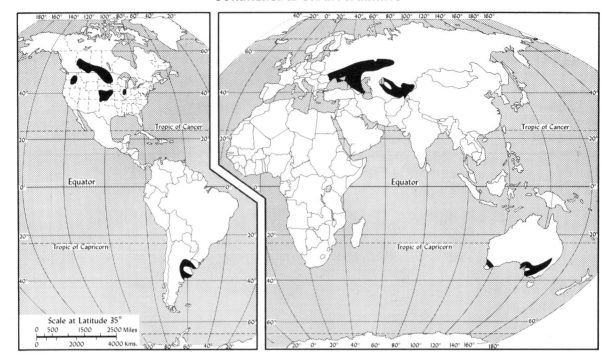

Figure 11-1

Figure 11-2

WHEAT

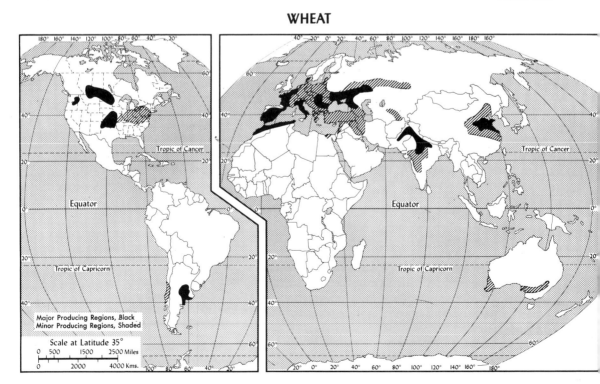

Major Producing Regions, Black
Minor Producing Regions, Shaded

rily on wheat for reasons that will be explained later.

LOCATION

The major world regions of commercial grain farming are shown on Figure 11-1. The largest one, in Eurasia, stretches for 2000 miles from Kiev in southern Russia to Omsk in western Siberia; at its widest it extends 700 miles, from the Caucasus to Saratov on the Volga River. A few hundred miles to the east is a second region including much of the Uzbek Republic.

In North America there are several grain areas, the largest running from Alberta, through Saskatchewan and Manitoba, to the Dakotas. Another area centers on Kansas and spills over into neighboring states. Smaller regions appear in eastern Washington and Oregon, eastern Illinois and northern Iowa.

South America has commercial grain farming in Argentina. Australia has two areas, one in the southwest and one in the southeast.

Commercial grain farming is a mid-latitude activity—it is all between 30° and 55° latitude in both the Northern and Southern Hemispheres. None of the regions devoted to it is very large compared to other agricultural regions. Altogether, they take up only a small fraction—less than 5 per cent—of the earth's surface.

In this chapter, we shall start with Anglo-America and then take a look at other countries to see how they differ.

CHARACTERISTICS: ANGLO-AMERICA

Specialization in One Single Cash Crop
Commercial grain farmers are highly specialized. They concentrate on crops instead of animals, and each usually selects one single grain as the main source of income. In most commercial grain regions that crop is wheat.

Wheat   There are two kinds of wheat— *soft* wheat and *hard* wheat—and they are grown in distinctively different regions. Soft wheat has a low gluten content; therefore, its flour does not rise well with yeast, and it spoils fast. Soft wheat is better for spaghetti, crackers, and pastry.

Hard wheat has a high gluten content; flour made of it rises well and makes good bread. Further, it stands transportation without spoiling readily. For these reasons hard wheat is the type used in international trade and is the more widely grown variety.

The locational pattern of wheat in the United States is shown in Figure 11-3. Wheat occupies 11 per cent of all cropland, but in the commercial grain regions sometimes over half the farm land is given over to it. Many people are surprised to see states outside the Great Plains on a map like Figure 11-3. Thinking only of Kansas, North Dakota, and other well-known wheat states, they fail to realize that the farmers of northern Missouri, southern Illinois, Indiana, Ohio, Michigan, Pennsylvania, and the Eastern Seaboard place a heavy emphasis on wheat.

The value of the United States' wheat crop comes to around $2 billion annually—about half the value of dairy products. The leading wheat-growing states are Kansas, North Dakota, Montana, Nebraska, and Washington. (However, the Canadian Province of Saskatchewan produces almost twice as much wheat as Kansas: a ratio of approximately 300,-000,000 to 150,000,000 bushels.)

Other Crops   There are two commercial grain regions in the United States where the farmers specialize in producing corn for sale: east-central Illinois and north-central Iowa. Frequently these are termed *cash-corn* areas because corn is the main crop grown—but grown for sale rather than for feeding animals on the corn-growing farm as is done through most of the corn belt. The reason for this apparent anomaly will be considered later under the topic of relationships. For the nation as a whole, corn sold is valued at $1.5 billion. Occasionally, some other grain may be the major cash product. Farmers, in southern Louisiana and the Sacramento Valley of California, for instance, specialize in rice. All other crops play secondary roles. A farmer may put in barley, oats, and rye in small amounts for consumption by his family, for feeding a few farm animals, or for supplementary income.

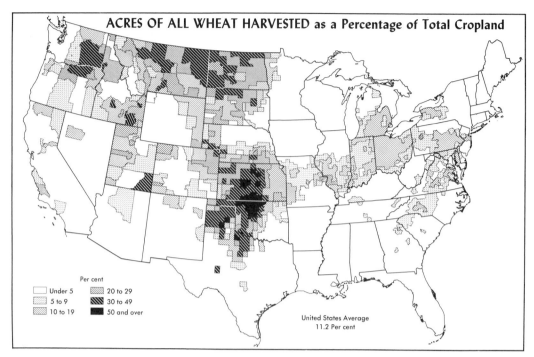

ACRES OF ALL WHEAT HARVESTED as a Percentage of Total Cropland

Per cent
- Under 5
- 5 to 9
- 10 to 19
- 20 to 29
- 30 to 49
- 50 and over

United States Average
11.2 Per cent

Figure 11-3 *(From U. S. Bureau of the Census.)*

Area Cropped   The proportion of land devoted to crops attains unusually high percentages in commercial grain regions. Cropland accounts for 80 per cent of the total in the Red River Valley of North Dakota and in parts of western Kansas. Over large stretches of the grain regions the figure surpasses 60 per cent (see Figure 9-6).

Role of Animals   Animals—some chickens, perhaps a dairy cow, and a few swine— are raised to meet the subsistence needs of the farm family though many wheat farmers raise no animals at all. There are, however, small anomalous areas where cash animals are important, but these usually surround large cities. At one time horses were essential on every grain farm for pulling wagons and machinery, but their number declined as farms became mechanized. Draft horses are absent from most grain farms today.

Mechanization   No other type of agriculture is as highly mechanized as is commercial grain farming. Indeed, the very birth of commercial grain farming is attributable largely to the invention of two pieces of equipment—the steel plow and the harvester—that enabled man to unlock the resources of handicapped land. Today the typical grain farm has a fleet of machines: tractors, plows, disks, harrows, drills, reapers, combines, wagons, and trucks. There is scarcely a job to be done for which a machine has not been designed. The distribution of farm machinery in the United States can be typified by a map of farms with tractors (see Figure 9-11). Note that over 80 per cent of commercial grain farms have tractors.

Number and Size of Farms   There are approximately half a million cash-grain farms in the United States—approximately the same number as dairy farms. But the cash grain farms cover an aggregate of 200 million acres—double that in farms specializing in milk production.

Commercial grain farms are the largest on earth. (Livestock raising takes up more acres, but it is based on natural vegetation rather than crops, so the holdings are more properly called ranches rather than farms.) Wheat

Commercial Grain Farming

farms average from 500 to 1000 acres in North Dakota, the Canadian provinces, and Washington, but many cover 2000 acres. Farther south, in Kansas, they are smaller, as small as 350 acres, and in the cash-grain area of Illinois, the average size of a farm is 200 acres.

Labor Force   The labor force on any farm is small, consisting of the farmer plus one or two hired hands—except for the brief period of harvest when large numbers of laborers are hired. The labor force totals approximately 750,000 farm residents (including the operator and members of his family) plus 200,000 hired workers. Were it not for mechanization, a farmer never could handle the tremendous acreage of commercial grain farms.

Wheat farming has one peak period for work: harvest time. Thousands of extra laborers had to be hired before the invention of *combine* machines (which cut and thresh wheat in one operation) and cornpicking machines (which pick and husk ears of corn). Today extra hands are still needed to man the fleet of combines that sweep northward beginning in May with winter wheat harvest in Texas and finishing in September with spring wheat harvest in Alberta.

Farmsteads   Structures on grain farms are small and unpretentious compared to farmsteads in regions of dairy farming or of mixed-farming. With so few animals there is little need for large barns and silos to store feed, or for barns and sheds to shelter animals, or for large feedlots. In addition to the family residence, the only building needed is a garage for the machinery. At harvest time the grain is sped to market so that the farmstead needs no structure to store or process the crop.

Value of Farms   Commercial grain farms are far above average in total value of both farm land and farm buildings—around $40,000 per farm. As Figure 11-4 shows, commercial grain regions stand out favorably compared to the national average of $35,000 per farm. The average farm value in North Dakota is $39,569 and in Kansas $49,046. But

Figure 11-4 (*From U. S. Bureau of the Census.*)

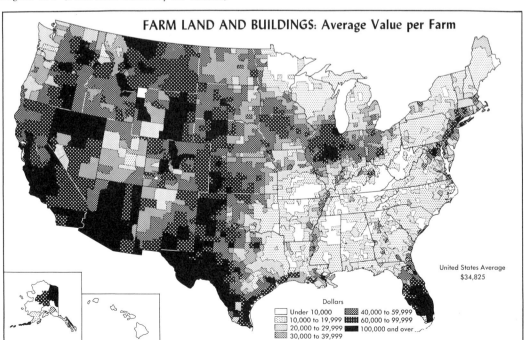

A farmstead in the expansive wheat lands of central Kansas. Trees are generally absent from wheat fields except where they have been planted around the farmstead to serve as a windbreak. (Courtesy of Kansas Industrial Development Commission.)

because these farms are so large their value per acre is low—approximately $100 per acre, considerably below that of farms in the Corn Belt (see Figure 9-14).

PHYSICAL RELATIONSHIPS

Precipitation   Commercial grain farming occurs usually where the annual rainful is between 10 and 20 inches. But the effectiveness of precipitation depends not only on number of inches but also on rate of evaporation; where evaporation exceeds precipitation, a *dry*, or *arid*, climate results. Regions of commercial grain farming usually are associated with subhumid climates, that is, the drier margins of humid climates.

More critical than annual amount of precipitation and evaporation rate, though, is the seasonal distribution. Since wheat is a grass, it begins to grow by sending up a tuft of green blades. Then stalks of straw shoot up that carry the seeds. In this formative period, moist weather is essential if numerous large heads of grain are to develop. At the next stage, however, the weather should be sunny and dry if the grain is to mature properly. Excess rainfall at that time causes the plant to grow straw instead of seeds, makes it vulnerable to fungus and wilt, and induces molding of the grain after harvest. Humid summer weather may be excellent for corn but it is undesirable for wheat.

Hard wheat does well in subhumid lands. *Soft* wheat, though, can tolerate more moisture; it is the prevailing type east of the Mississippi River. But in humid lands, soft wheat must compete with corn, which is better than wheat for fattening animals. Moreover, wheat produces a lower yield per acre than do corn, oats, rye, and barley (Table 11-1). Humid regions in the mid-latitudes do grow wheat (Figures 11-2 and 11-3), but only secondarily to some other specialty crop.

The cash-grain areas of Illinois and Iowa are exceptions to these generalizations about precipitation and specialization. Illinois and Iowa are humid enough for corn and farmers there specialize in growing that crop for sale. They do so because of relationships with other factors to be considered later.

Droughts   Since the variability of precipitation *increases* as the annual amount *decreases*, the threat of drought is serious in commercial wheat lands. In the chapter on livestock ranching, we observed that the grazing regions of the United States have often been invaded by farmers who thrived during humid years and went bankrupt during dry years. Most of these farmers were commercial wheat producers.

In drier country, *dry farming* (see p. 158) is commonly practiced. Over 40 per cent of all cropland in the Columbia Plateau (eastern

Washington and northeastern Oregon) lies fallow each year. In western Kansas this proportion varies between 30 and 40 per cent; in North Dakota it is 16 per cent. To put these figures in perspective, we can note that, for the nation as a whole, only 6 per cent of the cropland lies fallow any one year.

Temperatures   Wheat is widespread throughout the mid-latitudes (see Figure 11-2), being cultivated as far north as Finland and as far south as Argentina. Hardy strains of wheat need growing seasons of only 90 days. On the other hand wheat cannot stand excess heat, particularly in the formative period when the straw stalks are shooting upward and the cereal grains are developing. Therefore, little wheat is grown in areas where the average summer temperatures are over 68°. When both rainful and temperature are considered, the best wheat climate is one with a cool, moist season for early growth followed by a warm, sunny, dry period for maturation.

By temperature, there are two types of wheat region: winter wheat areas and spring wheat areas.

Winter wheat grows where winters are mild. Seed is sown in the autumn, begins to sprout before the growing season ends, lies dormant through the mild winter, and matures in early summer. Winter wheat predominates throughout the United States except in Montana, the Dakotas, Minnesota, Wisconsin, and Michigan.

Spring wheat grows where winters are too severe for wheat seedlings. Seed is sown in early spring and is harvested in the autumn. The spring wheat belt of Anglo-America starts in Minnesota and North Dakota, extends northwestward into Montana and the Prairie Provinces of Canada (Manitoba, Saskatchewan, and Alberta), and finally penetrates to the Peace River valley of Alberta, almost 60° north of the Equator.

Spring wheat is usually hard wheat. Winter wheat grown in dry areas is ordinarily hard, while that grown in humid areas is generally soft.

The yield of spring wheat in the United States averages 11.6 bushels per acre, of winter wheat, 20 bushels per acre. The states with the highest average wheat yields by bushel per acre are all in the winter wheat region: Washington 32, New York 31, Indiana 31, Illinois 30, Idaho 30, New Jersey 29, Oregon 29, Michigan 29, Missouri 28, Pennsylvania 28. The astonishing thing about these states is that none is in either of the two main commercial grain-farming regions! The highest yields per acre within those two major regions are 19 in Nebraska and 17 in Kansas. Minnesota averages 14 bushels per acre and North Dakota only 9! Obviously, farmers in a region do not specialize in wheat just because its yields per acre surpass those of competitive regions but because, among their alternatives, wheat is the most remunerative.

Flora   Nearly every present commercial-grain region originally had a natural cover of grass. The only exception is the area in the Soviet Uzbek Republic where commercial grain farming extends into a region of desert shrub. The contemporary significance of the original vegetation lies in both fertility of soil and ease of cultivation.

Fertility of Soil   Mid-latitude grasslands have developed some of the world's most fertile soils. Known as *chernozem*, these soils are extremely rich in plant nutrients for two reasons. First, a very high content of organic matter has been imparted by the grasses, so much so that their color is black. Second, leaching is limited because the rainfall in the grasslands is limited.

Chernozemic soils are so rich they can stand repeated cropping of the same grain year after year. Many fields have been in wheat for 20 consecutive years with no decline in yield. Wheat farmers accordingly practice very little crop rotation. Nor do they spend much money for fertilizer. In the United States the average expenditure is $2.35 per acre for commercial fertilizer. As Figure 11-5 (page 174) shows, commercial-grain areas are far below this average. The national average application is 309 pounds of commercial fertilizer per acre; the figure for Kansas is 117, and for North Dakota 64—the lowest in the nation. Low expenditures in Nebraska, Iowa, and Illinois

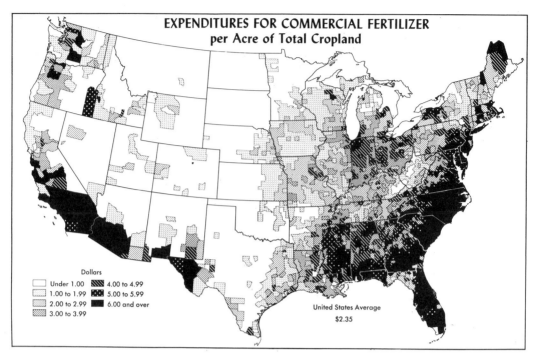

EXPENDITURES FOR COMMERCIAL FERTILIZER
per Acre of Total Cropland

Dollars

Under 1.00   4.00 to 4.99
1.00 to 1.99   5.00 to 5.99
2.00 to 2.99   6.00 and over
3.00 to 3.99

United States Average
$2.35

Figure 11-5 (*From U. S. Bureau of the Census.*)

are understandable in the light of large supplies of manure produced on the farms themselves. But commercial grain farmers have no such supply; their low investment in phosphates, nitrates, and potash can be understood only in light of the inherent matchless fertility of chernozemic soil.

Ease of Cultivation The original cover of mid-latitude grass has also influenced the amount of effort required to cultivate soil. In the days of the wooden plow the grasses were a curse; wooden plows simply could not cut through the sod mat of grass roots. It was easier for pioneers to clear forest lands. But things quickly changed when the steel plow was designed. Grasslands that were formerly avoided were now eagerly sought. Now, in fact, they could be cultivated more easily than tree lands! They had no stumps. Thus did a single cultural factor—the invention of the steel plow—completely reverse the relative merits of two environments.

Landforms Wheat will grow in rather rough land, but the major commercial wheat

regions occupy plains because mechanized methods, absolutely essential to successful commercial grain cropping, work best on flat land. The Columbia Plateau is no exception; although it is high land, its surface is that of a rolling plain.

It is landforms that seem to explain the presence of the two anomalous cash-corn areas in the midst of the American Corn Belt mentioned earlier. East-central Illinois and north-central Iowa are unusually flat areas endowed with fertile soils. On most farms in that region corn is the principal crop, and most of them are on rolling plains. Therefore there is a good deal of land with at least a gentle slope—enough to foster erosion when the land is devoted to corn, a crop that lays bare the soil for a considerable length of time. To combat erosion, Corn Belt farmers put the slopes in alfalfa, clover, or permanent pasture, the flats usually in corn. A Corn Belt farm with such a diversity of landform is likely to be a stock farm—the animals being sustained by crops from that farm. But if a Corn Belt farmer is blessed with a large farm that is entirely flat, he is likely to realize more profit from it by

Commercial Grain Farming

devoting it all to corn—and then selling the grain as a cash crop.

In summation, the hypothesis ... is that in the Corn Belt, and certain peripheral areas, even where permanent pasture is negligible, cash-grain farming will be found concentrated in those portions least subject to erosion, and livestock farming will prevail in the more rolling areas. Flat land will not dictate cash-grain farming, but it is the crucial factor which will permit cash-grain farming as a reasonable choice over long periods. On lands subject to erosion, good soil management suggests a crop rotation including alfalfa or clover. Cash-grain farming in such areas may not be impossible, but it certainly is not a wise choice.*

CULTURAL RELATIONSHIPS

Commercial grain farming occurs in areas typified by low population density, recent development, "frontier economies," a particular type of trade-center, milling industries, and intricate transportation networks. And some areas have odd freight-rate structures.

Population Density Population densities are low in areas specializing in commercial grain, ranging from 2 to 25 people per square mile. Densities are higher, though—up to 125 people per square mile—in the few areas specializing in corn. If the population continues to shoot upwards from its present three billion it will be interesting to see what happens to the man/land ratios in these grain regions, especially the wheat lands. Will the ratios increase, and if so, will wheat growing persist as the leading activity or will it yield to other types of farming that today are associated with higher man/land ratios?

Recent Development Commercial grain farming is a comparatively new economic activity, occurring in regions that have been settled, in general, within the last 150 years. One reason for this is the recent development of a large wheat market in Europe and America. A second reason is the recency of the mechanical revolution, which provided steel plows, harvesting machines, and other equip-

* Leverett P. Hoag, "Location Determinants for Cash-Grain Farming in the Corn Belt," *The Professional Geographer*, May 1962, pp. 6-7.

ment for grain farming. To appreciate the significance of these inventions, we must recall the limited rainfall in commercial grain regions. In their natural state, these subhumid lands may be exploited successfully by livestock grazing, but they can not be cropped commercially with hand labor. Unless they are irrigated, dry lands have low yields per acre; therefore, each farmer must work a great deal of land in order to earn a living. This requires machinery, that is, *extensive* farming methods in which the ratio of number of acres to number of workers is high.

Frontier Stage of Development Commercial wheat farming is particularly adapted to frontier areas. As waves of Europeans moved into the sparsely settled mid-latitudes of North America, South America, Australia, and Africa they invariably started raising wheat. With the following waves of settlers, wheat farming was displaced by other kinds of agriculture; but it took root again on the more distant frontier. At one time the leading wheat state in the United States was New York, then Ohio, then Illinois; now it is Kansas. Wheat is an ideal crop for frontier areas because it is worth more per weight and volume than other grain and therefore bears transport costs better over long hauls; it keeps well and can be easily stored; and the market is relatively stable (that is, wheat-eaters consume about as much wheat in depressions as in times of prosperity). Since 1850 most of the world frontiers have been settled by Europeans familiar with wheat, and European financiers investing in these frontiers were interested in developing new sources of the grain most wanted in Europe.

"Sidewalk Farmers" and "Suitcase Farmers" Farms are linked to settlements by an increasing percentage of people who operate commercial grain farms but reside elsewhere than on the farms they run. Sully County, South Dakota, for instance, was selected as a sample area for studying this phenomenon; it had a total of 516 farms in 1950; 418 (81 per cent) of these were operated by farmers who lived on the farm; but 44

(8.5 per cent) of them were operated by sidewalk farmers—those who lived in a nearby settlement; 54 (10.5 per cent) were operated by *suitcase farmers*, operators, that is, who live 30 miles or more from the nearest border of the county containing their farm. These last are not to be confused with absentee owners who reside elsewhere and rent their farms to tenants. Most suitcase farmers in fact own their farms as well as operate them. As late as 1948 there had been only 12 suitcase farmers in Sully County; by 1952 their number had jumped to 78. Their homes were dispersed through twelve states; Texas was home for 20, Oklahoma for 17, Kansas 16, South Dakota 6, Minnesota 5, Colorado 5, Nebraska 3. Two others lived in Canada. By 1952 suitcase farmers were operating one-third of Sully County's wheat land.

On the other hand there was little change in number of sidewalk farmers between 1948 and 1952.

The amenities of life in a large, even if more distant, city is apparently a stronger draw than those of the isolated farmstead or the nearby town. Automobiles and airplanes enable the farmers to commute. Wheat is peculiarly adapted to *suitcase* farming because the farmer need not be on hand all the time.*

Settlements and Their Employment Structures Most towns and cities in commercial grain regions are fundamentally service centers whose existence depends on surplus grain. On the one hand they serve as transportation centers, where carloads of grain are assembled for shipment to larger centers; on the other hand, they serve as distribution points to supply farmers with lumber, coal, repair services for machinery, financial and other services.

There is an inverse correlation between the spacing of these settlements and general population density. In the commercial grain area of North Dakota the settlements are 40 miles

---

apart; in that of Kansas they are 20 miles apart while in the Illinois cash-grain area the average is 7 miles apart.

Most of the jobs in small cities in commercial grain regions are in trade and services. Look at the employment structure of two sample settlements in Kansas (Table 11-2).

Table **11-2** *Selected Employment Structures in the Commercial-Grain Region of Kansas*

Type of Employment	Norton	Dodge City
Population	3,060	11,262
Total Employed	1,149	4,303
Percentage Employed:		
Total	100	100
Primary activities	5	5
Secondary activities	18	16
Manufacturing	5	7.1
Construction	13	8.4
Tertiary activities	77	79
Trade	33	34
Transportation	10	14
Business services	8	7
Public administration	6	4
Other services	20	20

Some settlements are also railroad division points and trucking centers.

The larger settlements have factories that transform a large portion of the grain output. Throughout the winter wheat region there are numerous flour mills, particularly in Kansas City, Topeka, Wichita, and Oklahoma City. In the spring wheat zone, Minneapolis and Winnipeg are the chief milling cities. Northeastern Illinois has several corn mills where starch and oil are made (in Argo, for instance). Decatur, Illinois, is the seat of the nation's biggest processors of soybeans—one of the secondary cash crops in commercial grain regions (as well as in mixed-farming areas). We shall have more to say about the milling industry in Chapter 17.

The largest settlements contain grain exchanges—places where buyers of grain contact sellers. The largest exchange is the Chicago Board of Trade.

Truck and Railroad Transportation The wheat moves to market (flour mills primarily) by a series of transportation links. Usually the grain is trucked directly from the

---

* A fascinating analysis of this new development has been written by Walter M. Kollmorgen and George F. Jenks, "Suitcase Farming in Sully County, South Dakota," *Annals of the Association of American Geographers*, 1958, pp. 27-40.

Commercial Grain Farming

Seven country elevators lined up between highway and railway at the Alberta town of Nanton (population 1047) on the Canadian prairies. (Courtesy of Elizabeth Worth Vinson.)

harvesting machinery to a grain elevator which serves not only as a huge storage facility but also as a place of testing and grading the grain. Elevators are also equipped to clean and dry the kernels. Elevator owners generally buy the wheat and provide the farmers with marketing information. From farms within a few miles' radius, grain is trucked in directly to flour mills, but most of the grain is first assembled at country elevators. Elevators are located alongside railways, and railway box cars serve as the carriers which transport the grain from country elevators to flour-mills, brewers, exporting points, or other terminals. In the flat, treeless plains of commercial grain country, such clusters of buildings are visible for miles. Indeed, the most conspicuous features of the landscape as one travels through the countryside of southern Saskatchewan, North Dakota, central Kansas, eastern Washington, or northeastern Illinois are the tall white elevators that mark each town and many a village.

At harvest season in wheat belts these settlements face a unique type of traffic congestion. The maturing of wheat crops cannot be scheduled evenly over a long time as can harvests of milk or vegetables. In any one area, all the wheat ripens simultaneously and must be harvested at once. All wagons and trucks in the area are pressed into service, some on 24-hour-a-day schedules, to move the wheat from farm to transportation center. There the wheat is dumped into the country elevators and then into railroad cars for shipment to the main milling centers. American railroads begin shifting boxcars into the wheat regions several days in advance of harvest dates. The subsequent trainloads of wheat invariably clog the railroad yards in Winnipeg, Kansas City, Topeka, and other centers where huge elevators await filling. During the peak week, Kansas City alone receives 11,000 loaded cars. In no other economic region do the cities have, relatively, such large rail yards for storing freight.

In all this movement the railroad plays a major role—indeed, commercial grain regions did not develop until railways were constructed to and through them. The surge of railroad building west of the Mississippi River between 1870 and 1890 contained several companies (termed *"The Granger Roads"*), which wove a tight net through the leading commercial grain states, Kansas, Nebraska, Iowa, Minnesota, and the Dakotas (see Figure 7-8), and were financed for purposes of developing these granger states.

Today, grain accounts for 4 per cent of the tonnage moved on United States railroads as a whole; the proportion reaches 10 per cent on the Union Pacific Railroad and 16 per cent on the Santa Fe Road.

Railroad Freight Rates The anomalous cash-grain region in east-central Illinois is related to a peculiar freight-rate structure. Freight rates on grain moving into Chicago are skewed considerably in favor of northeastern Illinois. Places 100 miles west of

RATES ON GRAIN TO CHICAGO

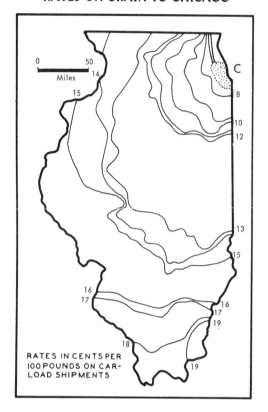

RATES ON LIVESTOCK TO CHICAGO

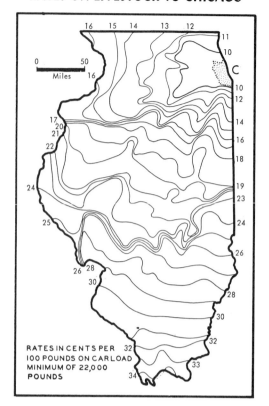

Figure 11-6 (*Courtesy* Economic Geography.)

Chicago pay half again as much to ship grain to Chicago as do places 100 miles south (Figure 11-6). Conversely, places 100 miles south of Chicago pay considerably more to ship animals to Chicago than do shippers 100 miles west of Chicago. Clearly, the freight-rate structures of Illinois encourage corn growers in the east to sell cash grain and those in western Illinois to ship their corn in the form of livestock.*

Water Transportation   Waterways play an important role in moving wheat from regions of surplus to deficit areas. Port Arthur, Fort William, Duluth, Superior, Milwaukee,

* A more detailed analysis of the Illinois freight-rate structures is found in the author's "Freight Rates as a Geographic Factor in Illinois," *Economic Geography*, 1944, pp. 25-30.

Chicago, New Orleans, and Houston—all have impressive dockside grain elevators for storing grain being transshipped from rail to boat (see illustration of Fort William, page 180). It costs about as much to haul wheat 20 miles by truck from farm to railway station as to haul it 500 miles by railroad or 3000 miles by water. A large part of the wheat then can be shipped cheaply from Great Lake ports to Buffalo (the nation's leading flour-milling city), and even on through the seaports of Baltimore, Philadelphia, and New York to Europe.

Market Regions   Most of the world's wheat is consumed as human food in Europe and Anglo-America. Most of the world's commercial grain regions are vitally linked with these two zones, which provide not only human

Commercial Grain Farming

consumers of wheat but also animal consumers of corn and oats. In 1800 these areas had a population of less than 200,000,000. Now their population is four times that figure. This population boom and the associated industrial revolution generated a tremendous purchasing power, a powerful stimulant to the development of commercial grain regions (as well as livestock ranching, dairy farming, and mixed farming) in distant regions of the world. Another linkage between commercial grain regions with Europe and with eastern Anglo-America involved the flow of capital funds that developed grain farms and serviced them with railroads. Moreover, Europe and eastern Anglo-America were the source regions of the settlers who opened up the world's commercial grain regions.

Most of the world's commercial corn is consumed as animal feed in the dairy belts, mixed-farming regions, and on poultry farms (Figure 13-1, page 202).

Government Price Support United States grain farmers produce more grain than the domestic and foreign markets are able to purchase. Normally this situation would produce such low prices that many a wheat or corn farmer would be confronted with bankruptcy. To avoid such a development, the federal government has guaranteed the farmers a minimum price which the Secretary of Agriculture establishes each year. The net effect of this arrangement is that the Government buys up surplus wheat and corn—and stores it in huge cylindrical steel bins which are common sights in many settlements within the commercial wheat and commercial corn areas. At present the government owns enough wheat to meet the domestic and export needs for two full years.

International Trade Table 11-3 indicates the volume of international trade in the six major grains. More tons of wheat circulate in this flow than the other five combined. Canada, the United States, and the Soviet Union are the major wheat exporters, with Canada, during most years, ranking first. Even

Table 11-3 *World Trade in Cereal Grains, Leading Nations, in Thousands of Metric Tons*

Exports		Imports	
Wheat—World: 30,455			
United States	9,723	United Kingdom	4,347
Canada	7,177	India	3,545
U.S.S.R.	6,052	Germany, West	2,472
Argentina	2,399	Japan	2,412
Australia	2,005	Brazil	1,820
		Czechoslovakia	1,638
Maize—World: 10,393			
United States	5,583	United Kingdom	2,970
Argentina	2,686	Netherlands	1,119
South Africa	409	Italy	1,065
Thailand	236	Japan	913
		Germany, West	863
Rice—World: 6,784			
Burma	1,692	Indonesia	604
China	1,661	Ceylon	583
Thailand	1,078	Malaya	535
United States	685	Hong Kong	347
Vietnam	328	India	295
Cambodia	190	Pakistan	291
Taiwan	160	Japan	277
Barley—World: 6,406			
United States	2,466	Germany, West	1,350
Canada	1,362	United Kingdom	1,013
Australia	890	Netherlands	526
Argentina	299	Denmark	500
		Japan	488
Oats—World: 1,547			
United States	640	Germany, West	402
Australia	398	Netherlands	330
Canada	139	Denmark	125
U.S.S.R.	131	Sweden	123
		United Kingdom	121
		Switzerland	117
Rye—World: 1,145			
U.S.S.R.	549	Germany, East	207
Germany, West	170	Czechoslovakia	158
United States	137	Netherlands	120
Canada	112	Finland	105

Source: United Nations, Food and Agriculture Organization, *Trade Yearbook 1960*, Tables 14, 15, 16, 17, 18, 19.

though all their wheat is spring wheat (which, as we saw, gives low yields per acre) Canadians export tremendous tonnages for several reasons. Their own population is small—about that of New York City plus suburbs; Canadian wheat is high-quality hard wheat; the Great Lakes provide a waterway across almost half

Terminal elevator at the mouth of Kaministiquia River on Lake Superior, Fort William, Ontario. The typical Great Lakes carrier alongside is 560 feet long and 59 feet wide, has a draft of 27 feet, and has a net capacity of 6180 tons. (Courtesy N. M. Paterson and Sons, Limited, Steamship Division.)

of the continent; and Canadians enjoy preferential trade privileges with the United Kingdom, the world's first-ranking wheat importer. Figure 11-7 shows the location of the major arteries in the world's wheat circulation.

COMMERCIAL GRAIN FARMING
IN OTHER REGIONS

Commercial grain regions on other continents are essentially similar to those in Anglo-America, but there are some differences that are worth noting.

U.S.S.R. The Soviet Union, with the largest grain belt, is now one of the world's foremost wheat producers. The western part of this belt is in the Ukraine, the most humid and productive wheat region of Russia. Winter wheat predominates there but in the rest of this expansive grain belt spring wheat does. All of it is hard wheat. Notice (Figure 11-2) that the region tapers off in Siberia, impinged on by low temperatures on the north and by low precipitation on the south. The Uzbek region, however, receives adequate rainfall for wheat, due to the influence of the Pamir and

Figure 11-7 *(From U. S. Department of Agriculture.)*

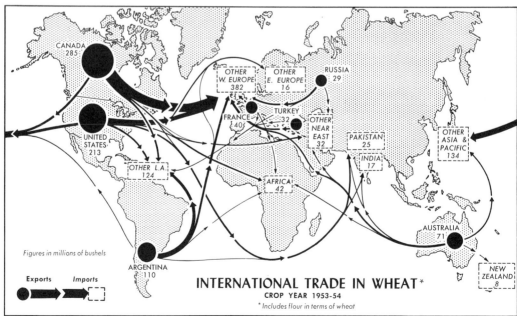

INTERNATIONAL TRADE IN WHEAT*
CROP YEAR 1953-54
* Includes flour in terms of wheat

Commercial Grain Farming

Harvest time on a mechanized wheat farm in the vast plains of the Ukraine. (Sovfoto.)

Tien Shan mountains. The Soviet wheat regions are distinguished by the Soviet system of collectivized farms on which thousands of acres are farmed by large labor forces, organized and managed by the government.

Argentina   The *pampas* of Argentina are vast flat grasslands west of Buenos Aires. The physical environment meets all the specifications for grain farming; it shows up clearly on a world map of wheat and of corn. In the east is the corn area, in the drier western portion is *the wheat crescent* (so-called because it bends around the populous area to the east). Because the region is near the sea, temperatures are so mild that farm buildings are few and small; instead of using elevators, distributors in some transport centers simply stack sacks of grain in huge piles. A railnet that is threaded through the pampas converges on the ports of Buenos Aires and Rosario. The propitious environment and good seaports have put Argentina in a competitive position for exporting grains. She ranks high in export of corn, wheat, and barley (Table 11-2).

Australia   Farmers in Australia's main commercial grain zone specialize in wheat. This zone extends 1000 miles inland from Adelaide in the general vicinity of the Murray and Darling river basins. A second zone is in the southwestern extremity of the continent. Australia's grain regions resemble Argentina's in both environment and nearness to the sea; they resemble Canada's in enjoying preferential trade agreements with Britain.

Suggested Readings

Hewes, Leslie, "Wheat Failure in Western Nebraska, 1931-1954," *Annals of the Association of American Geographers*, 1958, pp. 375-397.

———, and Schmieding, Arthur C., "Risk in the Central Great Plains: Geographical Patterns of Wheat Failure in Nebraska, 1931-1952," *Geographical Review*, 1956, pp. 375-387.

Hoag, Leverett P., "Location Determinants for Cash-Grain Farming in the Corn Belt," *The Professional Geographer*, May, 1962, pp. 1-6.

Jackson, W. A. Douglas, "Durum Wheat and the Expansion of Dry Farming in the Soviet Union," *Annals of the Association of American Geographers*, 1956, pp. 405-410.

———, "The Russian Non-Chernozem Wheat Base," *Annals of the Association of American Geographers*, 1959, pp. 97-109.

Johnson, Hildegard Binder, "King Wheat in Southeastern Minnesota: A Case Study of Pioneer Agriculture," *Annals of the Association of American Geographers*, 1957, pp. 350-362.

Kollmorgen, Walter M., and Jenks, George F., "Sidewalk Farming in Toole County, Montana, and Traill County, North Dakota," *Annals of the Association of American Geographers*, 1958, pp. 209-231.

——— and ———, "Suitcase Farming in Sully County, South Dakota," *Annals of the Association of American Geographers*, 1958, pp. 27-40.

Meinig, Donald W., *On the Margins of the Good Earth*, Chicago, 1962, 234 pp.

Morrill, Richard L., and Garrison, William L., "Projections of Interregional Patterns of Trade in Wheat and Flour," *Economic Geography*, 1960, pp. 116-126.

Schonberg, James S., *The Grain Trade: How It Works*, New York, 1956.

*Banana plantation in Ecuador. The headquarters buildings are in the center
with workers' houses in the foreground and background. The Andes mountains are in the distance.
(Courtesy Embajada del Ecuador.)*

TWELVE

The world has thousands of commercial crop farms that fit none of the agricultural types discussed so far. Many low-latitude farmers specialize in coffee, bananas, rubber, cacao, or other tropical crops. Their mid-latitude counterparts concentrate on cotton, tobacco, vegetables, or fruit. Some grow only flowers or bulbs. There is an increasing number of farmers in the higher latitudes who specialize in growing trees for wood. Clearly, there is quite a diversity. This chapter, however, will take up all these miscellaneous types of crop farms together, distinguishing only between farms in the tropics and farms in the mid-latitudes.

Tropical Commercial Crop Farming

LOCATION

Commercial crop farming, as Figure 12-1 shows, is widely dispersed throughout the tropics, those areas in which the average temperature for the coldest month is above 64°F. Three general tropical zones can be recognized: the American (extending through North America, South America, and the Caribbean Islands), the African (including Madagascar), and the Australasian (from India through Malaya and Indonesia to northeastern Australia).

All told, tropical commercial crop farming occupies only a small percentage of the earth's surface in both the Northern and Southern Hemispheres. It occurs in numerous small areas rather than in broad regions.

MISCELLANEOUS COMMERCIAL CROP FARMING

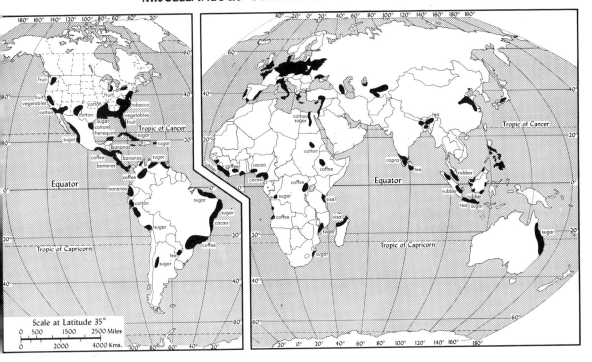

Figure 12-1

CHARACTERISTICS

Specialization in One Crop   Most farmers in these areas concentrate on growing a single crop for sale, such as bananas, cacao, pineapples, coffee, sisal, or rubber. A farmer may grow several other crops (often beans, yams, rice, corn, or manioc) for subsistence, but he selects one main source of revenue in an attempt to achieve the efficiencies of large-scale production.

There is regional specialization in each of the cash crops. For instance, most of the world's coffee is produced in the Western Hemisphere (see maps of world distribution of these crops in almost any economic atlas), but most of the tea comes from the Far East. Most of the cacao and palm oil come from Central Africa, whereas copra comes almost entirely from Southeast Asia. From tropical farms come three valuable fibers for making twine and rope: in the Far East abaca, in Africa sisal, and in North America henequen. Almost all natural rubber comes from Southeast Asia.

Two plants grow widely in the tropics: bananas and sugar. But in most sections these are grown either for subsistence or for local sale. Commercial operations are mostly confined to the Americas.

Hand Labor   A large amount of hand labor is required to plant, tend, harvest, and process the cash crop. Occasionally, machinery is used to clear the land, but other operations are done by hand. The hoe and the machete are typical tools.

Operating Units   The distinctive operating unit is the *plantation*, which is typified by large acreage, a small community of workers and families, a headquarters containing the central offices, and a processing plant in which the cash crop is prepared for shipment. The labor force often numbers several hundred people. This is *intensive* agriculture on a large scale.

But even taken all together plantations cover only a small part of the tropics. Extensive

Miscellaneous Crops

185

areas of natural vegetation usually surround each individual plantation; they constitute standby land that can be turned into fields as the soil in the old ones is depleted. In this respect, plantations resemble tropical subsistence farms; the subsistence farmers, however, shift their fields much more frequently.

Most plantation land is owned by foreign interests—a fact which, at times, has given rise to intense friction between indigenous people and the outsiders.

Not all commercial farms in the tropics are plantations, of course. Some small operations are run by individual farmers. These, though, are usually in the vicinity of large plantations, and they specialize in the same crops as do the plantations, and market their surplus during years of high prices through the same agencies as the plantations. They represent a transitional type between plantations and the small-scale primitive subsistence farms that cover most of the tropics (see Chapter 3).

PHYSICAL RELATIONSHIPS

Climate and Soil   Tropical plantations occur in regions where temperatures are relatively high and precipitation abundant throughout the year. With an uninterrupted growing season and plenty of moisture, the tropics are a natural greenhouse where crops can be harvested year around. But because of rainforest vegetation and rapid soil leaching, tropical soils usually contain little organic matter. To cope with the problem, some plantations even employ soil scientists whose main duty is to supervise the tending and fertilizing of the soil.

Diseases and Pests   Fungi, insects, and other forms of life thrive in this warm, humid environment. Plantations are sometimes shifted from one location to another not only to take advantage of fresh soil but also to escape infested areas. For instance, until 1930 the banana industry was centered on the *eastern* coast of Panama, Costa Rica, and Nicaragua. But about 1890 a wilt disease, known as *Panama Disease*, had begun to attack the root systems of banana trees. The banana companies, unable to check the spread of this blight, set about abandoning the infested plantations and clearing land for new fields. But within three or four years the new fields too began to display symptoms of the disease. Finally, around 1930, the banana-growers conceded defeat, abandoned the humid eastern coast of Central America, and shifted their operations to the western coast. Here, there was a regular annual dry season that, though it made irrigation necessary, did check the disease.

Another plant disease, *Sigatoka*, attacks the banana leaves and limits the crop to small bunches of poor fruit. This blight can be controlled, but only at great expense. The trees must be sprayed every three weeks; the harvested fruit must first be dipped in sodium acid sulfate to remove the spray and then in water to rinse off the sulfate. These spraying and washing operations account for one-fourth of the labor costs of a banana plantation in the affected areas. And the capital invested in pipes, pumps, and other spraying equipment almost equals the initial cost of preparing the land and planting the banana trees.

Winds and Landforms   Strong winds are also a serious menace, particularly to the larger fruits. Mature bunches of bananas, for example, fall in even a 25-mile-per-hour wind. The frequent hurricanes on the East Coast of Central America were a consideration, along with Panama Disease, in the relocation of the banana industry to the West Coast.

Most tropical plantations are situated on the lowland plains. There the alluvial soils are richer than the soils of the highlands, the land is easier to clear, the crops are easier to tend, and transportation is less costly.

Tropical plantations also tend to cluster along coasts or along navigable rivers, for water shipment is the main means of transportation in the tropics.

CULTURAL RELATIONSHIPS

Labor Supply   Since almost all the work on tropical plantations is performed by hand, commercial cropping in these regions is invariably associated with high population densities. For example, the Amazon Basin has

Miscellaneous Crops

an excellent physical environment for rubber growing but has few workers. By contrast, the coasts of Southeast Asia have both a satisfactory environment and many people. Consequently, most natural rubber comes from Malaya and Indonesia.

Transportation   Plantations that are not on natural waterways must be near to railroads that lead to ports, for virtually all the cash crops in the tropics are shipped to distant regions.

Regions of Demand   The commercial-farming regions of the tropics are intimately related to the populous northern mid-latitudes, specifically Europe and Anglo-America—the same regions that gave rise to livestock ranching, dairy farming, mixed farming, grain farming, in fact, almost every major commercial activity. Before 1300 A.D., very few tropical products were consumed in the mid-latitudes. Europe still had comparatively few people and eastern Asia, though it supported large masses, produced little purchasing power. Then with the cultural revolution that swept Europe in the fourteenth and fifteenth centuries, purchasing power increased and European traders scattered around the world. Tropical commodities now began to trickle back to Europe, but without exception they were the fruits of gathering rather than of agriculture. As the European market expanded, European settlers, in cooperation with native populations, launched agricultural enterprises to augment commercial gathering and increase the production of indigenous plants. Some plants were transplanted to other tropical regions, either to take advantage of a better labor supply, as in the case of rubber, or to be nearer the market regions, as in the case of bananas. (The details of these shifts will be explained below.) In the nineteenth century Anglo-America became the second major market for tropical crops.

Europe and the United States also supply the tropical farms with investment capital, (most plantations are foreign-owned), machinery for clearing and cultivating the land, personnel for managing the enterprises, soil scientists to tend the soil, fertilizers with which to replenish soil, chemicals for combating diseases and pests, railway facilities for hauling the crops to ports, and ships for transporting the cargoes overseas.

Tropical crops usually undergo the final stages of manufacturing in the market regions; thus, rubber refineries, sugar refineries, and copra oil factories are seldom in plantation country. The main reason for this situation is simply that it is cheaper to ship the raw materials than the finished products.

Political Factors   The heavy influx of plantation managers, settlers, and investment capital from Europe and the United States in the late 1800's and early 1900's led to their political control over many tropical lands. This type of development has already been discussed in the treatment of primitive agriculture (see Chapter 3).

The political factor has also been operative in government attempts to control the price of the tropical commodity. The clearest example of how this has influenced the regional location of an industry is the rubber industry. In the early 1900's, for example, Brazil had almost a monopoly on rubber; and the Brazilian government kept rubber prices higher than those charged by British companies in the Far East—thereby unwittingly aiding the development of the Malayan industry. In the 1930's the British producers similarly attempted to keep prices up, only to discover that the plantations in the Dutch East Indies could make severe inroads into the market by producing rubber at a lower price.

CHARACTERISTICS AND RELATIONSHIPS OF SPECIFIC CROPS

The general pattern of tropical commercial agriculture can be seen more clearly, perhaps, as it applies to individual crops.

Sugar Cane   Sugar cane requires a total of 50-65 inches of rainfall a year, with a dry period to allow for final ripening; continuous rainfall encourages stalk growth but discourages the formation of sucrose. Growth usually

Leading Exporters		Leading Importers	
Sugar—World: 14,583			
Cuba	4,878	United States	5,899
Philippines	904	United Kingdom	2,588
Hawaii	886	Japan	1,172
Puerto Rico	868	Canada	690
Australia	683	France	497
Taiwan	665	U.S.S.R.	335
Dominican Republic	632	Iran	305
Brazil	616		
Cacao (Cocoa Beans)—World: 777			
Ghana	254	United States	219
Nigeria	145	Germany, West	104
Brazil	80	United Kingdom	87
Ivory Coast	63	Netherlands	75
Cameroun	53	France	56
Bananas—World: 3,769			
Ecuador	891	United States	1,808
Honduras	357	Germany, West	430
Panama	290	United Kingdom	342
Canary Islands	251	France	341
Brazil	213	Argentina	205
Costa Rica	213	Spain	166
Natural Rubber—World: 2,663			
Malaya	1,221	United States	583
Indonesia	689	U.S.S.R.	242
Thailand	174	United Kingdom	212
Ceylon	93	Japan	171
Vietnam, South	78	China	156
Coffee—World: 2,600			
Brazil	1,046	United States	1,390
Colombia	384	France	196
Ivory Coast	104	Germany, West	187
Uganda	90	Italy	84
Angola	89	Sweden	68
Copra—World: 1,357			
Philippines	713	United States	320
Indonesia	174	Germany, West	163
New Guinea	50	India	91
Mozambique	37	France	76

Source: United Nations, Food and Agriculture Organization, *Trade Yearbook 1960*,
Tables 26, 38, 39, 40, 50, 58.

ceases when the temperature falls below 65°
and is best above 80°. Sugar cane is a peren-
nial. The first crop, which is called *plant cane*,
requires 15 to 24 months to ripen; thereafter,
the harvests are annual. Succeeding crops are
termed *ratoon crops*; they decline in yield as
the years go by. The sugar yield of the first two
ratoon crops is satisfactory, but then it falls
off. So, many planters set out entirely new
canes after the second ratoon crop. The variety
of sugar most widely grown today was indigenous to Melanesia, perhaps New Guinea. Until
the fifteenth century it was almost unknown in
Europe (honey was the main source of sweet-

Miscellaneous Crops

ening) and was regarded as a luxury until the nineteenth century. The Spaniards and Portuguese introduced sugar culture to the Caribbean area in the early years of western colonization. Today, though India produces more sugar cane than any other one nation, the Caribbean area provides almost two-thirds of the sugar in world trade. The leading exporters and importers of cane sugar are indicated in Table 12-1.

Cacao   These trees begin to bear at the age of five years and continue to do so for two decades. The plant demands a continuously warm and humid climate. Sensitive to temperatures under 60°, cacao trees do best in the warm lowlands. They are also sensitive to strong winds, which increase transpiration and cause the fruit pods to drop prematurely. Indigenous to remote areas of the Upper Amazon and Upper Orinoco valleys, cacao now comes mainly from tropical Africa, where the first seedlings were planted around 1880. Ghana, the world's leading producer, has over 1,000,000 acres in cacao farms. The average size of the Ghana cacao farms is four acres. In Nigeria, which produces only half as much cacao as Ghana, there are both small native farms (two or three acres) and plantations (exceeding 30 acres). Recently a virus has struck African cacao plants with a *swollen shoot* disease that may develop into a serious threat unless a remedy is found. The major exporters and importers of cacao are listed in Table 12-1.

Bananas   Native to southern Asia, bananas were brought to the Western Hemisphere in the early 1500's where they now serve as a subsistence food. Bananas had already become an important commercial crop in the lowlands, encircling the Caribbean Sea by the late 1800's. Since the fruit spoils rapidly, however, only with the advent of air-conditioned ships (which are cool in summer, warm in winter) has it been possible to ship bananas from the tropics to Europe and Anglo-America all year round. Since such transportation is costly, the regions nearest the major markets have won an advantage.

A rubber plantation in Malaya. Homes of the workers are aligned in rows in the clearing, surrounded by plantation trees. (Courtesy Natural Rubber Bureau.)

The banana tree, which matures in one year, demands from 75 to 100 inches of annual rainfall with no dry season (it responds well to irrigation when the rain is inadequate), uniformly high temperatures, and well-drained soils to keep the roots from becoming waterlogged. It depletes soil nutrients so rapidly that it is called a soil killer.

Rubber   This plant thrives best in a hot, humid environment where rainfall is at least 70 inches (preferably 100 inches) and average temperatures are above 75°. Temperatures above 95°, however, unless accompanied by high humidities, cause the plant to dry out and discourage the flow of *latex*, the sap from which rubber is made. The soil must be well drained, for rubber trees will not grow with wet feet. Rubber trees are lowland plants that become vulnerable to viruses and other diseases at elevations above 1000 feet. In virgin rainforests there is an average of one rubber tree per acre; plantations, though, average 100 rubber trees per acre.

The rubber tree is indigenous to Brazil. The Brazilian government, in an effort to preserve Brazil's monopoly over the rubber industry, banned the export of rubber seeds and rubber shoots. But in 1878 an Englishman, Henry Wickham, smuggled out several thousand rubber seeds. Planting them in Ceylon, he successfully launched the rubber industry in the Far East. In 1905, the year the first shipment of rubber left Malayan shores, Brazil was producing 99 per cent of the world supply; today she produces scarcely 2 per cent. Malaya, with a larger and more efficient labor supply, easy access to ocean shipping, and satisfactory environment, quickly gained a competitive superiority to Brazil in rubber production.

Although the synthetic rubber factories of the United States could produce most of the nation's domestic rubber needs, the United States deliberately encourages imports of natural rubber from the Far East. Natural rubber is better than synthetic rubber for most purposes. Moreover, if the nations of this area were deprived of their export trade, their economies would be severely jolted and, then (many Western statesmen believe), the national people would become more receptive to communist appeals.

Coffee   Coffee is an evergreen tree that originated in the highland forests of Ethiopia. The most widely grown variety (which demands uniform but moderate temperatures of from 60° to 80°) is a tropical highland crop that does best at altitudes between 3000 and 6000 feet. It requires from 50 to 90 inches of rainfall well distributed throughout the year, but with the least during the flowering period. Like other forests plants, it prefers shade; in fact, shade trees are planted to protect it in sunny regions where adequate protection is lacking.

Copra   Copra is the white lining of the nut of the coconut palm tree. Rich in both oil and protein, copra is mainly used for margarine, soap, and animal feed. The coconut palm requires a mean annual temperature between 72° and 88°, a daily temperature that never falls below 50°, and annual rainfall of at least 50 inches. It prefers a coastal lowland but it will grow inland at surprising altitudes—up to 5000 feet in the Philippine Islands, which are the world's foremost source of surplus copra (Table 12-1).

Drying coffee in São Paulo. Over 95 per cent of the coffee grown in Brazil belongs to the Coffee Arabica species originally from Ethiopia. In Brazil the plant attains a height of 8 to 15 feet, and reaches full production capacity in three to five years. Coffee beans, which are picked by hand, are spread over drying surfaces in the open air, where workers continuously rake them to assure maximum exposure to the sun. The dried berries are cleaned, graded, and sacked for shipment. Each tree yields an average of one pound of marketable quality. (Courtesy of Brazilian Government Trade Bureau.)

Mid-Latitude Commercial Crop Farming

The *mid-latitudes* (areas which are not always warm—in contrast to the tropics—or always cold—as are polar zones) are generally defined by these limits: an average temperature below 64° F for the coldest month and an average above 50° for the warmest month. Many crops will grow successfully under such conditions and several are produced commercially. Commercial grain farming, an outstanding example, has already been discussed in detail in Chapter 11.

LOCATION AND CHARACTERISTICS

The commercial production of crops (other than grains) in the mid-latitudes is restricted to small areas dispersed through broader regions that are typified by other forms of commercial bioculture, such as mixed farming, and livestock ranching. Most of these small areas occur in Anglo-America and Europe, though there are some in Asia and a few in other continents. The only really large example of this type is in the eastern United States along the Atlantic and Gulf coasts.

Some farmers concentrate on a single cash crop such as cotton, tea, or tobacco; others specialize in groups of vegetables or fruit; a large number sell a diversity of crops. In any case, the income derives mainly from crops.

Major World Crops The staple crops in mid-latitude commercial farms vary from region to region. Most of the *cotton*, for example, is grown in the southern United States, southern Soviet Union, northeastern China, western India, Pakistan, and the Nile Valley (Figure 12-2). *Tobacco* conforms to somewhat the same pattern, although it is grown in Europe but not in Egypt. *Tea* is essentially a Far Eastern product although one type of tea (called *yerba mate*) is produced commercially in South America. No single map is available

Figure 12-2

COTTON LINT

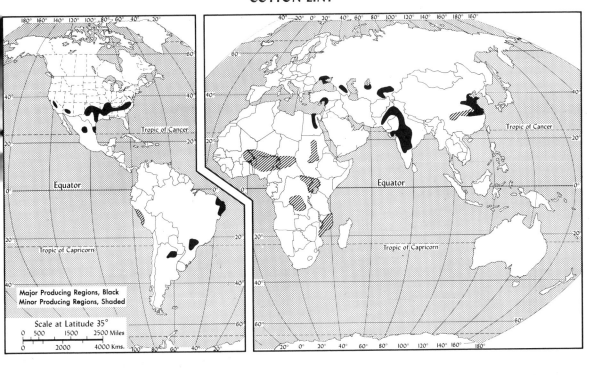

Major Producing Regions, Black
Minor Producing Regions, Shaded

Scale at Latitude 35°

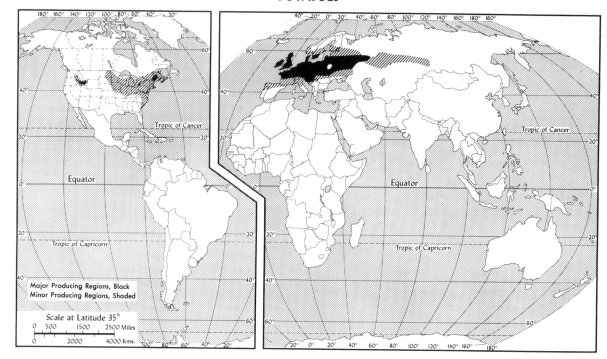

Figure 12-3

of all fruit- or vegetable-growing, but for *apples* Europe and Anglo-America are the most productive areas, and Europe and the Soviet Union dominate the world *potato* map (Figure 12-3). Europe and Anglo-America are the main areas of horticulture—flowers, flower bulbs, flower and vegetable seeds, potted plants, vines, shrubs, and nursery trees. (World maps of these and numerous other mid-latitude crops are available in the economic atlases recommended earlier.)

Major Crops within the United States The *National Atlas of the United States*, published by the federal government, breaks down in great detail the regions of commercial crops within this country. The chief categories (other than grains) are cotton, fruits, tobacco, vegetables, and horticultural specialties.

1. Cotton: The largest region of cotton farming in the United States (Figure 12-4) is in the middle portion of the Mississippi Valley, beginning at its confluence with the Ohio River

and spreading south. A second region swings eastward from Alabama through Georgia and the Carolinas. A third region, which consists of fewer farms and covers less area yet produces more cotton than the first two, is that in Texas and Oklahoma. In addition some cotton is harvested in California and Arizona. Texas accounts, by value, for one-fourth of the national total, more than twice as much as does Mississippi, the second-ranking state.

Figure 12-4 (*From U. S. Bureau of the Census.*)

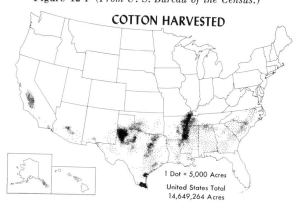

COTTON HARVESTED

1 Dot = 5,000 Acres

United States Total
14,649,264 Acres

Miscellaneous Crops

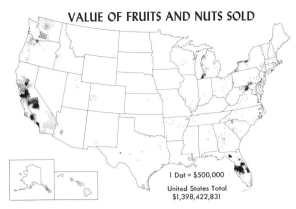

VALUE OF FRUITS AND NUTS SOLD

1 Dot = $500,000

United States Total
$1,398,422,831

Figure 12-5 (*From U. S. Bureau of the Census.*)

The total value of the cotton crop is 50 per cent greater than that of wheat.

2. Fruits and nuts: The regional pattern of commercial fruit and nut farming is very spotty (Figure 12-5). The West Coast states clearly predominate, but central Florida also produces a great deal, as do the Northeastern states. Small pockets of this activity are scattered elsewhere.

3. Tobacco: The major tobacco region (Figure 12-6) spreads over the eastern Caro-

linas and southern Virginia; it includes most of Kentucky and southern Georgia and northern Florida. Shares of the nation's tobacco crop by value are as follows: North Carolina 42 per cent, Kentucky 20 per cent, and Virginia 7 per cent.

4. Vegetables: Vegetables harvested for sale (Figure 12-7, page 194) occupy many small areas widely dispersed through the nation, particularly in the Northeast from Minnesota to New Jersey. Several sections appear throughout the Southern states. But most commercial vegetable production is in the Far West; California alone accounts for 30 per cent of all vegetables sold from the nation's farms.

5. Horticultural commodities: Flower growing also shows a spotty pattern (Figure 12-8, page 194). California is the leading state with 14 per cent of national sales, but the Northeast is the leading area and contains the next-ranking states.

6. Trees: Tree farming is a new activity that is difficult to classify. Does it belong with forestry or with bioculture? Indeed, some people would contend that these three para-

Figure 12-6 (*From U. S. Bureau of the Census.*)

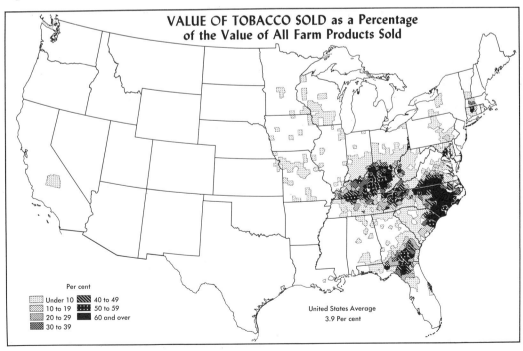

VALUE OF TOBACCO SOLD as a Percentage of the Value of All Farm Products Sold

Per cent

Under 10	40 to 49
10 to 19	50 to 59
20 to 29	60 and over
30 to 39	

United States Average
3.9 Per cent

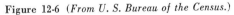

VALUE OF VEGETABLES HARVESTED FOR SALE

1 Dot = $500,000
United States Total
$739,626,458

Figure 12-7 (*From U. S. Bureau of the Census.*)

VALUE OF HORTICULTURAL SPECIALTIES SOLD

1 Dot = $500,000
United States Total
$615,338,081

Figure 12-8 (*From U. S. Bureau of the Census.*)

graphs belong in Chapter 6 on forest gathering. We are assigning tree farming to agriculture because, as in banana plantations and apple orchards, particular plots of land are set aside for a particular tree crop, seedlings are deliberately planted, the growing trees are tended and protected, and the harvest is carefully gathered. The main differences between tree farming and traditional types of agriculture are that the trees are grown not for fruit (like coconuts) or for leaves (like tea) but for wood, and that the crops require several decades rather than a few months to mature.

Tree farms now cover about 35 million acres of the United States, an area bigger than the State of New York. Over 21 million acres are in southern states from North Carolina to Texas. But the largest tree farms, planted mostly in Douglas fir, are in the Pacific Northwest, where the first large mass planting took place in 1941. It will probably be 2020 before the first large harvest is ready.

Figure 12-9 (*From U. S. Bureau of the Census.*)

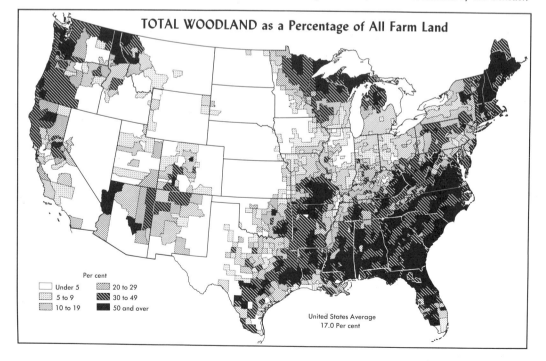

TOTAL WOODLAND as a Percentage of All Farm Land

Per cent

Under 5
5 to 9
10 to 19
20 to 29
30 to 49
50 and over

United States Average
17.0 Per cent

Miscellaneous Crops

Here is one reason why tree farming has not been conducted on a large scale in the past: The long time-lag between the date of investment and the date of harvest has disouraged risk capital.

There is no world or national map of *tree farms*; Figure 12-9, however, shows the location of woodlands on *farms* in terms of percentages of total *farm* acreage. (Note that this is not at all the same as a map of forests.) An enormous region in the Southeast contains numerous counties in which over half the farm acreage is devoted to woodland. Similarly high percentages typify New England; the northern portions of Michigan, Wisconsin, Minnesota, and the states of the Pacific Northwest.

Figure 12-10 (*From U. S. Bureau of the Census.*)

EXPENDITURES FOR COMMERCIAL FERTILIZER

1 Dot = $100,000
United States Total
$1,079,265,372

Figure 12-11 (*From U. S. Bureau of the Census.*)

FARMS WITH NO TRACTOR, HORSES, OR MULES

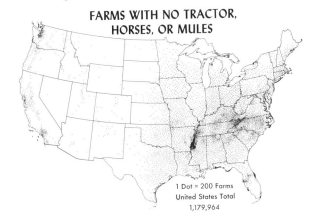

1 Dot = 200 Farms
United States Total
1,179,964

Operating Units   All these diverse commercial crops are grown on operating units that range from vegetable farms of ten acres to tree farms of a thousand acres. An average has little meaning with this kind of diversity. However, the biggest crop farm in the United States is a vegetable plantation covering 50,000 acres operated by Seabrook Farms in southern New Jersey. This plantation has 3000 workers who tend, harvest, and process over 100,000,000 pounds of 29 different vegetables and fruits a year. One thousand of these employees are field workers; the rest work in the plant—cleaning, freezing, and shipping the harvested items. There are 500 trucks in the plantation fleet.

Fertilization   Animals play a minor role on commercial crop farms; consequently, there is a dearth of manure, and plant food must be purchased. Most of the expenditure is for *commercial fertilizers* manufactured from phosphate rock, nitrate rock, potash rock, and limestone. In the United States, the average expenditure *per acre* of cropland for commercial fertilizer is $2.35 a year, but on vegetable, flower, fruit, tobacco, and cotton farms the figure sometimes exceeds $7.00. Figure 12-10 shows several conspicuous areas in which a good deal of money is spent for fertilizers; notice that all these areas are either in the Corn Belt or in those regions where cotton, tobacco, vegetables, and fruits are grown. See also Figure 11-5, page 174.

Draft and Motive Power   Few commercial crop farms are highly mechanized. In the cotton, tobacco, and orchard areas of the United States, for example, less than half the farms have tractors (Figure 12-11); that figure drops to below 10 per cent in the orchard districts of West Virginia. Furthermore, many farms in the South (particularly the Mississippi Valley), the Puget Sound Lowland, the Willamette Valley, and California have neither animals nor machines for power. On the other hand, a few large vegetable farms in California, Arizona, Texas, and Florida do have considerable amounts of machinery.

Plantations and Neoplantations The predominance of the plantation system in the American Cotton Belt before the Civil War is well known. There seems to be a widespread impression, however, that after the War this plantation system disintegrated with the abolition of slavery. To be sure, the nature of the plantation *labor force* did change radically, but the *landholdings* remained generally intact and have persisted to the present time. Indeed, the term *plantation* is still common coin in the South to apply to agricultural enterprises that meet the following criteria: (1) A landholding considerably larger (averaging between 700 and 800 acres) than "family farms" (those operated by a single family). (2) A division of labor and management duties. (3) Specialization in commercial production. Rarely, however, is the specialization in just one single item; rather, *groups* of two or three specialties are the norm today, principally some combination chosen from cotton, rice, sugar, soybeans, pecans, cattle, and hogs. (4) Location somewhere in the South where the plantation tradition is part of the cultural heritage: namely, the Mississippi Valley and a broad belt from the Brazos River in Texas to the James River in Virginia. (5) Centralized location of dwellings (in a "plantation village") and of farm operations. (6) A large input of cultivation power per acre.

The term *neoplantation* applies to a type of plantation operation that has evolved since World War II. What mainly distinguishes the type from regular plantations is a high degree of mechanization. This has been associated with migration of rural labor to cities in the North and the South in response to the lure of higher wages in industrial plants and an increase in labor costs and other production costs relative to market prices. To resolve these two problems, farm operators have mechanized. Such a solution has been expedited by the mass production of tractors selling at reasonably low prices. On one plantation, for example, three tractors replaced fourteen teams of mules and the labor force has decreased from sixteen to seven.

Merle Prunty has this to say about neoplantation development in the South:

Such evidence as exists suggests that mechanization has not displaced large numbers of laborers on plantations; on the contrary, landowners have been compelled to mechanize because of voluntary labor migrations. . . .

However, acquisition of tractors and cultivating implements alone customarily does not signify the inception of neoplantation occupance. . . . Neoplantation occupance is established when *harvesting* implements are added in sufficient numbers to justify large fields for their efficient use.

The functional focus of the neoplantation is the tractor station, which also shelters harvesting, cultivating and accessory machinery, spare parts, repair tools and fuel. Neoplantation occupance eliminates most share-paid labor. Cash-wage labor, which works machines under central direction, and which is applied as a unit to the whole acreage of the holding in a manner approximating the employment of gangs of slaves on large fields under ante-bellum occupance, predominates on these holdings today. The tractor station is always located close to the manager's or owner's residence, a locational factor suggesting the intimate interrelationship of centralized management and cultivating power. Thus its location approximates, closely, that of the mule barn under ante-bellum occupance.

The neoplantation differs from the ante-bellum unit in a few significant spatial aspects. The proportion of woodland is less, generally, than on the ante-bellum form . . . and beginnings of sensible legume-livestock rotations are implied by the crops now grown. There are fewer houses than on the ante-bellum unit of the same acreage, and their arrangement customarily is more linear (along roads) than rectangular or compact.*

PHYSICAL RELATIONSHIPS

The several crops dealt with in this chapter —cotton, tobacco, tea, vegetables, and fruits— are diverse enough in their environmental requirements to warrant separate mention. But in their cultural aspects, they are similar enough to be considered as a group.

Cotton requires a growing season of 200 frost-free days. Usually the longer the growing season, the longer the staple length (that is, the length of fiber). There must also be five months of high temperatures, preferably above 70°. Cloudy weather, though, prevents the cotton boll from ripening. At least 20 inches of rainfall are needed annually, with eight of them distributed through the growing season.

* Merle Prunty, Jr., "The Renaissance of the Southern Plantation," *Geographical Review*, 1955, pp. 459-491.

Miscellaneous Crops

Excess moisture in the growing season, however, promotes attacks by funguses and bollworms. Cotton grows on a large variety of soils; it does particularly well on less rich ones that limit excess vegetative growth at the expense of boll growth.

Tobacco is one of the most tolerant crops in terms of temperature requirements. Some varieties prefer warm humid conditions as in the Carolinas, while others thrive in more rigorous climates such as Wisconsin and Connecticut. High humidity produces thin leaves with low nicotine content—"mild" tobaccos.

Tea is an evergreen plant that grows best where temperatures stay above 55° and below 90°. Few plants require as much moisture as tea, which demands over 100 inches well distributed through the year. Humidity must be high to assure abundant leaf formation, consequently heavy dews and fogs are welcome.

Vegetables need only rather short growing seasons but they demand considerable moisture during the season. In California, Arizona, Texas and Florida the climate is warm enough to permit two and three crops a year of several vegetables.

The trees and vines that flourish in mid-latitude can endure severe winters; but their *fruits* are sensitive to frosts. The best locations, therefore, are those where the springs are cool enough to discourage blossoming until the threat of severe frost is past and the autumns are mild enough so that late summer growth can be completed before the winter cold sets in. These conditions frequently prevail on the *leeward* side of large bodies of water, where the water warms up more slowly than the land in spring and cools off more slowly in autumn. Notice how the leeward shores of Lake Michigan, Lake Erie, Lake Ontario, and central Florida stand out on Figure 12-8. This helps explain the contrast on this map between the West Coast states, on the leeward side of the Pacific Ocean, and the East Coast states, on the windward side of the Atlantic Ocean. (Remember that *prevailing* winds in the United States blow from the West).

Unfortunately, many regions with good environments for cotton, tobacco, tea, vegetables, and fruits are far from urban markets. As a result, low production costs are partially offset by the high transport charges due to both long hauls and air-conditioning. To overcome these disadvantages, producers in distant areas concentrate on large crops of a few commodities so that they can ship each in carload and trainload lots.

Regions of Mediterranean climate have particularly favorable environments for many of the crops discussed in this chapter. Consequently, the agriculture in such areas is now a mixture of traditional Mediterranean farming and commercial growing of vegetables, fruits, vines, and even cotton.

CULTURAL PHENOMENA

Market   Nearness to market saves both time and money in transportation—an advantage that is critically important in the case of perishables such as vegetables and fruits. Every large city is surrounded with vegetable farms intermixed with dairy farms.

But commercial crop farming on the outskirts of cities suffers certain disadvantages as well: The land is expensive, the growing seasons around many mid-latitude cities are short, the soils may be poor, and the terrain may be rough. Therefore, market gardeners must employ very intensive methods in order to squeeze out the maximum yield per acre. Usually they grow a multiplicity of crops, scheduling their plantings to insure a harvest of both early crops (such as radishes and lettuce) and later crops (such as carrots, tomatoes, and cabbages). They cram the greatest number of harvests they can into the growing season, which lasts for 189 days on the farms around New York City, 177 days around Detroit, and 162 around Chicago.

Farm Management   Even regions that enjoy easy access to markets and favorable environments do not automatically develop commercial crop farming, however. This activity develops only where the farmers recognize and exploit natural advantages. The role of this factor as well as market and the physical environment is analyzed by Clarence W. Olmstead as follows:

Three conditions were necessary for the development of orchard and vineyard regions: (1) a market demand for the produce, (2) a permissive, if not favorable, natural environment, and (3) recognition of the opportunity afforded by these conditions and the desire and ability to profit therefrom. In the early days of small, widespread kitchen and farm orchards, the market was correspondingly small and widespread; environmental conditions were not carefully evaluated. Then came the change which has stimulated the revolution in agriculture in America and the world—the multiplication and alteration of market demand.

Urbanization separated most householders from their kitchen orchards, as from their milk cows and vegetable gardens. Increase of population, especially in cities, multiplied demand for the product of farm orchards. As farm orchards were expanded to meet the demand for quantity, they became subject to new demands—for quality. Only those growers who took advantage of the new developments in plant improvement, pest control, pruning, thinning, tillage, fertilization, harvesting, and selling, could survive the competition that ensued.

Specialization resulted. The farmer with three or four acres of orchard and the remainder of his 80 acres devoted to field crops and livestock does not postpone corn-planting in order to spray apples, or interrupt haying so as to thin peaches. Unsprayed apples and unthinned peaches lost out in the increasingly quality-conscious market. Thus, the general farmer faced the alternatives of expanding and intensifying his farm orchard enterprise, or of abandoning it. Most were abandoned. Where the first alternative, specialization, was chosen, orchard regions began to emerge. The evolution occurred where one or a combination of three sets of conditions existed: (1) advantageous location with respect to market, (2) advantage with respect to natural growing conditions, especially climate, and (3) a particular desire to specialize in orchard or vineyard enterprise.

Successful development and maintenance of a regional orchard and vineyard specialty requires the expert attention of many people, not only farmers but also processors, packers, brokers, shippers, researchers, inspectors, laborers, labor recruiters, bankers, and handlers of equipment and supplies. A small farm orchard, or even a few large modern orchard establishments, may operate successfully on the basis of a limited local market. But such an individual operator is handicapped in meeting the keen competition offered in large, distant markets by established orchard and vineyard regions which have developed the organization and services not only for efficient production, but also for low-cost grading, packing, processing, advertising, shipping, and selling.*

* Clarence W. Olmstead, "American Orchard and Vineyard Regions," *Economic Geography*, 1956, pp. 189-236.

The appraisals farmers have made of the potentialities of various areas, of the costs of farming particular crops there, and of the profits available by marketing those crops in urban regions have led to pronounced specialization in many places: citrus fruit in Florida, southern Texas, and southern California; peaches in Georgia (for early marketing), in Arkansas, southern Illinois, and Colorado (for August marketing), and in western Michigan (for autumn marketing); tung trees (for vegetable oil) in southern Mississippi and Alabama; apples in the Yakima and Wenatchee valleys of Washington and in numerous Appalachian valleys of the eastern United States; cherries in western Michigan and Wisconsin's Door Peninsula; and strawberries in the Delmarva Peninsula (the land mass between Chesapeake Bay and the Delaware River). And as

Table **12-2** *International Trade in Selected Mid-Latitude Crops in Thousands of Metric Tons*

Leading Exporters		Leading Importers	
Apples—World: 1535			
Italy	503	Germany, West	524
Argentina	165	United Kingdom	200
Netherlands	123	U.S.S.R.	144
China	94	France	61
Australia	91	Germany, East	46
Cotton—World: 3233			
United States	834	Japan	607
Mexico	405	Germany, West	301
U.S.S.R.	344	United Kingdom	282
Egypt	317	France	249
Sudan	179	U.S.S.R.	190
Peru	115	Italy	166
Tea—World: 562			
India	214	United Kingdom	235
Ceylon	174	United States	50
China	39	Australia	27
Indonesia	27	Canada	20
Tobacco—World: 766			
United States	212	United Kingdom	137
Turkey	66	U.S.S.R.	96
Bulgaria	62	Germany, West	81
Greece	55	United States	69
Potatoes—World: 2805			
Netherlands	631	United Kingdom	538
Italy	281	Germany, West	472
France	238	France	284
Poland	183	Algeria	178
Czechoslovakia	150	Belgium	145

Source: United Nations, Food and Agriculture Organization, *Trade Yearbook, 1960*, Tables 27, 34, 41, 48, 62.

Miscellaneous Crops

for California—nearly every mid-latitude fruit and vegetable thrives in at least one of its several valleys.

Labor Supply The tending of most mid-latitude crops requires large numbers of laborers, particularly during the harvest season. Every year, with the coming of summer, thousands of migrant laborers (largely Mexican and Puerto Rican) travel north from the harvest fields of the southern United States as farm jobs open up in the higher latitudes. On most vegetables plantations, the migrant labor force is nearly 10 times the permanent force. For example, a 2000-acre "ranch" in Arizona has a permanent labor force of 25 (tractor drivers and irrigators) plus 200 seasonal migratory workers (mostly Mexican nationals) who weed and harvest the crop.

International Trade The leading exporters and importers of several of the crops discussed in this chapter appear in Table 12-2. Since so many mid-latitude vegetables and fruits (carrots, lettuce, onions, cabbages, potatoes, apples, pears, peaches) are grown in the general vicinity of their main markets, there is comparatively little international trade in these commodities. Most of what limited trade there is is within Europe or across the North Atlantic. Whereas only one per cent of the world's apples and potatoes cross international boundaries, 30 per cent of the cotton,

Table 12-3 *International Trade as a Percentage of Production of Selected Crops*

World Totals: Thousands of Metric Tons

Crops	Production	Trade	Trade as a Percentage of Production
Tropical			
Sugar (Cane)	371,000	14,583	4
Bananas	15,100	3,769	25
Coffee	4,605	2,600	56
Copra	2,800	1,357	48
Cocoa Beans	1,020	777	77
Mid-Latitude			
Cotton	10,900	3,233	30
Potatoes	276,000	2,805	1
Apples	14,000	1,535	1
Tobacco	3,660	766	21
Tea	1,110	562	51

Source: United Nations, Food and Agriculture Organization, *Production Yearbook, 1960* and *Trade Yearbook, 1960.*

51 per cent of the tea, and 21 per cent of the tobacco (Table 12-3) cross such borders.

Some countries appear in both the exporter and importer column for the same crop in Table 12-2. Thus, the United States exports almost 30 per cent of all tobacco yet imports almost 10 per cent. Such apparent incongruity is often explained by the fact that a country has a surplus of one specific *type* of a crop but is deficient in another type—in this case, considerable tobacco comes from Turkey for blending with domestic leaves.

Suggested Readings

Aschmann, Homer, "A Consumer Oriented Classification of the Products of Tropical Agriculture," *Economic Geography*, 1952, pp. 143-150.

Dahlberg, Richard E., "The Concord Grape Industry of the Chautauqua-Erie Area," *Economic Geography*, 1961, pp. 150-169.

Dyer, Donald R., "Sugar Regions of Cuba," *Economic Geography*, 1956, pp. 177-184.

Fryer, D. W., "Recovery of the Sugar Industry in Indonesia," *Economic Geography*, 1957, pp. 171-181.

Parsons, James J., "Bananas in Ecuador: A New Chapter in the History of Tropical Agriculture," *Economic Geography*, 1957, pp. 201-216.

Plantation Systems of the World, Social Science Monographs, Pan American Union, Washington, D.C., 1959, 212 pp.

Prunty, Merle, Jr., "Recent Quantitative Changes in the Cotton Regions of the Southeastern States," *Economic Geography*, 1951, pp. 189-207.

Tower, J. Allen, "Cotton Change in Alabama, 1879-1946," *Economic Geography*, 1950, pp. 6-28.

Weaver, John C., *American Barley Production, A Study in Agricultural Geography*, Minneapolis, 1950, 117 pp.

———, "Changing Patterns of Cropland Use in the Middle West," *Economic Geography*, 1954, pp. 1-47.

———, "Crop-Combination Regions for 1919 and 1929 in the Middle West," *Geographical Review*, 1954, pp. 560-572.

Winnie, William W., Jr., "The Papaloapan Project: An Experiment in Tropical Development," *Economic Geography*, 1958, pp. 227-248.

*This mink farm east of Janesville, Wisconsin, annually produces
30,000 mink, gives full time employment to twenty persons and requires 1500 tons
of dry feed—mainly meats, eggs, and high-protein products. The mink
are bred in March, born in May, and skinned in November. Mink farming was originated
and developed into a broad-scale industry in Wisconsin, which now produces over a third
of the nation's domestic mink. (Courtesy MacArthur Mink Farm.)*

THIRTEEN

Our purpose in this final chapter on bioculture is twofold: (1) to consider several branches of animal raising not taken up in previous chapters, and (2) to generalize about bioculture as a whole, now that we have examined individual types. The United States will serve as the case-study area, essentially because of availability of statistical measurement.

Miscellaneous Animal Farming

LOCATION AND CHARACTERISTICS

There is no satisfactory world map available showing the regions of commercial animal farming other than livestock ranching, dairying, and mixed farming. The reason for this deficiency is that the specialization of farms in producing other animals and products is a rather recent development, is still comparatively limited, and has not been widely studied by regional analysts. Nevertheless, from what information is available, it seems clear that commercial farms that specialize in the production of animals (other than cattle, sheep, and swine) are generally located in Anglo-America and western Europe.

Products Sold   Eggs and poultry, fur animals, and fish are all produced for sale on specialized farms. We have seen that some of these products, notably eggs and poultry, are minor sources of income on farms that specialize in other items, but in recent years a substantial number of farms have come to depend for their income *primarily* on the sale of these products. Let us take them up separately.

1. Poultry: Chickens are probably the most widespread farm animal. Almost every farm, regardless of type, whether subsistence or commercial, in tropical climates or in severe climates, has a few laying hens. And a sizable amount of commercial poultry is indeed sold from farms with other specialties. But we are concerned here with farmers who raise poultry for sale. Some specialize in poultry to such a degree that poultry sales account for at least half their revenue.

Actually, the United States has over 100,000 such farms. Although these make up less than 4 per cent of all the farms in the country, they constitute unusually high percentages in certain states: Delaware 30 per cent, New Jersey 29, Connecticut 19, Massachusetts 18, New Hampshire 16, and Rhode Island 15. In Delaware and New Jersey, in fact, poultry farms outnumber any other type of farm. As revealed in Figure 13-1, which shows the locational pattern of poultry farms, the major area is along the Middle Atlantic Seaboard from Maryland to New England. Poultry farms are thinly sprinkled through the Corn Belt and are concentrated in a few sections of the South, particularly the hill country of western Virginia, northern Georgia, and northwestern Arkansas. There are very few poultry farms in the western half of the country, with the conspicuous exception of southern California, central California, the Willamette Valley, and the Puget Sound lowland.

The value of poultry sold by United States poultry farms, augmented by the value of poultry sold by dairy farms, mixed farms, and other establishments, reaches the astonishing sum of $2 *billion* annually; this exceeds the value of corn and of wheat.

Figure 13-2, based on the value of all poultry sold, shows somewhat the same pattern as Figure 13-1. But notice that two different types of region are discernible: (1) The Corn Belt (from Ohio to the Dakotas) is a homogeneous area over which commercial poultry is uniformly distributed with no pro-

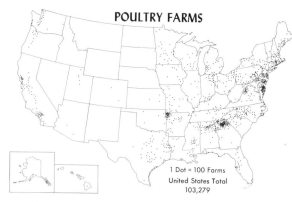

POULTRY FARMS

1 Dot = 100 Farms
United States Total
103,279

Figure 13-1 (*From U. S. Bureau of the Census.*)

nounced concentration. (2) Elsewhere in the nation the locational pattern is very spotty. The outstanding single poultry area is the Delmarva Peninsula; but also in New Jersey, West Virginia, and New Hampshire, poultry is the leading farm product sold.

Chickens and eggs are, of course, the main sources of income. Of the $2 billion in poultry sales in the United States, eggs account for half, chickens and turkeys make up the rest.

The pattern of egg sales differs from that of chicken sales. Most of the eggs are produced in the Northeast, especially in New Jersey and southeastern Pennsylvania (Figure 13-3). But the high productivity of California makes it the top egg-producing state—almost 10 per cent of all eggs sold. Although the Corn Belt has few poultry farms it supplies almost 40 per cent of the nation's eggs; Iowa and Minnesota are only slightly surpassed by California in egg production.

The map of chickens sold (Figure 13-4) reveals a highly unusual regional pattern. Notice that the map is extremely spotty, with numerous centers of intense activity surrounded by areas where scarcely any chickens are sold. The influence of a cultural factor, contract farming, is a major explanation of this pattern and will be explained below. Imagine a line drawn diagonally from central Maine to Oklahoma City and then straight south to Mexico. Southeast of this line lies the main chicken-selling region of the nation. Nearly two dozen concentrations stand out there, of which the most extensive are in north-

Miscellaneous Animals; Review of Bioculture

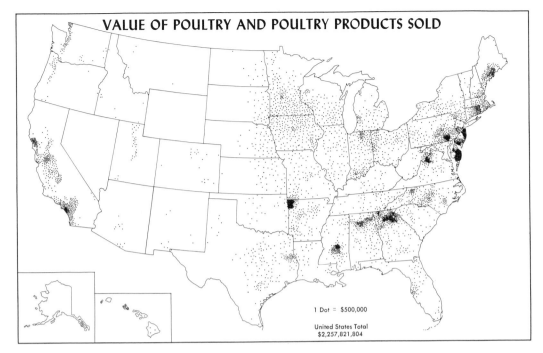

VALUE OF POULTRY AND POULTRY PRODUCTS SOLD

1 Dot = $500,000

United States Total
$2,257,821,804

Figure 13-2 *(From U. S. Bureau of the Census.)*

ern Georgia, Delmarva (see Figure 13-5, page 204, which shows the distributional pattern of broilers from that region), northwestern Virginia, and northwestern Arkansas. A few equally sharp concentrations appear on the West Coast. But again the Corn Belt is different; there the distribution is rather even, with few blank and yet few intense areas. By states, Georgia is the unquestioned leader; farmers there raise 13 per cent of the chickens sold in the United States.

2. Fur: Fur farming is a new type of bioculture less than 50 years old. The main emphasis is on silver foxes and mink, although rabbits, muskrats, racoons, and martens are also raised. Half the world's mink fur and all the silver fox fur now come from commercial farms. Where land is cheap, the animals are allowed to roam freely in a natural habitat enclosed by fences. But where land is expensive, the animals are kept in small pens or dens. In both cases, the animals

Figure 13-3 *(From U. S. Bureau of the Census.)*

CHICKEN EGGS SOLD

1 Dot = 1,000,000 Dozens

United States Total
3,330,265,407 Dozens

Figure 13-4 *(From U. S. Bureau of the Census.)*

CHICKENS SOLD

1 Dot = 500,000 Chickens

United States Total
1,620,241,266

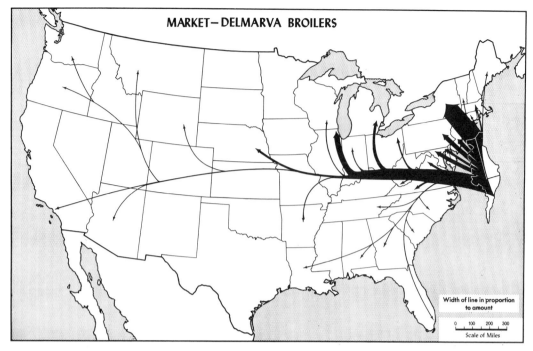

MARKET—DELMARVA BROILERS

Width of line in proportion to amount

0 100 200 300
Scale of Miles

Figure 13-5 (*After Kenneth Martin.*)

are bred, protected, fed, and handled like ordinary domestic livestock.

The major areas of fur farming in North America are Prince Edward Island (where this type of bioculture originated), the Adirondack hill country of northern New York, Manitoulin Island in Lake Huron, the upper peninsula of Michigan, northern Wisconsin, and southeastern Wisconsin. In Europe, fur animals are farmed in Russia and Scandinavia.

In the future, there will probably be a sharp increase in the relative importance of farming over hunting in satisfying the world's fur markets. At one time man procured all his furs from wild animals—just as he once gathered all his rubber from wild rubber trees. But farmed rubber now exceeds wild rubber, and the same thing is likely to develop in the fur business.

3. Fish: As yet there is very little commercial farming of fish—subsistence farming of fish in the Far East has already been cited in Chapter 3—for the natural supply of wild fish is still abundant enough to meet man's needs. In only a few places are fish farmed— that is, penned, fed, and protected—as if they were cattle or swine. Commercial fish farming is carried on in the U.S.S.R., Poland, Germany, Hungary, the Netherlands, Denmark, Italy, and Israel. The principal fish raised are carp, goldfish, and game fish fingerlings; in addition, oysters and pearls are cultivated in a few places.

The main species farmed commercially is the *carp*, which multiplies almost as rapidly as the tropical tilapia, and produces more pounds of meat per acre than any other edible fresh-water fish of the mid-latitudes. European immigrants to the United States brought along live carp for transplanting to streams and lakes. A few carp farms are now operated in Wisconsin, Illinois, and Iowa.

Many farms raise *game fish fingerlings* (especially trout, muskellunge, and pike) which are transplanted to lakes, rivers, and streams, to augment the natural supply. Most of these farms are operated by state governments; Wisconsin, for example, maintains a dozen trout farms and two muskellunge farms from which an issue of 50,000,000 fish a year is distributed to the state's rivers and lakes.

Many *oysters* are now quasi-farm products.

Miscellaneous Animals; Review of Bioculture

In Chesapeake Bay, for example, "fields" are staked out in shallow coastal waters and "prepared" by dumping in cement blocks, tile, and shells to provide surfaces to which the oysters can attach themselves, oysters being sedentary creatures that sift their food out of the water. *Pearls* are now produced artificially in oyster beds. The oysters are extracted from the water and small fragments of foreign matter are inserted inside their shells. The oysters are then placed in small cages or baskets which are replaced in the water. Japan leads the rest of the world in this type of pearl production.

Almost all *goldfish* in the United States are raised on a 150-acre farm two miles from Martinsville, Indiana, where 50,000,000 fish a year are scientifically bred, fed, protected, and harvested in 645 ponds with a water surface of 350 acres.

Size of Farms   Poultry farms, fur farms, and fish farms are usually small in size, often less than ten acres. Fur farms in northern Wisconsin, upper Michigan, and Canada are larger because few people live there, so land is less expensive, and because forests rather than grasslands serve as "pastures"—the point is that, generally acre for acre trees produce less animal food than grass or bushes.

National Fish Hatchery, Rochester, Indiana. Fish-culture ponds (more than two dozen in number) are within the town; Lake Manitou is in the background. This hatchery annually produces approximately 1,000,000 largemouth bass, 2,000,000 bluegills, and 300,000 channel catfish fingerlings, primarily for stocking farm ponds and new impoundments and for restocking streams. (Courtesy U. S. Fish and Wildlife Service, Department of the Interior, Minneapolis, Minnesota.)

Supplementary Feed Most of these farms produce at least some of the feed consumed by their animals. But an increasing number produce *none* of it (see Figure 13-6) serving only as a place of residence for the animals. In this respect, these farms are unique, and the question comes to mind whether such animal culture is "agriculture" or "manufacturing." For example, some poultry farms in Delmarva produce 10,000 chickens on no more than two acres of land. Crowded together in one long building, these birds spend their entire life on sawdust litter, never getting out from under the roof. (This way they are less vulnerable to disease than when they roam around on dirt.) To be sure, the "machine" that converts corn, soybeanmeal, menhaden-meal, food concentrates, and water into eggs and broilers is animate, while the machine that changes tin plate into tin cans is inanimate. But otherwise the operation of the two enterprises is rather similar.

Five Phases of Animal Culture On the basis of source of feed and degree of animal husbandry in a region, we are able to identify

five different phases of animal-producing economies.

1. Hunting: Animals subsist entirely on wild fauna and wild flora, with no supervision by man of the habitat or the animals.

2. Herding: Animals subsist entirely in the wild state, but man tends the animals and gathers them in for his purposes.

3. Ranching, or grazing: Animals subsist mostly on wildlife, but man tends them and also provides supplementary feed.

4. Animal farming: Animals subsist largely on feed grown on the farms where they reside.

5. Animal "manufacturing": The operating units simply provide a place of residence for animals that subsist entirely on feed, which, like raw materials arriving at a factory, comes from other places.

Here is an interesting hypothesis awaiting verification: As population density and the standard of living increase in a region, the production of meat (and perishable animal products) tends to move progressively from phase 1 toward phase 5. To prove this conten-

Figure 13-6 (*From U. S. Bureau of the Census.*)

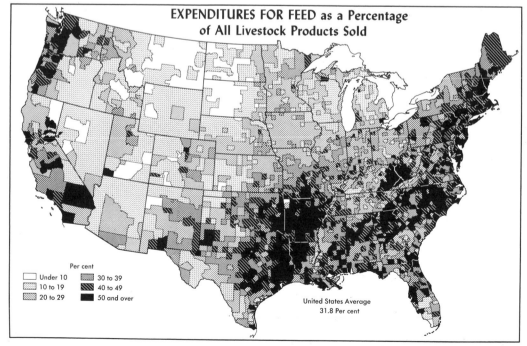

EXPENDITURES FOR FEED as a Percentage of All Livestock Products Sold

Per cent
Under 10
10 to 19
20 to 29
30 to 39
40 to 49
50 and over

United States Average
31.8 Per cent

Miscellaneous Animals; Review of Bioculture

tion, we would have to draw evidence that would support it and to consider carefully any that would refute it. The reader may wish to ponder the problem for himself.

PHYSICAL RELATIONSHIPS

The regional pattern of these animal-raising activities reveals very little association with any physical features.

There seems to be no critical growing season. Chickens thrive in the tropics and the mid-latitudes—almost everywhere that man lives. The best fox and mink fur do come from colder climates, but good muskrat fur is produced as far south as the Mississippi River delta.

These animal farms tend to be located in humid regions, but there is no evidence to suggest that they would be less successful in dry regions; indeed, southern California, one of the major poultry areas in the nation, has a climate that is subhumid at best and often dry.

The association between soil and poultry farming was once thought to be a critical factor in the success of Delmarva's poultry industry, for the sandy soil of this peninsula was said to discourage the spread of chicken diseases. Perhaps the most that can be said about the soil relationship is that enterprises that do not grow their own feed crops need not compete with commercial grain farms, dairy farms, and mixed farms for better soils.

No particular type of landform is associated with these farms. They thrive on the plains of Delmarva and on the hills of Arkansas, Georgia, and northern New York. All other environmental features being equal, these farmers seem to take the cheaper, rougher land, leaving the flatter, more expensive land to crop farmers.

All in all, there appears to be no other type of bioculture in which the regional pattern is so unrelated to the physical environment as is the commercial farming of these animals.

CULTURAL PHENOMENA

Specialized farming of poultry, fur animals, and fish is a very recent activity. It is associated with an agricultural revolution marked by: (a) increased output, and (b) intensified specialization—phenomena that are associated with the development of urban markets.

Growth of Urban Markets   This agricultural revolution was triggered by the amazing expansion of urban settlements in recent years. Millions and millions of city people are now totally dependent on commercial bioculturalists for food and fibers. Illustrative of how recent is the demand for these products is the trend in poultry sales (see Table 13-1).

Table **13-1**   *United States: Poultry Products Sold, 1919-1954*

Year	Billions of Dozens of Eggs Sold	Millions of Chickens Sold
1919	1.0	140
1929	1.9	284
1939	2.2	300
1949	2.4	588
1954	2.6	968
1959	3.0	1,618

Source: United States Bureau of the Census, *Census of Agriculture*, 1959, Vol. II, General Summary.

Distance to Market   Urban markets are naturally enough powerful influences on the location of commercial animal farms. The line of great metropolises stretching from Boston through New York, Trenton, Philadelphia, Baltimore, and Washington, D.C., is edged by poultry farms (as well as by vegetable farms and dairy farms). Notice on Figures 13-1, 13-2, 13-3, and 13-4 that many other cities also have a near-by concentration of poultry farming: for instance, Louisville, South Bend, Fort Worth, Austin, Los Angeles, and San Francisco.

This urban association seems to be particularly important in egg production (Figure 13-3). Scarcely any large city is far from an egg area. Accordingly, the northeastern quadrant of the United States has most of the nation's people and produces most of its eggs.

There is less correlation between cities and chickens grown for sale than between cities and eggs. To be sure, several large urban areas stand out on Figure 13-4. However, several large cities lack near-by chicken farms: Chicago, Detroit, Pittsburgh, St. Louis, Milwaukee, Minneapolis, and Buffalo. Moreover, many areas full of chicken farms are remote from large cities: the Shenandoah Valley of western Virginia, the Blue Ridge Mountains of northern Georgia, the Tennessee River Valley of northern Alabama, and northwestern Arkansas. Obviously, the farmers in areas adjoining certain cities have chosen not to specialize in raising poultry, since vegetable farming, dairying, and other agricultural activities are more rewarding. Yet farmers in remote rural areas have chosen this specialty. Much of the explanation of this pattern lies on *contract farming.*

Contract Farming   Sometimes known as *integrated farming,* contract farming is a new type of bioculture conceived by the managers of commercial feed corporations. In the 1930's these men, sensing the increasing demand for broiler chickens, began to line up farmers who would agree to buy the corporation's feed, to concentrate on raising broiler chickens, and to market all their birds through distributors with whom the feed corporations also had contracts. The term *integrated* describes the series of contracts between the feed manufacturer on the one hand, and the farmer, slaughterer, wholesaler, and retailer on the other. In a sense, then, the contract-broiler farmer is no longer an independent producer whose profit depends on the difference between expenses for feed (and other production costs) and income from an unpredictable market. Rather, he is like an employee in a factory, a hired technician who is paid a stipulated fee, regardless of whether prices rise or fall, by a company to whom he guarantees a certain output.

To save transportation and distribution costs and to expedite the shipment of birds to market, the commercial feed manufacturers contracted with many farmers in a few areas rather than with a few farmers in many areas. Poultry feed is shipped in carload lots to the farmers in these specialty areas; the largest farms even have their own railroad sidings, and several smaller farms are often serviced by one siding. In selecting the areas that would respond most readily to broiler specialization, the commercial feed manufacturers tended to choose regions of "problem farms."

Understandably enough, prosperous farmers in the Corn Belt and Dairy Belt were not very

This large poultry farm, a division of International Genetics Corporation, is located near Duluth, Georgia. It covers 406 acres, employs 80 full-time workers, has facilities for breeding 300,000 chicks and housing 90,000 mature hens. This particular farm concentrates on two markets: Florida and the Chicago area. The commercial development of chicken for meat began in this area in 1938. (Courtesy Charles Vantress Farms.)

enthusiastic about the idea of contract poultry farming. Most of the farmers who did respond to the scheme were located in areas characterized by rather backward farm methods, small acreage, rough terrain, or poor soil. This new scheme seemed an ideal solution to these farmers: Equipment would be provided and methods specified under the terms of the contract, small acreages would suffice, rough land would serve well enough for broiler houses, and the quality of the soil would be immaterial. Almost any part of the South, except the more lucrative cotton, tobacco, vegetable, and fruit areas, was perfectly suitable. Even an area located rather far from a sizable urban market was satisfactory, for the higher transport costs were offset by lower production costs.

For the nation as a whole, 90 per cent of the poultry is now produced by only 28,000 farms, a few of which are huge and most of which operate under integration contracts held by commercial feed corporations. Most California poultry production now comes from contract farms, which are known locally as *poultry ranches.*

The success of contract farming in the poultry business has led agriculturalists to scrutinize its possibilities for other types of production. Some mixed farms are already experimenting with integrated farming. What the advantages and the disadvantages might be of applying this concept to dairy farming, to livestock ranching, to wheat farming, to cotton farming are open to speculation.

Feed-producing Regions Most poultry feed comes from crops grown in the Corn Belt, and much of the feed for fur farms and fish farms comes from meat-packing plants in the same region. This is one reason for the dispersed pattern of poultry farming in the Corn Belt, where almost every farm has a few chickens, but where farmers have chosen to specialize in dairying, cattle fattening, swine raising, or cash-grain cropping rather than poultry.

Feed is expensive. In many of the chicken-producing areas the expenditure for feed exceeds 50 per cent of the value of animal products sold (Figure 13-6). (Notice the similarities between Figures 13-4 and 13-6.)

eneralizations about Bioculture

The several types of bioculture that have been discussed in Chapters 3, 4, and 7 through 13 may be diagramed as in Figure 13-7, page 210. By synthesizing these various activities, we can make certain generalizations about the geography of bioculture as a whole.

LOCATION

Less than half the land on earth is devoted to bioculture (in even the broadest use of the term), and a large portion of even this land is used for nomadic herding. Land under cultivation accounts for a considerably smaller proportion, about 20 per cent of the total. The pattern of cultivated land (Figure 13-8, page 211) shows a marked concentration in humid portions of the mid-latitudes. Four major regions loom up: western Eurasia, eastern Anglo-America, eastern Asia, and south-central Asia. Remember that these are also the four major regions of population.

A detailed map of the location of farm land is available for the United States (Figure 13-9, page 211). Notice the blanket of closely spaced dots sweeping northward from Texas to the Dakotas. The western boundary of this belt is very sharp. An eastward prong with a rather sharp edge on the north projects through Iowa, Missouri, Illinois, Indiana, and Ohio. East of the Mississippi River and south of the Ohio River the amount of farmland is high but the pattern is irregular.

CHARACTERISTICS

Unfortunately, we do not have enough accurate worldwide information to show the differences in the characteristics of bioculture from place to place. But enough data for this purpose are available for the United States, thanks to the federal Bureau of the Census and the Department of Agriculture, which has published detailed reports on such char-

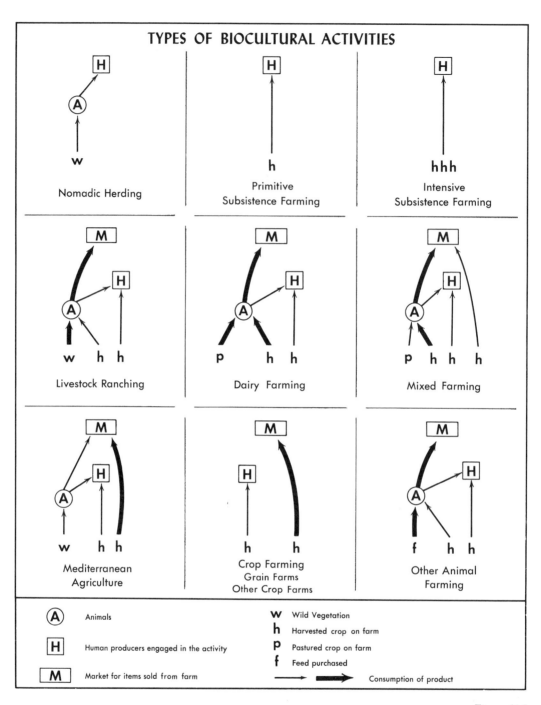

TYPES OF BIOCULTURAL ACTIVITIES

Nomadic Herding

Primitive
Subsistence Farming

Intensive
Subsistence Farming

Livestock Ranching

Dairy Farming

Mixed Farming

Mediterranean
Agriculture

Crop Farming
Grain Farms
Other Crop Farms

Other Animal
Farming

(A) Animals

[H] Human producers engaged in the activity

[M] Market for items sold from farm

w   Wild Vegetation
h   Harvested crop on farm
p   Pastured crop on farm
f   Feed purchased

⟶ ⟹ Consumption of product

Figure 13-7

acteristics as types of farms, sales of all farm products, and changes in agriculture.

Types of Farms in the United States What is a *farm?* The United States Census defines a farm as *any* piece of land under one management covering three or more acres producing at least $150 worth of agricultural products each year either for home use or for sale. Places of less than three acres are re-

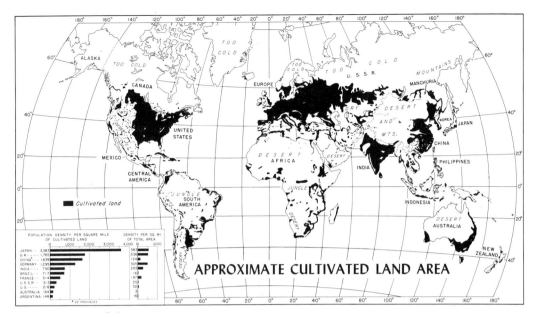

Figure 13-8 (*From Office of Foreign Agricultural Relations.*)

garded as farms only if the annual value of sales of agricultural products amounts to $150 or more. Places that produce less than this value of agricultural products because of crop failure or other unusual conditions are counted as farms if their normal production equals that amount. The Bureau of the Census defines three types of farms on the basis of commercial specialization: *commercial farms*, *part-time farms*, and *residential farms*.

Figure 13-9 (*From U. S. Bureau of the Census.*)

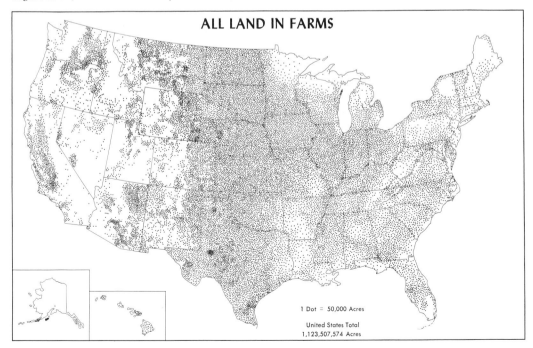

1. Commercial farms: These account for 65 per cent of the nation's total. They are defined as farms whose total annual value of agricultural products sold is $1200 or more. The definition is expanded to include farms selling only $250 worth of products, provided that the farm operator worked away from his farm less than 100 days and that his revenues from agricultural products exceeded the family income from other sources. Figure 13-10 shows the regional pattern of commercial farms.

The Census also classifies nine types of commercial farms by commodities sold. The criterion for classification is that sales of a given product must represent at least half the total value of all products sold. Otherwise the farm is regarded as a *general* farm. The number of commercial farms by type, expressed as a percentage of all United States farms, is shown in Table 13-2.

Table **13-2**   *Percentage of All United States Farms by Types*

Type	Percentage
Livestock farms	18.6
Dairy farms	11.7
Cash-grain farms	10.9
Cotton farms	6.6
Other field-crop farms	6.4
General farms	5.8
Poultry farms	2.9
Fruit and nut farms	1.7
Vegetable farms	0.7
All commercial farms	65.3

2. Part-time farms: These constitute 24 per cent of the nation's total. The value of products sold by these farms is from $250 to $1199, and either (a) the farm operator works away from his farm more than 100 days a year, or (b) nonfarm income received by him and his family exceeds the value of farm products sold. Figure 13-11 shows that part-time farms are widely distributed over the eastern half of the country.

3. Residential farms: Farms of this type, which account for 11 per cent of the national total, are defined as farms whose annual sales of farm products is less than $250. On some of these the operator works away from

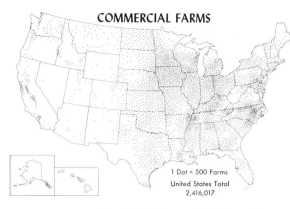

COMMERCIAL FARMS

1 Dot = 500 Farms
United States Total
2,416,017

Figure 13-10 (*From U. S. Bureau of the Census.*)

PART-TIME FARMS

1 Dot = 500 Farms
United States Total
884,785

Figure 13-11 (*From U. S. Bureau of the Census.*)

the farm more than 100 days a year; on some the income from nonfarm sources is greater than the income from sales of agricultural products; others are subsistence and marginal farms of various kinds. Figure 13-12 shows that the greatest concentration of residential farms is in the southern Appalachian highlands, particularly in eastern Kentucky and southern West Virginia, where thousands of coal miners live on farms and partially support themselves by farming.

Sales of All Agricultural Products from United States Farms   American farmers sell $30 billion worth of products annually. For decades the value of crops sold exceeded the value of animal products sold from farms. By the early 1950's the two were approximately equal. The 1959 Census of Agri-

Miscellaneous Animals; Review of Biocultur

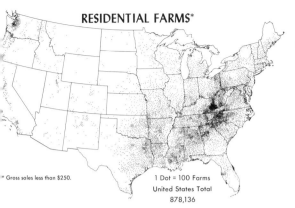

RESIDENTIAL FARMS*

* Gross sales less than $250.

1 Dot = 100 Farms
United States Total
878,136

Figure 13-12 *(From U. S. Bureau of the Census.)*

Table **13-3** *United States: Value of Farm Products Sold, 1954 and 1959 (in Millions of Dollars)*

Type of Product	1954	1959 *
TOTAL	$24,644	$30,337
Animal Products	12,292	17,025
Livestock	7,039	10,764
Cattle and calves	4,283	7,820
Hogs	2,279	2,431
Sheep	328	337
Wool	113	96
Dairy	3,334	4,010
Poultry	1,918	2,250
Eggs	916	1,055
Chickens	698	854
Crops	12,222	13,313
Field crops	9,925	10,492
Cotton	2,514	2,342
Corn	1,448	1,779
Wheat	1,715	1,736
Soybeans	777	981
Tobacco	973	947
Potatoes (Irish)	363	414
Rice	290	245
Barley	255	240
Sorghum	231	333
Alfalfa	216	277
Oats	246	178
Fruits and nuts	1,198	1,398
Citrus	378	494
Apples	241	204
Grapes	121	164
Peaches	107	126
Berries	100	112
Vegetables	645	739
Horticultural specialties	453	615
Forest Products	130	187

Source: United States Bureau of the Census, *Census of Agriculture,* 1954 and 1959.

* There is a slight but negligible discrepancy between this Census total and that on Figure 13-13, a Bureau of the Census map for 1959.

culture indicates that the value of animal products ($17 billion) finally has definitely surpassed that of crops ($13 billion). The relative importance of each product is shown in Table 13-3; the locational pattern of the nation's total agricultural output is shown in Figure 13-13, page 214. Perhaps some day such data will be available for the rest of the world; then it will be possible to construct maps showing regional patterns of *value* of farm products for the world as a whole, as Figure 13-13 now does for the United States. In studying this map, it will be helpful to recall the characteristics given in the preceeding chapters of each "white" area and of each area where dots are close together.

Changes in United States Agriculture
The number of farms in this country is steadily decreasing. The figure plummeted from an all-time high of 6,812,350 in 1935 to 3,703,894 in 1959, an amazing decline of 46 per cent in just 25 years. Much of this change is attributable to the amalgamation of many small farms into fewer larger ones, which, with improved machinery, can be operated by fewer persons. Consequently, thousands of farmers have left agriculture for other employment.

But acreage in farms is also declining, though only slightly—and only recently. The peak was reached in 1950 when our farm land totaled 1,158,565,000 acres. By 1959 the total was 1,120,158,000 acres, a decrease of 3 per cent. The drop in acreage of *cropland* is more striking—from 477,837,000 in 1950 to 447,-563,000 on 1959, a drop of 6 per cent. This trend seems truly astonishing when we recall that United States population increased from 150,000,000 to 179,000,000 between 1950 and 1960. Obviously, through improved agricultural methods fewer men can operate more acres (reducing the number of farms) and fewer acres can produce larger yields.

Change in acreage by states over the past quarter century reveals several clear-cut regions (Figure 13-14). The most striking contrast is between the eastern half of the nation, where every state lost (except Florida), and the western half, where every state gained. The severest reductions occurred in a belt

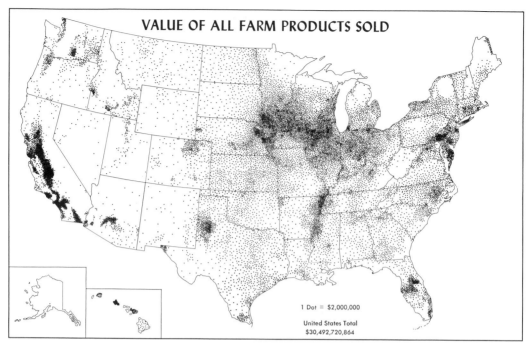

VALUE OF ALL FARM PRODUCTS SOLD

1 Dot = $2,000,000

United States Total
$30,492,720,864

Figure 13-13 (*From U. S. Bureau of the Census.*)

from Maine through Georgia and from the Atlantic Coast through Kentucky. The highest losses were in Rhode Island (down 65 per cent) and Connecticut (down 60 per cent). Decline in farm acreage in all these eastern states is attributable to (a) the transformation

Figure 13-14

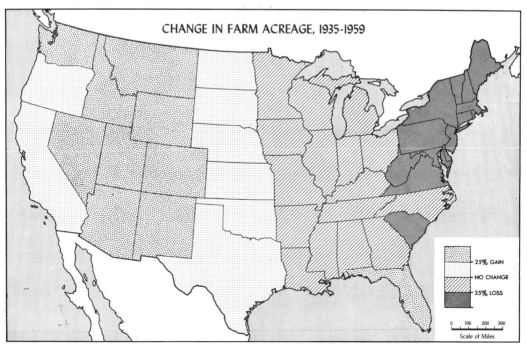

CHANGE IN FARM ACREAGE, 1935-1959

25% GAIN

NO CHANGE

25% LOSS

0   100   200   300
Scale of Miles

of marginal farm land (that is, handicapped land yielding small profits from farming) into forests or recreational areas, (b) the invasion of rural land by cities, and (c) the obliteration of farm acreage by new or widened highways. The only eastern state that did not follow the declining pattern was Florida, where reclamation projects produced new farm land from drained swamps.

Every western state experienced a gain in farm acreage. The most rapid expansion was in Nevada and Arizona where farm acreage increased 200 per cent and 190 per cent re-

spectively. Extension of farm land in the West was associated with (a) the expanding population and purchasing power of the western states, which created a larger demand for farm products, and (b) the appearance of new farm land in dry areas as a result of expanded irrigation facilities.

RELATIONSHIPS

Relationship of Biocultural Employment to Total Employment   For the world as a whole, approximately three out of every five breadwinners are in bioculture. Although pre-

Table **13-4**   *Employment in Agriculture,*
as a Percentage of Total Employment by Selected Countries

Continent	Countries under 33%		Countries from 33% to 50%		Countries from 50% to 66%		Countries over 66%	
Africa	Northern Rhodesia	23	Guinea	44	Zanzibar	64	Congo	85
			Southern Rhodesia	39	Egypt	64	Algeria	75
			Union of South Africa	33	Southwest Africa	57	Mozambique	74
							Morocco	71
							Tunisia	68
							* Ghana	68
Asia	Israel	16	Japan	40	Pakistan	65	Nepal	93
					Philippines	59	Thailand	88
					Malaya	58	North Borneo	85
					Taiwan	50	South Korea	80
							Turkey	77
							India	71
Europe	Austria	32	Spain	49	Bulgaria	64	Roumania	70
	Italy	30	Greece	48	Poland	57	Yugoslavia	67
	East Germany	29	Portugal	48	Hungary	53		
	France	26	Finland	46				
	Norway	26	Iceland	40				
	Denmark	23	Ireland	40				
	Sweden	20	Czechoslovakia	38				
	Netherlands	19						
	Switzerland	16						
	West Germany	15						
	Belgium	12						
	Scotland	7						
	England and Wales	5						
North America	Puerto Rico	25	Jamaica	49	Mexico	58	Honduras	84
	Canada	13	Cuba	42	Costa Rica	55	Haiti	83
	United States	12			Panama	50	Guatemala	68
	(Alaska	10)					Nicaragua	68
South America	Argentina	25	British Guiana	46	Brazil	58	Bolivia	72
			Venezuela	41	Colombia	54		
			Chile	30	Paraguay	54		
					Ecuador	53		
Others	New Zealand	16	* U.S.S.R.	47				
	Australia	13						

Source: United Nations, Food and Agriculture Organization, *Production Yearbook*, 1960, Table 5A. (*) The asterisk indicates nations not listed in Table 5A. Their percentage has been inferred from data in United Nations', *Statistical Yearbook*, 1958.

cise data are not available on total biocultural employment, the United Nations publishes data on agricultural employment. Table 13-4 is based on these figures and indicates that the proportion of the labor force in agriculture varies sharply from one part of the world to another, from a minimum of 5 per cent in England and Wales to 93 per cent in Nepal. An inspection of Table 13-4 makes one wonder whether there is any correlation between the variation in this ratio and the age of a country or a political unit, location, standard of living, or to some other variable.

Relationship of Land Area in Farms to Total Land Area   A somewhat different regional view of bioculture emerges when we compare the amount of agricultural land with the total amount of land. For the world as a whole, the percentage is 29, but the variation is considerable—from 2 per cent in Egypt to 82 per cent in the United Kingdom (see Table 13-5).

In the contiguous 48 states of the United

Table **13-5**   *Total Area and Agricultural Land Area: Continents and Selected Areas, in 1000 Hectares*

Location	Total Area	Agricultural Land Area	Percentage in Farms
WORLD (Land Masses)	13,529,000	3,975,000	29
Europe	493,000	232,000	47
Austria	8,385	4,052	48
Belgium	3,051	1,734	56
Bulgaria	11,093	5,630	51
Czechoslovakia	12,787	7,329	58
Denmark	4,304	3,142	72
Finland	33,701	2,911	9
France	55,121	34,633	63
Germany, East	10,799	6,448	60
Germany, West	24,692	14,332	58
Hungary	9,302	7,186	77
Italy	30,123	20,965	70
Netherlands	3,245	2,310	71
Norway	32,392	1,030	3
Poland	31,173	20,403	65
Spain	50,502	22,185	44
Sweden	44,966	4,350	10
Switzerland	4,129	2,172	52
United Kingdom	24,402	19,907	82
Yugoslavia	25,580	14,955	58
U.S.S.R.	2,240,300	591,055	27
North and Central America	2,426,000	615,000	25
Alaska	151,878	331	0.2
Canada	997,438	62,476	6
Cuba	11,452	5,867	52
Guatemala	10,889	2,055	19
Honduras	11,209	2,997	26
Mexico	196,927	87,307	44
Nicaragua	14,800	1,355	9
United States (48)	782,798	444,236	56
South America	1,776,000	364,000	21
Argentina	277,841	143,151	52
Bolivia	109,858	14,414	13
Brazil	851,384	126,728	15
Chile	74,177	5,968	8
Colombia	113,836	18,116	16
Paraguay	40,675	1,222	3
Peru	124,905	13,730	11
Uruguay	18,693	14,590	77
Venezuela	91,205	20,724	23

States, 56 per cent of all land is in farms, but this percentage varies sharply from region to region, as in Figure 13-15, page 218. Note how high the percentages are in the Plains and Corn Belt states, south-central Florida, and central California and how low they are in Maine, New Jersey, the northern reaches of Michigan, Wisconsin, and Minnesota, and in vast stretches of the western states.

Physical Phenomena That Deter Bioculture   The blank areas on Figures 13-8,

13-9, and 13-15 seem to be associated with regions that are cold, or dry, or have poor soils, or have rough topography. But these statements oversimplify the relationships, because they ignore the fact that land is cultivated not only in accordance with its physical attributes but also in response to human needs for crops and animals.

Human Needs for Biocultural Products
Man's need for crops and animal products varies spatially as surely as do climates, land-

Table **13-5**   (*Continued*)

Location	Total Area	Agricultural Land Area	Percentage in Farms
Asia	1,739,000	583,000	34
Afghanistan	65,000	12,229	19
Burma	67,795	8,614	13
India	328,888	171,852	52
Indonesia	149,156	17,681	12
Iran	163,000	26,760	16
Iraq	44,444	6,332	14
Israel	2,070	1,199	58
Japan	36,966	6,072	16
Malaya	13,129	2,186	17
New Guinea	41,600	20	0.0
Pakistan	94,625	24,825	26
Philippines	29,940	8,470	28
Thailand	51,400	9,898	19
Turkey	77,698	53,972	69
Africa	3,025,000	828,000	27
Algeria	238,174	45,496	19
Angola	124,670	29,900	24
Congo	234,493	51,430	22
Egypt	100,000	2,610	2
Ethiopia	118,432	70,211	59
Ghana	23,787	5,310	22
Kenya	58,265	2,798	5
Liberia	11,137	2,145	20
Libya	175,874	11,067	6
Nigeria	92,377	14,979	16
Southern Rhodesia	38,936	6,693	17
Northern Rhodesia	74,626	30,300	40
Sudan	250,582	31,100	12
Union of South Africa	122,341	97,366	80
Oceania	854,000	475,000	55
Australia	770,416	459,474	60
New Zealand	26,867	13,128	50

Source: United Nations, Food and Agriculture Organization, *Production Yearbook, 1960*, Table 1.

forms, and soils. Furthermore, it changes more swiftly than do the physical attributes of land. Two hundred years ago, Figure 13-8 would have shown most of Anglo-America as a blank area, not because it was too cold, too dry, too wet, or too rough, but because there was no active need to cultivate it. Since then the physical environment has remained essentially unchanged but the need for farms and ranches, generated by widespread settlement has changed markedly. It is interesting to speculate what a map based on the same criteria as Figure 13-8 will look like 200 years hence.

The intensity of human need for biocultural products varies with three major elements: the number of people in the area, their standard of living, and their cultural attitudes. The first two are obvious enough, but the third merits comment, since both the quantity of commodities demanded and the type of commodity consumed are closely related to such cultural factors as religion and dietary habits. Take attitude toward diet in the United States, for example. Americans have begun to watch their waistlines so closely that a change is being forced on the nation's pattern of food production. Consumers are buying less starch and fewer fats. In the 1930's Americans consumed 18 pounds of butter and margarine per capita; now they eat only 16 pounds. Per capita intake of potatoes has dropped from 131 pounds to 104 pounds per year; sweet potatoes are down from 22 to 10 pounds. Before World War II each United States citizen ate an average of 162 pounds of flour a year; now he eats only 135 pounds. On the other hand he is eating more eggs, chickens, turkeys, vegetables, and fruit. Further, the annual per capita consumption of beef rose from 49 pounds in 1930 to 85 pounds in 1960, of veal, from 7 pounds to 10 pounds; consumption of pork remained the same.

Impact of Bioculture Upon Soil   One of the consequences of man's use of land for growing crops is destruction of the soil—*if* the soil is not properly tended. Figure 13-16 is a dramatic expression of how farmers in the Southeast, the Midwest, and the Far West have laid bare the topsoil, over three-quarters of which has been carried away. If the rainfall

Figure 13-15 (*From U. S. Bureau of the Census.*)

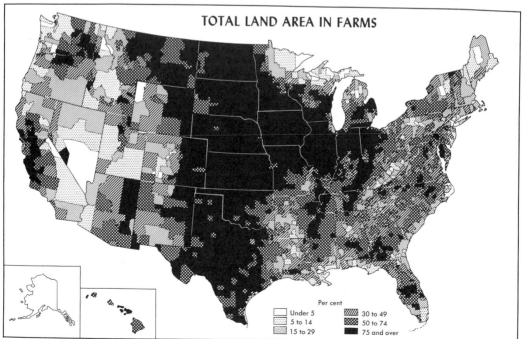

TOTAL LAND AREA IN FARMS

Per cent
☐ Under 5   ▨ 30 to 49
⬚ 5 to 14   ▧ 50 to 74
▨ 15 to 29   ■ 75 and over

Miscellaneous Animals; Review of Bioculture

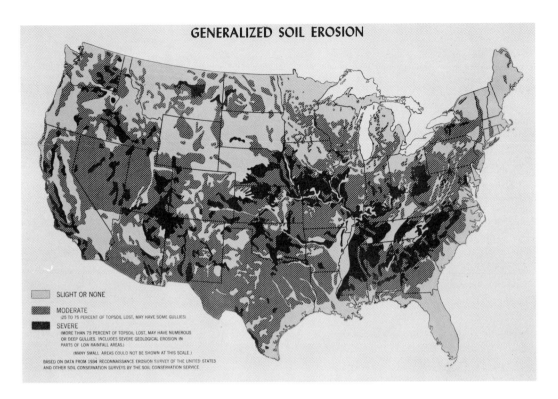

GENERALIZED SOIL EROSION

SLIGHT OR NONE

MODERATE
(25 TO 75 PERCENT OF TOPSOIL LOST, MAY HAVE SOME GULLIES)

SEVERE
(MORE THAN 75 PERCENT OF TOPSOIL LOST, MAY HAVE NUMEROUS
OR DEEP GULLIES. INCLUDES SEVERE GEOLOGICAL EROSION IN
PARTS OF LOW RAINFALL AREAS.)

(MANY SMALL AREAS COULD NOT BE SHOWN AT THIS SCALE.)

BASED ON DATA FROM 1934 RECONNAISSANCE EROSION SURVEY OF THE UNITED STATES
AND OTHER SOIL CONSERVATION SURVEYS BY THE SOIL CONSERVATION SERVICE.

Figure 13-16

in the eastern United States were of the gentle, drizzly type characteristic of western Europe, erosion would not have been nearly so severe. But the climate in America's most populous areas has a high incidence of thunder showers which dash torrents of water against the earth within a few minutes. The combination of tilled soil, thunder showers, and sloping land creates the worst possible conditions for maintaining topsoil.

Suggested Readings

Blaut, J. M., "Microgeographic Sampling: A Quantative Approach to Regional Agricultural Geography," *Economic Geography*, 1959, pp. 79-88.

Clark, Andrew H., "The Sheep/Swine Ratio as a Guide to a Century's Change in the Livestock Geography of Nova Scotia," *Economic Geography*, 1962, pp. 38-55.

Dovring, Folke, *Land and Labor in Europe 1900-1950*, The Hague, 1960, 480 pp.

Garrison, William L., and Marble, Duane F., "The Spatial Structure of Agricultural Activities," *Annals of the Association of American Geographers*, 1957, pp. 137-144.

Harris, Chauncy D., "Agricultural Production in the United States: the Past Fifty Years and the Next," *Geographical Review*, 1957, pp. 175-193.

Haystead, Ladd, and Fite, Gilbert C., *The Agricultural Regions of the United States*, Norman, 1955.

Helburn, Nicholas, "The Bases for a Classification of World Agriculture," *The Professional Geographer*, March 1957, pp. 2-7.

James, Preston E., "Pattern of Land Use in Northeast Brazil," *Annals of the Association of American Geographers*, 1953, pp. 98-126.

———, "Trends in Brazilian Agricultural Development," *Geographical Review*, 1953, 301-328.

Jasny, Naum, *The Socialized Agriculture of the U.S.S.R.*, Stanford, 1949, 837 pp.

Kerr, Donald, "The Physical Basis of Agriculture in British Columbia," *Economic Geography*, 1952, pp. 229-239.

Large, David C., "Cotton in the San Joaquin Valley: A Study of Government in Agriculture," *Geographical Review*, 1957, pp. 365-380.

Lewis, Robert A., "The Irrigation Potential of Soviet Central Asia," *Annals of the Association of American Geographers*, 1962, pp. 99-114.

Martin, Kenneth R., *An Analysis of the Broiler Chicken Industry on the Delmarva Peninsula,* unpublished Ph.D. dissertation, University of Wisconsin, 1955.

Mather, Eugene Cotton, and Hart, John Fraser, "Fences and Farms," *Geographical Review,* 1954, pp. 201-223.

Pepelasis, A. A., and Thompson, Kenneth, "Agriculture in a Restrictive Environment," *Economic Geography,* 1960, pp. 145-157.

Robinson, Arthur H., Lindberg, James B., and Brinkman, Leonard W., "A Correlation and Regression Analysis Applied to Rural Farm Population Densities in the Great Plains," *Annals of the Association of American Geographers,* 1961, pp. 211-221.

Sauer, Carl O., *Agricultural Origins and Dispersals,* New York, 1952, 110 pp.

Villmow, Jack R., "The Nature and Origin of the Canadian Dry Belt," *Annals of the Association of American Geographers,* 1956, pp. 211-232.

Weaver, John C., *American Barley Production, A Study in Agricultural Geography,* Minneapolis, 1950, 115 pp.

——, "The County As a Spatial Average in Agricultural Geography," *Geographical Review,* 1956, pp. 536-565.

Whitaker, J. R., "Erosion of Farmery Sites in the Nashville Basin of Middle Tennessee," *Economic Geography,* 1952, pp. 207-211.

Woytinsky, W. S., and Woytinsky, E. S., *World Population and Production: Trends and Outlook,* New York, 1953.

—— and ——, *World Commerce and Governments,* New York, 1955.

PART FIVE

COMMERCIAL MINING

The plant and animal kingdoms are not man's only sources of economic commodities. He also extracts goods from what we loosely call the mineral kingdom. Among geographers, the term *mining* applies to all endeavors by which minerals or other resources, whether solid or liquid, are extracted from the earth regardless of method, whether through shafts, open pits, quarries, or any other technique.

Several difficulties beset a geographer when he comes to the study of mining. In some respects, indeed, the geography of mining is more formidable than the geography of any other economic activity. One reason is that regions of mining are so hard to visualize. Forests, which cover extensive areas of the earth's surface, can be readily seen, as can dairy regions, wheat belts, and rice areas. Farms, like forests, take up appreciable stretches of land; so agriculture areas too can be apprehended rather easily. But mines are mere pinpoints on the earth's surface, for most of them are small holes in the ground through which men descend to the harvest realms below. Since mines are often dispersed through regions of farms or forests, an aerial photograph in mining country would show some other land use prevailing. Plainly, delimiting the regions of mining is an exacting task.

Moreover, the heterogeneous distribution of minerals makes it difficult to delimit types of regions. In some places coal alone occurs; elsewhere there is only iron ore; other localities have only petroleum. But there seem to be no combinations of minerals that distinguish kinds of mining regions, "typical associations" of minerals comparable to the "typical associations" of crops in intensive subsistence agriculture or to those of trees in mid-latitude softwood forests.

Nor is there any readily discernible regional association of mining techniques. Methods simply differ from place to place: Coal mining in Pennsylvania is highly mechanized, in Britain it is less so. But the regional associations of methods are missing that would permit us to delimit broad regions for mining as we can for, say, primitive subsistence farming.

Finally, there are at present few discernible correlations between areas of mining and the location of other phenomena. Mining is carried on in the high latitudes north of the Arctic Circle, in the mid-latitudes, and in the tropics; in mountains and in plains; in hot countries and in cold; in dry land and in wet; in densely populated areas and in sparsely settled ones; in regions of advanced cultures and in regions of culture which the advanced people consider backward.

For all these reasons it is difficult to regionalize mining activity very effectively. Consequently, we shall discuss the subject in terms of individual minerals. In Chapters 14 and 15 we shall deal with a few of the more important minerals; then, in Chapter 16 we shall endeavor to summarize the general geography of mining.

Two reference atlases are particularly recommended for use with Part Five: *The Oxford Economic Atlas of the World* from Oxford University Press, and *Atlas of Mineral Resources of the World* by Van Royen and Bowles.

*Coal mining at Gladbeck, near Essen, in the heart of the Ruhr area
and Westphalian coal field. Foreground of picture
shows apartments and houses, financed by the mining company, for occupancy
by mining employees. (Courtesy German Information Center.)*

FOURTEEN

Through the ages man has discovered in and on the earth's crust a wide variety of valuable minerals that meet his needs for fuels, lubricants, building materials, gems, coins, fertilizers, tools, weapons, synthetic fabrics, and medicines. Obviously we cannot go into the whole vast array of materials man has found in the earth. So we shall choose for discussion a few of the economically more important ones: coal, iron ore, ferro-alloys, copper, bauxite, diamonds, nuclear fuels, fertilizers, asbestos, building materials, and water.

Man places economic value on many additional minerals, of course. Some of these are located in relatively few places, they lend considerable geographic distinctiveness to their localities. Here are a few examples: the lead and zinc mines of Upper Silesia; the tin mines of Malaya, Indonesia, and Bolivia which together account for 66 per cent of the world total; the Broken Hill district of Australia which can boast of the richest lead and zinc ores on earth; the silver-mining belt that runs from Mexico to British Columbia; the famous Witwatersand of South Africa which produces much of the world's gold, notably in the vicinity of Johannesburg; and the Rustenberg district (also in South Africa) where a substantial share of the earth's platinum is extracted. But the minerals we are concentrating on are the most valuable.

Since we shall be dealing with these substances one by one—and for the sake of variety—the three basic questions of the geographic method will be implicit rather than explicit in our discussion.

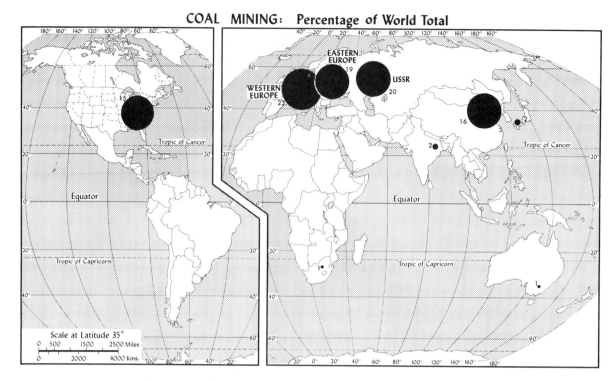

COAL MINING: Percentage of World Total

Figure 14-1

Coal Mining

The three main kinds of coal are anthracite, bituminous coal, and lignite. Anthracite is the hardest variety and is almost smokeless. Lignite is the softest, has the most impurities, and is the dirtiest. Bituminous coal is the all-purpose type that is most widely used.

Coals vary considerably in quality. Two regions may produce the same quantity of coal, but if one has high-grade bituminous coal and the other only lignite, the significance of the two areas will be quite dissimilar. Coals differ in three components: moisture, carbon, and volatile gases. As these vary, so do three potentials: heat energy, coking ability, and available by-products.

In 1960 the world's miners extracted from the earth's crust 2.9 billion tons of coal of which 708,000,000 tons were lignite. The regional patterns of the types of coal are distinctive. Bituminous coal is the most widespread, occurring in nearly every coal region. Lignite is mined chiefly in Europe and European

Russia (Germany alone accounts for two-thirds of the world's lignite—more in East Germany than in West Germany—and the U.S.S.R. accounts for one-fourth of the total, mostly from the Tula field south of Moscow). And three areas produce virtually all the world's anthracite—the Soviet Union, western Europe, and Pennsylvania.

PRODUCING REGIONS

The world's principal coal belt runs through the middle latitudes of the Northern Hemisphere (see Figure 14-1). Four major regions stand out: Europe, the Soviet Union, China, and Anglo-America, a quartet that accounts for 93 per cent of the world's coal harvest (see Table 14-1).

Western Europe   A distinct coal belt extends from the United Kingdom through

Table 14-1 *World Production of Coal and Iron Ore*

Region	Coal in Millions of Tons	Coal as Percentage of World Total	Iron Ore	Iron Ore in Millions of Tons	Iron Ore as Percentage of World Total
WORLD	2900	100		507	100
Western Europe	641	23		142	28
West Germany	264 (105*)	9		19	4
United Kingdom	216	7		17	3
France	64 (2*)	2		66	13
Belgium	24	—		—	—
Luxembourg	—	—		7	1
Sweden	—	—		21	4
Spain	17	—		5	1
Communist Europe	531	19		11	2
East Germany	252 (248*)	9		1	—
Poland	125 (10*)	4		2	—
Czechoslovakia	95 (64*)	3		3	—
U.S.S.R.	565 (154*)	20		105	21
North America	447	15		108	22
Canada	11	—		19	4
United States	434 (3*)	15		88	17
West Virginia	119	4	Minnesota	57	11
Pennsylvania	84	3	Michigan	13	2
Kentucky	67	2	Alabama	4	1
Illinois	46	1	Utah	3	—
Ohio	34	1	New York	2	—
Virginia	28	1			
Indiana	16	—			
Alabama	13	—			
South America	7	—		37	7
Venezuela	—	—		19	4
Brazil	2	—		5	1
Peru	—	—		7	1
Asia (except U.S.S.R.)	615	21		83	16
China	463	16		54	11
India	58	2		10	2
Japan	57	2		2	—
Africa	47	1		15	3
Union of South Africa	42	1		3	—
Algeria	—	1		3	—
Australia	42 (17*)	1		4	1

Source: United States Bureau of Mines, *Minerals Yearbook*, 1960, Vol. I, pp. 572, 584-585; Vol. II, pp. 57, 144-146, 151.

* Million tons of lignite included in total figure.

northern France, Belgium, and northern Germany, to southern Poland (Figure 14-2). The United Kingdom, although recently surpassed by West Germany, was for decades Europe's leading coal producer. Coal fields are widely dispersed throughout her territory, along the coast as well as inland. The chief mining areas are York, Derby-Nottingham, Northumberland-Durham, southern Wales, and the Scottish Lowland.* On the continent the richest areas are the Sambre-Meuse, which threads its way through the northernmost province of France into central Belgium; the Saar, which lies close by the French-German border; and the Westphalia (sometimes called the Ruhr), which is second only to the United States'

* An economic atlas should be consulted for the location of all fields mentioned in this chapter.

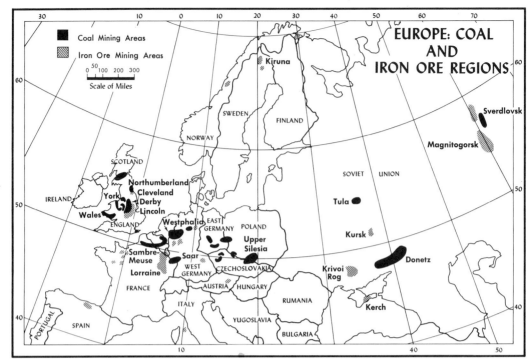

Figure 14-2

Appalachian field in volume of production. The quality of product in all these fields is high-grade bituminous coal. But beyond the Ruhr, the product changes character, for most of the coal in central and eastern Germany is lignite. Better coal appears again, though, in the Silesian field which straddles the Polish-Czechoslovakian border.

Figure 14-3

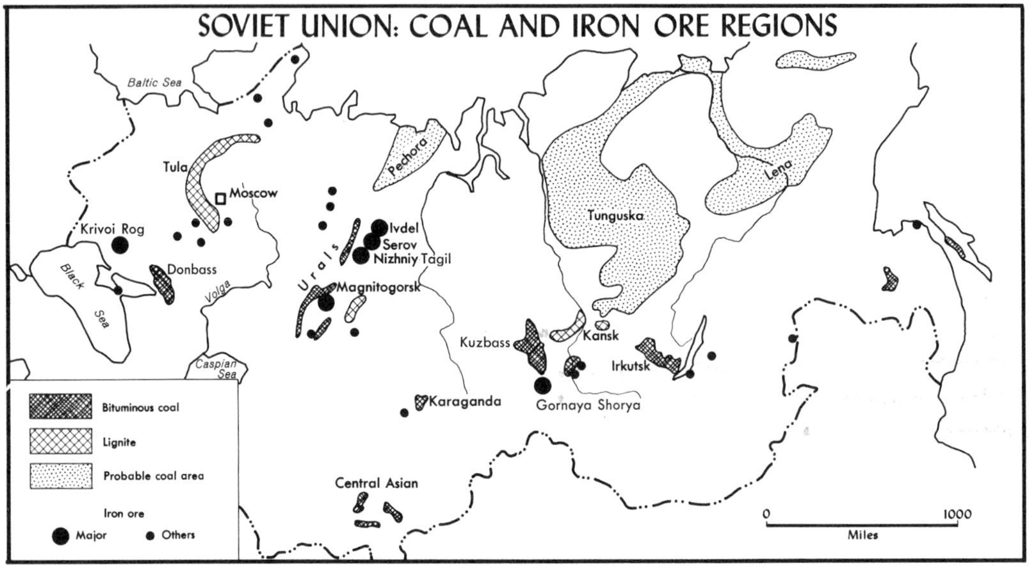

SOVIET UNION: COAL AND IRON ORE REGIONS

Selected Minerals

U.S.S.R. The Soviet Union is rapidly approaching western Europe and has overtaken the United States in quantity of coal mined. Indeed, when the satellite nations of eastern Europe are included, the Soviet bloc leads the world.

Within the U.S.S.R., coal mines are clustered in six areas separated from 600 to 1000 miles apart (Figure 14-3). The Donbass coal field in the Ukraine is the foremost producer. Not surprisingly, it was a prime target in World War II for the German army that stormed through the Ukraine to the Volga. Of less importance is the Tula lignite field near Moscow. The Ural field is a long linear area corresponding approximately in location with the Ural hills. One thousand miles to the southeast, the Karaganda area produces moderate amounts of a good product. Six hundred miles east of Karaganda is the Kuzbass field, which has been developed rapidly since 1930 to become the Soviet Union's second-ranking producer. Finally, almost 600 miles farther east is the Irkutsk coal field.

Anglo-America Almost all of Anglo-America's coal is mined in the eastern half of the continent. The Appalachian field, which extends from northwestern Pennsylvania to Alabama, is the most productive coal-mining region on earth; it accounts for 80 per cent of United States production. West Virginia is unquestionably the leading state (Table 14-2, and Figure 14-4, page 230). The East Central field, which produces 15 per cent of our coal, underlies Illinois, fringes of Indiana, and western Kentucky. A small amount is produced in the Western Central region, which stretches from Iowa to Oklahoma. Slightly more originates in the Rocky Mountain field, mostly in Utah, Wyoming, and Colorado. In Canada, which produces about as much coal as Indiana, Nova Scotia and British Columbia (at opposite sides of the country) are the leading coal-producing provinces.

Other Places China has surged rapidly into world prominence in coal mining and, if her published data are correct, she now is mining as many tons of coal as the United States. Within China, two fields dominate: the Manchurian field and the Shensi-Shansi field.

Elsewhere in the world only a few areas are conspicuous. Japan accounts for 2 per cent of the world's coal, mostly from the southern island of Kyushu and the northern island of Hokkaido. Most of India's coal is mined in the Northeast. Southeast Australia (Newcastle), southeastern Africa (Transvaal), and southern Brazil are the more prominent coal-producing areas in the Southern Hemisphere.

Table **14-2** *United States Coal*

State	Production (Million Tons) All Coal	State	Reserves (Billion Tons) All Coal	Anthracite	Bituminous Coal	Sub-bituminous Coal and Lignite
TOTAL	434*		1953	24	1093	836
West Virginia	119	North Dakota	350	—	—	350
Kentucky	67	Montana	222	—	—	222
Pennsylvania	65	Illinois	137	—	137	—
Illinois	46	Kentucky	123	—	123	—
Ohio	34	Wyoming	121	—	13	108
Virginia	28	West Virginia	116	—	116	—
Indiana	15	Colorado	100	1	90	9
Alabama	13	Pennsylvania	98	23	75	—
Tennessee	6	Utah	93	—	88	5
Utah	5	Ohio	86	—	86	—

Source: United States Bureau of Mines, *Minerals Yearbook*, 1960, Vol. II; 1955, Vol. II.
* Including 19 million tons of anthracite mined in Pennsylvania.

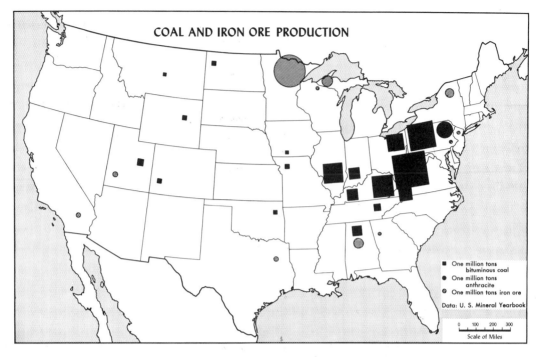

COAL AND IRON ORE PRODUCTION

■ One million tons
bituminous coal
● One million tons
anthracite
◎ One million tons iron ore

Data: U. S. Mineral Yearbook

0 100 200 300
Scale of Miles

Figure 14-4

RESERVES

The volume of the world's known coal reserves is tremendous—sufficient for another 1750 years at the present rate of consumption. Geologists have established that certain kinds of rock never contain coal; on this basis vast areas of the earth have little likelihood of ever yielding that fuel. But in extensive regions that geologists have not yet penetrated, the rocks might contain coal. As far as known reserves are concerned, the following observations seem to hold true. Coal reserves are unequally distributed, and the nations most favored with reserves are generally the very ones that now dominate coal mining. In order of coal assets, the leading areas are the United States, the Soviet Union, China, and western Europe (Table 14-3). China has in particular a tremendous reserve of high-quality coal in the provinces of Shensi and Shansi, probably the world's outstanding region of abundant good coal that is still only slightly tapped. The Soviet Union reports large reserves in the Tungas and Lena fields in northern Siberia, but as yet little mining is in progress.

Within the United States the leading states in reserves are not the leading states in production. Most of the reserve tonnage is in the West with North Dakota and Montana heading the list (Table 14-2). It is perhaps surprising that the principal producing state, West Virginia, is surpassed by five others in reserve tonnage; indeed, it has only a third as much coal as North Dakota. The Dakota and Montana stores, however, are mostly lignite. Of

Table 14-3 *World Coal Reserves Estimates (in Billion Metric Tons)*

Country	Anthracite, Bituminous and Sub-bituminous Coal	Lignite, Brown Coal	Total	Percentage of World Total
United States	1325	495	1820	36.3
Soviet Union	998	202	1200	24.0
China (mainland)	1011	1	1012	20.2
Germany	280	57	337	6.7
United Kingdom	172	—	172	3.4
India	62	3	65	1.3
Japan	16	—	16	0.3
World Total	4155	854	5009	100.0

Source: United States Geological Survey, *Coal Resources of the United States,* Circular No. 293, October 1, 1953.

Selected Minerals

bituminous coal, Illinois and Kentucky have the most abundant reserves.

RELATIONSHIP TO POPULATION

The main coal-mining regions tend to be comparatively densely populated. The correlation with population is not very high, however, since the reverse generalization definitely does not hold; that is, the world's two most populous regions (China and India) are not the two leading coal-producing countries (though China is making rapid progress).

RELATIONSHIP TO MANUFACTURING

Factories are the primary market for coal. To be sure, large quantities are used for other purposes—for instance, to heat buildings and to provide power for railroad engines. But to an increasing degree, coal is being consumed by factories, not only to heat water in boilers, to smelt metallic ores in blast furnaces, but also to be processed as a raw material. And since most of the world's manufacturing is situated in western Europe, Anglo-America, and the Soviet Union, the locational association between coal mining and manufacturing is immediately evident—it is, in fact, one of the most striking correlations in the economic geography of the world in the middle of the twentieth century. The correlation holds not only for the three great regions but elsewhere as well. Japan, Manchuria, India, and southeast Australia—all are mining areas *and* manufacturing areas.

INTERNATIONAL TRADE IN COAL

Since coal is consumed for the most part in the general vicinity where it is mined, the international flow of this commodity is meager. The leading exporters today are the United States, Poland, and West Germany (Table 14-4). But for almost three centuries the United Kingdom alone served as the world's coal bin. She began shipping coal abroad in the early 1600's, and for nearly 250 years was the only country that produced a surplus. We cannot overestimate the role of coal in the reign of Britain during that period as the world's leading commercial and maritime power. But the United Kingdom has

Table 14-4 *International Trade in Coal, in Thousands of Tons, 1958*

Leading Exporters		Leading Importers	
World Total: 119,700			
United States	47,730	France	15,000
Poland	17,750	West Germany	14,840
West Germany	16,230	Canada	12,530
U.S.S.R.	9,950	Italy	9,150
United Kingdom	4,440	Netherlands	9,060
East Germany	4,370	East Germany	8,580
Belgium	3,010	Belgium	5,720
France	1,920	Japan	4,510

Source: United Nations *Yearbook of International Trade Statistics*, 1958, pp. 28-33. Note: The *Yearbook* tabulated the Saar and Western Germany separately, but entries for Table 14-4 above have been revised to show the Saar as part of Germany.

skimmed off the cream of her coal supply and is mining deeper and thinner seams, many of which dip at steep angles. These handicaps make it difficult to use the mechanized mining methods widely employed in the United States and Germany. Indeed, the United Kingdom is now actually importing small amounts of highgrade coal from the United States.

The world pattern of international trade in coal is unusual. It is not surprising to see the United States, Poland, West Germany, and the U.S.S.R. listed among leading exporters in Table 14-4. Nor is it surprising to find France, Canada, Italy, the Netherlands, and Japan among the leading importers. But why are West Germany, East Germany, and Belgium on both lists? West Germany and Belgium are explained partly by the encouragement the European Common Market (discussed in Chapter 16) gives to trade in coal by removing tariffs on shipments among the member nations. Thus, coal fields in a country that are near an industrial concentration in another country can serve the latter easily. Now, most of West Germany's coal exports flow to France and the Netherlands; most of her coal imports come from the United States and East Germany. Strange as it may seem, United States coal can be sold on the markets of German *port* cities at a lower price than most German coal of comparable quality. The reasons for this anomaly are (a) much lower production costs in the United States due to mechanized mining methods, and (b) cheapness of ocean transportation. Belgium's exports go mostly to France, and her imports come largely from the United States. The case of East Germany is somewhat different. Her leading customer is West Germany, which purchases a great deal of lignite, but most of East Germany's imports are of bituminous coal from the U.S.S.R. and Poland. United States coal exports go mainly to Europe (leading customers being West Germany, Italy, the Netherlands, France, and Belgium in that order), Canada, and Japan. The Soviet Union's main customer for coal is East Germany.

In the foregoing discussion we have done little more than apply the first basic question of the geographic method to the topic of coal. The questions of characteristics and relationships, which normally should be considered at this point, will be postponed until Chapter 16; the same applies to the other substances taken up in this and the next chapter. We are doing so because many characteristics and relationships of coal mining are similar, in terms of geography, to those for iron ore mining, copper mining, and other mining activities. Consequently, it seems reasonable to treat of these topics in one chapter that can generalize for all mining endeavors grouped as one major economic activity.

Iron Ore

Iron is ubiquitous, being one of the most abundant elements in the earth's crust, which averages 47 per cent oxygen, 28 per cent silicon, 8 per cent aluminum, and 5 per cent iron. The catch to this abundance is that it costs too much to extract that 5 per cent of iron from a mass of crustal rock. In several places, however, geological processes have concentrated iron in proportions far above the average. Any mass of dirt or rock with a high enough concentration of a metal to pay for the cost of extraction is called an *ore*. Whether a material is ore depends, then, on *both* its chemical composition *and* the economics of the moment. The costs of extraction rise and fall as do the prices extracted metal will fetch, and what is iron ore today may be just so much dirt tomorrow, or vice versa. The principle tends to hold, then, that the *higher* the market price, the *lower* the percentage of metal content necessary to qualify a substance as *ore*.

The quality of iron ore depends not only on its percentage of iron but also on the absence of objectionable impurities. Thus, an ore may be half iron, but phosphorus or sulphur may make it unusable. In the early history of iron ore mining, some rocks rich in iron had to be bypassed because they contained considerable phosphorus; it was impossible by methods then known to separate the phosphorus from the iron. Not until 1878 did scientists discover that the two could be dissociated by the addition of calcium carbonate (in the form of limestone or dolomite) in the smelting operation.

PRODUCING REGIONS

Iron ore mining is concentrated in the same trio of regions that top the list for coal mining. Western Europe, Anglo-America, and the Soviet Union together account for 70 per cent of the world's iron ore production (Table 14-1 and Figure 14-5).

Western Europe   Here, iron ore mining is located in the same general pattern as coal except for the absence of Silesia and the presence of northern Sweden. The United Kingdom has several iron mining areas in unusually close proximity to coal. The Midland field, about 60 miles north of London and only 15 miles from the interior coal field, provides two-thirds of Great Britain's total; the Lincoln field to the north (also very close to coal) provides one-fourth; the remainder comes from the Cleveland field (near Durham coal) and the Oxford field to the south. No other nation has been favored with so much iron ore so close to so much good coal.

But Europe's largest quantities of iron ore are produced on the continent. The Lorraine field in northeastern France is less than 30 miles from Saar coal, 100 miles from the

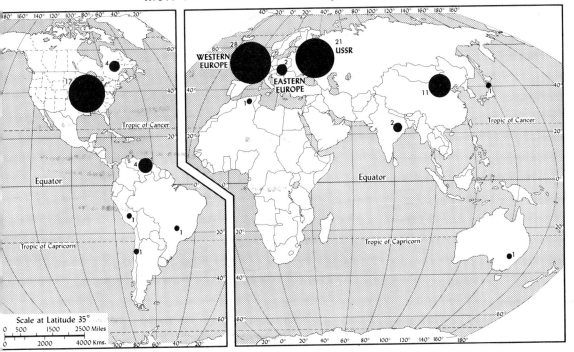

Figure 14-5

Sambre-Meuse field, and 150 miles from Westphalia. (The Lorraine ores were known but unused for decades because of their high phosphorus content. The largest known reserve of iron ore in Europe lay undeveloped in spite of its nearness to good coal fields. But shortly after the discovery mentioned above, the Lorraine became the foremost iron-mining region of Europe.) Lorraine ores are not unusually rich (they average 30 to 40 per cent iron), but in volume they constitute western Europe's most productive source and are a strong reason why France leads western Europe in iron mining, producing more than the next three nations—Sweden, Germany, and the United Kingdom—combined.

Sweden's foremost field is in the vicinity of Kiruna (north of the Arctic Circle), where remarkably high-grade ores—up to 60 per cent metal—are unearthed. Germany's major mines are in the Siegerland (southeast of Köln) and Salzgitter (near Braunschweig). Many smaller iron-mining areas dot the rest of the map of Europe; nearly every nation in fact produces a little.

The United States and Canada   For several decades the world's most prolific iron mines have been those in the Lake Superior district (see Figure 14-4), which consists of several iron ranges in Minnesota, Wisconsin, Michigan, and Ontario. This area yields over 80 per cent of United States ore (mostly from the Mesabi, Cuyuna, and Vermillion ranges in Minnesota, and the Gogebic and Menominee ranges in Wisconsin and Michigan). In addition to their abundance, Lake Superior ores have been uncommonly rich—as high as 60 per cent. Canada is represented here by Steep Rock and Michipicoten in Ontario. Elsewhere, the Alabama field, which produces less than one-tenth that of the Superior district, is unusual in the United States in that beds of iron ore lie close to those of good coal. The Quebec-Labrador field is new—the first ore was mined in 1954—but already 10,000,000 tons of ore are coming annually from this area. The Adirondack field in northern New York and the Wabana field in Newfoundland also provide a little iron ore. In the entire western half of North America the only notable mines

The many-tiered Sokolovo iron ore mine in Kazakhstan, U.S.S.R. (Sovfoto.)

Krivoi Rog; "Magnet Mountain" near Magnitogorsk and Nizhniy Tagil are the biggest producers. A thousand miles east lies the new field, Gornaya Shorya, the U.S.S.R.'s third-ranking source.

Other Places South America's foremost nation in iron ore extraction is Venezuela where, in the eastern forests, two new mining districts, Cerro Bolivar and El Pao, are achieving world prominence. Asia's leaders are China (with approximately the same tonnage mined as Minnesota) and India (comparable in volume to Michigan).

RESERVES

Unfortunately, we lack sufficient data for accurate mapping of world reserves of iron ore either by quantity or quality.

For the world as a whole, iron ore seems to have been deposited more widely than coal. Indeed, several countries that as yet mine comparatively little ore give promise of considerable endowments—notably India, Brazil, Cuba, South Africa, and the Philippines.

INTERNATIONAL TRADE

A substantial share (almost 30 per cent) of the world's iron ore crosses international boundaries, some of it being transported over long distances. Leading exporters are France, Canada, Venezuela, Sweden, and the U.S.S.R.; leading customers are the United States and West Germany (Table 14-5). This trade re-

Table 14-5 *World Trade in Iron Ore, in Thousands of Long Tons, 1959*

World Production: 431,709

Exports		Imports	
WORLD	130,486	WORLD	130,486
France	27,502	United States	35,724
Canada	18,552	West Germany	27,936
Venezuela	17,104	Belgium-Lux.	17,883
Sweden	15,224	United Kingdom	12,879
U.S.S.R.	13,234	Japan	10,526
Chile	4,193	Czechoslovakia	5,853
Brazil	3,895	Poland	5,645
Peru	3,267	Canada	2,707

Source: United States Department of the Interior, Bureau of Mines, *Minerals Yearbook*, 1960, Vol. I, pp. 586-587. (*The Minerals Yearbook* also indicates the major countries of destination for each nation's exports.)

are near Cedar City in southwestern Utah and Eagle Mountain in southern California.

The Soviet Union Most of the iron ore in the U.S.S.R. comes from three areas, the foremost of which is Krivoi Rog, approximately 250 miles west of the Donbass coal field. This general vinicity also yields iron ore in the Kerch peninsula. The Ural Hills boast extensive deposits and now rank close behind

Selected Minerals

flects the tendency of iron ore to move to coal—a tendency which greatly exceeds that in the opposite direction. The strongest reasons in support of this principle are these: (1) in the production of finished steel, more coal than iron ore is consumed—a fact with several ramifications to be considered in Chapter 20 on steel manufacturing. (2) The buyers of steel are largely fabricating factories that tend, themselves, to locate in areas which are nearer to coal than to iron ore (for reasons which will be analyzed in Chapters 20, 21, and 22 dealing with location of metal-processing industries). The general tendency is for iron ore to flow toward coal regions to join a raw material (coal) and to be near a market. Most of this flow is to western Europe (especially Germany, Belgium, and Great Britain) and to the United States. Also a heavy trade moves from the U.S.S.R. to Poland, Czechoslovakia, and Hungary.

Heavy movements of iron ore in international trade relate directly to the trend of the world's main industrial regions to reach out into distant places to procure this mineral. Arctic Scandinavia, Quebec-Labrador, and eastern Venezuela are three such remote areas that function as ore suppliers for industrial regions in the middle latitudes of Anglo-America and western Europe.

The United States is importing increasing quantities of iron ore because our best ores have been used up, and it is cheaper to smelt high-quality foreign ores than low-grade domestic ones. We import around 35,000,000 tons of ore annually—nearly 40 per cent of the tonnage produced by domestic iron mines. Such dependence on foreign ore is a new development. As recently as 1950 the United States imported only 9,000,000 tons—in a year when domestic production was 100,000,000 tons.

United States links to other areas for iron ore are changing not only in quantity but also in location. As recently as 1953 the main foreign sources were Chile and Sweden; 1954 brought an abrupt change as the newly discovered fields in Venezuela (Cerro Bolivar and El Pao) and Canada (Quebec-Labrador) began producing. Now 97 per cent of United

Table **14-6** Breakdown of United States Imports of Iron Ore

Sources	Thousands of Tons	Percentage of Total
South America	20,570	57
Venezuela	13,542	38
Chile	3,590	10
Peru	2,236	6
Brazil	1,200	3
Canada	13,458	38
Others		
Liberia	1,105	3
Sweden	136	—
TOTAL	35,724	100

Source: *Ibid.*, pp. 582 and 587.

States imports of ore come from the Western Hemisphere, principally from Venezuela and Canada (see Table 14-6).

CASE STUDY: ARCTIC SCANDINAVIA

North of the Arctic Circle in Sweden and Norway is a nest of five iron ore fields. The three most productive are in Sweden on the eastern slopes of the Kjölen highlands. The leader is the world-famous Kiruna district, which boasts large quantities of extremely rich ore (much of it is 66 per cent iron) so close to the surface that mining can be carried on in open pits. An initial handicap was distance. Kiruna is over 500 miles from the principal population cluster of Sweden and 1000 miles from the blast-furnace centers of Europe. But ore so rich and so easily mined can bear high transport costs and still compete with those that are closer to the furnaces but leaner in content and harder to mine. Although located in the Arctic, these Scandinavian districts have mild enough winters so that year-round operations are feasible.

A railroad extends all the way from the Swedish port of Luleå, through the Malmberget, Gällivara, and Kiruna ore fields, to the Norwegian port of Narvik. One might think that all the ore would pass through Luleå—the gradient is downhill all the way, the port is in the same political state as the mine, and the town is 200 miles *south* of Narvik. But the Gulf of Bothnia freezes during the winter, while the ocean at Narvik remains ice-free. Thus, in order to benefit from the lower costs accruing from *year-round* operations (in both mining and shipping), Kiruna ore is shipped in freight trains up through the backbone of the Kjölen Mountains, across an international border, and northward in virtually the opposite direction from the German and British steel mills for which most of it is destined. As a result, Narvik is well equipped with docks and ore-handling facilities while Luleå, although closer to and downhill from Kiruna and within the same country, is less well set up.

The Malmberget and Gällivaara minerals are less plentiful and poorer in quality than the Kiruna ore. And since the mines are farther than Kiruna from Narvik, little of their production can bear shipping costs through that port. So the ore goes to Luleå. There it is processed in a steel mill the government built shortly after World War II in an effort to bolster the economy of northern Sweden. This may appear, at first glance, to be dubious strategy since Luleå is so far from coal. But Scandinavia has a wealth of hydroelectric power—at Kiruna even the pit shovels are electrically powered—and Sweden tapped some of that energy for the Luleå mill, the largest electrified steel mill in the world.

Thus, in the flow pattern of ore in Arctic Sweden, the greater tonnage and the richer ore move north to Narvik for foreign mills and the lesser tonnage and lower quality move south to Luleå for domestic mills. Through the latter port, in addition, a small amount of ore is forwarded to central Europe.

The Norwegian ore fields in the Arctic show a contrast between an older area ravaged by war and a newer area just coming into production. The Bjornevatn (or Kirkenes) field is in the far northeast corner of Norway, only two miles from the Russian border. Mining operations began here in 1906; ore was shipped out to England and Germany; a population of 7000 was supported by this economy. But in World War II the works were all but obliterated. The last shipments moved out in 1944 and the subsequent destruc-

tion was so complete that it took eight years to reconstruct the mines, railroad, and port facilities. Outbound flow of ore resumed in 1952.[*]

Dunderland is a new ore field, 25 miles upstream from the fishing port of Moirana in a narrow valley only two miles from flanking mountain ice fields. The development here resembles that of Luleå in being a government project designed to bolster a national need for more job opportunities. The authorities have constructed a railroad through the valley, begun mining, and brought a hydroelectric plant into operation. Ore and power now converge in a new electric steel mill in Moirana, formerly a small fishing village.

CASE STUDY: QUEBEC-LABRADOR FIELD

The Quebec-Labrador field illustrates how the geography of a region can be transformed by new dynamic ties with distant places. The vast triangular land mass of northern Quebec and Labrador is a cold, bleak, barren plain, almost devoid of population except for a few Indians and white villagers along the southern margin. For centuries, caribou and fish were the main subsistence supports, though a little commercial trapping, fishing, and lumbering were practiced.

Nature set an inhospitable stage for human occupancy. Winter temperatures reach 50° below zero. The ice-age glaciers scoured this land severely and left very little soil, so much of the surface is bare rock. The first white man here dubbed it "the land God gave to Cain." As early as 1892 a Montreal geologist discovered an extensive vein of rich iron ore straddling the Quebec-Labrador boundary. But the resource was in a wilderness, 200 miles from even the smallest human settlement, 250 miles from Ungava Bay to the north, 250 miles from the Atlantic, over 300 miles from the St. Lawrence. Here lay lots of ore, good ore, but it was inaccessible—inaccessible, that is, in terms of what man was willing to pay to get at it. Elsewhere on earth there

[*] A fascinating analysis of this area is Trevor Lloyd's "Iron Ore Production at Kirkenes, Norway" in *Economic Geography*, 1955, pp. 211-233.

Selected Minerals

were plenty of good ore fields, easier to work and easier to reach. But these other mines began to give out. So in 1936 the first of two companies was formed to explore Labrador's ores. It received a concession from the government of 20,000 square miles. But not until 1943 did a full-scale exploration begin. Every man, every piece of equipment, every bit of food had to be flown in—the greatest civilian airlift in history. Harvesting this resource required importing to this wilderness workmen and tools for modern production, facilities for a community in which the labor force could enjoy the amenities of civilization, and a railroad that could transport the ore to civilization and bring back the food, clothes, fuel, books—in short, every single item—needed by the miners. The local region had absolutely nothing with which these various needs could be met.

A total of 6900 men and $250,000,000 was required to get this economic organism into operation. On October 2, 1950, a small steamer tied up at Seven Islands, Quebec, with the first load of equipment. Dock facilities were built here for shipping at least 10,000,000 tons of ore a year; tremendous storage areas had to be built too because winter restricts the mining season to 165 days, although the St. Lawrence is ice-free for shipping 220 days a year. Railroad classification yards were built so that cars containing ores of different grades could be sorted, thereby facilitating the loading of ships with homogeneous cargoes. In 1950 Seven Islands numbered only 1000 people—a fishing village that exported pulpwood and served as a trading center for the fur-trapping Montagnais Indians. Today the settlement numbers well over 5000 inhabitants. Population in the mining country is approximately 3500 in winter and 5500 in summer.

A mainline railroad 357 miles long was built between Seven Islands and Schefferville, the heart of the mining country. Few railroads on earth encountered such difficulty: Swamps, lakes, and streams cover half the land. Elsewhere, bare rock made it difficult to anchor the rails and ties. Tunnels required blasting. In December, 1953, the construction gang averaged two miles of road per day for ten consecutive days in 30-below-zero weather.

The full extent of the Quebec-Labrador ores is not known. Only a fraction of this wilderness has been explored, but evidence at hand indicates 44 bodies of proved ore totaling 420,000,000 tons of ore averaging 50 per cent or higher iron content. This does not include much larger tonnages containing less than 50 per cent iron. Most of these iron-rich rocks are concentrated in a band 80 miles long and six miles wide that lies in an unproved area 225 miles long and 30 miles wide; but explorations indicate the presence of good ores not yet accurately estimated. The average overlay of rock or dirt covering the known beds is only 15 feet, so they can be readily strip-mined. Ore formation extends downward an average of 300 feet. The deepest hole drilled goes down 596 feet—and is still in ore!

Equally impressive, although on a somewhat smaller scale, is the more recent effort of a second company to unlock the iron ore resources of northern Quebec. In 1958 this organization began constructing three installations: Port Cartier (an iron-ore shipping port on the St. Lawrence River, 50 miles upstream from Seven Isles), a 193-mile railroad connecting Port Cartier with a newly discovered ore field near Lac Jeannine, and Gagnon (a new settlement hewn out in the wilderness at the focus of mining operations, 200 miles southwest of Schefferville). Iron ore was first shipped from this area in 1960. Since the ore is comparatively lean (averaging 31 per cent iron content for the company's entire holdings, with the richest ores around 45 per cent), a concentrating mill has been built just east of Gagnon. When operations reach their planned stage, the two company towns of Gagnon and Port Cartier are expected to have populations of 4800 and 3200 respectively.*

* Additional insights to the development of these two Canadian ventures can be gleaned in Graham Humphry's "Schefferville, Quebec: A New Pioneering Town," *Economic Geography*, 1958, pp. 151-166, and in a special report entitled "Precambrian Mining in Canada, Special Report," dated April, 1961, by the Quebec Cartier Mining Company.

Ferro-alloys are metals that, in small amounts, are blended with iron to make steel. Each of these substances imparts a particular quality. Manganese provides tensile strength in rails and beams, and resistance to abrasives in rock-crushing machinery. Chromium renders iron resistant to corrosion from liquids. Nickel adds strength, ductility, and toughness to steels used in machinery. Tungsten is used in making high-speed cutting tools. The presence of molybdenum makes a steel that is useful in magnets and highly elastic steel. Steels containing cobalt resist rust and withstand high temperatures (as in jet engines). Springs, forgings, and high-speed tools require vanadium. To be sure, each of these metals is also used for many other purposes—but their main role in today's economy is as alloys with iron.

The world's combined annual ore yield of these seven metals is 15,000,000 tons, approximately 4 per cent of the figure for iron ore.

Most of the areas well endowed in coal and iron ore are *not* well endowed with ferro-alloys. For example, North America's major region of alloy minerals is in the western part of the continent, extending from Canada to Mexico, corresponding generally with the Rocky Mountains. This region leads the world in the mining of molybdenum and vanadium and has at least modest reserves of every other major alloy mineral. Colorado and Utah are predominant states. In eastern North America the ferro-alloys are neither as widespread, nor as numerous, nor as abundant as in the West. But one zone is notable for nickel: 75 per cent of the world's supply of that metal comes from the Sudbury area of eastern Ontario.

Europe is poorly endowed with ferro-alloys. For only one of them—tungsten—does it produce even as much as 5 per cent of the world total and for that one its leading producer is Portugal. What ferro-alloys Europe does possess are located in either the South or the North. The southerly belt begins at the Atlantic coast and runs eastward through the Soviet Union; it includes not only European nations but a fringe of northern Africa (Morocco) and a fragment of Asia (Turkey). Not many ferro-alloys appear here, but the region does produce appreciable amounts of chromium and tungsten. In northern Europe, ferro-alloys are restricted pretty much to Scandinavia.

The Soviet Union has a long belt that runs the length of southern Russia clear to the Pacific with branches northward along the Urals. It is notable for its diversity (all ferro-alloys are available) and for the prominence of manganese—nearly half of the world total. The leading manganese mines are at Nikipol and Chiatura near the Black Sea.

In eastern Asia ferro-alloys are found in an arc running from Hokkaido in the northeast around through southeast Asia to western Pakistan. Except for cobalt, all ferro-alloys are represented. China is the world's leading source of tungsten (25 per cent), notably in Kiangsi. The Philippines yield chromium. India accounts for 15 per cent of the world's manganese.

Africa, from the Congo (Leopoldville) to the Union of South Africa, has a spectacular share in the mining of cobalt: The former Belgian colony alone mines 63 per cent of the world total. Southern Africa (particularly Rustenberg in the Union of South Africa and Selukwe in Rhodesia) is the world's foremost chromium-mining zone. Africa also produces 20 per cent of the world's manganese. Indeed, southern Africa does extensive mining of a wide array of ferro-alloy ores; the industry has developed rapidly since 1940.

South America, like Europe and Australia, has few ferro-alloys. The ones mined there are scattered through the southern and western part.

Within the mining regions, ferro-alloy ores seem to be associated with igneous rocks and with hilly or mountainous terrain where the earth's crust has been subjected to folding and other forces associated with instability.

For the world as a whole, ferro-alloy ores

are mined much more widely than coal and iron. Indeed, the three outstanding areas for coal and iron (Europe, Anglo-America, and the U.S.S.R.) altogether only account for approximately 50 per cent of the manganese, 25 per cent of the chromium, 40 per cent of the tungsten, and 25 per cent of the cobalt. Only in nickel, molybdenum, and vanadium do the industrial leaders rank as high as in coal and iron ore.

The significance of this situation is that a lively foreign trade in ferro-alloys develops, virtually all in the direction of Europe and Anglo-America—the predominant miners and users of coal and iron. Some of the ores (or substances concentrated from them) travel long distances, indeed. Manganese moves 7000 miles from India to Europe, and over 3000 miles from Ghana to the United States. Chromium ore travels 8000 miles from the Philippines to the United States, and nearly 7000 miles from South Africa to Europe.

Copper

Western North America boasts the world's leading copper-mining region. It extends from Canada to Mexico and accounts for almost a third of the world total. Arizona is the prin-

The open-pit copper mine at Bingham Canyon, 20 miles southwest of Salt Lake City, Utah, resembles a huge amphitheatre. Operations here cover 1042 acres; the mine consists of many levels continuously connected by railways and switchbacks. The vertical distance from the bottom to the top of the pit on the west side is 1500 feet. Rock is mined by drilling 30-foot holes at intervals of 20 feet into the toe of each terrace. The holes are charged with blasting powder and detonated. Over 2000 tons of material are dislodged per drill hole. Electric shovels then load the broken rock into side-dump railway cars which are hauled in small trainloads (several are discernible in the picture) by electric locomotives to the pit exit. There they are assembled into long trainloads which are transported 16 miles to the concentrator. The mining area contains 166 miles of standard-gauge railway track, most of which is periodically moved as mining operations carry away terrace after terrace. The many small towers support electric overhead lines from which the shovels and locomotives draw their power. (Courtesy Kennecott Copper Corporation.)

cipal state, with important mines near Globe-Miami, Bisbee, and Jerome. The largest single copper mine in North America, though, is at Bingham, Utah, where operations have been continuous since 1865. The Bingham ores are near the surface, permitting inexpensive open-pit mining. This is fortunate since more expensive operations might not be worthwhile. For Bingham probably has the world's leanest copper ore. It averages only 0.9 per cent metallic content (that is, every 1000 tons of ore dug from the earth contain only nine tons of copper). Butte, Montana, is the northernmost important copper district. There, the mineral must be mined via shafts, the deepest of which is over 5000 feet. In eastern Canada, the Sudbury, Ontario, district yields copper as a by-product in refining nickel ores.

The interior of southern Africa, notably a zone straddling the Congo-Rhodesia boundary, has recently become one of the world's main copper zones—particularly the Congo's Katanga district. This area is second only to the western United States in the mining of copper ore. Rhodesia mines more copper than does the Congo. Kolwezi and Elizabethville are the centers of activity. A distinctive attribute of Katanga ores is their richness—nearly

7 per cent copper—the highest percentage in any of the world's major copper mines, and eight times as rich as Bingham's ore.

The South American copper belt extends from northern Peru to central Chile. Chile mines more copper than any other single nation except the United States, and her Chuquicamata district contains more ore reserve than any other deposit in the world. Already it produces almost as much as Bingham, and its ores are richer, averaging 2 per cent copper content.

The Soviet Union has ample copper in the Ural Hills, notably around Mednogorsk. But western Europe is almost barren of copper ore and has long been dependent on outside areas for its supply. Similarly, there appears to be little in Asia.

The locational pattern of copper ore mining is closely associated with a significant volume of international trade. Most of Africa's production goes to Europe while most of Chile's goes to the United States. In spite of being the world's leading producer, the United States is now a net importer. Sales of copper account for an astonishing 60 per cent of Chile's exports by value, 60 per cent of Rhodesia's, and 35 per cent of the Congo's.

Bauxite

The Caribbean area (notably Jamaica, Surinam, and British Guiana) has recently assumed world leadership in mining the aluminum ore, bauxite, and now accounts for over half the world total. Bauxite shipments constitute 30 per cent of British Guiana's sales abroad and fully 80 per cent of Surinam's.

Some bauxite is mined in Arkansas, the only portion of the United States that yields any significant quantity. Several European countries have bauxite, the most prominent being France (particularly the Var Valley), Greece, Yugoslavia, and Hungary. Hungary's bauxite, in fact, is an important reason for the tenacity with which the Soviet Union is holding on to that country, for along with Yugoslavia it produces more of that valuable mineral than the Soviet Union does in its own bauxite mines.

Whereas most nonferrous metals are associated with igneous rocks, bauxite tends to be associated with clay-limestone rocks which have been exposed to weathering in tropical climates. The presence of bauxite in Arkansas, France, Hungary and other such areas suggests that at one time they must have had a tropical climate which expedited the formation of bauxite. Rich bauxite ores have also been found recently in tropical Africa (Ghana) and tropical Asia (Indonesia). Aluminum is one of the most abundant elements in the earth's crust (averaging 8 per cent) but current methods for extracting the element are too expensive for ores that contain less than 20 per cent of the metal.

Diamonds

Of the several precious minerals—gold, silver, and platinum among them—we shall select the diamond for comment here because of its significance in the manufacture of machinery. Unlike the others mentioned, diamonds are not a metal but rather pure carbon in crystallized form.

By value, the gem trade takes most of the diamond harvest. But by weight the industrial trade predominates, since 85 per cent of the world's diamonds are built into cutting instruments, abrasives, and bearings in machinery. No other economically significant mineral is so geographically concentrated as the diamond. Virtually all diamonds are mined in Africa. The Congo alone accounts for nearly three-fourths; Ghana, the Union of South Africa, and Sierra Leone are also important. In most of these places diamonds are gathered by placer-mining methods, being washed out from alluvial gravels. Before the discovery of such gravels in 1867 (along the Orange River) diamonds had been mined by shaft methods in South Africa, especially around Kimberley. But alluvial diamonds are much cheaper to gather; consequently, many of the underground mines have been closed. The greatest alluvial deposits are in the Congo where the diamond-bearing gravels are scattered over an area 450 miles long and 300 miles wide along the courses of the Kasai and Sankuru rivers, which are southern tributaries of the Congo River.

Nearly all these African diamonds find their way to industrial Anglo-America, and Europe; many of the gem-quality stones go to Israel and Belgium for cutting and polishing before moving on to the consumer markets. Diamonds make up 5 per cent of the Congo's export trade and 7 per cent of the Union of South Africa's.

Nuclear Fuels

The most recent additions to the list of desirable items in the earth's crust resulted from the discovery that a pair of radioactive metals can be used to produce nuclear energy. Uranium is now the more important of these but thorium is a potential source. When one *ounce* of these nuclear fuels disintegrates, it yields energy equal to that produced in the burning of 100 *tons* of coal. When released rapidly, such energy explodes violently, as in a bomb. When slowly controlled and released, it can meet man's needs as does any other source of power.

Governments tend to keep secret the data on amount and location of uranium and thorium, but since uranium occurs mainly in veins associated with such metals as copper, silver, gold, vanadium, cobalt—and with some oil shales—it is possible to make estimates. The largest known uranium deposits are near Elizabethville in the Congo. In the Western Hemisphere the apparent richest reserves are around Port Radium (next to Great Bear Lake) in Canada's Northwest Territories. Most of the United States' uranium is in the vicinity of Grants, New Mexico. Europe's sources seem to be largely in Czechoslovakia and eastern Germany. Supposedly the Soviet Union has considerable uranium deposits in the Turkestan district.

The United Nations is trying to formulate a plan by which the major powers will agree to international control of uranium mining and the production of nuclear energy.

Asbestos

About 2,000,000 tons of asbestos are mined each year for use as fire-proof insulation. This mineral is unique. It occurs in the form of nonflammable fibers that can be spun and woven, these fibers making up 5 to 10 per cent of a rocky substance termed serpentine. In Canada, which is responsible for 60 per cent of the world's supply, all the product is taken from a narrow belt of serpentine rock that stretches for 150 miles near the Quebec-New York border. Some of the mining is open-pit. Most of the output is exported to the United States and Europe. The Soviet Union mines one-sixth of the world's asbestos, mostly in the Ural Hills and mostly for domestic markets. South Africa, the only other notable producer, ships its product to the United Kingdom and other European customers.

Fertilizer Mineral

Soil supplies plant rootlets with plant foods, some of which are consumed in only small amounts and are restored by natural processes. But there are four nutrients that are returned too slowly to maintain crop yields in regions of intensive farming: phosphorus, potassium, nitrogen, and calcium. Man must add these to the soil if high yields are to continue.

Most farmers depend on manure to convey plant foods back to the soil. But regions with inadequate manure supplies must rely on commercial fertilizers that are manufactured largely from pulverized rocks. Three different types of rock (one high in phosphorus, another in potash, a third in nitrate) are crushed, treated by several chemical processes, dried, ground up into pellets or finer grains, and blended together in measured proportions. Since in very wet areas the soil is also poor in calcium, calcareous rocks must be ground into the mixture or applied directly to the soil.

The market for manufactured fertilizers is found in those humid regions where pressure on the land is intense and where farmers have enough capital to buy plant food for supplementing their manure supply. Specifically, the main consumers are western Europe, eastern Anglo-America, central U.S.S.R., and Japan. Acre for acre, Japan, Holland, and Belgium are the leading nations in the application of commercial fertilizer (Table 14-7).

The source regions for most manufactured fertilizers are certain areas where ages ago there were deposited sediments from sea water containing high proportions of calcium, nitrogen, potassium, and phosphorus that are now suitable for mining.

Since *calcium* is available in the limestone that is widespread in many farming regions, local quarries can provide the rock for pulverizing and spreading on the fields. Because it is so widespread, limestone for fertilizer is not shipped very far; hence, no specific areas achieve renown for producing it.

Table **14-7** *Consumption of Manufactured Fertilizers* *

Country	Amount
Japan	215
Belgium	199
Netherlands	196
West Germany	135
Sweden	64
United Kingdom	52

Source: *Oxford Economic Atlas*, 1959, p. 85.
* In pounds of nitrogen, phosphates, and potash per hectare of agricultural land.

At one time most of the *nitrogen* for fertilizer came from a nitrate rock (known as *caliche*) of which the entire known world supply occurs in the Atacama Desert of Chile. Before World War I Chile monopolized world nitrate production and price-setting. And for many years nitrates constituted the major portion of Chile's sales abroad. But Chile's industry is now in trouble due to competition from chemical factories in other countries that are manufacturing nitrogen from the air, which is 78 per cent nitrogen, and from coal, which yields many volatile gases, including ammonia—composed primarily of nitrogen. Today only 15 per cent of Chile's exports are nitrates and only 5 per cent of the world demand is met by Chilean mines. Twenty per cent is now derived as a by-product of coal and 75 per cent is manufactured from the atmosphere.

Potash salts deposited from ancient seas are the prime source of potassium. Although useful in tanning leather and in making soap and a wide diversity of products, 90 per cent of the world's potash goes into fertilizer. For a long time Germany and France were the principal sources. In the vicinity of the Harz mountains (half-way between Berlin and the Ruhr) lie potash beds from 10 to 100 feet thick resting from 1000 to 2000 feet below ground level. Half the world's reserves of potash are here. The Iron Curtain bisects this potash field. So today 22 per cent of the world's potash comes from West Germany and 20 per cent from East Germany. Shortly before World War I, the Alsace district of France began producing potash from deep beds, but Germany controlled Alsace at that time and restricted its output. But since 1919 Alsace has been French and the French government has so stimulated the industry that French companies now mine 17 per cent of the world total. For years the United States was dependent on these European sources, but after World War I a series of potash deposits were discovered underlying thousands of square miles east of Carlsbad, New Mexico. Commercial mining began in the early 1930's; today the United States mines 26 per cent of the world supply. The worst handicap of the Carlsbad area is its location—far from the eastern demand for fertilizer. The Soviet Union has tremendous reserves in the vinicity of Solikamsk, just west of the middle Urals, and is self-sufficient.

Fertilizer factories procure some *phosphorus* from blast-furnace slag, but the bulk of their need is met by phosphate rock. About 30,000,-000 tons are mined a year, that is, roughly one-tenth the tonnage of iron ore. The United States is responsible for 45 per cent of that total and is self-sufficient. Florida produces three-fourths of our supply from open-pit mines widely distributed in a belt 100 miles long paralleling the western coast north of Tampa. Heavy movements of phosphate rock account for high percentages of the freight traffic on Florida's railroads (21 per cent of the tonnage on the Atlantic Coast Line Railroad and 24 per cent on the Seaboard Railroad), for they start the rock on its way to numerous fertilizer factories scattered widely

and evenly over the eastern United States, from the Gulf of Mexico to Minnesota, and from the Atlantic Coast to the Great Plains. Ocean carriers, too, transport much of Florida's phosphate to New York and other Atlantic ports; barges take it up the Mississippi. Although the Southeast is the principal mining region, the nation's biggest *reserve* of phosphate rock is in the West. Underlying Idaho, Montana, Wyoming, and Utah are deposits of much greater quantity and much higher quality than those in Florida and Tennessee. Yet little mining is done. For one thing, the deposits are deep and must be shaft-mined. Then once it is out of the ground, the rock is far from customers, most of whom are hundreds of miles to the east.

In Europe phosphate rocks are mined in numerous places, but a century of digging has depleted the resource; so it is now imported, mainly from Morocco and Tunisia, which together produce 25 per cent of the world supply. The Soviet Union, which accounts for 12 per cent of the world total, is self-sufficient; its mines are located in the Kola Peninsula and in southern Russia west of the Volga River.

Several Pacific islands (notably Nauru, Ocean, and Makatea) produce strip-mined rock to go to Japan, New Zealand, and Australia.

A unique source of phosphorus is guano from the arid Chincha Islands, a few miles off the coast of Peru. Guano is composed of the excrement and skeletal remains of millions of *guanay* birds and other ocean-birds which, for reasons still obscure, flock to these specific islands. When man discovered the islands, the guano deposits were several feet thick. Prized by the Incas, guano later became Peru's most valuable export, but the supply has been so depleted that the Peruvian government bans its sale abroad. Rich in nitrogen as well as phosphorus, guano today is consumed entirely by the sugar and cotton plantations of coastal Peru (see Figure 12-1).

Essential to the production of commercial phosphate fertilizer is another mineral— *sulfur*. Each year miners excavate about 8,000-000 tons of sulfur, the bulk of which goes into the manufacture of sulfuric acid. A large proportion of the acid is, in turn, used by the fertilizer industry in treating phosphate rock. Although pulverized phosphate rock can be effectively used without treatment, the phosphorus is more easily released to the soil if the rock is first treated with sulfuric acid. The result is termed "acid phosphate" or "superphosphate." More than a ton of sulfuric acid is required in the treatment of each ton of phosphate rock.

Sulfur comes from mines in two forms: sulfide ores and "native" sulfur. Sulfide ores contain a metal (say, iron or copper) that is actually the principal object of mining; sulfur is merely a by-product. But over half of the earth's sulfur is mined in the "native" form, not combined with metals. Nearly 90 per cent of all native sulfur comes from the fringes of the Gulf of Mexico, 10 per cent from Mexico, and 80 per cent from the United States. Texas and Louisiana are the leading states. Here the sulfur deposits have been concentrated, by rather complex geological forces, as caprock atop salt domes. These salt domes are massive affairs, sometimes 3000 feet in diameter, that rise to within 1200 feet of the earth's surface and are capped with a layer of sulfur-bearing rock 100 to 200 feet thick.

The prominence of the Gulf Coast in sulfur production provides an excellent example of how several advantageous relationships can work together in the economic geography of a region. The region naturally has large amounts of sulfur-bearing mineral, which fortunately is of high quality (around 40 per cent sulfur);

some rocks even have such a high content of that element that they can be used without further refining. Then, since the domes are located close to ocean ports, the mineral may be moved cheaply up the Mississippi River or to the Atlantic Seaboard, or to foreign ports. In addition, scientists were able to develop a peculiar mining technique that extracts the sulfur from the ground at a very low cost. Three concentric pipes are driven into the sulfur cap; hot water is forced down the outermost pipe and, escaping at the bottom, melts some of the sulfur. Compressed air is forced down the middle pipe and forces the water-sulfur mixture up the innermost pipe. At the surface this mixture is led to huge storage vats where the water evaporates, the sulfur hardens, and then is dug for transporting. Mining costs would be considerably higher if this area were not endowed with abundant water and abundant fuel (natural gas).

Other sulfur mines, widely dispersed through the western states, can scarcely compete with inexpensively mined salt-dome sulfur. But this supply is limited; four domes are already depleted, only ten remain in operation. Eventually, the United States will have to shift to lower-quality western resources.

Prior to discovery of the Gulf domes (around the turn of this century) Italy dominated the world mining of sulfur. The island of Sicily and the southern mainland have several deposits, averaging 26 per cent sulfur content, associated with old volcanoes.

Building-Materials Minera

In spite of the widespread occurrence of sand, gravel, and stone, few people appreciate their economic importance. For example, in the United States the value of sand and gravel mined is 80 per cent of the value of the iron ore mined; the value of crushed stone is almost that of copper.

A few places are endowed with distinctive stone resources. In this country, although limestone exists in every state, Indiana is blessed with masses of easily accessible stone that is solid yet easy to mine, is easy to cut in blocks,

resists weathering, and hardens with exposure. Bedford is the center of this industry in Indiana which mines over half the nation's building limestone. But stone is a heavy commodity in proportion to its value, which means that after a few hundred miles transportation costs begin to equal the original cost of the stone when loaded at the quarry. Quarrymen in the Alpena district of northern Michigan—world leader in the production of crushed limestone —ship stone via the Great Lakes to the industrial heart of Anglo-America.

Water

Water is perhaps the most versatile—and surely the least expensive—of all the economic minerals. The average price of municipal water to consumers (in the United States, for example) averages seven cents *per ton*. Water's versatility is demonstrated by its ability to meet man's need for nourishment, water power, navigation, recreation, irrigation, washing, air-conditioning, and in such industrial processes as forming solutions, cooling, and disposing of waste materials. In addition, sea water can serve as a raw material from which different chemicals are extracted. And steam is used to make electricity.

Clearly we cannot take the time to discuss the geographic aspects of each such individual use of water. Only two will be considered: water power and sea water as a raw material.

WATER POWER

Unlike coal, water has no capacity within itself for producing energy. But as a liquid which responds easily to the influence of gravity, water is mobile—and its *motion* does possess the ability to develop power. This ability varies with two major factors: (a) vertical distance of water fall, and (b) volume of water falling. Obviously, a large volume falling a great distance has the greatest power potential. Where one of these two factors is small, a small volume falling a great distance is to be preferred generally over a large volume falling a short distance—because of ease in harnessing the power. For it is easier to construct a narrow high dam than a broad low one. Accordingly, more power is produced by falling water of small rivers in the mountains than by the waters of giant rivers in the plains.

The ideal physical environment for the production of water power has (a) a steep gradient in the river, (b) a uniformly large supply of water from month to month, and (c) a narrows somewhere in the river's course than can facilitate dam construction. Uniformity of supply of abundant water cascading over a dam is enhanced by the following conditions: a vast drainage basin over which a humid climate prevails and through which an extensive network of tributaries feeds the major river trunk. In such a situation, droughts in one portion of the drainage basin may be compensated for by wet periods in other portions so that water flow in the main artery is maintained. Uniform flow is also favored by the presence of numerous lakes and swamps which serve as reservoirs in the drainage system, impounding water during unusually wet seasons and regulating its passage through the river network.

The ideal cultural environment for production of water power has large consumers of power (for example, factories and cities) located rather close to the power site. In the early days of water power such consumers had to be within a few yards of the waterfall or dam. Many a grist mill and saw mill were actually alongside a water wheel, turned by the falling water. The number of factories at a single dam was increased in the early days by the construction of *millraces*. A millrace was a channel dug to divert water from a river at a point upstream from a dam and then to lead it in a downstream direction parallel to the river, though at a distance of at least 100 feet. The intervening land was an ideal site —a factory could take water in from the millrace, conduct it to a water wheel within or beside its building, and then let it flow out into the river which was several feet (depending on the dam height) lower than the millrace. Many a small city grew up around an industrial district consisting of several factories straddling millraces. It was possible also for power thus produced to feed factories on the opposite side of a millrace. Such factories, however, could not possess their own water wheels; rather, they were serviced by overhead rotating shafts which extended to the millrace site where, via leather belts, they were rotated by power generated at the water wheels. Such overhead shafts, often extending 100 feet or more—sometimes crossing streets —made millrace districts noisy parts of town.

In the early days of water power development two major world areas stood out, distinguished by a myriad of small water power installations: western Europe and eastern Anglo-America. These were the areas where the Industrial Revolution first flowered, and part of its power requirement was met by a host of small water power developments. Many a good power site (with an excellent physical environment) was totally undeveloped because of a poor cultural environment; whereas many a poor power site (with a limited physical endowment) was fully exploited because of a favorable cultural environment.

The discovery of electricity opened a new era for water power. Prior to this discovery, power generated by water-driven wheels could be transported only by mechanical means which spanned comparatively short distances measured, at most, in yards. But the discovery of electricity—a form of energy into which water power could be converted—unshackled factories and cities from the necessity of being located right by water power sites. Electricity is transportable and can be conducted scores of miles. But shipping electricity is not like shipping coal; a volume of coal does not decline with distance transported (a hopper car loaded with 50 tons of coal departing from Pittsburgh will contain 50 tons of coal when it arrives at Indianapolis). Electricity, on the other hand, dissipates with distance. But inventions have enabled it to be shipped economically as far as 400 miles. However, the actual distance which electricity is transported in any given area depends upon the costs of competing fuels; if coal, oil, or gas is cheap, a region is likely to manufacture more electricity from steam plants and to transport hydroelectricity only short distances.

Water power is thus a competitor with fuels. Wherever the cost of generating electricity at a water power site plus the cost of transporting it to a market is more than the cost of building and operating a thermal plant at the market, the choice is likely to be made in favor of fuel-consuming power plants near the customers.

Thus, the principle holds that hydroelectricity (electricity generated by water power) tends to be consumed in the general region of production. Even with inventions for transporting electricity, many excellent water power sites are still undeveloped while many poor power sites are totally developed!

Today, water power itself is unimportant in the world's total power picture. Only as a generator of electricity is it significant in meeting the world's energy requirements. Even so, water power produces only 20 per cent of United States electricity, and only 5 per cent of the country's total power demand. Even if every potential water power site in the nation were fully developed, only 20 per cent of our power needs would be satisfied thereby. For the world it is estimated that 30 per cent of the electricity is water powered.

Regions of Developed Water Power Major areas measured in percentage of the world's developed water power are: western Europe 37 per cent, the United States 27, Canada 13, Japan 8, the Soviet Union 7. Mainland Asia exclusive of the Soviet Union accounts for 4 per cent, the continent of South America generates a little over 3 per cent, and Africa 2.

Figure 14-6 shows the general areal pattern of the world's developed water power. Southern Europe has numerous water power districts in the several nations through which the Alps and contiguous mountain ranges run. Indeed this part of Europe is distinguished by nations where water power development is so complete that the capacity (measured in horsepower) actually exceeds the potential power at ordinary minimum water flow. Examples of such nations are Italy and France (Europe's leaders in hydroelectric capacity— each accounting for around 8 per cent of the world total), Switzerland, and Austria. Developments in Norway and Sweden rank these nations right behind Italy and France in capacity.

Figure 14-6 also shows that eastern Anglo-America (from Canada to northern Alabama) is a major world region in the generation of hydroelectric power. The chief centers are the Shipshaw and Isle Maligne projects (in east-

Selected Minerals

DEVELOPED WATER POWER

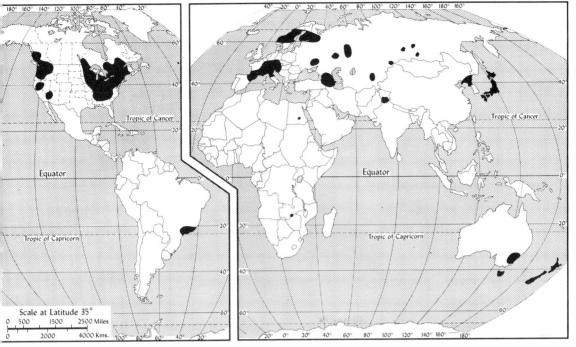

Figure 14-6

ern Canada, harnessing the Saguenay River), Niagara Falls, and the series of dams in the Tennessee Valley. The new St. Lawrence Seaway dams increase the power in eastern Anglo-America. The western part of the continent has several water power plants, from Kitimat (in British Columbia) to Hoover Dam. The state of Washington generates almost twice as much power as does the entire continent of South America. Oregon, New York, and California follow in that order. The

three Pacific Coast states, in fact, account for 40 per cent of the nation's developed water power. Although developed power sites are more numerous and widespread in eastern states, the power produced is less than that of the West.

The Soviet Union has both natural power sites (principally in the Caucasus Mountains and in the numerous mountain chains of eastern Siberia) and man-made sites, such as the Dnepropetrovsk dam on the Dnepr River in

The Bhakra Dam under construction on the Sutlej River in the Punjab, India. (Courtesy Press Information Bureau, Government of India.)

Table 14-8 *World's Largest Dams by Height*

Dam	Location	River	Height in Feet	Year Completed
Grand Dixence	Switzerland	Rhone	940	*
Vajont	Italy	Dolomites	870	*
Mauvoisin	Switzerland	Dranse	780	1958
Tachien	Taiwan	Tachia	780	1961
Bhakra	India	Sutlej	740	1960
Oroville	California	Feather	730	*
Hoover	Arizona-Nevada	Colorado	726	1936
Glen Canyon	Arizona	Colorado	700	*
Shasta	California	Sacramento	602	1945
Tignes	France	Isère	592	1953

Sources: *Encyclopaedia Britannica, World Atlas,* 1961, pp. 260-261 and Petrov, Victor P., *Geography of the Soviet Union:* 1V-B, Electric Power (Washington) 1959, p. 73; and Khruschchev, A. T. and Nikol'skiy, I. V., *The Development and Distribution of Industry and Transportation in the U.S.S.R. During The Seven-Year Plan.* (Moscow), 1960, p. 78.
* Under construction.

the rather flat Ukraine, and two new installations at Kuibyshev and Stalingrad (now Volgograd) on the Volga. Japan, Korea, and Manchuria dominate hydroelectric power production in the Far East. Indeed, Japan's developed capacity almost equals her potential waterpower at ordinary low flow. Elsewhere, a few hydroelectric projects are of great significance to their immediate hinterlands in nations that, in the over-all view, otherwise have comparatively little power development. Examples are the Kariba Dam in Rhodesia, the Aswan High Dam in Egypt, and the Bhakra Dam in India. The periphery of South America and of southeast Australia and New Zealand should also be mentioned in this category. (A detailed hydroelectric power map in an economic atlas will serve to pinpoint the location of the foregoing districts.)

Prominent in the world's waterpower installations are some very impressive dams several of which exceed 500 feet in height—and almost reach 1000 feet (see Table 14-8). However, the rivers flowing over these high dams are relatively small in comparison with those at certain other installations which have greater capacity. In terms of capacity for generating hydroelectricity the world's fore-

Table 14-9 *World's Largest Dams by Developed Power Capacity*

Dam	Location	River	Installed Kilowatts	Year Completed
Krasnoyarsk	U.S.S.R.	Yenesei	5,000,000	*
Bratsk	U.S.S.R.	Angara	4,600,000	*
Stalingrad (Volgograd)	U.S.S.R.	Volga	2,500,000	1960
Kuibyshev	U.S.S.R.	Volga	2,300,000	1958
Grand Coulee	Washington	Columbia	1,974,000	1942
Hoover	Arizona-Nevada	Colorado	1,249,800	1936
John Day	Oregon-Washington	Columbia	1,105,000	*
San Men Gorge	China	Yellow	1,000,000	*
Glen Canyon	Arizona	Colorado	900,000	*
McNary	Oregon-Washington	Columbia	740,000	1957
Kariba	Southern Rhodesia	Zambezi	600,000	1960
Bhakra	India	Sutlej	594,000	1960
Dneprostroy	U.S.S.R.	Dnepr	560,000	1932

Source: *Ibid.*
* Under construction.

Selected Mineral

most installations tend to be elsewhere (see Table 14-9).

Potential Water Power   The location of potential water power, however, is markedly different from the foregoing pattern. Africa, for instance, has 41 per cent of the world total. For other places the percentages are Asia 15, North America 12, U.S.S.R. 11, South America 10, and Europe 8. Notice that the world pattern of potential water power tends to correlate with areas with good physical environments but poor cultural environments for hydroelectric installations. Some of the world's greatest potential water power sites are the lower Congo River, the Parana River, the middle Yangtze, and some of the rivers in New Guinea—all of which are too far from customers demanding electric power. In contrast to the wet tropics of Africa, the Amazon basin has little potential water power. In spite of tremendous water volumes, the Amazon has a comparatively low water *head*, so it drops little in elevation along its course.

WATER FOR MINERAL CONTENT

The earth's surface embraces almost 200,000,000 square miles. Continents occupy 56,000,000 square miles (roughly 28 per cent of the total surface) including the rivers, lakes, and inland seas. This leaves the staggering figure of 144,000,000 square miles as the area of the ocean surface. For every square mile of continent, there are almost three square miles of ocean. Most of the wet acreage is concentrated in the Pacific Ocean—approximately 65,000,000 square miles. If we could shift all the land masses in the world into the Pacific, we would still have 9,000,000 square miles of water left—the area of North America. The other oceans, in order of size, are: Atlantic 32,000,000 square miles, Indian 28,000,000, and Arctic 6,000,000. In addition there are numerous smaller bodies such as the Mediterranean, Caribbean, China, Red, Yellow, Okhotsk, Bering, Baltic, and Japan seas, as well as Hudson Bay and the Gulf of Mexico.

Oceans are deep as well as vast. The greatest known depth, 35,640 feet, is south of the Mariana Islands in the western Pacific.

The water world is indeed gigantic and so are its resources. One single cubic mile of sea water contains, on the average, 166,000,000 tons of dissolved minerals. If we multiply this by the number of cubic miles in the world's seas, we get the staggering product of 50,000,000,000,000,000 tons of minerals!

The sea averages 96.5 per cent water and 3.5 per cent dissolved minerals. The figures vary from region to region—in the rainy tropics, for instance, the percentage of minerals is slightly lower, the ocean being diluted by rainfall, and in the dry subtropics the percentage is higher because of reduced rainfall and increased evaporation.

The most abundant *elements* dissolved in sea water are sodium, chlorine, magnesium, calcium, potassium, and sulfur; the most prevalent *minerals* are:

Sodium chloride	78%
Magnesium chloride	11
Magnesium sulfate	5
Calcium sulfate	3
Potassium sulfate	2.5
All others	0.5
Total dissolved minerals	100.0%

Extracting minerals from sea water is an expensive business, with few exceptions. Chemists have identified 50 elements in sea water, but technologists have succeeded in extracting only a few at costs that are competitive with the mining of these minerals from rocks. Sea water is evaporated in huge reservoirs in the open sunshine to produce residues of sodium chloride (common salt) on the shores of the Persian Gulf, China, Japan, and the Philippines. Bromine is now produced commercially by means of the same general technique. In 1941 scientists discovered methods for commercially extracting the strong light metal magnesium from sea water. During World War II much of the magnesium used in airplanes, star shells, incendiary bombs, boats, and even lightweight buildings was mined from the sea, a cubic mile of which contains 4,000,000 tons of the metal. A cubic mile of sea water also contains $90,000,000 worth of gold and $8,500,000 worth of silver, but the labor and complex equipment required for extracting these precious metals would cost more than they are worth. As for the other elements known to exist in the ocean—lobsters absorb huge quantities of cobalt and their blood contains copper; mollusks contain nickel; it was not known that vanadium even existed in the sea until zoologists discovered it in the blood of sea cucumbers. Someday man may devise techniques for commercially extracting other minerals from ocean water. When that day comes, world regions of mining may go through a major transformation, as "mines" line the seacoasts near the world's major markets of mineral consumption.

WATER CONSUMPTION

For the United States, information is available on the principal uses of water and the primary areas of consumption. The nation as a whole uses 1740 billion gallons of water *per day!* This is one and one-half times the average annual runoff of water from the entire surface of the United States! But little water is actually "consumed"; ordinarily, after it is used, whether by hydroelectric plants, cooling systems, or in soaking operations, it is forthwith passed on. Over 85 per cent of the usage is for power. The daily withdrawal of water, in billions of gallons, breaks down as follows: water power 1500, irrigation

110, industries 110, public water works 16, farms and rural users 4. Leading states in total water usage are Oregon and New York (Table 14-10) where most of the water is used for power. California and Texas are the leaders in nonpower consumption.

Table **14-10** *Withdrawal of Water, by Billion Gallons per Day*

State	Water Power	Other Uses	Total
TOTAL, U.S.	1500	240	1740
Maine	100	—	100
New Hampshire	31	—	31
New York	130	8	138
Pennsylvania	41	11	52
Michigan	60	6	66
Wisconsin	84	5	89
Minnesota	32	1	33
Illinois	27	9	36
West Virginia	27	4	31
North Carolina	41	2	43
Alabama	95	3	98
Tennessee	100	4	104
Kentucky	43	3	46
Texas	11	17	28
Montana	37	10	47
Idaho	61	15	76
Washington	110	6	116
Oregon	180	7	187
California	45	30	75

Source: United States Bureau of Mines, *Minerals Yearbook,* 1956, "Water," pp. 4-5.

Suggested Reading

Cole, Monica M., "The Rhodesian Economy in Transition and the Role of Kariba," *Geography,* January, 1961, pp. 15-40.

Cressey, George B., "Water in the Desert," *Annals of the Association of American Geographers,* 1957, pp. 105-124.

Deasy, George F., and Griess, Phyllis R., "Geographical Significance of Recent Changes in Mining in the Bituminous Coal Fields of Pennsylvania," *Economic Geography,* 1957, pp. 283-298.

Estall, R. C., "The Problem of Power in the United Kingdom," *Economic Geography,* 1958, pp. 80-89.

Hamming, Edward, "Water Legislation," *Economic Geography,* 1958, pp. 42-46.

Kish, George, "Hydroelectric Power in France," *Geographical Review,* 1955, pp. 81-98.

Lloyd, Trevor, "Iron Ore Production at Kirkenes, Norway," *Economic Geography,* 1955, pp. 211-233.

Marts, M. E., "Upstream Storage Problems in Columbia Power Development," *Annals of the Association of American Geographers,* 1954, pp. 43-50.

Pounds, Norman J. G., "The Spread of Mining in the Coal Basin of Upper Silesia and Northern Moravia," *Annals of the Association of American Geographers,* 1958, pp. 149-163.

Raitt, William L., "The Changing Pattern of Norwegian Hydroelectric Development," *Economic Geography,* 1958, pp. 127-144.

Roepke, Howard G., "Changing Patterns of Coal Production in the Eastern Interior Field," *Economic Geography,* 1955, pp. 234-247.

Rudolph, William E., "Chuquicamata Twenty Years Later," *Geographical Review,* 1951, pp. 88-113.

Thiel, Eric, "The Power Industry in the Soviet Union," *Economic Geography,* 1951, pp. 107-122.

Thomas, Trevor M., "Recent Trends and Developments in the British Coal Mining Industry," *Economic Geography,* 1958, pp. 19-41.

United States Bureau of Mines, *Minerals Yearbook* (published annually) and *Mineral Trade Notes* (published monthly).

White, Gilbert F., "Industrial Water Use: A Review," *Geographical Review,* 1960, pp. 412-430.

Selected Mineral

Petroleum mining near Sexton City in the East Texas oil field.
Wells are unusually close together in this view.
Later, in newer fields, wells were spaced farther apart so as to reduce the cost
of mining petroleum from any given area. (Courtesy World Oil.)

FIFTEEN

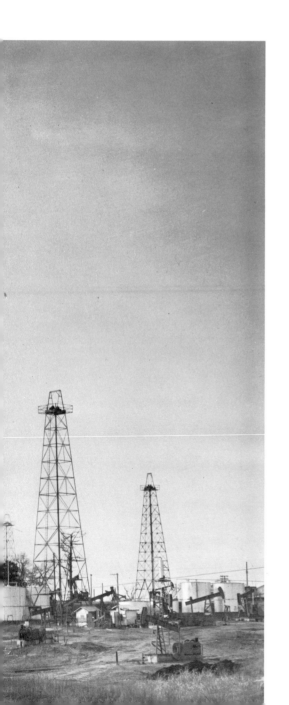

Petroleum is versatile in its uses; fuel; lubricant; source of illumination, wax, and tar; and raw material from which many chemicals can be extracted. Its high economic value automatically commends it to our attention. In addition, the mining of this liquid mineral is unusual in two respects that are of peculiar interest to the geographer. First, few other mining industries have experienced such abrupt locational changes in so few years as has that of petroleum. Second, of all mining, the petroleum industry provides the most complete collection of production records published year by year, country by country, and (in the United States) state by state.

For these reasons, petroleum mining is admirably suited to illustrate a particular type of geographic analysis which we have not touched on so far, but with which every student of geography should be familiar—historical geography.

Historical geography is not the history of geography nor the geography of history; rather, it is the geography of past periods. The historical geographer applies the basic questions of the geographic method to the past, age by age, in order to understand regions as they existed in whatever periods he wishes to study. Thus, historical geography adds a useful dimension of time to our understanding of world economic activity.

Petroleum

A complete portrayal of the location of oil mining in the world from one period of time to another would resemble a motion picture of a dynamic map showing the location of petroleum mining, a map that has been kept continually up to date ever since petroleum was first mined as a commercial venture. But such a movie, however informative, might run longer than "Gone with the Wind" and "Ben-Hur." So for our account we shall project individual frames from the total sequence of pictures. Each chosen frame will provide a view of the geography of petroleum mining at a particular time and will reveal some significant development. Occasionally, we may find we have to run our film forward and backward in order to bring a particular frame into meaningful focus.

1857

For thousands of years man had known about petroleum. In some places it bubbled to the surface in tar pits or small flows. From time immemorial people used the stuff to leakproof their boats, to make hot fires, or to burn for illumination. But not until 1857 was petroleum mined commercially. Although historical records unfortunately disagree about where and when the first commercial oil was produced, the author accepts the verdict of *World Oil* (a trade journal of the United States oil industry) that 1857 was the year and Romania the country. In that first year the wells, in the vicinity of Ploesti, 40 miles north of Bucharest, yielded 2000 barrels of petroleum—the entire world output—which was marketed in the surrounding hinterland. The rest of the world continued to use whale and other animal fats and vegetable oils for illumination, lubrication, and fuel.

1860

Three years later the world map showed two regions. Romania had increased her output to 9000 barrels, a respectable increase of 350 per cent. But her share of the world total had plummeted to 2 per cent! For another region, thousands of miles away, had burst upon the scene.

Since 1750 oil seepages had been observed in western New York and Pennsylvania. Several of these happened to be in the vicinity of salt wells. Several such wells near Tarentum, Pennsylvania, a few miles north of Pittsburgh, yielded not only salt but a nuisance product, oil. Many white people had adopted the Indian practise of using such oil for medicine, and since 1847 an astute druggist named Samuel Kier had been salvaging this discard and bottling it for sale under the following caption: [*]

Kier's Petroleum or Rock Oil, celebrated for its wonderful curative powers ... gets its ingredients from the beds of substances which it passes over in its secret channels. Its discovery is a new era in medicine.

Kier's advertisements carried a picture of a derrick, like those of the salt wells from which the oil had been taken, which caught the eye of a New York lawyer, George Bissell. Bissell got the idea that oil itself could be mined commercially. Under his leadership, the Seneca Oil Company was organized for the purpose of drilling for petroleum. The question of where to drill was decided in favor of Oil Creek (near Titusville in northwestern Pennsylvania) where seepage had been known for years not only to white settlers but earlier to the Indians. In late 1859 an experimental well struck oil here at a depth of 70 feet. In the very next year the wells of Pennsylvania yielded 500,000 barrels. Demand for this product came mainly from the illuminating-oil market in the northeastern United States, particularly the Atlantic Seaboard where most of the nation's populace resided.

1880

Twenty years later the total world production was up from 509,000 barrels to a surprising 30,000,000. The United States was the unrivaled leader (see Table 15-1, page 254). Within the United States, Pennsylvania still dominated; that state alone accounted for 80 per cent of the world's total. In addition, oil drillers began roaming, with success, into New York, Ohio, and West Virginia (Table 15-2, page 255).

In the rest of the world, Romania was still

[*] Wallace E. Pratt and Dorothy Good, *World Geography of Petroleum*, American Geographical Society, Special Publication No. 31, 1950, page 130.

Table 15-1 Crude-Oil Production by Leading Nations (for Selected Years) and Reserves (1960) (in Thousands of Barrels)

Region	Production 1860	1880	1900	1910	1920	1927	1940	1950	1960	1960 Percentage	Reserves 1960	Percentage
WORLD	509	30,019	149,137	327,763	688,884	1,262,582	2,149,821	3,802,995	7,663,184	100	266,249,992	100
Europe	9	355	4,346	23,480	13,751	33,038	61,494	65,293	205,683	3	2,820,741	1
Romania	9	115	1,629	9,724	7,435	26,368	43,168	32,000	85,169	1	903,532	†
Poland	—	229	2,347	12,673	5,607	5,342	3,891	1,205	1,442	†	25,228	†
Germany	—	9	358	1,032	246	663	7,371	8,107	39,262	†	489,800	†
Austria	—	—	—	—	—	—	2,808	10,200	16,619	†	205,000	†
U.S.S.R.	—	3,001	75,780	70,337	25,430	77,018	218,600	266,200	1,080,400	14	24,000,000	9
North America	500	26,636	64,534	213,507	600,194	965,727	1,405,983	2,075,217	2,865,824	38	37,749,753	14
Canada	—	350	913	316	196	477	8,591	29,044	191,841	2	3,678,542	1
United States	500	26,286	63,621	209,557	442,929	901,129	1,353,214	1,973,574	2,574,933	35	31,613,211	12
Mexico	—	—	—	3,634	157,069	64,121	44,036	72,443	99,049	1	2,458,000	†
South America	—	—	274	1,421	7,068	102,822	268,764	644,056	1,265,333	16	20,405,698	8
Peru	—	—	274	1,258	2,817	10,127	12,126	15,012	19,255	†	300,000	†
Colombia	—	—	—	—	—	15,014	25,593	34,060	55,770	†	625,000	†
Venezuela	—	—	—	—	457	63,134	185,570	546,783	1,041,675	14	17,353,558	7
Trinidad	—	—	—	143	2,083	5,380	22,227	20,632	42,357	†	390,000	†
Africa	—	—	—	—	1,046	1,275	6,532	16,702	103,508	1	8,374,000	3
Egypt	—	—	—	—	1,046	1,267	6,505	16,373	22,559	†	500,000	†
Algeria	—	—	—	—	—	—	—	—	67,226	†	4,600,000	2
Middle East	—	—	—	—	12,230	40,026	102,691	640,862	1,929,789	25	162,900,000	61
Iran	—	—	—	—	12,230	39,688	66,317	242,475	390,754	5	22,000,000	8
Iraq	—	—	—	—	—	338	24,225	49,726	354,591	5	24,000,000	9
Saudi Arabia	—	—	—	—	—	—	5,075	199,547	456,453	6	51,000,000	19
Kuwait	—	—	—	—	—	—	—	125,722	594,278	8	60,000,000	23
Far East	—	—	4,203	18,998	29,145	42,663	85,740	94,657	212,643	3	9,599,800	4
Japan	26	26	871	1,829	2,221	1,789	2,639	2,048	3,730	†	40,000	†
Indonesia	—	—	2,253	11,031	17,529	27,459	62,011	48,400*	150,510	2	8,200,000	3
North Borneo	—	—	—	—	—	—	—	—	34,004	†	410,000	†
China	—	—	—	—	—	—	—	—	12,810	†	500,000	†

Source: *World Oil*, August 15, 1957, pages 191-194 and August, 1961, page 76.
* In 1946 Indonesia's production had slumped to only 2,100 thousand barrels.
† Less than 1%.

Table 15-2 *Crude Oil Production by Leading States for Selected Years and Reserves (in Thousands of Barrels)*

Region	Production									Reserves as Percentage of U.S. Total
	1860	1880	1900	1910	1920	1927	1940	1950	1960	
U.S. TOTAL	500	26,286	63,621	209,557	442,929	901,129	1,353,214	1,973,574	2,574,933	100
Northeast										
Pennsylvania	500*	24,987*	13,258	8,795	7,438	9,626	17,353	11,859	6,213	†
New York	—	1,041	1,301	1,054	906	2,242	4,999	4,143	1,796	†
W. Virginia	—	179	16,196	11,753	8,249	6,023	3,444	2,808	2,306	†
Ohio	—	39	22,363*	9,916	7,400	7,593	3,159	3,383	4,886	†
Illinois	—	—	—	33,143	10,774	6,994	147,647	62,028	79,463	2
Mid-Continent										
Kansas	—	—	75	1,128	39,005	41,069	66,139	107,586	112,531	3
Oklahoma	—	—	6	52,029	106,206*	277,775*	156,164	164,599	191,553	6
Texas	—	—	836	8,899	96,868	217,389	493,209*	829,874*	932,321	47
Louisiana	—	—	—	6,841	35,714	22,818	103,584	208,965	392,712	15
New Mexico	—	—	—	—	—	1,226	39,129	47,367	108,383	3
Northwest										
Wyoming	—	—	6	115	16,831	21,307	25,711	61,631	134,441	4
Montana	—	—	—	—	340	5,058	6,728	8,109	30,135	1
N. Dakota	—	—	—	—	—	—	—	—-	22,010	1
California	—	—	4,325	73,011*	103,377	231,196	223,881	327,607	304,535	12

Source: *World Oil*, Feb. 15, 1958, pages 127, 166-167, and February 15, 1961, pages 81 and 100.
* Leading state for year indicated.
† Less than one per cent.

pumping oil, but several new areas had bobbed up on the map. Russia for one far surpassed Romania. The first oil in Russia was struck in 1863 at Maikop on the northern flanks of the Caucasus, 60 miles east of the Black Sea; in 1871 another field was found near Baku on the Apsheron Peninsula. Then a third field opened up in the vicinity of Grozny, midway between Maikop and Baku. Elsewhere, lesser flows were appearing in Poland, Germany, Japan, and Canada.

1900

Great changes are seen in our next frame, 1900 (Figure 15-1, page 256). Romania's yield had gone up steadily to 1,629,000 barrels. Much of her oil was now moving up the Danube River to the markets of western Europe, particularly the budding industrial power, Germany. Yet her share of the world total was only one per cent. Poland, now ahead of Romania, led in Europe.

Many new regions were furnishing crude oil, especially Peru and the Dutch East Indies. Peru's production was small, but several islands in the Indies were, taken together, yielding a great deal. The story in the Indies began in 1885 when Dutch farmers, clearing tropical forests on the northeastern coast of Sumatra for plantation sites, noticed oil seepages. They drilled, struck oil, and began to produce commercial petroleum. The same story was repeated on Java in 1896 and on Borneo in 1897.

Things were different also in North America. Canada appeared with a small yield, but the chief change was the dethroning of Pennsylvania as leader, a position she had held for a generation—from 1860 to 1895. Ohio now led the states (Table 15-2), and even West Virginia overtook Pennsylvania. But this was just a shift of focus within a single field—the Appalachian—that underlay all these states. More significant was the faint appearance of entirely new fields, one in the Southwest (Texas, Oklahoma, and Kansas), one in the Rockies (Wyoming), and one on the West Coast (California). All told, the United States flowed with 63,000,000 barrels of oil. Yet for all this volume, she could be credited with only 43 per cent of the world total—quite a comedown from her previous shares (98 per cent in 1860 and 88 per cent in 1880).

The most spectacular area on the 1900 map

PETROLEUM PRODUCTION, 1900

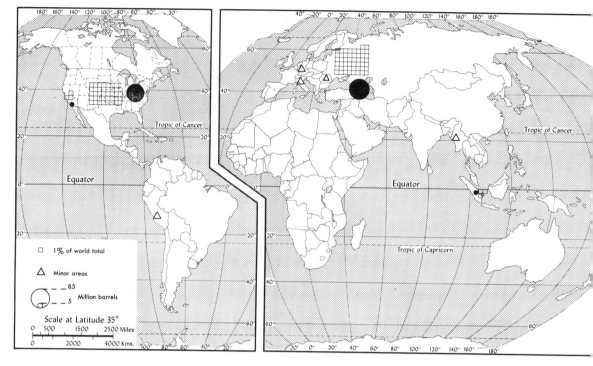

Figure 15-1

Figure 15-2

PETROLEUM PRODUCTION, 1910

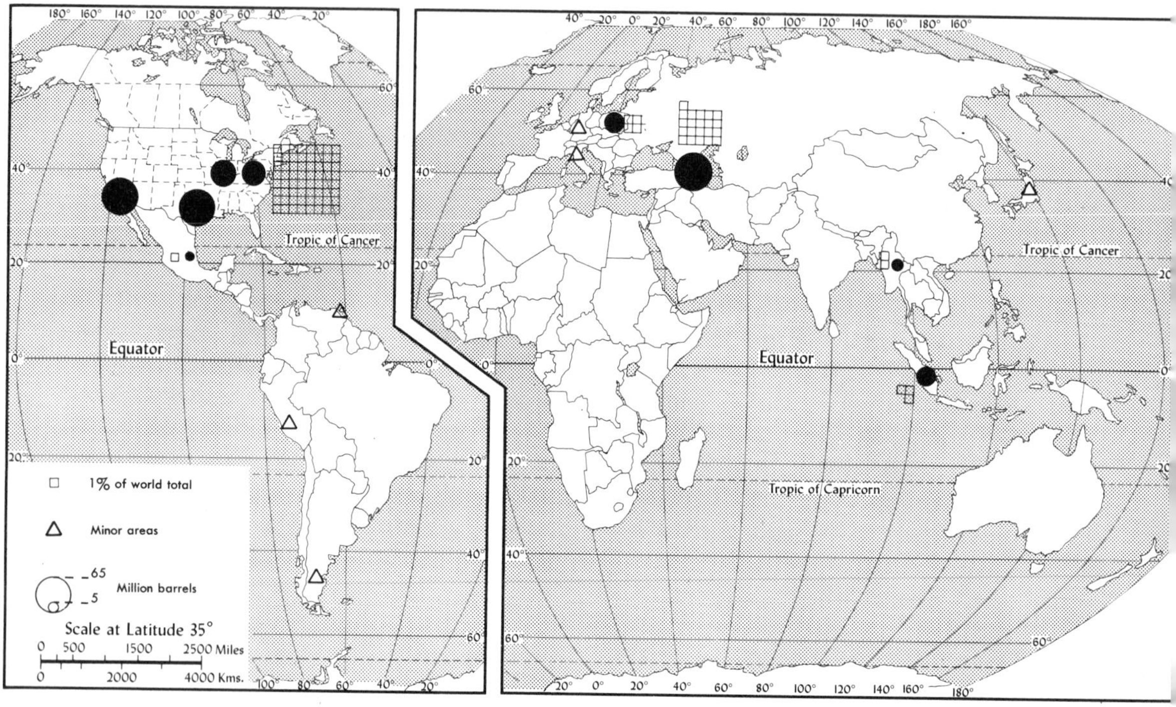

is southern Russia (Figure 15-1). The three Caucasian fields (Maikop, Grozny, and Baku) poured forth 75,000,000 barrels, an astonishing increase in 20 years that propelled Russia into first place among the nations. In fact, she was mining more crude oil—50 per cent— than the rest of the world combined. This period' marks the apex of Russian oil mining in percentage of the world total. Never since has her share attained that figure.

The market for Caucasian oil was partly in the Moscow area (some oil moved by water across the Caspian and up the Volga), partly in the Ukraine (to which oil moved by pipe, rail, and river), but mostly in western Europe where industry was now using petroleum for lubrication and fuel. To get the oil to market, a pipeline was constructed from the Grozny field through the Maikop field to Tuapse, a Black Sea port, where it then proceeded by barge and ship. Most of the Baku oil also moved to Europe by another pipeline along the south side of the Caucasus to Batum. Thus, the pipelines, the ports of Batum and Tuapse, and the three mining areas all functioned together in moving oil from the Caucasian wells to the western European customers.

By 1900, petroleum mining was under way in other widely separated areas that were also becoming related to the market of western Europe—a region with a large population and tremendous industrial capacity that meant a voracious demand for petroleum. So capital flowed out of western Europe as payment for petroleum and as investment in property and mining equipment in the Dutch East Indies, Peru, and even Russia (where the Russian economy under the Czarist regime was incapable of providing much investment capital). Not only money but also personnel moved out from Europe (Britain and the Netherlands in particular) to most of the oil-producing regions of the world. In the geography of petroleum for 1900 even the United States was a supplier to Europe.

1910

The year 1910 shows a still different picture. Virtually all the areas on the 1900 map increased their output. Russia was the chief exception (Figure 15-2). During the ten-year interval her annual yield shrank to 70,000,000 barrels, and from the biggest cut of the pie her share shriveled to 21 per cent of the world total. Political and economic turmoil within Russia was beginning to affect oil mining.

Some of the older fields expanded substantially by 1910. Polish wells on the northern flanks of the Carpathian Mountains were enjoying a mild boom. But this proved to be their peak period, for the resources soon faded. Few oil fields on earth have been so fragmented by national boundaries as this Carpathian field which, in 1910, was at the juncture of southern Poland, eastern Czechoslovakia, and western Russia.

During this time an unusual advance occurred in the United States, which strode beyond the 200,000,000-barrel mark—more than half again the volume of the rest of the world combined. The sharp contrast in ten short years from 1900 (Russia 50 per cent and the United States 43 per cent of the total) to 1910 (Russia 21 per cent and the United States 64 per cent) is one of the most abrupt changes ever seen in historical economic geography.

A new regional pattern also appeared within the United States. Pennsylvania's oil yield had shrunk to a third of that in her best years. Ohio, the nation's leader just a decade earlier, was down to less than half her peak. Booms were underway farther west, in Illinois and Oklahoma. But the biggest boom of all was in California, which now ranked first in the nation and actually outproduced every foreign nation except Russia.

Two newcomers to the map were Mexico and Trinidad whose yields were still small.

1920

At the close of World War I North America dominated the world in petroleum production. Mexico in particular had made notable gains. Mexico and the United States together accounted for 86 per cent of the world's oil yield. In the decade since 1910 Mexico's production shot up from 3,000,000 to 157,000,000 barrels —about 22 per cent of the world total—the largest volume coming from the gulf fields in the vicinity of Tampico on the eastern coast. But this was the high mark in the history of Mexican oil. For in 1921 there was an event with far-reaching consequences—the Queretaro Convention. It had been long-standing Mexican policy that subsoil rights were vested in the landowners. Accordingly, oil prospectors (representatives of companies from California, Britain, and the Netherlands) purchased subsoil rights far and wide from the individual owners. The Queretaro Convention reversed this policy and transferred all petroleum rights to national ownership. Moreover, it made the action retroactive. The upshot was lengthy litigation between the government and the oil companies, which eventually reduced operations in Mexico.

The United States likewise had made rapid advances, boosting her output to 442,000,000 barrels. Within the United States the regional pattern was different from that of 1910. Oklahoma was now the leading state, California had slipped to second, and Texas, riding the crest of the most vigorous expansion in the industry so far experienced in the United States, was a close third. It was actually in

1901 that oilmen prospecting in Texas struck a gusher just north of Beaumont. This gusher, the most productive in the nation's history, was on a small hill called "Spindletop." From that date, there began a frenzy of prospecting and drilling in southwestern states. Thousands of dry wells disappointed their drillers, but hundreds came through successfully. So feverish was the activity that by 1920 the Gulf Coast field (along coastal Texas and Louisiana) and the Mid-Continent field (in northern Texas, Oklahoma, and Kansas) had far outstripped all other fields in the nation. Indeed, Kansas and Louisiana joined Oklahoma, California, and Texas as the five petroleum leaders. For the first time, the nation's crude-oil industry was clearly centered in south-central states. West Virginia, Pennsylvania, and Ohio had slumped; their wells were literally running dry.

Another development in the Western Hemisphere, though not prominent in 1920, had significant implications for the future: Venezuela appeared for the first time on the world oil map. Seepages in the northern part of the country had been reported centuries earlier

Figure 15-3

PETROLEUM PRODUCTION, 1920

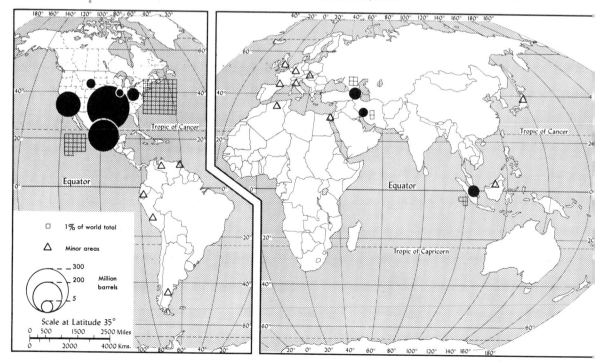

by the conquistadores, but it was not until 1917 that geologists of the Royal Dutch Shell company drilled successfully and developed the Mene Grande field, the first large oil field in Venezuela. This development occurred in the northwestern part of the country on the eastern shores of Lake Maracaibo. An unusual geographical relationship arose between Venezuela and Curaçao, a Caribbean island 50 miles off the coast and a colonial possession of the Netherlands. There was little choice of where the mining should be located, but there was a choice of where the refineries should be built. Curaçao was selected as the site of the latter for several reasons: A refinery would provide job opportunities for the citizens of the colony; it would provide tax revenues for the Dutch government of the island; and capital invested in refining equipment would be protected by Dutch law-enforcement agencies. Thus, a flow pattern was established whereby a mining venture (combining a Venezuelan physical resource with a European cultural resource) shipped crude oil to Curaçao which in turn shipped refined products to Europe.

Another significant debut in the decade between 1910 and 1920 was that of the Middle East. It appeared with a larger volume than Venezuela and was destined to play a larger role. The first entry was Persia—now Iran. Shortly after the turn of the century the Persian government granted a concession to an Englishman named William D'Arcy who made the first successful oil strike in 1909 in the southern part of the country at Masjed-I-Sulaiman. But this was nomadic herding territory having no demand for petroleum within hundreds of miles. Even the populated heart of Persia 400 miles to the north and the populous Tigris-Euphrates valleys to the west had little purchasing power. The market was thousands of miles away in western Europe. Ships could traverse that distance in a few weeks. But Masjed was 100 miles from the Persian Gulf—a distance that, for large oil movement, could *not* be conquered in a few weeks. Indeed, it required four years to overcome that 100-mile barrier—by constructing a pipeline to the port of Abadan. The year

1913 saw the initial shipment of Persian oil. That year she accounted for 1,000,000 barrels —not much in the world total (385,000,000 barrels), but a significant portent of things to come. Again, European capital and personnel interacted with the physical resource of Iran to give birth to an economic activity, most of which was administered by the Anglo-Iranian Oil Company.

Elsewhere, Indonesia, Trinidad, and Peru enjoyed increases. But yields in every European nation were down, reflecting depletion of the resource in some wells but, more importantly, the exigencies of war. The toll of conflict and disorganization was particularly severe in Russia, which was jolted by war and revolution. Volume was down to only 25,000,000 barrels, a mere 4 per cent of the world total—an astonishing decline in 20 years from the 75,000,000-barrel harvest which had exceeded that of all other nations combined. 1920 was the nadir of Russian oil mining. Not since 1889 had yields been that low; and they have never since been that low.

1927

Seven years later the United States and Mexico parted company in production trends. Mexico was in a nosedive not only in her share of world total (in seven years down to 5 per cent) but also in actual volume: from 157,000,000 down to 64,000,000. Some of her fields were giving out, and some of the gulf fields were being infiltrated by salt water, but the most serious factor was political strife— legal tangles between oil companies and the Mexican government that were precipitated by the Queretaro Convention and discouraged oil extraction.

By contrast, prospecting and drilling in the United States enjoyed a healthy gain; over 900,000,000 barrels flowed from her wells in 1927—71 per cent of the world total. Not since 1860 had a single country so dominated the world. But this was the last year that a lone nation was responsible for such a percentage. Since this 1927 apex, the United States' share has slipped steadily downward even though the volume has moved steadily upward.

Within the country, three fields, Mid-Continent, Gulf Coast, and California, were leaping far ahead of all others. Among the leading states, Texas was gaining rapidly on Oklahoma and California.

Even more remarkable, though on a smaller scale, was the boom in Venezuela. In seven short years output rocketed from 457,000 barrels to 63,000,000. She quickly overtook all other nations except the United States and Russia. By this time a second mining company —an American one—had struck oil in the Lake Maracaibo district. And, like its Dutch predecessor, it chose to locate refineries just outside Venezuela in Aruba, another possession of the Netherlands. Nearly all of Venezuela's oil was exported, mostly to European consumers.

Russia had recovered dramatically from her earlier decline; since 1920 her yield had risen sharply to 77,000,000 barrels. In the Middle East, Iran was up to 39,000,000 barrels. Although this was a respectable increase over 1920, it still was a very small fraction of the world total. Worth noting also is Iraq's first appearance on the world map.

Thirteen years later the world was going through a petroleum revolution. Consumption had reached the unprecedented figure of 2,000,000,000 barrels as the age of the internal combustion engine shifted into high gear. The world map of oil production in 1940 is substantially different from that of 1927.

For one thing, the United States was dropping—down to 63 per cent of the world total —despite a huge increase in production, now more than one billion barrels. Within the United States the most dramatic change was the emergence of Texas as national leader. Indeed, this single state now accounted for twice as much oil as any nation outside the United States. Hundreds of new wells were drilled in north, northwest, and coastal Texas, and in the Gulf itself. Derricks and wells were marched out to sea several miles from shore. At this point Texas and Louisiana found themselves enmeshed in an unusual and complex relationship with the United States government; many states contended that oil underlying the Gulf (that is, the "tidelands") was

Figure 15-4

PETROLEUM PRODUCTION, 1940

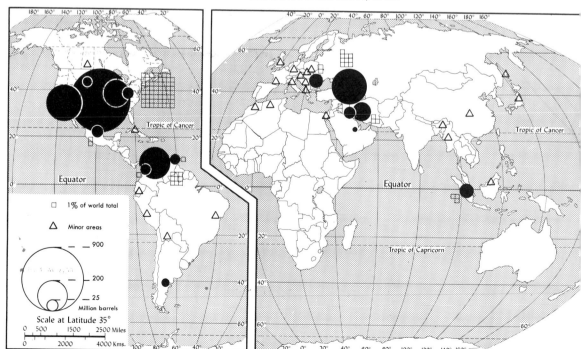

A portion of the Bolivar coastal oil fields along the northeastern shore of Lake Maracaibo in Venezuela. Wells have been drilled in an orderly arrangement as far as 15 miles into the lake in depths up to 100 feet of water. There are over 2000 wells in the lake and 1000 miles of pipeline threaded on the lake bottom, carrying oil from the wells to storage facilities ashore at such collecting points as the one shown here—Lagunillas—which contains many storage tanks, company offices, and houses for employees. From this settlement, pipelines carry the crude oil 145 miles north and east to refineries at Amuay which has a deep-water harbor accessible to ocean tankers. (Courtesy Creole Petroleum Corporation.)

the property of the United States as a whole rather than the state off whose shores the wells were situated. California, now the second-ranking state, was also involved in this hassle because she too had wells reposing on stilts in the Pacific Ocean. The debate over tidelands oil raged for several years until, in 1953, the federal government enacted legislation recognizing state ownership of the tidelands as far out as 10½ miles from shore.

Southern Illinois had boomed into prominence with 147,000,000 barrels in 1940, only slightly behind third-ranking Oklahoma. But Illinois turned out to be a fast starter but slow in the stretch, for her wells dried up within a decade to yield less than half that volume.

For the United States as a whole, consumption was increasing more rapidly than production. Yet the country still had a surplus for sale abroad, primarily to three deficit areas: Europe, Japan, and Canada.

Russia, at the start of World War II, had climbed to second place in oil mining—with 10 per cent of the world total, nine-tenths of it still being mined in the Caucasus. But exploration in the '30's had uncovered another field west of the Urals, in the heart of the Volga drainage basin. The extent of this field was roughly 300 miles from east to west and 600 miles from north to south, approximately two-thirds as large as the state of Texas. In addition, just northeast of the Caspian Sea Russia had the Emba field, and far to the east there were wells on Sakhalin Island.

Venezuela also was enjoying successes in oil. Fortunately the government took an attitude that is fundamental to a successful mining economy. Broadly speaking, the Venezuelan government position was formally cast in the Petroleum Law of 1922, which charted a course followed assiduously by succeeding governments. The sturdiest planks in the Venezuelan platform are these: (1) Any person, national or foreigner, may freely explore and carry on geological investigations in the national territory. (2) A specific governmental department (Inspectoria Tecnica de Hidrocarburos), supervises the oil industry and encourages all efforts to develop it. The effectiveness of this department has been demonstrated by its miraculous ability to maintain a continuity of action even during convulsive political changes and its ability to preserve cordial relations between the industry and the government. (3) The tax burden in oil is kept comparatively lenient, a policy that has helped to make Venezuelan oil the cheapest on earth.

Although the Venezuelan government both owned and controlled the production of all subsoil minerals in the nation, it realistically recognized that a strong mining economy requires both natural resources and the aptitudes needed to develop them. In the early days of her petroleum production, she had only the former, and western Europe had only the latter. So Venezuelan authorities permitted the two to interact. Without this enlightened policy, crude-oil mining in Venezuela would surely be considerably behind its present pace. And the Venezuelan economy, in turn, would be less developed.

The Venezuelan policy is clearly expressed as follows:

A nation in an initial stage of her development from a backward and disorganized agro-pastoral economy in which there suddenly appears, like an unnatural growth, the enormous creation of riches produced by the oil industry and which, in twenty years, changes from being the world's fifth or sixth exporter of coffee to its leading exporter of petroleum, finds herself faced with an upheaval so intense and so dangerous that out of it may come genuine and enduring greatness, or subjection to the fortunes of fuel and oil. This, expressed summarily and even brutally, is the way we should plan in what we may call Venezuela's fundamental economic problem: we must use petroleum to develop Venezuela instead of permitting her future and the course she follows to be diverted and unnaturally displaced by the violent torrents of wealth produced by that industry and by all the special conditions that its existence brings about day after day.*

Before 1920 Venezuela was not wealthy but was self-sufficient in food. The oil boom reversed this situation. The country gradually became more and more wealthy, attaining the highest per capita government budget in Latin

America. Oil provided the government with over half its revenues, which were expended rapidly in an effort to give all Venezuelans a higher standard of living. But meanwhile, paradoxically, Venezuela was losing its ability to feed and clothe itself, and began to import rice, corn, wheat, flour, sugar, meat, textiles, and garments: commodities desired by a people with an increasing purchasing power, no longer satisfied with the modest diet accepted by their forebears.

The Venezuelan story stands in sharp contrast to that of Mexico where the government discouraged oil exploration by foreign technicians. The feud between Mexico's government on the one hand and the American and European oil concerns on the other depressed oil output through the 1920's and the 1930's (notice Table 15-1) until finally, in 1938, the Mexican government took the bold and unprecedented step of expropriating all property and equipment of foreign oil companies, whose activities were thereby abruptly terminated. The 1940 picture shows Mexico, which 20 years earlier had mined 157,000,000 barrels—23 per cent of the world's share—down to 44,000,000, a mere 2 per cent of the world total.

Almost as outstanding as Venezuela's expansion was that in the Middle East. Here, as in Venezuela, the mining economy was based on the blending of resources from two regions: the Middle East contributed the material and the Western world contributed the knowledge to exploit it. The very company names—Anglo-Iranian and Aramco (Arabian-American Company)—epitomize the forces at work. About 40 per cent of the crude oil was piped westward to ports on the Mediterranean Sea for shipping to Europe; a slight amount was moved by tanker from Persian Gulf ports to the same destination. But over half the oil was refined in large factories in new Gulf settlements and then moved by tanker—mostly through the Suez to Europe. Some of the refined product, though, was dispersed widely to markets in Africa and eastern Asia.

Indonesia was progressing, becoming one of the more prolific exporters. Since its market was almost entirely in the Far East, par-

* From Uslar Pietri as quoted by Guillermo Zuloaga in Wallace E. Pratt and Dorothy Good, *op. cit.*, pp. 74-75.

ticularly China and India, where refineries were only scarcely developed, Indonesia processed all its oil before export.

Europe showed a few changes. Romania was still the leader, thanks to the Ploesti fields which in World War II were destined to be a goal for Nazi invasion and then a prime target for Allied aircraft. Germany's petroleum industry showed growth by 1940 in the Hanover district. This area (termed by oilmen as the North German Basin) is underlain by sedimentary rock somewhat like that of the American Gulf Coast field. Austria appeared for the first time; production in the vicinity of Vienna almost equalled home consumption.

The over-all world circulation of oil between nations in 1940 fell, in general, into the following pattern. Major exporters (with percentage of world exports) were:

Venezuela, Trinidad, and Colombia	37%
United States	35
Middle East	17
Indonesia	6
Others	5
	100%

From the three principal export areas, the destination of most of the product was western Europe; but as we noted above, Indonesia's oil went to the Far East.

1950

The economic geography of crude oil in 1950 showed some striking changes. There were no new nations on the scene but there were a variety of new relationships among established producers.

At mid-century the United States maintained its position of leadership, reaching the astonishing record of two billion barrels, but there were two significant developments. First, for all its boom, the United States was slipping in degree of world leadership; other regions were developing even more rapidly and closing the gap, so that for the first time in nearly half a century the United States could not claim appreciably greater production than the rest of the world combined. (The actual percentage in 1950 was 51 per cent—quite a drop from the 71 per cent peak of 23 years earlier.)

The second development was that, for all its production, the United States was now an importer of petroleum. The consumption of gasoline, diesel oil, and other petroleum products had skyrocketed. The number of automobiles in the United States had jumped from 8,000,000 in 1920 to almost 35,000,000 in 1950; diesel engines had displaced steam engines on railroads; millions of homes had discarded coal furnaces and stoves for oil furnaces and heaters; World War II had brought with it an airplane revolution, and the chemical industry now consumed millions of barrels of crude oil as raw material. Thus, the uses of oil for energy in driving engines, for heat, and as a raw material, all shot up so rapidly that they finally exceeded domestic production. Tankers began carrying oil in the opposite direction. From an exporter of oil, mostly to Europe, the United States turned into an importer, mostly from Venezuela.

The most conspicuous novelty on the 1950 map is the Middle East, which now surpassed Caribbean America (Venezuela, Colombia, and Trinidad). Not only did the older fields (Iran and Iraq) enjoy healthy gains, but Arabia's ten-year increase was fabulous (from 5,000,000 to 199,000,000 barrels). Most astonishing of all was the unparalleled debut of a little country whose name was practically unknown outside the Arab World: Kuwait, tucked in between Arabia and Iraq on the Persian Gulf. As late as 1945 Kuwait, a flat, sandy, treeless, hot stretch of desert about the size of Massachusetts, supported on a subsistence economy an unknown number of nomadic herdsmen and a few thousand settlers in villages along the coast. The main export business was pearl fishing. Then in 1946 British and American geologists struck oil. After four short years Kuwait was pumping more oil than any other country in the world except for the United States, Venezuela, the U.S.S.R., and its own neighbors, Iran and Arabia. Rarely in history has so small an area burst so dramatically upon the stage of the world's economy. Being of such recent vintage, the Kuwait oil industry had the advantage of modern methods and equipment so that the average oil well yielded 3700 barrels a day.

The average for each well in Venezuela was 200, in the United States, 11. And the reserves awaiting future mining were enormous, estimated to be half those of the United States.

Another noteworthy development occurred in the Soviet Union, where the Volga-Ural field had experienced a soaring oil boom. This area, located about 450 miles east of Moscow, underlies a vast amount of land in the upper Volga River basin and extends upward into the western foothills of the Urals. Production is centered in the vicinity of Tatar, Bashir, and Kuibyshev, with lesser wells near Saratov and Stalingrad (Volgograd) to the south. Although a little petroleum had been drawn off here before 1940, it was not until 1950 that the field came into its own, accounting for 30 per cent of the Russian total. The opening up of this field was significant in that it occupies a strategic location in the heart of the Soviet Union between two great industrial regions, the Industrial Center and the Urals (discussed in Chapter 25 and shown on Figure 25-1). Moreover, this new field is in an area served by Russia's main railway and waterway systems, and costs of distribution are low.

By 1950, Indonesia's oil mining was recovering from a severe experience. When World War II broke, crude oil was flowing from Indonesian wells at the rate of 60 million barrels a year. War strife cut her production down to 22 million as the Japanese moved in. But when the Japanese evacuated in 1945 they so thoroughly demolished the facilities that the 1946 yield trickled off to only 2 million barrels. Yet recovery was fast (Table 15-1).

Africa's only oil mining was in the far northeastern extremity of the continent, in the Sinai Peninsula. From the standpoint of landform configuration, these small oil fields are really outliers of the Middle East fields. But politically they lie within the boundaries of Egypt, and Egypt (at least for the keeping of statistics) is part of Africa. Yields were small, though, and provided Egypt with only a third of her own needs.

The 1950 pattern of world circulation showed only one minor and two major regions of surplus oil. The Caribbean area provided 50 per cent of the world surplus, the Middle East 45 per cent, and Indonesia a trace. The most profound change since 1940 in this aspect of the industry was the disappearance of the United States from the list of exporters.

Figure 15-5

PETROLEUM PRODUCTION, 1960

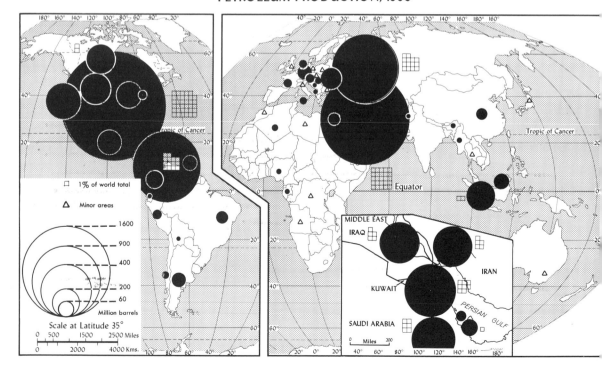

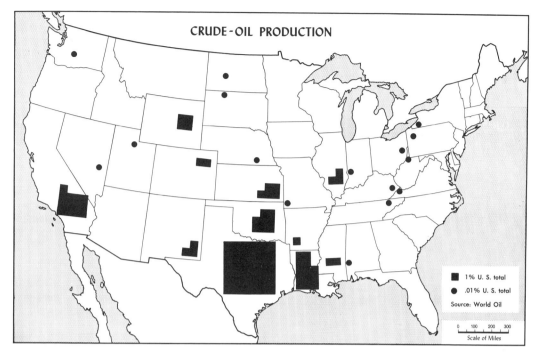

CRUDE-OIL PRODUCTION

■ 1% U. S. total
● .01% U. S. total

Source: World Oil

0 100 200 300
Scale of Miles

Figure 15-6

The world pattern for 1960 was basically the same as that for 1950. Old established areas continued to dominate, although some of the small areas were making unusual progress, notably Canada and western Europe. All told, the world's oil wells yielded over seven billion barrels—more than twice the 1950 output. Practically every producing nation showed an increase. Distinction depended not on growth, but on rate of growth.

The United States retained first rank and reported yields in two-thirds of the states. Texas alone produced almost one billion barrels. Other important oil states were Louisiana, California, Oklahoma, and Wyoming in that order. But the mining of crude oil was expanding not only in terms of barrels from leading states but also in terms of numbers of states mining any oil at all. Thirty-two of the 48 contiguous states were producing some crude oil.

But United States production had begun to slip—both absolutely and relatively. A peak of 2,617,283,000 barrels had been attained in

1956, and 1960 marked the fourth consecutive year in which production had been less than that maximum. Moreover, the United States percentage of world total had steadily dropped —to 35 per cent. But this is not surprising. In an economic activity like petroleum mining, with reserves widespread among several countries, only the most naive would expect that any single nation could long maintain so disproportionate a share of world production as did Russia in 1900 or this country in 1927.

Canada is enjoying an oil boom in her prairie provinces—particularly Alberta. Unfortunately, since Canada's petroleum is considerably farther from her center of population than is the case in the United States, great transportation problems must be overcome.

The most eye-catching advance is going on in the Middle East with Kuwait now the leader there. Only three other nations (United States, U.S.S.R., and Venezuela) produce as much oil as does this amazing little nation.

Within the Soviet Union the Volga-Ural field, which had overtaken the Caucasian field in the early 1950's, was rocketing upward and by 1960 was accounting for 67 per cent of

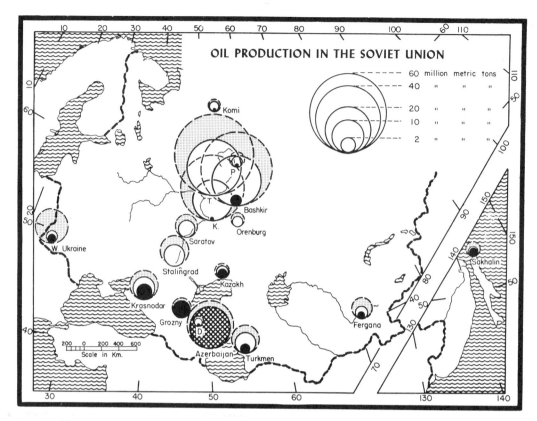

Figure 15-7 *Black circles = 1940 production; white circles = 1958 production; outermost circles = 1965 plan. For the Azerbaijan area 1958 production (crossed lines) was less than 1940 which equaled the 1965 plan. (Courtesy Paul Lydolph, Theodore Shabad and Annals of the Association of American Geographers.)*

Russian petroleum production. This astonishing performance ranks the Volga-Ural area as one of the world's foremost producers of crude oil and suggests that this will be Russia's main source of supply for many years to come. As recently as 1940 it appeared that 80 per cent of Russian oil reserves were in the Caucasus; but by 1955 the evidence provided by new discoveries showed that 80 per cent of Russian oil reserves were in the Volga-Ural area, which is closer to both Russian consumer and producer markets than is the Caucasus.

Western Europe has shown a surprising development since 1950. Thirteen European nations now mine oil, and their combined production almost equals that of the Far East.

REGIONS OF CONSUMPTION

Most of the world's petroleum is consumed in Anglo-America; the United States and Canada together take 56 per cent of the world total. Western Europe takes 18 per cent and the Soviet Union 9. That leaves only 19 per cent for the rest of the world. Petroleum consumption plainly correlates with a high degree of industrialization—the bulk of the product is used up in regions that are rich in both producer goods (such as factory machines, railroads, trucks) and consumer goods (such as automobiles, oil furnaces, and so on). This relationship will be more apparent after we have studied the chapters dealing with manufacturing (Chapters 17-25).

INTERNATIONAL TRADE

Because of the marked discrepancy between regions of production and regions of consumption, a tremendous volume of oil moves between regions—this transfer is one of the great movements in international trade in the

Table 15-3 *World Petroleum: Demand and Supply Regions, 1960*
(in Thousands of Barrels per Day)

Region	Domestic Demand	Domestic Supply	Excess Demand	Excess Supply	Percentage of World Total Demand	Percentage of World Total Supply
WORLD	20,466	20,641		175	100	100
North America	10,830	8,813	2,017		49	40
United States	9,677	7,977	1,700		44	36
Canada	860	542	318		4	2
South America	1,431	3,492		2,061	7	16
Venezuela	164	2,866		2,702	*	13
Europe	4,539	651	3,888		21	3
U.S.S.R.	2,500	3,020		520	11	13
Africa	495	285	210		2	1
Middle East	589	5,247		4,658	3	24
Far East, Oceania	1,654	649	1,005		7	3

Source: *World Oil*, August 1961, p. 72.
* Less than one per cent.

mid-twentieth century. The main supply and demand areas are tabulated in Table 15-3. Just two regions produce much surplus petroleum: the Middle East and Venezuela. Oil accounts for a staggering 95 per cent of all export revenues for Venezuela; similarly, almost all of the sales abroad made by businesses in Iran, Iraq, Arabia, and Kuwait are petroleum and its derivatives. In Arabia and Kuwait oil payments to local authorities go directly to the ruling power. During the pre-oil era in Arabia, Ibn Saud had an annual income of $16,000,000, mostly from tourists (pilgrims to Mecca); in 1955 it was $125,000,000, mostly from oil. Sheik Abdullah of Kuwait gets royalties of $200,000,000 a year—by far the largest annual income of any man on earth. Overnight these economies have seen the Cadillac take its place alongside the camel as a means of transportation.

As Table 15-3 also indicates, Europe and the United States are the most significant deficit areas. The resulting flow pattern encompasses two chief arteries: from the Middle East to western Europe and from the Caribbean to Anglo-America.

Notice particularly the setting in the Middle East. Two-thirds of the oil moves out by tanker as a processed product from Persian Gulf refining centers—including Abadan in Iran, the world's largest refinery in capacity, Ras Tanura in Arabia, Bahrein in the Persian Gulf 15 miles from Arabia, and Mina-Al-Ahmade in Kuwait. But the other third moves in crude form westward via several pipelines. The older ones link the northerly fields of Iraq (in the vicinity of Kirkuk) with Banias in Syria and Tripoli in Lebanon—two other lines formerly connected Kirkuk with Haifa and Acre in Israel, but these are no longer in use. A newer line connects Persian Gulf fields with Sidon in Lebanon. These pipelines must go through one or more of the following nations: Jordan, Syria, and Lebanon, none of which produce much oil. But the economies of these countries are bolstered by revenues from transit fees and income from transshipping services at the ports. Jordan, for example, buys ten times as much from abroad as she sells; revenues from pipeline rights make up most of the difference. Lebanon imports four times the value of her exports; the deficit is largely compensated for by income

Drilling for oil in northern Kuwait. The Kuwait Oil Company is owned jointly by Gulf Oil Corporation of the United States and British Petroleum Company, Limited, of Great Britain; it operates on a concession from the government of Kuwait. Wells in this area are drilled to depths of 10,000 feet. (Courtesy World Oil and British Petroleum Co.)

from the oil transport business. But another consequence is that if the nations that lie between the oil and the market are so disposed, they can disrupt that flow whether by tanker through the Suez Canal (the canal was blocked for almost a year, 1956-57, by Egyptian-European friction) or by pipeline. Cessation of flow over the two older pipelines from Kirkuk to Haifa and Acre is attributable to strife between the Jewish state and Arab nations.

For the United States, the pendulum continues to swing. Until after World War II (except for the brief period of 1920-1922) our exports always exceeded our imports. As recently as 1942 we shipped out three times as much oil and oil products as we imported. Then things changed; 1947-48 saw the pendulum pass the point of balance. Since then our deficit has steadily increased. Today we produce only 80 per cent of our demand. Two-thirds of the inbound crude oil and refined products originate in Venezuela; but 15 per cent of our imports of *crude* oil come from Canada. We also receive a little oil from the Middle East. Foreign oil can be marketed in the United States more cheaply than much

of the domestic product because of (a) lower labor costs, (b) newer efficient wells abroad, and (c) savings in production costs abroad, and (d) cheap ocean transport (the cost is so low it does not cancel out the savings attributable to the foregoing factors). Domestic producers suffer from this competition and have put pressure on Congress to restrict imports. In 1957 the Office of Defense Mobilization responded by ordering a 10 per cent reduction on crude oil imports into all areas except the West Coast.

THE FUTURE

In volume, the known world reserves of petroleum in 1960 totaled 266 billion barrels —enough to last 35 years at the 1960 rate of consumption (quite a contrast to the world coal situation).

In location, the world's petroleum *reserves* conform to a different pattern from that of production (see Table 15-1). An astounding 60 per cent of known reserves are in the Middle East! Little Kuwait has the nearly unbelievable portion of 23 per cent—more than any other country in the world and over half again as much as the entire United States!

Oil and Gas: A Study in Historical Geography

Saudi Arabia ranks second. Iraq has approximately as much in known reserves as the Soviet Union. Iran's reserves equal those of all South America. No other facts portray so telling a story of the future significance of the Middle East to the world's economy.

Within the United States most of the known petroleum reserves are located in the very regions that now mine it. Texas has almost half our crude-oil resource.

Prophets of doom cry that what remains in United States pools (some 30 billion barrels) will be used up in 12 or 13 years at the present rate of mining (Table 15-4). This is indeed a gloomy prospect. But in 1924 our known reserves were only 7½ billion barrels—in a year when we mined 713,000,000 barrels; even

then the wail might have been that we had only enough oil to last ten years! Had no new oil been discovered, the wells would have run dry in 1934. Fortunately, a trend has prevailed so far that, as oil miners increased their production, oil prospectors discovered more new oil than was mined. So the United States now has more oil than she has known at any previous time. Table 15-4 (Column D) documents this principle. But Table 15-4 is worth closer scrutiny. It tells a fascinating story. What, for example, is the implication of the data in column E (which is an index number of years which the known reserve would have lasted if (a) consumption had remained constant, and (b) no new reserves had been discovered)?

Table 15-4 United States: Estimated Proved Resources of Crude Oil, by Selected Years (in Thousands of Barrels)

Year	A Reserves at Start of Year	B Additional Reserves Discovered That Year	C Mined That Year	D Reserves at End of Year	E Index: Column D/C
1920	6,700,000	942,929	442,929	7,200,000	16.3
1930	13,200,000	1,298,011	898,011	13,600,000	15.1
1940	18,483,012	1,893,350	1,351,847	19,024,515	14.1
1945	20,453,231	2,110,299	1,736,717	20,826,813	12.0
1950	24,649,489	2,562,685	1,943,776	25,268,393	13.0
1955	29,560,746	2,870,724	2,419,300	30,012,170	12.4
1960	31,719,347	2,468,797	2,574,933	31,613,211	11.8

Source: *World Oil,* February 15, 1958, p. 126, February 15, 1961, pp. 81 and 100, and August, 1961, p. 76.

Natural Gas

Crude oil generally occurs with natural gas. But the geography of mining natural gas is quite different from that of crude oil for the simple reason that whereas oil is easily trapped at the wells and lends itself to shipment via barrels, tank cars, trucks, barges, or ocean tankers, gas readily escapes at the wells, and what is trapped can be transported feasibly only by pipelines. Gas is an economic product only in those mining areas that are close enough to market to be connected by pipeline. Accordingly, most of the world's natural gas is "produced" in the United States, Russia, and Europe.

Within the United States, natural gas has experienced a dramatically growing role in the nation's total production of inanimate energy. In 1900 it accounted for about the same volume of energy as water power—3 per cent of the national total. In those days coal was responsible for almost nine-tenths of such energy production. Subsequent years have seen a rapid shift in relative importance of energy sources. Table 15-5, page 270, reveals that by 1960 coal's share had dropped from 88 to 27 per cent, water power had remained steady at around 3 or 4 per cent, while petroleum and natural gas had soared from 8 to 69 per

Table 15-5 United States:
Inanimate Energy Production

Source of Power	Trillions of BTU's			Percentages		
	1900	1930	1960	1900	1930	1960
Bituminous coal and lignite	5,563	12,249	10,886	71	55	26
Anthracite	1,457	1,762	478	18	8	1
Crude petroleum	369	5,208	14,935	5	24	36
Natural gas	254	2,148	13,822	3	10	33
Water power	250	752	1,723	3	3	4
Total	7,893	22,119	41,844	100	100	100

Source: United States Department of the Interior, Bureau of Mines, *Minerals Yearbook 1960*, Volume II, pp. 4-5.

cent. Today, crude oil and gas have almost equal shares of the nation's total inanimate power output.

In view of the foregoing indication of the importance of natural gas, its treatment in these pages is disproportionately brief. Two reasons may be cited. First and foremost, very little research has, as yet, been done in analyzing the geography of natural gas. Secondly, although natural gas has overtaken coal as a source of energy in the United States, gas is still far behind coal and oil in meeting the world's energy demands.

Within the United States, 14 per cent of the natural gas "produced" (that is, removed from the ground) is either lost to the atmosphere, is burned for energy on the producing property, or returned to the underground reservoir for repressuring. Consequently, only 86 per cent of the production is available for commercial sale. Production of commercial gas occurs in 27 states, but the great bulk comes from wells in Texas and Louisiana, which, together, account for almost 70 per cent of the national total. See Figure 15-8 and Table 15-6.

In the United States, the major use for gas, the heating of residences and commercial buildings, accounts for 40 per cent of natural gas consumption. Furthermore, gas now has overtaken both coal and oil in providing heat to these customers. Indeed, in some states, gas outsells all other fuels combined in meeting this market—particularly in the states listed in Table 15-6. At the other extreme are New England, the Carolinas, and Florida, which

Figure 15-8 (*After James Lindberg.*)

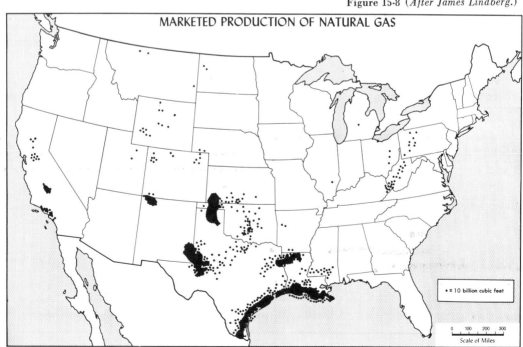

MARKETED PRODUCTION OF NATURAL GAS

• = 10 billion cubic feet

0 100 200 300
Scale of Miles

Oil and Gas: A Study in Historical Geography

Table **15-6** *Production of Natural Gas for Sale, by Leading States*

Area	Billions of Cubic Feet	Percentage
United States	12,771	100
Texas	5,892	46
Louisiana	2,988	23
Oklahoma	824	7
New Mexico	798	6
Kansas	634	5
California	517	4
West Virginia	208	2

Source: United States Bureau of Mines, *Minerals Yearbook 1960*, Volume II, p. 321.

neither produce gas nor are well-served by gas pipelines (see Figure 26-12). These states, however, are well served by oil tankers and, accordingly, depend for space-heating more upon petroleum derivatives, or (to a steadily decreasing degree) upon coal, which is more costly and less convenient than oil.

About 15 per cent of the marketed gas is consumed by thermal-electric generating plants. Indeed, almost all the electricity produced by public utilities in the Southwest is from generators driven by gas-fired boilers.

Suggested Readings

Abrahamson, Sherman R., "The Shifting Geographic Center of Petroleum Production and Its Effect on Pricing Systems," *Economic Geography*, 1952, pp. 295-301.

Alexandersson, Gunnar, "The Oil Refineries Of The World—A Case Study," *Proceedings of IGU Regional Conference in Japan 1957*, pp. 260-266.

Jordan, Constantin N., *The Romanian Oil Industry*, New York, 1955, 357 pp.

Lindberg, James, *Selected Aspects of the Geography of Natural Gas in the United States*, unpublished Ph.D. dissertation, University of Wisconsin, 1962.

Lydolph, Paul E., and Shabad, Theodore, "The Oil and Gas Industries in the U.S.S.R.," *Annals of the Association of American Geographers*, 1960, pp. 461-486.

McNee, Robert B., "Centrifugal-Centripetal Forces in International Petroleum Company Regions," *Annals of the Association of American Geographers*, 1961, pp. 124-138.

Melamid, Alexander, "The Geographical Pattern of Iranian Oil Development," *Economic Geography*, 1959, pp. 199-218.

————, "Geographical Distribution of Petroleum Refining Capacities: A Study of the European Refining Program," *Economic Geography*, 1955, pp. 168-178.

————, "Geography of the World Petroleum Price Structure," *Economic Geography*, 1962, pp. 283-298.

Netschert, Bruce C., *The Future Supply of Oil and Gas*, Baltimore, 1958.

Parsons, James J., "The Geography of Natural Gas in the United States," *Economic Geography*, 1950, pp. 162-178.

————, "The Natural Gas Supply of California," *Land Economics*, 1958, pp. 19-36.

Pratt, Wallace E. and Good, Dorothy, editors, *World Geography of Petroleum*, Princeton, 1950, 464 pp.

Spangler, Miller B., *New Technology and the Supply of Petroleum*, Chicago, 1956.

The Berkeley Copper Pit cuts deep into the earth by Butte, Montana.
Butte, 32 per cent of whose workers are employed in mining, is one of the few American
cities that has been losing population; from a peak of 41,611 in 1920, it has dropped
to 39,532 in 1930, 37,081 in 1940, 33,251 in 1950,
and 27,877 in 1960. (Courtesy The Anaconda Company.)

SIXTEEN

In the two preceding chapters we considered the mining of selected minerals, giving major attention to location, making only occasional remarks about characteristics and relationships. The purposes of this chapter are to make some observations about location and characteristics of mining activities in general and then to give closer attention to the topic of relationships.

LOCATION

Regions of the World   When we assemble all our jigsaw pieces of fact about the location of each individual mineral and fit them into a world-wide composite view of all mining, we can discern several regions of concentration. In the Western Hemisphere a wide zone spans the North American continent from the Atlantic to the Pacific and extends from southern Canada to central Mexico. A second region runs like a ribbon from Nicaragua to Chile; there are outlying clusters in northern Venezuela, the Guianas, and southeastern Brazil. In the Eastern Hemisphere a broad region that begins at the Atlantic coast of Europe runs eastward into southern U.S.S.R. and southward through the Balkan nations into Arabia and Iran. The Ural Hills stand out conspicuously as a north-south mining belt. A narrow band also runs east-west through the center of Asia. In southeastern Asia mining is found all the way from Japan and Manchuria on the east through southern China to India on the west. Burma, Malaya, and Indonesia can be included in this region. Australia, like South America, is almost encircled with a peripheral pattern of mining. Africa has a long and wide zone that extends from South Africa to Ethiopia, with a secondary section along the Guinea Coast. Elsewhere there are scattered mining operations, though they are small in scale.

Thus, commercial mining appears on every continent, but mostly in the mid-latitudes, primarily in those of the Northern Hemisphere.

Regions in the United States   We can construct a more accurate map of mining for the United States than for the world because more information is available. Figure 16-1 shows the location of mining in terms of numbers of people employed. The most conspicuous region is the Appalachian belt which stretches 500 miles from western New York to northeastern Alabama. Luzerne and Schuylkill counties, in northeastern Pennsylvania's coal district, exceed all other counties in the nation in terms of mining employment. Figure 16-1 is an example of the type of map that can be constructed when employment data are available for areal units as small as counties.

It is based on data in the United States *Census of Population*, Volume II, "Characteristics of the Population," one of the world's most detailed sources of published facts on the numbers of people engaged in specific economic activities in small areal units. The United States Government also publishes the *Census of Mineral Industries* that gives figures on other measurements, such as value of product mined. But this census withholds data on counties where publication would reveal information about individual companies.

CHARACTERISTICS

Two key characteristics for distinguishing mining regions are source of employment and value of mined product.

Employment in Specific Types of Mining   The combinations of minerals that support mining employees differ widely from place to place in the United States. Texas and Pennsylvania are the leading states in number of employees, but they are markedly unalike in the distribution of workers in mining industries: 97 per cent of Texas's miners are

Figure 16-1

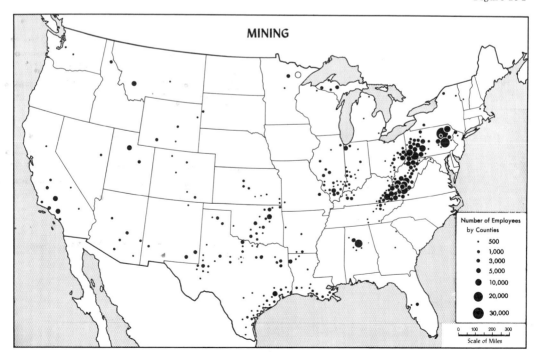

Mining: General Observations

engaged by the petroleum and natural gas industries while 82 per cent of Pennsylvania's are connected with coal. Oklahoma, Kansas, Louisiana, and California report that employment in oil and gas accounts for over 80 per cent of their total mining labor force. Other high percentages appear in Minnesota (95 per cent in iron ore), Arizona (92 per cent in copper), West Virginia (87 per cent in coal), Massachusetts (95 per cent in sand, gravel, and crushed stone), and Florida (75 per cent in phosphate rock). For the United States as a whole, employment in specific mining industries is shown in Table 16-1. Unfortunately, comparable data for the rest of the world are unavailable.

Value of Types of Products Mined

We have inadequate information for measuring the value of each mined product by individual nations; however, such figures are available for the United States. Statistics on

Table 16-1 United States Mining

Product	Number of Mines, Quarries, or Wells	Value of Shipments in Millions of Dollars	Thousands of Persons Engaged
U. S. TOTAL	513,128	$14,906	825
Metallic ores	3,356	1,506	103
Iron	298	547	34
Copper	201	508	28
Lead and zinc	491	175	17
Gold and silver	528	46	5
Ferro-alloys	1,042	153	9
Fuels	440,330	9,118	438
Bituminous coal and lignite	6,841	2,068	226
Anthracite	1,263	408	39
Crude oil and gas	432,226	6,642	173
Gas only	53,681	427	12
Nonmetals, nonfuels	8,054	1,582	119
Sand and gravel	3,949	466	40
Crushed stone	1,882	465	38
Chemical minerals	298	457	21
Potash	20	107	6
Phosphate	73	117	5
Sulfur	16	140	4
Clay	673	103	8
Dimension stone	352	18	3

Source: United States Department of Commerce, *Census of Mineral Industries, 1954*, General Summary, Table 2.

value of shipments for the leading products are given in Table 16-1. By value, petroleum (with natural gas) is three times as important as the nation's next-ranking mineral, coal, which is almost four times as valuable as iron ore or copper. Coal and oil also provide the most jobs. But perhaps surprisingly, sand and gravel support the third largest payroll— more even than iron. And the mining of crushed stone employs more people than does either iron or copper mining. Indeed, the mining of nonmetallic solids (sand, gravel, stone, sulfur, phosphate, clay) collectively provides employment to more people and yields as valuable shipments as does the mining of all the metallic ores.

During the last four decades, mining in the United States has shown contrasting trends. The number of employees has declined from an all-time peak of 1,084,000 in 1919 to 800,-000 in the early 1960's. But the number of mines increased in that time from 14,417 to 20,736 and the value of shipments shot up from $3,158,000,000 to $15,147,000,000.

PHYSICAL RELATIONSHIPS

Mining in any region is related with many physical factors, such as the resource pyramid, depth of mineral deposit, surface topography, subsurface conditions, natural waterways, and climate.

The Resource Pyramid

In the distribution of mineral resources, quantity and quality are inversely related. The pattern is like a three-tiered pyramid. The base of the pyramid consists of tremendous quantities of low-grade deposits widely distributed around the world. In the middle are moderate amounts of moderate-grade deposits which are less widely scattered. At the apex there are small amounts of high-grade deposits located in only a few areas. The rule holds that the higher the quality the less the reserve and the more restricted in location.

Herein lies a problem, for man is skimming the cream from the top of this resource pyramid. In the future he may face increased costs of exploiting the low-quality deposits in the mines now in operation, or else face high transport charges if he taps remote but rich sources. Still, there is always the hope that science will discover new techniques for cheaply processing the poor residue in mines from which the best has already been taken.

Depth of Mineral Deposits

Minerals at the earth's surface are obviously less costly to mine than those far underground. For the shallow deposits, *strip* or *open-pit* methods can be used whereby miners simply carry away the surface materials, digging downward and outward for as far as the mineral is rich enough and property rights can be acquired at a reasonable cost. Surface deposits are a large part of the explanation of the success of the Mesabi Range (where the mines are a series of tremendous open pits, some 300 feet deep and several hundred feet wide), of Bingham Canyon copper mines, and of the southern Ohio coal fields. These places have some of the most mechanized mining on earth; in some of them huge electric shovels scoop out 16 tons of ore per bite. In the United States, one out of every four tons of bituminous coal is mined in open pits, and in some states open pits yield more coal than do underground mines. For the leading states, here is the amount of coal in millions of tons mined by each type of mine annually:

Table 16-2 *Coal Mined, in Millions of Tons*

State	Open Pit	Underground
West Virginia	9	126
Pennsylvania	20	64
Kentucky	13	54
Illinois	18	27
Ohio	23	12
Indiana	11	4

Certain foreign areas, such as the Kiruna iron mines, also enjoy the savings of strip-mining methods. Kiruna, however, faces costly readjustments because the most accessible ore is nearly gone. Shortly after World War II the first shaft-mines began producing; about 10 per cent of the ore there is now shaft-mined, and by 1975 probably all of it will be.

Surface Topography

Flat topography expedites strip-mining, but a rough surface can also simplify operations by permitting *drifting*. In this method, horizontal tunnels are driven into the side of a hill in which mineral deposits occur in nearly horizontal strata (see Figure 16-2). The erosion of valleys performs the same function as the construction of mine shafts by providing access to mineral deposits too deep for strip-mining.

Subsurface Conditions

A combination of generally flat topography and unusual subsurface structure has given the East Central coal field of the United States a distinctive pattern of mining. Subsurface rock strata have been warped into the shape of a bowl. At this bowl's edges where the coal seams meet the earth's surface, strip-mines are numerous. But shaft-mines typify the interior of this area.

Shaft-mining is undertaken most easily where subsurface conditions meet the following specifications: rock layers are horizontal, there has been little or no *faulting* (the movement of rock masses vertically along fractures), and minerals occur in thick layers. Horizontal layers facilitate the blasting, cutting, loading, and hauling of minerals in underground work rooms. Such operations are obviously awkward and hazardous in rock layers that dip at steep angles. But even where the seams are horizontal, faulting prevents continuous mining on the same floor and necessitates changes in level of operation. Thick seams are of course easier to work than thin, for in one, say, two feet thick, miners must either work flat on their stomachs or expend effort in digging out dross rock to make work room.

Subsurface water is a nuisance in most mines. Strip-mines can become temporary lakes after heavy rains, and shaft-mines can turn into drainage channels where underground water collects. So a big item of expense is pumping out water. In this matter drift-mines, which enter hills on a slight upgrade, have a peculiar advantage—for ground water simply runs out of the tunnel by gravity flow.

Mining: General Observations

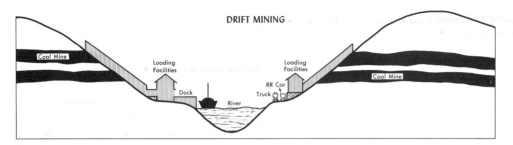

DRIFT MINING

Figure 16-2 *This sketch diagrams the position of* drift *mines in horizontal rock strata in areas of hilly terrain.*

Figure 16-3 *This sketch suggests some of the difficulties in mining of rock formations which have been deformed by folding and faulting.*

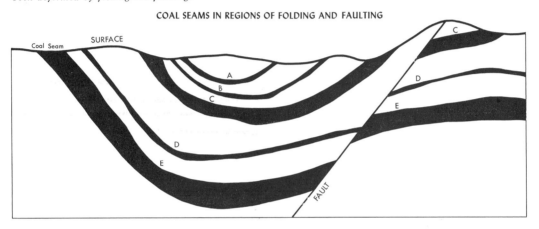

COAL SEAMS IN REGIONS OF FOLDING AND FAULTING

Natural Waterways Drift-mines often enjoy another peculiar advantage because their mine entrances, on valley sides, are adjacent to valley bottoms, some of which contain navigable rivers.

Water transportation routes, indeed, are sometimes the critical factor in transforming a region from a mineral reserve to a mining center. We have already encountered many contemporary examples of this point. The Great Lakes link the iron ore of the Lake Superior district with the coal of Appalachia. Who can tell what the status of Sweden's Kiruna would be were it not for the ocean highway that runs from Narvik to the coal belt of central Europe? Fortunately for Venezuela, her newly discovered ore fields lie close to the Orinoco waterways and not far from the greatest waterway of all, the ocean. Quebec-Labrador iron ore moves up the St. Lawrence River to the manufacturing heart of Anglo-America and down that river to the Atlantic Ocean and eastern United States ports. For nearly three centuries before 1900, Great Britain was the world's leading coal producer, partly because, being surrounded by the sea, her mines were all close to ocean shipping. Three of her major coal fields—Northumberland-Durham, the Scottish Lowlands, and South Wales—actually front on tidewater. The ports of Newcastle in the first-named area and Cardiff in the third became the world's leading coal suppliers.

Climate Climate relates to mining in two different ways. Historically, certain types of climate favored the formation of mineral deposits. Two examples are coal (vegetative growth of the type favorable to coal requires a warm moist climate) and bauxite (formed by weathering of feldspar rock in tropical moist climates.

Currently, climate affects both extraction and transportation. Obviously, surface mines have trouble operating in freezing temperatures—the new Quebec-Labrador mines, for instance, are *closed* 200 days a year because of weather. Moreover, there seems to be some correlation between stormy weather and mine explosions. For example, the air in shaft coal mines contains two compounds which are particularly prone to ignite: methane gas and coal dust. In a revealing article, C. B. McIntosh reports evidence that the passage of low pressure areas over mining regions correlates closely with increased methane in the air within the mines and that atmospheric *fronts* correlate with increased coal dust.*

Finally, severe winter climates block many waterways. As we saw, this is the main reason why Kiruna ore is exported through Narvik instead of Luleå. Transportation from Lake Superior's ranges is icebound four months of the year. And that which moves by rail in winter must be specially treated to keep it from freezing solid in the hopper cars.

CULTURAL RELATIONSHIPS

The relationships of mining and culture are reciprocal. Such relationships are discernible in population distribution, manufacturing, prices, technical discoveries, railroads and canals, mining settlements, economic bases, problems of land-use, political boundaries, and conservation problems.

Population Distribution From the world viewpoint, regions of mining tend to be comparatively densely inhabited. Yet the correlation is not perfect since some populous areas have little mining; for instance, China and India. Other factors appear to be more strongly associated with mining, notably manufacturing.

Manufacturing Since most minerals must be processed before man can use them, there is a rather close world-wide locational correlation between mining and manufac-

turing. This correlation holds particularly well if our unit of measurement is the nation: The countries that are the manufacturers are also the leading miners. (We shall elaborate on this relationship in Part Six.)

But on a finer areal scale, manufacturing correlates more closely with coal mining than with any other type of mining. This is because of coal's versatility as a fuel, as a source of power, and as a raw material. Consequently, many minerals are shipped toward coal-mining regions for final manufacturing. Some minerals, though, do go through preliminary stages of manufacturing in factories located near the mines, particularly low-grade metallic ores. Much of the dross can be separated by crushing the mined rocks and sorting out the mineral-bearing particles by washing, filtering, and precipitating. Such separation of dross by *mechanical* methods is termed *concentration*, and the factories that perform such operations are called *concentrators*. Mechanical methods however do not remove impurities in chemical union with the metal; such purification requires more elaborate techniques that are often applied in factories located far from the mines (see Chapters 19 and 20).

The significant fact for the geographer is that concentrators tend to locate in mining areas in order to avoid paying transport charges on dross. This tendency is well illustrated by the copper industry. Of every 100 tons of most copper ore, 98 tons are dross and only two tons are copper. Why pay freight on those 98 tons? Generally, the *lower* the percentage of metal contained in the ore, the *stronger* the tendency for concentrators to locate near mines. This principle holds for all ore mining, including iron ore and ferro-alloys. For some minerals, like copper, which average a very low percentage of metal, virtually every mining area has concentrators. But for other ores, like iron, which may yield high percentages (up to 70 per cent) of metal, very few mining areas support concentrators.

In some iron-mining localities man has proceeded to remove all the high-grade ores and is down to the low-grade ones. In the Lake Superior region, for example, 64 billion

* "Atmospheric Conditions and Explosions in Coal Mines," *Geographical Review*, Vol. 42, April, 1957, pp. 155-174.

tons of ore remain, but only one billion tons are as rich in iron as 50 per cent; less than three billion tons have a 30 to 50 per cent iron content; but there are 60 billion tons of low-grade iron ore (20 to 30 per cent iron content) called *taconite*, much of which is silica. Traditional methods for processing are too costly to apply to taconite, so the Lake Superior iron region faced a dark future until technologists devised a process for crushing taconite and removing the silica, leaving a residue that is 60 per cent iron and can be profitably shipped to distant blast furnaces. Taconite processing mills (or concentrators) have been constructed recently in northeastern Minnesota and are now in operation.

Prices The value that factories place on minerals largely determines whether mining authorities judge a rock to be an ore or not. The general situation is clear enough, though few precise details are available. Geographers need to do a good deal more research on the geography of prices not only for minerals

A large taconite processing plant at Silver Bay, Minnesota. Low-grade iron ore comes from mines in the eastern end of Minnesota's Mesabi Range. The rock is first crushed into small sizes (three-inch diameter) at Babbitt for shipment by private railroad 47 miles to Silver Bay. Here the rock is pulverized, the ore-bearing particles being separated from sand, clay, and other dross and then formed into pellets. Large stockpiles of pellets (in the left center of the picture) await shipment on lake freighters, one of which is shown approaching the loading dock. In what was formerly almost unsettled wilderness, Silver Bay has been laid out as a new town (in background) with over 700 homes plus shopping centers, schools, churches, and other urban attributes. (Courtesy Reserve Mining Company.)

but for all economic items.* But price alone is only part of the story; for mining soon ceases when production costs exceed prices (whether consumer payments or government supports). The point is emphasized here because the demand for minerals as expressed in *price* is such a clear-cut example of this force at work.

Technical Discoveries For over three centuries western Europe was the unquestioned world leader in mining because it had a large number of people, extensive manufacturing, and a consequent demand for minerals reflected in high prices. But another force was at work too—discovery and invention. Human beings first learned to use iron about 1400 B.C. in China. If "early start" were the main factor in a region's economy, China should be a major market for iron ore today. But those early techniques were unable to process very large amounts of iron, which remained for many centuries a precious metal. It was in the minds of men in western Europe that the ideas unfolded for making large masses of iron available. Around 1300 A.D. Catalonian artisans in northeastern Spain developed the *Catalan Forge*, a furnace large and strong enough for developing high temperatures capable of separating large quantities of iron out from ore.

When the Moors invaded Spain, the ironmasters fled northward to the Meuse Valley in Belgium, a metal-working center. Here they developed the Catalan forge into a full-fledged blast furnace, using charcoal as the fuel. But charcoal supplies became scarce as oak and chestnut forests disappeared. A new fuel was needed. The process for making coke from coal finally solved the problem—another discovery of a European, this time an Englishman. (The first record of making coke from coal was in 1590 when a patent was granted to John Thornborough of York, England. Its first use was in the drying of malt.)

The idea for the steam engine, which un-

leashed a tremendous demand for both iron and coal, also flowered in Europe—in the mind of James Watt in 1776. It was in Europe also that the idea was born in the mind of England's Henry Bessemer for converting large amounts of iron into steel. Then in 1878 Sir William Siemens of England invented the electric furnace for making steel. That same year Gilchrist and Thomas (two Welshmen) discovered the technique for recovering iron from ores blighted with phosphorus.

These inventions strongly emphasize the truth that the origin and spread of ideas is as significant to the geography of mining as is variation in the physical environment. For inventions played fundamental roles in Europe's development as the leading region in world mining.

Railways and Canals Hand in hand with mining has gone the construction of railways and canals. Western Germany, northern France, and Belgium are interlaced with canals that carry heavy tonnages of coal, metallic ore, petroleum, sand, gravel, stone, and other minerals. A strong impetus in the construction of the Sault Saint Marie canals between Lakes Superior and Huron was the demand for ore shipment. For decades the St. Lawrence Seaway along the Ontario-New York boundary was proposed; yet time after time it was approved by the Canadian government only to be rejected by the United States. Then two developments in iron ore caused the United States government to change its mind: a decline in quality of Lake Superior ores and the opening up of the Quebec-Labrador field. America's steel mills in Chicago, Detroit, Cleveland, and Pittsburgh, long dependent on Superior ores, could still feed off rich ore if a waterway linked them to the St. Lawrence as the Great Lakes linked them to Superior.

One impulse for railroad-building, too, was the need to link mines with waterways. Witness the net of railways in northeastern Minnesota and in the Appalachian coal fields (Figure 26-1) and the 357-mile railway that links Quebec-Labrador iron with Seven Islands, its terminal port on the St. Lawrence. In Russia, too, prospects for coal and iron mining in the

---

* A solid beginning is William Warntz's "The Geography of Prices and Spatial Interaction," The Regional Science Association, *Papers and Proceedings*, 1957, pp. 118-136, and his *Toward a Geography of Price* (Philadelphia, 1959), 117 pp.

Sewell, Chile, the settlement at the El Teniente copper mine in rugged terrain of the Andes Mountains. (*Courtesy of Kennecott Copper Corporation; photo by Bob Borowicz.*)

Karaganda, Kuznetzk, and Irkutzk areas played a potent role in the construction of the Trans-Siberian Railway.

For United States railways, minerals constitute 65 per cent of revenue tonnage and generate 22 per cent of freight revenues. Coal, the single most important commodity, accounts for 32 per cent of the tonnage and 16 per cent of the revenue.

Mining Settlements Within mining regions distinctive settlements take root. The small ones contain the homes of a few miners who commute out to the mines just as fishermen and foresters commute out from fishing villages and forest communities. The large mining settlements include, in addition, company headquarters and railroad yards for joining loaded gondola and hopper cars (a few from each of many mines) to make complete trains. Beyond these bare statements, there is little we can add. For, as with fishing or forest villages, the geographer encounters a dearth of information. What are the characteristics of mining towns that distinguish them from other types of settlement? Do mining communities differ enough among themselves to distinguish coal towns from iron ore towns, or are they all essentially the same regardless of the mineral mined? The questions await careful analysis. What we need is a system of classification so that we can map the United States, and the world, showing regions by types of *mining settlement*. It should be possible to devise such a classification in terms of observable features, of functions in regional economic life, and of local problems.

We do know something about the simpler

matter of location, though. Northeastern Minnesota is an excellent example of a region where mining makes a conspicuous impact upon the location of settlements. The over-all population density is low and there are few cities. But the Mesabi, Cuyuna, and Vermillion iron ranges have lured those few to locate in a pattern closely corresponding to the distribution of the ore. In the 60 miles from Grand Rapids at the southwest to Aurora in the northeast there are 30 settlements strung out like beads in a necklace. Hibbing (17,700 inhabitants) and Virginia (14,000) are the largest of these communities. To encounter another city at least as large as Hibbing one would have to travel 60 miles southeast (to Duluth), 160 miles south (to Minneapolis), 180 miles west (to Fargo), and 250 miles northwest (to Winnipeg).

Economic Base   This is a convenient point at which to illustrate the concept of *economic base*. A region's *economic base* consists of the activities that support the livelihood of its inhabitants.

The importance of mining in the economic base can be measured by means of a simple ratio, say, of the number of mining employees relative to the total number of workers. This ratio is one expression of the importance of mining in the economy of that area.

Data on mining employment for most countries that have been collected by the United Nations reveal considerable variation in the proportion of jobs in mining (see Table 16-3). In most political units, mining accounts for less than 10 per cent of total employment: The only exceptions are Rhodesia and the Union of South Africa. Highly industrialized nations are at first glance paradoxical with such low percentages as 2 per cent in the United States and Japan, 3 in France, 4 in Germany, 5 in England, and 7 in Belgium and Scotland. Yet these are all countries with high absolute employment in mining. What is the explanation?

There seems to be a tendency, at least in today's economy, for regions with an expanding mining economy to go through two stages: in the first stage, mining provides a large proportion of jobs; in the second, the

Table **16-3** *Mining Employment*

Place	Thousands of Mining Employees	Percentage of Total Employment
Rhodesia	5	35
Union of South Africa	499	14
East Germany	416	9
Bolivia	39	8
Belgium	188	7
Scotland	101	7
Chile	99	6
England, Wales	746	5
West Germany	583	4
France	374	3
Venezuela	41	3
United States	945	2
Japan	485	2
Yugoslavia	106	2

Source: United Nations, *Statistical Yearbook*, 1957, Table 6.

proportion shrinks as other secondary and tertiary endeavors (manufacturing, trade, and services) expand more rapidly.

Within the United States we have enough information to measure the mining-employment ratio on three scales: by states, by counties, and by cities.

By *states*, the mining-employment ratio varies from a minimum of 0.1 per cent to a maximum of 21 per cent. The six lowest and six highest states are as follows:

New Hampshire	0.1%	New Mexico	5.1%
Massachusetts	0.1%	Nevada	5.2%
Rhode Island	0.1%	Oklahoma	5.3%
Connecticut	0.1%	Kentucky	7.3%
Delaware	0.1%	Wyoming	8.1%
Maine	0.2%	West Virginia	21.6%

The relationship between mining employment and total employment by counties is shown in Figure 16-4. On this basis, mining is plainly the foundation stone in the economic base of such counties as Harland and Letcher (Kentucky), and McDowell (West Virginia) with ratios of 58 per cent, 60 per cent, and 65 per cent respectively.

Among the larger cities mining employment varies from zero to 41 per cent—in Shenandoah, Pennsylvania (see Table 16-4). Within the United States there are 897 urban settlements having a population of at least 10,000 inhabitants, and their average ratio of mining employment is 1.6 per cent. By computing

Mining: General Observations

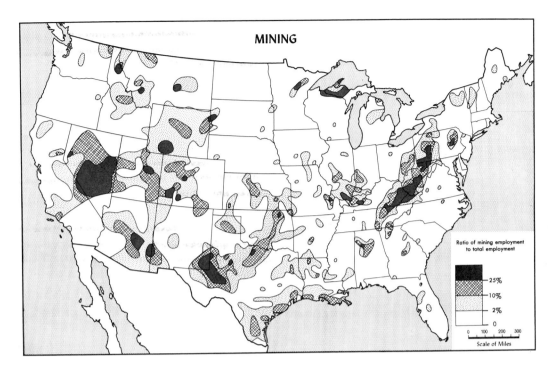

MINING

Ratio of mining employment
to total employment

25%

10%

2%

0

0   100   200   300
Scale of Miles

Figure 16-4

Table **16-4**   *Leading American Cities (Over 10,000 Population) in Ratio of Mining Employment to Total Employment*

City	Percentage	City	Percentage
Shenandoah, Penn.	41	Hobbs, N.M.	27
W. Frankfurt, Ill.	39	Tamaqua, Penn.	27
Snyder, Texas	38	Ironwood, Mich.	26
Mt. Carmel, Ill.	35	Rock Springs, Wyo.	26
Hibbing, Minn.	35	Odessa, Texas	25
Bartlesville, Okla.	34	Midland, Texas	25
Butte, Mont.	32	Wilkes-Barre, Penn.	23
Mahanoy City, Penn.	32	Madisonville, Ky.	23
Carlsbad, N.M.	28	Virginia, Minn.	23
Duncan, Okla.	27		

Source: United States Bureau of the Census, *Census of Population,* 1950, Vol. II, Characteristics of the Population.

the standard deviation (see Chapter 31) of cities from this average, Howard Nelson* classified mining cities into three categories: those that exceeded the average by at least one deviation, those that exceeded it by two deviations, and those that exceeded it by three. Figure 29-4 distinguishes regions by degree of mining employment in cities according to the Nelson System.

* "A Service Classification of American Cities," *Economic Geography,* 1955, pp. 189-210.

The ratios in smaller cities within mining regions can be remarkable, as Table 16-5 shows (see page 284).

When the mineral "downstairs" gives out, or when the market price drops excessively, a city's economic base may collapse, causing employment to drop. People may even emigrate, causing the total population to decline. In 1960 there were 212 metropolitan areas in the United States and almost all had gained population since 1950. Only eight, indeed,

Table 16-5 *Mining Employment in Selected Cities with Under 10,000 Inhabitants*

City	Population	Percentage
Kenvir-Redbud, Ky.	3420	88
McComas, W.Va.	2999	88
Gary-Ream, W.Va.	2858	80
Omar-Barnabas, W.Va.	3073	79
Lynch-Benham, Ky.	7952	78
Dragerton, Utah	3453	75
Bingham, Utah	2569	72

Source: *Ibid.*

contained fewer people in 1960 than in 1950; and of these, the two that had suffered the severest percentage losses were in mining areas: Scranton and Wilkes-Barre, Pennsylvania, in the midst of depleting anthracite fields, lost respectively 8.9 per cent and 11.5 per cent of their population.

If collapse of the economic base is complete, a city may well-nigh disappear to become a ghost town. Many cities in the western United States that formerly had thousands of people are mostly empty now. For example, Silver City, Nevada, once had 35,000 people but now numbers only 700.

Problems of Land Use   Mining influences man's use of land in several respects. Strip-mines ruin the terrain for farming. This may not matter at Bingham, Utah, where the land being chewed up is too rough and rocky for cultivation. But a real problem develops in parts of Ohio, Indiana, Illinois, and elsewhere where coal and gravel pits are eating their way into farm land. Open-pit iron mines in Minnesota have bitten off not only farm land but also some urban land. Forty years ago the center of Hibbing, Minnesota, was moved two miles to the south to make way for the mines. Shaft-mines also blight the land by depositing *tailing* piles, cone-like hills of rock and other unsalable substances hauled up from the ground. Cave-ins of underground tunnels and mine rooms, years after mining has emptied them, cause the surface to sink and shift. The washing of coal at mine entrances fills streams with coal dust and mud. For example, the Schuylkill River, which drains the anthracite region of Pennsylvania into the Delaware River at Philadelphia, was once a navigable river. But years of debris accumulating from coal mines filled the channel with black mud, spoiling its appearance and impeding navigation.

In recent years man has begun to combat some of these problems. As one remedy to blight he is planting trees in rough strip-mined areas. Although written off for traditional farming, they will eventually yield crops of trees, serve as habitat for wild life, and create a recreational area for hunting, fishing, and hiking.

This is an important question for any land-owner who has legal control of subsurface

St. Elmo, Colorado, is one of several ghost towns, former mining settlements, now preserved as tourist attractions by the state of Colorado. This particular settlement, incorporated in 1880, attained a peak population of 2000; at one time it had five hotels and its own newspaper. (Courtesy Colorado Department of Public Relations.)

rights to consider: In view of such adverse effects, is it worthwhile to sell mineral rights? A short-term gain may be realized, but in the long run the surface of the land may be ruined for further use.

Political Boundaries   Within mining regions, international boundaries sometimes impede mining activities. Europe's best coal (Westphalia) and one of her best iron ore fields (Lorraine) are only 200 miles apart. A single political boundary separates the two. America's best coal field (Appalachia) and her best iron-ore (Lake Superior) are 800 miles apart, with half a dozen state boundaries in between. Yet that lone boundary in Europe separates sovereign nations whereas those between Lake Superior and Appalachia delimit states that yielded their sovereignty to a federation. Had it not been for that boundary, Lorraine and Westphalia might have functioned together as do Superior and Appalachia. But the political boundary between France and Germany has cleft these two mining regions apart with severe repercussions. The new-born Germany, victorious in the Franco-Prussian war of 1870, occupied Lorraine, and for nearly 50 years both Westphalian fuel and Lorraine ore were controlled by a single political power which had the technological knowledge for processing, and the economic demand for consuming, large quantities of iron. During this period Germany made enormous strides as a world industrial leader.

With Germany's defeat in World War I its western boundary was quickly pushed eastward, the Lorraine returned to France, and Europe's two main mineral regions were split asunder.

This cleavage was reflected in trade restrictions. German steel mills had to seek elsewhere than the Lorraine for ore and came to depend largely on Swedish ores, 1700 miles away. French steel mills were denied Ruhr coal. The relationships were more complex than this, of course, but essentially it was a case of neighboring, naturally complementary regions being sundered by man's political decisions.

A history-making experiment is now underway to erase the economic handicaps of these political boundaries. In 1953 six nations (Germany, France, Belgium, the Netherlands, Luxembourg, and Italy) launched the *Schuman Plan* whereby the sextet functioned as one areal unit insofar as the steel industry was concerned. There were no tariffs or trade restrictions on the movement of coal, coke, ore, limestone, scrap iron, pig iron, or steel between these countries. Moreover, the six states functioned as one in competing for sales on the world market. It was as if steel mills in Pennsylvania, Maryland, Alabama, and other American states once fought with one another for sales abroad, and then organized a United States of America for purposes of competing as a team on the world market. J.A. Coker analyzes the geography of the Schuman Plan region in an informative article, an excerpt from which is as follows:

Nowhere else in the world do labor, capital equipment, raw materials, communications, and finishing industries coincide in such a small compass. France has the ore, Germany the coke, and Holland and Belgium the ports. The Schuman community has therefore a potential strength greater than the aggregate of the individual countries. It is a case of two and two making five.*

The Schuman Plan was so successful that subsequently its principles were applied to other phases of international trade among these six nations. Thus the European Common Market was formed (to be discussed in Chapter 27).

An ironic twist in the relationship of iron ore and political areas occurred after the Gilchrist-Thomas invention in 1878 of techniques for cheaply processing large volumes of phosphoric iron ores. Since the early 1700's, Britain had been the world's leading steel producer. Fortunately, her ores contained little phosphorus, and her supremacy in steel was unchallenged—until this discovery by two of her own scientists turned out to be the very key to unlock the huge Lorraine field. Remember that Germany at that time had *both* the Lorraine and the Ruhr. So, aided by this

* "Steel and the Schuman Plan," *Economic Geography*, Vol. 28, October, 1952, pp. 283-294.

English discovery, Germany rapidly rose to challenge England in steel production.

Problems of Conservation Nature produces economic minerals very slowly—so slowly that man terms them *nonrenewable* resources. The only notable exception is water. Because minerals are nonrenewable they are also *exhaustible*. Some economically important minerals (for instance, coal) are so abundant that the supply will endure for hundreds of years. But others (such as copper) are rationed in small measures. This scarcity assumes political significance because the reserves of these minerals are unequally parcelled out among the nations. Take copper and petroleum in the United States, for instance. Known petroleum will be gone in perhaps 12 years, although new petroleum discoveries are being made every year. By contrast, known copper ores in the United States will be gone in 25 years, but few new ores are being discovered. This process of depletion leads to a fundamental question: How should these limited resources be handled? Some persons advocate *preservation*. Under this policy a nation would seal up reserves and buy from abroad what she needs, withholding her own stores until a day when she may be unable to import. Others advocate *conservation*. This approach aims at extracting minerals with the least possible waste, processing them carefully, using the products fully, and then salvaging what remains after they have been used. (In forestry, this concept led to *tree farming*; but of course since minerals can-

not be "grown," there can be no counterpart in commercial mining.) Still others seem to advocate neither preservation nor conservation; ignoring the obligation of the present generation to the future, they prefer whatever policy is "best" for today.

Ninety per cent of the world's mining today has come into existence within the past 150 years. This cannot be claimed for fishing, or forestry, or most bioculture. Indeed the Industrial Revolution has correlated with a mining revolution. Our tools, weapons, utensils, buildings, sewer systems, machines, ships, and trains: all are made now principally of minerals. Moreover, the *energy* that does our work is now mostly mineral in origin. For evidence, consider the astonishing developments in power within the last century. In the United States in 1850, animals, humans, and minerals generated 80, 15, and 5 per cent respectively of man's economic energy, but in 1960 those figures had changed drastically to 3, 3, and 94 per cent. The wave of industrialization sweeping the earth today is calling for minerals at a rate unprecedented in all of human history.

But the *geography* of mining still wants a system for classifying by regions those many places where men are engaged in commercial mining. Extensive field work and research will be needed to get the answers from specific areas to specific questions: What is their mining like? How is it related to other phenomena there? And how does it link those areas with other regions?

Suggested Reading

Alderfer, E. B., and Michl, H. E., *Economics of American Industry*, New York, 1957.

Bateman, Alan M., *Economic Mineral Deposits*, New York, 1950, 916 pp.

Brown, J. Coggin, and Dey, A. K,. *India's Mineral Wealth*, London and Bombay, 1955, 761 pp.

Doerr, Arthur, and Guernsey, Lee, "Man as a Geomorphological Agent: The Example of Coal Mining," *Annals of the Association*

of American Geographers, 1956, pp. 197-210.

Jones, Stephen B., "The Economic Geography of Atomic Energy. A Review Article," *Economic Geography*, 1951, pp. 268-274.

Kohn, Clyde F., and Specht, Raymond E., "The Mining of Taconite, Lake Superior Iron Mining District," *Geographical Review*, 1958, pp. 528-539.

Miller, E. Willard, "Changing Patterns In the Mineral Economy

of the United States, 1939-1954," *The Professional Geographer*, May 1961, pp. 1-7.

Resources for Freedom, Vol. 3, *Outlook for Energy*, President's Material Policy Commission, 1952.

Shimkin, Demitri, *Minerals—A Key to Soviet Power*, Cambridge, 1953, 452 pp.

Thoman, Richard S., *The Changing Occupance Pattern of the Tri-State Area: Missouri, Kansas, and Oklahoma*, Chicago, 1953.

PART SIX

COMMERCIAL MANUFACTURING

Scarcely any of the products of commercial gathering or commercial bioculture are in usable form when they come from forests, fields, mines, or water. Logs must be converted into wood pulp, ores must be smelted, wheat must be milled, hides must be tanned. This conversion of commodities into a more useful form is called *manufacturing*.

For thousands of years manufacturing was conducted on a subsistence level in the homes of the consumers. The specialization of large numbers of people in commercial manufacturing is a phenomenon of the past 200 years.

As we shall use the term, *commercial manufacturing* includes all activities whereby man (a) assembles raw materials in an establishment (whether cottage workshop or factory building), (b) upgrades their usefulness by changing their form, and (c) ships out these more valuable commodities to other places. The focal point of this process is the factory, for it serves as a link between the source regions in which the raw materials originate and the market regions in which the products are consumed (see the accompanying figure). For convenience, we shall call every establishment that fulfills this function a *factory*.

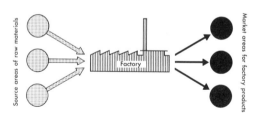

In considering factories, we shall often take location factors into account. The term *location factor*, as used in the geography of manufacturing, is applied to any phenomenon that influences the location of a factory. Examples of location factors are source areas of raw materials, market areas, sources of labor supply, regions providing fuel and power, transportation lines, terrain, taxes, and city zoning codes.

The ideal manufacturing region provides its factories with four essential requirements: raw materials, fuel and/or power, labor, and customers. But since such ideal locations rarely exist, most factories must choose among locations that are well endowed in some but not all of these elements. The *orientation* of an industry determines which single requirement will be deemed most important in establishing the location of a factory. For example, a factory that is raw-material oriented tends to locate nearer to raw-material regions than to either markets or power sources; and if the raw-material region is sparsely inhabited, labor must be imported. A market-oriented factory places a premium on location nearer to customers than to the other factors. A power-oriented industry chooses a site near dams or supplies of mineral fuels even though it may be necessary to pay freight to bring in raw materials from afar, to ship products long distances to customers, and to lure labor from distant places. Finally, a labor-oriented industry responds primarily to the availability of an abundant or particularly skilled work force.

There are numerous ways in which we might answer the question, "How much manufacturing is there in a region?" We could reply in terms of number of people *employed* by manufacturing companies. This would include production workers (those engaged directly in manufacturing processes), supervisors, foremen, researchers, janitors, stenographers, and other personnel. Another criterion is number of *production workers* only. Still another is number of *factories* (or "establishments"). Value of *employee payrolls*, number of *production-worker man-hours*, value of *wages paid to production workers, value added* in the manufacturing process (that is, the differential between the value of a product as it leaves the factory and the value of raw materials, including purchased parts): All these are examples of criteria that might be used in quantifying the amount of manufacturing.

At this point we could indulge in a lengthy discussion of the question "Which criterion is best?" However, the author has chosen to skip such comment here in favor of recounting a recent report which indicates that there is close correlation among all these criteria. A study was conducted in the United States in 1954 (a year in which a Census of Manufactures was taken); the objective was to see whether the several manufacturing criteria varied similarly or dissimilarly from place to place. The United States was divided into 166 metropolitan areas (each of which consisted of at least one county containing at least one major city) plus 2791 other counties, making a total of 2957 areal units in the entire nation. Of these, 811 counties had either no manufacturing or too little to be thoroughly tabulated in the Census. The remaining 2146 areal units were quantified in terms of different manufacturing criteria. Coefficients of correlation (explained in Chapter

Table A Coefficients of Correlation of Criteria for Measuring Manufacturing for 2146 Areal Units (Metropolitan Areas and Counties) in the United States

	1 Number of Establishments	2 Number of Employees	3 Value of Payroll	4 Number of Production Workers	5 Number of Man-Hours	6 Value of Wages	7 Value Added
1. Number of Establishments	1.00	.94	.92	.94	.93	.91	.92
2. Number of Employees		1.00	.99	.99	.99	.99	.99
3. Value of Employee Payroll			1.00	.99	.99	.99	.99
4. Number of Production Workers				1.00	.99	.99	.99
5. Number of Production Man-Hours					1.00	.99	.99
6. Value of Wages Paid						1.00	.99
7. Value Added							1.00

Source: John W. Alexander and James B. Lindberg, "Measurements of Manufacturing: Coefficients of Correlation," *Journal of Regional Science*, Vol. 3, Summer 1961, pp. 71-81.

31) were then computed for several criteria as each varied from place to place among the 2146 areal units. Table A indicates that every correlation in which the criterion *number of establishments* was involved had a rather high coefficient—over .90; but that all correlations involving the other six criteria had an astonishingly high correlation of .99, regardless of what pair of criteria were compared.

These coefficients give considerable support to the belief that, when it comes to measuring manufacturing for purposes of an over-all geographic pattern of the nation, it is immaterial which criterion we choose—since the probability is extremely high that we would get essentially the same pattern no matter which measurement we selected.

For this reason, we shall not take time in the following pages to quantify each manufacturing topic in terms of all possible criteria. Generally we shall adopt only one—number of employees, for the reasons that it is readily comprehended and, in some instances, is the only criterion for which data are available.

Nobody knows for certain how many people in the world are engaged in commercial manufacturing, but the number lies somewhere in the vicinity of 95,000,000, approximately 3 per cent of the world's total population, and probably no more than 10 per cent of the world's employed labor force. A breakdown of industrial employment by nations and regions such as Table B, demonstrates unmistakably that the world's outstanding manufacturing region is western Europe with almost 30,000,000 factory workers. This figure exceeds by over 10,000,000 the number of manufacturing employees in either the United States or the Soviet Union. Even if we add the workers behind the Iron Curtain in eastern Europe to those in the U.S.S.R., the total is little more than that for western Europe.

Table B *Employment in Manufacturing: Leading Nations*

Region	Thousands of Employees	Region	Thousands of Employees
Western Europe	29,500*	*U.S.S.R.*	23,000
United Kingdom	7,634		
West Germany	7,090†	*East Asia*	14,000*
France	4,398	Japan	6,042
Italy	3,463	China	no reliable data
Netherlands	1,263	India	1,813
Belgium	1,144	Pakistan	343
Switzerland	889	Indonesia	338
Sweden	841	Taiwan	310
Austria	826	Korea	260
Greece	508	Philippines	228
Denmark	353	Thailand	189
Finland	347	Burma	168
Norway	286		
		Southwest Asia	580*
Eastern (Soviet-Controlled)		Turkey	295
Europe	9,520*	Israel	109
East Germany	2,603	Iraq	82
Poland	2,496		
Czechoslovakia	1,987	*Africa*	1,400*
Hungary	867	Union of South Africa	652
Yugoslavia	857	Egypt	251
Bulgaria	368**		
Romania	337**	*South America*	4,000*
		Brazil	1,547
North America	19,000*	Argentina	1,462
United States	15,949	Colombia	230
Canada	1,305	Chile	216
Mexico	1,477	Uruguay	184
		Venezuela	138
Australia	1,071		
New Zealand	168		

Source: United Nations *Statistical Yearbook,* 1960, Table 66.
* Totals of major areas are not given in the source, but are tallied in this table as estimates.
† Includes data for West Berlin.
** Data given in 1958 *Statistical Yearbook* but not the 1960 edition.

Commercial manufacturing as a whole, as the map on page 292 portrays, is highly concentrated within the middle latitudes of the Northern Hemisphere, especially in four rather clearly defined places: Europe, the Soviet Union, Anglo-America, and eastern Asia.

Like the other economic activities we have studied, manufacturing exhibits regional variation. Our purpose is to identify the location, characteristics, and relationships of manufacturing regions. In doing so we shall adopt two approaches.

For the first few chapters, we shall deal with selected *industries* (for instance, vegetable canning and petroleum refining), considering *many areas* in which each *industry* appears. Then we shall investigate *selected areas* (such as the Ruhr or New England), considering many *industries* that exist in each area.

We begin with industries that process the products of farms and forests whether they come from gatherers or bioculturalists—food manufacturing in

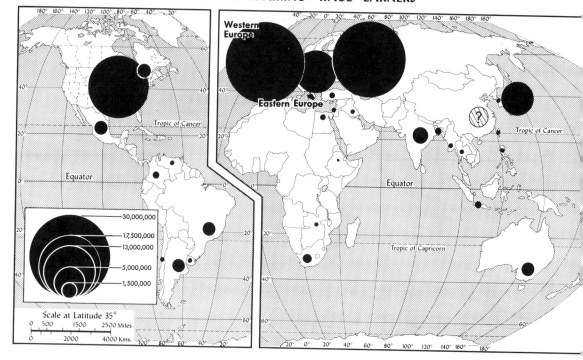

Chapter 17, and the processing of fiber and wood products in Chapter 18. Then, in Chapters 19 and 20 we cover industries that transform the products of mines. Now, these are instances of *primary manufacturing*—that is, industries that process raw materials from *primary* economic activities. In Chapters 21 and 22 we turn to selected types of *secondary manufacturing*—that is, factories that process materials produced by other factories. Finally, Chapters 23, 24, and 25 are devoted to the principal manufacturing regions of the world.

Tomato cannery in Indiana. Raw tomatoes are stored in five-eighths-bushel hampers in foreground. Pond in center has cooling water, those in far right background are for sewage. (Courtesy Kenneth N. Rider Co., Inc., Trafalgar, Indiana.)

SEVENTEEN

Food processing was one of the last types of manufacturing to advance from the subsistence to the commercial stage, from home kitchen to business enterprise. The development of the industry has progressed rapidly, though, so that today, most of the food that the millions of people in the highly developed countries consume has passed through some sort of factory.

The eight food industries selected for individual discussion in this chapter illustrate different *types* of location in manufacturing. The *canning* industry exemplifies location that is determined almost entirely by nearness to perishable raw materials. In the second type, which is represented here by the *baking* industry and *soft-drink bottling* works, location is determined almost solely by proximity to customers. *Meat packing, flour milling,* and *sugar refining* are specimens of enterprises whose location is determined partly by the location of raw materials and partly by the location of markets. The distribution of the *brewing* and of the *distilling* industries illustrates the operation of still other forces which, for the present, can be termed "human factors."

Commercial Canning and Freezing

LOCATION AND CHARACTERISTICS

In the distribution of vegetable and fruit canneries in the United States, as Figure 17-1 shows, the chief region is the Northeast, where the pattern reveals several clusters, rather than a broad dispersal. Other concentrations

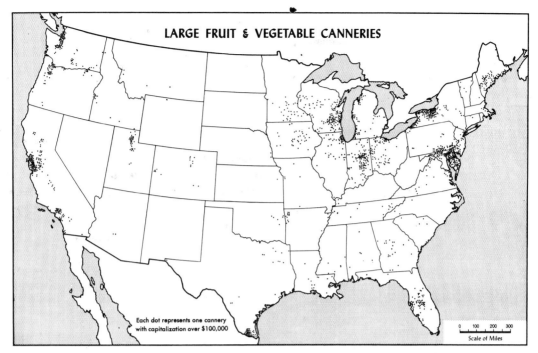

LARGE FRUIT & VEGETABLE CANNERIES

Each dot represents one cannery with capitalization over $100,000

Scale of Miles

Figure 17-1 (*After Robert Young.*)

have developed in central Florida, southern Texas, northern Utah, southern California, central California, and western Oregon and Washington.

In terms of number of employees or value added, it is impossible to construct a map on a county basis as detailed as Figure 17-1, but the United States Census of Manufactures does provide information by *states* which indicates that of the nation's total of 100,000 employees in the canning and freezing of fruits and vegetables, California has 26,000 and New York 8000.

Regional specialties in canning reflect regional preferences in agriculture. The fattest cluster on the map is along the East Coast (Delmarva and the adjacent flanks of New Jersey, Pennsylvania, Maryland, and Virginia) and constitutes the nation's leading area for its specialties, tomatoes and beans. In southern Maine the emphasis is on berries and beans. Western New York canners process both vegetables (tomatoes, cabbage, pickles) and fruits (grape juice, peaches). Their counterparts in western Ohio and eastern Indiana specialize in sweet corn and tomatoes.

Factories in Wisconsin and neighboring states are the main centers for sweet corn, green peas, and cherries. Central Florida and southern Texas boast a huge volume of citrus fruit juices, and the Western states specialize in various fruits.

In all these areas canning tends to be a small-scale industry. Few canneries employ over 100 people and few cover as much as two acres of land. Moreover, since the equipment required is comparatively simple, the capital investment is low. The industry is highly seasonal; most plants operate for only a few weeks each year. The technique of preserving food by heating it in air-tight containers was discovered in 1795, but the technique of preserving food by freezing was discovered only about 1920. Yet despite its great head start, canning is losing ground to freezing throughout the country. In 1937 the value of frozen fruits and vegetables was one-eighty-fourth the value of canned products; in 1954 it was one-fifth; and in 1958 it was almost one-half! Many plants are now dual-process factories that engage in both canning and freezing.

Sources of Raw Materials The strongest influence on the location of the canning and freezing industry is the nearness of the perishable raw materials. Without exception, all the regions shown on Figure 17-1 are also notable for the cultivation of vegetables and fruits. Some of them are market-garden zones. There, the harvests are canned and consumed in the nearby markets. Many, however, are truck-farming areas, from which the canned goods must be shipped to distant markets. This relationship suggests a principle: If the raw materials that a factory processes are perishable, the factory will gravitate toward wherever the raw materials originate. We will encounter this principle again and again. Of course, another force also attracts factories to the source of raw materials: the desire to avoid shipping substances that will eventually be discarded (like corn cobs and pea pods). But perishability is the critical element. Any industry like canning that tends, for whatever reason, to locate mainly where its raw materials are is said to be *raw-material oriented.*

Contract Farming Canneries do not, of course, simply take a chance on whatever produce might be available. They deliberately influence farmers' choices of crops. In fact, most farmers, before they put seed into the ground, make firm contractual arrangements with canneries for specified acreages of beans, tomatoes, sweet corn, and other crops.

Tin-can Factories Canneries require still another basic material: tin cans. Because freight charges are higher on empty tin cans than on sheet steel, tin-can factories locate where the canneries are. Geographers call such a relationship *symbiosis*. The term, borrowed from biology, applies here to the tendency of dissimilar factories to locate near one another for mutual advantage, in this case because the finished product from one serves as a raw material for the other. The regional pattern of tin-can factories, as Figure 20-8 reveals, is in many places highly similar to that of canneries.

Small Settlements Since the labor requirements of canneries are usually quite modest, and since the plants tend to gravitate toward the farms that supply them, most canneries are situated in small rural settlements. These settlements have the added advantage of relatively low tax rates, a decided advantage in an industry that pays taxes on installations that are idle much of the year. Canning is rarely an important activity in large cities. For example, in California, which has 51,000 cannery workers (including those engaged in canning seafood), the two largest metropolitan areas, Los Angeles and San Francisco, have only 9000 and 8500 respectively—merely a third of the state total.

Sources of Labor Since local labor forces often cannot meet the highly seasonal demand of canners, migrant laborers are employed by the thousands. Workers from Mexico and Puerto Rico find jobs not only in the harvest fields but also in the canneries as far north as New York and Wisconsin. Few other industries choose their locations with so little regard to labor supply.

Market Regions The main market area is the northeastern United States. Scarcely any cannery goods are shipped abroad, and comparatively little canned food is imported.

Thus, canneries in the Lake Ontario lowland of New York, in New England, in Maryland, and other eastern locales are fortunate in being near both their customers and raw material sources.

Commercial Baking

Bakeries provide jobs for over 300,000 people in the United States. Few industries are so ubiquitous, for commercial bakeries tend to follow population. Table 17-1 indicates that there is a strong tendency toward the following relationship: the more populous

Table **17-1** *Population and Employment
in Commercial Baking by Leading
Metropolitan Areas*

Metropolitan Area	Population 1960	Employment in Bakeries, 1958
1 New York-Northeastern New Jersey	14,114,927	37,153
2 Los Angeles	6,488,791	11,897
3 Chicago-Northwestern Indiana	5,959,213	19,044
4 Philadelphia-Camden	3,635,228	13,411
5 Detroit	3,537,709	6,944
6 San Francisco-Oakland	2,430,663	6,369
7 Boston	2,413,236	6,798
8 Washington, D.C.	1,808,423	1,663
9 Pittsburgh	1,804,400	4,546
10 Cleveland	1,784,991	4,382

Sources: United States Bureau of the Census, *Census
of Population, 1960*, Vol. I, Part A, pp. 1-50 and *Census
of Manufactures*, 1958, each state's volume, Table 5.

the settlement, the larger the employment in commercial baking.

Bakers settle near their markets because of at least three considerations.

1. Their products are more perishable than their raw materials. Indeed, the stress some customers place on the freshness of bread has led many bakeries to stamp on the loaf wrap- ping the day of manufacture. "Day-old" bread fetches a lower price than fresh bread.

2. The baking industry has a low *weight-loss ratio*. This ratio expresses the relationship between the weight of raw materials consumed by a factory and the weight of the finished products. In the case of commercial baking, these weights are roughly equal—that is, 1000 pounds of raw material (flour, salt, yeast, and so on) are transformed into approximately 1000 pounds of bread and pastry. There is little weight loss. Herein is another geographic principle: Other things being equal, the *lower* the weight loss the *stronger* the tendency for the industry to locate near its customers.

3. Transport costs for moving finished products are greater than those for moving raw materials. Flour, salt, sugar, and yeast can be handled in bulk form; consequently, freight charges are much lower per 100 pounds than are the charges on bakery goods, which must be handled more carefully and fill more shipping space. This leads us to still another geographic principle: Other considerations aside, the *higher* the transport costs on finished products (relative to transport costs on their raw materials) the *stronger* the tendency for the industry to locate near its customers.

Soft-Drink Bottling

Soft-drink bottling factories are dispersed in a pattern which, like that of bakeries, reflects a high positive correlation with population. But the reasons in each case are somewhat different. In contrast to bakery goods, bottled drinks do not spoil quickly, so perishability is not a factor. But easy availability of raw materials is. One principal ingredient, fresh water, is virtually ubiquitous; so no matter what city a bottling factory selected, it would most probably find fresh water available locally. The other main raw material is the syrup, a sweetened, flavored, concentrated substance. Since it is usually manufactured according to a private formula, it is produced only in a few key places, so it does not affect the location of plants. For example, the Coca-Cola Company manufactures its syrup in At- lanta, Georgia, and ships the concentrate to its bottling works throughout the nation as well as abroad. For an additional factor— relative transportation charges—baking and bottling are alike. The transport costs on a bottling works' products are much higher than those on drums of syrup. The principle observed with bakeries holds again: Factories tend to locate near their customers if transport costs on product exceed those on raw material.

CORRELATION WITH POPULATION

The association with population of both baking and bottling affords us an excellent opportunity to illustrate the principle of covariation. Two phenomena are said to covary positively if both reach their high values in

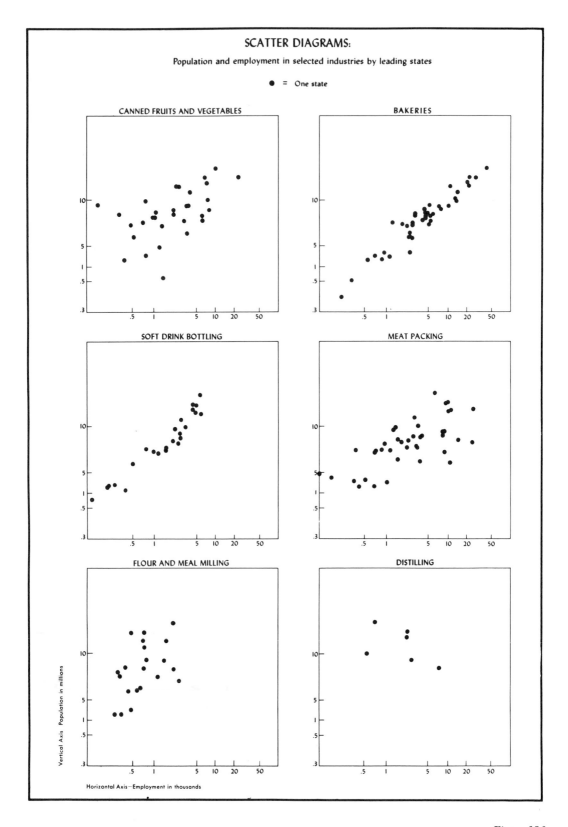

SCATTER DIAGRAMS:

Population and employment in selected industries by leading states

● = One state

CANNED FRUITS AND VEGETABLES

BAKERIES

SOFT DRINK BOTTLING

MEAT PACKING

FLOUR AND MEAL MILLING

DISTILLING

Vertical Axis Population in millions

Horizontal Axis—Employment in thousands

Figure 17-2

Commercial Food Manufacturing

the same places and their low values in the same places. Thus, when we observe that the soft-drink bottling industry or the bakery business tends to correlate positively with population, we can say that the higher the population the greater the amount of commercial baking or of soft-drink bottling.

We can portray such correlations visually by means of a *scatter diagram,* a graphic device that depicts the variation of one phenomenon *in relation to* a second.

In Figure 17-2 there are six scatter diagrams, one for each of six industries. Each shows the correlation by states between *population* and *employees in the industry.* Each state is represented on the diagrams by a single dot, the position of which is determined by the state's number of inhabitants and by the number of employees in the particular industry. Some diagrams in Figure 17-2 contain no dots for certain states because the Census of Manufactures failed to report any data.

If a *positive* correlation exists, the dots on a scatter diagram will tend to align along a sloping line that rises from left to right. If a *negative* correlation exists, the dots tend to align along a line that slopes downward from left to right. The line along which they tend to conform is known as the *regression line.* The closer the dots to this line, the *stronger* (or *higher*) the correlation. If the dots are widely diffused over a scatter diagram, the correlation is *weak* (or *low*) and it is difficult to discern any regression line.

Of the industries plotted on the scatter diagrams of Figure 17-2 the ones that reveal the highest correlation with population are baking and soft-drink bottling. For these two, the dots are most closely oriented along a clear line. The weakest correlation with population is shown by the distilling industry; on that scatter diagram the dots are widely dispersed.

Mathematical formulas have been worked out for measuring the closeness of dots to the regression line. Such measurements which permit a more accurate (or more scientific) appraisal of the strength of correlation, will be discussed in Chapter 31.

Meat Packing

LOCATION AND CHARACTERISTICS

Meat packing takes place in every state (see Figures 17-3 and 17-4, page 300), but most of the industry is located in the northeastern quadrant. Notice that slaughter houses tend to cluster in the large cities, such as New York, Philadelphia, Cincinnati, Chicago, St. Louis, and Milwaukee.

Meat-packing plants are disassembly plants in which animals are broken down into meats, hides, tallow, and waste products, some of which are used by other factories in making glue, fertilizer, and animal feed.

There is no typical size. Many small plants employ half a dozen people to make sausage, for example; some large plants employ 5000 people to process hogs, cattle, lambs, and horses into numerous products. But regardless of size, each slaughtering factory, or slaughter house, adjoins a *stockyard* where animals are penned, watered, and fed before being killed. Often these yards occupy as much land as the factory buildings themselves.

Meat-packing plants tend to specialize in processing one type of animal: hogs, cattle, calves, or sheep. And whole cities also display a tendency toward specialization: The St. Louis Metropolitan area is the nation's center for hog-slaughter, Omaha ranks first in cattle-packing, Milwaukee in the processing of calves, and Denver in handling sheep and lambs (Table 17-2, page 301).

And there are over-all regional patterns of specialization, too. Hog slaughtering, for instance, is largely concentrated in the Midwest (Figure 17-3), from the cities along the Missouri River to those in Illinois and Indiana. The center of cattle slaughtering is farther west (Figure 17-4), especially in the Missouri River Valley.

RELATIONSHIPS TO MARKETS

Originally, meat-packing plants were located near their customers, because the salable product is more perishable than the live animals. Here is an obvious principle which we have

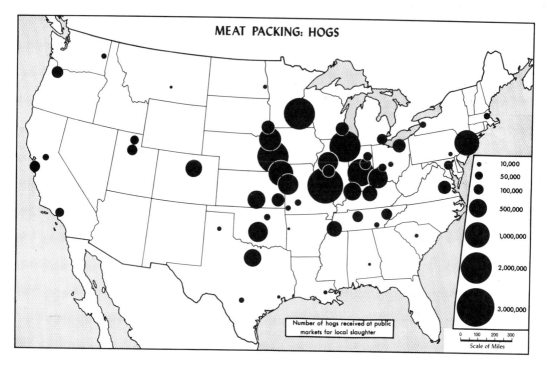

Figure 17-3

Figure 17-4

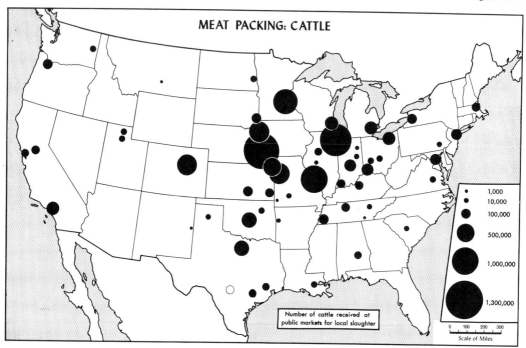

Commercial Food Manufacturing

Hogs		Cattle		Calves		Sheep and Lambs	
St. Louis	3100	Omaha	1335	Milwaukee	550	Denver	894
Omaha	2370	Chicago	1252	St. Paul	329	Ft. Worth	717
Chicago	1987	St. Louis	979	St. Louis	211	St. Paul	522
Indianapolis	1357	St. Paul	886	Houston	145	Omaha	513
St. Joseph, Mo.	1186	Sioux City	659	Kansas City	104	New York	424
New York	926	Kansas City	649	Detroit	76	St. Joseph	395
Sioux City	769	Denver	632	Chicago	74	St. Louis	343

Source: U.S. Department of Agriculture, Agricultural Marketing Service, Livestock Division, *Livestock Receipts and Disposition at Public Markets,* February, 1958, pp. 3-6.

already encountered with baking: Factories that turn out products *more perishable than the raw materials* gravitate toward their markets.

In the early days, livestock had to be driven overland to the slaughter houses. This was a costly maneuver because the animals walked off pounds of weight en route. Then, with the expansion of railroad service in the latter half of the nineteenth century, most of the animals were shipped in railway cattle cars. Not only did the journey take less time, but the animals also lost less weight in the process. But the influence of railways alone did not effect any great change in the location of the meat-packing industry. That came only with the invention of refrigeration.

RAW MATERIALS

The refrigeration of perishable goods in railway cars was introduced around 1870. This innovation greatly increased the pull of the animal-producing areas upon the location of meat-packing plants. Transporting live animals has its drawbacks. For one thing, freight charges are high for shipping live beasts—they must be watered and fed by the carriers unless they are delivered within a certain time limit after departure. (Today, it is 40 hours.) Then, in addition to some loss of weight by each animal, there often is some loss through injury. Moreover, in transporting live animals, freight charges are being paid on hides, skulls, hoofs, and other parts that, at the factory become waste products at least and by-products at best. On all these counts, savings result if the slaughter house locates near the farms and ranges that raise the livestock. But such

an arrangement was not feasible before refrigeration prevented spoilage en route to market.

To be sure, freight rates are higher per 100 pounds on refrigerated meat than on live animals. But the rates paid are for the moving of meat alone, not for meat plus half again as much weight in bones and waste.

Once it became possible to transport meat to the market from distant plants, another factor came into play that further strengthened the lure of raw-material regions on the plants. This factor is the very high percentage of production costs that go into the purchase of raw materials—nearly 85 per cent. The other 15 per cent represent expenditures for such things as labor, fuel, and taxes. Now, a geographic principle tends to hold that, in the absence of other compelling considerations, the higher the ratio of raw-material costs to total production costs, the stronger the tendency of a factory to locate near its source of materials.

Still another factor is the increased consumption of *canned* meat in recent years—further enhancing the pull of the ranch and farm areas on the meat-packing industry. About 10 per cent of all meat packed is now put up in cans.

For all these reasons, several meat-packing plants abandoned the centers of population for communities within the stock-raising regions. The New York urban area, the nation's largest metropolis, with nearly one out of every ten United States citizens, once led the nation in meat packing; but it has now fallen far behind western cities. New York still ranks fifth in the slaughtering of sheep and lambs,

This meat-packing plant at Rio Santiago (just outside the city of La Plata), 40 miles southeast of Buenos Aires, produces a full range of products for domestic as well as export trade. Ocean-going refrigerator ships load directly at the factory, the chief exports being frozen beef, frozen lamb, and a wide variety of canned meats and by-products. This plant manufactures its own tin cans, operates its own wool house for drying, grading, and baling wool, generates its own power and steam, and normally employs 4000 people. (Courtesy International Packers, Limited.)

probably because of her large kosher market, but even this branch of the industry has gravitated to grazing regions. Hog packing and cattle packing are now largely clustered in the Corn Belt and along the eastern borders of the grazing regions, and calf packing is found largely in the Dairy Belt.

Some meat-packing factories are illustrative of *bridge industries,* factories that are located *between* their raw material and their market.

Small packers depend entirely on trucks. Large packing plants, however, are near railroads and many even have their own railway sidings. About half the animals arrive by rail at the large packing centers, and 70 per cent of the product leaves in trains. Even for the giant concerns, trucks carry most of the transport burden within a radius of 150 miles of the factory. But meat destined for longer shipments generally moves by carload lot in factory-owned refrigerator cars. These cars receive top priority from the railroads, and every evening whole trainloads of refrigerated-meat cars speed eastward from Omaha, Sioux City, Waterloo, and other great packing centers.

The United States engages in little export or import of meat products. Western Europe is the largest world market for meat; a large proportion of its needs is satisfied by the packing plants of Argentina, Australia, and New Zealand.

Commercial Flour Milling

The United States flour-milling industry exhibits a complex locational pattern (Figure 17-5). Ninety-five per cent of the mills are located in the eastern half of the country. Buffalo, New York, is the leading city, followed by Kansas City (Missouri) and Minneapolis. If in delimiting milling regions, however, we take into account the smaller plants in nearby communities, Buffalo quickly loses its lead, for very little flour is processed elsewhere in western New York. Kansas City, on the other hand, is surrounded by a host of milling cities in nearby Kansas, Missouri, Nebraska, Oklahoma, and northern Texas. Together they form the nation's most productive zone of flour milling. The second-ranking region is southeastern Minnesota, and lesser concentrations appear in southwestern Illinois (notably East St. Louis) and northern Ohio (particularly Toledo). Notice that several cities stand out conspicuously in the midst of extensive blank areas: Chicago, Denver, Spokane, and Seattle. By contrast, many eastern states (from Indiana to Pennsylvania and from Michigan to South Carolina) have numerous small mills flung across the countryside, with no pronounced concentration in any one city.

Flour milling is so highly mechanized—several machines can be supervised by one man—that labor accounts for only 5 per cent of total production costs. Operations of this sort lend themselves to large-scale enterprises carried on in enormous buildings. Indeed, the flour mills at Buffalo, Kansas City, and Minneapolis are visible for miles around. Adding to their size is the need to maintain tremendous storage facilities for the wheat that cascades out of the fields every harvest time.

RELATIONSHIPS

Raw Materials   Wheat-growing regions exert a strong pull on flour mills. For one thing, 85 per cent of the production costs go for grain purchases. Yet this alone would not necessarily lend the farming regions any particular attraction were it not that 40 per cent of the weight of the grain is "lost" in the manufacturing process: 100 tons of wheat make only 60 tons of flour. Thus the weight-loss ratio is high. Consequently, there is some correlation between the locations of flour milling and of commercial wheat farming—notice that most of the areas that stand out in Figure 17-5 appear also in Figure 11-3.

But some milling centers are located hundreds, even thousands, of miles from their raw-material sources. Buffalo and Liverpool

Figure 17-5 (*After Robert Anderson.*)

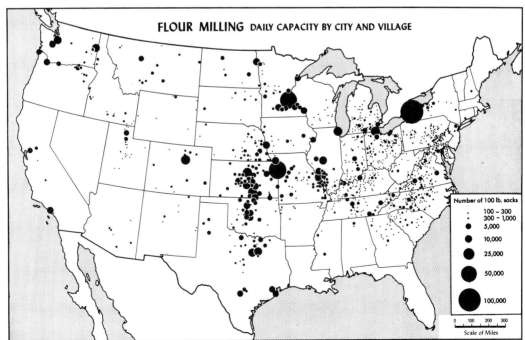

are prime examples of how other relationships are operative in determining the location of this industry.

Markets   The myriad of small mills and many of the medium-sized ones represented in Figure 17-5 are located close to their markets. These are the old mills, relics of a bygone day when the nation's wheat regions and market areas were both situated in the eastern half of the country. These mills have lost their competitive advantage to newer and larger operations in the West, but they persist in processing local grain for local consumers. In terms of market relationships, mills in dairy and poultry regions have fared somewhat better because they suffer less from the weight-loss ratio—the 40 per cent waste can be sold as poultry and animal feed to nearby farmers. Of course, this does not bring as high a price as flour but the added revenue reduces the effect of the loss in weight.

The main milling centers in the West (especially in the winter and spring wheat belts) are far removed from their markets, and most of their flour is funneled off to the East. To avoid back-hauling, the mills in this area have been built on the eastern, marketward margin of the grain-growing zone—in Figures 17-5 and 11-3, notice for instance, the position of Kansas City and Minneapolis relative to the two wheat areas for which they serve as milling capitals.

The prominence of Buffalo as a milling center illustrates the composite influence of several factors. It is located near the most populous market region of the nation. Although far removed from their major sources of wheat, Buffalo millers do enjoy extremely low transportation costs on the Great Lakes. Notice that Buffalo occupies a favored location at the eastern end of Lake Erie—the deepest penetration by the Great Lakes into the nation's main domestic market. At the other end of the Great Lakes chain, Lake Superior reaches almost to the edge of the spring wheat region and Lake Michigan almost halfway to the winter wheat region. Such easy access to different *kinds* of wheat gives Buffalo an advantage over other centers by enabling the

millers to blend a variety of grain types into a variety of flours. A disadvantage for Buffalo, though, is that most Great Lakes shipping comes to a dead stop in winter; however, this drawback is partly offset in that, since the western ports freeze over before the harbor freezes over in Buffalo (if it freezes at all), the fully loaded freighters end up their last trip each season serving as storage bins in the Buffalo harbor, thus reducing the grain-elevator capacity needed there. This city is centrally located not only among urban markets but also among dairy and poultry farms that consume the by-products mentioned above. Buffalo is untypical in another respect: It depends to a slight degree on distant outlets in foreign countries, for about 20 per cent of the city's flour is exported. Some of it is even manufactured from Canadian wheat and sold to Europe. Normally, tariff charges would make it impossible for Buffalo to engage in this international commerce, but a milling-in-bond privilege granted by the government permits Canadian wheat to be imported, milled, and exported tariff-free.

Transportation Costs   Were proximity to markets and materials the only elements involved, flour mills would probably be either in the growing regions or in the consuming centers. There are, however, three considerations in transportation costs which help explain why certain places that are near neither one nor the other have achieved such eminence in the industry. These three considerations are bulk-break point, rate-break point, and milling-in-transit rate.

1. Bulk-break point: This term refers to any transportation center where commodities are transferred from one type of carrier to another. Wheat moves by truck from farms to railroad centers; there, numerous truck loads are consolidated into fewer rail carloads. A considerable volume of freight moves by rail to lake or sea ports where the wheat is further consolidated into shiploads. At the other end of the journey, ships deliver the wheat at ports where the bulk is broken down into carloads. It could even move by train to

further destinations before being split up into truckloads. All these transportation centers are bulk-break points. Such centers punctuate the movement not only of wheat but also of petroleum and other bulky substances.

In the flour business, the significance of a bulk-break point is that it could support considerable milling even though its immediate hinterland grew little wheat or consumed little flour. If such a point, Y, were on the line of movement between wheat-growing region X and flour market Z, it would be at no disadvantage, insofar as transport costs are concerned, compared with mills in X that ship flour through Y to Z or with mills in Z that receive wheat from X via Y. Buffalo and Toledo are examples of cities where flour mills enjoy the advantages inherent in location at bulk-breaking points.

2. Rate-break points: A principle of transportation economics is that charges increase with distance but at a decreasing rate. Thus, the charge for hauling wheat by rail 500 miles may be $25.00, while the charge for hauling it 1000 miles is $40.00. Although the distance is twice as great, the charge is less than twice as much. This would hold true even when no bulk-break is involved. Imagine a wheat region 1000 miles from a flour market; flour mills would tend to locate either with the wheat (and pay one through rate on flour) or with the customers (and pay one through rate on wheat), rather than at an intermediate point that would call for a joint rate—two separate lesser rates which, added together, would exceed either of the through rates. But in fact the system does not inevitably work so simply, for through rates may not always apply. To understand why, we must take into account freight-rate territories. (This topic is investigated more fully in Chapter 27.) These territories have arbitrary boundaries that are significant for this reason: The shipping cost from point X in territory A to point Y in adjoining territory B is not computed as one through rate but as the joint rate of the fee from X to the boundary and the fee from boundary to Y. This practice applies even in situations where the same railroad company runs from the point of origination to the point

of destination. Cities that are located where transport arteries cross rate-territory boundaries are called rate-break points. What matters here is that flour mills located at rate-break points can often compete equally, insofar as freight rates are concerned, with mills located in the wheat lands and those in the markets. One of the main rate-break lines parallels the Illinois River and the Mississippi River; several flour mills along this line are conspicuous on Figure 17-5.

3. Milling-in-transit: This is a privilege granted by railroads to milling centers that, although neither bulk-break points nor rate-break points, are located on the line of flow between raw material and market. Normally, the mills in such centers would be saddled with joint rates, but milling-in-transit permits them to pay through rates and yet stop the grain en route for milling purposes. This practice is similar to the feeding-in-transit privileges mentioned in the discussion of mixed farming (see Chapter 9).

The Role of an Invention   As late as 1850, commercial flour mills were able to grind only soft wheat, for the mill stones wore out too rapidly when kernels of hard wheat were ground. Almost all the wheat grown in this country was of the soft variety produced in the humid East. Then in the latter half of the nineteenth century wheat lands opened up out West; although the new western producers enjoyed potential competitive advantages over their eastern brethren, the only variety they could grow was the unmillable hard wheat. Finally, though, in 1870, a design for steel *rollers*, instead of stone *discs*, was introduced from Hungary, and the hard-wheat flour-milling industry began to boom in Minneapolis. This city held first place in United States flour milling until it was surpassed by Buffalo in 1929.

The Sources of Power   In the early days of commercial flour milling, the mill stones were turned by power transmitted mechanically by waterwheels. Most of the small older mills in the eastern United States are still situated close to dams along small streams. This is one reason why, in the early 1800's, the leading flour city in New York was Rochester on the Genesee River rather than Buffalo on the Lake Erie lowland. Water-power was also a factor in the early start of Minneapolis as a milling center on the St. Anthony Falls in the Mississippi. But water-power no longer plays a significant role.

Sugar Manufacturing

Sugar manufacturing involves three types of factory: sugar-cane *centrales*, cane-sugar refineries, and beet-sugar refineries.

Sugar-cane centrales are located right on the sugar plantations. Here the cane stalks are put through the initial stages of manufacturing in order to take advantage of a tremendous reduction in weight. For cane-sugar stalks consist of 74 per cent water, 10 per cent cellulose, and 2 per cent waste fibers; only 14 per cent is raw sugar. The other 86 per cent of the weight of the stalks can be eliminated right at the plantation. The cellulose (termed bagasse) serves as fuel on some *centrales* and, it has recently been discovered, is a usable material for paper pulp. Our mainland *centrales* (all in Gulf States, mostly Louisiana) produce only 5 per cent of our needs.

Cane-sugar refineries are located in three general areas. The leading one, which extends from Boston to Philadelphia, refines half the sugar consumed in this country. Metropolitan New York alone processes a fourth of the nation's total. These mills draw all their raw sugar from *centrales* in Latin America: Cuba (until recently), Puerto Rico, and other Caribbean islands. A second area, along the Gulf Coast, absorbs the raw sugar from domestic *centrales* plus an even larger amount from the Caribbean. The third center is Crockett (California), whose refineries process Hawaiian raw sugar. Although we grow very little sugar cane in continental United States, we refine most of the sugar we consume because (a) it is cheaper to ship raw sugar in bulk than to ship pure sugar in sacks, (b) there

Sugar factory at Halfweg, North Holland, which is supplied with beets by canal barges. (Copyright Foto-Reclame, J. G. Van Agtmaal.)

is very little weight lost in purifying raw sugar (a larger weight-loss factor would encourage the industry to locate near the plantation), and (c) the government protects domestic refineries by a rigid quota system that limits the volume of refined sugar that can be imported. The Secretary of Agriculture determines the quotas each year according to a complex formula that gives priority to the refineries in Hawaii, Puerto Rico, and the Philippines. In sum, imports of refined sugar account for only about 10 per cent of our total sugar consumption.

Beet-sugar refineries are located in California, Colorado, Idaho, Montana, Michigan, and the other northern states that grow sugar beets. These factories locate near beet farms because (a) beets are of such little value per pound that transport charges quickly exceed it on long hauls, and (b) beets are a perish-able, seasonal crop that cannot be stored for very long. Beet-sugar mills, like vegetable canneries, tend to be small and numerous within the growing area. About 15 per cent of the sugar consumed in this country is refined from domestic beets.

No better industry than that of beet sugar could be chosen to reveal the contrast between the *Census of Agriculture* and the *Census of Manufactures* in giving locational detail. See Table 17-3. Surely this difference in availability of information is one reason why geographers have made more progress in analyzing agricultural than manufacturing regions and why economic atlases generally contain more maps of the one than the other.

The United States is divided into three sugar market regions. The eastern part of the country (east of a line running from western Texas to Lake Superior—except for much of

Table 17-3   *The Beet Sugar Industry as Presented in United States Census Publications*

| | 1959 Sugar Beets Harvested on Farms [1] | | 1958 Value of Beet Sugar Shipments From Factories [2] |
	Value (in thousands)	Tons (in thousands)	(in thousands)
By Leading States			
United States Total	$191,186	17,015,000	$392,212
California	56,672	4,928,000	no data given
Colorado	29,000	2,437,000	no data given
Idaho	22,066	1,886,000	no data given
Nebraska	13,505	1,107,000	no data given
Michigan	11,301	1,299,000	no data given
Montana	9,841	827,000	$23,924
Washington	8,927	763,000	no data given
Minnesota	8,800	880,000	no data given
Wyoming	7,629	616,000	no data given
Utah	6,399	551,000	$14,225
By Counties: California [3]			
California Total		4,314,422	
Imperial	no	919,217	no
Yolo	data	591,447	data
San Joaquin	given	540,950	given
Monterey		532,716	
Solano		359,020	

(Data are given for 27 other counties in California. Similar data are given for counties in Colorado, Montana, Utah, and other states.)

Sources: [1] United States Bureau of the Census, *Statistical Abstract of the United States*, 1961, p. 672.
[2] *Census of Manufactures*, 1958, Bulletin MC58(2)-20F "Sugar, Confectionery and Related Products," Table 2, and also the individual state sections in Bulletin MC58(3).
[3] *Census of Agriculture*, 1959, Vol. I Part 48: "California," pp. 232-237. The Census presents county data in tons, not in value.

Michigan, which has its own beets) is served by cane-sugar refineries on the Eastern and Gulf Seaboards. The Pacific Coast states constitute a market served by both beet-sugar and cane-sugar refineries in California. Between these two regions is a large zone that extends from Canada to Mexico and is served by beet sugar refineries only.

Commercial Brewing

A comparison of the map of the brewing industry (Figure 17-6) with a map of population suggests that, on a broad national scale, the brewing industry is *market-oriented.* Thus, the northeastern quadrant of the United States contains most of the nation's people, and most of the nation's breweries are there, too. Moreover, New York is the nation's leading state and metropolitan New York the leading urban area in brewing production. In a broad view of the nation, then, breweries tend to correlate in location with population.

When we turn to a finer scale, however, examining specific states and cities, the correlation with population seems much weaker. California, Pennsylvania, Ohio, and Texas, the states that rank after New York in population, do not rank in that order in brewery production. Nor do Chicago and Los Angeles rank as runners-up to New York City in the brewing industry. Wisconsin produces almost as much beer as New York State, and Milwaukee, although only one-fifteenth as populous as metropolitan New York, brews nearly as much beer.

Here the location of a particular type of people who have both an unusual desire for the beverage and a peculiar aptitude for making it is a determining influence on the location of this industry. Germans have long been recognized as adept braumeisters, and many brewery companies bear German names. A large concentration of German immigrants and their descendants is a major reason why the business settled in New York, Milwaukee, and St. Louis rather than elsewhere. Few other industries in the United States have a locational pattern that illustrates so well the power

Figure 17-6 (*After N. E. Battist.*)

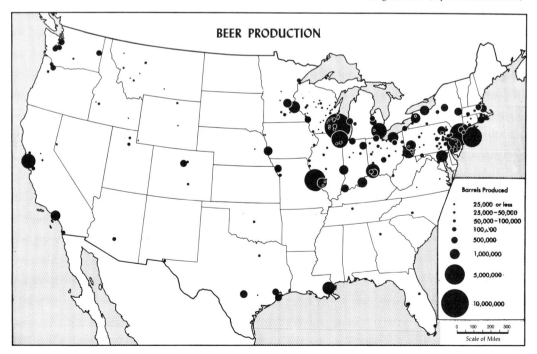

Commercial Food Manufacturing

of an ethnic factor in influencing location. The major raw material (by volume) is water; barley and hops, the other ingredients, can be grown widely in the Northeast.

Distilleries of Alcoholic Beverages

The final food industry we shall examine, the distilling business, is still something of a geographic conundrum. Its locational pattern (Figure 17-7) suggests a slight correlation with population, since most of the production is in the northeastern states and on the West Coast. Yet New York and Pennsylvania are not the leading states; indeed, very little distilling is done in New York. Kentucky is unquestionably the leader with Illinois ranking second. The inordinate concentration of the industry in these two states has puzzled analysts. Why here instead of dispersed among the populous centers of the nation?

One suggestion is that distilling is a raw-material oriented industry, and therefore would naturally locate in the Corn Belt. But, Kentucky is not a leading corn state, and her distillers import the grain from states to the north. Moreover, the *weight-loss ratio* is so low that, on this count, there would be little advantage in a location near raw materials. Another suggestion is that Kentucky water possesses "unusual" qualities; but this claim has never been demonstrated, and Illinois distillers laugh at the suggestion.

Perhaps there is something in the costs of distilling liquor and of marketing it that gives Kentucky and Illinois an advantage. But a glance at the relationship of selling price to production costs shows that federal *taxes* are the largest component in the price of liquor. The federal government assesses a tax of $2.10 on each fifth (of a gallon) of 100-proof whiskey (100-proof means 50 per cent alcoholic content). Nearly every state adds an additional tax, varying from 55 cents in Minnesota to 15 cents in South Dakota. The combined federal and state taxes make up well over half the retail price in every state; in Wisconsin, for instance, the combined taxes are $2.50 on a fifth that retails for $4.00. The

Figure 17-7 (*After John Mader.*)

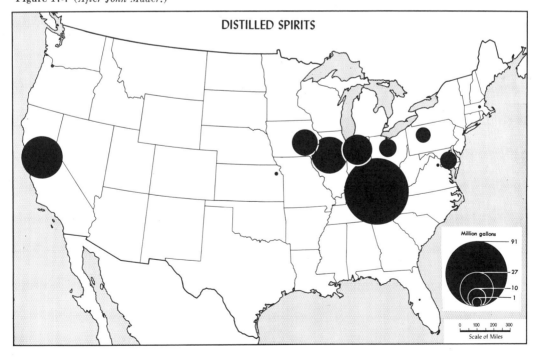

DISTILLED SPIRITS

Million gallons
91
27
10
1

0 100 200 300
Scale of Miles

total production and distribution costs account for $1.50, only 37 per cent of the retail price.

Thus, the cost of actually distilling liquor is unusually low compared to its final value. Indeed, aging the product (including insurance and loss through evaporation) runs higher than raw materials, labor, and overhead combined. But taxes overshadow all other costs. Therefore, within the nation, Kentucky and Illinois would seem to have no particular advantage over other states.

Nobody has yet explained why the distilling industry is so highly concentrated in Kentucky and Illinois rather than in Ohio and Indiana, say, or in Michigan and Wisconsin, or in Missouri and Iowa. Perhaps it is a case of locational inertia—historically speaking, the industries got an early start in these places—and have maintained their position. But might it also be that distilling is a type of industry whose location is explained largely by the "reputation of an area"? Unless it can be demonstrated that Kentucky whiskeys are actually "better" than those distilled elsewhere, may it not be that clever national *advertising* which vaunts the rolling green pastures, the white rail fences, and the purebred horses of Kentucky has been able to weave an element of charm into the very name "Kentucky," and so has had a strong, though immeasurable, impact on the minds of whiskey drinkers? At first glance, this explanation may seem highly implausible, but social scientists may someday discover ways of measuring customer reaction accurately enough to put it to the test.

In this chapter we have dealt entirely with the United States, using it, in effect, as a case study area to illustrate how certain food industries have developed definite types of locational patterns. For the world as a whole, the regions of commercial food manufacturing conform to the same principles just observed within the United States, as will be seen in Chapters 24 and 25.

Suggested Readings

Alderfer, E. B., and Michl, H. E., *Economics of American Industry*, New York, 1957, chapters 27-33.

Bergsmark, D. R., "Minneapolis, the Mill City," *Economic Geography*, 1927, pp. 391-396.

Durand, Loyal, Jr., "The Migration of Cheese Manufacturing in the United States," *Annals of the Association of American Geographers*, 1952, pp. 263-282.

Moke, Irene A., "Canning in Northwestern Arkansas," *Economic Geography*, 1952, pp. 151-159.

O'Day, Laura, "Buffalo as a Flour Milling Center," *Economic Geography*, 1932, pp. 81-93.

Pickett, V. G., and Vaile, R. S., *The Decline of Northwestern Flour Milling*, Minneapolis, 1933.

Shaw, Earl B., "United States Restrictions on Argentine Beef," *Scientific Monthly*, 1945, pp. 101-108.

White, Langdon, "The Argentine Meat Question," *Geographical Review*, 1945, pp. 634-646.

FIBER, LEATHER, AND WOOD PRODUCTS

*Textile mill in Kamyshin, on the Volga. This division
has 4000 automatic looms in operation. On completion in 1965, it is claimed,
this will be the largest in the world.* (U.S.S.R. Magazine, *from Sovfoto.*)

EIGHTEEN

The purpose of this chapter is two-fold: (a) to emphasize a special adaptation of the geographic method that is particularly appropriate to *manufacturing*, and (b) to consider the geography of a few selected industries that process the nonfood products of farm and forest.

A Special Adaptation of the Geographic Method to Manufacturing

In Chapter 1 it was suggested that the third basic question in the geographic method (involving relationships) could be approached from four alternative viewpoints which considered (1) physical and cultural factors, (2) causes and consequences, (3) internal and external relationships, or (4) correlations. A fifth alternative is available when one studies manufacturing—he can choose to emphasize the relationships which link a factory (a) to areas which supply its raw materials, fuel and power, and (b) to areas which consume its product.

Recall that the basic function of a factory is to perform an intermediate function between raw-material producers and finished-product consumers. Thus, the role of a factory, which upgrades the value of existing items of wealth, is generally different from that of a farm, a forest, or a mine.

Now we will take up separately the textile, apparel, leather, lumber, furniture, pulp, paper, and printing industries. In each case the United States will serve as our case-study area, after which we shall trace the general world patterns.

LOCATION

There are two outstanding regions of textile manufacturing in the United States (Figure 18-1), both on the Atlantic Seaboard. Few other industries are so concentrated in that part of the country. A southeastern strip running from Virginia through the Carolinas, Tennessee, and Georgia is the home of 45 per cent of the nation's textile industry, 20 per cent of it in North Carolina alone. Most of the textile mills here are located in the Piedmont, a transitional landform of rolling plains and hills between the Appalachian Mountains and the Atlantic Coastal Plain. A northeastern belt stretching from Pennsylvania to southern New England encompasses 42 per cent of U.S. textile production. A less important area is in the upper Midwest.

CHARACTERISTICS

Textile workers spin fibers (plant, animal, or synthetic) into yarn, weave or knit the yarn into fabrics, and then finish the fabrics by bleaching, dyeing, and sometimes printing patterns.

It is a declining industry in the United States: Between 1947 and 1958 employment in textile factories fell from 1,232,293 to 901,677, and the value added to materials in processing declined from $5,322,000,000 to $4,857,000,000. During this same period every other notable industry increased its value added, and almost every other one increased the size of its payroll. Yet for decades, the textile industry, in both categories, led the country, reaching its apex in 1920. But World War II, with its heavy demand for mechanized equipment, catapulted the machinery industry into the lead. Textiles now have also been surpassed by metals, chemicals, apparel, and printing.

The textile industry has changed not only in size but also in situation. For over a century New England paced the nation. Then, shortly before the turn of the present century,

Figure 18-1 (*After Alan Eberhardt.*)

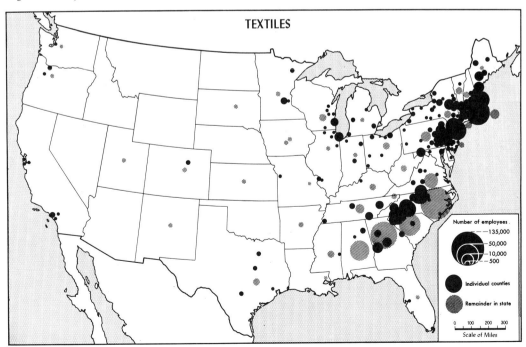

er, Leather, and Wood Products

textile mills began to spring up in the Piedmont, and in 1925 New England lost her supremacy to this new competitor. The older mills of New England were poorly equipped and poorly designed. Typically three or four-story buildings, they required the vertical movement of materials during the manufacturing process. The new southern mills, by contrast, were equipped with modern machines and were efficiently designed so that all operations can be conducted on one level, the materials moving horizontally from step to step.

The two regions also differ in what they produce. The Piedmont supports largely cotton manufacturers, whereas New England and the Middle Atlantic states (Pennsylvania, New Jersey, and New York) have a balance between woolens, cottons, and synthetics. Still, the Piedmont is rapidly increasing its share of all three fabrics, and now accounts for 70 per cent of the nation's cotton textiles, 52 per cent of the synthetics, and 25 per cent of the woolens.

EXTERNAL RELATIONSHIPS

What is the orientation of the textile industry? To raw materials? To markets? Or is its locational pattern determined by something else? Let's look first at the three principal raw materials—cotton, wool, and synthetics.

Raw Materials   Most of our raw cotton comes from the Mississippi Valley and Texas. In addition, small amounts originate near the factories in Georgia and South Carolina, and some cotton comes from California and Arizona (Figure 12-4). A very small quantity of long-staple cotton is imported for blending with the domestic variety, all of which is short-staple.

Most of our domestic wool originates in the western half of the country, particularly Texas and the Rocky Mountain states (Figure 18-2), though a little is shorn from sheep in the Corn Belt. But the United States imports twice as much wool as it produces, largely from Argentina, Australia, and New Zealand.

Synthetic fibers originate almost entirely in chemical factories on the East Coast.

WOOL SHORN

1 Dot = 50,000 Pounds
United States Total
230,689,709 Pounds

Figure 18-2 (*From U.S. Bureau of the Census.*)

Clearly, there is little correlation between the locational pattern of textiles and that of raw materials, otherwise Texas, the leading state in both cotton and wool shipments, would have a similar leading position in cloth manufacturing.

Markets   Markets are a more powerful draw than raw materials on textile mills, because little weight is lost in the manufacturing process and because transport costs on fabrics exceed those on fibers.

Since the cotton and synthetic-fiber mills produce both yarn and consumer goods, the market for these fabrics consists partly of apparel factories and partly of wholesalers. Both of these markets are also essentially eastern, the apparel factories being located according to the pattern in Figure 18-4 and the textile wholesalers corresponding generally with the distribution of population. Domestic demand takes care of most of the output of the mills. Foreign markets take scarcely any of it, because United States manufacturers cannot compete with the textile makers in Europe and Japan where labor costs are markedly lower.

Notice New England's changing position relative to cotton markets. Does this provide us with a clue to the forces behind the region's decline? In the late 1700's and most of the 1800's New England had the core of the United States market near at hand. But for many years the center of population has been moving steadily westward and is now in southern Illinois. So the Piedmont is now somewhat closer than New England to the national market. In fact, though, the mills of neither New England nor the Piedmont are located very near the bulk of their customers. Other forces are apparently at work, as we shall see.

The market for woolen textiles is more restricted than that for cottons or synthetics, for it consists largely of apparel factories in New York and Philadelphia. This has been the strongest bulwark for New England and the Middle Atlantic states in retaining the woolen mills.

RELATIONSHIPS WITHIN THE TEXTILE REGIONS

Within each of the areas shown in Figure 18-1, there are certain common relationships between textile manufacturing and labor supply, power supply, tax rates, and the economic base of settlements. Let us examine each in turn.

Labor Supplies   New England, with its early start in textile manufacture, developed a highly skilled work force. But the cost of labor there has always been higher than in the Piedmont. The gap was great in the early years of this century but has gradually narrowed so that today northern wage rates average only 10 per cent above those in the South. Moreover, the workers are less widely organized in the South, and are willing to work more hours per shift, more shifts per day, more days per week. As one consequence of spotty unionization, there are fewer restrictions on the number of machines an operator handles; southern workers tend half again as many looms as do their northern counterparts.

The resulting contrast in labor costs between New England and the South effected a competitive disadvantage to the northern mills. On this score, witness what an official commission appointed by the Commonwealth of Massachusetts had to say:

The Commission finds that ... probably the major factor in causing competitive disadvantage in the Commonwealth is wages and cost of labor.

The Commission is of the opinion that a reduction of wages in the northern mills is no solution to the problem as it feels that any reduction would be followed by a similar reduction of wages in the South.

Unionization in the southern industry is tending to narrow the gap in wage rates and will probably continue that trend in the future.

The Commission finds that the differential in productivity is one of the two major factors causing competitive disadvantage to the textile industry in the Commonwealth.... The Commission finds that the individual work load of the northern worker is not as great in many instances as that of the southern worker....

The Commission finds that certain existing Massachusetts laws tend to prevent the most effective and economical use of machinery by rendering third shift operations difficult.*

This discrepancy in labor costs has been reflected in two developments. First, it has led New England textile companies to close their mills, move their supervisors south, and build new mills with modern machinery that southern workers have quickly learned to operate. Second, the mills that have remained in New England have begun to specialize in high-quality textiles for which their highly skilled and expensive workers may be used to better advantage.

Since woolen textiles, more than cotton, require more skillful workmen—largely because the patterns must be woven into the fabrics rather than simply stamped on them— the woolen industry has been slower than the cotton industry to leave New England's reservoir of expert labor. But improved machinery is now reducing this advantage, southern labor is developing the requisite abilities, and the woolen industry is beginning to shift south, too.

Power Supply   In the 1700's and 1800's numerous textile mills were constructed along New England streams, for dams ten feet high developed enough fall to meet the power requirements of small factories. Besides a dam, a millrace (see Chapter 14) was necessary for waterpower. Any factory located downstream from the dam and between the millrace and the stream would be in a favorable position for generating waterpower. Then, if the dam

* The Commonwealth of Massachusetts, *Report of the Special Commission Relative to the Textile Industry and to Prevent Removal Thereof from the Commonwealth,* House Document No. 2590 (Boston, 1950), pp. 44-45.

were ten feet high, the factory could have the equivalent of a ten-foot waterfall turning a water wheel in its basement; water could be channeled into the factory from the upper millrace level on one side and be drained out on the other side into the lower stream below the dam. Thus, although the southern New England area got an early start in textiles because of closeness to market, specific sites were chosen primarily for water power.

Access to water power has also been an asset of the Piedmont area. By the time the textile industry began to develop there, though, the electrical revolution had dawned, and hydroelectric power became feasible. Therefore, there are few millraces in the Piedmont.

For the textile industry as a whole, power and fuel account for 4 per cent of the total cost of manufacture.

Taxes   Both municipal and state taxes on factories are lower in the South than in the North. Indeed, many southern communities have lured northern factories with the promise that no municipal taxes will be imposed for stipulated periods of time. Some mills have been built in rural areas outside the taxing limits of municipalities.

Economic Base of Settlements   Textile mills are important components of the economic base of many communities because they provide large percentages of the local jobs. In Fall River, Massachusetts, for instance, textile mills afford work to a fifth of the city's employed residents; in Kannapolis, North Carolina, the figure is an astonishingly high 68 per cent. (For the nation's urban population as a whole the ratio of textile employment to total employment is only 2 per cent.)

The overriding position of the textile industry in Kannapolis has made that community the nation's most industrialized city: Manufacturing accounts for 70 per cent of all jobs in Kannapolis, nearly three times the national average.

THE WORLD PATTERN

Four regions dominate the world production of textiles. They are, by percentage of

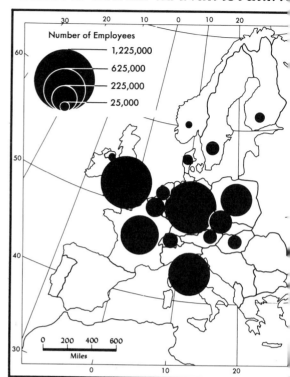

EUROPE: TEXTILE MANUFACTURING

Figure 18-3

world total: Europe (33 per cent), the United States (30 per cent), the U.S.S.R. (14 per cent), and the Far East, mainly India and Japan (14 per cent). In Europe the top nations, as shown in Figure 18-3, are Germany, the United Kingdom, Italy, and France.

As for raw materials, Europe and Japan import almost all their cotton and wool. The United States, as we saw, imports most of its wool and some high-grade cotton, but has a tremendous surplus of short-staple cotton for export to Japan and Europe. The U.S.S.R. produces all her own fibers.

The four leading manufacturing areas are the leading market areas as well. In addition, Europe, Japan, and India are the dominant exporters to the world market. Half the world's cotton textiles are exported from Europe, 35 per cent from the Far East, and only 15 per cent from the United States. But 95 per cent of all woolen exports originate in European mills.

Fiber, Leather, and Wood Products

In general, the same basic factors are involved in the location of textile manufacturing in the other countries as have just been observed in the United States. Rather than repeat the story at this point, we shall postpone a discussion of textile manufacturing in other portions of the world until Chapters 24 and 25, on general world regions of manufacturing.

Apparel

The manufacture of clothing is highly concentrated in a small strip between metropolitan New York and Philadelphia, along with several communities in eastern Pennsylvania (Figure 18-4). Measured in terms of value added, half the nation's apparel industry is in this small zone. Other conspicuous clothing centers are Chicago, St. Louis, Boston, Baltimore, Rochester (New York), Dallas, Los Angeles, and San Francisco. Elsewhere, the distribution is spotty.

The apparel industry is a small-scale industry; in fact, the average number of employees in the nation's 29,297 clothing factories is only 40. Compare this with a national average of 118 in textile mills. One reason for this dissimilarity is differing degrees of mechanization; spinning machines and looms can manufacture the fabric, but no machine has yet been designed to make a suit of clothes. Another reason is that, by virtue of its tremendous variety in sizes, styles, and quality, clothing is difficult to mass-produce. Thus there is little advantage in large assembly lines manned by hundreds of workers. Factories that make women's clothing are even smaller than those that turn out men's. In keeping with the small scale of the operations, the machines themselves are small (for instance, sewing machines and cutting machines). A good deal of the work requires high skill. It takes years to learn the art of sewing neat seams and making trim shoulders on coats. Accordingly, labor costs account for 33 per cent of the value of the shipments that leave apparel factories.

Figure 18-4

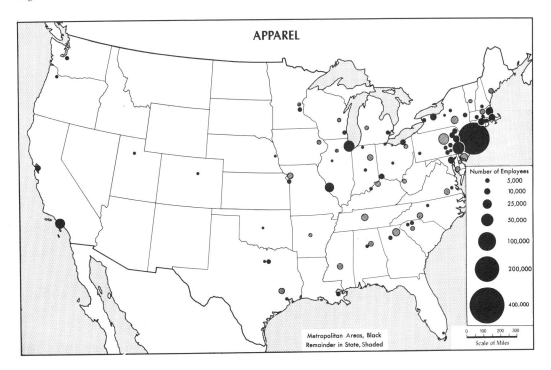

The industrial area of Preston, one of the leading cotton textile centers in Britain's Lancashire County. (Courtesy British Information Services.)

RELATIONSHIPS

Raw Materials   The New York-Pennsylvania apparel region is close to the northern textile factories and 300 miles from those in the Piedmont. These are its chief sources of material. Comparatively small quantities of fabrics are imported from abroad. Thus, nearness to raw materials is a major consideration in the location of factories.

Market Regions   There is a rather close correlation between the location of garment factories and urban markets. Notice that virtually every large city appears on Figure 18-4 and that the main concentrations of clothing factories are all close to large cities, where most of the consumers are. Very little apparel is exported to foreign markets, since the competition of European and Japanese clothing manufacturers (with their lower labor costs) is intense.

Labor Supply   The large labor pools of the nation's metropolitan areas are essential to an industry in which machines have augmented but not replaced the human hand. New York City had a particular advantage in this respect because, as the nation's main port of entry, it was able to tap the flow of European immigrants looking for work, many of whom had years of experience in European apparel factories. Even today, thousands of New York City's 360,000 clothing workers are foreign-born.

Style Centers   All the leading designers of men's, women's, and children's clothes are in cities, principally New York. Since apparel manufacturers maintain constant contact with these designers, they are a powerful force in keeping clothing factories in New York. For this reason, the most expensive clothes are made in large cities while simpler garments (overalls, work shirts, and wash dresses), whose style is not so important, are made in smaller, distant communities, such as those in Ohio, Wisconsin, and, increasingly, the southern states.

Central Business Districts within Cities

The garment business is one of the rare industries that tend to locate in the downtown sections of cities. In New York City, for example, there are 150,000 apparel workers in scores of small factories in Manhattan alone. In Chicago also, thousands of garment workers operate in the Loop and its periphery. Land in central business districts is expensive, and these factories cannot afford first-floor space. Often the ground floor in a building is occupied by a clothing retailer; sometimes the second floor is devoted to clothing wholesalers; while the clothing manufacturers occupy the upper stories, thereby winning the name of "loft" industries.

The main reason for the downtown concentration of garment manufacturing is labor supply. The downtown area, having a central location to the local population, is therefore in a good position for assembling a working force. In the case of New York City more workers can gather with less effort in Manhattan than in any other part of the city because most of the city's transportation arteries converge upon the island.

METROPOLITAN NEW YORK

The foregoing relationships all combine to make the New York metropolitan area the outstanding center of clothing production in the United States. This one urban area contains 54 per cent of the nation's garment factories, supports 31 per cent of the industry's employees, and accounts for 38 per cent of the value added (see Table 18-1). Rarely has any one industry become so highly localized.

Manhattan Island, containing New York City's central business district, can boast the greatest concentration of manufacturing of any area on the face of the earth, measured in terms of employment. And on the island, apparel-making is the leading type of manufacturing.

The core zone covers 150 acres in an area bounded by the Pennsylvania Railroad station on the south, Times Square on the north, Seventh Avenue on the east, and Ninth Avenue on the west. Here are the lofts that house the hundreds of small enterprises which constitute the garment business. In the neighboring streets are the buyers and sellers of high-style fabrics, feathers, furs, and other materials used in the manufacture of clothing. Though the following description was written in the 1930's, it is still remarkably applicable to the industry as it continues to function:

Because it is built upon fashion and behaves accordingly, the district looks to the casual visitor more like a madhouse than anything else. To pass through its streets at lunch time is an unforgettable experience. Its sidewalks are so jammed with throngs of garment workers who have poured out of its buildings for a breathing spell that through traffic is virtually stopped. The buildings house a jumble of showrooms, workrooms, storerooms, and offices. Through them passes a stream of buyers looking for goods they can sell to the customers of the retail stores they represent. Boys push little carts around through from one workshop or showroom to another. In offices scattered throughout the section, employers and workers argue out their recurring disputes over wages. Throughout all these operations runs a high nervous tension.

Madhouse though it may seem, the garment center and its way of doing business are a logical answer to the fundamental force which brought them into ex-

Table 18-1 *Apparel Manufacturing: United States and Greater Metropolitan New York*

| Criteria | United States | Metropolitan New York | |
		Quantity	Percentage of U.S. Total
Number of factories	29,297	15,814	54
Number of employees	1,180,517	361,638	31
Value added (thousands of dollars)	6,003,853	2,316,898	38
Payrolls (thousands of dollars)	3,585,646	1,302,578	36

Source: United States *Census of Manufactures*, 1958, Bulletin MC58(1)-1, Table 3 and Bulletin MC58(3)-31, Table 5.

Fiber, Leather, and Wood Products

istence—fashion. It provides two fundamental needs: First, it enables everybody to keep in touch with what everybody else is making and with what the consumers of the country and the storekeepers who represent them in this market are buying. Second, it makes possible great speed in setting up facilities to produce a particular style while the demand for it is good, closing them down when demand falls off, dropping styles quickly before stocks have been accumulated if they fail to win demand, and copying immediately anything any competitor devises which consumers like.*

THE WORLD PATTERN

The manufacture of garments on a commercial basis for world export is largely centered in western Europe. To be sure, considerable clothing is shipped from Japan and the United States; nevertheless, most of the apparel which moves through the arteries of international trade comes from factories in the United Kingdom, France, Germany, Italy, Belgium, the Netherlands, and Switzerland. The same factors that have operated in the United States have likewise operated elsewhere, influencing the apparel industry to locate primarily in the more industrially advanced areas. Further comment about apparel production in these other countries will be reserved for Chapters 24 and 25.

Leather

LOCATION AND CHARACTERISTICS

There are two major and three minor regions of leather manufacturing in the United States (Figure 18-5). The northeastern states from Pennsylvania to Maine constitute the foremost of these; eastern Massachusetts is the outstanding state area, but New York is the predominant city. The second-ranking region centers around St. Louis and includes numerous small settlements in Missouri and neighboring parts of Illinois, Kentucky, Tennessee, and Arkansas. The minor areas appear in eastern Wisconsin, southern Ohio, and the Piedmont.

The leading leather-manufacturing centers are, in terms of employment: New York 44,000, Boston 23,000, Binghamton (N.Y.)

* Reavis Cox, *The Marketing of Textiles*, The Textile Foundation (Washington, D.C., 1938), p. 312.

Fiber, Leather, and Wood Products

10,000, St. Louis 9,000, Chicago 8,500, and Philadelphia 6,500.

Leather manufacture has two principal phases: *tanning* and *fabricating*. Each process has a different locational pattern.

Tanneries process hides and skins, first soaking them to remove the hair and flesh, then treating them with tannic acid and oils to preserve the leather. Within the United States there are 578 tanneries which employ 37,130 people, an average of 64 workers per plant. The tanning phase is heavily concentrated in the Northeast: Massachusetts' plants perform a quarter of the nation's tanning. Boston is the chief tanning city, although Philadelphia is a close second.

The factories that fabricate the tanned leather into shoes, luggage, gloves, and belting employ 270,000 people and are much more widely distributed (Figure 18-5). Metropolitan New York is paramount in this stage with 40,000 leather-workers.

RELATIONSHIPS

Since about half the skins and hides for tanning are imported, largely from Argentina and South Africa, tanneries in Boston and Philadelphia are advantageously located. But the tanneries in interior cities such as Chicago, St. Louis, Milwaukee, and Omaha are also fortunately situated relative to raw materials, for they are near the large slaughter houses. Indeed, almost every large meat-packing center (Figures 17-3 and 17-4) is also a leather-tanning center (Figure 18-5).

For centuries, the foremost source of tannin was the bark of oak trees, principally the cork oak. Since it was more expensive to ship bark than hides (considering the relative volumes of each required in the tanning process), tanneries tended to locate in regions with oak forests (Chapter 6) and the hides were shipped in from animal-raising areas elsewhere (Chapters 7 and 9). Then, in the late 1880's, it was discovered that tanning chemicals could be extracted from chrome-bearing minerals. These chemicals proved less expensive than oak bark, and tanneries began abandoning forest locations in favor of places closer to their sources of hides and skins. A few tanneries, however, have lingered on in some Piedmont and northern communities, which

Figure 18-5 (*After Earl Lentz.*)

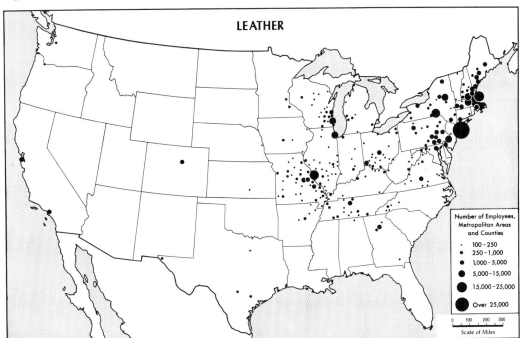

originally had nearby stands of oak trees. Their persistence demonstrates the power of an early start (or of subsequent *locational inertia*) in perpetuating an industry in a place which at one time promoted an association that is no longer predominant.

Markets   Today, the location of the leather industry is influenced more strongly by the pull of markets than of materials. It is much cheaper to ship leather to shoe, glove, and belt factories located near consumers than to ship shoes, gloves, and belts from factories located near tanneries. As the center of the nation's population has been shifting steadily westward, the leather industry in general and shoemaking in particular have also gradually moved westward from New England, which, as late as 1900, dominated the nation in the manufacture of shoes. Several New England firms subsequently moved their supervisors to St. Louis to train a new labor force. This was a planned regional shift in response to a moving market.

Labor Supply   Shoemaking and other forms of leather fabrication require considerable skill, and for years New England has had the nation's best reservoir of leather workers. This was a powerful factor in New England's long dominance in leather-working. But, as with the textile industry, labor rates there were higher than in other areas, so the shoe industry also tended to move away, in effect, creating its own labor supply in its new locations.

Machinery-leasing Systems   The movement from New England was expedited by an unusual trend in mechanization begun in 1852 with the adaptation of sewing machines to shoemaking. Other inventions followed, as a result of which a new industry was born: the manufacture of shoemaking machinery. At first there were several small specialized companies, some making cutting machines, some stitching machines, and so on. Gradually these small companies began to merge, to evolve one giant firm, the United Shoe Machinery Corporation, which today controls 90 per cent of the shoe machinery business. This corporation originated the unusual policy of renting rather than selling machines. The geographic impact of this policy was that small shoe factories sprang up in Wisconsin, Illinois, Missouri, Ohio, and other states, for a large capital investment was no longer needed for purchasing machinery. The combination of mechanization and machinery leasing reduced New England's attraction because the role of skilled labor, though not eliminated, was substantially reduced in importance.

"Jobbing - Out" Practices   The large leather manufacturers in Boston, New York, Philadelphia, St. Louis, Chicago, and Milwaukee frequently "job out" some of their work to factories in smaller cities. Soles, inner soles, heels, and uppers are often cut in outlying communities and trucked into the parent factory for final assembly. This practice enables the parent factory to combine the distribution advantages of a large city with the lower wage rates prevailing in smaller cities. Sometimes children's shoes and less expensive brands of adult shoes are completely assembled in outlying towns and trucked for distribution to a central factory that itself specializes in more expensive footwear.

THE WORLD PATTERN

Tanneries are widely distributed throughout the world, but they are concentrated in the industrial nations of Europe, the United States, the U.S.S.R., and Japan. To most of these countries comes a steady supply of hides and skins from Australia, South Africa, South America, and other ranching areas. All the industrial nations are large importers except for the U.S.S.R., which produces an adequate quantity of hides and skins to meet its demand.

Leather fabricators also tend to be located in Europe, U.S.S.R., and the other industrialized regions of the world (Figure 18-6). They sell most of their product to customers within their own countries, but they ship some products, particularly shoes, back to the very nations from which they import the hides. More information on the world pattern of the leather industry is in Chapters 24 and 25.

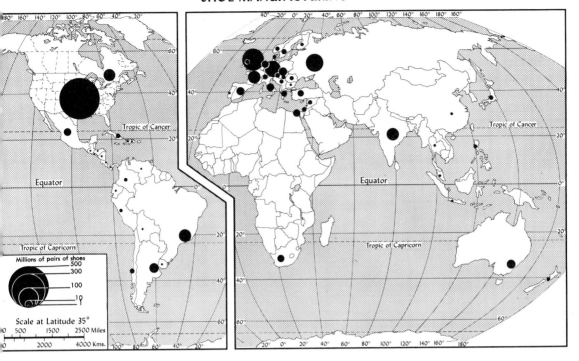

Figure 18-6 (*After Alfred Usack.*)

umber and Wood Products

LOCATION AND CHARACTERISTICS

Lumber manufacturing is one of the most widely distributed industries, as Figure 18-7, page 324, reveals, and one of the smallest in scale, averaging 16 employees per factory.

Over half the factories fall in the category of *primary* manufacturing. This category includes all industries whose raw materials come from the *primary* forms of economic production—forestry, fishing, bioculture, or mining. In the lumber business, the typical primary factories are sawmills and veneer mills, which process logs into boards, plywood, shingles, and excelsior. Many of the sawmills are actually portable factories that are moved about from week to week. But large sawmills are permanent. The *secondary* factories, whose raw materials come from the primary ones, are typically mills that manufacture sash, doors, trim, wooden containers, furniture, and prefabricated houses.

RELATIONSHIPS

Raw Materials Most lumber factories are located in forest regions as Figures 18-7 and 6-3 show. This is particularly true of the primary factories, for two reasons: (1) Logs are difficult to transport, not only because of their bulkiness but also because of their low value compared to the cost of moving them, especially by truck or rail. (2) The weight-loss ratio is high; at least half of each log ends up as sawdust, bark, or odd-shaped boards—items for which there is little sale. This combustible waste matter presents a problem since it cannot simply be dumped all over the countryside. The larger mills have so much that they build specially designed bee-hive furnaces to destroy it. In addition, in a few localities that are far from coal, the mills can sell sawdust for heating houses. Yet sawdust is not entirely a bother since the mills can burn some of it to meet their own fuel

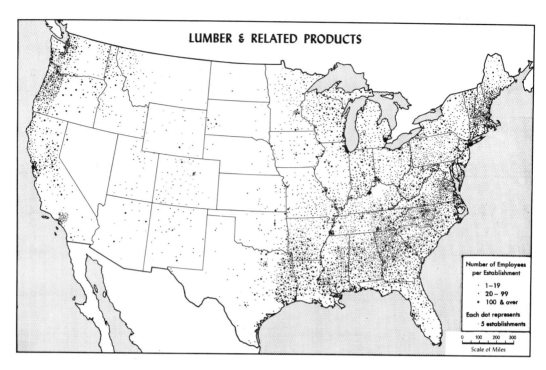

LUMBER & RELATED PRODUCTS

Number of Employees
per Establishment
· 1–19
· 20 – 99
• 100 & over
Each dot represents
· 5 establishments

0   100   200   300
Scale of Miles

Figure 18-7 (*After E. Maki.*) *This map is of interest for it not only shows the locational pattern of an industry but also illustrates a particular mapping technique. It endeavors to present a detailed pattern on a county basis. It is based on figures from the* Census of Manufactures. *This source of data, however, has a definite drawback since it does not indicate the precise number of employees in a given industry in every county; the reason for this limitation is the so-called "disclosure rule" which the Census authorities follow in order not to reveal confidential information about individual factories. Still, this Census does indicate for each county the number of factories in each of the 20 major industries (as established by Census authorities) by three size groups: (a) those employing 1 to 19 people, (b) those employing from 20 to 99, and (c) those employing over 100. This system is not altogether satisfactory, since a factory employing 100 people counts for as much as one employing 2000 people; nevertheless, it makes possible some sort of real description on a county basis of each major industry within the United States.*

requirements. And some dust is chemically treated, heated, and compressed into salable sheets of "Prestwood."

Providing a large sawmill with raw materials requires several logging camps. These camps are usually moved from time to time through the forest as one area after another is harvested. Thus, a sawmill serves as a sort of nucleus for the numerous logging operations conducted in the region around it.

Frequently a similar relationship exists between a single planing mill and several sawmills that supply it with rough-sawn boards for planing and finishing down to precise measurements. Planing mills are not portable like some sawmills, so they tend to be larger than the sawmills that feed them.

Waterways   Permanent sawmills are invariably located at the confluences of rivers or along the coast. Because of the low costs of water transportation, mills at such sites can usually tap a vast source of logs upriver so as to produce a steady flow of raw materials. By contrast, the small portable sawmills, which work the interfluves, must bring their logs overland. This is, of course, more expensive than floating them down watercourses; consequently, the overland hauls must be comparatively short. That is why portable mills are moved close to where logging is going on.

Markets   Most products of United States lumber mills are destined for the northeastern

Fiber, Leather, and Wood Products

part of the country. Until a few decades ago, this population heart of the nation was heavily forested. Indeed, lumbermen were in the vanguard as the pioneers moved through Ohio, Indiana, and Wisconsin. And the manufacture of wood products continues on in this great market region even though forests are severely depleted. One reason why the industry persists in the northeastern portion of the country is that freight rates on sash, door, and other wood products are 20 per cent higher than those on wood. Another reason is that the long-established mills enjoy an unusual freight-rate advantage, the fabrication-in-transit privilege. Under this arrangement, the railway companies permit lumber from the West Coast to be turned into doors in the Midwest and then shipped for sale into the East at a single through rate rather than at two joint

rates. For example, Wisconsin is dotted with dozens of sash-and-door factories dating back to the 1800's, when Wisconsin was a forested state. These businesses would collapse if in-transit schedules were abolished. The fabrication-in-transit rates are to the wood-products industry what the milling-in-transit rates are to flour milling.

THE WORLD PATTERN

Almost all the world's lumber manufacturing is carried on in the industrial nations of the Northern Hemisphere. By percentage of world total, the leaders are as follows: United States 40 per cent, Canada 8, Europe—mainly Scandinavia and Germany—20, U.S.S.R. 19, and Japan 6. The principal exporters, however, are Canada 40 per cent, Sweden 18, and Finland 17.

urniture

LOCATION AND CHARACTERISTICS

The manufacture of furniture (including office equipment, prefabricated cabinets, and restaurant fixtures) is highly localized in the

Northeast (Figure 18-8). Over half the industry is situated east of the Mississippi River and north of the Ohio River, although there are concentrations in the Piedmont and in California. When measured by states, furniture

Figure 18-8 (*After Walter Treece.*)

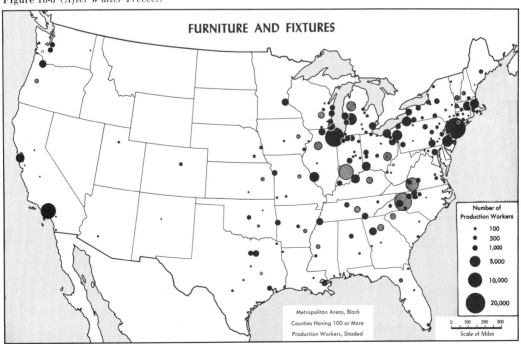

FURNITURE AND FIXTURES

Number of Production Workers
- 100
- 500
- 1,000
- 5,000
- 10,000
- 20,000

Metropolitan Areas, Black
Counties Having 100 or More
Production Workers, Shaded

0   100   200   300
Scale of Miles

manufacturing shows a rather positive correlation with population since the most populous states tend to be leaders in this industry. Measured in millions of dollars of value added, the top states are: New York 271, California 215, North Carolina 210, Illinois 188, Ohio 159, Michigan 159, and Pennsylvania 154.

Furniture factories generally are small, averaging only 34 employees per plant, one of the smallest-scale industries in the nation. The main reason for the modest scale is that many styles of furniture require extensive hand work that can be performed in small establishments as efficiently as in large ones. Other styles, however, particularly the cheaper ones, can be mass-produced on assembly lines. Consequently, large-scale plants, averaging 150 employees, have recently come into being, particularly in North Carolina, which now leads the nation in making wood furniture.

RELATIONSHIPS

Markets   The dominant position of the Northeast in Figure 18-8 strongly suggests that furniture factories are market-oriented. This generalization is further supported by the amount of furniture-making in metropolitan areas, many of which appear conspicuously on the map. Metropolitan New York alone manufactures more furniture than any state (except New York). Chicago and Los Angeles follow New York in that order. For these three metropolitan centers, the value-added figures for the furniture industry are $220,000,000, $161,000,000, and $158,000,000, respectively.

In response to market, the furniture industry originally was settled in New England and along the Atlantic Seaboard. Then, as the center of the United States market moved westward, so, like the leather industry, did much of the furniture industry. However, some furniture companies moved south to the Piedmont where other powerful attractions were less-costly labor, lower taxes, and Appalachia's hardwood forests. The advantage of hardwoods is their strength; most softwoods make poor furniture.

Raw Materials   Today, most furniture factories are not located very close to their raw materials. Hardwoods, for instance, which are harvested and sawed into boards mostly in the South, are then shipped to northern factories. In recent years an increasing amount of furniture is being made of metal. For this material, the northeastern factories are somewhat closer to the source, since most metal-producing factories are in the same area.

THE WORLD PATTERN

The manufacture of furniture as a commercial venture is widespread throughout the world. Small chairs, tables, and chests made from wood and woven fibers are made, at least in limited quantities, in a diversity of places such as the Philippines, Pakistan, India, South Africa, Colombia, and Britain. Yet most of the furniture that enters the channels of international exchange originates in the factories of Europe, Japan, and Anglo-America. This is particularly true for metal furniture, which has begun to account for an increasing, although still small, proportion of the total output.

Wood Pulp

LOCATION AND CHARACTERISTICS

Most of the United States' pulp mills, including the largest ones, are in southern states, particularly along the Gulf of Mexico and the Atlantic Ocean and in the Appalachian highland (see Figure 18-9). Elsewhere, northern New England, upper New York, the upper Midwestern states, and the Puget Sound-Willamette Valley region have sizable clusters of mills. Washington, Mississippi, and Wisconsin are in that order the three principal states in the manufacture of wood pulp.

The transformation of logs into pulp requires both mechanical and chemical processes. These are diverse, depending on the type of paper desired. The logs are peeled to remove the bark and then, in the most fre-

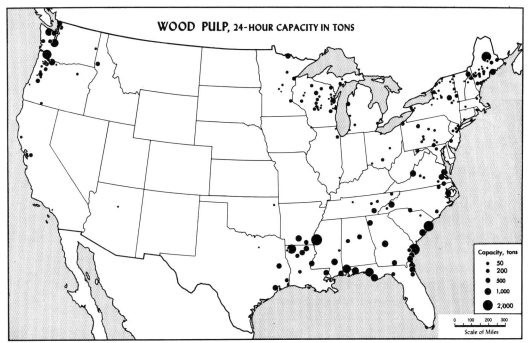

Figure 18-9 (*After Ray Hargreaves.*)

quently employed process, are chopped into small chips. The chips are boiled and treated with calcium bisulfite (or sometimes with caustic soda and sodium sulfide) to separate the woody fibers, which are discarded, from the cellulose fibers, which are sent through "beater engines" that mix them into a homogeneous mass known as *wood pulp*.

Pulp-making establishments are large, covering several acres. Adjacent to the factory structures are storage spaces where logs are piled in huge stacks 30 to 40 feet high. The average dimensions of pulpwood logs (termed "bolts" by men in the industry) are in length from six to eight feet, and in diameter from six to ten inches. There are 60 pulp mills in the country, which employ 14,000 people—an average of 230 per plant. This makes pulp mills one of the larger types of factory in the nation.

RELATIONSHIPS

Most pulp mills use softwood. Softwood is a term used by woodsmen to distinguish trees (such as the pine, larch, spruce, hemlock, and poplar) that are less dense and more easily worked than hardwoods (such as the oak, elm,

maple, and walnut). It is possible to make paper from the cellulose material of hardwood, but the process is expensive and the resulting paper is unsatisfactory for many purposes. Pulp mills invariably locate in or near softwood forests for precisely the same reasons that sawmills locate near timber stands: a high weight-loss ratio.

In order to insure a steady supply of bolts, many a pulp company has gone into the business of tree farming. First it purchases vast tracts of land, often *marginal* farm land, with poor soil or some other handicap. These tracts are then planted with a specific type of tree good for pulping. The company then husbands the trees, protecting them against fire, insects, and diseases. Finally, the trees are harvested carefully by means of selective cutting—only the mature trees are cut for bolts, deformed and scraggly ones are thinned out, and only the promising saplings are permitted to remain.

One reason the southern states loom up so large on Figure 18-9 is that their mild humid climate permits trees to reach maturity more rapidly than in the North (see Chapter 6).

Another raw material pulp factories con-

The Kaukopää Mills of the Enso-Gutzeit Corporation are the largest pulp- and paper-making installations in western Europe, with a capacity for producing 450,000 tons of sulphate pulp and paper board annually. (Courtesy Embassy of Finland.)

sume in tremendous quantities is water. Water is necessary for washing logs, boiling chips, and treating cellulose fibers. Since it must be fresh, every large-scale pulp mill is on a river or a lake. In many instances the river or lake performs two additional functions: It provides a means of transportation (bolts are simply floated or towed to the mill) and it provides sorting ponds, in which bolts are classified in terms of size, or ownership, or any other criterion of significance at the moment.

Waste disposal is a problem. Liquid waste from pulp mills is abundant and smelly. Channeling such stuff into a municipal sewage system is usually discouraged by the community. In the past most mills have simply dumped the waste into the rivers from which they got their water. But this practice polluted many rivers, and in recent years several states have passed laws requiring pulp mills to treat their waste with chemicals to make it less obnoxious before dumping it into streams. Mills situated where streams enter salt water

are often freed from these restrictions, however.

Pulp mills use great quantities of power in operating the machinery that removes bark, splinters the logs, and chips the splints. Large streams with rapids, falls, or enough of a drop to encourage dam construction can thus exert the added attraction of water power in the location of pulp mills.

Because rivers within forested regions can perform several functions (floating the bolts, providing fresh water for pulp-making processes, removing wastes, and generating power), it is not surprising that the locations of several rivers are discernible on Figure 18.9: for examples, the Fox, Wisconsin, St. Croix, Tennessee, Penobscot, and Kennebec.

THE WORLD PATTERN

Most of the world's wood pulp is produced in those nations that are both highly industrialized and endowed with softwood forests. The leading manufacturing areas, by percent-

Fiber, Leather, and Wood Products

age of total world pulp manufacture, are: United States 44 per cent, Canada 22, Europe 28, U.S.S.R. 3, and Japan 2.

In international trade the United States exports almost no pulp. The leading exporters are Scandinavia—Sweden, Finland, and Norway in that order—63 per cent and Canada 31 per cent.

Paper and Allied Products

LOCATION AND CHARACTERISTICS

Over two-thirds of the nation's paper, envelopes, bags, cartons, bread wrappers, stationery, decorations, and other paper products are made in the Northeast (Figure 18-10). The front-ranking states in order are New York, Pennsylvania, Massachusetts, Illinois, and New Jersey. The foremost cities are New York, Chicago, Philadelphia, and Boston.

Paper factories convert pulp, waste paper, and rags into paper. The material is washed, soaked, and pulverized into a homogeneous fibrous mass which is then run through long machines—some a city block in length—which extract the water and roll the fibrous mixture into a uniform sheet. About half the solid raw material is pulp, a third is waste paper, and much of the remainder consists of cotton and linen rags. But the proportion of these constituents varies, depending on the quality of paper being made. The best writing papers, for example, are made entirely from cloth rags. Coarser paper can be made from other fibers such as bagasse (sugar cane), straw, jute, and abaca.

RELATIONSHIPS

The paper industry as a whole is more market-oriented than raw material-oriented. Most of the paper mills in the United States are near their consumers, not only the manufacturers of stationery and printing paper but also those that make wrapping papers, decorating papers, and paperboard. The main reason for this pattern is that the value of most paper is low compared to its weight; consequently,

Figure 18-10 (*After Donald Schneider.*)

PAPER & ALLIED PRODUCTS

Number of Employees
- less than 500
- 500
- 1,000
- 5,000
- 10,000
- 20,000
- 25,000

0   100   200   300
Scale of Miles

it does not pay to ship it very far, since freight charges would eat up too large a percentage of its selling price. As a result, most paper factories are within 300 miles of most of their customers.

Many paper factories find it possible to locate near both their raw-material sources and their customers. This is particularly true for paper mills in the northeastern quarter of the country, for that is the foremost source region for waste paper (the main raw material used in making corrugated paper and packing boxes) and for rags (for stationery).

Factories that make newsprint and wrapping paper are exceptional. They tend to be raw-material oriented because they depend almost entirely on pulp, and it is usually more feasible to ship the papers than the pulp.

The world pattern for paper manufacture is similar to that for pulp. Leading areas by world share are United States 50 per cent, Canada 15, Europe 26 (with the United Kingdom and Germany the leaders), the U.S.S.R. 4, and Japan 3. But the leading exporters are Canada 64 per cent and Scandinavia 20 per cent (with Sweden and Finland predominant).

Printing and Publishing

The locational pattern of the United States printing and publishing industry is portrayed on Figure 18-11. Almost three-fourths of the nation's printing is done in the Northeast; in order of importance the foremost states are New York, California, Pennsylvania, Ohio, and Illinois. New York, Chicago, and Los Angeles are the leading cities.

Printing and publishing make up a highly diversified industry: Some plants specialize in newspapers, others in periodicals, books, or telephone directories, while others concentrate on advertising materials. Newspaper factories employ a third of all those in the printing industry, but commercial print shops are the most numerous—and also the smallest—for the nation has 12,000 of them averaging only 16 employees each.

Printing is closely associated with urban settlements where most of the nation's readers

Figure 18-11 (*After Sol Levin.*)

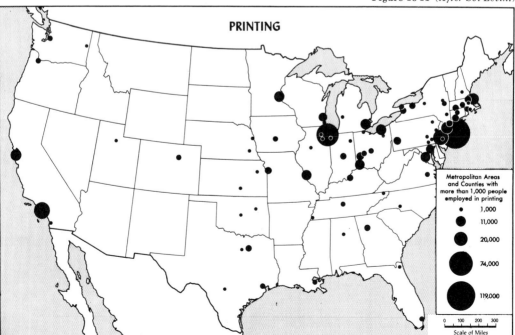

PRINTING

Metropolitan Areas and Counties with more than 1,000 people employed in printing

- 1,000
- 11,000
- 20,000
- 74,000
- 119,000

0 100 200 300
Scale of Miles

Fiber, Leather, and Wood Products

Table **18-3** *Employment in the Printing and Publishing Industry*

Type of Printing	United States	New York Number	Percentage of U.S.
Total	864,101	171,269	20
Newspapers	294,258	31,596	11
Commercial printing	287,803	48,877	17
Books	68,694	21,675	32
Periodicals	66,028	29,978	46
Printing trades services	42,021	11,940	29
Bookbinding	40,032	13,545	33
Greeting cards	21,777	5,024	23

Source: United States Bureau of the Census, *Census of Manufactures,* 1958, Bulletin MC58(1)-1, Table 3 and Bulletin MC58(3)-31, Table 5.

live and where most of the businesses are located that need advertising brochures and letterheads. Most publishers of textbooks, novels, and trade journals tend toward large cities. The New York City vicinity is unquestionably the nation's capital for the printing and publishing industry; Table 18-3 clearly illustrates the stature of New York in various segments of the business. It is because the printed products are highly valuable in relation to shipping costs that they can bear transport charges over long distances and therefore can be marketed throughout the nation from publishers in a few large cities.

We can generalize, then, by saying that there is a high correlation between population and the printing industry; as a whole, this endeavor tends to be market-oriented. There is one important additional relationship of daily newspapers with a raw material: If we consider "local news" to be a basic "raw material," then the same region that constitutes the newspaper's market has another function in generating one of the prime ingredients.

THE WORLD PATTERN

On a world basis, the location of printing and publishing correlates closely with economic advancement and high rates of literacy. When information is available for all parts of the world, it may be possible to measure a high correlation between the location of printing and publishing with that of commercial apparel production, number of telephones, educational level of the populace, and standard of living indices.

Suggested Readings

Airov, Joseph, *The Location of the Synthetic Fiber Industry,* Cambridge, 1959.

Alderfer, E. B., and Michl, H. E., *Economics of American Industry,* New York, 1957, chapters 19-26.

American Pulp and Paper Association, *The Statistics of Paper,* New York, 1959.

Burgy, J. Herbert, *The New England Cotton Textile Industry: A Study in Industrial Geography,* Baltimore, 1932, 246 pp.

Cooper, S. G., "The Canadian Woolen and Knit Goods Industry," *Canadian Geographical Journal,* 1946, pp. 174-185.

Eddison, John C., *A Case Study in Industrial Development—The Growth of the Pulp and Paper Industry in India,* Cambridge, 1955.

Herman, Theodore, "Cultural Factors in the Location of the Swatow Lace and Needlework Industry," *Annals of the Association of American Geographers,* 1956, pp. 122-128.

Herring, Harriet L., *Passing of the Mill Village: Revolution in a Southern Institution,* Chapel Hill, 1949.

Hsieh, Chiang, "Post-War Development in the Japanese Textile Industry," *International Labour Review,* 1950, pp. 364-388.

Lemert, Ben F., *The Cotton Textile Industry of the Southern Appalachian Piedmont,* Chapel Hill, 1933.

Manger, John E., "Pakistan's Cotton Textile Industry," *Foreign Agriculture,* 1951, pp. 274-276.

Prunty, Merle, Jr., "Recent Expansion in the Southern Pulp-Paper Industries," *Economic Geography,* 1956, pp. 51-57.

Rees, Henry, "Leeds and the Yorkshire Woolen Industry," *Economic Geography,* 1948, pp. 28-33.

Rodgers, Allan, "Changing Locational Patterns in the Soviet Pulp and Paper Industries," *Annals of the Association of American Geographers,* 1955, pp. 85-104.

Smith, Thomas R., *The Cotton Textile Industry of Fall River, Massachusetts: A Study of Industrial Location,* New York, 1944, 175 pp.

Stafford, Howard A., Jr., "Factors in the Location of the Paperboard Container Industry," *Economic Geography,* 1960, pp. 260-266.

Stanford Research Institute, *The Future for Paper in the United States,* Menlo Park, 1956.

United States Department of Agriculture, Marketing Research Division, *Changes in the American Textile Industry,* 1959.

Wolfbein, S. L., *The Decline of a Cotton Textile City: A Study of New Bedford,* New York, 1944.

The Lubumbashi copper smelter near Elisabethville in Katanga, Congo,
has an actual capacity of 125,000 tons of blister copper. Nearly all the concentrates
smelted come from the concentrator at the Prince Leopold
Mine. The first furnace here was fired in 1911. (Courtesy Union Minière du Haut-Katanga.)

NINETEEN

Few minerals are in usable form when they are dug out of the ground. Consequently, mining is closely related to manufacturing. In Chapters 19 and 20 we shall take up the industrial activities associated with several important minerals. Chapter 20 is concentrated largely on steel. But the present chapter deals with a trio of mineral-processing industries, chosen to illustrate different ways of upgrading the value of substances by changing their form. These industries are: copper processing, aluminum processing, and petroleum refining. For each, the United States will serve as a case-study area, after which we shall take a look at the world pattern.

Primary Copper Manufacturing

Copper is not abundant in the earth's crust, and rarely does it occur in pure form. Usually the atoms of copper are chemically combined with other elements (particularly oxygen and sulfur), and these compounds in turn are mechanically mixed with numerous other substances. To extract usable copper metal from copper ore—*primary manufacturing*—requires three steps: concentrating, smelting, and refining.

COPPER CONCENTRATING

The first step in transforming ore to metallic copper is *concentrating*. The rocky mass excavated from mines is hauled to concentrating mills where it goes through the "froth-flotation process": The material is crushed, soaked in water, and mixed with oils. When that mixture is agitated, the copper-bearing materials float

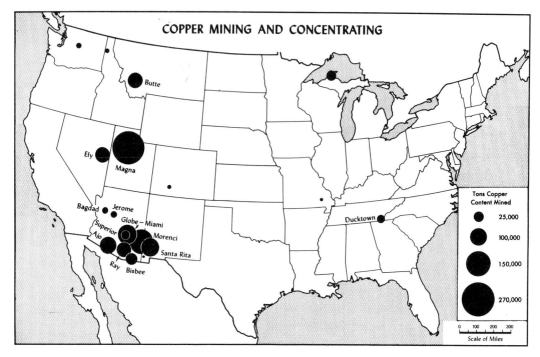

COPPER MINING AND CONCENTRATING

Figure 19-1

to the top and are separated.* The discovery of the froth-flotation process in 1914 opened up many new regions of copper mining by making it economically possible to process low-grade ores.

The location of copper concentrating mills in the United States is shown on Figure 19-1. From that map we learn that almost all this phase of copper manufacturing takes place in a copper belt running from Arizona to Montana. Several Arizona mills alone—the largest is near Bisbee—perform 50 per cent of the country's copper concentrating. But the distinction of having the largest single mill in the nation belongs to Magna, Utah (a settlement of 4000 persons ten miles west of Salt Lake City), which shows up prominently on Figure 19-1.

* More detailed information on the technology of this process, as well as the numerous other technological processes that will be mentioned in these chapters, appears in William Van Royen's *Atlas of the World's Resources*, Vol. I: *Mineral Resources of the World* (New York, 1952), and in textbooks on industrial engineering.

The locational pattern of concentrating mills correlates closely with that of copper mining. Indeed, nearly all concentrating takes place within a few miles of the mines. The reason for such close affinity is a high weight-loss ratio: Of every 100 tons of copper ore processed, an average of 97½ tons is worthless waste. Even the remaining 2½ tons consist of various impurities in chemical union with copper.

Thus, copper concentrating provides an excellent example of a raw-material-oriented industry, again illustrating the principle: The higher the weight-loss ratio, the stronger the tendency for the factory to locate near its raw material.

COPPER SMELTING

The purpose of smelting is to separate other elements, especially sulfur and oxygen, from the copper atoms. Chemically, the procedure is to convert copper sulfides (which survive the concentrating process) into oxides which are then reduced under great heat to relatively

Mineral-Processing Industries

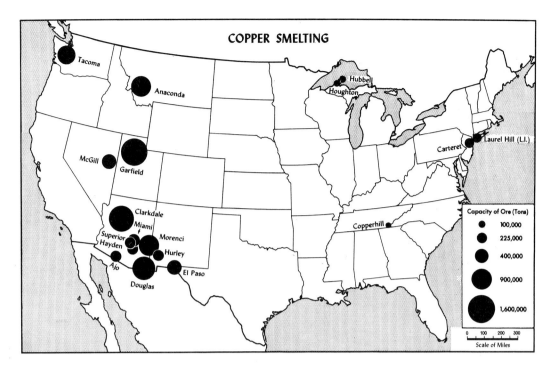

Figure 19-2

pure metal. The weight-loss ratio for copper smelters is 60 per cent; the 2½ tons of material which remain of the 100 tons that entered the concentrators are smelted into 1½ tons of waste and one ton of "blister copper," which is 99 per cent pure metal. The impurities in blister copper are usually gold, silver, lead, and zinc, which cannot be smelted out. Since the weight-loss ratio is fairly high, smelters usually locate rather close to concentrators. Most of the 18 copper smelters in the United States (Figure 19-2) are so situated. Arizona alone has seven of the 18. All told, the copper-mining states contain 15 of the nation's 18 smelters and account for 90 per cent of its copper-smelting capacity.

Yet, since the smelting weight-loss ratio of 60 per cent is considerably lower than the 97 per cent ratio that prevails in concentrating, the location of smelters correlates less closely with the location of their raw-material sources (the concentrating mills) than does the location of the concentrating mills with the location of their raw-material sources (the copper mines). Accordingly, some smelters are hundreds of miles from concentrators. Both the Atlantic Seaboard (New York City area) and the Pacific Seaboard (Tacoma) boast copper smelters, though they have no concentrators. These coastal smelters depend on foreign supplies of copper concentrate.

COPPER REFINING

Even though blister copper is 99 per cent pure metal, it is not suitable for manufacturing electric wires, cooking utensils, and other products. The gold, silver, lead, and zinc impurities must be extracted—and this must be done through electrolysis. In this process, blister copper is immersed in a bath of acidulated copper sulfate through which an electric current is passed. The ratio of weight loss in copper refining is extremely small, scarcely one per cent of the weight of the refinery's raw material.

Not only is the weight-loss ratio low, but what is "lost" is valuable. So, it is worthwhile to pay freight on it along with the copper.

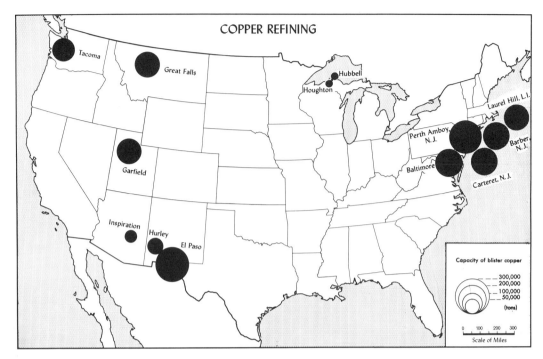

COPPER REFINING

Figure 19-3

Consequently, the attraction of copper-mining regions is substantially less for refineries than for smelters.

The nation has 14 copper refineries (Figure 19-3); the most productive are on the East Coast, with metropolitan New York as the leading center. One large refinery is located on Long Island (on an East River tributary) while three still larger ones are in the New Jersey suburbs of Perth Amboy and Carteret. This New York group accounts for 40 per cent of the United States' total copper-refining capacity. A fifth eastern refinery, in Baltimore, raises the Atlantic seaboard's capacity to exactly half the national total. Five refineries are located in the western copper belt; Arizona and New Mexico have only one apiece (two of the smallest refineries in the nation, in fact). Close by, however, is El Paso, Texas, with the largest refinery in the country. Utah has a

Figure 19-4

FLOW DIAGRAM: MANUFACTURE OF AMERICAN COPPER ORE

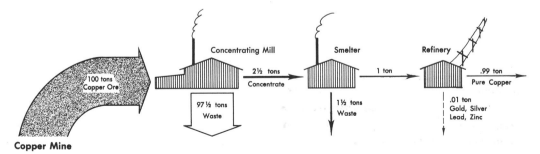

Mineral-Processing Industries

refinery at Garfield, and Montana has one at Great Falls. The capacity of these five copper-belt refineries is 40 per cent of the nation's total. Finally, there are one refinery in Tacoma and three small ones in upper Michigan.

The location of the copper-refining industry illustrates two principles: (a) Factories with low weight-loss ratios tend to be less raw-material-oriented than factories with high ratios, and (b) if the weight lost consists of valuable substances (such as gold and silver, in this case), then the attraction of the raw-material region for locating the factory is further weakened. For these reasons, in the matter of location, refineries correlate even less with their raw-material sources (the smelters) than smelters do with theirs. Smelters, in turn, correlate less closely with the source of their raw materials than do concentrating mills. These principles are illustrated by the data in Table 19-1.

Table 19-1   United States:
Copper-Manufacturing Industries

Industry	Weight-loss Ratio	Coefficient of Correlation*
Copper concentrating	97.5%	+0.98
Copper smelting	60 %	+0.35
Copper refining	1 %	−0.72

Source: Computed from data in *Minerals Yearbook* published by the United States Government, Department of the Interior, Bureau of Mines.
* Between tons of raw material produced and tons of product produced, on a state basis. A coefficient of correlation measures the strength of relationship between two variables. It will be discussed more fully in Chapter 31. In these computations, the figures employed to measure "tons of raw material produced" are as follows: For refineries, tons of smelter product were used; for smelters, tons of concentrate product were used; for concentrators, tons of copper ore mined were used. States with no production in any of these three items were omitted from the calculations.

COPPER MARKET

With completion of the refining process, primary manufacturing is over. The copper has been brought to a form that is workable for fashioning many objects of utility. The production of these items constitutes *secondary* manufacturing. It transpires in the diverse factories that fabricate electric wire, electric generators, electric motors, hardware, cooking utensils, and so on. These industries, hence the market for the refineries, are located largely in the northeastern quadrant of the nation (Figures 20-6 and 20-7), particularly in Connecticut. In the early 1800's, that state became the nation's leader in brass and copper fabrication and indeed, for many decades, copper prices on the national market have been synonymous with prices in the Connecticut Valley, the "hardware heart" of the United States.

PRIMARY COPPER-MANUFACTURING REGIONS

When the regional patterns of concentrating, smelting, and refining are synthesized, two regional types emerge. One is close to copper-mining areas, the other on the margin of fabricating areas.

Within Mining Country   Most regions of copper mining embrace all three stages of copper manufacturing. The western copper belt in particular contains almost all the concentrating in the country, 90 per cent of the smelting, and half as much of the refining. In some places all three types of factories are close to the local mine as in northern Utah and upper Michigan. Some localities have only two factories: for instance, a concentrator and smelter in eastern Nevada, or smelter and refinery in El Paso. Elsewhere factories are isolated: In Montana the concentrator is at the mines in Butte, the smelter is at Anaconda 20 miles to the west, and the refinery is at Great Falls, 100 miles to the northeast on the Missouri River. Where the smelters and refineries are in different settlements from those of the concentrators but still within the general mining region, they tend to locate on the line of movement from mine to market. For instance, most of Arizona's and New Mexico's copper moves eastward, and much of it is refined at El Paso, which is on the eastern edge of the copper area and on a mainline railroad toward eastern fabricators.

Near Fabricating Regions   Manufacturing regions far from copper mines account for 10 per cent of the nation's smelting and 55 per cent of its refining. Smelters in these areas are invariably alongside refineries (compare Figures 19-2 and 19-3). These refineries enjoy three favorable relationships: (1) They are close to their market, the fabricating mills. (2) They are close to foreign sources of copper. This is significant because the United States is now a net importer of copper. For example, this country's refineries annually consume 900,000 tons of domestic blister and 300,000 tons of foreign blister, virtually all of which is transported on ocean-going freighters. This is why a *port* location on the margin of the nation's main fabricating region is advantageous for a copper refinery in a nation whose mines do not meet its copper needs. (3) They are close to scrap copper. In addition to blister, United States refineries also consume 450,000 tons of scrap, most of which is "produced," so to speak, in northeastern states.

RELATIONSHIPS TO FOREIGN AREAS

Before 1939, the United States exported more copper than it imported. World War II, with its tremendous demand for electrical equipment, abruptly reversed that relationship. United States exports now total 170,000 tons of copper in pure form, but her imports total 700,000 tons, measured by copper content, of which 40 per cent is pure copper from foreign refineries, 45 per cent is blister copper from foreign smelters, and 15 per cent is "matte" (a product which has been only partially smelted). By percentage of total copper imports, these are the principal areas of supply: Chile 40 per cent, Canada 20 per cent, and Peru 17 per cent.

THE WORLD PATTERN

Types of Region   The world can be divided up in exactly the same manner as the United States. One type of region refines more copper than it concentrates and therefore must import semiprocessed materials. As Table 19-2 indicates Anglo-America and western Europe belong to this first type since they refine considerably more copper (almost three-fourths

Table 19-2   Copper Manufacturing: Percentage of World Total, by Leading Areas

Area	Concentrating*	Smelting	Refining
North America	35	35	47
United States	24	25	47
Canada	10	9	—
Mexico	1	1	—
South America	17	15	11
Chile	13	11	11
Peru	4	4	—
Western Europe	2	8	20
West Germany	—	7	—
Eastern Europe and U.S.S.R.	13	13	12
U.S.S.R.	11	11	11
Africa	24	21	5
Northern Rhodesia	14	13	5
Congo	8	7	—
Union of South Africa	1	1	—
Asia	7	7	5
Japan	2	4	3
China	2	2	—
Philippines	1	—	—
Australia	2	1	—

Source: United States Department of the Interior, Bureau of Mines, *Mineral Trade Notes*, October, 1961, pp. 17-18.
* Expressed by ore content recorded at mines.

of the world's total) than they concentrate (less than half). Europe, in fact, is almost devoid of copper ore, and much of Canada's copper is a by-product of her nickel industry at Sudbury (Chapter 14).

A second type of area concentrates more ore than it refines. The Katanga district (straddling the Congo-Rhodesian boundary) and Chile belong to this type. Most of the former's copper moves to Europe; most of the latter's to the United States. Katanga is the biggest exporter of blister copper, Chile of refined copper. But since central Africa has the greatest potential hydroelectric power on the globe (Chapter 14), it will probably not be many years before enough dams are built to harness the power needed to feed refineries with adequate electricity to take care of Katanga's copper.

There is a third regional type, one where concentrating and refining are nearly equal. The U.S.S.R. and Japan fall in this category. They refine what they concentrate, and neither

Mineral-Processing Industries

export or import very much concentrate or blister.

Control of the Copper Industry The regions that consume the most copper are the home bases for the companies that control the mining and manufacturing. American firms oversee about half the world's production, principally in the United States, Mexico, Chile, Peru, and other Western Hemisphere nations. British companies control a quarter of the total with operations largely in Africa, Canada, and Australia. Belgian companies control nearly 10 per cent, entirely in Africa. This pattern of control conforms with a principle of geography that investment capital and entrepreneurs tend to move from the markets to areas of primary production.

Primary Aluminum Manufacturing

Aluminum constitutes 8 per cent of the earth's crust, a larger proportion than that of any other metal or element except silicon and oxygen. However, it never occurs in pure form, always in combination with oxygen and often with other elements in a variety of minerals, only one of which—bauxite—contains enough aluminum to pay for the cost of extraction.

There are two types of plants engaged in the primary manufacturing of aluminum: (a) *alumina factories*, which separate out most impurities from bauxite, leaving aluminum oxide, or alumina, and (b) *aluminum factories*, which break down aluminum oxide into its two constituents. Because these two industries differ in both location and spatial relationships, each merits separate consideration. (A word about terminology: In the aluminum industry and the copper industry the terms *concentrate* and *refine* are used dissimilarly. Thus, alumina factories refine bauxite and aluminum factories concentrate alumina.)

ALUMINA FACTORIES

Alumina factories are clustered in the central part of the United States (Figure 19-5, page 340). Five are strung along the Gulf Coast from Texas to Alabama. Two mills are in western Arkansas, one in southern Illinois, and one in Ohio. These factories consume three types of raw materials: bauxite, fuel, and caustic soda. The fuel is burned to supply heat in the mechanical separation of impurities from bauxite, which is crushed and baked in rotating kilns. The aluminum-bearing residue is then soaked in caustic soda, which removes all other impurities with the exception of oxygen.

The weight-loss ratio is high enough—100 tons of bauxite make 40 tons of alumina—to discourage long hauls of bauxite by expensive forms of transportation such as trucks and trains. Therefore, *inland* bauxite mines tend to have alumina factories close by, as in western Arkansas, where 98 per cent of the nation's bauxite is mined. But the weight-loss ratio is still low enough to encourage long shipments of bauxite by water. The Gulf Coast mills, the Illinois mill (at East St. Louis on the Mississippi River), and the Ohio mill (at Clarington on the Ohio River) all feed on bauxite arriving by water, the main source regions being Jamaica, British Guiana, and Surinam. In fact, for every ton of domestic bauxite mined, the United States imports three tons of Latin American ore, which helps explain the role of coast and river mills.

If importing aluminum ore to coastal mills is feasible, why isn't copper ore shipped to coastal concentrators? The answer lies in the ratio of dross to metal: 5000 tons of dry cargo would yield 1000 tons of metal from average bauxite but only 50 tons of metal from average copper ore.

From the standpoint of time of development, the East St. Louis mill was the first to be constructed, in 1902. Not until 1938 was a second one built—in Mobile, Alabama. Then, during World War II, three more were put up (Hurricane Creek, Arkansas; Baton Rouge, Louisiana; and Listerhill, Alabama). Since the war five more have been built, one in

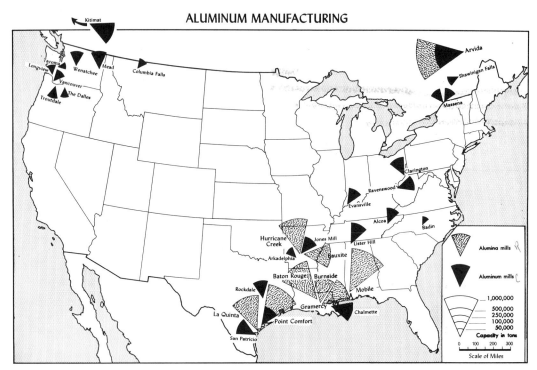

Figure 19-5

Arkansas, two in Texas, one in Louisiana, and one in Ohio. Thus, since its inception, alumina manufacturing in the United States has been a phenomenon of the south-central portion of the country.

ALUMINUM FACTORIES

These are located in three widely separated areas: the Pacific Northwest, the South, and the Northeast (Figure 19-5). The geography of aluminum manufacture may be understood more easily with an historical orientation, because different factors operated at different times to influence the location of aluminum production.

1895-1940 The nation's first aluminum mill was constructed at Niagara Falls in 1895; all the alumina processed was imported from Germany, and the electricity required was generated at the falls. In 1903 a second and smaller refinery was built at Massena, New York, adjoining a hydroelectric power plant on the St. Lawrence River. This was the year that the United States began to produce its own alumina (at East St. Louis, where

Illinois coal and South American bauxite were brought together) which was then shipped to Niagara Falls. During World War I two additional concentrators (that is, aluminum factories) were constructed near hydroelectric plants in the southern Appalachians (Alcoa, Tennessee, and Badin, North Carolina). These four concentrators, operated by a single company, The Aluminum Company of America ("Alcoa"), supplied all the nation's aluminum until World War II broke out.

1940-1946 The sudden demand for light-weight metals in warplanes caused an intense shortage of aluminum. Alcoa hastily constructed a new mill at Vancouver, Washington; but the United States government, convinced that one lone company could not meet the nation's need, took a rare step—it itself hurried into the business. The government built and then operated seven new concentrators, one in Arkansas near bauxite, one in northern Alabama near hydroelectric plants on the Tennessee River, one in Massena, New York (a large new mill replacing the one built in 1903, which had been closed) and *four* in the Pacific Northwest where several power installations had been constructed in major river beds. During the war the aluminum industry consumed one-fifth of the electricity produced in the Pacific Northwest. These northwestern mills were far from alumina factories, and all the alumina they processed was (and still is) hauled by rail from Arkansas and the Gulf—one of the longest rail hauls of bulk goods in the United States.

1946-Present   Since World War II the federal government has either sold its concentrators to private companies, new competitors of Alcoa, or closed them. Alcoa dismantled its Niagara Falls plant, which was obsolete, and built a new one on the Texas coast. Other companies have constructed or are in the process of constructing new aluminum mills—all of them in the South and the Ohio Valley.

Power Supply   To understand the locational patterns in these three periods, we must be familiar with the single dominant relationship in the placement of aluminum refineries: access to electric power. For electrolysis is the only method for separating aluminum atoms from oxygen atoms in the alumina molecule. In this process, electricity is passed between carbon anodes and cathodes through the mineral cryolite. The mineral melts, forming a bath to which the alumina is added. Under these conditions, the oxygen in the alumina unites with the carbon in the anodes, forming carbon dioxide and leaving the aluminum to puddle at the bottom and be drained off as crude castings called "pigs." To produce one ton of aluminum requires 2 tons of alumina, $\frac{3}{4}$ ton of carbon anodes, and 20,000 kilowatt-hours of electricity—enough to service an eight-room house with six persons, electric washing machine, dishwasher, mangle, roaster, toaster, and other conventional electric gadgets for a full decade. Because the power must be both electric and abundant, aluminum concentrators have tended to settle near the cheapest available source—thus, the mills at Niagara Falls, in

the Tennessee River Valley, and in the Pacific Northwest: all areas of extensive hydroelectric power production. In the past decade, however, improvements in techniques for manufacturing electricity from steam explain the birth of concentrators in the South, where natural gas serves as the fuel, and in the coal-rich upper Ohio Valley. Plans for future expansion call for increases in the East and South—near coal and gas. Apparently the era of supremacy of hydroelectric power sites for aluminum concentrating in the United States is over.

Market Regions for Aluminum   The market for refined aluminum consists of airplane manufactures and a wide variety of fabricators—those who make storm windows, ladders, hardware, and a rapidly increasing number of other items. Indeed, the increase is so great that United States factories now use more aluminum than any other metal except iron. Most of these factories are located in the northeastern part of the country (see Chapter 20, Figures 20-6, and 20-7). Notice the contrast in locational pattern between aluminum concentrators and copper refineries: The former have displayed much less inclination than the latter to be near their market. Aluminum mills can afford to keep their distance, though, because the value of aluminum sheets, tubes, bars, and other forms is high relative to their weight, upon which freight rates are assessed. Besides, it is cheaper to ship aluminum from concentrator to market than to "ship" electricity (or tremendous tonnages of fuel for generating electricity).

Relationships with Foreign Areas   The United States exports scarcely any aluminum and imports three-quarters of her bauxite requirements. Of her imports, almost half comes from Jamaica and almost a third from Surinam. Before World War II we mined almost as much as we imported, but since then our degree of dependence on foreign regions has steadily increased.

THE WORLD PATTERN

Three areas account for over 90 per cent of the world's aluminum manufacture (see

Table 19-3): (1) Anglo-America produces over half the total. The United States is the world leader, and Canada accounts for a perhaps surprisingly large amount. (2) Western Europe refines a little more than Canada. (3) The Soviet Union refines somewhat less than western Europe.

Canada Though lacking in bauxite, Canada has aluminum mills at the extreme eastern and western parts of the country (Figure 19-5). In the East, Canada can boast it has the largest aluminum mill on the face of the earth. In 1901 a concentrator was built 60 miles southwest of Quebec City at Shawinigan Falls on the St. Maurice River, a few miles upstream from its confluence with the St. Lawrence River. Alumina was imported from Germany. This mill is still in operation, but limited water power restricts its expansion. In 1926, Aluminium Limited of Canada ("Alcan"), which operated the Shawinigan Falls concentrator, built a new plant in a forested wilderness 120 miles northeast of Quebec on the Saguenay River. The attraction of that remote spot was tremendous hydroelectric potential, for the water drops 300 feet between Lake St. John and the St. Lawrence River (Figure 19-6). Total power development here on the Saguenay is now 2,580,000 horsepower. At first, alumina was imported, but in 1928 an alumina mill was added. Bauxite arrives by ocean freighters from Jamaica and the Guianas at Port Alfred, 40 miles up the Saguenay at the head of navigation; thence, it is taken by rail 20 miles to the mills. Personnel to operate the port facilities, the railroad, the refinery, and the concentrators were all brought in from elsewhere, and a new community, Arvida, displaced the forest surrounding the mills. The city now numbers 13,000 people, and the alumina and aluminum factories employ over 1000 people.

Figure 19-6

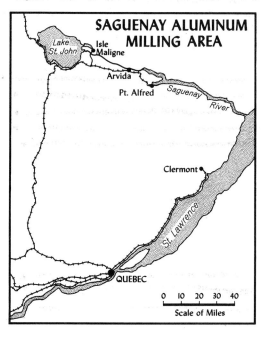

SAGUENAY ALUMINUM MILLING AREA

Arvida, Quebec, is a planned city (population 13,000) laid out in the wilderness around a huge aluminum smelter and refinery built along the Saguenay River (background). The Arvida mill, with an annual capacity of 373,000 tons of aluminum (7 per cent of the world's total), is the world's largest aluminum concentrator and refinery. (Courtesy Aluminum Limited Sales, Inc.)

Western British Columbia also has a large aluminum mill, a new development lured to a wet, rugged wilderness by potential water power resources. An initial handicap was that most of the water drained along gentle gradients to the east, whereas the steep western slopes had very few streams. But by an ingenious plan, the Canadians reversed the direction of flow of a stream to fall down the precipitous western side of the mountains. This was accomplished by damming the Nechako River (which flows east) and creating a lake 120 miles long (Figure 19-7, page 344). At the lake's western end a 25-foot tunnel was drilled 10 miles to drain the lake *westward* to Kemano where a power house was constructed 2585 feet below the level of the lake. The potential for power development from a large volume of water with so great a waterhead exceeds the potential of that on the Saguenay. Electricity generated at Kemano is transmitted 50 miles to Kitimat (on the shores of Douglas Channel) which is accessible to ocean-going vessels delivering alumina from mills in Jamaica. Plans also call for eventual construction of an alumina mill at Kitimat using Canadian gas for heating the rotary kilns.

Canada is a prize demonstration of how a region with absolutely no native ore and scarcely any domestic market (she exports almost all her aluminum to the United States and Europe) can be a dominant world figure in an industry that requires large amounts of power. The Canadian experience again illustrates the principle that aluminum production is a power-oriented industry.

Europe The aluminum industry was born in Europe in 1886, France and Germany being the early leaders. Today, France, along with Greece, still supplies most of the bauxite for western European mills. (Yugoslavia and Hungary actually yield more ore than Greece, but most of the former's and all of the latter's is snapped up by the Soviet Union.) In the production of alumina and aluminum, West Germany paces the continent. Germany is the largest link in a chain of aluminum nations that encircles the Alps. The others are France, Italy, Austria, and Switzerland. A second, lesser area crops up in Norway which, like

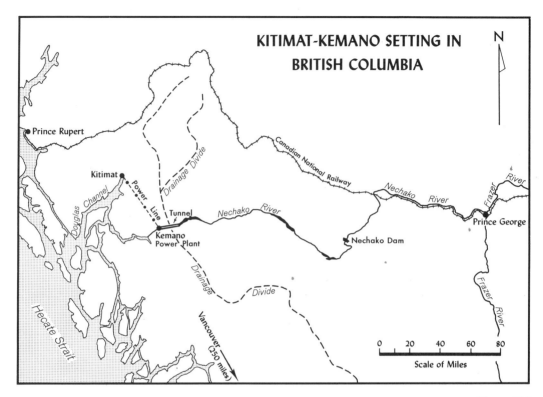

KITIMAT-KEMANO SETTING IN BRITISH COLUMBIA

Figure 19-7

Canada, lacks both ore and market but is blessed with power. All told, western Europe accounts for 12 per cent of the world's bauxite and 19 per cent of the refined aluminum, so she does not figure nearly as much as Anglo-America in long ocean movements of materials.

U.S.S.R. Before World II, the Soviet Union's largest aluminum factory was at Zaporozhye near the large dam in the Dnieper River at Dnepropetrovsk. This mill depended almost entirely on Hungarian bauxite. A smaller mill at Volkhov used low-grade ores that came from east of Leningrad. Both of these factories were destroyed by the German army in World War II. But just before the war started, at Kamensk on the eastern flanks of the southern Ural Mountains, the Russians built a third plant to take advantage of Ural bauxite and local lignite for thermal electricity. Later, far to the east in Stalinsk a fourth mill was constructed, equipped with machinery hastily evacuated from Volkhov, and based on bauxite from the Kuzbass field.

After the war, the Russians rebuilt the Volkhov and Zaporozhye mills, using machinery expropriated from Germany. A large new mill was built at Kraznoturinsk in the northern Urals to process the bauxite there, the richest in the U.S.S.R.; electricity is generated thermally from local lignite. But the largest Soviet mill today is at Yerevan in the Cauasus where hydroelectricity is abundant. Hungarian and Yugoslav bauxite sustain this plant. Unless the Soviets have made some very recent discoveries of bauxite, they must continue to depend on Hungary and Yugoslavia, each of which produces almost as much bauxite as Russia herself.

Petroleum Refining

The locational pattern of petroleum refining in the United States (Figure 19-8) reveals a few places with large refineries—Philadelphia, Los Angeles, Chicago, and Port Arthur—while numerous small refining centers are scattered elsewhere—in Texas, Oklahoma, Kansas, and the Rocky Mountain states in particular.

Refineries have several distinguishing characteristics that set limits on their location. They require a lot of land (particularly for storage tanks), they emit an obnoxious odor, and they present some danger of explosion.

Accordingly, they are usually located on the outskirts of settlements or even in rural areas. Indeed, although many of the symbols on Figure 19-8 are identified by names of metropolitan areas, the refineries may be actually in lesser-known suburbs such as Whiting (Chicago) and Marcus Hook (Philadelphia).

Petroleum refining is one of those rare industries in which the weight-loss ratio is zero. Besides, there is a volume-gain, for 1000 barrels of crude oil, when heated and distilled, yield more than 1000 barrels of kerosene, gasoline, fuel oil, or many other products that vaporize at different temperatures.

Figure 19-8 (*After Gunnar Alexandersson.*)

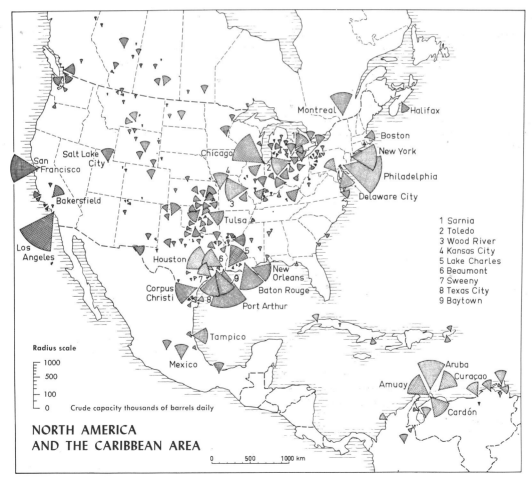

NORTH AMERICA AND THE CARIBBEAN AREA

Radius scale

1000
500
100
0

Crude capacity thousands of barrels daily

0   500   1000 km

1 Sarnia
2 Toledo
3 Wood River
4 Kansas City
5 Lake Charles
6 Beaumont
7 Sweeny
8 Texas City
9 Baytown

A petroleum refinery processes only one raw material but over one hundred products result. The steps for processing crude oil are so highly mechanized that few employees are needed. Indeed, labor accounts for only 6 per cent of the production costs of the industry. On the other hand, payments for crude oil account for no less than 75 per cent of refinery production costs.

RELATIONSHIPS

Petroleum refineries can be classified by location into two types: those within (or on the margin of) resource regions and those within (or on the margin of) markets.

Refineries near Oil Fields   Here is a clear capsule description of the installations in the oil regions:

Many refineries are located on or near the oil fields. They are usually rather small. In Anglo-America inland refining centers of this type are numerous. They roughly outline the main oil field. Compare [on Figure 19-8] northern Texas, Oklahoma, and Kansas in the large Mid-Continent field [see Chapter 15] with the denser populated southeastern states which have virtually no oil production and very little inland refining capacity. Several . . . refining centers located on or near oil fields are . . . rather small compared to centers located in areas of maximum market potential or in shipping ports.*

In addition to the Mid-Continent field, refineries have been established in the oil fields of western Pennsylvania, Ohio, Michigan, Illinois, the Gulf Coast, the Rocky Mountain states, and the prairie provinces of Canada.

One reason that refineries within oil fields tend to be small is that the life of an individual oil pool tends to be short (approximately 25 years), discouraging companies from investing capital in the construction of large works. Besides, since transport costs on crude oil are slightly lower than those on petroleum products, firms are discouraged from establishing many large refineries within oil fields that have no large contiguous market. Most of the products of

* Gunnar Alexandersson, "The Oil Refineries of the World—A Case Study," *Proceedings* of IGU Regional Conference in Japan, 1957, p. 266.

the small inland refineries move to market by truck or rail. Because of the expense this represents, their customers are principally in the immediate hinterland.

There are only a few enormous refineries within or on the edge of oil fields. Invariably, these few have three attributes: (1) They are in or near huge fields that produce large volumes of crude oil—volumes greatly exceeding the demands of local customers. (2) They are in port cities with access to deep-water shipping. Port Arthur, New Orleans, Baton Rouge, Houston, and Corpus Christi are examples of this type. (3) They are sustained by sales to numerous distant markets that lack oil resources and sufficient demand, as yet, to support a large refinery of their own. It is cheaper for such localities to import refined products from an efficient large refinery elsewhere than to run a less efficient small operation of their own.

Refineries within Market Areas   The northeastern quadrant of the United States is by far the nation's biggest market for petroleum products. Although the oil industry started there—in Pennsylvania—the Northeast today is relatively unimportant in oil production. Consequently it is an oil-deficit region and millions of barrels of petroleum are shipped in. Some of it arrives in processed forms, but most of it arrives as crude oil to be refined within the market region. The Delaware River estuary downstream from Philadelphia supports the largest single concentration of refineries in the world. Several other seaports between Massachusetts and Virginia stand out on Figure 19-8, and all receive crude oil by ocean-going tankers, mostly from Texas, Louisiana, and Venezuela.

Within the northeastern market region a few centers are inland, however—Chicago, East St. Louis (Wood River), and Toledo. These places are served by pipelines from the Mid-Continent field; in addition, the first two cities, being on the Mississippi-Illinois waterway system, receive large volumes of crude oil by barge.

Elsewhere in the nation other refining centers have also come into existence to serve

Mineral-Processing Industries

surrounding markets: for instance, Kansas City, Denver, Salt Lake City, and San Francisco. Los Angeles is unique in that it is endowed with both a substantial urban market and extensive oil resources; accordingly, Los Angeles is one of the nation's major refining centers.

There are four over-all reasons why large refineries are set up in large markets, even when such areas are barren of oil. First, it is easier to bring in one material and distill it centrally into 100 different products for subsequent distribution to surrounding consumers than to bring in 100 different products from refineries in distant oil fields. A second reason is the volume-gain factor mentioned earlier; it is cheaper to ship a small volume of crude oil than a larger aggregate volume of all its derivatives. Third, tanker shipping rates are lower on crude oil than on its products because "dirty" carriers can be used to haul crude oil whereas tankers carrying gasoline and kerosene must be clean. Fourth, there is a greater *evaporation loss* in transporting refinery products than in transporting crude oil. For example, for every 1000 barrels of crude oil shipped from the Gulf Coast to the Eastern Seaboard, the evaporation loss is approximately ten barrels, but for refinery products it averages about 50 barrels.

Products Demanded   For the United States as a whole, the demand for petroleum products breaks down as follows: gasoline 45 per cent, domestic fuel oil 25 per cent, industrial fuel oil 15 per cent, and kerosene, lubricants, and other derivatives 15 per cent. These figures reflect the ubiquity of the automobile. The demand for the foremost petroleum product is nation-wide, so refineries are rather widespread through most of the country. We shall note a revealing contrast to this when we discuss European refineries.

Role of Waterways   Waterways play a critical part in the location of petroleum refineries because of the low cost of barge and tanker transport. Few commodities can be loaded and unloaded from ships as easily as crude oil, and tankers are unquestionably the

most economical means for moving crude oil. The index of costs per ton-mile on crude-oil movements in the United States are: truck 75, railroad 22, pipeline 4, and ocean tanker 1. In short, ton-mile costs by ocean tanker are only $\frac{1}{75}$ as much as those by truck.

Water is a big factor in the success of large refineries near Galveston, Corpus Christi, and other port cities adjacent to large oil fields. One might suppose that only crude oil would move through these ports. Actually, however, these Gulf Coast refineries ship refined products by barge and tanker to myriad small market areas where demand, until now, has been too small to support a refinery. This is especially true of the southeastern portion of the United States, which is almost devoid of refineries. Some of the products move from Texas and Louisiana refineries by barge along rivers, but most of it moves along the coast by tanker to Tampa, Savannah, and other ports.

Clearly, the ideal locations for huge refineries are port cities, whether they are near oil fields or market.

Relationships to Foreign Areas   The United States no longer exports very much refined oil. In fact she is importing a gradually increasing amount of crude oil to meet a voracious domestic demand that now exceeds domestic production. Indeed, crude oil is now the second-ranking commodity, after coffee, imported into the United States.

THE WORLD PATTERN

By percentage of world totals, the chief areas are Anglo-America 54 per cent, western Europe 15, the Caribbean 12, the U.S.S.R. (and eastern Europe) 9, and the Middle East 7. The world pattern of refining gives evidence of the same locational factors as we observed in the United States.

Markets and refining regions tend to coincide even though some yield no oil at all. The best example of this relationship is Europe. Figure 19-9 emphasizes the role of port cities encircling a region that consumes large quantities of oil although it mines very little. Industrial Europe depends on imports, most of which come from the Middle East. And Rotter-

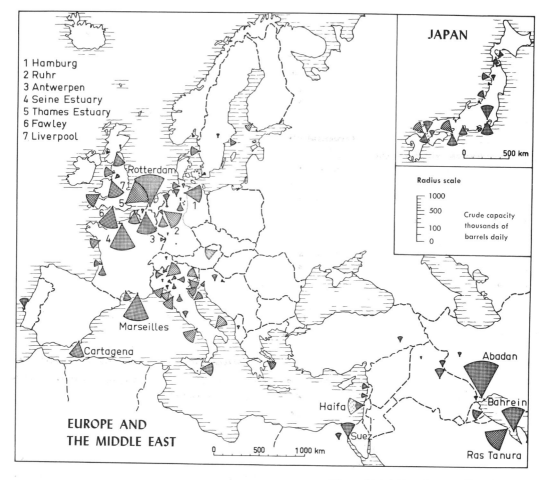

Legend:
1 Hamburg
2 Ruhr
3 Antwerpen
4 Seine Estuary
5 Thames Estuary
6 Fawley
7 Liverpool

JAPAN

0   500 km

Radius scale

1000
500
100
0

Crude capacity
thousands of
barrels daily

Rotterdam

Marseilles

Cartagena

Haifa

Suez

Abadan

Bahrein

Ras Tanura

EUROPE AND
THE MIDDLE EAST

0   500   1000 km

Figure 19-9 (*After Gunnar Alexandersson.*)

dam, gateway to the industrial heart of the continent, is the foremost refining center; but the Thames estuary, the Seine estuary, Marseilles, Antwerp, and the Ruhr are not far behind. There is a closer locational correlation between refining and manufacturing in Europe than in the United States because most of Europe's refinery production is industrial fuel. The European demand for petroleum derivates breaks down as follows: industrial fuel oil 65 per cent, gasoline 20 per cent, other uses 15 per cent. Compare these figures with those cited earlier for the United States. They help explain the difference in the two areas. Europe's refining is largely concentrated in its west-central area, which is her industrial heart. Likewise northern Italy, another industrialized zone that possesses scarcely any

crude oil, supports several market-oriented refineries (Figure 19-9).

As for other places, Figure 19-8 demonstrates that Canada's largest refineries (Montreal and Sarnia) are in the East—precisely where the majority of Canada's population and market is. And Japan, an important buyer of crude oil, has refineries in several port cities (Figure 19-9). None of these is very large compared with the world's major refineries.

Oil-field regions of consequence that also contain refineries are the Middle East, Venezuela, and Indonesia. Virtually all the large refineries are in port cities close by the oil fields. Examples in the Middle East (Figure 19-9) are Abadan (the world's single largest refinery), Ras Tanura, and Bahrein. In Venezuela (Figure 19-8) the principal refineries

Mineral-Processing Industries

Shell Nederland Raffinaderij, one of the petroleum-receiving ports in the Netherlands. Crude oil arrives by ocean tankers (mostly from the Middle East), which, well-down in the water, tie up at the docks (right foreground). At specially designed docks (as in left-center foreground) the oil is pumped from the ships through numerous pipes to storage facilities on land where nearby refineries (as in center background) process the crude oil. Some oil is piped inland (the Ruhr, for instance) to refineries closer to consumers. A little crude oil is transferred from ocean tankers to barges which service inland refineries via inland waterways. At the extreme left of this picture, a tanker with bow riding high in the water is nearing the end of pumping operations. (A Shell Photograph.)

are in the ports of Amuay and Cardon. Indonesia's counterparts are Balikpapan (on Borneo) and Palembang (on Sumatra). Sarawak has a large refinery at Lutong. The largest refinery in the Soviet Union is at Baku, a major port on the Caspian Sea.

A third type of refinery location is discernible: at intermediate *transport focal points* between oil fields and markets. Aruba and Curaçao (Figure 19-8), for instance, refine considerable oil pumped up in the environs of Lake Maracaibo (see Chapter 15). The lake is too shallow for ocean tankers, but the ports of Aruba and Curaçao can handle large

ships. Furthermore, these islands fly the Dutch flag, and Dutch investors preferred to install refinery equipment in a place that was under the protection of the Netherlands government. Refinery products from these small islands are exported to Brazil, Argentina, other Latin American countries and Europe.

In the eastern Mediterranean area (Figure 19-9) are several refining centers (for instance, Suez and Haifa) which conform to the intermediate-location type, as also do the refineries in southern Italy, particularly at Naples, that process oil from the Middle East en route to European and African customers.

Suggested Readings

Alderfer, E. B. and Michl, H. E., *Economics of American Industry,* New York, 1957, chs. 6, 7 and 16.

Duncan, Craig, "The Aluminum Industry in Australia," *Geographical Review,* 1961, pp. 21-46.

McNee, Robert B., "Functional Geography of the Firm, With An Illustrative Case Study From the Petroleum Industry," *Economic Geography,* 1958, pp. 321-337.

Pearson, Ross, "The Jamaica Bauxite Industry," *Journal of Geography,* 1957, pp. 377-84.

Shabad, Theodore, *The Soviet Aluminum Industry,* New York, 1958, 25 pp.

The Lorraine-Escaut steel mill at Longwy (Lorraine), with a huge slag pile in the background. (Photo Henrard, courtesy France Actuelle.)

TWENTY

The purposes of this chapter are (1) to consider two classes of *location factors*, (2) to examine the primary manufacturing of iron, man's favorite metal, and (3) to investigate the geography of a few secondary manufacturing industries that fabricate steel products. As before, we shall examine the United States intensively before turning to survey world regions.

Location Factors

There are two distinctly different types of location factors: initial and survival.

Initial location factors explain how a factory comes into existence in a particular place. Perhaps a local citizen invents a commodity and, wishing to abide in familar territory, sets up his factory on home grounds. Perhaps available raw material convinces investors of the worth of processing it on the spot. Perhaps a local market, previously served by a distant factory, becomes prosperous enough to support a local outfit. Perhaps local power sources, such as the mill races in many New England cities, initially lure several factories to their sites. In some instances, a labor pool of skilled artisans gives birth to an enterprise. Such factors answer the question, "Why was the factory first located *there?*"

Survival location factors, which pertain to costs, explain how a factory continues to exist where it is. After it is in operation, a plant, to survive, must be favorably located relative to two kinds of costs: (a) *overhead costs* (such as real estate taxes), which continue regardless of whether the factory is operating full-time or half-time or is idle, and (b) *production costs* (such as labor, freight charges, and income taxes), which vary with the amount of manufacturing.

To answer the question, "Why is this factory where it is?" calls for inspection of both initial and survival factors. And that inspection requires extensive digging into the present and past relationships of individual factories —a task on which researchers have barely scratched the surface.

The problem is complicated because location factors may, of course, change with time. What was once a favorable factor in locating a plant may disappear. For instance midwestern sash-and-door mills were at first right in the middle of surrounding forests, but as the forests were cut over, the surviving mills had to draw lumber from distances as great as 2000 miles, as we said in Chapter 18. Thus an initial location factor is no longer a survival location factor.

The Steel Industry

Iron is an abundant element that constitutes 5 per cent of the earth's crust. Man uses iron in far greater quantities than any other metal—as Table 20-1 shows, nearly sixty times as much as the next-ranking element.

In the United States the iron-and-steel industry employs over half a million people, ten times the number engaged in the primary production of all other metals combined (Table 20-2).

Table **20-1** *World Production of Metals*

Metal	Tons
Pig Iron	285,000,000
Aluminum	5,010,000
Copper	4,590,000
Zinc	3,390,000
Lead	2,530,000

Source: United States Bureau of Mines, *Mineral Trade Notes*, November, 1961, p. 29, October, 1961, p. 17, September, 1960, p. 49, September, 1961, p. 30, August, 1961, p. 7.

Figure 20-1 (*After Gunnar Alexandersson, courtesy* Economic Geography.)

RAW STEEL CAPACITY IN ANGLO-AMERICA, 1948 and 1959

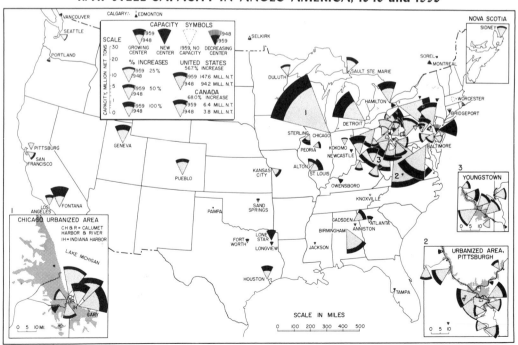

Steel and Fabricated-Metal Products

Industry	Number of Employees	Value Added
Blast furnaces and steel mills	511,392	$6,062,227,000
Other metals	47,086	700,431,000
Primary aluminum	17,381	383,836,000
Primary copper	14,561	158,122.000
Primary zinc	8,923	71,653,000
Primary lead	3,563	36,325,000
Other primary metals	2,658	50,495,000

Source: United States *Census of Manufactures*, 1958, Bulletin MC58(1)-1, pages 1-16.

LOCATION

The heart of United States steel manufacturing is a triangular area, 250 miles on a side, that is marked off by Johnstown (Pennsylvania), Detroit (Michigan), and Buffalo (New York) (Figure 20-1). Within this steel triangle are mills capable of making over 60,000,000 tons of steel a year—almost half the United States total (Table 20-3). The leading municipality in the triangle is Youngstown, Ohio, whose plants have an annual capacity of nearly 7,000,000 tons. Pittsburgh itself can produce only 3,400,000 tons. But its suburbs—such as Braddock, McKeesport, Duquesne, and particularly, Munhall, which has a capacity of 4,000,000 tons—raise the potential product of the Pittsburgh urbanized area to 18,000,000 tons. Most of these towns are in the Monongahela Valley, whose residents can boast of the largest number of steel mills in the country. Other outstanding communities in the steel triangle are Buffalo and Cleveland (Table 20-3).

At the southern tip of Lake Michigan a few huge mills in East Chicago, Chicago, and Gary, have a combined capacity of 27,000,000 tons, almost a fifth of the national total. Though the regional total is less than that of the steel triangle, these cities, in the order mentioned, are the three leading steelmaking municipalities in the United States (Table 20-3). All three repose within the Chicago urbanized area, which at last has wrested from Greater Pittsburgh the honor of being the na-

Table **20-3**   Steel Centers Arranged by Areas, 1959

Areas and Leading Centers	Net Tons Capacity (in 000)
Appalachian Coal Valleys	55,260
Pittsburgh and suburbs	18,345
Other centers along the Ohio, Monongahela, and Allegheny Rivers	13,218
Monessen	1,560
Donora	1,015
Midland	1,362
Weirton	3,300
Steubenville	2,400
Ashland	1,022
Portsmouth	1,500
Other centers in western Pennsylvania	4,612
Johnstown	2,425
Farrell	1,268
Other centers in eastern Ohio	13,664
Youngstown and suburbs	11,155
Canton	1,829
Southern Appalachian district	5,421
Birmingham	4,178
Gadsden, Alabama	1,209
Great Lakes (Southern Shores)	50,512
Chicago and suburbs	26,970
Detroit and suburbs	7,942
Lorain, Ohio	2,648
Cleveland	5,435
Buffalo and suburbs	7,200
Atlantic Seaboard	
Atlantic Seaboard	12,176
Baltimore	8,382
Morrisville, Pennsylvania	2,687
Inland centers, eastern Pennsylvania	8,445
Steelton	1,500
Bethlehem	3,900
Inland Centers, Eastern Ohio, Indiana, and Illinois	6,919
Middletown, Ohio	2,557
St. Louis (Granite City)	1,440
Lake Superior Ore Ports	
Duluth	973
The South, Outside of the Appalachian Coal Fields	3,027
Lone Star, Texas	800
Houston	1,343
The West	
Large coastal cities	5,234
Fontana, California	2,933
Inland Centers	4,868
Geneva, Utah	2,300
Pueblo, Colorado	1,800
United States Total	147,634

Source: Alexandersson, Gunnar, Changes in the Location Pattern of the Anglo-American Steel Industry: 1948-1959, *Economic Geography*, 1961, pp. 99-100.

tion's foremost urbanized area in steel production. Impressively enough, Chicago and its suburbs make almost as much steel as the entire United Kingdom (see Table 20-5) while Pittsburgh and its suburbs manufacture almost as much steel as France.

The Middle Atlantic steel district contains several mills in various communities in eastern Pennsylvania and Maryland. The regional capacity is roughly equal that of Pittsburgh and suburbs. The leading centers here are Sparrows Point (a suburb of Baltimore) and Bethlehem, Pennsylvania.

The Middle Ohio Valley district (from Middletown, Ohio, to Ashland, Kentucky, and Huntington, West Virginia) has several small mills with an aggregate capacity of around 5,000,000 tons. Additional small steel centers appear in southern Indiana, southern Illinois (particularly the suburbs of St. Louis), and Duluth, Minnesota.

All told, 90 per cent of United States steel is made east of the Mississippi River and north of a line running from St. Louis to Baltimore. Elsewhere, steel districts are small and widely separated. The capacity of mills in southeastern states is 5 per cent of the national total, mostly in Fairfield and Ensley (suburbs of Birmingham, Alabama). The southwestern states account for a little, particularly at Houston. Pueblo (Colorado), Provo (Utah), Fontana (California), and the San Francisco area each can produce at least 1,000,000 tons.

CHARACTERISTICS

The manufacture of steel involves three general steps: smelting the ore into pig iron, refining the pig iron, and adding alloys.

Ore is smelted in blast furnaces. Four raw materials go into the process and three products result (see Figure 20-2). The solid raw materials—ore, coke, and limestone—are dumped in from above; then the coke is ignited, and a draft of forced hot air is introduced from the bottom. Gases (mostly

Figure 20-2 (*After American Iron and Steel Institute.*)

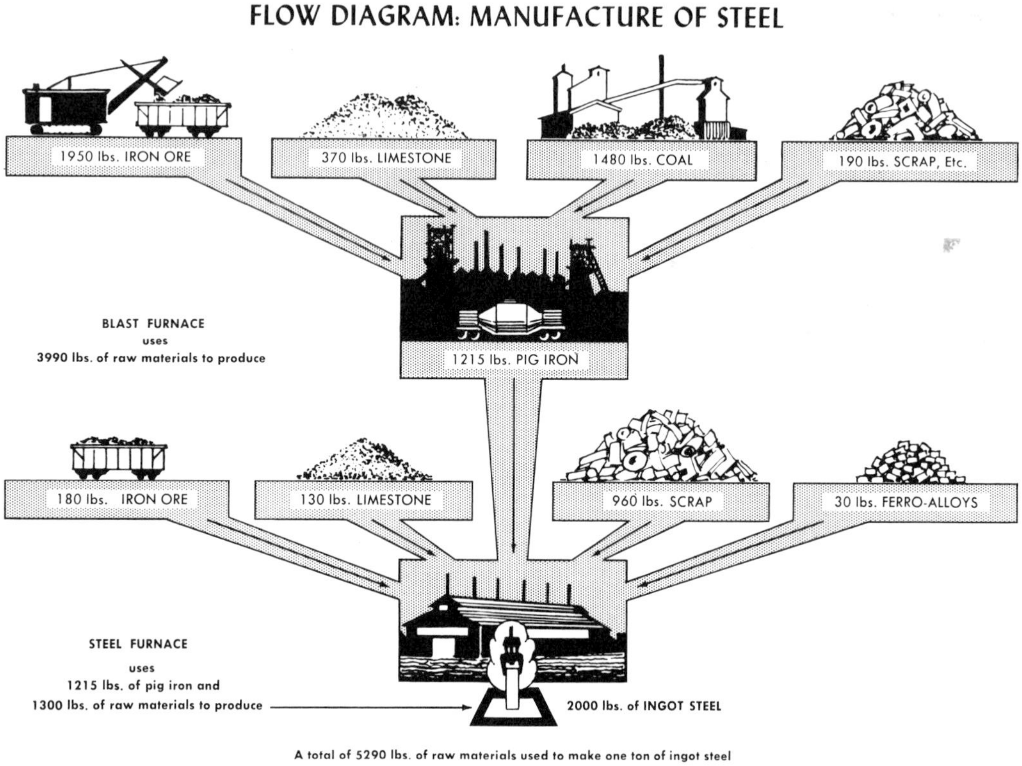

FLOW DIAGRAM: MANUFACTURE OF STEEL

| 1950 lbs. IRON ORE | 370 lbs. LIMESTONE | 1480 lbs. COAL | 190 lbs. SCRAP, Etc. |

BLAST FURNACE
uses
3990 lbs. of raw materials to produce

1215 lbs. PIG IRON

| 180 lbs. IRON ORE | 130 lbs. LIMESTONE | 960 lbs. SCRAP | 30 lbs. FERRO-ALLOYS |

STEEL FURNACE
uses
1215 lbs. of pig iron and
1300 lbs. of raw materials to produce ⟶ 2000 lbs. of INGOT STEEL

A total of 5290 lbs. of raw materials used to make one ton of ingot steel

Steel and Fabricated-Metal Products

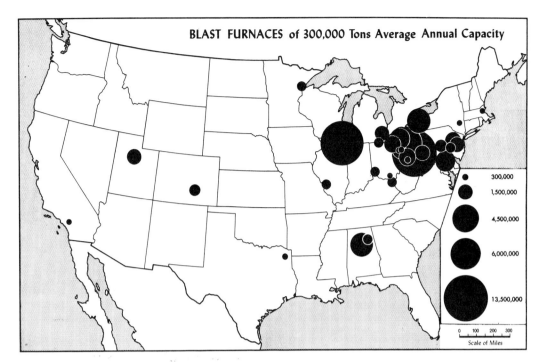

Figure 20-3

carbon dioxide) are drawn off the top while molten iron and molten slag are drawn from the bottom. The lighter slag floats on top of the heavier liquid iron. In addition to the four ingredients already mentioned, tremendous quantities of cold water (ten tons of water for every two tons of iron ore) are pumped through the jackets around the blast furnaces to keep them from melting.

Coke is the most common fuel in blast furnaces, although charcoal may be used. Coke itself is a manufactured product made from bituminous coal. The coal is heated in order to drive off volatile gases that are undesirable in smelting ore. The residue, the coke, is a light carbon substance that is still strong enough to bear the weight of ore and limestone in a blast furnace without being crushed. Were it not so strong, it would become so compact under the weight of rocky iron ore and rocky fluxing stone that the passage of hot air upward through the burning charge would be obstructed. The function of coke in a blast furnace is two-fold: It provides heat to melt the iron-oxide ore with the fluxing stone, which unites with many of

the impurities, and it provides carbon, which unites with much of the oxygen in the iron oxide to form carbon dioxide, thus releasing the iron. But in accomplishing these two objectives the coke unfortunately supplies an excess of carbon which combines with the iron. One of the main purposes of the next step—the refining process—is to separate iron and carbon atoms.

The locational pattern of smelters is shown in Figure 20-3. Notice that the general distribution conforms to that of steel mills. A closer inspection of Figures 20-1 and 20-3, however, reveals (1) that fewer places make pig iron than make steel, and (2) that most of the places that make steel but not pig iron are outside the prominent steel districts.

Many companies operate blast furnaces and steel furnaces side by side. But where only one plant exists, it is invariably a steel mill. For reasons which will be seen later, steel mills can thrive in places that lack blast furnaces, but blast furnaces can rarely subsist without the mills.

Pig iron is 95 per cent pure metal, but it contains certain other elements (mostly carbon and silicon) that must be eliminated before the iron is usable. These impurities are extracted by refining processes in special furnaces. Some furnaces (for instance, the open hearth or the Bessemer converter) burn them out under very high temperatures with jet streams of forced superheated oxygen. Such furnaces are able to handle scrap iron as well as pig iron in one batch. Again, coke is the main fuel (although gas can be used). Typical proportions of these materials in refining operations are: 1 ton pig iron + 1 ton scrap iron + 1 ton fuel = 2 tons steel + 1 ton gas. The electric furnaces that have been perfected in recent years are now competing successfully with the other two types. Although more costly to operate, these electric furnaces can be controlled with more precision, so they are being used in making a higher-quality product.

After pure iron is obtained, certain alloys, such as carefully determined small quantities of carbon, manganese, nickel, and cobalt, are added to the refined pig iron to give specific qualities such as ductility, malleability, elasticity, and endurance under heat. The resulting product is *steel*. About 10 per cent of our steel is now made in electric furnaces.

Two other characteristics of steel manufacturing deserve citation: scale and nuisance.

Blast furnaces and steel mills are typically large-scale operations, averaging 176 employees per plant. Large tracts of land are required not only for the structures (such as the blast furnaces, ovens for preheating air, refining furnaces, rolling mills, and soaking pits) but also for huge storage piles of ore, coal, and limestone. The Bethlehem Steel Corporation's plant at Sparrows Point, Maryland, the largest single steel factory in the world, covers 4,000 acres and employs 30,000 people (see photo, page 359).

Regardless of size, steel plants have certain nuisance attributes. All blast furnaces and most steel mills (except those that use electricity) are notoriously dirty and often smelly. Their belching smoke stacks throw plumes of smoke into the atmosphere, and the fallout of dust particles over steelmaking centers is tremendous. When atmospheric conditions are favorable, the plume of reddish smoke from steel centers at the southern end of Lake Michigan trails away to the east in a streamer 40 miles long. Some cities have passed anti-smoke measures requiring that all chimneys be equipped with devices to arrest escaping dirt particles. This scheme has worked with outstanding success in Pittsburgh.

RELATIONSHIPS

The four principal relationships of steel-making are those with sources of raw material, with markets, with transportation, and with certain site features.

Raw Material The steel industry consumes six raw materials in huge amounts. In order of tonnage, they are cool water, preheated air, coke, iron ore, scrap iron, and fluxing stone. Other raw materials—alloy metals or refractory brick for lining furnaces —are used in very small amounts.

1. Cool water: Since fresh water must be flushed through the jackets of the furnaces to keep them from melting, most mills select sites along rivers or lakes. Where several steel plants are clustered in one valley, the river water, being used and reused repeatedly, absorbs so much heat that its temperature rises. Water in the Mahoning River, for instance, below the final mill in Youngstown frequently registers a temperature above 90° F. Sometimes, other considerations take precedence over the availability of fresh water in locating a plant. In such cases, clever solutions have been devised to supply the necessary coolant. The Sparrows Point mill, for one, has adapted its cooling system to permit the use of sea water. And in the semi-arid Los Angeles basin, the Fontana steel mill has set up an elaborate and complex water reclamation system. Waste water from near-by municipal sewage systems and from other industries is treated and then recirculated 40 times through the furnace jackets. There is not enough waste water to meet all the needs of this mill, but by using what is available, the plant only draws 3,000,000 gallons a day, rather than 130,000,000 from California's limited supply of fresh water. For the United

Steel and Fabricated-Metal Products

States as a whole the steel industry makes use *each day* of the staggering total of four billion gallons of water, not only to cool furnaces but to generate steam and to quench coke.

2. Hot air: To make a ton of steel requires four tons of air, heated to 1500° F and blown up through the coke and ore in the furnace. Some blast furnaces swallow 50,000 cubic feet of air a minute. Although air is free, *hot forced* air must be manufactured. So every blast furnace is flanked by a series of tall ovens (usually more conspicuous than the furnace itself) in which the air is warmed under pressure.

Although air and water are items used in greatest quantities by blast furnaces and steel mills, the industry cannot be said to be "air-oriented" or "water-oriented." For these materials—the one world-wide and the other widely available—are less costly to assemble than other raw materials that are consumed in smaller amounts.

3. Coke: To manufacture a ton of coke requires 1½ tons of bituminous coal. In the early days of coke manufacture, beehive ovens were used for heating the coal. The first beehive was built in the 1840's (before then, charcoal had served as the fuel for smelting ore and making steel). But beehive ovens had two shortcomings: They could handle only high-grade bituminous coal, and they lost all the volatile gases. Because Appalachian coal was the only satisfactory raw material for these ovens, and because so much weight was lost in the process, virtually all the nation's coke was made in the mining areas of western Pennsylvania, West Virginia, and eastern Ohio. Connellsville, Pennsylvania (40 miles south of Pittsburgh), was the unrivaled capital of coke production.

Then in the 1890's a new technique was devised—the by-product oven—which could use lower-quality coal and salvage all the volatile gases, which in turn could be used not only as fuel in making more coke but also as raw materials for chemical factories. Now that there was no weight loss, since the total weight of coal had value in one form or other, coke manufacturing quickly moved next door to the steel plants. Today, since the steel industry gobbles up most of the nation's coke the pattern of coke production coincides closely with that of steel.

4. Iron ore: When ore that is one-half iron is used in blast furnaces, there is a 50 per cent weight loss. This would tend to pull blast furnaces toward iron ore regions. But the strength of this attraction is neutralized by the pull of coal, since it takes two tons of coke (which require three tons of bituminous coal) to make one ton of steel. The lower the percentage of iron content, of course, the stronger the drawing power of iron-mining regions on the location of ore-processing factories. In all likelihood, however, such factories will be concentrators (taconite mills) rather than blast furnaces (see Chapter 16). The movement of iron ore to steel plants is shown in Figure 20-4, page 358.

5. Fluxing stone: Limestone (or dolomite) is used in blast furnaces to attract and combine with the impurities that are mechanically mixed with iron in the ore; the mixture is slag. Some slag can be used as a raw material in cement factories or as a surface on rural roads. Yet much of it is useless, and disposing of it is an appreciable cost item for steel plants because it must be transported, sometimes considerable distances, to dumping grounds.

Both limestone and dolomite are widely distributed. Mills in western Pennsylvania procure the stone from limestone quarries a few miles to the east. Mills along Lake Michigan and Lake Erie receive theirs in lake freighters from huge quarries in northern Michigan, where Alpena and Calcite are the major shipping ports. Certain plants need no limestone, for some ores contain enough lime to be almost entirely self-fluxing, such as those in Alabama and Lorraine in France.

6. Scrap iron: On the average, for every one ton of pig iron going into a steel furnace, there is one ton of scrap iron. Some small electric steel furnaces, however, subsist entirely off scrap. Most of this material comes from junk yards and secondary factories (for example, steel shavings and cuttings from machinery factories). Since these suppliers are chiefly located in the Northeast, that is the nation's major source region of scrap iron.

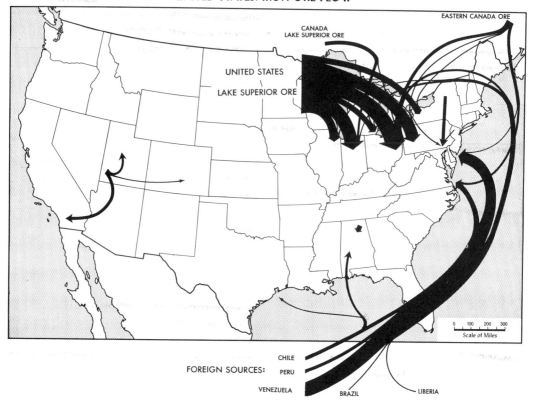

CANADA
LAKE SUPERIOR ORE

EASTERN CANADA ORE

UNITED STATES

LAKE SUPERIOR ORE

0   100   200   300
Scale of Miles

CHILE

FOREIGN SOURCES: PERU

VENEZUELA   BRAZIL   LIBERIA

Figure 20-4

Comparison of Steel Centers in Their Relationships to Raw Materials   At this point it is possible to appraise the several steel regions in terms of their relationships to the source areas of raw materals. The steel triangle is well off vis-à-vis coal; indeed, to the south it coincides with a portion of the Appalachian coal field. But for iron ore, the triangle must depend entirely on distant sources—mostly Minnesota, to a lesser degree upper New York, and increasingly the Quebec-Labrador fields.

Southern Lake Michigan mills are far from coal—coking coal, that is. For the near-by Illinois and Indiana coal is not of good coking quality. Consequently, the big mills in Gary and Chicago depend on Appalachia for most of their fuel. Much of it arrives by lake freighters which have been loaded at Toledo and other Lake Erie ports. Lake freighters also transport 95 per cent of the ore to these mills,

which depend entirely on Lake Superior mines.

The Middle Atlantic steel region gets its coal from West Virginia and other Appalachian states by way of rail to Newport News, thence coastal waterways up Chesapeake Bay and the Delaware River. For its iron ore this region is becoming increasingly dependent on foreign imports, notably from Venezuela and Canada; some domestic ore, though, comes from eastern Pennsylvania, northern New Jersey, and upper New York (Figure 20-4).

The blast furnaces in Alabama are unique among United States mills in that their immediate environs have abundant natural resources of coking coal, iron ore, and fluxing stone. For this reason, steel can be manufactured more cheaply in Birmingham than anywhere else in the nation.

The Pueblo, Colorado, mill subsists on coal from western Colorado and ore from eastern Wyoming, and the one in Provo, Utah, keeps

Steel and Fabricated-Metal Products

View looking northwest over the Bethlehem Steel Company at Sparrows Point, Maryland. The plant is located 12 miles downstream from Baltimore (background) on the Patapsco River near its entry into Chesapeake Bay. Covering 4000 acres, with a normal work force of 30,000, an annual payroll of approximately $190 million, and an annual capacity of 8.2 million tons of steel, Sparrows Point is the world's largest steel producer.

The first pig iron here was poured in 1889. The tidewater location allows incoming ships, carrying iron ore, mostly from Venezuela and Quebec, to dock directly at the plant. Coal mined in Kentucky and West Virginia as well as Pennsylvania arrives by water from Hampton Roads, Virginia; a little arrives by rail. Limestone also comes in by rail from quarries in Pennsylvania and West Virginia. Substantial quantities of scrap iron come from the Patapsco Scrap Corporation's plant, where old ships, old machinery, and other equipment are broken up for smelting. Daily rates of water consumption are 115 million gallons of fresh water and 540 million gallons of salt water.

Finished steel is shipped from the plant docks to points on the Atlantic, Gulf, and Pacific coasts and to ports in foreign countries. In addition, this is one of the world's few steel mills adjoined by shipyards (extreme left of picture). Cargo vessels and passenger-cargo vessels of several types, utilizing many products of the steel mill, are built here. (Courtesy Bethlehem Steel Company.)

going on coal from the eastern part of the state and ore from Cedar City in the southwestern part.

If this were a raw-material-oriented industry we might expect it to be concentrated more heavily near coal fields or ore fields, for these are the raw materials that cost the most to assemble. But only a small percentage of the nation's steel is made in coal-mining regions and an even smaller share in iron-mining regions. Notice how little steel is made in West Virginia, the leading coal-mining state, and in Minnesota, which mines three-fourths of the country's iron ore. Clearly, other relationships are operative that influence the location of the steel industry.

Relationships to Market Regions

Over 95 per cent of the steel made in the United States is sold domestically. Domestic customers are (1) secondary fabricators who purchase ingot steel and pig iron (to make castings) or steel sheets, tubes, wires, and bars for use in further manufacture, and (2) direct consumers who use I-beams, pipes, and rails as they come from the mill without further fabrication.

By percentage of steel they take, the leading domestic consumers are listed in Table 20-4. The significance of this table to the geographer is that most of the secondary manufacturers who process the steel, most of the warehouses that distribute steel sheets and other forms of the metal, and most of the contractors who use I-beams and other construction materials are located in the northeastern quadrant of the nation. We shall develop this point later in this chapter and in the chapters on urban economic activity.

It is in market relationships then that the leading steel regions have their advantage. The steel triangle, for example, provides steel to a market consisting of thousands of foundries, hardware factories, plumbing-equipment producers, and automotive manufacturers in Pittsburgh, Cleveland, Detroit, Buffalo, and scores of other places in the Northeast.

Chicago, too, is centrally located within a large market, in her case the midwestern steel-using industries. Middle Atlantic steel mills are close by manufacturers dispersed all the way from Baltimore to Boston. Alabama mills supply southern markets. And steel mills have sprung up in Texas, California, and the Pacific Northwest to meet local needs for steel.

Thus, it appears that within the United States, steel is essentially a market-oriented industry, since all the largest markets have steel mills close by and all the large-scale steel mills are close to substantial markets. This fundamental relationship explains why Birmingham, Alabama, with good supplies of all three major raw materials, has less of a steel industry than either Chicago or Baltimore with none of the three. And even though the cost of making steel is less in Alabama than anywhere else in the United States, that state produces only 4 per cent of the national total.

A by-product market is frequently provided by cement mills that settle near steel mills, for they can use slag from blast furnaces as a raw material. In fact, the same general region that takes most of our steel also uses most of our cement. This is another example of *symbiosis*.

Transportation

Steel companies select plots of land along water bodies for blast furnaces and steel furnaces not only for access to cooling water but also for cheap water transportation to link the mills to iron mines, to coal fields, to limestone quarries, and to customers. An ideal situation exists where waterways penetrate deeply into market regions, thus permitting water transport of the bulky raw materials into the middle of the steel-consuming area. Mills at the southern end of Lake Michigan have just such a setting as do the Sparrows Point Mill of Bethlehem Steel Corporation on Chesapeake Bay and the Fairless Hills mill that the United States Steel

Table 20-4 *Markets for Steel Shipped from United States Mills, 1960*

Market		Percentage of U.S. Total
Secondary manufacturing	56	
Automotive industries		20
Container industries		9
Industrial equipment and tools		6
Railway equipment industries		4
Forge, screw, and bolt industries		3
Electrical machinery industries		3
Appliance and utensil industries		3
Agricultural machinery industries		2
Shipbuilding industries		1
Others		5
Direct consumers	40	
Warehouses and distributors		18
Construction industry		14
Railroads		4
Others		4
Domestic Market	96%	
Foreign Market	4%	

Source: United States Bureau of Mines *Minerals Yearbook, 1960*, Volume I, p. 607.

Corporation constructed in 1956 in the rural countryside of eastern Pennsylvania. This mill is alongside the Delaware River, convenient for bringing in raw materials, and on the main lines of railways and highways to Philadelphia, New York, and other eastern customers.

Site Features The most desirable topography for blast furnaces and steel mills is expansive flat land. Such terrain facilitates the construction of buildings and allows for future expansion. In this respect western Pennsylvania and eastern Ohio, despite their other attractions, faced a handicap. The terrain is rough and valley bottoms are narrow. Even so, the mills were located in the valley bottoms, not only for access to water for coolant and for barge transportation but also because the railroads follow the rivers. Other industries subsequently flocked to these valley bottoms, which are now built up solidly around the mills.

Quite the opposite is the setting of mills at the edge of Lake Michigan. There the land is flat and swampy, undesirable for residential areas but ideal for steel mills which need elbow room for expansion and vast dumping grounds for slag that cannot be used in cement milling or road building.

STEEL REGIONS OF THE WORLD

Worldwide, steel production is highly concentrated in three places—Anglo-America, western Europe, and the Soviet Union (and her European satellites). Together, these regions account for 80 per cent of the world's

Table 20-5 *World: Production of Pig Iron and Steel, 1960*

Area	Pig Iron		Steel	
	Million Tons	Percentage of World Total	Million Tons	Percentage of World Total
WORLD TOTAL	285	100	381	100
North America	74	26	107	28
United States	68	24	99	26
Canada	4	1	6	2
South America	2	1	3	1
Brazil	1	—	2	1
Western Europe	85	30	118	31
West Germany	28	10	38	10
United Kingdom	18	6	27	7
France	16	6	19	5
Belgium	7	3	8	2
Luxembourg	4	1	5	2
Italy	3	1	9	3
Eastern Europe and U.S.S.R.	69	24	96	25
U.S.S.R.	52	18	72	19
Poland	5	2	8	2
Czechoslovakia	5	2	7	2
East Germany	2	1	4	1
Africa	2	1	3	1
Union of South Africa	2	1	2	1
Asia	50	17	50	13
China	30	11	20	5
Japan	13	5	24	6
India	5	2	4	1
Australia	3	1	4	1

Source: United States Bureau of Mines, *Mineral Trade Notes*, November, 1961, pp. 29-30.

pig iron and 84 per cent of its steel. Outside the three main regions, China and Japan are the most conspicuous. Tonnage and percent-

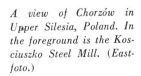

A view of Chorzów in Upper Silesia, Poland. In the foreground is the Kosciuszko Steel Mill. (Eastfoto.)

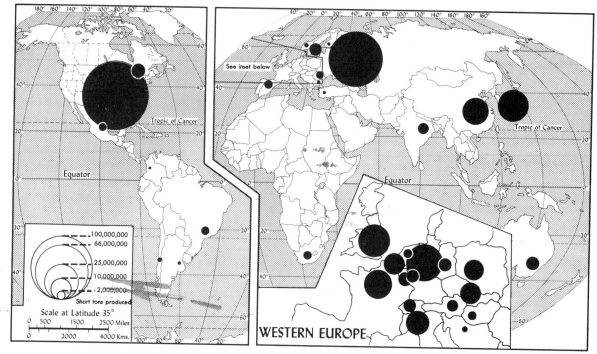

Figure 20-5

ages by nation are given in Table 20-5; the locational pattern is shown in Figure 20-5.

The world pattern of steel gives evidence of the same relationships that we observed in the United States: The steel industry tends to locate where the demand for steel products is vigorous, and of all the raw materials coal exerts the most powerful lure. Indeed, most of the individual foreign areas that are outstanding for steel manufacture have already been identified in Chapter 14 as major coal-producing zones: In Western Europe, Germany's Ruhr, northeastern France, the Midlands of Britain centering on Birmingham, and the Scottish Lowland; in the Soviet Union, Stalino (now Donetsk) in the Donbass, Magnitogorsk and Chelyabinsk (in the Urals), and Kuznetsk, 1000 miles east of the Urals; and in Japan, the Yawata district of Kyushu Island.

The steel zones outside the United States are treated in more detail in Chapters 24 and 25.

Metal-Fabricating Industries

Before reaching the final consumers, most of the steel that primary factories produce is fabricated by a large number of secondary factories into machinery and an extensive variety of consumer goods. We shall now make a few comments on the manufacture of fabricated-metal goods, and give a closer look to the manufacture of machinery in Chapter 21.

As revealed by Figure 20-6, which shows the locational pattern of the fabricated-metal industry, New York, Chicago, Pittsburgh, Philadelphia, Cleveland, and Detroit are the leading centers, principally because it is cheaper to ship steel sheets, bars, and ingots to these centers of population than to make hardware grills, stampings, and so on in the steel regions and then pay high freight rates on them to the wholesale centers. Thus, fabricated-metal factories are near their customers and many steel mills have been drawn to these fabricators.

Metal fabricating is a big business: There are 25,000 factories employing over a million people (Table 20-6); hardware and metal

Steel and Fabricated-Metal Products

stamping support the largest payrolls and add the most dollar value. Space does not permit us to discuss the geography of all these industries, but we can provide maps of some of them along with a few brief comments.

HARDWARE

Most hardware (Figure 20-7, page 364) is produced in large cities, but a good deal comes from smaller settlements, such as New Britain and Hartford, Connecticut, Grand Rapids, Michigan, and Rockford, Illinois. The surprising thing about such places is that they produce no steel, so all face *backhauls* on freight, shipping most of their hardware back in the very same direction from which their steel came! This peculiar situation can be explained in terms of three factors. (1) Tools, cutlery, and other hardware items are highly valuable relative to their weight (on which freight charges are assessed) so that a few extra miles does not price factories in these cities out of competition with hardware producers who have the locational advantages of being near steel mills or markets. (2) Many of these towns, those in the Connecticut Valley in

Table **20-6** *Fabricated-Metal Industries*

Industry	Number of Employees	Value Added (Thousand Dollars)
UNITED STATES TOTAL	1,057,986	$9,412,183
Structural metal products	340,622	2,962,860
Hardware	135,718	1,202,227
Stampings	125,567	1,049,311
Bolts, nuts, screws, etc.	85,106	754,706
Plumbing and heating equipment	71,775	671,914
Wire products	55,476	439,940
Plating, coating, etc.	52,151	362,163
Others	137,333	1,300,456

Source: United States *Census of Manufactures, 1958,* Bulletin MC58(1)-1, pages 1-16.

particular, got an early start in making not only tools but also firearms, clocks, and many other kinds of hardware. Local entrepreneurs in these settlements recognized the hardware market and risked some capital in starting hardware factories. This force, which might be termed "whim," is one of the most difficult influences to study scientifically, but there is

Figure 20-6 (*After Eugene Krell.*)

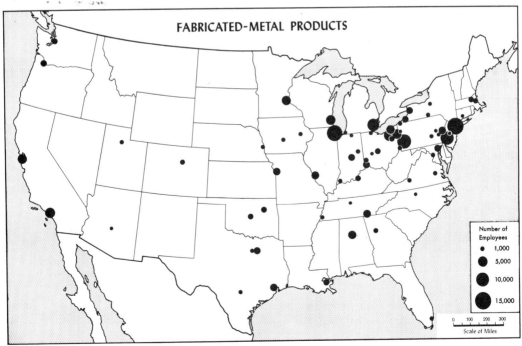

no doubt that it is operative. Surely it is a strong reason why Rockford and Grand Rapids—instead of Fort Wayne and Indianapolis or Saginaw and Dayton, or Peoria and Pittsburgh—are outstanding centers of hardware production in the Midwest. An early start provides a powerful impulse in perpetuating manufacturing in any region. (3) Finally, production costs—expenses for labor, rent, municipal taxes—are slightly lower in small cities than in large ones, an advantage that helps neutralize the possible drawback of higher freight costs.

TIN CANS

The pattern of tin can factories (Figure 20-8) correlates strongly with the market for tin cans, which is, of course, the packers of vegetables, fruit, beer, and a host of other perishable items. Compare Figure 20-8 with Figure 17-1, which shows the location of the fruit and vegetable *canning* industry. Rarely do tin can factories locate near the steel mills that make tin plate, since it is much cheaper to ship the plate from mills to can factories than to ship tin cans from steel mills to the

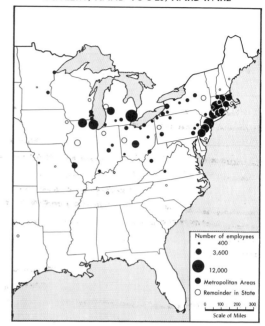

CUTLERY, HAND TOOLS, HARDWARE

Figure 20-7 (*After Peter Harings.*)

agricultural area. Take New York for example —there are more canneries and more can factories in the vegetable and fruit area south of

Figure 20-8 (*After Charles Ahner.*)

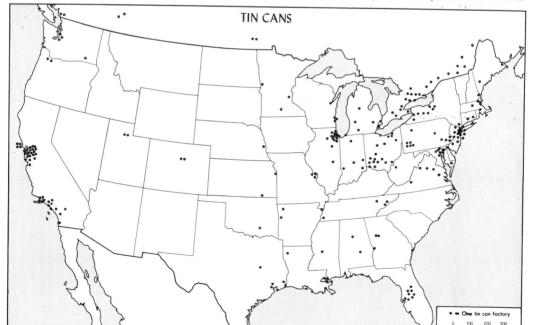

TIN CANS

Steel and Fabricated-Metal Products

INSTRUMENTS

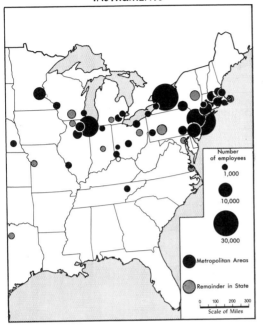

Number
of employees

1,000

10,000

30,000

Metropolitan Areas

Remainder in State

0   100   200   300
Scale of Miles

Figure 20-9 (*After Eugene Musolf.*)

medical instruments, scientific instruments, and ophthalmic equipment has an unusual pattern (Figure 20-9). It is extremely localized in just a few cities; the leaders are listed in Table 20-7. It is not unexpected that New York

Table **20-7** *United States: Manufacture of Instruments by Leading Metropolitan Areas, 1958*

Area	Number of Employees	Value Added in Thousands of Dollars
United States Total	296,558	$2,906,390
New York Metropolitan Area	58,548	540,955
Rochester Metropolitan Area	39,560	544,438
Chicago Metropolitan Area	24,115	250,233

Source: United States *Census of Manufactures*, 1958, Bulletin MC58(1)-1 and Bulletin MC58(3) each states volume, Table 5.

Lake Ontario than in steelmaking Buffalo. Similarly, New England, which produces hardly any steel, has more tin can factories than does the steel district straddling western Pennsylvania and eastern Ohio. There are many tin can factories in California, a state which produces scarcely 3 per cent of our nation's steel but has the largest number of canneries, putting up a third of our canned fruits and vegetables.

Within canning regions, tin can factories locate in large cities for easy distribution to the myriad of canneries in the hinterland. Most packing plants are too small to support a tin can factory individually, hence can factories locate at transport centers. Thus, Wisconsin's can factories are in Milwaukee and Green Bay; California's are in San Francisco and Los Angeles.

INSTRUMENTS

The manufacture of photographic equipment, mechanical measuring instruments,

and Chicago, the two largest cities, both with longstanding reputations as centers of learning and scientific development, should dominate the map. The surprises are Rochester, New York, and several communities in southern New England. Other cities, too, loom up astonishingly large: Binghamton, New York, and Knoxville, Tennessee. Here is an industry that is neither power-oriented nor raw-material-oriented. To be sure, it does tend to develop within the broad framework of its market; but the precise location of a factory seems to be due to chance. It was merely coincidence, for instance, that a particular invention, George Eastman's *Kodak* camera, was the prime stimulus to the development of manufacturing in the particular city of Rochester. One cannot help but speculate whether, if George Eastman had lived in Columbus, or Erie, or any one of dozens of cities in the populous heart of the nation, that city would not loom up on Figure 20-9 as conspicuously as Rochester in fact does.

Alderfer, E. B., and Michl, H. E., *Economics of American Industry,* New York, 1957, chapters 2-5.

Alexandersson, Gunnar, "Changes in the Location Pattern of the Anglo-American Steel Industry: 1948-1959," *Economic Geography,* 1961, pp. 95-114.

Brush, John E., "The Iron and Steel Industry in India," *Geographical Review,* 1952, pp. 37-55.

Clark, M. Gardner, *The Economics of Soviet Steel,* Cambridge, 1956, 400 pp.

Coker, J. A., "Steel and the Schumann Plan," *Economic Geography,* 1952, pp. 283-294.

Cunningham, William Glenn, "The Tin Can Industry of California," *Yearbook of the Association of Pacific Coast Geographers,* 1953, pp. 11-16.

ErSelcuk, Muzaffer, "The Iron and Steel Industry in China," *Economic Geography,* 1956, pp. 347-371.

Isard, Walter, and Cumberland, John, "New England As A Possible Location For an Integrated Iron and Steel Works," *Economic Geography,* 1950, pp. 245-259.

Kerr, Donald, "The Geography of the Canadian Iron and Steel Industry," *Economic Geography,* 1959, pp. 151-163.

Pounds, Norman J. G., *The Geography of Iron and Steel,* London, 1959, 192 pp.

———, "World Production and Use of Steel Scrap," *Economic Geography,* 1959, pp. 247-258.

———, and Parker, William N., *Coal and Steel in Western Europe,* Bloomington, 1957.

Rodgers, Allan, "Industrial Inertia—A Major Factor in the Location of the Steel Industry in the United States," *Geographical Review,* 1952, pp. 56-66.

———, "The Iron and Steel Industry of the Mahoning and Shenango Valleys," *Economic Geography,* 1952, pp. 331-342.

———, "The Manchurian Iron and Steel Industry and Its Resource Base," *Geographical Review,* 1948, pp. 41-55.

Roepke, Howard G., *Movements of the British Iron and Steel Industry—1720 and 1951,* Urbana, 1956, 198 pp.

Stocking, George W., *Basing Point Pricing and Regional Development,* Chapel Hill, 1954.

University of Maryland, Bureau of Business and Economic Research, "The European Coal and Steel Community," *Studies in Business and Economics,* Vol. 9, No. 3, 1955, pp. 1-19, and Vol. 10, No. 1, 1956, pp. 1-16.

White, C. Langdon, "Water—A Neglected Factor in the Geographical Literature of Iron and Steel," *Geographical Review,* 1957, pp. 463-489.

*Assembly berths and slipways along the River Clyde at Glasgow. In the
foreground is a passenger ferry being built for Canada, to its left, a cargo ship being built
for Norway. Since World War II, the British have built almost one-third of
all new shipping. Nearly 20 per cent of all commercial ships
(over 100 gross tons) are registered in the United Kingdom, which has the
largest merchant marine. (Courtesy British Information Services.)*

TWENTY-ONE

Machines are power-driven instruments that perform work for man. Machines are both savers of work and makers of work, since the manufacture of machines provides employment to millions of people. In the United States more than 4,000,000 people are at work making machinery—a larger number than in any other type of manufacturing (a breakdown of the machinery industry into its component parts is given in Table 21-1). Never before has man

Table **21-1** *United States: Leading Machinery-Making Industries*

Type	Number of Employees	Value Added (Thousands of Dollars)
Transportation machinery and equipment	1,557,759	$15,283,694
Aircraft and parts	765,482	6,924,338
Motor vehicles and equipment	577,188	6,750,675
Ships and boats	144,442	1,070,996
Railway equipment	39,591	319,662
Electrical machinery	1,122,284	10,395,369
Other machinery	1,348,245	12,391,190
Total, all machinery	4,028,288	38,070,253

Source: Bureau of Census, *Census of Manufactures,* 1958, Bulletin MC58(1)-1, Table 3.

had so many labor-saving devices at his command, and never before have so many workers earned their livelihood by making them.

Since different machinery industries conform to different locational patterns, we shall direct our attention separately to particular industries, beginning with those that make machines for transporting people and freight.

More persons (1,500,000) are employed in making machines to save man time in transporting himself and his goods than in any other industry (except food manufacturing) in the United States. Nearly half of these workers are in the booming aircraft industry with automobile, truck, and bus manufacture a close second (Table 21-1).

Aircraft

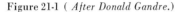

LOCATION AND CHARACTERISTICS

The aircraft industry is concentrated in a few widely separated places in the United States (Figure 21-1), mostly in large metropolitan areas. The leading centers in terms of employment are: Los Angeles, 160,000; New York, 58,000; Seattle, 50,000; San Diego, 45,000; Wichita, 40,000; and Hartford, 30,-000.

Notice the position of Los Angeles (Figure 21-1), which provides jobs for nearly one of every five persons employed by aircraft plants. By states, California accounts for 30 per cent of the national total of jobs in this industry, followed by New York with 10 per cent and Ohio with 9 per cent.

A Few Large Companies In the early days of the airplane industry there were numerous small companies, but they gradually merged or faded from the picture so that today there are only 30 companies in all. By far the largest are the trio of Douglas, Lockheed, and Boeing.

Limited Mass-Production Methods Plane makers have adopted some of the mass-production methods typical of the automotive industry but with only partial success. Several characteristics of airplane production limit the applicability of such methods: Many models are produced in small numbers, designs change rapidly, and over-all airplane production is sporadic. Still, during periods of large output

Figure 21-1 (*After Donald Gandre.*)

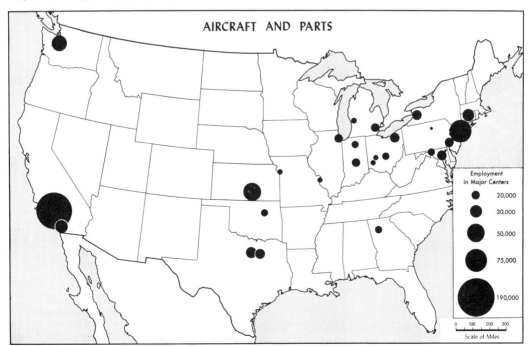

—as in the later years of World War II—mass production can be highly successful indeed.

Subcontracting   The 30 airplane companies purchase engines, propellers, instruments, and parts from many other firms. So an airplane plant is usually a combination of (a) an air-frame factory where aluminum sheets and other metal forms are manufactured into wings and fuselages, and (b) an assembly plant where engines, radios, compasses, wheels, and a host of other parts are brought together from far-flung factories. Los Angeles, Baltimore, Philadelphia, and Greater New York are the only areas where at least a portion of the engines, propellers, and parts required by their assembly plants are also produced. Elsewhere, there is regional specialization: Cities in the northeastern states specialize in engines (especially Paterson, Hartford, Detroit, Indianapolis), propellers (Hartford), and electrical equipment (Cleveland, South Bend, Chicago), which are shipped to assembly plants in Buffalo, Detroit, Cleveland, Chicago, St. Louis, Wichita, Oklahoma City, Dallas, Fort Worth, Atlanta, Seattle, as well as to Los Angeles, Baltimore, Philadelphia, and New York. The manufacture of frames usually occurs in the same locality (often the same factory) as the final assembly. Yet there have been instances in which fuselages have been shipped long distances from factory to assembly plant. In 1953, for example, fuselages (or "hulls") for giant "Albatross" seaplanes were manufactured in Evansville, Indiana, and hauled on huge trailers 1000 miles to the Grumman Aircraft Engineering Corporation at Bethpage, Long Island, New York.

Size   Aircraft factories have enormous payrolls. The nation's 18 propeller factories average 860 employees each, the 223 engine factories average 710, and the 127 assembly plants 300 people. Airplane factories are also large in terms of acreage, for they require huge parcels of land for hangars and adjoining airstrips where planes are flight-tested.

Intense Fluctuations   Aircraft production is a highly fluctuating industry, which experiences its greatest booms in wartime. Before World War I the industry scarcely existed; but by the time of the Armistice, the nation's factories were making planes at the rate of 20,000 a year and employing 200,000 people. Then the industry (based entirely on military demands) collapsed overnight as peace dawned. Lindbergh's flight across the Atlantic in 1927, however, stimulated interest in commercial aviation, and rearmament in the late 1930's revived orders for military planes. By 1940 the industry employed 100,000 people making 5000 planes a year. In the next four years the production skyrocketed to a wartime peak of over 2,000,000 employees and 96,000 planes a year.

The experience of Los Angeles epitomizes these fluctuations in aircraft employment (Table 21-2). In three short years (from 1940-1943) Los Angeles plane makers created 222,000 new jobs as their payrolls leaped from 40,000 to 262,000. The pendulum then swung

Table **21-2**   *Aircraft and Parts Manufacturing: Number of Wage and Salary Workers, Los Angeles and United States, 1940-1961*

Year	Los Angeles Metropolitan Area (in Thousands)	United States Total (in Thousands)	Los Angeles Percentage of Total
1940	40	148	27
1941	93	347	27
1942	170	831	20
1943	262	1345	19
1944	218	1296	17
1945	145	788	18
1946	74	237	31
1947	66	239	27
1948	59	237	25
1949	65	264	25
1950	70	283	25
1951	109	468	23
1952	151	670	23
1953	167	796	21
1954	180	783	23
1955	191	761	25
1956	209	837	25
1957	213	896	24
1958	175	784	22
1959	170	755	23
1960	147	674	22
1961	134	669	20

Source: Compiled by Research Department, Security First National Bank, Los Angeles 34, California.

Transportation Machinery

This large aircraft factory in Santa Monica, California, produces airplanes and missiles. (Courtesy Douglas Aircraft Company.)

back almost as sharply, and by 1948 there were less than 60,000 on the payrolls.

Change in Location   The aircraft industry has been characterized by an unusual change in locational pattern. In the early days it grew up largely on the East Coast and in the Midwest; New York, Dayton, Buffalo, and Detroit were the focal points. After World War I the industry began to move west—San Diego, Seattle, Wichita, Dallas, and Fort Worth now loomed up large, and Los Angeles soon became the airplane capital of the country. With this locational change there developed the regional specialization already noted. Some assembly plants remained in the East, particularly those making small' planes, for both private and military purposes (for instance carrier-based Navy planes). The Martin plant in Baltimore was the largest one to resist the westward movement.

RELATIONSHIPS

Raw-Material Source Regions   Since aircraft are rarely assembled in areas where aluminum, engines, propellers, radar, elec-

tronic devices, and other materials are produced, those components are shipped long distances. Therefore, we may conclude that the pull of raw-material source regions upon the location of aircraft assembly plants is weak.

Market Regions   The market for airplanes is three-fold: military, commercial, and private. In 1960 the armed forces purchased 2700 planes, private customers bought 7800, and 250 planes went to commercial air lines. But private planes are small and less complex than commercial planes or fighting craft so that by value the private plane market is by far the smallest. Over 90 per cent of the aircraft industry sales, in terms of dollars, are to the armed forces. (The United States Department of Defense purchases annually *five billion dollars'* worth—"flyaway value"—of airplanes.)

To some degree, the location of customers does affect the location of plants. The military market is nationwide, of course, for air bases occur in all parts of the country; however, since there are more large air bases in the West and South than in any other part of the nation, factories in Los Angeles, Wichita, and Dallas have an advantage. Then too, the civilian market for commercial and for private planes, being largely in the Northeast has served to attract factories there. And a considerable factor in the growth of Wichita's industry was the demand of oilmen in Kansas and Oklahoma for small planes with which to visit their oilfields. But for the nation as a whole it does not appear that market is the dominant influence upon the location of airplane manufacturing. Southern California, for prime instance, makes a fourth of the nation's planes, but does not provide that proportion of customers. What other factors might be in play?

Climate   For one, a warm dry climate, as in southern California, is ideal for airplane manufacture, for it enables substantial savings in costs of storage, assembly, and testing. Engines, propellers, aluminum, and other parts can be stockpiled outdoors; much of the assembly work can be done outdoors; the heating requirement for what few hangar-buildings are required is small; and the assembled planes can be flight-tested nearly every day of the year.

Entrepreneurs   The term "entrepreneur" here stands for all the intangible factors that have motivated enterprising men to start manufacturing. In Seattle a wealthy lumberman named Boeing operated a private plane as a hobby during World War I. After a minor accident he himself repaired the damage to the plane and became so interested in its construction that he decided to build a new one himself. The experiment was a success, and from this chance event grew the nation's largest single airplane factory. May we not wonder as with Eastman and Rochester: if Boeing had lived in Portland (or in San Francisco, or in any other town) would it instead of Seattle be the conspicuous dot on Figure 21-1?

Similarly, Donald Douglas was a Los Angeles citizen and an airplane fan. In 1923, backed by local capital, he set up a small factory to make planes. His ideas worked, his

operation succeeded, and from this chance start emerged the largest airplane factory in Los Angeles.

Risk Capital   "Risk capital" applies to the supply of money in the hands of investors who are willing to invest in new enterprises. It was the juxtaposition of risk capital and men with ideas in Seattle, Los Angeles, and Wichita that led to the start of aircraft making there.

Labor   But ingenious enterprises and daring capital cannot develop a large industry by themselves. Thousands of productive workers are needed to turn out the items designed. All the steps in the manufacture of airplane frames (cutting aluminum sheets, riveting, and so on) and the assembly of engines, propellers, and wires can be performed in large measure by semiskilled labor. Even so, the assembly plants that sprang up during World War II in Los Angeles, Fort Worth, Dallas, Wichita, and Seattle were hopelessly unable to procure labor from local sources. But the nature of the work was such that farmers, salesmen, schoolteachers, and housewives could be recruited from all parts of the nation and quickly trained in large numbers to augment a few highly skilled technicians and supervisors.

Noticeably different is the manufacture of engines, propellers, radar devices, compasses, and various electronic equipment. This requires highly skilled workers who cannot be quickly recruited and trained. Skilled machinists in particular must serve long apprenticeships. Now, one of the principles of labor location is that skilled labor tends to be more immobile than unskilled labor. This offers a persuasive explanation of why assembly plants dispersed (or sprang up) widely whereas engine production plants remained rooted in the northeastern states where most of the nation's skilled machinists are.

"Security"   During World War II the government encouraged aircraft plants to expand less in coastal cities and more in inland centers. Boeing set up a branch in

Wichita, and eastern producers moved to Dallas and Fort Worth. Defense contracts were awarded to producers in the interior— such as the contract for "Albatross" hulls, mentioned earlier, that was awarded to an Evansville company. With the advent of missile production, the government is even establishing factories in barren western deserts.

Because aircraft have such strategic significance, data on world production are almost as difficult to procure as those for uranium. There is no doubt, however, that the United States and the U.S.S.R. make the most planes. Still, Germany, the United Kingdom, France, and Japan each produce quite a large number of aircraft.

All these leading manufacturing countries export at least a few airplanes. For the United States, the export value of aircraft is twice that of wheat and almost equal to that of cotton, which is our number-one agricultural export.

Motor Vehicles and Equipment

LOCATION

The manufacture of automobiles, buses, and trucks is highly concentrated within a midwestern region we might well call "the automotive triangle" (Figure 21-2). If we drew three imaginary lines from Buffalo to Cincinnati to Janesville (Wisconsin) and back to Buffalo we would delimit an area containing over nine-tenths of the nation's automotive employees. The southern half of Michigan alone accounts for almost 50 per cent of the employees in this industry. No other large industry is so highly concentrated in a single state. And on an even finer scale, Detroit and its suburbs can boast of nearly a third of the automotive jobs in the country. Of large industries only the apparel business is so highly concentrated in one metropolitan area. Flint, Michigan, is second only to Detroit in terms of automotive employment.

The automotive triangle is revealed in

Figure 21-2 (*After Donald Hirschfeld.*)

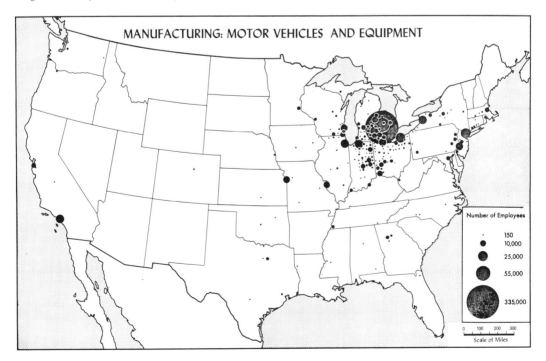

Figure 21-2 as a virtually continuous cluster of large cities: Detroit, Flint, Lansing, Saginaw, Grand Rapids, Pontiac, Jackson—all in Michigan—and Cleveland, Buffalo, Toledo, South Bend, Chicago, Milwaukee, Indianapolis, and Cincinnati in neighboring states. But the triangle also contains numerous smaller settlements, such as Janesville and Kenosha (Wisconsin), Rockford (Illinois), Muncie and New Castle (Indiana).

Outside this triangle automotive manufacture is small-scale and widely scattered. It appears in small places such as La Crosse, Wisconsin and Decatur, Illinois, but generally in large cities, notably New York, Philadelphia, St. Louis, Kansas City, Atlanta, Los Angeles, and San Francisco.

CHARACTERISTICS

Two Factory Types The automotive industry has two types of plants: factories where *parts* are made (engines, transmission systems, axles, wheels, and frames) and factories where *assembly* takes place. The regional patterns of these two components are somewhat different.

Nearly all parts are manufactured within the automotive triangle or on the Middle Atlantic Seaboard. Several cities have even specialized: Flint, Michigan, on engines, Rockford, Illinois, on universal joints, and Oshkosh, Wisconsin, on axles.

Assembly plants, on the other hand, are scattered in a few spots throughout the nation. Detroit still assembles more cars than any other city, Michigan than any other state; the automotive triangle is still the main assembly area. But more and more assembling is being done elsewhere—on the East Coast, in the South, and on the West Coast. Examples of such assembly points are Boston, Framingham (Massachusetts), Tarrytown (New York), Bloomfield (New Jersey), Chester (Pennsylvania), Norfolk, Atlanta, Louisville, Memphis, St. Louis, Kansas City, Minneapolis, Los Angeles, San Jose, and Oakland. Invariably, each assembly plant has a body-making factory close by, because transportation costs cn long-distance shipments of bodies almost exceed their value.

Large Scale There are nearly 2300 factories in the United States that make motor vehicles and parts; they average 250 employees apiece. Large corporations predominate. In 1960 the United States manufactured 6,701,279 passenger cars—all of them the output of just six companies (Table 21-3). And of that group, General Motors alone produces almost as many automobiles as the other five combined. Of the individual makes of car, the names Chevrolet and Ford identify over half of the cars that roll off the factory lines.

Clearly, the tendency is toward gigantism. The largest manufacturing enterprise in history is, in fact, an automotive company, General Motors. GM provides jobs for half a million people who work in 83 parts plants, 43 assembly plants, 103 warehouses, 79 sales offices, and 46 management offices. This one enterprise pays almost one billion dollars annually into the national treasury in federal taxes. The head offices are in Detroit, where General Motors operates nine factories for making parts and two factories for assembling vehi-

Table **21-3** *United States: Passenger Car Production by Companies and Selected Leading Makes, 1960*

Company and Make	Amount	Percentage of Total
UNITED STATES, TOTAL PASSENGER CARS PRODUCED	6,701,279	100
General Motors Corporation	3,193,180	48
Chevrolet	1,873,617	28
Pontiac	450,206	7
Oldsmobile	402,612	6
Buick	307,804	5
Cadillac	158,941	2
Ford Motor Company	1,890,234	28
Ford	1,509,733	23
Comet	198,031	3
Mercury	161,787	2
Chrysler Corporation	1,019,238	15
Plymouth	483,964	7
Dodge	411,614	6
American Motors	485,745	7
Rambler	485,745	7
Studebaker-Packard Corporation	105,902	2
Studebaker	105,902	2
Checker Cab	6,980	—

Source: Automobile Manufacturers Association, *Automobile Facts and Figures*, 1961, p. 10.

Transportation Machinery

cles. In Flint it runs four parts-factories and four assembly plants.

The largest single *factory* in the country belongs to the Ford Motor Company. It occupies 1200 acres along a small stream named River Rouge in southwestern Detroit. It is so vast that one hundred miles of company railroad tracks thread their way through the establishment. This one plant provides employment to 75,000 people to the tune in payroll of $1,250,000 *per day*. This is one of the few *integrated* metal-industry factories in the world—that is, in this plant all the manufacturing is carried out in both the primary and secondary steps. Almost 1,000,000 tons of iron ore, 2,500,000 tons of coal, and 500,000 tons of limestone arrive each year at company docks along the widened Rouge at its confluence with the Detroit River. Two blast furnaces and two coke ovens begin the long line of processes by which these raw materials are ultimately transformed—along with many other materials—into automobiles and trucks. But not all parts manufactured at the Rouge are assembled there. A large proportion is shipped out to 17 Ford assembly plants dispersed across the nation.

Mass-Production Methods   The manufacture of automobiles is an excellent example of the mass-production method. Thousands of engines, pistons, bearings, shafts, and wheels are produced by specially designed tools with such precision that craftsmen can fit any one of a thousand axles with any two of a thousand wheels and achieve a smoothly functioning unit. These multitudes of parts are then assembled along complex assembly lines on which each of dozens of workers specializes in a comparatively simple task, such as affixing a wheel, welding a joint, or securing a few screws. The result of this system, developed to a large extent by Henry Ford, is greater aggregate production than would be possible if each worker endeavored to assemble a complete car by himself.

The latest development in the mass-production technique is *automation*, whereby machines turning out the manufactured product are operated, not by human operators, but by other machines. In not only the automotive industry but many other industries as well, automation is accounting for a slowly increasing percentage of output.

Changing Location   The automotive industry today is changing its location—it is leaving Michigan in general and Detroit in particular. This is such a recent phenomenon that many people do not realize it is under way. Between 1939 and 1947 (years in which Censuses of Manufactures were taken) jobs in automotive factories jumped by 200,000, of which 130,000 accrued to Detroit alone! But a different story began to unfold in the 1950's. The 1958 Census of Manufactures revealed that since 1947 the nation's automotive industry as a whole lost jobs, from 693,000 to 580,000—a decline of 113,000 positions. But Michigan lost almost 140,000 jobs as her automotive employment shrank from 370,000 to 231,000. Detroit's loss was staggering: down 120,000 jobs from 250,000 to 130,000! All the while, the other states collectively increased by 26,000 employees. For the first time in decades, Michigan now provides less than half the jobs in our production of automobiles, trucks, and buses.

RELATIONSHIPS

Market Regions   Today, assembly plants are located primarily in cities that are centrally situated among customers. Originally, though, this was not true; automobiles were made mostly in Michigan and shipped throughout the country. But shipping costs on an automobile are now extremely high (for instance, almost $500 by rail on a sedan from Detroit to Los Angeles). It is much less expensive to ship carloads of engines, transmissions, wheels, and other parts to Los Angeles, Dallas, Atlanta, and Boston for assembly there. This principle holds not only for distant cities but also for assembly points close to the automotive triangle, such as Minneapolis, Janesville, St. Louis, and Tarrytown. From these dispersed assembly points, finished automobiles have shorter, cheaper distances to travel to dealers. They are usually carried on specially designed trailer trucks that, rolling along the highways, are conspicuous features of the landscape throughout southern Michigan and on the roads radiating outward from other assembly plants.

The location of the market corresponds closely with that of population. In 1960 Americans purchased nearly 7,000,000 motor vehicles. The leading buying states, as indicated in Table 21-4, are those where most assembly work is now performed.

It is in this relationship to market that we find part of the explanation for Michigan's losses in automotive job opportunities. To be sure, Michigan has a rather good location in relationship to the domestic market, but her relationship in this respect is probably less favorable than that of Ohio, Indiana, or Illinois. The foreign market buys 266,000 vehicles (less than 5 per cent of the United States' automotive output)—about the same number as was purchased by Florida residents. But the value of motor vehicles is such that they constitute our first-ranking export! This foreign market consists chiefly of Latin America and Canada. Major customers in terms of numbers of United States vehicles purchased are Brazil 47,000, Mexico 35,000, Venezuela 33,000, Canada 30,000, and the Union of South Africa 11,000. Some producers are recognizing the attraction of the foreign market by locating assembly plants in foreign nations. General Motors, for example, has two assembly plants in Canada and others in Mexico, Venezuela, Brazil, Argentina, and

Peru; Britain, Sweden, Denmark, Belgium, France, and Germany; South Africa; India and Indonesia; and Australia and New Zealand.

The pull of market areas on the location of parts factories is weaker than its effect on assembly, because parts can be shipped much more economically than can finished vehicles. Of the many parts that go into an automotive vehicle, only one is usually manufactured near the assembly plant: the body. This is by far the bulkiest component of the vehicle and it is costly to transport. Therefore, sheet steel is shipped to assembly centers and manufactured into bodies in factories that often adjoin the assembly plant. Notice the similarity in this respect between airplane frames and automobile bodies.

Raw-Material Regions   Assembly plants are evidencing less and less of a tendency to locate where the parts they assemble are made. But factories that make engines, carburetors, and gears show a definite disposition to settle near steel centers. Compare the pattern of the automobile industry (Figure 21-2) with that of the steel industry (Figure 20-1). Admittedly, Pittsburgh has scarcely any automotive manufacturing; but, on the other hand, many of the leading automotive areas do have steel mills: for instance, Detroit, Chicago, Cleveland, and Buffalo. No part of the automotive triangle is very far from sources of steel.

An example of how a single assembly plant is functionally related to diverse localities for raw materials is illustrated in Figure 21-3, which shows that the Buick assembly plant in Flint, Michigan, is involved in the following "linkages": It is linked to 35 localities between Wisconsin and New England supplying it with machinery, to 34 settlements providing it with metal parts, to nine places widely dispersed between California and Massachusetts providing tires and tubes, to 26 communities scattered between Colorado and New England supplying other rubber parts.

Up to this point it seems logical to expect that the heart of the automotive industry would naturally be somewhere in the Mid-

Table 21-4   *New Motor Vehicle Registration by States, 1960 (in Thousands)*

State	Amount
UNITED STATES TOTAL	6966
California	704
New York	546
Illinois	452
Michigan	438
Ohio	419
Texas	413
Pennsylvania	383
Florida	247
New Jersey	245
Indiana	206

Source: Automobile Manufacturers Association, *Automobile Facts and Figures*, 1961, p. 17.

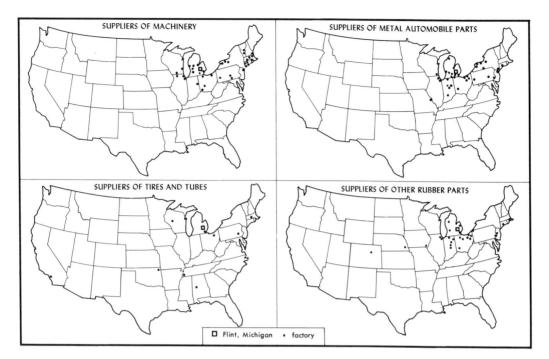

Figure 21-3 (*Courtesy G. Rex Henrickson. See text for explanation.*)

west, a region that has the advantage of being centrally located both to the bulk of the market and to the principal raw material—steel. But why should Detroit rather than Pittsburgh, Chicago, or a dozen other midwestern cities have become the automotive capital of the world?

An Early Start   Part of the answer lies in Detroit's early start. Even before the day of the large corporation, in the late 1890's and early 1900's when cars were made by numerous small companies, Detroit was the leading center. (This statement applies only to gasoline-burning vehicles; in 1900 the United States produced 4000 horseless carriages, about half of which came from New England shops. But over 3000 of these vehicles were powered by either steam or electricity—types of motive power that soon disappeared. It was the gasoline burners that won the competition, and by 1900 southern Michigan was ahead of all other regions in this phase of the industry.)

But the concept of "early start" is only a partial answer to the query and, in a sense, begs the question. It certainly leads to others.

Why did Detroit get such an early start? Moreover, why has Detroit persisted for so many years as the outstanding automotive center? Many an industry has started in one region and subsequently moved to another which outstripped the original site. What other advantages did Detroit have to begin with, and which ones have persisted?

Favorable Environment   Many authorities point out that since southern Michigan has a comparatively flat and gently rolling topography, horseless carriages did not encounter discouraging gradients in the early days. Moreover, the glacial soil with a high proportion of sand and gravel made for more "navigable" roads in inclement weather; though horse-drawn vehicles can make their way through mud roads, horseless ones cannot. Then, too, Detroit's location along the Detroit River, a major link in the Great Lakes thoroughfare, supposedly stimulated the development of factories to make internal combustion engines for boats, a factor which then combined with the manufacture of carriages to give natural birth to the automobile industry. All this is true and unquestionably played a part in the early start of automobile making in Michigan. But these conditions are essentially true for eastern Wisconsin and northern Ohio. What did Michigan have that these other states lacked?

Inventive Genius The birth of the automotive industry occurred in 1886 with the invention (by Gottlieb Daimler in Germany) of the first internal combustion engine using petroleum. But several years elapsed before anybody successfully harnessed the engine to a wheeled vehicle. By 1895 though, several inventors had built experimental vehicles, with Ford, Hanes, and Duryea each claiming to have built the first successful one in the United States. By 1900 there were a large number of manufacturers making cars. The products were somewhat like houses in that very few were exactly alike. Each manfacturer made a variety of vehicles at a variety of prices.

Then Henry Ford conceived three ideas that were to catapult his company to fame and give his home town, Detroit, a tremendous lead over all other places in the manufacture of automobiles. First, he designed an extremely simple internal combustion engine that was also unusually durable and easy to operate. The vehicle built around this power unit was called "the model T," and it immediately caught the fancy of the American buyer. Ford's second idea was to abandon the strategy of many models at many prices and concentrate on one model in order to produce the most efficient car at the lowest price, "a motor car for the multitude." The third idea was to manufacture these cars, not piece by piece as one builds a house, but by mass-production methods whereby all parts of the car were standardized and produced by extremely specialized machine tools and then fitted together on assembly lines. These two technical innovations combined with the marketing innovation were so successful that in 1909 Ford turned out 10,000 vehicles. By 1923 production hiked past 2,000,000. At the same time, selling prices dropped steadily in response to efficiencies of the mass-production

system, from $950 per car in 1909, to $295 in 1922.

Now, Henry Ford had been born on a farm a few miles from Detroit. We can only speculate, of course, about where the automobile industry might have taken root had this inventive genius resided in Pittsburgh or in Chicago. But if he had, might not Pennsylvania or Illinois instead of Michigan have dominated the geography of the automotive industry this past half-century?

Ford was not the only maker of automobiles, of course. Numerous other companies were in the business, but most of them followed Ford's basic ideas, and most of them were started in Michigan. Lansing was the home town of R.E. Olds, a young mechanic who launched the Oldsmobile company in 1901. Flint was the home town for a carriage producer, W.C. Durant, who founded Buick.

Just as Iowa was blessed by a natural endowment of rich soil for corn agriculture, Michigan was blessed by an unusual group of bright, inventive minds.

Risk Capital Henry Ford had the ideas but not the money for launching an automotive factory. And most people who had the money lacked the disposition to risk it on so novel a venture as manufacturing a horseless carriage. But Detroit investors were willing to gamble their dollars on Ford's ideas. Again we can wonder: If Detroit money had said "no" to Ford and Milwaukee money or Cleveland money had said "yes," would the mass of black circles on Figure 21-2 be hovering over southern Wisconsin or northern Ohio instead of southern Michigan?

Productive Labor We have exposed Michigan's advantageous relationships to market, environment, human inventiveness, and so on. What about that other essential, an adept work force? Southern Michigan in the early days had a flock of carriage factories, wagon factories, and machine shops where mechanically trained men had gathered experience which fitted them well for making automobiles. And yet the whole agricultural heart of the Midwest, from Ohio to Iowa, had just as many wagon factories and machine shops—enough to supply a labor pool as wide and deep as that in southern Michigan. Without question, Michigan's labor force was fundamental to her automotive industry, but this relationship in itself scarcely explains why Michigan instead of Ohio should have become so prominent.

Indeed, not many years elapsed before the new industry exhausted Michigan's supply of labor and began attracting workers from other states, from as far distant as Alabama and Mississippi. Thousands of Southerners, many of them Negroes, flocked to Michigan, primarily Detroit, to work for General Motors, Ford, or Chrysler. Regardless of origin, race, or sex, these workers did not have to be highly skilled; the widespread use of machinery on the production line enabled semi-skilled labor to turn out acceptable cars.

Highly developed skills are required, however, in the design and manufacture of the machinery, in its supervision and maintenance, and in the organization of a production line. The highly trained mechanics required for these jobs take years to develop; they are a fruit of the Midwest's long experience in producing machines, and they are a powerful force in perpetuating the boundaries of the automotive triangle.

Wage Rates   The automotive industry pays one of the highest wage rates of any manufacturing industry. The Bureau of Labor Statistics, which publishes data on the average hourly earnings of production workers in 140 different types of manufacturing industries, shows that the automotive business, which averages $2.81 per hour per production worker, is surpassed by only six other industries (Table 21-5), none of which employs nearly as many people. Consequently, Michigan leads all other heavily industrial states in the hourly earnings of factory workers, and Detroit enjoys a high rating among cities for its average hourly earnings of production workers in manufacturing; indeed, of the top ten cities in Table 21-6, five are in the automotive triangle and three are in Michigan.

Table **21-5**   *Average Hourly Earnings of Production Workers in Manufacturing, 1960*

Leading Industries	Annual Hourly Average
Flat glass	$3.16
Blast furnace and steel products	3.04
Petroleum refining	3.02
Tires and inner tubes	2.96
Newspaper publishing and printing	2.87
Industrial chemicals	2.82
Motor vehicle and equipment	2.81
Railroad equipment	2.78
Aircraft and parts	2.70
Ships and boats	2.64

Source: United States Bureau of Labor Statistics, *Monthly Labor Review,* January 1962, pp. 101-109.

Table **21-6**   *Average Hourly Earnings of Production Workers in Manufacturing, December, 1961*

Ten Highest States		Ten Highest Urban Areas	
Nevada	$2.82	Sacramento, California	$3.03
Michigan	2.76	Charleston, West Virginia	2.96
Washington	2.68	Detroit, Michigan	2.95
California	2.67	Flint, Michigan	2.92
Ohio	2.62	Youngstown, Ohio	2.91
Oregon	2.57	Casper, Wyoming	2.90
Indiana	2.54	Baton Rouge, Louisiana	2.88
Wyoming	2.51	Lansing, Michigan	2.87
Arizona	2.49	Akron, Ohio	2.87
Utah	2.49	San Francisco-Oakland	2.85

Source: United States Bureau of Labor Statistics, *Employment and Earnings,* Vol. 8, February, 1962, Table C-8.

"Agglomeration"   As used in geography, "agglomeration" means the tendency for enterprises to locate near one another. Automotive factories have shown a strong tendency to do this in Michigan, particularly in Detroit. At first glance this may seem surprising; one might expect that a new company would locate in a different region from the seat of an already existing company in order to get away from the competition. Yet in any mass-production industry, large factories have an advantage over small ones, and a city that has attributes attractive to one large producer may be equally attractive to another. Thus, apart from competing for the same labor pool, there is no particular disadvantage in two or more manufacturers locating in the same state —or city. Indeed, there are certain advantages, such as nearness to local trained technicians; the combined influence of two or more companies in turn can lure even more potential technicians from other places. Besides, the interests of other establishments in the region (such as banking, financing, vocational schools) become geared to the industry. And other industries that specialize in servicing the agglomerated one also cluster round.

Unionization   The automobile business is one of the most highly unionized industries in the country; furthermore, its union, the United Auto Workers, is one of the most powerful labor organizations. Its local #600 (at the Rouge) is, indeed, the largest labor union local in the world. At this point we encounter a phenomenon about which there is violent difference of opinion. Some persons believe that the strength of the U.A.W. in Michigan is one reason for the exodus of the industry from Michigan. Others reply that the industry is inevitably destined to become more evenly dispersed through the northeastern quadrant of the nation, and that only the momentum of Michigan's early start has kept her ahead this long.

The Economic Base   Employment in automotive factories constitutes a large segment of the economic activity in several places. Michigan's jobholders in the automotive industry make up 30 per cent of her employment in manufacturing and about 15 per cent of her total employment. In Detroit those percentages are roughly 50 per cent and 20 per cent respectively. In Flint they are unbelievably high: 90 and 50 per cent. Think what it means to the economic life of Flint and Detroit—and Michigan—when the automotive industry is in trouble.

THE WORLD PATTERN

The great majority of the world's automotive vehicles are manufactured in Anglo-America and western Europe. Nearly 14,000,-000 passenger cars, trucks and buses roll off the world's factory lines each year, almost half coming from United States producers. Table 21-7 suggests that there are two types of areas in terms of emphasis on passenger car and truck output. One type produces many

Table **21-7** *World Motor Vehicle Production by Leading Nations, 1959 (in 000)*

Region	Passenger Cars	Trucks	Buses	Total
WORLD	10,772	3,099	45	13,916
Anglo-America				
United States	5,600	1,121	2	6,723
Canada	300	67	1	368
Western Europe				
West Germany	1,356	355	7	1,718
United Kingdom	1,190	370	*	1,560
France	1,085	195	3	1,283
Italy	470	28	2	500
Sweden	95	15	2	112
Spain	53	3	—	56
Austria	15	5	*	20
Netherlands	4	3	—	7
Eastern Europe				
East Germany	53	18	—	71
Czechoslovakia	50	15	1	66
Poland	14	15	1	30
Yugoslavia	4	3	1	8
U.S.S.R.	125	405	10	540
East Asia				
Japan	79	335	7	421
India	12	19	5	36
Others				
Australia	247	16	—	263
Brazil	15	80	1	96
Argentina	4	24	—	28

Source: Automobile Manufacturers Association, *Automobile Facts and Figures,* 1961, p. 15.
* Number of trucks and buses not distinguished.

This air view of the Peugeot auto assembly plant at Sochaux, France, gives an idea of the enormous scale of an automotive enterprise. (*Courtesy Peugeot.*)

more trucks than passenger cars—the U.S.S.R. Poland, Japan, India, Argentina, and Brazil. The other type emphasizes passenger cars more than trucks—the United States, Canada, most of the countries in western Europe, and Australia. There may be a correlation between such variation and standard of living, so we might hypothesize that the higher the standard of living, the higher the ratio between output of passenger cars and output of trucks—assuming, of course, that the area in question manufactures both.

International trade in motor vehicles is a somewhat different story from that of production. Western Europe is by far the leading source region of vehicles that figure in international trade. West Germany, the United Kingdom, and France are far ahead of all others. Even Italy exports about as many vehicles as the United States. For the ten leading exporters and importers, see Table 21-8.

Imports are a still different story since the United States imports more than three times as many vehicles as any other nation—and almost three times as many as she herself exports. Thousands of Americans have come to prefer the smaller, more economical European cars.

Table 21-8   *Motor Vehicles: Exports and Imports by Leading Nations, 1959 (in Thousands)*

Ten Leading Exporters		Ten Leading Importers	
West Germany	870	United States	690
United Kingdom	697	Belgium	188
France	603	Canada	165
United States	266	Sweden	118
Italy	221	West Germany	117
Belgium	62	Netherlands	104
Sweden	51	Australia	93
Japan	19	Switzerland	87
Canada	11	Austria	74
Netherlands	10	France	14

Source: Automobile Manufacturers Association, *Automobile Facts and Figures*, 1961, p. 15.

Only one-seventh the number of persons are engaged in the manufacture of watercraft in the United States as are in the aircraft industry (Table 21-1), and scarcely half the number as make automobiles in Detroit alone.

The main region of watercraft manufacture, as Figure 21-4 shows, is a belt along the Middle Atlantic Coast. Five places predominate: Newport News, Sparrows Point, Chester, Camden, and Quincy. Smaller tidewater producers are found in Pascagoula, Port Arthur, San Diego, San Francisco, and Seattle. In addition a line of small centers fringes Lake Erie, Lake Michigan, and the Detroit River. Finally, a handful of boat-building cities are inland, the largest being Pittsburgh, where barges are made to haul the heavy coal traffic on the Monongahela River.

The location of shipbuilding has gone through a pronounced change. For nearly two centuries before 1900 the industry was centered in New England. During colonial days New England had all the requirements for shipbuilding: a location at one end of a major avenue of ocean shipping, a thriving maritime trade, a brisk whaling industry which demanded ships, a resourceful people with the ingenuity and productivity for making ships, rich stands of timber for making hulls, masts, spars, and decks, and satisfactory harbors along which "ways" (for building ships) could be constructed. The industry thrived and the United States led the world in launching ships until 1860. The famous "Yankee Clippers" designed and built in American yards were the world's fastest ships; numerous foreign shippers bought and operated them in all the world's major seas. Then American shipbuilding ran into stormy weather which changed both its location in the United States and this nation's position in world production.

A technological revolution saw steel displace wood as the material for construction and steam replace wind as the propelling force. New England, rich with trees, had scarcely any steel mills, so it quickly lost out to harbor cities farther south that were close to the steel mills in Pennsylvania and Maryland. Indeed, Baltimore developed shipyards immediately adjoining a steel mill at Sparrows Point. The change from wood to steel also played a role in America's loss of first place to the United Kingdom. Although severely limited in timber resources, Britain was well-endowed with coal and iron ore; indeed she led the world in coal mining, iron ore mining, and steel manufacture. She had a 50-year head start on the United States in the large-scale production of steel.

Even more important in the decline of the United States in shipbuilding though, was a rise in this nation's wage rates. Today, hourly wages in our shipyards are $2.00. Compare this to the 80 cents in Norway, 50 cents in Britain, 33 cents in Italy, and 10 cents in Japan. Such discrepancies can be overcome by industries that are adaptable to mechanization. But shipbuilding is the antithesis of mechanized production. Ships are simply too large to produce on assembly lines; the demand is too small to justify mass production, and the few orders that do come in are from shippers who stipulate different specifications. For these reasons, shipbuilding—in peacetime —defies mass production and simply does not fit into the present scheme of American manufacturing. The nation that manufactures 51 per cent of the world's automobiles today makes only 7 per cent of the world's ships (Table 21-9).

Things are different in wartime, however. During World Wars I and II the call for military and merchant ships was tremendous. Orders for large numbers of similar ships permitted the use of a few mass-production methods. Steel mills, for instance, turned out beams and plates cut to specification for Victory ships, Liberty ships, and destroyers. Overnight, during the second war, the United States became the world's leading shipmaker again. In 1943 our yards turned out ships totaling 12,499,000 tons. But just as quickly, with peace, the industry collapsed; in 1948 our production was down to 164,000 tons!

THE SHIPYARDS OF THE WORLD

LAUNCHED TONNAGE, 1959

Figure 21-4 (*From Gunnar Alexandersson.*)

Country	All Vessels	Percentage of World Total	Tankers Only
WORLD TOTAL	8746	100	4375
Japan	1723	20	912
United Kingdom	1373	16	529
West Germany	1202	14	344
Sweden	857	9	568
Netherlands	607	7	383
United States	597	7	522
Italy	518	6	350
France	408	5	229
Norway	307	3	187
Denmark	225	3	120
Poland	184	2	—
Belgium	165	2	73
Yugoslavia	162	2	45
Spain	112	1	38
Finland	109	1	13
Canada	88	1	27

Source: United Nations, *Statistical Yearbook*, 1960, page 253.

Still, the government recognizes that for defense purposes shipyards must not close completely and the labor force must not be allowed to disappear. A nucleus must be maintained around which wartime production—if necessary—may be quickly rallied. Accordingly, the government is now heavily subsidizing the construction of not just men-of-war but also merchant tankers, freighters, and liners. Even so, American yards still launch less than 600,000 tons of ships a year.

Currently, American coastal shipyards are concentrating on tankers, which constitute nearly nine-tenths of the annual launched tonnage of merchant vessels. Great Lakes yards make ore and coal carriers and barges; inland centers limit themselves to barges, yachts, and small craft.

The world picture (Figure 21-4) shows that Japan, the United Kingdom, and West Germany now lead in the construction of merchant vessels (Table 21-9).

Rail Vehicles

Virtually all the United States' transportation machines with flanged wheels are manufactured in the northeastern quadrant of the country. For decades steam locomotives came mostly from Philadelphia, Schenectady, and Lima (Ohio) where, in early railroad history (the mid-1800's) designers of locomotives got a head start, just as Henry Ford did later in Michigan in automobile production. But the steam locomotive industry is dead now, having been replaced by electric-diesel engines. It was not the steam-engine makers who made the change, however, but competitors from quite different industries such as the electromotive

division of General Motors in La Grange, Illinois, and Fairbanks Morse in Beloit, Wisconsin. Such firms got the jump on the older manufacturers in making diesel engines and now lead in locomotive production.

Factories in Chicago, St. Louis, and Altoona make most of the nation's railway cars, although some railroad companies make their own cars in various places—all in the northeastern states. Such locations have the dual advantage of being near steel mills and in the most densely trafficked railway region of the country (Figure 26-3).

The world pattern of the manufacture of

railway equipment is familiar, since there is a very close correlation by nations between the production of steel and the production of railway equipment. So the steel regions indicated in Figure 20-5, page 362, are approximately those where vehicles are produced.

uggested Readings

Alderfer, E. B., and Michl, H. E., *Economics of American Industry*, New York, 1957, chapters 9-11.

Boas, Charles W., "Locational Patterns of American Automobile Assembly Plants, 1895-1958," *Economic Geography*, 1961, pp. 218-230.

Cunningham, William Glenn, *The Aircraft Industry: A Study in Industrial Location*, Los Angeles, 1951, 247 pp.

Goodwin, William, "Relocation of the British Motor Industry," *The Professional Geographer*, July 1962, pp. 4-8.

Henrickson, G. Rex, *Trends in the Geographic Distribution of Some Basically Important Materials Used at the Buick Motor Division, Flint, Michigan*, Ann Arbor, 1951, 72 pp.

Hurley, Neil P., "The Automotive Industry: A Study in Industrial Location," *Land Economics*, 1959, pp. 1-14.

Rae, John B., *American Automobile Manufacturers: The First Forty Years*, New York, 1959.

Vent, Herbert J. and Monier, Robert B., "The Aircraft Industry in the United States and the USSR," *The Professional Geographer*, May 1958, pp. 2-8.

This huge machine tool, with a man sitting on top, is an adjustable rail-milling machine manufactured in Rockford, Illinois. It weighs 265 tons and requires a concrete foundation 21 feet deep. (Courtesy Ingersoll Milling Machine Company.)

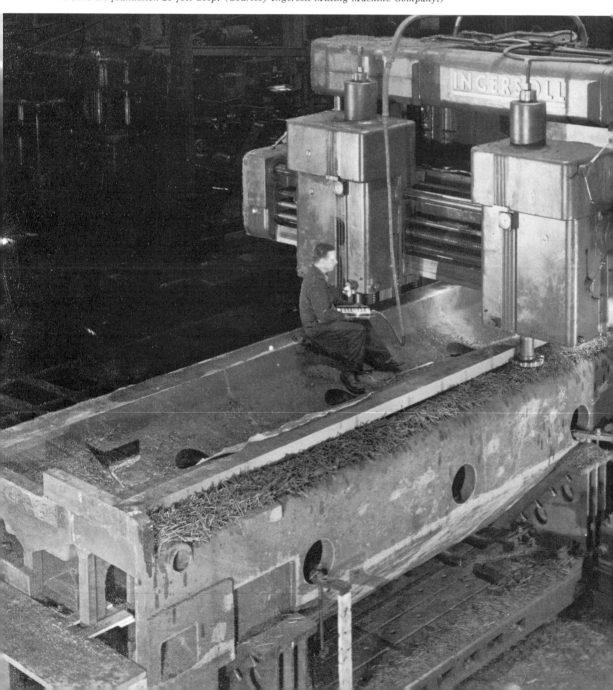

TWENTY-TWO

Since the Industrial Revolution began, inventive men have devised machines to perform so many different jobs, and the demand for such machinery has become so great, that in the United States today there are almost 2,500,000 people who earn their living by manufacturing engines, motors, lathes, typewriters, and a host of other machines—besides the nearly 1,500,000 workers who produce transport machines that we discussed in the previous chapter. The machinery industries we shall examine in this chapter are extremely diverse, so, for better understanding, we shall separate them into two broad groups: electrical machinery and nonelectrical machinery. A breakdown of the number of jobs provided by these industrial groups is listed in Table 22-1 (page 388) according to the classification system of the Bureau of the Census.

Electrical Machinery

As Table 22-1 shows, approximately 1,000,000 people are at work making generators, transformers, motors, appliances, bulbs, lamps, telephones, radios, electronic tubes, storage batteries, X-ray apparatus, and other categories of electrical machinery. And as Figure 22-1 (page 388) shows, most are in the northeastern part of the country, within an area marked off by Boston, Philadelphia, St. Louis, and Milwaukee. The two outstanding centers are New York and Chicago, which between them account for a quarter of the nations' makers of electrical machines. Other focal points of this industry in the Northeast

Table **22-1**   *United States: Leading Machinery Manufacturing Industries*
            (Other than Transportation Equipment)

Type	Number of Employees	Value Added ($000)
Electrical Machinery	1,122,284	$10,395,369
Communication equipment	215,059	2,038,438
Household appliances	142,251	1,548,808
Electrical control apparatus	134,395	1,338,652
Motors and generators	93,541	813,124
Nonelectrical Machinery	1,348,245	$12,391,190
Metalworking machines	233,523	2,058,049
Construction and mining machines	199,711	2,054,841
Office and store machines	121,615	970,529
Farm machines	108,586	1,087,836
Service-industry machines	100,059	918,151
Engines and turbines	95,572	1,067,971

Source: United States Bureau of the Census, *Census of Manufactures, 1958*, General Summary, Table 3.

are Philadelphia, Boston, Pittsburgh, and Milwaukee. Los Angeles is the most conspicuous spot outside of the Northeast; indeed, it is surpassed only by New York, Chicago, Philadelphia, and Boston.

By either states or metropolitan areas, there seems to be a correlation between the manufacture of electrical machinery and size of population (see Table 22-2). The fourteen

northeastern states do contain the bulk of the nation's population as well as the bulk of employment in electrical machinery production. But the correlation is very gross, for those fourteen states contain 80 per cent of the electrical-machinery industry but only 46 per cent of the population. If this industry correlated precisely with population, California, now the most populous state, would

Figure 22-1 (*After Donald Dallman.*)

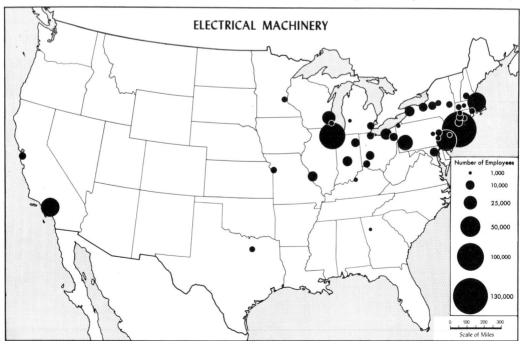

ELECTRICAL MACHINERY

Number of Employees

- 1,000
- 10,000
- 25,000
- 50,000
- 100,000
- 130,000

0 100 200 300
Scale of Miles

Electrical and Other Machinery

Table **22-2**   *United States: Leading Areas of Employment in Electrical Machinery Manufacture and of Population*

| | Employees in Manufacture of Electrical Machinery | | Population |
| | Number in Thousands | Percentage of U.S. Total | Percentage of U.S. Total |
Area			
UNITED STATES	1122	100.0	100.0
New England States			
Massachusetts	73	6.5	2.9
Connecticut	31	2.8	1.4
Rhode Island	3	—	0.5
Middle Atlantic States			
New York	138	12.3	9.4
New Jersey	107	9.6	3.4
Pennsylvania	96	8.5	6.3
East North Central States			
Illinois	162	14.4	5.6
Ohio	108	9.7	5.4
Indiana	75	6.7	2.6
Wisconsin	40	3.6	2.2
Michigan	27	2.4	4.4
Others			
California	85	7.5	8.8
Missouri	21	1.9	2.4
Maryland	16	1.4	1.7

Source: Computed from United States *Census of Manufactures,* 1958, Bulletin MC58(3), Table 4 in each state's volume and *Census of Population,* 1960, General Summary, Table 10.

make considerably more electrical machinery, in which it now ranks sixth, than it does.

Similarly with metropolitan areas: The correlation between population and employment in the electrical-machinery industry tends to hold—but there are conspicuous exceptions. San Francisco, sixth in population, does not appear among leading machinery makers (Table 22-3, page 390). But the most glaring exception is Detroit, the fifth largest American city. It has over 3,700,000 inhabitants but only 6,000 electrical-machinery workers. Why this major manufacturing city should have so little of the electrical-machinery industry is, so far, a mystery. Milwaukee, by contrast, ranks higher in making electrical devices than it does in population.

Such concentration in the Northeast suggests that this region is still riding on the momentum of an early start in this industry. Manufacturers in the region could get an early start because the Northeast early had four qualifications essential for industrial development: (1) the nation's largest group of potential customers; (2) the nation's most abundant supply of steel (as we saw in Chapter 20), copper (Chapter 19), and other required raw materials; (3) the nation's biggest supply of adaptable labor; and (4) abundant supplies of electricity.

As Figure 22-1 shows, there is an unusually heavy concentration of plants along the Atlantic Seaboard (particularly New York, Philadelphia, Boston, Baltimore, Bridgeport, and other cities in New England and eastern Pennsylvania). Now, this area is favorably located to one additional factor: the export trade. Since over one billion dollars worth of electrical machinery is exported from the United States annually, a volume exceeded only by that of automobiles and cotton, the foreign market is not an inconsiderable influence. And for this export trade the Atlantic Coast states in general and their coastal cities in particular have a tremendous locational advantage.

Thousands of Employees Making Electrical Machinery		*Thousands of Inhabitants*	
New York	149	New York	14,759
Chicago	133	Los Angeles	6,742
Los Angeles	64	Chicago	6,649
Philadelphia	46	Philadelphia	4,342
Boston	42	Detroit	3,762
Milwaukee	24	San Francisco-Oakland	2,783
Dayton	23	Boston	2,589
Cleveland	21	Pittsburgh	2,405
Pittsburgh	20	St. Louis	2.060
St. Louis	16	Washington, D.C.	2,001

Sources: United States Bureau of the Census, *Census of Manufactures,* 1958, Bulletin MC58(3), and *Census of Population,* 1960, General Summary, Tables 36 and 37.

COMMUNICATION EQUIPMENT

One subtype of electrical machinery is particularly outstanding for the payroll it supports: communication equipment. This industry provides jobs for over 200,000 people (Table 22-1). In its broad locational pattern (Figure 22-2) it resembles that of all electrical machinery, but it is more highly localized in fewer places; for example, the two main centers (Chicago and New York) together account for a third of the nation's total employment in the industry. Chicago (with 75,000 employees) has more people producing radios, television sets, electronic tubes, telephones, telegraph equipment, and other communication supplies than any other city. One reason for Chicago's predominance over New York is that since telephones, radios, and other communication equipment are used throughout the nation, Chicago is more centrally located to the market than New York is; by contrast, since other electrical machinery is used to a large extent in the Northeast,

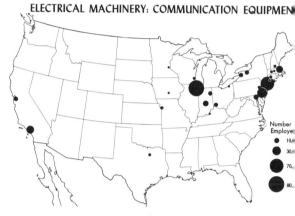

ELECTRICAL MACHINERY: COMMUNICATION EQUIPMENT

Number Employed
10,0
30,0
70,0
80,0

Figure 22-2

New York is more favorably located to that market (Figure 22-1). Another contrast between the two maps is the absence of the Pittsburgh-Youngstown-Cleveland-Toledo zone from Figure 22-2. Manufacturers in this region have tended to concentrate on making electrical industrial apparatus such as generators, motors, transformers, and batteries.

Nonelectrical Machinery

More than 1,500,000 people are involved in producing machines that are neither electrical nor for transportation: steam engines, turbines, tractors, grain combines, corn pickers, milking machines, bulldozers, road graders, steam shovels, mining machinery, oil-

drilling equipment, lathes, drills, sewing machines, looms, printing presses, power saws, pumps, elevators, conveyors, typewriters, scales, comptometers, washing machines, and dozens of other mechanical devices. (To be sure, some of these machines are driven by

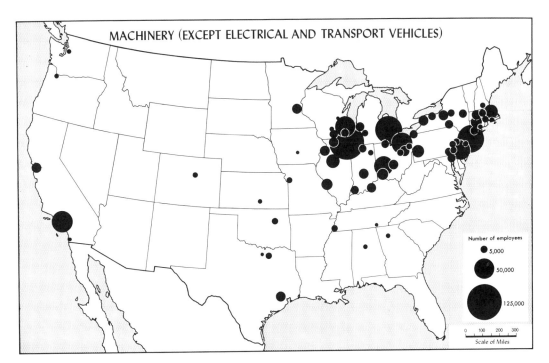

MACHINERY (EXCEPT ELECTRICAL AND TRANSPORT VEHICLES)

Number of employees
● 5,000
● 50,000
● 125,000

0 100 200 300
Scale of Miles

Figure 22-3 (*After John Meyer.*)

electric motors, but their distinction lies in their use rather than their motive power.) This myriad of machinery industries, which supports almost as many wage earners as does the transportation-equipment industry (compare Tables 22-1 and 21-1), is located according to the pattern drawn on Figure 22-3.

Six general areas stand out: (1) The Atlantic Seaboard from Maryland to southern New England. (From the consistency with which this area looms up in almost every industry studied so far, it would seem to be the nation's number-one manufacturing region.) (2) Middle New York State, from Albany to Buffalo. (3) The Detroit-Cleveland-Pittsburgh belt. (4) The Middle Ohio Valley, especially Dayton and Cincinnati. (5) Chicago and environs bounded by Milwaukee, Moline, Peoria, South Bend, and Muskegon—this is the machinery heart of the country, principally because of Chicago's prominence. (6) Los Angeles, which leaps out strikingly as the principal center west of Chicago.

As is true for electrical machinery, so for the nonelectrical, there seems to be an over-all similarity between the location of people and the location of factories, as Figure 22-3 reveals. Another view of this correlation (see Table 22-4, page 392) also supports the conclusion that the northeastern states (consisting of the three groups of states, East North Central, Middle Atlantic, and New England) are the nation's main machine shops. In fact, the northeastern states are credited with 80 per cent of the employment in this industry although they support only 45 per cent of the population.

THE QUESTION OF "LEADING REGION"

At this point, we want to direct our gaze at a question that often confronts the student of geography: "How does one determine the location of the leading region of an economic endeavor?" The machine industry can be used to illustrate this problem. If we take a map, say, Figure 22-3, and the measurements of employment in individual states (or metropolitan areas), as in Tables 22-4 and 22-5, we can discern at least five general ways of proceeding to answer our question. Let's see what we find in this particular case. (1) By individual metropolitan areas, Chicago is the

Table 22-4 *United States: Leading Regions of Nonelectrical Machinery Manufacture and of Population*

| Region | Employees in Manufacture of Nonelectrical Machinery | | Population |
	Number in Thousands	Percentage of U.S. Total	Percentage of U.S. Total
UNITED STATES	1348	100.0	100.0
New England			
Massachusetts	66	4.9	2.9
Connecticut	59	4.4	1.4
Rhode Island	8	0.6	0.5
Middle Atlantic			
New York	139	10.4	9.4
Pennsylvania	112	8.3	6.3
New Jersey	57	4.3	3.4
East North Central			
Illinois	164	12.2	5.6
Ohio	157	10.7	5.4
Michigan	124	9.3	4.4
Wisconsin	81	6.0	2.2
Indiana	45	3.3	2.6
Others			
California	78	5.8	8.8
Texas	37	2.7	5.3

Source: United States Bureau of the Census, *Census of Manufactures*, 1958, Bulletin MC58(3), each state's volume, Tables 4 and 5 and *Census of Population*, 1960. General Summary, Table 10.

unrivaled leader, accounting for nearly 10 per cent of the national total. (2) By groups of neighboring metropolitan areas, the leading region surrounds southern Lake Michigan and extends into northern Illinois. This region consists not only of Chicago but also of Milwaukee, Peoria, Moline, Rockford, Beloit, South Bend, Muskegon, and Grand Rapids.

Table 22-5 *Leading Metropolitan Areas in the Manufacture of Nonelectrical Machinery*

City	Thousands of Employees
Chicago	98
New York	78
Detroit	72
Los Angeles	50
Milwaukee	45
Philadelphia	43
Cleveland	37
Dayton	25
Boston	25
Pittsburgh	20

Source: *Ibid.*

Nearly 20 per cent of the nation's employment in making nonelectrical machinery is here. (3) By single states, Illinois ranks first, clearly ahead of Ohio. (4) If we choose groups of neighboring states as our basis, the leading region consists of five midwestern states—Ohio, Michigan, Indiana, Illinois, and Wisconsin. This quintet accounts for almost half the nation's machinery fabrication. (5) By major segments of the whole country, the northeastern quadrant (east of the Mississippi River and north of the Ohio River) accounts for 81 per cent of the jobs in this industry.

So, to answer the question, "What is the leading region of economic activity," we must first select the *scale* in which we want the answer given. *Coarse* scale involves large areas, such as the northeast quadrant of the United States; *fine* scale involves small areas, such as metropolises. Between these two extremes are transitional magnitudes of scale from which we may choose, and the choice depends upon the degree of accuracy which we desire. For some purposes, a "coarse" gen-

Electrical and Other Machinery

eralization will suffice; for other purposes, a "fine" scale answer may be required.

To understand the locational pattern of the machinery industry as a whole it will help to look at the location of leading regions in a few individual industries: metal-working machinery, service and household machinery, farm equipment, construction and mining machinery, office machinery, engines, and turbines.

METAL-WORKING MACHINERY

"The Metals Revolution" Until very recently in the long span of history, man used metals to a severely limited degree. He made his boats of skin or wood, his wagons of wooden bodies and wooden wheels; he built his shelters of skins, timber, stone, or other earth materials, and the furniture in them mainly of wood; he even fashioned plows, rakes, hoes, and tools from wood. Metals were always scarce enough to be precious. But in the last century and a half man has unlocked the earth's metallic storehouse and discovered methods for cheaply producing steel, aluminum, copper, zinc, and lead. As a result, metals have displaced wood as the most prominent raw material in the manufacture of consumer and producer goods.

Consumer goods are items that we use directly, in satisfying our needs—such personal items as watches, fasteners on clothing, furniture, automobiles, toys, washing machines, refrigerators, stoves, and such public ones as rails, bridges, and buildings, whether they be cottages or skyscrapers. Today all of these are exclusively or partly made of metal.

Producer goods are items that manufacturers use in making consumer goods or other producer goods. Nearly all producer goods are made of metal: looms and spinning machines in textile mills, cutting and sewing machines in apparel factories, milling machines in flour mills, ovens in bakeries, bottling machines in beverage plants, machines that convert sheets of steel into automobile fenders, and machines that form steel or aluminum panels for new office buildings.

"The Power Revolution" Concomitant with the *metals revolution* was a *power revolu-* *tion* in which steam and then electricity displaced animal power in doing our work for us. Without an abundance of cheap metals, this power revolution would have been impossible since no nonmetallic substance can withstand the tremendous pressures of steam or transmit electricity in large quantities.

Inventions of Metal-Working Machines The combined effect of the metals revolution and the power revolution enabled man to invent many different machines to perform a hitherto unbelievable number of jobs, from heating his house in winter to cooling it in summer, from transporting wheat to transmitting voice, from plowing soil to baking his bread, from grading his roads to balancing his ledgers. Whether the goods he manufactures be consumer or producer, whether they be for generating power or using it, man needs machines that will take metal in the shape of sheets, bars, rods, or plates, and change its form by cutting, drilling, boring, planing, grinding, or pressing it. Machines that do such work are known collectively as *metal-working machinery*. To be sure, man can perform these steps manually, but the cost of such effort is excessive. A high economic standard of living is utterly dependent on machines that can process metals (a) in large quantities, (b) in short time, and (c) with high accuracy.

This third point—accuracy—is of central importance, for metal-working machines exceed by far what the human hand can do. Forges and stamping machines rapidly process thousands of automobile fenders with such accuracy that any one of them fits the auto body for which they were designed. Some metal-working machines are so precise that they can cut and form metal to within one ten-thousandths of an inch (0.0001 inch), which is about 1/20 the diameter of a human hair. This interchangeability enabled by accuracy is the secret of mass production in which thousands of parts are formed to precisely the same dimensions and then assembled into finished products. And mass-production, of course, is a foundation stone of our prosperous industrial economy.

Machine-tool manufacturers, observing the high standard of living made possible by mechanization, declare proudly, "We make not only the machinery used in all metal-fabricating factories; we also make the machine tools that make machine tools."

A note on nomenclature is in order here. Sometimes the general public uses the term "machine tool" to identify these machines that process metal. But the men in the industrial world restrict the term to those machines that perform six basic jobs in shaping metal: turning, drilling, planing (when cutting is done by a fixed cutting tool), milling (when cutting is done by a rotating cutter), grinding, and shearing.

Location of Metal-Working Machinery Factories More than a quarter of a million people are now engaged in making metal-working machines in the United States; Figure 22-4 shows their locational pattern. Detroit stands head and shoulders above all other cities; the leading *region* can be bounded by a line encircling Detroit, Milwaukee, Rockford, Cincinnati, Pittsburgh, and Cleveland. Nearly two-thirds of American metal-working machinery comes from this region. Another third comes from New England, New York City, and Philadelphia. Elsewhere, however, except in California, very little metal-working machinery is made.

The industry is essentially market-oriented. Now, the market for lathes, drills, dies, and other metal-working machines consists entirely of factories, most of which are in the northeast quadrant of the country. Therefore, the western half of that quadrant is an ideal location for three reasons: (1) The five states of Ohio, Michigan, Illinois, Wisconsin, and Indiana are themselves the nation's biggest market. They contain thousands of factories that produce metallic products and therefore require metal-working machinery. Since the automotive industry is the single largest buyer of metal-working machinery, Detroit is prominent in both (note the correlation between Figures 22-1 and 22-4). (2) The Midwest is centrally located for shipments to metal-working factories in the East, South, and

METAL-WORKING MACHINERY

Number of Employees
● 10,000
● 20,000
● 40,000

Metropolitan Areas, Black
Remainder in State, Shaded

Figure 22-4

West. (3) The Midwest is well-endowed with steel. Compare the map of steel production, Figure 20-1, with 22-4, noting visually the correlation between midwest steel centers and midwest centers in the production of metal-working machinery.

On the East Coast the metal-working machinery factories of New England and New York may not have the fortunate location of those in the Midwest but they are advantageously situated for the foreign market. Machine tools are a lucrative export of the United States ($300,000,000 worth a year), some machine-tool companies selling over 25 per cent of their production to foreign buyers.

As the regional pattern portrayed by Figure 22-4 evolved, these leading regions assumed critical significance in the military strategy of the nation, for they produce the machines that make airplane engines, radar units, guns, tanks, ammunition, ships, and torpedoes. Indeed, one of the most paralyzing blows that can be dealt a nation's industrial life is to knock out its machine-tool factories.

Metal-Working Machinery and the Level of Industrial Development This is an opportune time to introduce a vital principle in the relationship between a region's level of manufacturing in general and its level of machinery-making in particular. *The higher the level of industrial development, the greater the production of metal-working machinery.* We can examine this principle in several ways, first in terms of time-periods within a

Electrical and Other Machinery

given region. Let us continue to use the northeastern United States as our example.

Four periods are discernible in the development of *commercial* manufacturing. First comes the *handicraft* period in which manufacturing processes are performed by hand with aid of simple equipment. At this stage in the United States, furniture, cloth, clothes, whale oil, ships, harnesses, nails, and numerous other items are made essentially by machines made. In stage two, which can be called the *imported-machinery* period, thread is spun, cloth is woven, garments are sewn, and many other items are made essentially by machines —but by machines imported from a region that is industrially advanced. The northeastern United States entered this second stage in the latter years of the eighteenth century, and imported its machines from Europe. Stage three is the *machinery* period. In the northeastern United States, manufacturers began to make their own spinning jennies, weaving looms, sewing machines, and an increasing number of machines that had previously been imported. But Americans made these products with machine tools and other metal-working machinery that they purchased across the Atlantic. The United States entered stage three early in the nineteenth century. The fourth and final stage is the *metal-working machinery* period. The northeastern United States, since the late 1800's, has not been dependent on other regions for machine tools but has made its own—plus a surplus for export. Maturity in a region's industrial development is attained when it becomes capable of making the tools that make the machines that fill its factories. Table 22-6 portrays this sequence in diagrammatic form.

Table **22-6** *Periods in Development of a Major Manufacturing Region*

Period	Items Made by Hand	Items Made by Imported Machinery	Machinery Made by Imported Machine Tools	Machine Tools Made
4	Very few	Yes	Yes	Yes
3	Few	Yes	Yes	No
2	Yes	Yes	No	No
1	Yes	No	No	No

The principle we are discussing also applies at any one time to different regions. Take the world pattern today. Four types of manufacturing regions are discernible. The first includes those countries whose manufactures are largely handmade from materials produced by their farms, forests, mines, and fisheries. Very few countries are still completely in this stage, although substantial portions of China, India, Indonesia, Philippines, much of Africa, and parts of Latin America, Spain, and Greece are in the latter phases of it. The second type of region is more dependent on mechanization than on handiwork, but machinery is largely imported. Venezuela, Brazil, Argentina, South Africa, Australia, Iceland, and Austria are in this category. The third stage has been reached by Canada, northern Italy, Sweden, France, Switzerland, Japan, and other countries that manufacture machinery. The fourth and final stage has been attained in Germany, the United Kingdom, and the United States, all of which make machine tools and have surpluses to ship to other areas. Japan too is beginning to qualify as a stage-four region. And the Soviet Union, which shot up rapidly from stage one to stage three in 40 years, is probably nearing stage four, although she still does not produce a very large exportable surplus of machine tools. Indeed, metal-working machinery is one of the most coveted items the U.S.S.R. wants to get from the free world through trade.

SERVICE AND HOUSEHOLD MACHINERY

The manufacture of vending machines, laundry equipment, dry-cleaning equipment, vacuum cleaners, garbage grinders, sewing machines, refrigeration machinery, pumps and a wide diversity of household and service mechanisms support approximately 250,000 employees. In Figure 22-5, page 396, on the locational pattern of employment, we see again the familiar prominence of northeastern states that has distinguished all our maps of machinery production.

Note, however, that the manufacture of service and household machines does not coincide very closely with large metropolitan areas. Dayton, Ohio, dominates the map, clearly outranking New York, Chicago, Los

Angeles, and Detroit. Moreover, there are many factories that turn out this equipment in cities not even identified in the Census of Manufactures. Consequently, it has been necessary on Figure 22-5 to represent a rather sizable component of this industry by means of shaded rather than black circles, with one shaded circle per state standing for the employment that remains after metropolitan area employment is subtracted. Even so, the east-north-central states dominate the map.

Dayton's prominence is attributable to three organizations—Frigidaire, General Motors' Delco Division, and Chrysler's Airtemp Division—that have moved from Detroit within the past 40 years. Dayton's main advantages over Detroit are, in the opinion of these companies, as expressed in correspondence with the author, (a) more satisfactory labor conditions, and (b) more central location to most of the nation's customers.

FARM MACHINERY

The manufacture of no type of machinery is so highly concentrated in the Midwest—or in a single state, Illinois—as is that of farm machinery (Figure 22-6). From Ohio to Iowa and from Kentucky to Minnesota are a group of communities that constitute the farm machinery heart of the nation. Illinois, the leading state, has 27,000 employees—25 per cent of the nation's total. Peoria is the leading city in the nation. Other conspicuous centers are Chicago, the "Tri-Cities" (Davenport-Rock Island-Moline), Rockford, Milwaukee, and Racine. Figure 22-6 maps one of the rare machinery industries in which the East Coast in general and New York City in particular are insignificant. Several factors have operated to produce this midwestern dominance.

Markets   One cannot miss the obvious locational correlation between makers and users of farm machines. For instance, compare Figure 22-6 with Figure 22-7, which shows the distribution of tractors on farms. A common sight on freight trains outbound from Milwaukee, Chicago, Beloit, Rockford, Peoria, and the Tri-Cities are flat cars loaded with tractors, corn-pickers, and other brightly

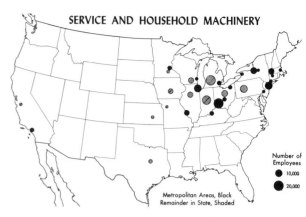

Figure 22-5

painted farm machines bound for customers in diverse parts of the nation. Many of them are too large to be shipped bodily and are shipped knocked-down from the factory for assemblage by the hundreds of dealers who are located in a widely dispersed pattern through the farming regions of the nation.

The nearness of midwestern cities to mechanized farms has long attracted manufacturers from other parts of the country. For example, it was in the Shenandoah Valley of Virginia that, around 1830, Cyrus McCormick invented the reaper, the first successful device for mechanically harvesting grain; but McCormick constructed his first factory in Chicago in order to be near the greatest number of reaper-using farms.

Today, new markets for farm machines are growing on the West Coast and in the South. Yet the demand in these areas, being relatively

Figure 22-6 (*After Marvin Wagner.*)

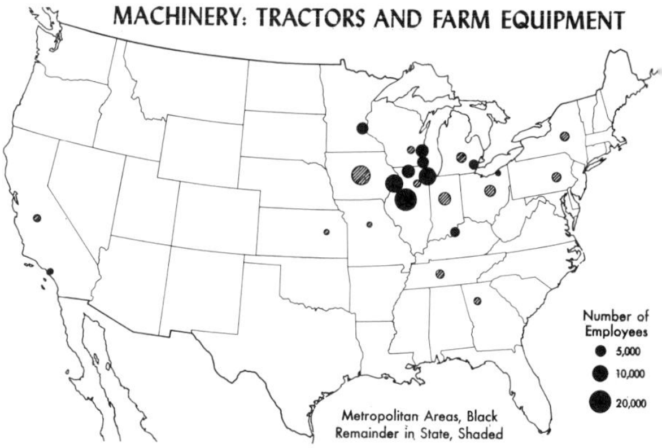

MACHINERY: TRACTORS AND FARM EQUIPMENT

Electrical and Other Machinery

View of a sewing machine factory, in the foreground, and a part of the city of Geneva, Switzerland, in the background. One of the world's largest sewing machine producers, this plant exports nine of every ten machines to a world-wide market. (Courtesy Elna Corporation, Tavaro.)

recent, is still not great enough to overcome the head start the midwestern manufacturing cities enjoy. Nevertheless, a few companies have responded to the pull of the new market

Figure 22-7 *(From U. S. Bureau of the Census.)*

TRACTORS ON FARMS

1 Dot = 500 Tractors
United States Total
5,138,921

areas and have opened plants that make small items such as (a) attachments to farm machines, (b) some of the simpler machines (for instance, harrows and discs), and (c) special machines only used locally (for example, the special hay balers manufactured in Stockton, California and cotton-picking machines in Memphis, Tennessee). One company turns out harrows and discs at Oxnard, California, for the California market. A competitor has a similarly oriented factory in Fowler, California.

Inventions The Midwest has not only had the nation's best market for farm machines but also an abundant supply of human inventiveness, from the time in 1855, when a citizen of Moline, Illinois—John Deere—designed a plow with a steel moldboard. The significance of this invention to midwestern America cannot be overemphasized.

For centuries farmers had successfully used *wooden* plows to turn furrows in the soil of their fields. But throughout those ages they were cultivating soils in humid regions where *trees* had been the native vegetation; wooden plows were capable of turning over forest-land soils once the trees and stumps were removed. The world's great clusters of population up until 1800 (China, India, and western Europe) coincided with areas of native forest vegetation, and the first populous belts in the United States were in forested New England, the tree-covered Middle Atlantic states, and the wooded southeastern states. But grasslands have a different history. Through the centuries they had been used for grazing, not for cultivating. The tough sod of heavily interwoven grass roots is too tight for wooden plows to cut. Accordingly, the first settlers in the Mississippi Valley, lower Ohio Valley, and other midwest areas clung to the ribbons of woodland along streams or to the pockets of trees on the interfluves. One reason for this was that tree-cleared land could be worked by the only earth-turning tool they had. Grassland soils, although they are richer than forest soils, were avoided.

Then came Deere's invention. Steel moldboards easily sliced through grassland turf, exposing the dark rich face of prairie soils that, when sown with wheat or planted in corn, delivered abundant yields. There followed, simultaneously, a boom in homesteading and sales of prairie land and a demand for plows with steel moldboards. Deere set up production in Moline, not only because it was his hometown, but also because it was situated so near the center of the American prairie. Moline boomed and, along with neighboring Rock Island and Davenport, became one of the world's foremost centers of farm machinery as other items were added to the Deere company's production line and other companies moved into the area.

There were other midwestern inventions, too. In the late 1840's a Rockford machinist, John H. Manny, invented a reaping machine that won numerous medals and cups in con-

tests with other reapers. By the early 1850's the city's factories were turning out hundreds of these machines, earning for Rockford the nickname, "Reaper City." Another Rockford industrialist, Marquis L. Gorham, invented three agricultural machines—a seeder, a corn cultivator, and a binder. In Beloit, Wisconsin, just north of Rockford, John Appleby designed the first twine binder, which freed farmers from the use of wire binders. Nearly all the farm machinery industry in the Midwest can be traced to inventions by local designers of tractors, harrows, drills, cultivators, harvesters, pickers, and binders.

The invention of farm machines in this region was stimulated by three concurrent conditions during the 1800's and early 1900's when the Midwest was being settled: (a) land was abundant, (b) labor was scarce, and (c) the market for agricultural products was large, particularly in Europe and the eastern United States where the Industrial Revolution was increasing the purchasing power of thousands of people who were leaving the farms for higher-paying jobs in cities. The thrust of American invention, therefore, was toward labor-saving devices. By contrast, very few farm machines were invented in Europe because (a) farm population remained so large that there continued to be an abundance of labor, and (b) agricultural land was scarce. Accordingly, the ingenuity of European inventors was directed more toward land-saving devices such as weed control, improved fertilizers, better strains of seeds for crops, and scientific breeding of animals.

Raw Materials   In addition to their central location (relative to markets) and the supply of inventive minds, the Midwestern farm machinery centers are close to the steel mills that manufacture their main raw material. Much of the steel is produced in Gary and Chicago itself, although some comes in from Youngstown and Pittsburgh.

Size   Farm machinery companies tend to be large, each making a diversity of implements. A strong reason for this diversity is the competitive advantage in selling a *com-*

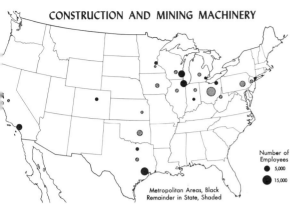

CONSTRUCTION AND MINING MACHINERY

Number of Employees
● 5,000
● 15,000

Metropolitan Areas, Black
Remainder in State, Shaded

Figure 22-8

plete line of implements. And this advantage in turn encourages the development of a few large companies that manufacture for a nation-wide market instead of a host of smaller companies each specializing in one implement. Thus, if he chooses, a farmer can get his tractor, plow, disk, drill, and harrow in one package deal from a single company.

CONSTRUCTION AND MINING MACHINERY

Construction and mining machinery will be considered together mainly because statistics on their location are lumped together in Census publications. Earth-moving equipment, bulldozers, cement mixers, oil-drilling equipment, and coal-loaders are typical examples. As Figure 22-8 shows, most of this industry is also in the Midwest, with Ohio the leading state. The principal cities in this business are Milwaukee, Chicago, and Cleveland. This

Figure 22-9

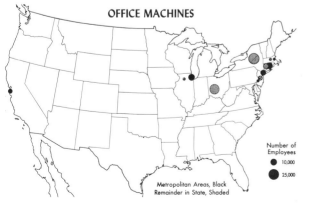

OFFICE MACHINES

Number of Employees
● 10,000
● 25,000

Metropolitan Areas, Black
Remainder in State, Shaded

rather diverse industry seems to conform with two principles: (1) that machinery factories tend to locate near their markets, and (2) that if the machines are manufactured in relatively small numbers but used throughout the country, the factories tend to settle in a central location.

The latter principle happens to apply particularly to earth-moving and construction machinery, whereas the former principle holds for equipment used in iron-ore mining, coal mining, and oil-drilling, the markets for which are not nationwide. Consequently, the location of factories correlates well with the location, respectively, of iron ore in Wisconsin and Minnesota (Figure 14-4), of coal in Ohio, Pennsylvania, and West Virginia (also 14-4), and of oil mining in Texas, Oklahoma, and California (Figure 15-6). Texas manufactures almost as much of the machinery in this category as does Ohio; indeed, Houston's is the largest solid circle on Figure 22-8. From Houston factories, oil-drilling machinery is shipped not only to Gulf Coast states but to Venezuela, Mexico, the Middle East, and other foreign oil-mining areas.

OFFICE AND STORE MACHINES

Typewriters, scales, balances, adding machines, comptometers, bookkeeping machines, and complex mechanisms that sort and compute statistics are manufactured almost entirely within the northeastern quadrant of the nation. Prominent cities are Chicago, New York, Hartford, Dayton (home of National Cash Register), and Binghamton-Endicott, New York (home of International Business Machines).

This industry serves a nation-wide market, therefore it looks with favor upon being located in the Midwest. Even so, the Eastern Seaboard stands out in Figure 22-9 because the most intense use of office and store machines in the nation coincides with the highly commercialized belt running from Boston, through New York, Philadelphia, and Baltimore, to Washington, D.C. In no other comparable portion of the earth do so many commercial and government offices and stores use office machinery.

Electrical and Other Machinery

Steam engines, turbines, and internal combustion engines are produced almost entirely in those states east of the Mississippi and north of the Ohio rivers. Philadelphia, Chicago, and Milwaukee are the prominent cities, while Wisconsin, Illinois, Michigan, New York, Pennsylvania, and Massachusetts are the leading states (see Figure 22-10).

These places are within the very region that demands most of the nation's power and so uses the power-production machines. Logically enough, the machines that convert energy from fuels (coal, petroleum, gas) into usable power are made there. To be sure, there is a demand for turbines at hydroelectric power dams, but only 4 per cent of the power generated in the United States is hydroelectric; 96 per cent is generated from the burning of fuel that is transported into the regions where it is used. It is there that fuel and power-making machinery converge; it is there that most of that machinery is manufactured.

SPECIAL-INDUSTRY MACHINES

There are 160,000 persons in the United States who make textile machines, printing machines, and other equipment designed specifically for particular trades (see Table 22-5).

Figure 22-11 shows the regional pattern of these special-industry machinery makers. The familiar Northeast again stands out: fittingly

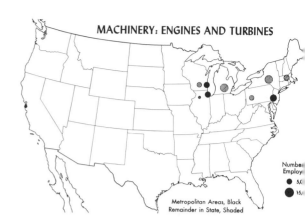

MACHINERY: ENGINES AND TURBINES

Metropolitan Areas, Black
Remainder in State, Shaded

Number
Employ
● 5,0
● 15,

Figure 22-10

for the publishing capital of the country, New York is the world's leading maker of printing presses and other printing-trades machinery. From southern Pennsylvania to New Hampshire, we find most of the nation's textile machinery is made, although some textile machinery is beginning to come from southern factories, particularly in the Carolinas. Most of the paper-industry machines are made in Wisconsin, New York, and Washington. Woodworking machines come from Illinois, Ohio, and Michigan. Food-processing machines are made throughout the areas shown on Figure 22-11. Clearly, these industries are all market-oriented.

UNITED STATES MACHINERY MANUFACTURING: CONCLUSIONS

Inspection of the foregoing series of maps leads to the conclusion that the United States

Table 22-5   United States: Manufacture
of Special-Industry Machinery

Type	Number of Employees	Value Added ($000)
Total	162,262	$1,339,530
Textile Machinery	34,313	214,199
Food-products Machinery	27,715	268,639
Printing-trades Machinery	21,453	188,881
Woodworking Machinery	21,219	112,936
Paper-industries Machinery	15,713	123,758

Source: United States Bureau of Census, *Census of Manufactures*, 1958, General Summary, Bulletin MC58(1)-1, p. 18.

Figure 22-11

SPECIAL-INDUSTRY MACHINERY

Number o
Employee
● 5,000
● 20,00

Metropolitan Areas, Black
Remainder in State, Shaded

Electrical and Other Machinery

contains *one* single outstanding *machinery zone*, a region extending from the Mississippi River to the Atlantic Coast. The northern boundary of this belt roughly coincides with a line from Milwaukee through Buffalo to Boston, while the southern margin runs from St. Louis through Cincinnati to Baltimore. The significance of this machinery belt in the nation's economic life can scarcely be over-emphasized, for in it we make most of (a) our transportation machines for both freight and passengers, (b) the machines that perform work for us in our kitchens and living rooms, forests and mines, farms and building projects, (c) the machines that perform most of the work in the nation's factories making shoes, clothes, tires, chemicals, flour, and a host of other consumer commodities which stream from factories in massive quantities thanks to mechanized methods of manufacturing, and (d) the machines that make all the machines just mentioned.

Within this main machinery belt, three clear subregions are conspicuous: a western area dominated by Chicago and Milwaukee; a central area led by Detroit, Cleveland, and Cincinnati; and an eastern one highlighted by New York, Philadelphia, and Boston.

Access to Customers   The single most important reason for the prominence of this great region is its nearness to machinery users. A basic principle prevails here that pertained to other industries discussed in previous chapters: For any given factory, if transport charges on its finished product *exceed those on its raw materials, that factory will tend to locate near its customers*. Freight rates on machinery are half again as much as those on the steel from which machines are made. Moreover, very little weight is lost in the conversion of steel to machinery. Therefore, users lure makers to their regions.

The customers who constitute the market for machinery are diverse indeed, but whether they be trucking companies, railroad companies, private automobile operators, whether they be housewives using vacuum cleaners and washing machines or business firms using typewriters and comptometers, whether they

be factories using machines to make consumer goods or factories that manufacture machines —most of these customers are located in the northeastern part of the nation. This is chiefly why most machinery factories are there.

Access to Ideas   New machines and improvements on old machines are conceived not only by designers in machinery-making factories but also by operators who use those machines, whether in factories, mines, farms, or homes. Close association between maker and user stimulates inventions and improvements—another reason for the Northeast's prominence.

Time-lag Principle   In recent years new markets for machinery have developed in other parts of the country, notably the southeastern states for textile machinery and California for a diversity of equipment. These new markets are relatively small compared to the Northeast; they have fewer people to buy the consumer-machinery and fewer factories to buy the producer-machinery. Consequently, as yet they have attracted few machinery-making factories. We can explain this by the *time-lag principle: A maker of machines tends to locate in the same region as the industry that uses those machines; but when that industry moves elsewhere, the machinery maker lags behind*. Take textiles for example. For decades New England and the eastern parts of the Middle Atlantic states manufactured nearly all of this nation's textiles, and Massachusetts and Pennsylvania became the leading producers of textile machinery. Then the textile industry moved south so that today over three-fifths of its workers are in southern states. Yet these southern factories operate with machinery that is largely northern-built; four-fifths of United States textile machines are still made in the North.

In such situations there is a conflict between (a) the lure of the new market region where transport charges on finished machinery would be less, and (b) the lure of the established region where, due to its *early start*, companies have built up an experienced labor force. Sometimes the hold of an established region is termed *industrial inertia*; it is a psychological factor, very difficult to measure scientifically, but nonetheless real in maintaining *momentum* in a region where factories continue to operate for awhile, sometimes long after one would expect.

Access to Steel   Customers may have been the chief initial attraction, but the machinery belt has within its borders the world's most productive steel mills to supply the basic ingredient for its factories. If we compare the map of steel production (Figure 20-1) with the machinery maps in this chapter we can see how centrally located the Pittsburgh-Youngstown-Cleveland steel district is for supplying the factories of the machinery belt.

MEASUREMENT
OF GEOGRAPHIC ASSOCIATION

The machinery industry was chosen as the "laboratory specimen" in a recent research project that is noteworthy as the first systematic attempt (as far as the author knows) to measure association in industrial geography. This analytical effort is so significant that we shall reserve it for careful treatment in Chapter 32, which deals with *methods of measuring* the location of manufacturing and the association of manufacturing with other phenomena.

THE WORLD PATTERN

Most of this chapter has dealt with locational patterns and locational principles of machinery-making in the United States.

But the same basic principles are observable in the world pattern, that machinery-making

Table **22-6**   *International Trade: Machinery*
(*in Millions of United States Dollars*)

Leading Exporters		Leading Importers	
United States	$6,307	Canada	$1,757
West Germany	3,956	United States	1,147
United Kingdom	3,800	U.S.S.R.	1,082
France	1,164	Netherlands	704
U.S.S.R.	837	France	678
Italy	680	Sweden	605
Japan	627	United Kingdom	602
Sweden	625	Belgium	588
Netherlands	537	West Germany	583
Canada	452	Norway	540
Belgium	426	Australia	522

Source: United Nations, *Yearbook of International Trade Statistics*, 1959.

tends to locate primarily within its main market region and secondarily near steel centers. The leading nations in machinery production are the countries in which there is both a great demand for machines and considerable production of steel. Specifically, the foremost machinery-makers are the United States, West Germany, the United Kingdom, France, and the U.S.S.R.

International trade in machinery displays a distinctive pattern: the world's major exporting regions are likewise its major importing regions (see Table 22-6). This contrasts rather markedly with the patterns of international trade for wheat, wool, wood, iron ore, fish, and most other commodities—for which the leading export nations are rarely the leading import nations.

Major areas of machinery manufacture in other parts of the world will receive attention in Chapters 24 and 25.

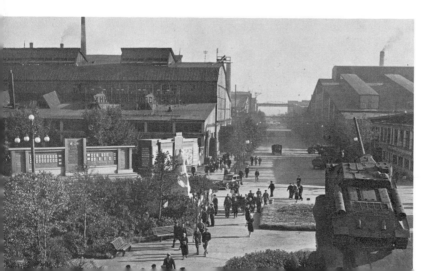

The Urals Heavy Machinery Plant. The last tank produced here during World War II is on a pig-iron pedestal at the right. (Sovfoto.)

A cluster of three different industrial establishments to the east of Port Arthur, Ontario: grain elevators alongside loading docks, shipyards (behind the elevators), and a pulp and paper plant with its vast log-storage pen in Lake Superior. (Courtesy National Film Board, Ottawa.)

TWENTY-THREE

In the last six chapters we have taken an industry approach to the geography of manufacturing—that is, taking individual industries one by one, we have identified the many different areas in which they are located. In the next three chapters we shall adopt a *regional approach*—that is, taking regions one by one, we shall consider the many different industries that are located in them. For one example, southern New England as a type of manufacturing region is different from northeastern Ohio; for another the Ruhr thrives on a different aggregate of industries than does the London area.

In Chapter 23 we apply the regional approach to manufacturing in the United States and Canada, in Chapter 24, we deal with western Europe, and in Chapter 25, we consider the Soviet Union, Asia, and selected areas in other parts of the world.

The United States

All told, the United States has over 400 different types of manufacturing industries, according to the classification system devised by the Census of Manufactures. Together they employ 15,393,000 people, who are tabulated by industry in Table 23-1 and are distributed according to the pattern shown in Figure 23-1. Each circle on this map represents either one county or one metropolitan area—which may consist of several counties. For example, the single circle for the New York metropolitan area represents 17 counties, nine in New York State and eight in New Jersey. The

Table 23-1   United States Industrial Structure, 1958

Census Code Number	Industry	Number of Establish-ments	Thousands of Employees	Annual Payroll ($ Millions)	Value Added by Manu-facture ($ Millions)	1947 Thousands of Employees
20	Food	41,619	1,698	7,553	17,532	1,441
21	Tobacco	504	84	294	1,413	111
22	Textiles	7,675	901	2,938	4,857	1,233
23	Apparel	29,297	1,180	3,585	6,003	1,081
24	Lumber and Wood	37,789	581	1,986	3,176	635
25	Furniture and Fixtures	10,160	347	1,388	2,349	322
26	Paper	5,271	555	2,779	5,707	449
27	Printing and Publishing	35,368	864	4,479	7,922	715
28	Chemical	11,309	699	3,947	12,270	632
29	Petroleum and Coal	1,608	179	1,116	2,518	212
30	Rubber and Plastics	4,462	347	1,723	3,276	259
31	Leather	4,534	349	1,145	1,897	383
32	Stone, Clay, Glass	15,022	554	2,594	5,528	462
33	Primary Metal	6,446	1,096	6,303	11,671	1,157
34	Fabricated Metal	24,782	1,057	5,412	9,412	971
35	Machinery (except electrical)	29,839	1,348	7,303	12,391	1,545
36	Electrical Machinery	8,091	1,122	5,605	10,395	801
37	Transport Equipment	6,607	1,557	9,164	15,283	1,181
38	Instruments	3,526	296	1,578	2,906	231
39	Miscellaneous	14,273	571	2,847	4,754	464
TOTAL		298,182	15,393	73,749	141,270	14,294

Source: United States Bureau of the Census, *Census of Manufactures*, 1958, General Summary, and 1947, General Summary.

Figure 23-1

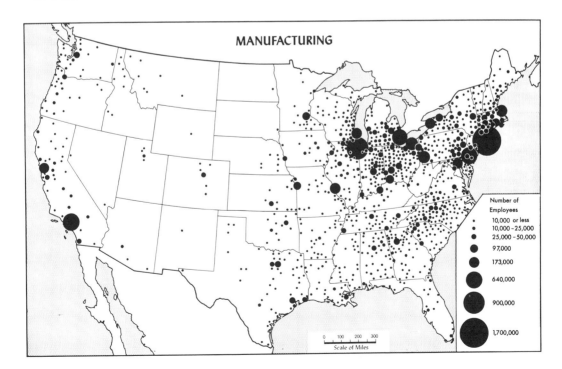

smallest circles stand for counties with from 1000 to 9999 manufacturing employees. Counties with fewer than 1000 such employees do not show up on Figure 23-1.

In terms of employment in manufacturing, the United States can be split in two along a line running from the southern tip of Texas northward to the Minnesota-Dakota border. East of this line, most counties have at least some manufacturing, west of the line, most counties have too little manufacturing to figure on the map.

The industrialized eastern half of the country in fact supports almost 90 per cent of the nation's employment in manufacturing. And most of these jobs—almost 70 per cent of the total—are in the northeastern states (east of the Mississippi River and north of the Ohio River). A closer inspection of the Northeast reveals that all but two—California and Texas —of the nation's ten leading manufacturing states are there, as are all of the ten major industrial metropolises except for Los Angeles (Table 23-2).

Actually there are several clearly identifiable manufacturing areas: the New York metropolitan area, New England, the Middle Atlantic states, middle New York State, the Midwest, the South, and the Pacific Coast. We shall pursue our investigation of the national pattern in those regional categories.

Before inspecting these regions, it will be helpful to consider four concepts that shed light on the industrial characteristics of a region and help one to distinguish between regions: *location quotient, light industry and heavy industry, industrial structure,* and *index of diversification.*

LOCATION QUOTIENT

The *location quotient* measures the degree to which a specific region has more or less than its share of any particular industry. Using the greater New York metropolitan area as the illustrative region and the number of manufacturing employees as the illustrative criterion, we can derive the quotient as follows.

1. Compute New York's employment in manufacturing (1,660,000) as a percentage of the national total (15,393,000). The answer is 10.8 per cent.

2. Compute New York's share of the national employment in each individual industry. For example, here are the New York and national figures for certain leading industries:

Industry	A. Employment in New York	B. Employment in the United States	Percentage of A/B
Apparel	361.638	1,180,517	30.5
Printing	171.269	864,101	20.0
Foods	129,503	1,698,000	7.7
Chemicals	99,182	699,166	14.3
Textiles	63,393	901,677	7.2
Primary Metals	40,821	1,096,359	3.7
Toys and Sporting Goods	29,280	98,704	29.9
Grain Mill Products	1,533	118,984	1.3

3. Compare the above percentage for each industry with 10.8 per cent (New York's share of the nation's total). If the percentage exceeds 10.8 per cent, New York has more than its share. To express this relationship precisely, divide 10.8 per cent into the percentage value for each industry. The results will be the New York metropolitan area's *location quotients* for those industries. Here are the figures and computations for our selected industries:

Table 23-2 *United States Manufacturing:*
Leading States and Metropolitan Areas,
(in Thousands of Employees)

States		Metropolitan Areas	
New York	1782	New York	1660
Pennsylvania	1337	Chicago	911
California	1181	Los Angeles	712
Ohio	1162	Philadelphia	515
Illinois	1139	Detroit	405
Michigan	809	Boston	285
New Jersey	761	Pittsburgh	269
Massachusetts	658	Cleveland	253
Indiana	544	St. Louis	243
Texas	466	Baltimore	195

Source: United States Bureau of the Census, *Census of Manufactures,* 1958, General Summary, Table 5.

Industry	A. New York's Percentage Share of National Employment in Each Industry	B. New York's Percentage Share of Nation's Total Manufacturing Employment	New York's Location Quotient: A/B
Apparel	30.5	10.8	2.8
Toys	29.9	10.8	2.7
Printing	20.0	10.8	1.8
Chemicals	14.3	10.8	1.3
Foods	7.7	10.8	0.7
Textiles	7.2	10.8	0.6
Primary Metals	3.7	10.8	0.3
Grain Mill Products	1.3	10.8	0.1

The maximum a location quotient could be in the New York metropolitan area is 9.2 if this region (which contains 10.8 per cent of the nation's manufacturing) had all (100 per cent) of any given industry. The minimum a location quotient could be anywhere is, of course, zero.

A location quotient of 1.0 means that a region has neither more nor less of the national industry than its over-all volume of manufacturing would suggest. A quotient over 1.0 indicates a high particular concentration in that locality, relative to local industrial development. A quotient less than 1.0 suggests that an industry is less developed in that region than is manufacturing in general.

Location quotients can be computed for any region and for any industry, not only for metropolitan areas but for cities, counties, states, or any other areal unit one cares to investigate. They are useful in comparing different industries with one another in the same region and in comparing different regions with one another.

LIGHT INDUSTRIES AND HEAVY INDUSTRIES

Another frequently useful approach to studying industrial regions is to categorize industries as light and heavy.

Light industry is a rather loosely defined term applied to factories that use comparatively light-weight machinery, or that consume small quantities of raw material, or that are free of nuisance qualities such as offensive odors, noise, or dirt. *Heavy industry* is also loosely defined but, in general usage, is applied to factories that use bulky machinery and consume copious quantities of raw materials, thus necessitating water or rail transport. Accordingly, heavy industries are often located along railroads, canals, rivers, or ocean inlets and often have their own docks and/or railway sidings with conspicuous piles of raw materials adjoining factory buildings. Furthermore, heavy industries often have severe nuisance qualities, emitting dirt, noise, or unpleasant odors.

INDUSTRIAL STRUCTURE

A region's *industrial structure* can be defined as the aggregate of individual industries that account for all the manufacturing in the region ranked by magnitude. The magnitude of each industry is measured proportionately in terms of some given criterion. For instance, if employment is the criterion we choose, and we want to measure the significance of the printing industry in the New York metropolitan area's industrial structure, we divide 1,660,000 (the total number of manufacturing employees in New York factories) into 171,269 (the number employed there in the printing and publishing industry), giving us a quotient of 10.3, which is one measure of the relative importance of the printing industry in New York. If we proceeded to make similar computations for each industry, we would arrive at a measure of New York's *industrial structure*. In other words, a region's industrial structure is a proportionate listing of all industries, rated according to a given criterion. Table 23-5 illustrates this concept.

INDEX OF DIVERSIFICATION

If most of a given region's manufacturing employees are in just one industry, then obviously that region is much less diversified than a region where employment is spread rather evenly among many different industries. The one region has all its money on one horse, industrially speaking; the other is playing the field. In an effort to measure such differences, the *index of diversification* has been devised.

This index was developed by Allan Rodgers and is computed as follows, using United States Census data:

1. For each industrial region being studied, Rodgers constructed a table that ranks all manufacturing industries in terms of employment, by number and percentage, as in columns 1 and 2 in Table 23-3, which uses Indianapolis, Indiana, as an example. There are 22 entries in the table, the number of major manufacturing categories recognized by the Census.

2. Computation was made of "progressive totals" of the percentages that appear in Table 23-3, column 2. These were then entered in column 3.

3. The progressive totals were added. The result was termed the *crude diversification index*. In the illustration, Indianapolis has a crude index of 1698. The highest possible crude index would be 2200, which would pertain if 100 per cent of a region's manufacturing employment were in one industry. Under such circumstances the first industry listed in Table 23-3 would show 100 in column 2 and 100 in column 3; thereafter each entry would show zero in column 2 and 100 in column 3. The lowest possible crude

Figure 23-2 (*Courtesy Allan Rodgers and* Economic Geography.)

INDEXES OF INDUSTRIAL DIVERSIFICATION

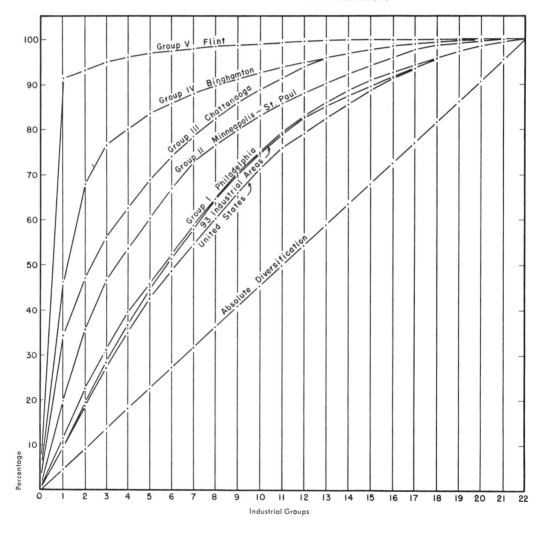

index would be approximately 1150. This would result if there were *absolute diversification*, that is, if employment were equally divided among the 22 industries so that each entry in column 2 would be 4.54.

At this point, the graphs in Figure 23-2 illustrate the principle involved in computing the crude diversification index. Flint has a very steep curve because her leading industry accounts for over 90 per cent of all her employment in manufacturing. Binghamton's curve is much less steep since her leading industry accounts for 46 per cent of her manufacturing total. Curves for a few other cities are shown as well as a curve for the United States as a whole and one for a hypothetical area in which *absolute diversification* prevailed.

4. The next step was to convert the crude index into the *refined index of diversification*.

The aim was to express the crude index in relationship to an average or norm. The norm Rodgers selected was the totality of employment for all metropolitan areas with at least 20,000 manufacturing workers. There were 93 such places, and the crude diversification index for the group was 1553. The formula he devised for computing the refined index for Indianapolis was as follows:

$$\frac{1698 - 1553}{2200 - 1553} = \frac{145}{647} = .224$$

In the above formula, the numerator represents the *difference* between the crude index of the city being measured and that of the norm; the denominator represents the *difference* between the crude index for the least possible diversity and the index for the average.

The refined diversification indexes for sev-

Table **23-3** *Computation of Index of Diversification (Example: Indianapolis)*

Manufacturing Industries	Employees in Manufacturing		
	(1) Number	(2) Percentage	(3) Progressive Totals
Total	76,945	100.00	—
Electrical Machinery	10.256	13.33	13.33
Other Machinery	9.596	12.47	25.80
Foods	8.712	11.32	37.12
Motor Vehicles	7,488	9.73	46.85
Chemicals	6.300	8.19	55.04
Fabricated Metals	6,256	8.13	63.17
Printing and Publishing	5,101	6.63	69.80
Transport Equipment (except motor vehicles)	4,444	5.78	75.58
Primary Metals	4.092	5.32	80.90
Paper	2,262	2.94	83.84
Rubber	2,210	2.87	86.71
Textiles	1,996	2.59	89.30
Miscellaneous Durables	1,571	2.04	91.34
Apparel	1,524	1.98	93.22
Stone, Clay, Glass	1,200	1.56	94.88
Furniture	1,085	1.41	96.29
Lumber and Wood	831	1.08	97.37
Not specified	744	0.97	98.34
Professional Equipment	636	0.83	99.17
Petroleum and Coal	424	0.55	99.72
Leather	173	0.22	99.94
Tobacco	43	0.06	100.00
Sum of progressive totals (Crude Diversification Index)			1697.71

Source: Allan Rodgers, "Some Aspects of Industrial Diversification in the United States," *Economic Geography* (January, 1957), pp. 16-30.

eral American cities computed by the Rodgers formula are listed in Table 23-4.

Two generalizations can be drawn here: (1) The higher the percentage of manufacturing employment accounted for by a region's leading industry, the higher is its refined index of diversification. (2) Large cities tend to have lower indices than do small cities, because they tend to have more diversification.

nated by the apparel industry. As Table 23-5 shows, clothing factories provide nearly one out of every four manufacturing jobs in New York, more than half of them in the making of women's clothing. Printing (including publishing) runs second. Newspaper, periodical, and book publishers as well as thousands of commercial printers, lithographers, bookbinders, and greeting card printers

Table **23-4** *Refined Diversification Indices of Selected American Cities*

Philadelphia	.039	Columbus (O.)	.298	Fort Worth	.580
St. Louis	.090	Cleveland	.301	Pittsburgh	.600
Los Angeles	.114	Des Moines	.355	Fort Wayne	.606
Boston	.118	Milwaukee	.363	Birmingham	.615
New Orleans	.152	Grand Rapids	.369	Wichita	.629
Cincinnati	.167	Toledo	.372	South Bend	.641
New York	.173	Miami	.383	Binghamton	.651
San Francisco	.173	Salt Lake City	.388	Galveston	.652
Memphis	.215	Houston	.393	New Britain	.655
Dallas	.218	Racine	.397	San Diego	.689
Chicago	.224	Providence	.402	Detroit	.700
Indianapolis	.224	Syracuse	.416	Youngstown	.709
Atlanta	.229	Chattanooga	.456	Akron	.717
Baltimore	.235	Seattle	.458	Fall River	.742
Denver	.238	Erie	.462	Peoria	.773
Buffalo	.243	Hartford	.462	Durham	.793
Kansas City	.257	Rochester	.498	Lansing	.848
Louisville	.261	Kalamazoo	.575	Flint	.934

Source: Allan Rodgers, *op. cit.*

THE NEW YORK METROPOLITAN AREA

With 1,660,000 industrial workers, the greater New York metropolitan area (consisting of nine counties in New York State and eight counties in New Jersey) comprises the world's single largest concentration of manufacturing employees, a group that makes up 11 per cent of the manufacturing labor force of the United States. This one metropolitan area contains the astonishing total of 51,645 factories. (Unless otherwise indicated, the name "New York" will be used in this section to identify this whole great metropolitan area.)

Manufacturing is the largest single endeavor in New York's economic life, providing jobs for 30 per cent of her employed labor force. And New York's *industrial structure* is domi-

provide New York with over 170,000 jobs. This combination of apparel and printing is unique. (A clarifying comment is in order here concerning types of people who are "employees in manufacturing." A garment district salesman is *not* so counted whereas an editor in a publishing firm *is* counted, because the latter, in contrast to the former, is engaged in *changing the form* of something into a more valuable product—the very definition of manufacturing adopted in Chapter 17.)

Other major industries are electrical machinery (especially communication equipment), which supports a payroll of 149,000 individuals, miscellaneous machinery (such as sewing machines and printing machines), food products (particularly bakeries and beverage works), chemicals (notably the manufacture of drugs and medicines), fabricated

Manufacturing Regions: Anglo-Americ

Table 23-5 *New York Metropolitan Area Industrial Structure*

| Manufacturing Industries | Employees | | Percentage of National Total | Location Quotient |
	Number	Percentage		
Total	1,660,404	100	10.8	—
Apparel	361,638	22	30.5	2.8
Printing, Publishing	171,269	10	20.0	1.8
Electrical Machinery	149,113	9	13.4	1.2
Food Products	129,503	8	7.7	0.7
Chemicals	99,182	6	14.3	1.3
Fabricated Metals	93,657	6	8.8	0.8
Machinery	78,226	5	5.7	0.5
Textiles	63,393	4	7.2	0.6
Aircraft and Parts	57,948	3	7.5	0.7

Source: United States *Census of Manufactures,* 1958, Bulletin MC58(3)-31, Table 5.

metal goods (with structural steel items the leading product), aircraft (and aircraft parts), and textiles (knitting mills). Numerous other industries are represented in some degree, but a few are conspicuously absent. For example, New York has no blast furnaces as do Pittsburgh and Chicago; scarcely any farm machinery is manufactured; and the region does comparatively little flour milling.

New York's index of diversification is .173 which identifies it as one of the most diversified manufacturing metropolises in the nation (see Table 23-4).

Factories are located in many parts of New York. The greatest concentration is on lower Manhattan Island as was discussed in Chapter 18. Numerous factories have sprung up on the Jersey side of the Hudson River. Many are light industries that were originally located in New York City but have migrated to the suburbs to the west in search of space for expansion, lower taxes, room for parking lots, and the chance to build new factory structures designed for their particular needs. Printing, textile, apparel, and light-machinery makers are in this category. But New Jersey also has much of metropolitan New York's heavy industry, for example, copper smelters, petroleum refineries, shipyards, chemical plants, and meat-packing establishments.

The New York metropolitan area also spreads eastward onto Long Island, which contains a large volume of industry in its western third, especially in Brooklyn and the suburbs. Industry here is highly diversified, both light and heavy, from factories that produce electrical machinery (gyroscopes, radios, and computers) to airplane plants.

This great metropolis can offer numerous advantages to a manufacturer. Foremost is the tremendous population and concomitant purchasing power that make it the largest domestic market for bread, dresses, books, radios, pencils, telephones, and almost every other consumer item you can name. In addition, New York is the headquarters for numerous business that "consume" typewriters, computing equipment, and printed material in greater volume than their counterparts in any other city. Besides its desirability as a market, New York City's huge labor force is an attraction for factories. Thousands of individual immigrants during the great influxes in the late nineteenth and early twentieth centuries brought their industrial skills with them from Europe; and New York, functioning as the port of entry, had an initial advantage over the rest of the nation in bidding for their services. Yet there are also some industries that do not need and cannot afford highly skilled labor; for them New York contains thousands of people, many just arrived from nonindustrial areas, with as yet few skills developed. Moreover, New York, being the

The New Jersey portion of metropolitan New York contains many industrial developments. This view (looking northeast) shows a portion of this area with its several advantages: diversity of transportation (ocean shipping, railways, highways, and airways), open flat land, and location near Manhattan (background), the primary commercial center in the world. (Courtesy Port of New York Authority.)

monetary nerve-center of the Western Hemisphere, is crammed with large amounts of the investment capital so necessary before a factory can even begin operations. As a transportation center, too, New York City provides its factories with excellent inland facilities and with superb ocean shipping not only to foreign countries but also to other coastal ports of the United States. Its excellent harbor system is lined with miles of docks along the Hudson River, East River, Upper Bay, and Newark Bay. And the Hudson River lowland leads to the Mohawk Valley, which provides

New York with the easiest access of any eastern port to the interior of the continent.

On the other hand, New York has two pronounced drawbacks for manufacturing; it lacks both power and raw materials. Scarcely any water power is generated along its rivers and all its fuel (coal, petroleum, gas) must be imported from far away. Likewise, the territory encircling New York produces very few raw materials for factories. The wool, cotton, paper, food, and metals they require originate hundreds (and sometimes thousands) of miles away.

New York is the prime example of the principle that market and labor are more powerful than raw material and power in determining the location of factories.

The New York metropolitan area is the pivotal zone of a large manufacturing region that extends along the Atlantic Coast from Maryland to Maine (Figure 23-1). For clarity in our discussion, however, we shall examine the remainder of this region under two headings: New England and the Middle Atlantic states.

NEW ENGLAND

In the six *New England* states (Connecticut, Rhode Island, Massachusetts, Vermont, New Hampshire, and Maine) there are about 1,500,000 factory employees—a figure somewhat less than that for metropolitan New York. The hub is Boston (Figure 23-1), which is, in fact, the nation's sixth-ranking industrial metropolis (see Table 23-2). Within New England the bulk of manufacturing is located toward the south, in Connecticut, Massachusetts, and Rhode Island with a northern fringe extending along coastal Maine.

The chief components of New England's *industrial structure* are shown in Table 23-6.

clusion is borne out by diversification indexes (Table 23-4): Boston has an index of .118 to New York's .173.

Eastern New England   There are two zones of manufacturing within New England: an eastern area and a western area. The eastern section focuses on Boston and includes the Merrimac Valley, Providence, Fall River, New Bedford, and Brockton, with an extension into Maine. Textiles, for a long time were the dominant industry. Leather industries, such as tanning and shoe making, also figured heavily in the economy of the region. But both of these have slumped in New England, and in the last 30 years many textile and shoe factories have moved south and west. Their places have been taken though, by others— electrical machinery and plastics plants. In addition, most of our domestic jewelry and silverware is made in Providence.

Eastern New England got a head start in manufacturing on all other parts of the nation. In the late 1700's and early 1800's her population made up one of the chief markets in the Western Hemisphere; the supply of capital, reaped from exports of timber and from successful operation of ships, both commercial

Table **23-6**   *New England: Industrial Structure*

Industry	Employees		Percentage of National Total	Location Quotient
	Thousands	Percentage		
Total	1398	100.0		
Electrical Machinery	148	10.7	13.2	1.4
Textiles	123	8.9	13.6	1.5
Machinery	115	8.3	8.5	0.9
Leather	106	7.7	30.0	3.3
Fabricated Metals	94	6.8	8.9	0.9

Source: United States *Census of Manufactures*, 1958. Bulletin MC58(1)-1 and Bulletins MC58(3), individual states volumes.

Since the leading industry makes up only 10 per cent of the industrial structure, we can say that New England's structure is more *diversified* than that of metropolitan New York where the single leading industry accounts for 22 per cent of all factory jobs. This con-

vessels and fishing boats, was good. Numerous streams flowing over the rocky terrain were easily dammed to provide scores of water power sites and millraces. Entrepreneurs flocked there to build factories. Another advantage of eastern New England lay in its location near the sea and its several good harbors which facilitated the import and export trade. Then, too, Yankee settlers had either a background of industrial experience in Europe or else displayed a quick propensity for grasping factory skills.

A key development was Samuel Slater's choice to emigrate from England to Providence, Rhode Island, in 1789. What is significant is this: Since New England was a lucrative market for textiles, England had banned the export of textile machinery and blueprints of textile machinery as well as the emigration of textile workers—lest consumer regions such as New England establish textile factories of their own. But Slater, born in 1768 in Derbyshire, England, was apprenticed in 1782 in a textile mill and became a skilled mechanic—and he memorized the design of textile machines! In 1789 he left England disguised as a farm youth, migrated to America, settled in Rhode Island and contracted with a Providence firm to build and operate cotton-spinning equipment. A site near a waterfall on the Blackstone River (in Pawtucket, five miles northeast of Providence) was selected. A factory housing 72 spindles was built and began operations in 1790. Slater is generally acknowledged as the father of the American cotton industry.

As time elapsed, however, eastern New England lost much of its competitive advantage. As the nation's population grew and moved west, New England manufacturers found themselves an increasing distance from the center of the national market, though they were still ideally situated relative to foreign markets. In cutting over their forests, too, New Englanders exhausted the supply of their one abundant raw material. With the development of electricity, the numerous small water power sites lost their advantage because electrically driven motors were cheaper to operate and easier to control. Moreover, electricity is more economically produced at large water power installations than at small ones. But unfortunately, most New England sites for high dams in sizable streams are far from industrial cities. The regional problem was compounded by inventions that generated thermal-

electric power (in power plants driven by steam) at less cost than most hydroelectric plants. Coal was the most desirable fuel for such steam plants—but New England has no coal. Most of industrial New England's power is now produced with imported coal (from Virginia ports on Hampton Roads), most of the factories depend on raw materials that are shipped in from other parts of the nation, and the market is now largely to the west. Consequently, New England industrialists face the handicap of *backhauls*. The major assets of New England's factories today are enterprising directors, skilled labor, access to ocean shipping, and local capital.

Western New England In western New England, manufacturing is located largely in the Connecticut Valley. No large city dominates this zone as Boston does to the east. Springfield, Hartford, Bridgeport, New Haven, and New Britain-Bristol are the main industrial centers. Metal products make up two-thirds of all manufacturing: machinery, hardware, tools, guns, screws, bolts, and clocks are typical commodities. This is the nation's "copper" belt, that is, of finished copper goods (such as electric wire, cooking utensils, and decorative hardware). Manufacturing in the western zone is expanding much more rapidly than in the eastern zone, largely because throughout the United States the consumption of textiles and leather items is increasing much less rapidly than that of metal goods.

THE MIDDLE ATLANTIC STATES

Eastern Pennsylvania, southern New Jersey, Delaware, and Maryland support extensive manufacturing (Figure 23-1), Philadelphia and Baltimore being the dominant cities here, although smaller places such as Allentown, Bethlehem, and Reading each provide around 20,000 factory jobs.

Diversity is the hallmark of this region. Virtually every industry is present in at least small amounts, from the heaviest industries (for instance, blast furnaces at Sparrows Point) to the lightest (such as the apparel plants and optical instruments factories in Philadelphia). Shipyards and petroleum refineries line the Delaware River below Philadelphia, and one of the nation's largest airplane factories is at Baltimore. Yet Baltimore and Camden have the greatest number of food canneries on the Eastern Seaboard. The leading industry is clothing manufacture, but even it accounts for only 15 per cent of the jobs. The diversification of the Middle Atlantic region is epitomized by Philadelphia's index of diversification of .039—the lowest in the nation (Table 23-4).

The Middle Atlantic area has several advantages for manufacturing. As one of the country's thickest concentrations of population and purchasing power, it provides a ready market for its own factories. It produces some raw materials—coal and iron ore, for instance, although neither in adequate amounts for the region's factories. Consequently, coal for industry must be brought in; but fortunately the bituminous coal fields of western Pennsylvania and West Virginia are not far away. Eastern Pennsylvania coal is closer, but being mostly anthracite it is more costly and so little used by factories. Iron ore is still mined in both eastern Pennsylvania and nearby northern New Jersey. Originally, local mines supplied the steel mills in this region, but today most of the ore comes from Canada and Venezuela. For such imports, the Delaware River and Chesapeake Bay serve as convenient waterways for ocean vessels. Frontage on the Atlantic Coast combined with good harbors along the Chesapeake and Delaware estuaries give this region easy access to foreign markets. Equally effective transportation, via the Pennsylvania and the Baltimore and Ohio railroads as well as the Pennsylvania Turnpike, links these states with the markets in the interior of the continent.

MIDDLE NEW YORK STATE

A band of manufacturing runs through New York State from Troy to Buffalo. Rochester, Syracuse, and Utica, all good-sized towns, along with Binghamton and several smaller places in the south-central portion of the state are the chief points of concentration (Figure 23-1).

This is a transitional zone. The range is between Troy, whose industrial structure resembles that of New England, to Buffalo, whose structure resembles that of Cleveland and Pittsburgh in its emphasis on heavy metal industries. In between lies Rochester, one of the most unusual industrial cities in the nation. Of its 111,000 manufacturing employees, two-fifths make instruments (cameras, optical equipment, thermometers, and so forth). Indeed, for the instrument industry, Rochester's location quotient is an astounding 23.1. This is attributable in large measure, of course, to the Eastman Kodak Company.

Buffalo's prominence stems basically from its location at the eastern end of Lake Erie; it is a vital point of trans-shipment for goods flowing from Atlantic ports, through the Mohawk-Hudson Valleys to the interior of the continent, and vice-versa. Prior to 1825 the west-bound traffic moved along the Hudson River to Albany, then overland via the Mohawk Valley and Ontario Lowland to Buffalo. Then in 1825 the Erie Canal was opened to link Lake Erie with the Hudson River. In 1851 a railway route was completed, which is now the main line of the New York Central Railroad running from New York City to Chicago. In the early 1900's highways were threaded through this same route, climaxed today by U. S. Route 20 and the New York State Thruway. The line of industrial cities through middle New York is one of the nation's best examples of alignment of manufacturing centers along a transportation route.

THE MIDWEST

Another appreciable manufacturing region (Figure 23-1) extends from western Pennsylvania to southeastern Wisconsin and from central Michigan to the Ohio River. An imaginary line connecting Pittsburgh, Louisville, Rockford, Green Bay, Flint, Detroit, and Cleveland would encircle what is, in fact, the industrial heart of the nation. The counties within this boundary share an unusual industrial consistency; for nearly every one of them has at least 1000 manufacturing employees, thereby rating a dot symbol on Figure 23-1. Dots are particularly closely spaced in Ohio, northern Indiana, southern

Michigan, northern Illinois, and southeastern Wisconsin because counties are small and close together. Somewhat detached from, but essentially part of, the core of the Midwestern area are St. Louis, Minneapolis, St. Paul, and Kansas City, and smaller manufacturing centers sprinkled through Iowa, southern Minnesota, central Missouri, and eastern Kansas.

The Midwest is a conglomeration of a few huge industrial centers (such as Chicago and Detroit) and scores of highly industrialized small cities, such as Hamilton (Ohio), Anderson (Indiana), LaSalle (Illinois), Midland (Michigan), and Kenosha (Wisconsin), where the proportions of jobs in manufacturing reach the unusually high figures of 50, 54, 50, 55, and 58 per cent respectively. The Midwest has a diverse mixture of industries. Nearly every type of manufacturing is represented, from the blast furnaces of Pittsburgh and Chicago to the auto factories of Detroit to the paper mills of the Miami Valley.

Within the Midwest, several zones stand out clearly. From Pittsburgh to Cleveland, including Youngstown, Akron, Canton, Wheeling, Steubenville, and Weirton, runs a band of heavy industry—the steel center of the nation. Metal industries dominate the industrial structures here, accounting for an astonishing 75 per cent of the industrial jobs in Pittsburgh,

burgh, whose location quotient for primary metal factories exceeds 6.

This metal works zone has an ideal setting for manufacturing. First of all it possesses the best location in the country relative to the domestic market.* Cleveland in fact is at the center of gravity for transportation costs to United States cities; that is, shipping costs to all parts of the nation, weighted in terms of population in each part, are lower from Cleveland than from any other city. In addition, this zone has excellent transportation advantages: the Great Lakes, all the major railroads running from the Middle Atlantic (including New York City) to the Midwest, major highways, and a network of pipelines and air routes (Chapter 26). Furthermore, the area is rich in coal. Notice that the manufacturing belt does not run northeast-southwest as does the coal field; rather it runs *northwest*, forming a bridge between the Appalachian coal region and the Great Lakes.

A second subzone is made up of Detroit and southeastern Michigan, the automotive capital of the United States. Detroit, the fifth-ranking industrial metropolis in the country, has a very asymmetrical (in contrast to diversified) industrial structure. It rates a diversification index of .700 (Table 23-4) and is largely dominated by the production of motor vehicles and parts (Table 23-7). The leading ma-

Table **23-7** *Detroit: Industrial Structure*

Industry	Employees		Percentage of National Total	Location Quotient
	Thousands	Percentage		
Total	405	100	2.4	—
Motor Vehicles	141	35	24.5	10.2
Machinery	72	18	5.3	2.2
Fabricated Metals	41	10	3.8	1.6
Primary Metals	37	9	3.4	1.4

Source: United States *Census of Manufactures*, 1958, Bulletin MC58(3)-21, Table 5.

68 per cent in Cleveland, and 79 per cent in Youngstown. *Primary* metal works (where metallic ores are converted into metal and where that product is refined) account for 40 per cent of all manufacturing jobs in Pitts-

* Access to market is a very difficult concept to measure. An excellent analysis of market influence in Cleveland is by Chauncy D. Harris, "The Market as a Factor in the Localization of Industry in the United States," *Annals* of the Association of American Geographers (December 1954), pp. 315-348.

Manufacturing Regions: Anglo-America

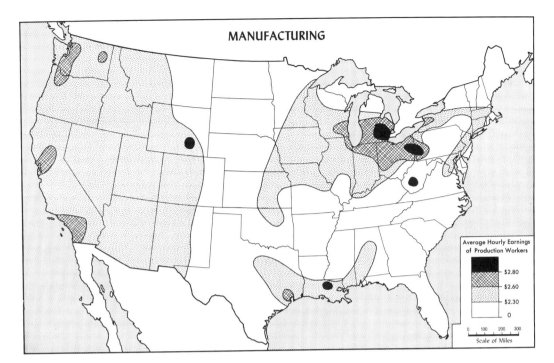

MANUFACTURING

Average Hourly Earnings
of Production Workers

$2.80
$2.60
$2.30
0

0   100   200   300
Scale of Miles

Figure 23-3

chinery product is (after motor vehicles), metal-working machinery. Located along the Detroit River, this metropolis is on the main stream of Great Lakes shipping, with easy access to iron ore from Lake Superior ports and coal from Lake Erie ports. But location alone was not enough to produce an industrial giant the size of Detroit in eastern Michigan, especially since it is considerably north of the main land-routes (rail and highway) between Chicago and Atlantic port cities. Surely another major factor was the presence of the automotive inventors in Detroit (Chapter 21).

There is some correlation between the locational pattern of wage levels and the industrial structure of the Midwest since the automotive, machinery, and steel industries are, comparatively speaking, industries that pay high wages and so raise the pay level of the Midwest to the top spot in the nation (see Figure 23-3).

The third important subregion is the *Southern Lake Michigan Hinterland,* a horseshoe-shaped industrial area wrapped around the lower end of Lake Michigan. The greater Chicago metropolitan area (comprising 6 counties in Illinois and 2 in Indiana) and Milwaukee dominate the area, but there are several other highly active cities close by, such as Green Bay (Wisconsin), Rockford (Illinois), South Bend (Indiana), and Muskegon (Michigan).

Machinery is unquestionably the foremost industry, for the region as a whole and for such metropolitan areas as Chicago (Table 23-8, page 418) and Milwaukee.

In Milwaukee 42 per cent of the factory workers are employed in making many different types of machinery. The cities of this region produce a major portion of the nation's machine tools, farm machinery, radios, and industrial appliances.

But the most spectacular factories are the steel mills lined up along a twelve-mile strip of Lake Michigan shoreline from Gary, Indiana, to southern Chicago. Towering above flat plains, the blast furnaces, coke ovens, gas ovens, and rolling mills (with associated stock piles of black coal, rust-brown iron ore, and gray limestone) give a striking impression of *heavy industry.* Plumes of reddish smoke from

Table **23-8** *Chicago: Industrial Structure*

Industry	Employees		Percentage of National Total	Location Quotient
	Thousands	*Percentage*		
Total	911	100.0	6.0	—
Electrical Machinery	133	14.6	11.9	1.9
Primary Metal	117	12.8	10.6	1.8
Fabricated Metals	106	10.8	10.1	1.7
Machinery	98	10.6	7.3	1.2
Foods	90	9.9	5.3	0.9
Printing	81	8.9	9.3	1.6

Source: United States *Census of Manufactures, 1958*, Bulletin MC58(3)-12, Table 5.

the rows of chimneys draw attention from miles around.

Elsewhere in Chicago there is considerable baking, meat packing, and candy manufacture. As a printing center, Chicago turns out a major share of the nation's telephone directories, mail-order catalogs, and weekly magazines.

Representative indices of diversification in this region are Chicago .224, Milwaukee .363, and Racine .397—these are in harmony with the principle that the smaller the industrial city, the greater the possibility that its index will be high. Manufacturing is prominent in the Lake Michigan hinterland for four basic reasons: (a) This being the most productive agricultural region in the nation, there is plenty of purchasing power, engendered by agricultural surpluses, for manufactured commodities; (b) this being a densely populated area, there are not only numerous customers but also a numerous labor supply for factories; (c) being toward the center of the entire United States, this region is well-served by rail and highway transportation; and (d) this is conveniently the point of deepest penetration by the Great Lakes into the densely populated interior of the nation. These factors combined advantageously with another: the favorable coincidence of level terrain, fertile soils, and favorable climate which supported successful ventures in commercial agriculture as soon as peoples with the cultural potential for such an economy moved in. Another, if less vital, consideration was the coal field underlying Illinois, Indiana, and Kentucky.

Actually, though, the manufacturing region is on the edge of, rather than atop, this resource (compare Figure 23-1 with Figure 14-4), which is not adequate for making coke; coking coal comes largely from Appalachia.

Southwestern Ohio (notably Cincinnati, Hamilton, Middletown, and Dayton), east central Indiana (particularly Indianapolis, Anderson, and Fort Wayne), and Louisville constitute a fourth area of diversified manufacturing, with machinery, aircraft, and paper the most conspicuous products. Cincinnati is a national leader in making machine tools, the Miami Valley in paper, and Dayton and Indianapolis in household machinery, office machinery, and airplane parts.

Outliers of the Midwest region are: Peoria, famous for tractors; the Tri-Cities (Moline, Rock Island, Davenport), equally famous for other farm machinery; Minneapolis and St. Paul, where diversity prevails; Omaha, where meat packing is the number-one industry, Omaha now being the nation's foremost meat-packing city; and St. Louis, whose structure is well diversified, the leading industry (foods—particularly meat packing) accounting for only 12 per cent of all manufacturing jobs. An outlier on the southeast is the Kanawha Valley and adjacent stretches of the upper Ohio River where the chemical industry has already taken root and where other industries (such as primary aluminum) using large amounts of coal may move in. (Some people may question the inclusion of West Virginia in the Midwestern manufactural region. Granted, West Virginia is considered by some to be a southern state; but on the basis of the pattern portrayed by Figure 23-1, West Virginia's manufacturing is generally located in those counties nearer to northern than to southern industrial areas.)

There is one portion of the Midwest which serves to illustrate a principle of manufacturing geography. The area in question is the Rock River Valley, and the principle involves the relationship between labor costs and transportation costs. The Rock River Valley extends in a north-south direction from southern Wisconsin into northern Illinois and includes several cities in which manufacturing constitutes the main component of the economic base; Rockford, Illinois, is probably the best known.

The Rock Valley stands out somewhat conspicuously on Figure 23-1 and might be said to mark the western margin of "the manufacturing parallelogram"—a region bounded by four imaginery lines connecting Portland (Maine), Green Bay (Wisconsin), St. Louis, and Baltimore—which constitutes the industrial heart of the nation. At first glance the Rock Valley seems to be a conundrum insofar as manufacturing is concerned: Its major industries produce machinery, but the Valley mines no metals, it smelts no ores and must therefore call upon other areas (principally Chicago and Pittsburgh) for the raw materials used by its machinery makers. Neither does the Valley have, nor has it ever had, any peculiar power resource. In the late 1800's, small dams in the river generated a little waterpower, but for years its power requirements have been met by local thermal electric plants burning coal hauled in from Illinois mines to the south. Nor has the Valley ever been a major transportation corridor, like the Mohawk Valley in New York. Finally, the region has no major market—its machinery output is shipped to diverse parts of the nation and even abroad, with 80 per cent of it moving to the *east*, the very direction from which comes most of the raw materials. The question thus becomes: How can Rock Valley manufacturers pay freight on steel shipments of 90 miles from Chicago steel mills, then pay freight on machinery moving back the 90

miles to Chicago, and still quote a price—to eastern buyers—which is competitive with that charged by Chicago firms. The answer lies in savings on other items, principally in labor costs. The explanation of this factor is presented in Chapter 32 under the general heading "A Theory of Labor Differentials and Transport Costs."

THE SOUTH

The South contains 20 per cent of the nation's employees in manufacturing. There are no large agglomerations of workers and factories comparable to those in the North. The largest concentrations are Dallas (91,000 manufacturing employees), Houston (89,000), and Atlanta (82,000). These figures are surpassed in nearly two dozen localities in the Northeast. Nevertheless, the South presents a rather continuous display on Figure 23-1, with a broad swath of counties blanketing the territory from southern Virginia through the Carolinas into northern Georgia, Alabama, and Tennessee. A second belt, rather fragmented, can be discerned running northward from Houston to Wichita.

Texas and North Carolina are the South's leading industrial states, with 466,000 and 455,000 industrial employees respectively. But each is dwarfed by several northern states. Indeed the New York metropolitan area alone supports almost four times as many manufacturing employees as Texas or North Carolina.

In the *Southeast* (from Virginia to Mississippi), four industries overshadow all others: textiles, lumber, furniture, and tobacco. Look at the industrial structure of North Carolina (Table 23-9, page 420), where textiles provide 46 per cent of factory jobs. Few states have so skewed an industrial structure.

The Southeast has several valuable attributes for manufacturing. Its moderately large population offers a potential labor force. Although originally the skills of the people were directed largely to agriculture, mining, and other nonindustrial pursuits, in recent years they have quickly learned the industrial arts. A related advantage is that the wage rates here are lower than in the North. Numerous factories have transferred operations from North

Table 23-9   North Carolina: Industrial Structure

Industry	Employees		Percentage of National Total	Location Quotient
	Thousands	Percentage		
Total	455	100	2.9	—
Textiles	211	46	23.5	8.1
Furniture	39	9	11.3	3.9
Lumber	31	7	5.3	1.8
Foods	29	7	1.7	0.6
Tobacco	26*	6	31.5	10.8

Source: United States *Census of Manufactures*, 1958, Bulletin MC58(3)-32, Table 4.

* Estimate. The Census refuses to divulge the number of employees in the tobacco industry in North Carolina "to avoid disclosing individual company figures."

to South in order to realize savings in wages. The average hourly earnings received by factory workers are $1.62 in North Carolina, $1.61 in Mississippi, and $1.92 in Tennessee. Compare these with the $2.42 in New York, $2.21 in Massachusetts, and $2.39 in Pennsylvania (Figure 23-3). Living costs, too, are lower in the South. And municipal and state taxes are lower. The milder climate means lower factory overhead expenses than in the North for winterizing and heating expenditures. The Southeast has many raw-material advantages too: Some cotton is grown, it has the nation's most vigorous forests, most of the

Kannapolis, North Carolina. James Cannon, a young Carolina cotton broker, started a small yarn spinning mill in Concord in 1888. Shortly afterwards operations were expanded to include cotton cloth and then flat-weave towels. To enlarge the facilities in 1905, Cannon bought a 600-acre farm seven miles from Concord and built a new mill and homes around it for workers. Production in the mill began in 1908. The new town that sprang up around it was named Kannapolis. With a 1960 population of 34,647, it is the state's largest unincorporated settlement. The mills occupy the rear half of this photo. (Courtesy Cannon Mills Company.)

nation's tobacco is produced, and a few minerals are mined (such as iron ore in Alabama, phosphate in Florida, and kaolin in Georgia). Moreover, the Southeast has two excellent power resources: water power and coal. Two important hydroelectric locations are the Piedmont and the Tennessee Valley. Water power sites are abundant in the Piedmont and in the late 1800's men started building factories along them. On the other side of the Appalachian highlands, the Tennessee River and tributaries have been dammed in 27 places, mostly by the Tennessee Valley Authority—a gigantic experiment in regional planning launched by the federal government for the purpose of upgrading the economy of a region. In addition to controlling floods, reducing soil erosion, and providing recreational environments, the T.V.A. generates a tremendous amount of electricity.

The Southeast also has coal; two-thirds of the great Appalachian coal field lies in West Virginia, Kentucky, Virginia, Tennessee, and Alabama. But notice that the southeastern manufacturing belt does not coincide with this, the world's major coal field. Indeed, the coal area is amazingly devoid of manufacturing! Obviously, the relationship to coal—although very important in some regions—is not the major factor determining the location of factories either in the Northeast (else West Virginia, our leading coal mining state, would be a leader in manufacturing) or in the Southeast.

The recent industrialization in the Southeast has had an impact on life there in two significant ways: (a) The standard of living has increased, and (b) the rate of both white and Negro emigration to the North has declined.

The *Southwest*, from the Mississippi River to Texas and Oklahoma, including southern Kansas, reveals a different locational pattern and a different industrial structure. There is no extensive industrial zone, but rather a series of nodes, such as Houston, Beaumont, Dallas, Fort Worth, and Wichita. The region as a whole has only 850,000 industrial employees, roughly comparable to the number in Chicago.

The industrial structure is rather diversified; nevertheless, two industries—foods (meat packing and flour milling) and aircraft—far exceed the others. Petroleum refining and the manufacture of chemicals join aircraft and foods to make a distinctive quartet of leading industries as illustrated by the industrial structure of Texas in Table 23-10.

The Southwest does not have as abundant a labor pool as the Southeast, nor as much water power or coal. But it does have a sound agricultural base plus most of the petroleum in the country. Astute industrialists moving onto such a scene quickly linked this region (via Gulf Coast shipping, the Mississippi River traffic, railways, and pipelines) with the nation's main market to the north and east.

The main drawback for manufacturing in both Southeast and Southwest has been the lack of a local market. This stems from the low population in the Southwest and the low purchasing power (in spite of rather high population) in the Southeast. But other attributes are drawing manufacturers so that the South, at least in certain well-favored localities, is currently going through a period of rapid industrial growth. Still, it is easy to overemphasize the "boom in the South";

Table **23-10** *Texas: Industrial Structure*

Industry	Employees		Percentage of National Total	Location Quotient
	Thousands	*Percentage*		
Total	466	100	3.1	—
Foods	75	16	4.4	1.4
Aircraft	50	11	6.5	2.1
Petroleum Products	42	9	23.5	7.6
Chemicals	38	8	5.4	1.7

Source: United States *Census of Population, 1958*, Bulletin MC58(3)-42, Table 4.

some southern areas are actually suffering a decline in manufacturing, as we shall see.

A vast, nearly blank area on Figure 23-1 occupies much of the western half of the United States. The eastern margin of this void runs generally from Minneapolis through Omaha to Houston. Its western margin runs parallel to, and 100 miles inland from, the Pacific Coast. Within this enormous space there probably are not more than 300,000 manufacturing employees, or about triple the number in Rhode Island and less than that in Pittsburgh. Denver's 55,000 industrial workers form the one outstanding concentration.

The absence of manufacturing in this large realm is due basically to the dearth of population. With little local market to be served, factories must depend mainly on processing local raw materials for distant consumers. Foods, lumber, and primary metals are the distinctive trio. Specifically, meat products are processed from beef cattle and sheep; sawmills and planing and veneer mills convert mountain stands of timber into lumber and plywood; and copper, lead, zinc, silver, and gold ores are put though primary processing.

THE PACIFIC COAST

A spotty pattern of small industrial developments characterizes many western counties of Washington, Oregon, and California. But the Los Angeles and the San Francisco metropolitan areas are prominent on not only the regional but also the national manufacturing scene. These are, in fact, the largest industrial centers outside the northeastern quadrant of the nation. Factory employment in major West Coast urban areas are: Los Angeles 712,000 (ranking third in the nation—Table 23-2), San Francisco 178,000, Seattle 114,000, and San Diego 70,000. For the West Coast's industrial structure, see Table 23-11.

The advantages of the Pacific Coast for aircraft production have already been outlined in Chapter 21. The large lumber industry is based on the most voluminous stands of timber in the nation; West Coast mills ship boards, shingles, veneer, millwork, pulpwood, and paper to nationwide markets utilizing rail, highways, and even the Panama Canal for reaching eastern customers. The foods industry is represented largely by the canning or freezing of the myriad of fruits and vegetables that flourish in the mild Pacific Coast climates.

The Pacific Coast is a rapidly growing manufacturing region because of a new factor —the emergence of the West Coast as a substantial market in its own right. This growth of course correlates directly to the population boom in western states. The emergence of this market has led to the appearance of machinery and fabricated metals in the Pacific Coast's industrial structure.

CONCLUSION

The United States Census Bureau recognizes nine arbitrary regions in publishing data on industrial structures. Figure 23-4 outlines these regions and identifies the three leading manufactures in each region. Notice that the map graphically illustrates the characteristics of regions discussed in this chapter and depicts such regional differences as degree of diversity and distinguishing industries.

Table 23-11 Pacific Coast: Industrial Structure

Industry	Employees		Percentage of National Total	Location Quotient
	Thousands	*Percentage*		
Total	1565	100	10.2	—
Foods	202	13	11.9	1.2
Aircraft	176	11	23.2	2.3
Lumber	160	10	27.4	2.7
Fabricated Metals	96	6	9.0	0.9

Source: United States *Census of Manufactures*, 1958, Bulletins MC58(3)-4, -36, and -46.

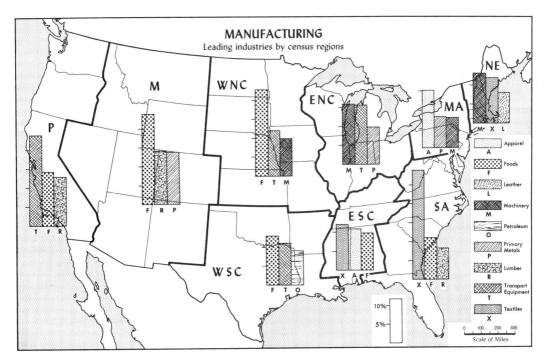

Figure 23-4 (*Census regions are: Pacific, Mountain, West North Central, East North Central, West South Central, East South Central, New England, Middle Atlantic, South Atlantic.*)

Figure 23-5

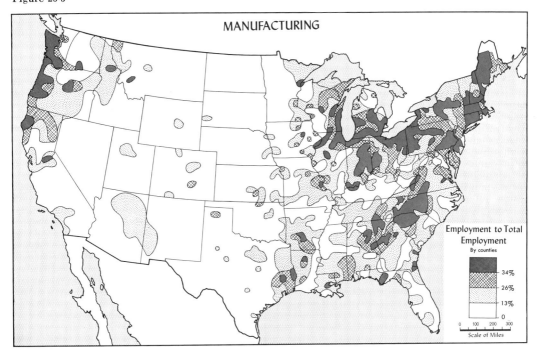

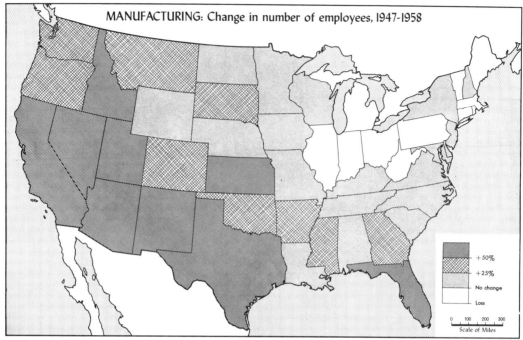

MANUFACTURING: Change in number of employees, 1947-1958

+50%
+25%
No change
Loss

0   100   200   300
Scale of Miles

Figure 23-6

Relation to Total Employment In Figure 23-1 we mapped manufacturing in the United States in terms of one variable: number of employees. In Figure 23-5, we present still another view, showing the location of manufacturing employees as related to workers in all economic activities. For the nation as a whole the ratio is one in four. For Figure 23-5, the median was determined of all counties that exceed the national average—it is 34 per cent. Of these above-average counties, those above the median are the darkest shade in the map, those below it are criss-crossed. Below-average counties were similarly handled. Notice how the Pacific Northwest stands out. Otherwise, the areas with high percentages correlate rather closely with the conspicuous regions on Figure 23-1.

CHANGES IN THE LOCATION
OF MANUFACTURING
BETWEEN 1947 AND 1958

Manufacturing employment in the United States increased by 7 per cent, from 14,294,000 to 15,393,000 people. But this growth was not uniformly distributed throughout the nation.

Some areas enjoyed healthy gains, some had moderate increases, and some suffered losses. Of the 48 contiguous states, 11 experienced a reduction in manufacturing jobs.

Figure 23-6 shows the location of change in employment by states. All 11 of the losing states are in the Northeast, and some suffered severe declines: Michigan 17 per cent, West Virginia 10 per cent, and Rhode Island 23 per cent. Nor were these losses offset by gains in other northeastern states, so that the Northeast as a unit dropped from 9,750,000 manufacturing jobs to 9,325,000 (a loss of 4 per cent). Clearly, the nation's foremost industrial region stands out as its foremost region of loss in manufacturing job opportunities. Most western and some southern states enjoyed vigorous gains, with New Mexico, Arizona, and Florida more than doubling their jobs; however, both had such small payrolls in 1947 that only a few thousand more jobs made a sizeable percentage gain.

Clearly, manufacturing is moving west and south. One reason for the western growth— beginning roughly at the Mississippi River— is that there are now relatively more people

Manufacturing Regions: Anglo-America

in these states than in 1947 and factories have followed them. Another reason is the somewhat popular policy of *decentralization* by which some companies decide to build branch plants in less-developed areas. Another factor, especially in the booming southern states, is increased use of local labor, power, and materials—as well as Southern purchasing power.

Canada

Canada has around 1,200,000 people who earn their livelihood in manufacturing, about two-thirds as many as in metropolitan New York, and just as many as in Illinois.

LOCATION

The locational pattern of Canadian manufacturing is, in some respects, similar to that of the United States. The preponderance of activity is in the eastern half of the country, and within the eastern half it is concentrated in a few outstanding zones. Furthermore, Canada's chief manufacturing cities are also her principal ports.

The main manufacturing zone of Canada runs through the St. Lawrence Valley and southern Ontario (Figure 23-7), between the two cities of Quebec and Windsor. Probably 90 per cent of Canadian manufacturing takes place in this zone; this is where the country's two largest industrial concentrations and all but two of her cities with at least 10,000 industrial workers are. The two exceptions are Winnipeg and Vancouver.

The two principal metropolitan areas far outrank all others: Montreal, with 200,000 manufactural employees, and Toronto, with 160,000. Hamilton, the third-ranking center, only supports 60,000 industrial workers. Montreal is in the same category as Buffalo, and Toronto in that of Cincinnati.

CHARACTERISTICS

Canada's industrial structure is headed by three groups of industries: foods, forest products, and machinery. Food factories process a wide diversity of Canadian products, notably dairy goods, meat, and flour. Fruit, vegetable, and fish canneries are numerous. But the most numerous type of factory is the sawmill, thousands of which dot the forested countrysides, especially on the southerly margin of the great forest zone (see Chapter 6) extending from British Columbia to Quebec. Although individual sawmills tend to employ few persons, their total payroll in Canada ranks them as a major industry. Pulp mills provide almost as many jobs as do sawmills, although

Figure 23-7

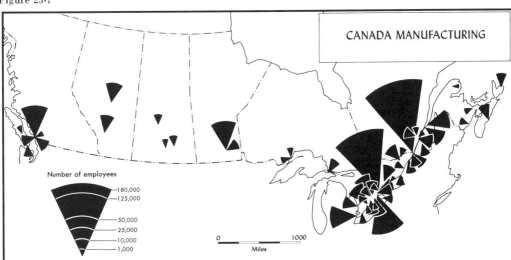

CANADA MANUFACTURING

Number of employees
180,000
125,000
50,000
25,000
10,000
1,000

0   1000
Miles

A manufacturing district in Ville St. Laurent on the fringe of Montreal, Quebec. (Courtesy Canadian National Railways.)

the mills are much fewer in number and much less widespread, being concentrated in Quebec and Ontario. Canadian machinery factories produce a wide line of merchandise: agricultural implements, railroad equipment, automobiles, electrical apparatus among others. Indeed, the machinery industries have expanded rapidly in the last two decades and are in process of assuming front rank in Canada's industrial structure.

Other industries are numerous and diverse. Virtually every type of manufacturing is represented: metal smelting and refining, petroleum refining, chemicals, textiles, clothing, rubber goods, furniture, printing, publishing, shipbuilding, shoes, and so on. We already gave Canada's prominence in the manufacture of aluminum special attention in Chapter 19.

In steel production, now around 5,000,000 tons per year, Canada ranks tenth in the world. Blast furnaces are concentrated in three very widely separated cities: Hamilton alone accounts for almost one half the jobs in this industry, and Sault Ste. Marie for almost 40 per cent; a lesser number is found in Sydney, Nova Scotia, These three cities also turn iron into steel; additional steel is produced from scrap iron in electric steel mills of Montreal, Welland, Selkirk, Edmonton, and Vancouver.

RELATIONSHIPS

The location of all these industries harmonizes with the same set of forces as operate in the United States. Correlation with markets is the most apparent relationship, since most

Canadians with purchasing power live in the peninsula of southern Ontario and along the St. Lawrence lowland. Similarly, this area provides the largest labor force. Raw material supplies, however, are meager in many respects and this region must import a lot: coal from the Appalachian field to the south; iron ore from the Lake Superior ranges to the west and the Labrador-Quebec field to the east; and wheat mostly from the Prairie Provinces to the west (Chapter 11). On the other hand, Ontario farms yield a surplus of dairy produce, fruits, vegetables, and tobacco. Without this successful agricultural base, there would be considerably less population and much less industry there today.

Canada has been signally well endowed in forests and potential water power, resources that lured certain types of manufacturing to the Pacific Coast and to the northern fringe of the main manufacturing belt. The presence of nickel, copper, and other metallic ores have favored the development of primary metal manufacturing industries in the sparsely settled zone lying between Lake Huron and Hudson Bay; here the settlements of Sudbury, Cobalt, Kirkland, Cochrane, and Noranda are cities whose manufacturing to a large degree is of this type. The name of the settlement of Asbestos (75 miles east of Montreal) identifies its mineral resource. Recent discoveries of petroleum in Alberta have stimulated the location of refineries not only in this province, to serve hinterland markets, but also in the manufacturing belt to which the crude oil is passed by pipeline and tanker.

The role of the Great Lakes and the St. Lawrence River cannot be overemphasized in the industrial development of Canada. Indeed, where good agricultural land borders these water bodies, population is heavy, and that is where we find the great preponderance of Canadian manufacturing. These water bodies function as a sort of main street for Canadian industry, linking her industrial zone with not only the rest of the country but also with foreign sources of many raw materials and with foreign markets.*

---

* Additional information on Canadian manufacturing is presented in Donald Kerr's "The Geography of the Canadian Iron and Steel Industry," *Economic Geography* (1959), pp. 151-163. Several portions of *Canadian Regions* (edited by Donald F. Putnam) discuss manufactured areas.

Suggested Readings

Alderfer, E. B., and Michl, H. E., *Economics of American Industry*, New York, 1957, chapters 34-36.

Alexander, John W., "Location of Manufacturing: Methods of Measurement," *Annals of the Association of American Geographers*, 1958, pp. 20-26.

Clark, W. A. V., and Boyce, Ronald R., "Brain Power As A Resource For Industry," *The Professional Geographer*, May 1962, pp. 14-16.

Deasy, George F., and Griess, Phyllis R., "Factors Influencing Distribution of Steam-Electric Generating Plants," *The Professional Geographer*, May 1960, pp. 1-4.

de Geer, Sten, "Delimitation of the North American Manufacturing Belt," *Geografiska Annaler*, 1927, pp. 247-258.

Harris, Chauncy D., "The Market as a Factor in the Localization of Industry in the United States," *Annals of the Association of American Geographers*, 1954, pp. 315-348.

Hartshorne, Richard, "A New Map of the Manufacturing Belt of North America," *Economic Geography*, 1936, pp. 45-53.

Jones, Clarence F., "Areal Distribution of Manufacturing in the United States," *Economic Geography*, 1938, pp. 217-222.

McGovern, P. D., "Industrial Development in the Vancouver Area," *Economic Geography*, 1961, pp. 189-206.

McKnight, Tom L., "The Distribution of Manufacturing in Texas," *Annals of the Association of American Geographers*, 1957, pp. 370-378.

Miller, E. Willard, "The Industrial Development of the Allegheny Valley of Western Pennsylvania," *Economic Geography*, 1943, pp. 388-404.

Rodgers, Allan, "Some Aspects of Industrial Diversification in the United States," *Economic Geography*, 1957, pp. 16-30.

Thompson, John H., "A New Method for Measuring Manufacturing," *Annals of the Association of American Geographers*, 1955, pp. 416-436.

Wallace, William, "Merrimack Valley Manufacturing: Past and Present," *Economic Geography*, 1961, pp. 283-308.

Wright, Alfred, "Manufacturing Districts of the United States," *Economic Geography*, 1938, pp. 195-200.

Zelinsky, Wilbur, "A Method for Measuring Change in the Distribution of Manufacturing Activity: the United States, 1939-1947," *Economic Geography*, 1958, pp. 95-126.

The city of Birmingham in the heart of industrial England. Factories in an arc at the left press in on the commercial city. (Aerofilms and Aero Pictorial Ltd.)

TWENTY-FOUR

Now we turn our gaze across the ocean to the birthplace of the Industrial Revolution, the locale where commercial manufacturing first developed as a major economic activity, the area that still today ranks as the world's foremost manufacturing region—Europe.

Within Europe manufacturing conforms to the pattern presented in Figure 24-1, page 430. The prominent countries there—the United Kingdom, West Germany, and France—although comparatively small in square mileage, together have an industrial labor force approximating that of the United States and the Soviet Union (Table B, page 291).

The United Kingdom

In some respects, the distribution of the 7,600,000 manufacturing workers in the United Kingdom resembles that in the United States: The largest city is the core of the leading manufacturing zone; a few industrial areas front on the coast, some are inland; some specialize in heavy industry, others are diversified. For discussion purposes five distinctly separated areas will be delimited (see Figure 24-2, page 431).

London, the foremost center, has Britain's most diversified industrial structure. Located on the Thames River 25 miles from the sea (and only 150 miles from the mouth of the Rhine River), the city has factories in two types of areas. Downstream from the city proper along the Thames are the port industries—heavy manufacturing, such as chemical plants, oil refineries, tanneries, soap factories,

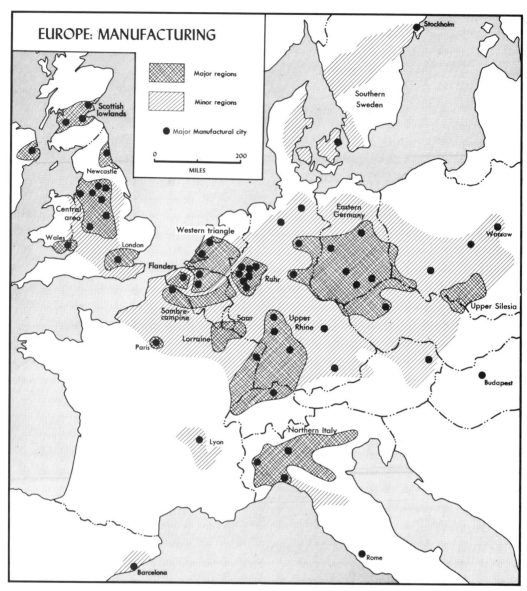

Figure 24-1

and shipyards. Elsewhere in the metropolis, especially in the north section, are the lighter industries that manufacture food, clothing, automobiles, cameras, furniture, books, and glassware. For all her industry, London has no blast furnaces or steel mills, mainly because she is farther from both coal and iron ore than are most of Britain's other industrial centers (Figure 14-2).

The bombings of World War II destroyed a large portion of London's industry, thereby stimulating a decentralization program. A conspicuous, although minor, proportion of the metropolitan area factories were moved as far as 30 miles into the hinterland. Entirely new towns took root around some of these transplantings. In all, eight such new towns have been established within a radius of 40

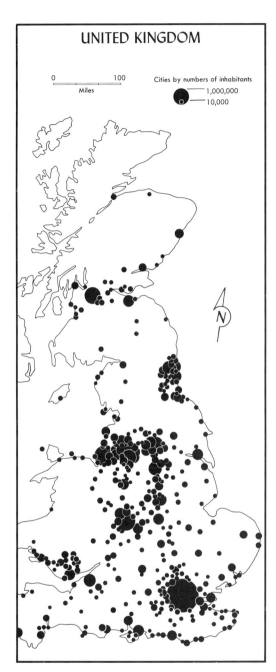

UNITED KINGDOM

0   100
Miles

Cities by numbers of inhabitants
1,000,000
10,000

Figure 24-2 (*After William-Olsson.*)

Table **24-1**   *New Towns in London Hinterland*

Town	Corporation Appointed	Population Dec. 1961	Factory Employees December, 1961
Basildon	Feb. 1949	56,000	9,540
Bracknell	Oct. 1949	21,563	5,656
Crawley	Feb. 1947	55,000	13,778
Harlow	May 1947	56,700	12,000
Hatfield	June 1948	21,500	654
Hemel Hempstead	Mar. 1947	56,500	14,102
Stevenage	Dec. 1946	44,000	11,900
Welwyn Garden City	June 1948	36,000	5,255
TOTAL		347,263	72,885

Source: "Planning Commentary," *Town and Country Planning,* Vol. XXX, No. 1, January, 1962, pp. 27, 28.

endowed with water power resources, neither has any blast furnaces; however, in its nation, each is the foremost city, each contains the largest labor pool, each has the greatest number of customers for manufactured items. In addition, each has good harbor facilities, is a major world port, and is the commercial and banking hub of its continent.

The *central* part of England contains several manufacturing cities, no one of which approaches London in factory output, but which together constitute the industrial heart of the United Kingdom. This region is bounded roughly by a line connecting Preston, Leeds, Leicester, Birmingham, and Liverpool. Much of the area, from Leeds and Bradford in the north through Nottingham and Derby to Birmingham in the south, is underlain by coal (Figure 14-2), which explains in part the region's prominence in manufacturing. For this is the United Kingdom's most productive coal zone. In addition, Britain's foremost iron ore field swings in an arc around the eastern and southern portions of the region. The locational correlation of these two resources has long helped make this the leading steel region in England, and numerous types of machines, automobiles, railway equipment, hardware, and other metal products are made here. Birmingham, in particular, is comparable to Pittsburgh in its blast furnaces and steel mills. But, since Britain's iron ore mines can no

miles from London; most of them have considerable manufacturing (Table 24-1) and their aggregate factory employment is 72,885.

In many of her relationships as a manufacturing center, London resembles New York City: Neither is in a coal region, neither is in an important raw-material region, neither is

longer keep pace with the domestic demand for steel, iron ore must be brought in, largely from Sweden and Spain, and the Birmingham area is suffering. For the city is poorly located for imports, being comparatively far from the sea. Consequently, this area is gradually declining in importance in the heavy steel industries and is expanding in the secondary industries which produce machine tools, railway equipment, automobiles, and hardware. The whole region is changing similarly.

The northern reaches of this central region contain numerous manufacturing cities. Sheffield long has been famous for high-grade steels and hardware. Most of the other cities specialize in textiles and constitute the textile center of Britain. Leeds and Bradford are the seats of the foremost woolen makers. This section, which has for decades been famous for its wool production, is well endowed with power resources. The Pennine Hills running northward from Stoke-on-Trent are lined with streams whose gradients are steep enough for numerous water power sites. Early in the Industrial Revolution, dams were built and millraces were constructed in many cities and villages to harness water power to drive machinery in the textile mills. Those on the eastern side of the Pennines specialized in woolen textiles, fabrics from the abundant wool of Britain's flocks. Britain is still, in fact, one of the world's leading sheep-raising countries, but her supply is now inadequate to sustain the mills, so wool is imported from Australia, New Zealand, South Africa, and Argentina.

Liverpool is the main point of arrival. This great port, with its excellent harbor in the Mersey estuary, functions as the ocean gateway to the whole central manufacturing region and is second only to London as an English port. Although the United Kingdom grows no cotton, British textile men, with lessons learned from spinning and weaving woolens, soon devised machinery for processing cotton lint which was becoming increasingly available as an import from America, Egypt, and elsewhere. Dams on the western slopes of the Pennines in southern Lancashire County were developed to power textile mills, and soon this area led the world in the production of cotton textiles. Numerous cities within a radius of 30 miles of Liverpool, particularly Manchester, sprouted spinning, weaving, and finishing mills. Manchester, 20 miles up from the Mersey estuary, is connected via the Manchester Ship Canal with Liverpool. It functions as the hub of Lancashire County's cotton business, being the distribution point for raw cotton to Bolton, Oldham, and other nearby cities and the collection point of manufactured cotton goods, most of which are then exported through Liverpool. Grain, hides, petroleum, and other raw materials also come in through Liverpool, to sustain the flour mills, tanneries, refineries, and other factories in the central manufacturing region.

The *northeastern* manufacturing district surrounds Newcastle, which is located ten miles upstream from the sea on the Tyne River. Industrialized suburbs line the Tyne valley, which is notable for a combination of advantages: The navigable river provides access to the ocean and protection to ships against rough seas; the region sits atop the Northumberland-Durham coal field; and only a few miles to the south is the Cleveland iron ore field. In this setting we find Britain's single largest steel district, where 20 per cent of the nation's steel is produced. Other local factories live off the steel mills, such as shipyards, railway plants, and numerous light industries. Newcastle's position on Britain's East Coast is favorable for trade with continental Europe. A leading import, for instance, is Swedish iron ore, brought in from Narvik, Newcastle being closer to that Norwegian port than any other English steel center is.

Although most United Kingdom manufacturing takes place in England, there are two districts of prominence in Scotland and Wales. The former is closely coextensive with the *Scottish Lowland* stretching from the Firth of Clyde to the Firth of Forth. Glasgow, Edinburgh, and Dundee are the chief industrial nodes. Scotland's largest city, Glasgow, is located astride the Clyde River, a few miles upstream from the estuary, so only the smaller ocean freighters can dock at Glasgow; larger sea vessels must berth downstream. Edinburgh,

Scotland's capital, is 50 miles east of Glasgow on the southern shore of the Firth of Forth. The two cities are connected by a canal, railways, and highways that parallel the Lowland, which is about 20 miles wide. This Scottish manufacturing belt correlates closely with coal fields (see Figure 14-2). Small amounts of iron ore and clay occur locally; wool and flax from the agricultural environs supply the textile mills. But most raw materials must be imported. Foreign sources of iron ore, cotton, grain, and petroleum, among other items, are particularly accessible by way of the North Atlantic trade route (see Chapter 27) on which Glasgow is favorably situated. In this setting the Scottish Lowlanders have developed a diversified industrial structure including blast furnaces, steel mills, woolen and cotton textiles, lace factories, and bakeries. Shipyards along the Clyde constitute Britain's most important concentration of shipbuilding. Dundee is Scotland's top textile town.

Southern Wales is another industrial district where good coal is mined near the sea (Figure 14-2). For years the Welsh have had plenty of coal to export, but have had to import ores for processing in local factories. Although steel is the leading product, this area smelts and refines considerable amounts of copper, zinc, and tin from ores and semirefined ores shipped in from abroad. The tin industry got its start on the basis of British ores that long since have given out; but the momentum of an early start and nearness to the European market have enabled the factories of the district to continue, although today most of the tin ore comes from Malaya. Cardiff, on the river Severn, is the industrial center of Wales.

Ireland has comparatively little manufacturing except in Belfast, where there are some manufacturers of linen and woolen fabrics.

For the United Kingdom as a whole the manufacturing districts are located either on coal fields or in the principal port cities (or close to them). This pattern, of course reflects both England's need to import so many factory raw materials from abroad and her heavy sales of factory products abroad. In few other nations does manufacturing depend on international trade for so much of both.

Continental Europe

The industrial heart of continental Europe occupies the west-central portion of the mainland, from the North Sea shores eastward to central Poland, and from the Po Valley northward to southern Sweden (Figure 24-1). This great territory is comparable in many respects to the northeastern quadrant of the United States: Each contains most of the manufacturing plants of its continent; each shows a strong correlation between high population density and manufacturing, and between manufacturing and transportation (waterway, railway, and highway); each contains most of the large cities and most of the leading ports of its continent. Both regions have highly productive farmlands and rather expansive stretches of forest, the latter in rough terrain or stretches of poor soil. Moreover, both have a similar range in the manufacturing ratio (of manufacturing employees to total employees) between different areas. For instance the most heavily industrialized states in Europe have the following percentages of their labor force engaged in manufacturing: Switzerland 44, Belgium 42, Great Britain 40, Germany 40, Netherlands 35, Austria 35, Czechoslovakia 35, France 31, Sweden 30, and Italy 27. The most industrialized states in the United States report the following percentages: Rhode Island 44, Connecticut 43, New Hampshire 40, Michigan 40, New Jersey 38, Massachusetts 37, Ohio 37, Pennsylvania 35, and Indiana 35.

We can mark off for individual discussion eight distinct subregions within the European heartland: the Western Triangle (including the Ruhr), Soviet-controlled Germany, Upper Silesia, Paris, Lorraine-Saar, the upper Rhine area, northern Italy, and southern Scandinavia.

THE WESTERN TRIANGLE

No other part of the world of equal size is so heavily industrialized as a triangular area that can be drawn in northern France, northern Belgium, southern Netherlands, and western Germany (Figure 24-3). The base of this triangle runs 250 miles from Lille, France, to Dortmund, Germany. The apex is in the vicinity of Amsterdam 100 miles to the north. Within this area is the astonishing number of nearly 250 cities, each with 10,000 or more inhabitants, in which manufacturing is the leading economic pursuit. However, none of the cities approaches the size of such metropolitan giants as London, New York, Paris, or Berlin, although three (Amsterdam, Brussels, and Köln) do have approximately 1,000,000 residents.

There are nearly 7,000,000 manufacturing employees in this region, which embodies nearly every type of industry, from smelting ores to polishing lenses, from tanning hides to making shoes, from sawing wood to finishing furniture. Ships, autos, airplanes, engines, turbines, shirts, coats, tablecloths, and lace are only a few of the items made here, in the most diversified zone of manufacturing on earth. With so large a volume of industry and so great a diversity of effort, it will be helpful to break the Triangle down into four distinctive subareas: the Ruhr, the Sambre-Campine zone, Flanders, and the Low Country zone.

The Ruhr   The label "The Ruhr" is a loosely defined term which is applied to an oblong area of land measuring 75 miles from east to west and 40 miles from north to south as shown in Figure 24-4. For so small an area there are an astonishing number of cities; 14 of them exceed 100,000 inhabitants and three (Essen, Dortmund, and Düsseldorf) have populations of over half a million. Altogether the population of the Ruhr exceeds 6,000,000 people.

The position of the Ruhr relative to other countries and to transportation routes is significant. The Rhine, the most heavily trafficked river in the world, flows along the Ruhr's western end, which is only 10 miles from the Dutch border and 110 miles from the mouth of the Rhine at the North Sea. Within the Ruhr, about ten miles apart, three parallel

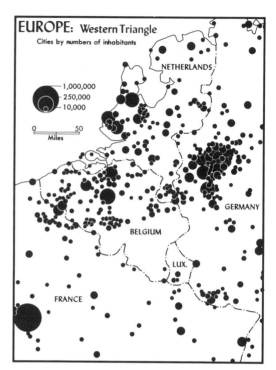

Figure 24-3 *(After William-Olsson.)*

small rivers flow into the Rhine from the east—the Ruhr, the Emscher, and the Lippe. South of the Ruhr River the terrain is hilly and most of the land is forested; northward the country is lower and gently rolling with most of the land in farms. Canals have been built along the flat land in the Emscher and Lippe Valleys eastward to Dortmund and to Hamm respectively. Near their eastern ends they are connected by the Dortmund-Ems Canal which runs northward to Bremen, Emden, and other German ports. On their western ends, these canals connect with the Rhine River.

The Ruhr—now the industrial core of Germany—has grown up comparatively recently, within the past 100 years. The first industrial effort was iron refining in the hills (just south of the Ruhr) where small amounts of ore from local deposits were smelted in furnaces burning charcoal from local forests. Then an important discovery launched the Ruhr on its path to world prominence; coal was discovered under the Ruhr itself—coal of excellent coking quality and tremendous

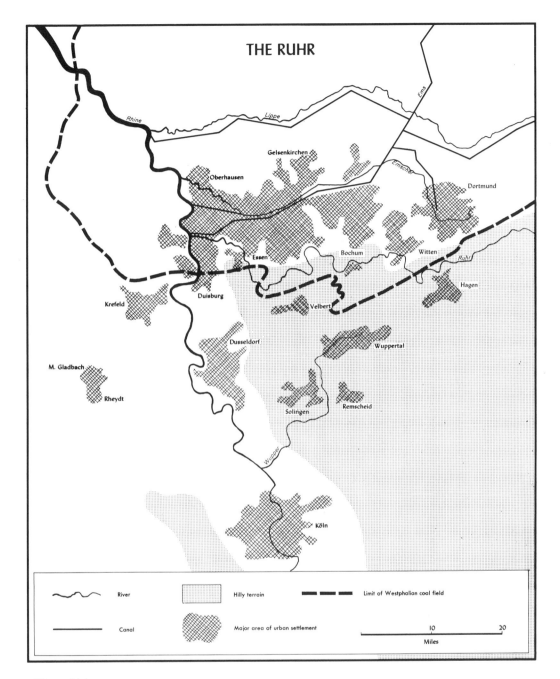

THE RUHR

Gelsenkirchen

Oberhausen

Dortmund

Rhine

Lippe

Emscher

Ems

Essen

Bochum

Witten

Ruhr

Krefeld

Duisburg

Velbert

Hagen

Dusseldorf

Wuppertal

M. Gladbach

Rheydt

Solingen

Remscheid

Wupper

Köln

	River		Hilly terrain		Limit of Westphalian coal field

| | Canal | | Major area of urban settlement | | |

10   20

Miles

Figure 24-4

quantity. The geologic structure dips northward so that the coal seams become progressively deeper. But at the outcrop line running generally east-west only a few miles south of the Ruhr River, they lie at the surface, veneered only with a mantle of soil. For obvious reasons, the first coal mines were dug along the southern edge and in the Ruhr valley. Subsequently, mining operations have moved steadily northward (necessitating ever deeper mines) so that today most of the coal is mined in the valley of the Emscher. Since the Ruhr is in the German province of Westphalia, the coal field is frequently termed the Westphalian field. Its several seams vary in type: A little coal in the south is anthracite, some seams in the north yield gas or heating coals, but most of the seams provide excellent coking coals. Westphalian coal is processed in numerous Ruhr factories that manufacture gas, coke, pig iron, steel, and oil. Of all the coal mined in the Rhur, 40 per cent is used there, 30 per cent is shipped to other German areas, and 30 per cent is exported, largely to France, Belgium, Netherlands, Italy, Switzerland, and Scandinavia.

The iron and steel industry quickly exhausted its original supply of Westphalian iron ore and began drawing upon Siegerland ores 50 miles to the south. But these also were inadequate to feed the voracious blast furnaces being built in the Emscher Valley, and Germany began to depend more and more on foreign sources of ore. Today, three-fourths of the ore smelted in the Ruhr comes from abroad, chiefly Sweden. The reason why Lorraine ores—only 150 miles to the south—are not much used will be explained later in connection with the Lorraine-Saar industrial region.

Primary mills produce pig iron and steel—sheets, wire, rods, and beams. Secondary factories that employ these items in the manufacture of tubes, boilers, bridges, castings, and other fabricated metals are more numerous and are sprinkled throughout the Ruhr. Dortmund, Essen, and Oberhausen are the chief cities in this belt of heavy industry.

Lighter metallurgical industries abound in the older industrial area to the south, where the hilly terrain provided numerous water power sites for many mills in the early days of industrial development. Small factories, and small cities typify this part of the Ruhr; Solingen and Remscheid are the leading towns. Since manufacturers of hardware, screws, nuts, machine tools, and electric motors are more dependent on skilled labor than on large quantities of fuel and raw materials, smallness is no drawback.

Although not in the Ruhr River Valley, Köln—40 miles up the Rhine from the Ruhr confluence—is generally considered to be the southern outpost of manufacturing in the Ruhr industrial area. Köln is in the Ville lignite field, which supports a wide array of indus-

Duisburg, Germany, is located at the western end of the Ruhr industrial region, where the Rhine and a labyrinth of canals come together. Duisburg is one of the major manufacturing and transportation centers in the Ruhr. (Courtesy German Information Center.)

tries—with the conspicuous exception of iron and steel. Some of the lignite is compressed into briquettes which are shipped out as fuel to other regions. And considerable amounts are burned in thermal plants to generate electricity for the main industrial centers of the Ruhr.

The chemical industry is rather widely distributed here, particularly among larger cities such as Duisburg and Düsseldorf. The textile industry, however, is highly concentrated in two areas: Wuppertal, the foremost city in all Germany for textiles and textile machinery, lies to the east of the Rhine, while ten miles west of the river is a cluster of textile cities led by München-Gladbach and Rheydt.

During World War II, the Allied military strategy was to pulverize the Ruhr. As peace dawned, some Allied strategists called for dismantling what Ruhr factories had survived the bombings. Others held that a spirited Ruhr was essential for peace. The latter group reasoned that the industries of too many regions (such as iron mining in Sweden, watch factories in Switzerland, metal works in Italy) and too many ports (for instance, Rotterdam and Antwerp) depended on the Ruhr to justify a decision to suppress the section. This group triumphed in the end. Although recovery in the Ruhr was slow immediately after the War, it soon picked up momentum, and by 1950 the Ruhr was back to prewar production levels; since then it has surged above them. This astonishing recovery epitomizes the ideal interplay of numerous geographic factors: central location to large population, location atop a high-grade coal field, land for easy transportation, especially by rivers and canals, and nearness to the sea. Above all, the Ruhr is peopled with an unusually energetic and ingenious folk. With such endowments, the Ruhr could hardly be repressed.

The Sambre-Campine Region This district derives its name from two coal fields which underlie it: the Sambre-Meuse field and the Campine field. The region extends along a line from Auchel in northern France through central Belgium and the southern tip of Netherlands to Aachen in western Germany. This is a belt of small cities, the largest of which is Liège with around 300,000 inhabitants. The location of the cities closely correlates with that of the coal field. Because of the abundant, good-quality coal considerable heavy industry has developed here to process several metallic ores, particularly those of iron, lead, and zinc, which are shipped in. Originally the iron industry was also based on local ores; indeed, as far back as the thirteenth century, this area was producing iron from its own ore and charcoal. Then this became the first area on the continent to use blast furnaces fired with coke; the breakthrough came in Charleroi and Liège in 1827. The mighty Ruhr was at that time still in the agricultural stage. Today, the mills of the region depend for most of their ore on France's Lorraine field to which it is conveniently connected by rail and waterways, including canals and the Meuse and Sambre rivers.

An array of secondary metal fabricators has taken position along this industrial strip. Liège, for instance, is famous for the manufacture of firearms (for one, the Browning rifle).

Another physical resource of the region is sand from which high-quality glass can be manufactured. Charleroi is the world's leading city in glass manufacturing, specializing in both plate and crystal. Local coal along with the glass sand favored this industry, but the key development was the immigration of Venetian glass blowers who settled in Charleroi in the fourteenth century.

The Campine field (eastern Belgium, southern Netherlands, and a corner of Germany) does not yield coking coal. Therefore, it supports no steel industry. But it has satisfactory heating coal useful in making pottery, cement, and chemicals. Cement production is encouraged not only by the coal but also by local limestone deposits. So much so that the cement industry in Belgium and northern France produces the greatest surplus of cement in the world, and Belgium is the world's top-ranking cement-exporting nation. Zinc ores close by are processed here.

Textiles (a somewhat limited industry

which is dependent on foreign sources of cotton and wool), machinery, chemicals, leather, and paper are products that typify the versatility of this manufacturing region.

Flanders Flanders is the name for northwestern Belgium and the contiguous part of France (including Lille). An area 50 miles long and 25 miles wide, it encompasses at least 25 cities of 10,000 or more inhabitants whose main industries are the manufacture of woolen, cotton, and linen materials. Ghent, at the confluence of the Lys and Scheldt rivers, is the economic pivot of the region.

The textile industry began here centuries ago with the manufacture of linens from the abundant flax from Belgian farms. The water of Flanders, curiously enough, also favored the linen business. One process in linen manufacture, called "retting," is to soak the flax in large vats of water to separate the soft tissue from the hard fiber. It so happens that water in the Lys River is peculiarly well suited for retting flax, because, some authorities believe, of its lime content; and for decades flax mills have lined the Lys. Flemish technologists added the manufacture of woolens to their skills, and during the Middle Ages Flanders was Europe's leading zone of wool manufacturing. In the past century, the textile manufacturers have added cottons to their line, depending entirely on imported fiber and on the Belgian Congo for some of the market. Belgian lace is the most expensive of Flanders textiles. In recent years the textile industry here has added another product—synthetic fibers, such as rayon.

The Low Country Zone Here is a region of diversified industry that extends 100 miles from Amsterdam on the north to Brussels on the south and varies in width from 40 to 60 miles. It lacks the closely spaced pattern of cities found in the other portions of the Western Triangle. Yet it has some of the largest metropolises in Europe: Brussels, Antwerp, Rotterdam, and Amsterdam. In contrast to the Ruhr and Sambre-Campine, this area has no coal and scarcely any raw materials for manufacturing. But it is well located:

For in it the Rhine, Meuse, and Scheldt rivers —the water routes into the entire Western Triangle—enter the North Sea. In such a strategic location, great port cities have evolved that support numerous types of characteristic port factories: sugar refineries, oil refineries, and mills processing wheat, copra, rubber, leather, and dozens of other foreign imports. The ships that leave these ports carry automobiles, machinery, textiles, and hundreds of other manufactured items. One unusual industry is diamond cutting—Antwerp is the world's number-one diamond-cutting city employing 20,000 people; an additional 5,000 workers cut diamonds in Amsterdam.

In summary, the Western Triangle is clearly the manufacturing nucleus of Europe, and, with its counterpart across the English Channel, constitutes the most heavily industrialized region on earth. Its natural-resource bases consist of coal, iron ore, limestone, glass sands, and a few minor ores, some water power, prosperous agriculture, and natural waterways. These latter consist not only of numerous rivers but also the North Sea and English Channel, which play a role in transport comparable to that of the Great Lakes in Anglo-America. The flat terrain has facilitated the construction of canals, the network of which has been interwoven so extensively throughout the Triangle that most large factories are adjacent to barge docks. Most of the local manufacturing traffic is waterborne; indeed, much of it is seaborne. However, the bombings of World War II seriously battered the waterways. Since they take much longer than railways to repair, the railway system (which came into existence *after* the canal system) is gradually moving more and more of the freight traffic.

SOVIET-CONTROLLED GERMANY

The second-ranking manufacturing region in continental Europe is in Soviet-controlled Germany and northwest Czechoslovakia. It covers about as many square miles as the Western Triangle but is much less densely settled, the cities being farther apart and smaller. This zone can be outlined roughly by a line drawn from Hanover southward to Kassel, eastward to Prague, and north to Berlin, and back to Hanover. The Iron Curtain falls just inside its western edge.

Heavy iron and steel industries are virtually absent. Otherwise, though, there is considerable diversity. The natural power sources for manufacturing are varied. An extensive coal field has the greatest reserve tonnage in all Europe. Yet the coal is lignite, which discourages heavy metal industries but is attractive to chemical and other factories that require considerable heat. In the south, the hilly terrain offers numerous water power sites.

As to raw materials, one of the world's richest potash beds underlies the northern part of this area. These reserves, along with salt beds and the lignite, are the basis of a considerable chemical industry. Clay with good characteristics for porcelain supply china factories in Dresden. High-quality glass sands contribute to the eminence of the optical industry at Jena. The fertile farms on the plains of Saxony, Anhalt, and Braunschweig supply sugar beets and grains for mills and breweries. Finally, several metallic ores are mined in the Ore Mountains separating Germany from Czechoslovakia.

On such an array of natural resources, the industrially inclined German people have built a sizable and diverse manufacturing economy. As early as the 1700's, water power sites of southern Saxony were being developed for woolen mills whose textile products were major items of sale at such markets as the famous Leipzig Fair. Today Chemnitz is the core of numerous small cloth-making cities tucked away in the Ore Mountain foothills. In addition, Chemnitz and a few of the small cities now manufacture textile machinery.

Although eastern Germany is short on steel, it is long on skilled labor. Accordingly, machine tools, which depend more on the latter than the former, can be successfully produced here, in Dresden particularly.

Farther north, Leipzig, Magdeburg, Braunschweig, and Hanover have developed as industrial centers serving the agricultural hinterland with the manufacture of farm tools.

Hanover is a leading rubber tire producer as well.

Thuringia (in the southwestern corner of Soviet-controlled Germany) is one of those unusual manufacturing regions that seems to have few physical bases but a high degree of cultural assets for industry. Originally local ores and local charcoal supported a metal industry, but these resources are of little significance now. It is the human skills built up through the years that today make this region famous for cameras and microscopes (at Jena), typewriters, clocks, firearms, hardware, and other precision goods.

Throughout southern Germany, a significant minority of total factory output is accounted for by an unusual type of manufacturing: *household industries*. A word on them may be in order at this point.

The production of surplus goods beyond the needs of the producer takes place in two types of organized efforts: household (or homecraft) industries and factory industries. *Household industries* are *light* industries that are conducted in private dwellings. Lace, watches, and toys are examples of items that are often produced commercially in households; Europe (particularly eastern Germany and Switzerland) and the Far East are the world's main areas of commercial household manufacturing. *Factory industries*, which we have been considering throughout these chapters, may be either *light* or *heavy* and are conducted in structures that are not primarily residential. Therefore, workers in factories must commute. In the early stages of commercial manufacturing, homecraft industries predominated. But the Industrial Revolution, with its mechanical harnessing of power, soon gave factory industries a competitive advantage (for most items) because of the efficiencies of mass production.

For Soviet-controlled Germany as a whole, the import and export trade moves mostly on the Weser and Elbe rivers; these streams are connected by canals, the largest of which is the famous Mittelland Canal stretching 300 miles across Germany from the Dortmund-Ems Canal on the west to the Oder River on the east. Near the eastern end of this canal lies Berlin, which has an industrial structure typical of metropolises. Bremen and Hamburg, the chief ports at the mouths of the Weser and Elbe, are typical manufacturing ports somewhat detached from the industrial regions to the south.

UPPER SILESIA

"Upper Silesia" refers to a region in southwestern Poland and north-central Czechoslovakia and includes the upper Oder River Valley. Katowice, Sosnowiec, and Gleiwicz are leading factory cities.

Upper Silesia possesses the best coal on the European continent except for Germany's Westphalia and Russia's Donbass. The reserve is abundant, but the quality is not as good as Westphalia's for coking; on the other hand, the beds are less difficult to mine. Upper Silesia also has some metallic ores. At one time iron ore was mined, but the deposits were limited in amount and vastly inferior in quality to Swedish ore which, arriving by barge up the Oder River, is now the main supply for the Upper Silesian steel industry. Local ores of lead and zinc, however, are good and can support considerable manufacturing. Chemical industries based on the by-products of the coke and blast furnaces have also prospered here.

Heavy industries predominate. There is little light manufacturing. The function of Silesian industry is largely to provide eastern Germany and Poland with semiprocessed metal for finishing into machinery and other objects.

There is some activity in textiles and apparel—shirts, trousers, and dresses—but the textile center of Poland, Lodz, is not in Silesia but 80 miles to the north.

Upper Silesia marks the eastern end of large-scale manufacturing in non-Russian Europe.

PARIS

The western end is marked by the industrial capital of France—Paris and its suburbs—a node that stands out conspicuously in a countryside which is essentially agricultural. This metropolitan area has no coal, no water power,

and no significant raw materials. But it is inhabited by approximately 7,000,000 persons who are at once the main national source of labor and the main national market. Automobiles, aircraft, electrical machinery, fabricated metals, engines, and railway equipment are the products of the largest metal-goods industries; in addition, printing, food processing, and clothing manufacture, which crop up in the chief city of every industrialized nation, prosper in Paris.

Paris depends on other regions for steel and power. Some electricity is transmitted from hydroelectric plants 200 miles to the south in the mountainous region known as the Massif Central; the rest is generated thermally from coal shipped in to Paris. As to transportation, the city is enmeshed with Europe's waterway system by the Seine, Marne, Oise, and Aisne rivers plus numerous canals connecting with the Sambre, Meuse, Moselle, Rhine, Doubs, Saône, and Loire rivers. Located 150 miles inland from the sea on the greatly meandering Seine river, Paris is not an important port, however. Parisian manufacturing is pushing more toward the north and northwest where land is flatter so access is easier to the Sambre coal field, to the canals leading to the Western Triangle, and to English Channel ports. There is comparatively little incentive for factories to expand on Paris' southern side toward the heart of France.

THE LORRAINE-SAAR REGION

A small but productive zone of intense manufacturing extends from Nancy in northern France through Luxembourg to the Saar. The French portion of this area lies within the ancient province of Lorraine, a term which is no longer current in identifying a political unit but nevertheless lingers on in common usage to identify this industrial area. Lorraine is rich in iron, the Saar in coal. High industrial development would seem to be inevitable. But the relationships are not quite what we might expect.

Without question the predominant industry is the primary processing of iron and steel for which the natural resources are abundantly at hand. Lorraine iron ore (Chapter 14) is noteworthy on several counts: the greatest quantity of any European deposit; a peculiarly high lime content which makes the ores *self-fluxing* in the blast furnace; and an unfortunately high phosphorus content. It was this handicap that defied scientists for years and prevented Lorraine ores from being utilized on a large scale. Not until Gilchrist and Thomas invented the *basic* process (discussed in Chapter 14) were these abundant ores usable. The principal mines are at Briey, Thionville, and Metz.

Fifty miles to the east lies the Saar coal field. It is smaller in extent than Westphalia's and much lower in quality. The coal makes unsatisfactory coke, which, if used at all in blast furnaces, must be blended with Westphalian coke. But Saar coal does work in steel-fabricating, glass, and machinery industries in several communities, of which Saarbrucken is the leader.

Contrary to a widely circulated myth, Europe's chief coal and iron ore regions are not in reciprocal relationship; that is, the Ruhr coal and the Lorraine iron ore do not complement each other. The Ruhr *does* ship coal to Lorraine—in fact, 60 per cent of the coke for Lorraine mills comes from the Ruhr. But scarcely any Lorraine ore finds its way to the Ruhr. Ores from Sweden are so much richer than that from Lorraine that they render production costs for steel in the Ruhr actually less than they would be if the closer but leaner ores were used. Consequently, Lorraine ore is disposed of as follows: 50 per cent is smelted locally, 25 per cent in the Saar, 8 per cent in Luxembourg (all three areas depending on the Ruhr for coke), and 17 per cent in Belgium.

THE UPPER RHINE REGION

From central Germany to western Switzerland is an area (somewhat coextensive with the drainage basin of the upper Rhine River) that contains a good many industrial cities, none of which is very large and a few of which are located close together. Some of the cities in this dispersed manufacturing region are on the Rhine itself, a few are in eastern France, several are in the highlands of Germany, and many are on the northern plateau of Switzerland. Particularly prominent are Frankfurt, Mannheim, Stuttgart, Strasbourg, and Zurich.

Few of Europe's industrial regions seem so handicapped in natural resources for manufacturing. There are no appreciable fuel or ore resources. Originally timber was abundant, and several woodworking industries flourished. Not long ago these were threatened by the imminent extinction of the forests, but they have been saved by a wise forest conservation program. There is waterpower, too. But the main assets are (a) the skills of the people (who have developed numerous light industries, making such commodities as watches and clocks, toys, electrical machinery, textiles, and textile machinery), and (b) the nearby dense population. In many respects this area resembles New England in the United States.

Homecraft industries still abound here, too.

SOUTHERN SCANDINAVIA

The Swedes are singularly well endowed with two raw materials—timber and iron ore —upon which wealth they have built several manufacturing cities. A few of these front on the Gulf of Bothnia, but most are south of a line from Stockholm to Lake Vänern. Sawmills, pulp mills, paper mills, match factories, and furniture plants are numerous. The steel industry is based largely on local southern ores, not curiously enough, on Kiruna ores, which are, as we saw, exported. For decades the Swedes have smelted ores with charcoal from the abundant timber. But some coke is imported, too. In either case, steel-making here is an expensive process compared to the large-scale methods of the Ruhr and Britain. Consequently, the Swedes have specialized in high-quality steels that cannot be mass-produced, that, indeed, are required only in small amounts and with characteristics fitting them for high-speed work or for cutting. The skills of Swedish labor have also developed a textile industry, processing imported cotton and wool for manufacture into cloth and garments, principally for the Swedish market.

Eastern Denmark is almost as highly indus-

The Fiat Motor Company integrated Mirafiori plant at Turin, Italy. (Courtesy FIAT.)

trialized as southern Sweden. Wood and metal industries are again the léading pair.

NORTHERN ITALY

Italy has 3,500,000 factory workers, nearly all of whom are in northern Italy, mostly in the Po Valley. With an extremely high ratio of population to arable land, Italians must industrialize ever more rapidly and extensively or else face a very low standard of living. But Italy is confronted with serious handicaps for manufacturing. The country has virtually no coal or metallic ores. So she is entirely dependent on other regions for steel, copper, aluminum, scrap metal, and coke. Offsetting these deficits to some extent is the enormous water power resource in the humid, mountainous Alps. But southern Italy lacks even this advantage, being hilly enough but too dry. The populace of northern Italy responds well to factory work and turns out such products as motor scooters, small automobiles, and textiles, all of which sell successfully on the world market. Milan and Turin are the leading manufacturing cities. Most cities in the Po Valley have diversified industrial structures except for a nest of small communities just above Milan that specialize in silk fabrics and cotton textiles made of cotton from the United States, Brazil, and Egypt.

OTHER REGIONS

In a brief survey such as this, we can merely mention other manufacturing regions. Here are a few.

Central France early had a steel industry

based on local ores and charcoal; a highly developed but small metal industry has persisted, specializing now in quality steel products. During recent hostilities the armament center of France was St. Etienne. Another early industry was the manufacture of silk textiles using locally produced silk augmented by imports from Japan. Other textiles were later added. The textile workers labored in hundreds of households and in small factories in several communities, of which Lyon is the largest. A large dam being constructed at Genissiat (in the Rhone River 50 miles east of Lyon) will rise 320 feet to be the highest in Europe; it will provide hydroelectric power for aluminum refineries and other industries.

Hydroelectricity from the Pyrenees powers a limited amount of manufacturing in southwestern France. It is here in the sunny Mediterranean-type climate, that scientists are experimenting with solar power in an effort to help relieve France's chronic shortage of energy.

The Barcelona district of Spain has developed a minor textile industry.

Elsewhere in Europe there are occasional concentrations of factories, nearly every one of which coincides with a large city, for instance: Rome, Naples, Budapest, Warsaw, Madrid, Lisbon, and Dublin.

TRADE ASSOCIATIONS

No discussion of manufacturing in western Europe would be complete without recognizing the role of the two great trade associations: the European Common Market and Europe Free Trade Association. These will be discussed in Chapter 27. Suffice it to say at the moment, however, that these trade associations involving 15 nations have stimulated manufacturing by enabling freer movements between nations of raw materials, fuel, finished products, and labor.

A final word: Little has been said in this chapter about such concepts as location quotients, indices of diversification, and industrial structures. There are two reasons for such omissions: For several countries data are unavailable in sufficient detail for such computations; secondly, where data are available researchers simply have not as yet invested the long hours required in the laborious computations exacted by these concepts.

uggested Readings

Heiden, Noland R., "Odda and Rjukan: Two Industrialized Areas of Norway," *Annals of the Association of American Geographers*, 1952, pp. 109-128.

Held, Colbert C., "The New Saarland," *Geographical Review*, 1951, pp. 590-605.

———, "Refugee Industries in West Germany After 1945," *Economic Geography*, 1956, pp. 316-335.

Pounds, Norman J. G., "The Industrial Geography of Modern Poland," *Economic Geography*, 1960, pp. 231-253.

———, "Lorraine and the Ruhr," *Economic Geography*, 1957, pp. 149-162.

———, *The Ruhr: A Study in Historical and Economic Geography*, Bloomington, 1952, 283 pp.

———, *The Upper Silesian Industrial Region*, Bloomington, 1958, 242 pp.

———, and Parker, William N., *Coal and Steel in Western Europe: The Influence of Resources and Techniques on Production*, Bloomington, 1957, 381 pp.

Smith, Wilfred, *An Economic Geography of Great Britain*, London, 1948, 747 pp.

Thomas, Morgan D., "Manufacturing Industry in Belfast, Northern Ireland," *Annals of the Association of American Geography*, 1956, pp. 175-196.

United Nations, Economic Commission for Europe, *Economic Survey of Europe*, Geneva, 1960.

Villmow, Jack R., "Notes on the Industrial Economy of West and East Berlin," *The Professional Geographer*, January 1961, pp. 11-14.

*Part of the Yawata Iron and Steel Works on Dokai Bay, the largest
integrated iron and steel operation in the Orient. Originally built by the Japanese
government, it stimulated subsequent development of other industries and thus
was a major factor in northern Kyushu's becoming one of Japan's biggest industrial concentrations.
(Courtesy John H. Thompson, the Geographical Review, and Mainichi newspaper.)*

TWENTY-FIVE

Anglo-America and Europe account for 20 per cent and 40 per cent respectively of the world's manufacturing workers. Most of the remaining 40 per cent live in the Soviet Union and in the Far East, with smaller numbers of them dispersed through South America, Africa, and Australia.

South America, Africa, Australia

In all the Southern Hemisphere (plus those portions of Africa and South America that extend into the Northern Hemisphere) there are probably fewer than 4,000,000 people engaged in commercial manufacturing. The most industrialized nations, Argentina and Australia, each barely exceed 1,000,000 manufacturing employees (less than the number in New York City and its suburbs). Industry in Australia is confined for the most part to an arc around the southeastern lobe of the continent. In Argentina it is concentrated largely in Buenos Aires and environs. Brazil and the Union of South Africa have entered the period of industrialization characterized by the primary steps of processing products of mines, farms, and forests and the beginnings of a consumer-goods industry to supply local markets. Machinery for all these areas, though, is still largely imported from Europe and Anglo-America.

On each of these three continents, the relative importance of manufacturing is increasing in the over-all economy. As yet, however, their roles in the world economy are too limited to warrant extensive or detailed comment here.

Information about manufacturing in the Soviet Union is difficult to compare with that for the rest of the world since Russia has not made public as much data on economic activity as have other industrial nations. Latest published statistics from the U.S.S.R. declare that approximately 23,000,000 people are engaged in commercial manufacturing. Russia thus provides more jobs in manufacturing than the United States but has lower labor productivity in industry.

Before we investigate the distribution of Soviet industry, it will be helpful to make a few general observations about manufacturing in Russia. The Socialist Revolution of 1917 marked a turning point in Russian industry. Before that date the Russian economy was agrarian; an extremely high percentage of the workers were farmers, and most farming was at a subsistence level. What little commercial manufacturing there was consisted mainly of food and textile industries. Victorious in their Revolution, the Communist rulers formulated a long-range industrial strategy: first, to increase the role of manufacturing in the Russian economy, and second, to enlarge the role of steel and machinery industries within the

industrial structure. These goals were eventually combined with goals for agriculture, mining, and all other phases of the economy in a series of five-year plans, the first of which was launched in the late 1920's. The first target has been reached for some time. By the end of the Second Five-Year Plan (1937) the Soviet Union apparently had surpassed every other nation in Europe in terms of total industrial output. Since World War II, manufacturing has continued to move ahead at an impressive tempo; no other nation of comparable size has ever experienced such a rapid pace of industrialization. Still, at the starting point the country was so primitive that even with such high rates of advancement, Russia has a long way to go before her 216,000,000 people will enjoy the refrigerators and automobiles and other consumer luxuries typical of western nations.

Likewise, the Russians achieved their goal in the industrial structure, for heavy industry has become the prime component and machine-building the leading type of heavy industry. The manufacture of consumer goods has been given a lower priority. For example, few automobiles are produced compared to the

Figure 25-1

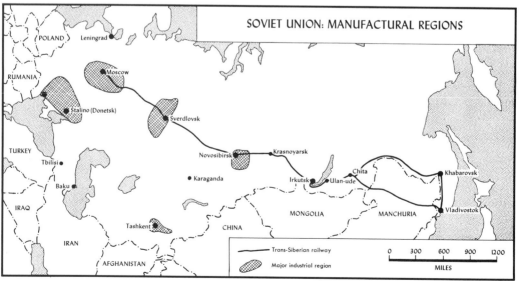

SOVIET UNION: MANUFACTURAL REGIONS

large numbers of tractors and trucks that roll off the assembly lines. But one major objective is still unattained—to surpass the United States in per capita industrial production. The Russians hope to take a gigantic stride in this direction during a new Seven-Year Plan which will end in 1965. But even the most optimistic Soviet planners believe the output of high-priority industries producing capital goods will not reach present United States levels until around 1970.

Locationally, there has been a pronounced shift to the east. Before the Revolution there was comparatively little manufacturing east of the Moscow area; now there are two major industrial regions and a few smaller ones that are results of government planning and execution. Even so, roughly 80 per cent of Soviet manufacturing takes place in European Russia and the Urals. Manufacturing is not highly concentrated in any one region comparable to the northeastern quadrant of the United States, or in the west-central portion of Europe. Instead, there are several rather dispersed regions (Figure 25-1). Five are particularly noteworthy: The Industrial Center, the Ukraine, the Urals, the Kuznetsk Basin, and Leningrad.

THE INDUSTRIAL CENTER

Perhaps one-fourth of Russia's factories are within what the Soviets term "The Industrial Center," an oblong territory centering on Moscow and extending from Shcherbakov at the north to Bryansk at the south, and from Smolensk on the west to Gorki on the east (Figure 25-2, page 448). The region is 450 miles long and over 200 miles wide at the extremes.

The Industrial Center does not have a strong physical base for manufacturing. The southern portion overlies the Tula coal field which contains substantial reserves—but the coal is low-quality lignite and it is difficult to mine, requiring relatively deep shafts. The zone is also poor in raw materials. Little oil is produced within this region, only a little iron ore, and some phosphates, though there is an abundance of sand and gravel in the glacial moraines. There are no significant water power resources, since the terrain is comparatively

flat. Swamps are numerous, and the rivers are rather small—here are merely the headwaters for several streams that flow into the Volga and Don systems. Nor does the region possess a port.

On the other hand, the Industrial Center does include Moscow, which is both the largest metropolis (7,500,000 inhabitants) and the center of government in the Soviet Union. For centuries this city has been the nucleus of the Russian state since it is comparatively secure from foreign invasion, is central to European Russia's land, has access (at least for small boats) to these hinterlands via the rivers which radiate outwards in all directions and is located in one of the most populous parts of the nation. All these factors have resulted in cultural forces that outweigh the natural handicaps for industry.

The first industries to develop were flax spinning, linen weaving, leather tanning, woolen manufacturing, wood processing, and a little iron refining—all based on small amounts of natural resources in the hinterland. Moscow, as Russia's trading hub, soon attracted other industries, even though they depended on using cotton, oil, and metals from other regions.

This was the first region in Russia to evolve from the domestic subsistence stage of manufacturing through the homecraft stage into the factory stage. The main encouragement to this development came not from abundant local natural resources (as in the Ruhr) or a good harbor (as at Rotterdam) but rather from the clustering of population, trade, and government in the geographical center of Russia's most populous territory. In the Soviet era, the Industrial Center, abounding with Russia's technical intelligentsia and skilled workers, has led the way in all the five-year plans.

When the first five-year plan was launched, the textile industry employed 66 per cent of the manufacturing workers in central Russia. Today, however, machinery and other metal-working industries account for almost one-half of industrial employment. Moscow is the nation's number-one city in the manufacture of electrical equipment, scientific instruments,

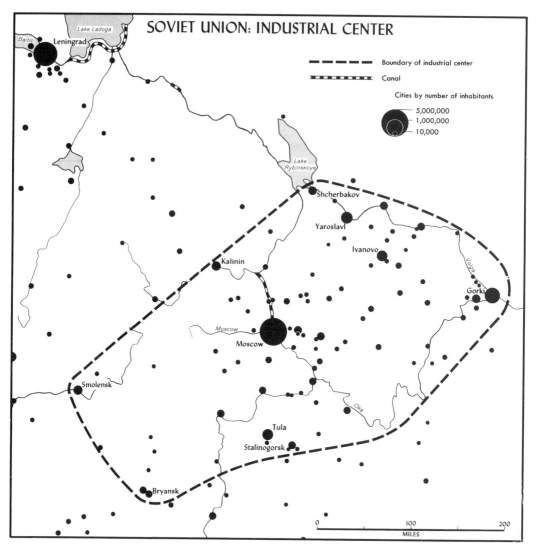

Figure 25-2 *(After William-Olsson.)*

and machine-tools. But the metals required come primarily from the south (the Ukraine) and the east (the Urals). Textile factories now employ less than one-fourth of Moscow's manufacturing labor force.

Textiles are still important, though. Moscow and Ivanovo are the two busiest places, and they also make most of the textile machinery, but there are three dozen smaller nearby settlements where textile-making is the livelihood of most of the workers. All the requisite cotton lint and wool fibers originate in agricultural regions of the U.S.S.R. to the south.

The chemical industry is also an old one,

but until recently it consisted mainly of dye production for the textile mills and depended on imported raw materials. Today the bulk of the chemical industry processes local raw materials (lignite, phosphates, and potatoes) to manufacture gases, alcohol, acids, fertilizers, and synthetic rubber.

Saw-milling, wood-processing, and furniture factories use local timber resources.

The Industrial Center's huge power requirements are satisfied largely by electricity produced in thermal factories that burn lignite and peat. Needs for bituminous coal are met by shipments from the Donbass. In the future,

Manufacturing Regions: U.S.S.R., Asia, Other

additional power will be supplied by (a) electricity produced at two new hydroelectric plants to the southeast on the Volga at Stalingrad (new name is Volgograd) and Kuibyshev (which, as per Table 14-8, are among the most powerful hydroelectric installations in the world), and (b) petroleum from the newly discovered and highly promising Volga oil field.

The transportation system of the Industrial Center consists primarily of a railway network with 11 routes radiating outward from Moscow. By far the heaviest tonnage is carried by the double-tracked line through Kharkov to the Ukraine, moving coal, steel, cotton, grain and other agricultural products. A highway system has been slow in developing, although trucks are beginning to move an increasing volume of freight. Waterborne freight travels mainly on an 80-mile canal running northward from Moscow to the Volga headwater. Counter to a widely held fallacy, the Moscow River *is* navigable in Moscow which contains several large river docks.

Moscow is unquestionably the dominant manufactural metropolis of this region as well as of all Russia; it accounts for more than 10 per cent of the U.S.S.R.'s total industrial output. As in London, Paris, and Berlin, its industrial structure is one of the most diversified in its nation. Although it is a region of farm and forest, the Industrial Center does have several cities that have taken on an industrial tone. These, however, are vastly farther apart than are those in the heavily urbanized Ruhr (Compare Figure 25-2 with Figure 24-3 and 24-4). Tula for years was a metallurgical center (there was a modest local supply of iron ore), but with the later development of more efficient operations in the Ukraine, the Tula metal industry has been concentrating more and more on hardware and other steel products; consequently, it now is only a minor pig-iron producer. Plants in Stalinogorsk process local coal and clay into chemicals and building materials. Ivanovo, one of the leading textile centers, is also the seat of research studies on textile techniques. Yaroslavl manufactures synthetic rubber and supplies rubber tires to its own truck factory

as well as to the nearby automotive factories in Moscow and Gorki. Yaroslavl also is a seat of tractor and farm machinery plants. Gorki, a booming industrial city on the Volga, is often referred to as "The Detroit of the Soviet Union" because of its automobile and truck factories. In addition, the large-scale manufacture of river vessels and railway equipment further strengthens the specialization of Gorki industry on transportation machinery. Being on the southern margin of the coniferous forest, Gorki also makes wood products and paper. Kalinin on the western boundary of the Industrial Center has cotton and linen mills; it is surrounded by Russia's most productive flax fields.

THE UKRAINE

In the southwestern portion of the Soviet Union lies the Ukraine, an area possessing the richest farmland and the most concentrated rural population in the country. But it also has an extensive manufacturing region, marked out by Odessa, Kiev, Kharkov, and the Donets River (see Figure 25-3, page 450).

The natural landscape of most of the industrialized portion of the Ukraine resembles the northern Great Plains of the United States, the vegetation being mostly grasslands. The area was sparsely inhabited until 1800 when colonists began moving in. As was true in the American Great Plains, the first agricultural endeavors were pastoral. Not until railways were built in the 1870's from Moscow to Black Sea ports did the Ukraine economy enter the grain-growing stage. At that time, Russian capital was insufficient to develop the mineral resources that had been discovered. French and Belgian investors, however, chose to risk money in Ukrainian enterprises, and by 1900 the Ukraine led the rest of Russia in metal processing and other heavy industry. Development was slow but generally upward for the next 40 years, and by the outbreak of World War II the Ukraine contained 20 per cent of the Soviet Union's population and perhaps 20 per cent of her manufacturing. Hitler's armies spearheaded their drive toward this region and overran it completely. Anticipating the invasion, however, Russian strategists dismantled

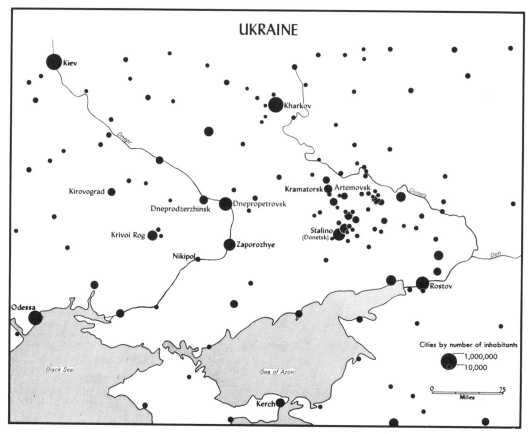

UKRAINE

Kiev
Kharkov
Dnepr
Kirovograd
Kramatorsk Artemovsk
Dneprodzerzhinsk Dnepropetrovsk
Krivoi Rog
Stalino (Donetsk)
Zaporozhye
Nikipol
Donets
Don
Rostov
Odessa

Cities by number of inhabitants
1,000,000
10,000

Black Sea
Sea of Azov
0   75
Miles
Kerch

Figure 25-3 *(After William-Olsson.)*

entire factories and, in the greatest industrial transplanting in history, moved them to the Urals and to Siberia. A few years later, as the Russians recaptured the Ukraine, the retreating Germans demolished what was left of the industrial capacity. Although totally destroyed, Ukrainian manufacturing has been rapidly rebuilt since 1945, a feat rivaling that in the Ruhr. Today the Ukraine is again the most productive steel region in the Soviet Union and accounts for 40 per cent of the national steel output.

The physical resources of the Ukraine are most impressive, and it is one of the best-equipped places on earth for heavy industry. There are large quantities of coking coal in the Donets River basin (that is, the Donbass) as we saw in Chapter 14; however, this coal has a serious qualitative defect for coking—a very high sulfur content ranging between 2.8 and 3.2 per cent. There are enormous re-

serves of high-grade iron ore at Krivoi Rog; one of the world's foremost manganese mines is at Nikopol; and in many parts of the Ukraine there is an abundance of limestone, salt, kaolin, and building clay. Less than 500 miles to the northeast lies the Volga-Ural oil region, which now produces over two-thirds of Soviet petroleum. And at Zaporozhye on the Dnepr river is one of the world's greatest hydroelectric installations adjacent to a dam which is 200 feet high and almost half a mile long.

Within the Ukraine, manufacturing activities have sprouted in two principal fertile zones and several outlying fields.

1. The number-one zone, to the east within the bend of the Donets River, comprises a cluster of closely spaced cities of which Donetsk (formerly Stalino) is the largest. Manufactured goods are of the heavy type: pig iron, crude steel, pipe, sheet steel, bar steel,

The Kirov works in Makeyeva, one of the biggest iron and steel plants in the Donbass. The region was heavily damaged by the Germans; but the Russians have restored the installations and steadily increased output ever since. (Sovfoto.)

rails, railroad equipment, farm machinery, and earth-moving equipment. Fertilizer factories and chemical factories are typical here, too.

The physical basis for industry here is Donbass coal—bituminous coal (with even some anthracite) which serves as the primary source of coking coal for the Soviet iron and steel industry despite the high sulfur content and increasingly difficult mining conditions. Before World War II this field accounted for over half of Russia's coal output. Although the volume mined in the Donbass has reached an all-time high of 185,000 tons a year, the percentage of the national total has dropped to 37 per cent because of the rapidly increasing outputs from Siberian fields. The iron ore is brought in primarily from Krivoi Rog, 200 miles to the west. The iron and steel industry supplies not only steel to a great many local fabricating industries but also by-product gases (from the coke ovens) for chemical plants. These factories have recently begun also to process an increasing volume of crude oil piped in from the Volga-Ural field and the Caucasus. Salt mines near Artemovsk constitute a third local resource for chemical industries.

Although most of the steel stays on home grounds, a substantial portion is shipped northward to the Industrial Center, particularly Moscow.

2. One hundred miles to the west lies the second major zone: the Dnepr Bend area, which extends from Dnepropetrovsk and Zaporozhye to Kirovograd. In contrast to the Donbass, the Dnepr Bend has no coal and it has few industrial cities; the few there are not very close together, either. But the region has three distinctive resources: hydroelectric power (at Zaporozhye), the Soviet Union's most abundant supply of rich iron ore (at Krivoi Rog), and a huge deposit of manganese (at Nikopol).

The principal industry in the Dnepr Bend is the manufacture of pig iron and steel. Railroad cars shuttle Krivoi Rog iron ore to the Donbass and return with coking coal—a perfect example of what is termed the *complementarity* of economic regions. Most of the pig iron made here is refined into steel and then fabricated, although some of the pig iron is shipped up to the Industrial Center. The manganese from Nikopol supplies both Dnepr Bend and Donbass steel mills with the single most important ferro-alloy metal.

Three cities along the Dnepr River (Dneprodzerzhinsk, Dnepropetrovsk, and Zaporozhye) are especially favorably situated for steel making and steel fabrication. With electricity from the Dnepr Dam and pig iron from either the Donbass or Krivoi Rog, finished steel is turned out in some of the largest rolling mills on the European continent. Other industries in these three towns are also based on electric power—the production of aluminum, fertilizers, and explosives.

Of the outlying cities, Kharkov, Kiev,

Rostov, and Odessa are the largest (Figure 25-3). Kharkov has the advantage of location at the convergence of two double-track railway routes to Moscow, one from the Donbass and the other from the Dnepr Bend. Surrounded by highly productive farm land, Kharkov has plants that specialize in making farm machinery, locomotives, and railway equipment. The industrial structures of Odessa and Rostov are diversified; their food and leather industries reflect the surplus production of their agricultural hinterlands. Agricultural machines are made in both cities. Moreover, Odessa and Rostov are the Ukraine's principal seaports.

Kiev, capital of the Ukraine Republic, is rather distant from other manufacturing centers. Surrounded by vast fields of sugar beets, Kiev is the chief sugar-refining city in Russia; it also has a diversity of industries pouring out products to serve its hinterland.

With an abundance of certain mineral resources, productive agriculture, favorable terrain for railway construction, frontage on the Sea of Azov and Black Sea for ocean shipping, and a cultural capacity for welding these resources into an industrial complex, the Ukraine with almost one-fifth of the national total is today Russia's second-ranking manufacturing region.

LENINGRAD

With 3,000,000 inhabitants, Leningrad is both the second largest metropolis and the second most important manufacturing city in the Soviet Union. Its highly diversified industrial structure is a response to a complex of factors unique in Russia. Located 60° north of the Equator and nearly surrounded by forests, Leningrad would seem to lack all the requirements for industrialization other than for wood working or paper making. Its hinterland has traces of iron ore, and a smattering of bauxite, but little else in the way of minerals. But Leningrad does have access by sea to the west—and that means imports. It is in fact Russia's prime industrial area that depends on imports. Leningrad has the best location in Russia for foreign trade with western Europe. At the head of the Gulf of

Finland (Figure 25-1), the city was founded by Peter the First, in the early 1700's, as a "window cut through on Europe." The city quickly became Russia's foremost port. On its landward side, St. Petersburg, as the city was then called, was linked with Moscow and the Volga system by a waterway network consisting of several rivers, lakes, and canals (Figure 25-2), which were easily constructed across the flat landscape. Since St. Petersburg served as Russia's capital for nearly 200 years, it became the metropolis for culture and education as well as for foreign trade. This development too had economic effects. For it was here that ideas were first born to develop manufacturing in Russia; it was here that the Revolution of 1917 first exploded. Thus, the cultural attributes of the place combined with its advantages as a transport center gave rise to factories processing imported cotton, wheat, tobacco, and metal. Today Leningrad factory hands specialize in making such items as maritime vessels (an atomic-powered ice-breaker was recently completed here), turbines and engines; as well as typewriters, cameras, telephone and radio equipment, motorcycles, and light machinery. Textiles, formerly the leading product, are still important. Power needs are met by burning timber and peat from the city's environs and coal from several distant fields and by using hydroelectricity produced in the hinterland.

During World War II, most of Leningrad's factory equipment was whisked away to the Urals before the Germans invaded. As in the Ukraine, factories in Leningrad have had to be rebuilt from the ground up. Today the city stands alone as an industrial giant surrounded by a vast hinterland in which scarcely any other manufacturing takes place.

THE URAL HILLS

Stretching north to south along the Ural Hills in a strip 500 miles long and 200 miles wide is a group of widely dispersed industrial cities. This manufacturing zone is 800 miles from Moscow (Figures 25-1 and 25-4). On the basis of what is probably the greatest variety of mineral wealth in any comparably large region on earth, the Russians have built up in

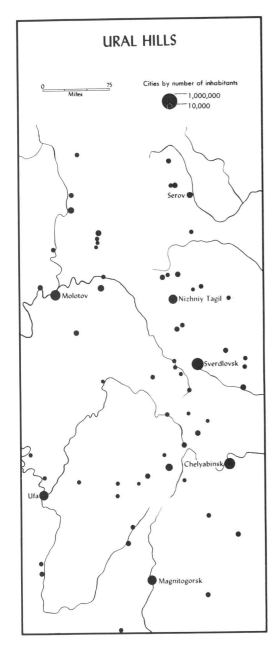

URAL HILLS

0   75
Miles

Cities by number of inhabitants
1,000,000
10,000

Serov

Molotov   Nizhniy Tagil

Sverdlovsk

Chelyabinsk

Ufa

Magnitogorsk

Figure 25-4 (*After William-Olsson.*)

Urals have been seriously depleted in recent years, the iron and steel industries of this region will not be hampered by a shortage of ore because of the recent discovery of enormous deposits of iron ore at nearby Kustanay in the northwest tip of Kazakhstan. Several ferro-alloys also occur, principally nickel, chrome, and manganese. Copper, too, is mined in many places throughout the Urals. Additional resources are potassium, salt, phosphate, pyrites, gold, platinum, asbestos, magnesium, bauxite, and building materials. The power picture is somewhat less spectacular. Although there is a good deal of low-grade coal, which is useful for heating and for making gas or thermal-electricity, coking coal must be hauled in from distant fields. And, oddly enough, water power is not abundant. The *local relief* (elevation differential between highest and lowest points) in the Ural Hills is not very great, and the climate is not humid enough to maintain a large flow of water in the rivers. So hydroelectric plants are not very feasible. A tremendous oil pool, however, has been discovered on the western flanks of the Urals, extending out under the plains. Known as the Volga Basin, this field will become a fundamental power prop for Soviet manufacturing. In addition, Urals industry will receive natural gas piped in from Central Asia through two 40-inch pipelines spanning more than a thousand miles of intervening arid territory.

The first major industry in the Urals was the smelting of local iron ore with charcoal from Ural forests. During the 1700's, in fact, this region was one of the world's leading localities in pig-iron production and actually exported metal to foreign nations, including Germany and Britain. But, when western Europeans discovered the art of smelting iron ore with coke, the Urals lost their importance, and by 1890 were surpassed by the Ukraine.

In 1930 Soviet authorities launched an unusual scheme to modernize the Ural steel industry and to develop other resources of the area. Since the chief deficiency was coking coal, the choice was either to haul Donbass coal 1200 miles from the southwest or the newly discovered Kuznetsk coal 1400 miles

the Urals what is now their third-ranking manufacturing region. Flanked by vast stretches of farm lands to the west and east, by broad sweeps of forest to the north and grazing lands to the south, the Urals stand out as a belt of mining and manufacturing. Even though the high-grade deposits of iron ore (among the richest in the U.S.S.R.) in the

from the east. Because the Donbass area was already tied in with the Dnepr Bend and the Industrial Center, while the Kuznetsk field was not, and because the latter was the less vulnerable to enemy invasion, the decision was made to gear the Ural development in with that of the Kuznetsk. The result was a reciprocal arrangement known as the *Ural Kuznetsk Combine* whereby the railways carried Kuznetsk coal to the Urals and Ural ores back to the Kuznetsk. Such reciprocation stimulated modern metallurgical industries in both regions. Shortly before World War II, however, the development of the Karaganda coal field, only 600 miles east of the Urals, was undertaken. Coincidentally, an iron ore deposit was discovered at Gornaya Shorya south of the Kuznetsk. Accordingly, very little iron ore now moves from the Urals to the Kuzbass, but considerable Kuznetsk coal still moves to the Urals because its coking quality exceeds that of Karaganda coal, which has a high ash content. Ural blast furnace operators mix Karaganda and Kuzbass coals in smelting iron ore. Of coal consumed for all purposes in the Urals, 57 per cent is mined within the region, 27 per cent comes from the Kuzbass, and 16 per cent arrives from Karaganda.

The program launched in 1930 to modernize the Urals has been singularly successful. From small-time operations with only one metal, the Urals have developed into an area that produces large volumes of many metals; in addition there are now a great array of industries that fabricate those metals into machinery and a wide line of metallic products. Fortunately for the Soviets, the Ural development program proceeded at such a pace that, by the time of the German invasion, the Urals could carry the burden of Soviet metallurgical manufacturing when the Ukraine was lost.

Today, the industrial structure of the Urals is heavy with metal industries. All told, Ural factories account for 35 per cent of Soviet steel output. Iron and steel foundries are located in several cities, but Magnitogorsk turns out more pig iron than all the other Ural cities combined. Despite the approaching depletion of the once-rich deposits of ore at nearby Mount Magnitayana, Magnitogorsk

can boast of the single largest steel mill in the U.S.S.R. Yet when the Soviets set up this huge mill and built around it an entirely new city, which now numbers more than 300,000 inhabitants, the site was utterly devoid of human habitation.

A profusion of smelters and plants that process nonferrous metals dot the Urals. A large percentage of Russian copper comes from these mills. Zinc, nickel, aluminum, magnesium, and asbestos are other products from Ural factories.

Living off the primary metal industries are the secondary ones, especially machinery manufacture, which account for 60 per cent of all industrial production in the Urals today. The largest cities in the Urals thrive on machinery production: Sverdlovsk, Chelyabinsk, and Nizhniy Tagil. Molotov and Ufa, cities of the plain at the western base of the Urals, are likewise machinery towns. Mining machinery, metal-working machinery, tractors, and trucks are typical products.

The chemical industry in the Urals gets its supplies partly from by-products of the coke ovens but largely from by-products of the smelting of nonferrous ores. Petroleum refining is a new industry in the Volga oil field to the west.

Since the Urals penetrate Russia's vast stretch of forests, the northern reaches are dotted with sawmills, plywood factories, and wood-chemical plants.

The nexus of this whole Ural complex is Sverdlovsk, a city of 800,000 people. Seven railways radiate from this transportation center, which is situated in a low section of the hills. Within the past 30 years this site has been transformed by Soviet planning from a small trade center to become not only a transportation and industrial center but also the educational and cultural capital of the region. Second only to Sverdlovsk in the Ural group, is Chelyabinsk, with about 700,000 inhabitants. It is the main gateway to Siberia.

The Urals are a superb example of a region that has been deliberately molded into a manufacturing area by a totalitarian government. The main asset here was an abundance of metallic ores; the chief handicaps were lack of coking coal, low population (which resulted in both a small labor supply and a small number of buyers for consumer goods), and remoteness from Russia' biggest markets to the west. Soviet strategists handled these problems by (a) hauling first Kuznetsk and then Karaganda coal to the Urals, (b) transferring people into the Urals to fill jobs in the new factories, (c) setting up machinery and fabricating factories in the Urals to process Ural metals, and (d) moving millions of people into Siberia to develop forests, farms, and mines, and to constitute a new market for the commodities made in Ural factories.

THE KUZNETSK BASIN

Within the past generation, an entirely new industrial area has sprouted in the Kuznetsk River basin (Kuzbass for short) tucked in among the northwestern foothills of the Altai Mountains (Figure 25-5), 1400 miles east of the Urals. Industrial production here is considerably less than that in the Urals, of course, mainly because the Kuzbass is so far from the agricultural, industrial, domestic, and commercial markets of the nation. The main resource base is the Kuznetsk coal field, which has an astonishing reserve, more than even the Donbass and probably 40 per cent of all Soviet proven bituminous coal reserves. The quality of the fuel is entirely satisfactory for industrial purposes, yet for years it was used only to fire locomotives on the Trans-Siberian railway (which runs across the northern end of the field).

Soviet planning called for a modern industrial complex here to complement that in the Urals. The first step was to construct a large iron and steel mill at a site upon which the city of Stalinsk (new name is Novokuznetsk) subsequently developed. This new city has mushroomed in the past three decades to the extent of almost 400,000 persons; they find their livelihood in mines, iron and steel mills, and a diversity of other new businesses in the vicinity. Today, this area accounts for 9 per cent of Soviet steel output. Originally, the steel mills worked Ural iron ore but now they depend partly on mines in Gornaya Shorya (which are being rapidly depleted) and to an increasing degree on newly discovered ores in eastern Siberia.

Expanding settlement in Siberia means an increasing demand for machinery (tractors, plows, locomotives, and mining machines), a large part of which is now made of Kuzbass steel. A chemical industry produces fertilizers for nearby collectivized farms. The efforts of a great many factory hands go into making cement, bricks, and structural timber for the expanding construction industry of western Siberia, where settlement is proceeding rapidly, partly due to an influx of refugees during World War II and partly due to peacetime migrations planned by the government.

Other Kuzbass industries process organic products raised in the hinterland. For example, this area produces Russia's greatest butter surplus. Sugar beet refineries, flour mills, distilleries, and tanneries are other examples of primary industries. Tranformed by textile mills into fabrics is the wool of Turkestan flocks and cotton grown by irrigation. But fundamentally, the Kuzbass industrial structure is based on coal, and the Russian strategy

Figure 25-5 (*After N. Baransky.*)

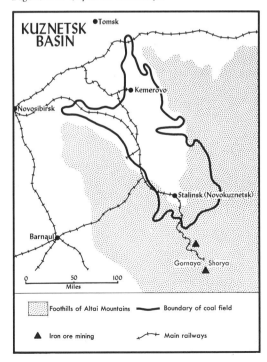

is to build here a second Donbass, a region of heavy industry.

Such economic development has nurtured several large cities within the past three decades. Novosibirsk, with nearly 900,000 citizens, is the metropolis of Siberia. It is the transportation pivot of the Kuznetsk industrial region, being located on both the Trans-Siberian railway, at a junction of lines to Novokuznetsk and Barnaul, and the Ob River, which is navigable to the north and to the south. Novosibirsk also has the greatest extent of manufacturing in these parts, with a wide variety of both producer and consumer goods. its shops turn out more machinery than any place else east of Chelyabinsk. Kemerovo, the largest mining city, has several chemical factories and produces thermal electric power. Stalinsk accounts for the most steel. Barnaul was the destination of thousands of factory workers from western Russia during the War; today it hums with numerous industries, particularly textiles, tanning, clothing, and food processing.

It seems certain now that the Kuzbass, whose remote location protects it from enemy attack, will experience substantial industrial growth in the years to come.

OTHER RUSSIAN MANUFACTURING AREAS

In line with Soviet policy, which seems bent on intensifying Siberian industrial development, new manufacturing centers are springing up far to the east of the Kuzbass. In several cities along the Siberian railway (such as Krasnoyarsk, Irkutsk, Ulan-Ude, Chita, Khabarovsk, and Vladivostok) factories are being built to process timber, minerals, and other primary products from the hinterlands or to manufacture items needed by settlers in those hinterlands, such as mining equipment, farm machinery, forestry equipment, and clothing. Petroleum requirements of these places are being met by a pair of pipelines (one for crude oil and one for refinery products) now under construction, paralleling the entire length of the Trans-Siberian Railway. By the end of 1961 they had been completed from Tuymazy (in the Volga-Ural field) to Krasnoyarsk.

The movement of Russians into Siberia since 1930—one of the great migrations of recent times—has stimulated the growth of a score of new cities in the vicinity of Krasnoyarsk and Irkutsk near Lake Baikal. Any number of industries are being developed, on a foundation of hydroelectric power which will come from the world's largest dams and inexpensive thermal power obtained from burning coal extracted economically from open-pit coal mines. A humid climate and rugged terrain provide excellent locations for hydroelectric installations and several are under construction. One of them is at Bratsk on the Angara River, which flows out of Lake Baikal. When completed, this dam will have the astonishing power capacity of 4,500,000 kilowatts, which is more than twice as great as the largest American dam at Grand Coulee. In addition, the Soviet Union may also have substantial atomic power projects hidden in the rugged countryside of this power-rich region.

Khabarovsk is rising as the industrial focus of southeastern Siberia wth a booming business in petroleum refining (oil from Sakhalin and the Volga-Ural region) and timber processing.

Detached from all the regions discussed so far are the industrial developments in the Causasus and in central Asia. The Caucasus foothills are the scene of Russia's oldest oil-drilling operations. Oil refineries and chemical factories are the basic industries here, Baku and Tbilisi the principal industrial cities.

In Central Asia, 800 miles east of the Caspian Sea, there is a narrow band of industrialization along the foothills of the Tien Shan mountains. The region's attractions for industry consist of water power from the lofty mountains to the southeast, vast reserves of natural gas from deposits recently uncovered near Bukhara, modest reserves of coal, some oil, and a few nonferrous metals. Furthermore, this region grows by far the bulk of the cotton in the Soviet Union—it is credited with 90 per cent of the Soviet output. A wide variety of industries have sprung up, especially cotton textiles and chemical fertilizers. Clearly, the dominant center of manufacturing is the city of Tashkent, with 930,000 people and the major machinery factories of Central Asia.

With so many industrial regions separated by such vast distances, the Soviet Union's transportation system is heavily strained. Railways now connect all these regions with one another, and waterways serve some of them. Probably 20 per cent of all the inanimate energy consumed in Russia is expended on transportation to overcome these vast distances; compare this with 12 per cent in the United States and 7 per cent in Britain.

Southeast Asia

From the standpoint of industrial development, eastern Asia is something of an enigma. Here is an area where peoples had attained a high level of culture thousands of years ago at a time when the inhabitants of Europe and Anglo-America were still in the Stone Age, or scarcely out of it. And there is persuasive evidence that the Chinese did the first melting and casting of iron. Yet, the steps upward into industrialization were first taken by men elsewhere, and the Far East has persisted through the past couple of centuries as an agricultural realm where most production remains on the subsistence level.

Today, the major nations of southeast Asia are endeavoring to change the nature of their economic activity. Specifically, they are endeavoring to industrialize an economy which, at present, is distinguished by three main attributes.

1. An exceedingly high percentage of the labor force is in agriculture, reaching such proportions as perhaps 80 per cent in China, 70 per cent in India, and 40 per cent in Japan. The comparable figure for the United States is 9 per cent.

2. Productivity per farm worker is low. The main reason for this is that readily arable land is scarce. There simply is too little land and too many people trying to earn a living off it. Land holdings, divided through generations and parceled out among progeny, have become exceedingly small, with two serious consequences: (a) even under intense hand tillage, production per worker is meager, and (b) there is not enough farming to do to keep a man busy full time. The result is a vast amount of agricultural underemployment, which means that a country's *total* agricultural production *could* be maintained by a much smaller labor force working *full* time. Some authorities estimate that in Japan there are 5,000,000 "underemployed" farmers; the estimate for India is an astonishing 25,000,000! One sobering consequence of the population explosion in the Far East is that much of the population increment is swelling the numbers of already underemployed agricultural laborers. The significance of all this to manufacturing is, of course, that agricultural underemployment constitutes a potential labor force for industry.

3. Average per capita income is low. Mainland China, with nigh onto 700,000,000 inhabitants has a total net national economic product no larger than that of West Germany with 1/13 as many people. India's 450,000,000 people produce, altogether, a national product about the size of that produced by Canada's 16,000,000 inhabitants. In Table 25-1, we see the per capita national product of the three largest Far Eastern nations compared to selected industrialized nations elsewhere. The facts of this table point up what John E. Orchard describes as the "contrast of wealth

Table **25-1** *Per Capita National Product (in United States Dollars)*

Far Eastern Nations	
China	57
India	62
Japan	229
Selected Industrialized Nations	
Italy	380
West Germany	673
United Kingdom	897
United States	2051

Source: John E. Orchard, "Industrialization in Japan, China Mainland, and India," *Annals*, Association of American Geographers (1960), p. 196.

and poverty between ... Western nations and most of the rest of the world ... the most important and fateful fact of the world today."

For these three reasons the Far Eastern nations have launched programs to increase the roles played by manufacturing and primary production in their total national economic life.

Industrialization will undoubtedly increase the number of jobs in these countries. The question is: Will the number of such jobs be enough to absorb the steady increase in the number of employable human beings? Can job opportunities match that number *and* absorb some of the agriculturally underemployed? The answers to both questions are likely to be negative for a good many years to come.

It is unrealistic, therefore, to anticipate any significant reduction in the absolute numbers of workers engaged in agriculture in China or India. For an indefinite period they will remain high. Indeed, those countries will be fortunate if capital formation and industrial expansion can proceed at a rate sufficiently rapid to absorb the new additions to manpower. The experience of Japan in the modern period would seem to substantiate such a prospect. From the opening of the country in the middle of the nineteenth century, the absolute number of farm workers has maintained, until the abnormal years immediately following World War II, a constant level of about 14 million. Industrialization has not broken into this hard core. Though it has succeeded in keeping pace with the increasing population and has absorbed the greater part of the new manpower, it has not solved the problem of the underemployed and the unemployed in the rural sector....

The over-all average productivity has improved. Agriculture itself has also benefited through some of the accompaniments of industrialization in the form of more scientific methods of cultivation, more effective application of fertilizer, some mechanical equipment, better seed selection, and the use of insecticides, all improvements contributing to greater productivity per worker. The urbanization resulting from industrialization has had the effect of providing a cash market for agricultural products.

These same trends are likely to hold also for China and India: expanding manufacturing will strive to absorb the new manpower; the percentage of gainfully employed in agriculture will then drop gradually as total population increases; urban centers will provide cash markets for agricultural produce; more capital will be employed on the land; agriculture will become somewhat more productive; the country's av-

erage per capita productivity will rise appreciably; the absolute numbers engaged in agriculture will undergo little change unless the commune organization of Mainland China can bring about more drastic shifts in occupations and in employment than have occurred in Japan.*

In undertaking their programs for industrialization, Far Eastern nations have both advantages and disadvantages. We can consider these under four general headings: manpower, technical skills, capital formation, and natural resources.

Manpower   Without question, the single greatest asset for industrialization in China, India, and Japan is their abundant labor supply. At present, much of this human asset is a wasted one, but it has tremendous productive potential. When properly trained, Far Eastern workers have demonstrated their ability to compete successfully on world markets for sales of textiles, apparel, nails, cameras, and many other items.

Technical and Administrative Skills   For now there is a deficiency in technical and administrative skills. To a certain extent this shortcoming can be ameliorated by importing foreign specialists. But an ever-increasing number of Far Easterners are studying abroad to acquire some of these skills and then returning home either to apply their skills directly to economic productivity or to pass them on to fellow countrymen in colleges and training schools. For years, Japan has sent young people to Europe and the United States for such training; China is now relying on Russia and her satellites for this type of education; India sends students to both camps. The magnitude of the movement of young scholars from the Far East to schools and training institutions in the United States is indicated in Table 25-2.

Capital Formation   No area can industrialize without available capital for purchasing machinery and other equipment and for

* John E. Orchard, "Industrialization in Japan, China Mainland, and India," *Annals*, Association of American Geographers (1960), pp. 196-197.

Table 25-2 Foreign Students
in the United States

Area	Number	Percentage
Total	48,486	100
Far East	17,175	35
China	4,546	9
India	3,772	8
Korea	2,474	5
Japan	2,168	4
Philippines	1,722	3
Thailand	1,000	2
Middle East	7,110	15
Iran	2,507	5
Turkey	835	2
Israel	807	2
Latin America	9,428	20
Mexico	1,356	3
Venezuela	1,126	2
Cuba	935	2
Jamaica	902	2
Africa	1,959	4
Egypt (U.A.R.)	490	1
Nigeria	258	—
Europe	6,362	13
Greece	1,095	2
United Kingdom	993	2
Italy	443	1
Canada	5,679	12

Source: Institute of International Education, *Open Doors* 1960, New York, pp. 21-23.

building factories and transportation systems. The Far East is even more seriously deficient in capital than in administrative and technical skills. Nor can it expect to procure enough capital from foreign sources. Capital is something that results from years of surplus productivity, first in such primary endeavors as farming, forestry, and fishing, and then in manufacturing and trade. History shows that surplus capital was slow in forming both in Europe and in Anglo-America. But accumulate it did, and the Industrial Revolution was partly a result of it and then a cause for more accumulation. "Money makes money" is true for societies as well as individuals. The question in the Far East is: Can present productive efforts generate enough surplus to start the chain of events that leads to adequate capital formation?

Natural Resources   None of the three largest Far Eastern countries has a particularly rich resource base for manufacturing. Japan is poorer than either China or India, and yet she preceded the other two in starting along the industrialized pathway. We shall mention some of the specific resource attributes of the three countries individually in the paragraphs to follow.

In China, the goals of industrialization are being pursued by a totalitarian government which has assumed complete control over practically all economic endeavor. Japan is employing different means—private enterprise —to reach the same end. India is following a middle-of-the-road philosophy; the state will be responsible for public utilities and industries of basic and strategic importance while remaining enterprises will be privately operated.

JAPAN

Japan is one of the more highly industrialized nations of the world. Most of her 5,000,-000 industrial workers are located in a manufacturing belt that runs through central Japan from Tokyo to northern Kyushu. This belt contains 80 per cent of Japanese factory workers and accounts for 90 per cent of the nation's steel. Within the last century, the Japanese economy has passed rapidly from the agrarian into the manufacturing stage in spite of several handicaps.

As we said, Japan does not have a strong resource base for manufacturing. To be sure, her water power and timber resources are considerable; she mines coal (especially in northern Kyushu), yet must import coking coal. Japanese iron mines (largely in Hokkaido) supply only a fraction of the iron ore required by blast furnaces; and these in turn are unable to supply the demand of the steel mills and fabricating factories. Some copper and a few other metals do come from Japanese mines, but again the local supply is inadequate. Japan is a spectacular example of a nation that has reached industrial eminence on the basis of cultural aptitudes. For the role of her factories in general is to process imported raw materials for export to foreign markets.

Home workshops and small factories are characteristic. Probably half of Japan's industrial manpower works in shops of five or less employees. Western-style factories appear, for the most part, only in the large cities.

For years, textiles were the outstanding industry, with silk and cotton fabrics the principal products. Silk fibers were produced in Japan but cotton fibers all were imported, mainly from the United States. Two main markets (East Asia and the United States) absorbed most of the product. In recent years, though, metal processing has expanded rapidly, as has the manufacturing of cameras, precision tools, and scientific instruments.

Four nodes punctuate Japan's industrial belt: the Kinki Plain, the Kwanto Plain, Nagoya, and northern Kyushu (Figure 25-6), all of which are tucked in among rugged hills and mountains.

The *Kinki* node centers on the three cities of Osaka, Kobe, and Kyoto. Textiles, secondary metal fabrication, shipbuilding, and chemicals as well as many of the artistic crafts are typical enterprises here.

The *Kwanto* plain industrial area consists mainly of Tokyo and Yokohama. Machinery, other metallic items, cameras, chemicals, textiles, and foods appear in this, the most diversified industrial part of Japan.

Nagoya is the least diversified of the four regions, being essentially a textile town.

Northern Kyushu, which is the only region with enough coal to support much manufacturing, is characterized by heavy industries: blast furnaces, steel mills, cement mills, and machinery producers. Manufacturing is dispersed through many small settlements rather than in large cities, partly because there is little level land here. Yawata manufactures 75 per cent of the nation's steel.

CHINA

Until recently China has been the least industrialized of the world's large nations, yet her resources for manufacturing appear to be substantial even if not outstanding.

China has noteworthy coal reserves, apparently exceeding those of the Soviet Union and almost equaling those of the United States. Most of the coal is located in two fields: Shensi-Shansi and Manchuria. The Manchu-

Figure 25-6 (*After John H. Thompson, from* Annals, *Association of American Geographers.*)

rian field is now the most productive, but the less accessible Shensi-Shansi field is vastly greater, containing 85 per cent of China's coal reserve, most of which is high-grade bituminous coal. Iron ore appears to be scattered in several places, notably southern Manchuria; lesser quantities occur in the lower Yangtze valley. Much of the ore has a low metal content however. Apparently, there are large deposits of bauxite. And several minerals (for instance, tungsten, antimony, tin, and kaolin) repose in the hills of southeastern China. China's water power potential is considerable; several power sites exist in the Yellow, Yangtze, Yalu, and Sungari river basins. As a percentage of China's total power production, water power rose from 9 per cent in 1949 to 20 per cent in 1962 and is expected to reach 40 per cent by 1970.

Most Chinese industrial employees live in the lower Yangtze area, particularly Shanghai, which is China's largest city and leading port. Cotton and silk textile plants, flour mills, and small machine shops are found there. The industrial area of the North China Plain contain Tientsin, China's second port, and Peiping, the Communist capital. Southern Manchuria is where most of China's iron and steel is produced. The totalitarian government now in power is endeavoring very rapidly to drive

Manufacturing Regions: U.S.S.R., Asia, Other

The first large-size open-hearth furnace, completed in 1959, in the Wuhan iron and steel works in central China. The Chinese report that it has the latest Soviet equipment, has a volume of 250 tons, and is only one of nine to be installed in the complex. (Eastfoto.)

the Chinese economy up from a primitive agrarian stage to an industrial level, duplicating the experience of western Europe, the United States, Japan, and the Soviet Union, all of which, at an earlier date and in different political climates, experienced the same transformation.

INDIA

India has almost 2,000,000 industrial employees. They are distributed, as mapped in Figure 25-7, page 462, in a dispersed pattern, with thick concentrations around the periphery of the country. The major zone is the large triangular southern peninsula, from Ahmadabad in the north to Tirunelveli in the south to Vishakhapatnam in the east. Bombay, with nearly 400,000 workers, is unquestionably the predominant industrial district. Cotton textiles form the leading Indian industry; and Bombay and Ahmadabad are the foremost cities in that business. The so-called "engineering" industries (machinery, electrical goods, trans-

port vehicles, and shipbuilding) rank second. Food processing predominates in the southernmost districts of India.

India's second zone runs northwest for a thousand miles from Calcutta across the border to Jammu in Pakistan. At the eastern end of this belt most of the world's jute is made. With a wide array of additional industries typical of port cities the Calcutta district provides as much employment as Bombay. Nowhere else in India do such large concentrations of manufacturing appear. Within 200 miles to the west of Calcutta we find virtually all of India's primary metal operations; local iron ore is smelted with local coal. The association of these two resources with such low labor costs makes pig iron from this locale the cheapest mass-produced raw iron on earth. Jamshedpur outproduces the other Indian iron centers. Many secondary metal fabricators have gone into business in Calcutta and nearby cities, thus setting this area apart as India's leading zone for "engineering" industries. Light manufactures (principally textiles and food—rice, flour, sugar, canned foods, and vegetable oils) typify the remainder of the industrial belt paralleling the Ganges and reaching far into West Pakistan; Kanpur, Delhi, and Jammu stand out here.

India's resource base is strong in some respects but weak in others. She has tremendous reserves of extremely rich iron ore, much of which is near enough to the surface for strip mining. Coal reserves, which exceed those of Japan but are much less than China's, are concentrated in the Northeast. India has considerable deposits of bauxite, manganese, mica, and chromite. As a basis for nuclear power developments, she has one of the world's best caches of uranium and thorium. The water power potential of the Himalayas is tremendous and the new Sutlej Dam (Table 14-8) will be among the twelve most powerful installations in the world. But unfortunately, the mountains are far from the heavy population and other resources that foster manufacturing.

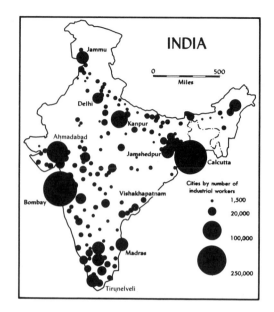

Figure 25-7 (After P. P. Karan, from Economic Geography.)

...history may record the industrialization of Japan, Mainland China, and India as the great economic event of the twentieth century...as the Industrial Revolution marked the eighteenth century, and the great expansion of world commerce, begun much earlier, marked the nineteenth. In effect, these two revolutionary developments, industrial and commercial, which spanned more than two centuries in their unfolding for the Western world, are now being brought in their full impact, in the brief space of a few decades, upon the three countries of Asia with 40% of the world's people. The results must be far reaching.

Here, in Japan, Mainland China, and India, is a laboratory for the economic geographer of magnificent proportions. It presents an infinite number of absorbing problems all inviting his study. If he is interested in man's utilization of his environment in meeting his economic needs, particularly if he is interested in changes in that utilization over time, a case study is unfolding for him in the three countries of East and South Asia and in their neighbors on a scale and with a speed never before witnessed in history.

More than half of the world's people are entering upon the task of altering, within a brief span of years, relationships with their surroundings that have persisted for centuries. Land and agriculture as the bases of economic life are giving way to energy sources, industrial raw materials, machines, manufacturing industry. Fundamental changes in the way of life of millions of people are inevitable.*

* John E. Orchard, ibid., pp. 201 and 215.

Suggested Readings

Brush, John E., "The Iron and Steel Industry in India," Geographical Review, 1952, pp. 37-55.

Estall, R. C., and Buchanan, R. O., Industrial Activity and Economic Geography, London, 1961, 232 pp.

Karan, P. P., and Jenkins, William M., "Geography of Manufacturing in India," Economic Geography, 1959, pp. 269-278.

Lonsdale, Richard E., "Industrial Location Planning in the Soviet Union," The Professional Geographer, November 1961, pp. 11-15.

———, and Thompson, John H., "A Map of the U.S.S.R.'s Manufacturing," Econ. Geog., 1960, pp. 36-52.

Shabad, Theodore, China's Changing Map, A Political and Economic Geography of the Chinese People's Republic, New York, 1956, 295 pp.

Thompson, John H., and Miyazaki, Michihiro, "A Map of Japan's Manufacturing," Geographical Review, 1959, pp. 1-17.

United Nations, Economic Commission for Asia and the Far East, Economic Survey of Asia and the Far East, Bangkok, 1959.

United Nations, Economic Commission for Latin America, Economic Survey of Latin America, New York, 1959.

Wu, Yuan-li, An Economic Survey of Communist China, New York, 1955, 566 pp.

PART SEVEN

TRANSPORTATION AND TRADE

Transportation is quite simply the movement of goods and people from place to place. Some persons also hold that communication, the movement of ideas from place to place, is a type of transportation.

From the standpoint of value, there are two types of transportation. The first is *economic* transportation by which goods and people are carried for the purpose of economic profit. The economist sometimes says that such transportation is a change in *place utility*—that is, the value of a commodity is worth more after it has been transported from its region of production to that of consumption. Grain pouring out of harvesting machinery in Kansas wheat fields has a certain value, but that wheat is worth more after it has been transported to Kansas City flour mills. Flour streaming from the milling machines in those factories has a certain value, but it is worth more after being transported to Chicago bakeries. Transportation accounts for such increase in value by moving commodities to locations of demand.

Noneconomic transportation includes all movements which are carried on for some purpose other than economic profit. Recreational travel and military logistics are two examples.

The significance of transportation in economic geography cannot be over-emphasized. In its own right transportation is an important *geographic element*—a spatial variable by which regions can be delimited and their characteristics studied, and in terms of which relationships can be analyzed, such as relationships among route location, traffic flow, and other phenomena. In addition, organized transportation is a *geographic factor*—an *influence* on the location of other economic activities; for without means of transport there would be no commercial coal mining, no production of surplus wheat, and no commercial lumbering. Without commercial transportation, in fact, the world's economy would remain at a subsistence level and regional specialization yielding exchangeable surpluses would be impossible.

We are all familiar with transportation in a practical way, but in Part Seven we shall consider the topic in terms of the basic categories of geographic method—location, characteristics, and relationships. Chapter 26 deals with the various means of transportation—railways, roads, waterways, airways, and pipelines. Chapter 27 covers international trade. Transportation hubs, however—places where routes converge that function as the nerve centers of trade—are reserved for Part Eight, which deals with service centers.

Ras Tanura, Saudi Arabia. This marine terminal is situated on a strip of sand that extends far into the Persian Gulf. The pier is enough off shore to allow the larger tankers to dock here. (Courtesy Standard Oil Company of New Jersey.)

TWENTY-SIX

In a sense, the transportation system of the world is analogous to several vital systems within the human body. One might say that the body keeps functioning by virtue of the finely adjusted co-ordination of several different transportation media, each with its own network: The nervous system conveys electrical impulses from the brain to the spinal cord and other parts of the body; the circulatory system keeps the blood cells moving; the lymph system circulates lymph; the alimentary system passes food and wastes along; and the respiratory system exchanges air between the lungs and the atmosphere.

The world's economy likewise depends on the interplay of several transportation systems: railways, roads, waterways, airways, and pipelines, plus the communication media—radio, telephone, telegraph, postal systems, and publications.

Because of this analogy with the human body, some economic geographers refer to transportation as the *world's circulation system*.

Railways

LOCATION

Distributed very unevenly over the surface of the earth are 780,000 miles of commercial railways. By the standard of *railway tracks*, we can readily discern two major regions and six minor ones. (See a map of world railways in almost any economic atlas.)

In Europe a remarkably dense network

spreads eastward from the Atlantic shores through the middle of the continent, gradually thinning out in the Soviet Union. Approximately 250,000 miles of track (nearly one-third of the world total) constitute this European network (*railnet* for short). In terms of track density (miles of line per unit of land, for instance, per every 100 square miles), western Europe is the foremost railway region of the world. Belgium, most notably, is interwoven with an average of 26 miles of railway line for every 100 square miles of land; comparable averages in other countries are 22 for United Kingdom, 21 for Switzerland, and 20 for West Germany. On the outer edges of this railnet, the national ratios drop to 2 in Norway, 6 in Sweden, 11 in Poland, 6 in Bulgaria, Rumania, and Yugoslavia, 12 in Italy, and 6 in Spain. Although her over-all ratio is less than one, the U.S.S.R. has approxmately 60,000 miles of railway, far more than France's 25,000, Britain's 20,000, and West Germany's 19,000.

Almost 280,000 miles of railway (37 per cent of the world total) stretch westward across North America from the Atlantic,

thinning out abruptly along the 100th meridian. With approximately 225,000 miles of track, the United States (Figure 26-1) has 29 per cent of the world total, or almost four times the density of the U.S.S.R. In the continental United States, there are 8 miles of track per 100 square miles, but by states this ratio varies widely, from 21 in Ohio to 1.5 in Nevada. Canada's network of 42,000 miles is surpassed in size, if not density, only by that of her neighbor to the south, and by the one in Russia.

The rest of the world has less than one-third of the total—roughly 250,000 miles. This track is distributed for the most part in six places. (1) In southern Asia, railways appear almost exclusively in India and Pakistan. The combined mileage is that of Canada, and the ratio of 2.6 approximates that of the European sector of Russia. (2) Railways are congested in eastern Asia (Japan, Korea and Manchuria). Japan has only 11,000 miles of line, but the area of the country is so small that the density exceeds seven. (3) Australia's 32,000 miles of track are almost entirely confined to the eastern and southern

Figure 26-1 (*From Association of American Railroads.*)

RAILWAY MAP OF THE UNITED STATES: 1960

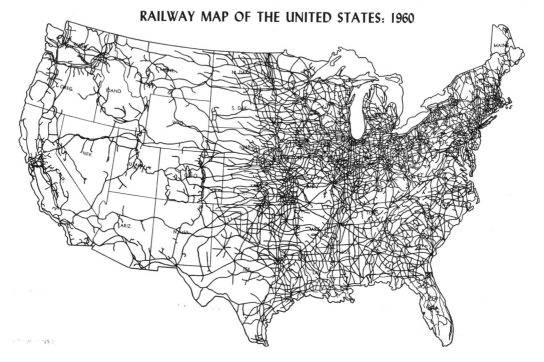

This view of Winnipeg, Manitoba, typifies the concentration of facilities in the major railway centers of the world. (*Courtesy Manitoba Department of Industry and Commerce.*)

fringes of the continent. (4) The southern tip of Africa is criss-crossed by a network as close as that of southeastern Australia. (5) Eastern Argentina, however, stands out with the densest railway pattern in the Southern Hemisphere. (6) Finally, a small but thick mesh of railway tracks spreads inland from coastal Brazil.

Elsewhere, railways are few and far between. The tropics have comparatively few rail lines and the Equator itself is crossed by less than half a dozen railroads. Most of South America, Africa, inner Asia, northern Asia, inner Australia, and northern North America are literally trackless.

CHARACTERISTICS

We could refine our picture of world railway lines *if* we could introduce into our maps information on such matters as: number of tracks (whether a line is four-track, double-track, or single-track makes a huge difference in its capacity for traffic), gauge of track (that is, the distance between the rails, which varies from six feet in a few countries to two-and-one half feet in others), weight of rail (heavier rails can support heavier carloads), type of traffic control (more traffic can move over an automatic central traffic control system than over one with few signal devices), and type of motive power (whether electric, coal-fired steam, wood-fired steam, or diesel-electric). Unfortunately, such data, and the maps derived from them, are extremely hard to come by.

Rights-of-way, however, are not the principal objects of analysis; at best they make up only the anatomy of the world's railways system. What we might call the physiology of the system is traffic, the flow of commodities and passengers. This constitutes the life of the railway. Fortunately, good maps do exist to show us some of the regional differences in freight and passenger traffic.

Freight Traffic   Figure 26-2 portrays the regional pattern of *freight* traffic quantified by means of the ratio of annual ton-miles of freight and miles of route. Ton-mile figures are determined by multiplying the tons of freight in each shipment by the mileage over which that shipment moves. A region's miles of route is a measure of miles of right-of-way regardless of number of tracks. As Table 26-1 and Figure 26-2 show, the Soviet Union is far ahead of any other nation—more than 6,500,000 ton-miles of freight traffic for every single mile of rail route. This astonishing

volume reflects both the large number of manufacturing areas separated by vast distances and the Soviet railway pattern of several main lines but few branch lines; thus, the traffic is concentrated on fewer miles of *route*. It is a principle of railway geography that of regions that are comparable in economic activity, the areas with a *fine* railway pattern (many lines close together) tend to have lower traffic densities than do areas with a *coarse* pattern (few lines far apart). China does not have many railways but if recent reports are accurate, freight now moves there with an intensity exceeding that of every nation except the Soviet Union (Table 26-1).

Most European nations report freight densities between one and two million ton-miles per route-mile. The highest densities (outside Russia) occur in Czechoslovakia and Poland whose surprisingly high figures exceed even those of West Germany. The main reason for this is that waterways carry more of the traffic burden in western Europe than in eastern Europe. Density in Canada approximates that of western Europe, whereas that of the United States is a little higher. Elsewhere in the world the only nations with over 1,000,000

Figure 26-2 (*After William Wallace and* Annals of the Association of American Geographers.)

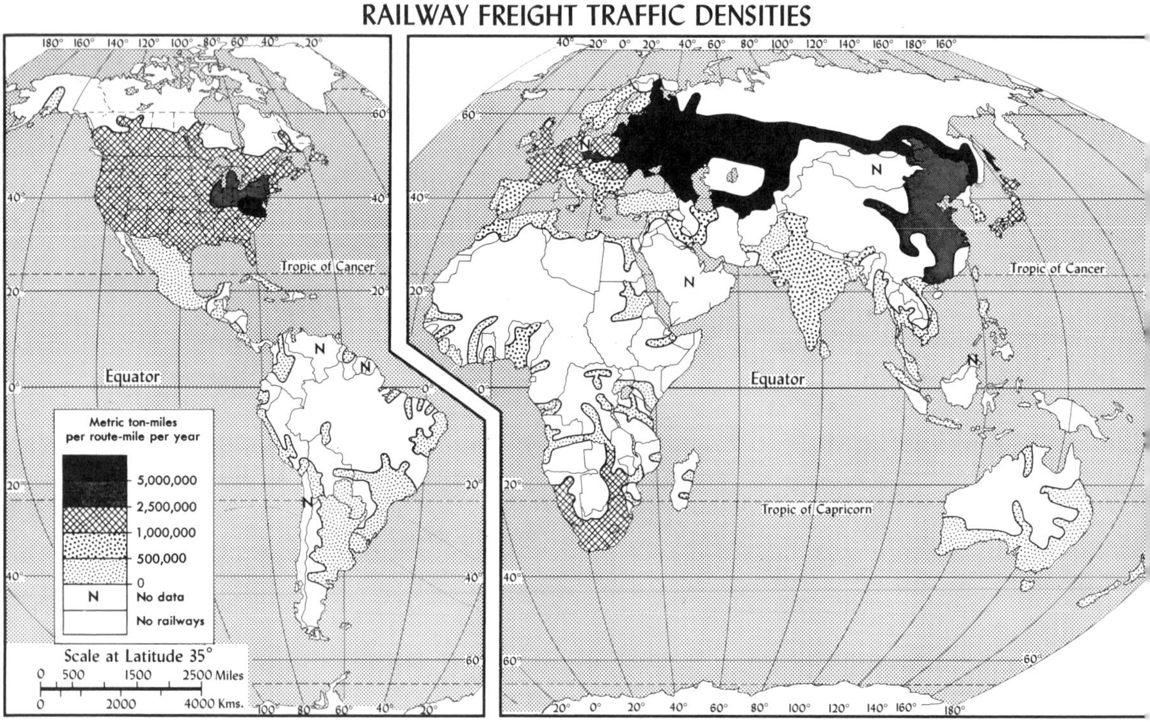

RAILWAY FREIGHT TRAFFIC DENSITIES

Table **26-1** *World Railroad Traffic Densities (Selected Nations)*

Rail System	Date	Thousands of Freight Ton-miles per Route-mile	Thousands of Passenger-miles per Route-mile
North America	1954		
Canada		1228	67
United States (total)		2223	130
Pocahontas		5118	73
Central Eastern		3377	300
Great Lakes		2906	200
Central Western		2211	128
Southern		2018	98
Southwestern		1718	50
Northwestern		1386	61
New England		1259	380
Mexico		427	136
South America			
Argentina	1954	361	321
Brazil	1953	238	300
Western Europe	1954		
West Germany		1705	1088
Great Britain		1179	1088
Belgium		1146	1538
Luxembourg		1065	520
Netherlands		1058	2214
France		1044	668
Austria		1008	862
Finland		849	429
Italy		785	1321
Sweden		613	407
Switzerland		520	1347
Denmark		268	710
Eastern Europe	1954		
Czechoslovakia		2149	no data
Poland		1777	1321
Romania		1150	1018
Bulgaria		894	590
Yugoslavia		824	558
Hungary		715	906
U.S.S.R.	1954	6652	no data
Asia			
China	1954	3617	607 (1948)
Japan	1954	1961	4341
India	1953	909	1139
South Korea	1954	715	1483
Indonesia	1954	639	155
Pakistan	1954	473	805
Africa	1954		
Rhodesia (N. and S.)		1310	no data
Union of South Africa		1087	no data
Morocco		912	342
Nigeria		579	185
Egypt		189	423
Australia	1953	250	no data

Source: William H. Wallace, "Railroad Traffic Densities and Patterns," *Annals of the Association of American Geographers*, Vol. 48, December 1958, pp. 354-356.

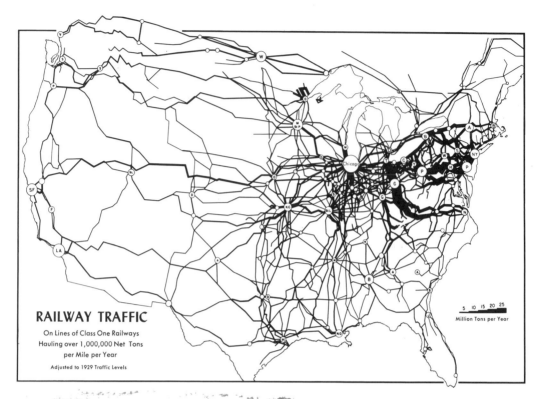

RAILWAY TRAFFIC

On Lines of Class One Railways
Hauling over 1,000,000 Net Tons
per Mile per Year

Adjusted to 1929 Traffic Levels

5 10 15 20 25
Million Tons per Year

Figure 26-3 (*Courtesy Edward L. Ullman, from* American Commodity Flow.)

ton-miles per route-mile are Japan (a bit ahead of West Germany), Rhodesia, and South Africa (where the boom in mining accounts for a heavy movement of ores), also Morocco and India.

Within the United States the Interstate Commerce Commission publishes traffic information for the eight regions listed in Table 26-1. Freight densities in these areas vary strikingly from over 5,000,000 in the Pocahontas region (which stretches from southeastern Ohio to eastern Virginia) to barely 1,000,000 in New England.

Figure 26-3 shows, by width of line, the freight density for the principal rail lines in the U.S. and Canada. The single most heavily trafficked *route* runs from the Pocahontas region through Columbus, to Toledo, Ohio. This represents, however, the combined flow of two parallel lines (the Norfolk and Western and the Chesapeake and Ohio) neither of which, alone, equals the tonnage carried by the Pennsylvania Railway between Harrisburg and Pittsburgh. The chief traffic item on

these routes is coal from Appalachian mines enroute to ports on the Great Lakes. Toledo is the foremost coal-shipping port in the country, and lake freighters pick up coal from its docks for delivery to Chicago, Milwaukee, Buffalo, and other lake ports, including those on the Canadian side. The heaviest railway traffic to and from the Atlantic Coast is concentrated in a very few routes that fall within a wedge bounded on the north by Boston and Buffalo and on the south by Norfolk and Cincinnati. A dearth of passes through Appalachia restricts the number of eastwest routes in this part of the country.

The Midwest has a different pattern. Traffic here is also heavy, but because of the flat terrain lines can run easily in many directions without much impediment. Consequently, the routes are more numerous and densities are lower than to the east. Because of so many routes, transport centers in the Midwest stand out sharply on a flow map: for instance, Chicago, St. Louis, and Kansas City. Northern Minnesota, too, looms up as a conspicuous

Means of Transportation

island of high density; this is attributable to shipments of iron ore from the iron ranges of Minnesota to Lake Superior ports.

Passenger Traffic   Spatial variation in passenger traffic is as striking as that in freight traffic. The total number of passenger-miles travelled in a region divided by that region's miles of right-of-way gives a ratio (passenger-miles per mile of route) by which regions can be compared. Thus, one passenger taking a 1000-mile trip would account for 1000 passenger-miles; 20 persons each taking a 50-mile trip would also produce 1000 passenger miles. Passenger traffic densities quantified in this manner range from a low of 1000 in Australia's Northern Territory to an astonishing 4,341,000 in Japan. Japan is in a class by herself, however, for the density there is twice that in the second-ranking country, the Netherlands (Table 26-1). Outside of Japan there are one small and two large areas of high passenger density: South Korea, Europe, and India (Figure 26-4). High rates prevail in the Netherlands, Belgium, Switzerland, Italy, Poland, West Germany, Britain, and Romania. France, perhaps unexpectedly, ranks rather low because of sparse travel in the southwestern half of the country. Traffic in India approximates that of Britain and Germany, and in South Korea exceeds it.

Within the United States the greatest amount of rail travel takes place in New England and between the East Coast (especially New York and Washington) and the Central states (notably Chicago and St. Louis). All are areas where commuters abound. For the country as a whole, railway passenger density is only 1/33 that of Japan, one reason—besides vast underpopulated stretches—being that over half the railway tracks in the United States no longer carry passenger trains.

Railway Rates   One might suppose that the price paid by customers for shipping freight would be commensurate with mileage. Although no world-wide study has been made to test the validity of this assumption, studies within the United States reveal that freight rates themselves are remarkably variable and that they do not vary consistently with either length or direction of shipment. Five aspects of freight rates illustrate this

Figure 26-4 (*After William Wallace and* Annals of the Association of American Geographers.)

RAILWAY PASSENGER TRAFFIC DENSITIES

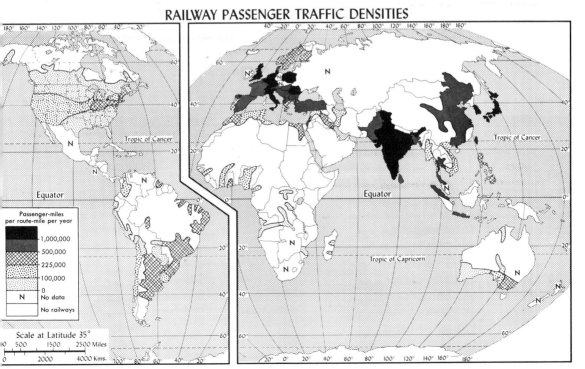

Passenger-miles per route-mile per year

- 1,000,000
- 500,000
- 225,000
- 100,000
- 0
- N No data
- No railways

Scale at Latitude 35°

UNITED STATES FREIGHT-RATE TERRITORIES

Index of Relative Levels	
Eastern or Official	100
Southern	139
Western Trunk-Line	147
Southwestern	175
Mountain Pacific	171

Figure 26-5 (*Source: U. S. Government, 75th Congress, First Session. The Interterritorial Freight-Rate Problem of the United States. House Document number 264, 1937, chart 4.*)

point: freight-rate territories, the rate-group principle, class rates, commodity rates, and in-transit rates.

1. *Freight-rate territories:* The freight rates charged by railways in the United States are regulated by the Interstate Commerce Commission. This agency divides the nation into five regions (see Figure 26-5). For several decades before 1937, when this map was constructed, the Commission authorized lower rates in the Eastern (or Official) Territory than anywhere else. As the map shows, prices were highest in the Mountain-Pacific Region, averaging 90 per cent more than those in Eastern Territory. The Interstate Commerce Commission defended this policy on the grounds that traffic was so heavy in the Eastern Territory that lower operating costs (per ton-mile) produced by the efficiencies of mass movement should be passed on to shippers in the form of lower rates. But this policy came under increasing attack from traffic agents in other parts of the nation arguing that the

rate structure of Figure 26-5 was discriminatory in favor of the Eastern Territory. In response to such pressure, spearheaded by the governors of southern states, the federal government in 1940 began gradually to reduce the differentials among the five regions. By 1952 all regions east of the Rockies were on equal footing.

2. *The rate-group principle:* One might suppose that along a railway radiating outward from a transportation center, rates would gradually increase with distance. But this is not true. Instead, the places along each route are divided up into groups, all the points in one group having the same rate. Consequently, profiles of freight-rate structures follow a stair-step pattern (Figure 26-6), not a curve.

3. *Class rates:* The Interstate Commerce Commission authorizes two types of rates: *class rates,* which apply to all items that move in small quantities, and *commodity rates,* which are applicable to a few items that move in large quantities. The rate-group principle is usually applied to class rates in such a

Means of Transportation

PROFILE OF RAILROAD CLASS-I FREIGHT RATES
to/from Milwaukee, 1953

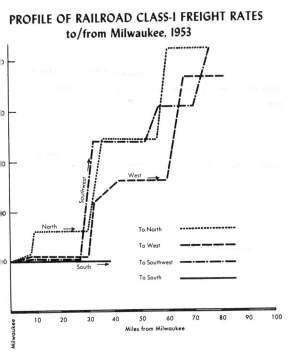

To North ········
To West ── ── ──
To Southwest ─·─·─·─
To South ─────

Miles from Milwaukee

Figure 26-6 (Courtesy Economic Geography.)

manner that there is at least a loose correlation with distance. Consequently, class-rate structures tend to be somewhat symmetrical;

Figure 26-7 (Courtesy Economic Geography.)

this is illustrated by Figure 26-7, which shows the pattern of class rates between Milwaukee and all points in Wisconsin. The lines on this map that connect points with equal freight rates are called *isophors*.

4. *Commodity rates:* Where the tonnage of a particular item is consistently large, the Commission permits a commodity rate that is lower than the class rate would be. For instance, in the rate structure within Wisconsin (Figure 26-8) on loads of coal from Milwaukee (Appalachian coal that has come in by ship), the northern part of the state enjoys a more favorable position than does the western part—because of competition from railroads linking the northern area with other ports on Lakes Michigan and Superior.

Clearly, railway freight charges do not always increase at the same rate in all directions around a shipping terminal (isophors are not circular) nor do they increase consistently with distance in any one direction. (Figure 11-6 is another illustration of this principle operative in the structure of commodity rates in Illinois on grain and cattle to Chicago.)

5. *In-transit rates:* These are privileges granted by the I.C.C. to factories located be-

Figure 26-8 (Courtesy Economic Geography.)

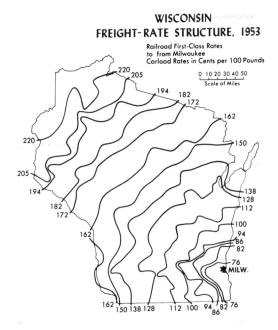

WISCONSIN
FREIGHT-RATE STRUCTURE, 1953

Railroad First-Class Rates
to from Milwaukee
Carload Rates in Cents per 100 Pounds

0 10 20 30 40 50
Scale of Miles

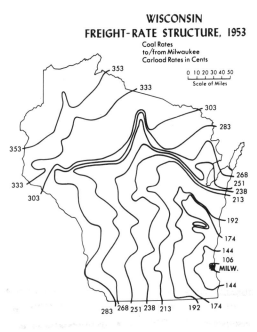

WISCONSIN
FREIGHT-RATE STRUCTURE, 1953

Coal Rates
to/from Milwaukee
Carload Rates in Cents

0 10 20 30 40 50
Scale of Miles

tween the origin and destination of a commodity. Sash and doors sold on the East Coast at one time were manufactured largely in Wisconsin factories from local pine. When Wisconsin's pine forests were cut away 50 years ago, these factories began buying raw material from saw mills in Oregon and Washington. But this resulted in two separate rates, one from the Pacific Northwest to Wisconsin and another from Wisconsin to the East. *Since freight costs tend to increase with distance but at a decreasing rate*, the through charge on a 3000-mile trip is less than the combination of one fee on the first 2000 miles plus a second on the final 1000 miles. The "in-transit" privilege permits a stop-over of raw material for processing before being shipped on to market—all at a *single through rate*. Such privileges are granted by the I.C.C. in only a few instances, but they spell the difference between life and death for factories located midway between raw materials and markets by enabling them to compete with factories located within the market areas. Most of Wisconsin's sash and door factories, for example (Chapter 18), would have vanished with the pine forests but for in-transit rates.

Advantages and Disadvantages of Railways The transportation advantages of railroads lie in their capacity for carrying *large volumes* of *heavy items* in comparatively *short time* at rather *low cost.* A five-man crew and a locomotive can haul a load of 100 or more cars averaging 40 tons per car. A drawback, however, is that it takes a good long time to assemble cars in a freight yard and then to link them together in proper sequence to form a train. Still, once underway, such a train moves at a relatively high speed. Again at the end of the journey it takes time to disconnect the cars and switch them around to the proper sidings for consignees. Consequently, railways are much better fitted for handling long shipments than they are for short hauls.

RELATIONSHIPS TO OTHER PHENOMENA

The relationships between rail transportation and other phenomena are essentially the same as those involving road, water, air, and pipeline transport. For this reason, we shall postpone a discussion of them until we have taken a look at the locations and characteristics of other media.

Roads and Highways

LOCATION

It is difficult to find or work up a map of the world's roads because concepts of just what constitutes a road vary so widely. In some places roads are wide and well-paved; elsewhere they are narrow and poorly, if at all, surfaced. One thing is sure, though, most roads are unsurfaced—mere ribbons of dirt track over the landscape. And yet such tracks constitute the major "highways" in vast underdeveloped regions. In general, though, the world pattern of surfaced roads resembles that of railroads, the main difference being that the road network covers a larger area, penetrating into areas where traffic is insufficient to demand a railway. The regions with the most highly developed road systems are Anglo-America, Europe, India, Pakistan, eastern Asia, southern Africa, and southeastern South America. At the other extreme are the great stretches of the earth's surface that are virtually unmarked by any semblance of a road: the vast northern expanses of North America and Eurasia, inner South America, inner Asia, inner Australia, and the islands of New Guinea and Borneo.

Within the United States the density of roads averages almost exactly one mile of road for one square mile of area. The highest ratio—2.1 to 1—obtains in Ohio where 41,000 square miles of land are interlaced with 85,000 miles of rural and intercity roads. The thinnest density—0.47—is in Nevada, where 23,000 miles of road serve 109,000 square miles.

CHARACTERISTICS

We can use numerous criteria to reveal differences among roads: width in feet, num-

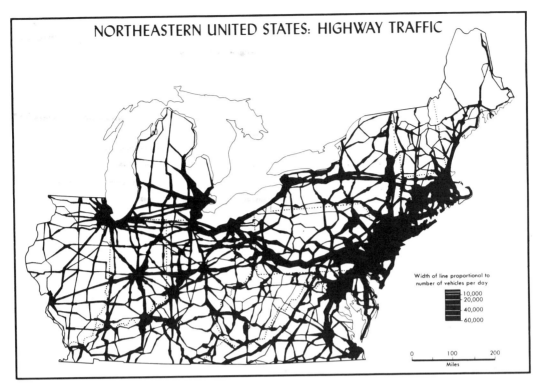

NORTHEASTERN UNITED STATES: HIGHWAY TRAFFIC

Width of line proportional to
number of vehicles per day

10,000
20,000
40,000
60,000

0   100   200
Miles

Figure 26-9

ber of lanes, type of surface, sharpness of
curves, and whether they are toll or free.
Depending on our objective, we could suggest
other criteria. But the most significant variable
for economic geography is traffic. In the
United States, the volume varies from hardly
any on some rural routes to about 60,000
vehicles a day on U.S. Highways 1 and 9
southwest of New York City. Traffic on the
major roads in the northeastern states, the most
heavily traveled road system in the world, is
shown in Figure 26-9. Within this region, the
densest belt extends from Washington to
Boston. Notice the close correlation between
large cities and high traffic densities. Traffic
thins out abruptly west of the 100th Meridan.
Between there and the West Coast, Denver
and Salt Lake City are the major convergence
points for highway traffic. Indeed, if we swept
our eye northward from El Paso, Texas, to
the Canadian border and made traffic counts
on all east-west highways encountered, the
total would not be much greater than that on
highways linking Buffalo and Albany. Representative counts of traffic on the three most
heavily traveled transcontinental highways in

the West are as follows: 2000 vehicles a day
on U.S. Highway 30 in southern Wyoming,
3000 and 4000 a day on Route 66 and Route
80 respectively in western New Mexico.

Roads are particularly adapted to moving
light loads *short* distances in brief *time*. On
short hauls, road transport actually costs less
than rail. In countries where the government
builds and maintains roads (but not railroads), shippers sometimes find it cheaper also
to send long shipments by truck. The contrasting advantages of the road for short
hauls and of the railroad for long ones has
led to the *piggy-back* practice which combines
the advantages of both forms. When the origin
of a shipment is several hundred miles from
its destination and neither is at a railway
terminus (thereby necessitating transfer between truck and rail at both ends), it is
practical to load the shipment in a truck,
drive the truck to the nearest railway terminal,
load the truck onto a railway flatcar which
carries it to the railway terminal nearest its
destination, and drive the truck off the flatcar
to complete the journey to the consignee.
Long trainloads of scarcely anything but

piggy-back flat cars are daily sights on railways between pairs of traffic centers such as Los Angeles and San Francisco, and Chicago and New York.

The discussion of road transportation in this chapter is markedly briefer than that for railroads, the main reason being dearth of data. It is much easier to collect, tabulate, and publish statistics on rail traffic. For instance, there are comparatively few railroad stations between which freight shipments and passenger journeys are made. Counts of passengers and tons can be made at these points. Moreover, there are no private carriers which use the railroad right-of-way; consequently, each railroad company—one single agency—can easily tabulate all the traffic that moves on its routes. Moreover, in the United States, the federal government has required railroads to submit complete reports of both freight and passenger traffic.

Traffic data on road transportation are much more difficult to come by. For one thing, the number of "terminals" which originate and terminate freight shipments (by truck) and passenger movements (by automobile) are

almost infinite. Moreover, there are millions of private carriers (passenger cars and private trucks) in addition to the common carriers (bus lines and commercial truck lines) operating on roads. This means that for road transportation there is a multitude of terminals and of operators. Finally, at least in the United States, the federal government does not require private operators (of either automobiles or trucks) to report on the location of trips or cargo carried. This is frustrating to the transport analyst in more ways than one, for it means that most road traffic cannot be measured (except by spot checks) and also that it is virtually impossible to segregate data on freight traffic from passenger traffic as is done so precisely for rail transportation.

The Interstate Highway System   A new era in highway transportation was opened in 1956 when the United States Government passed the Federal Aid Highway Act which made provision for construction of a 41,000-mile network of high-speed, limited access, divided super-highways threading throughout the 48 contiguous states (Figure 26-10).

Figure 26-10

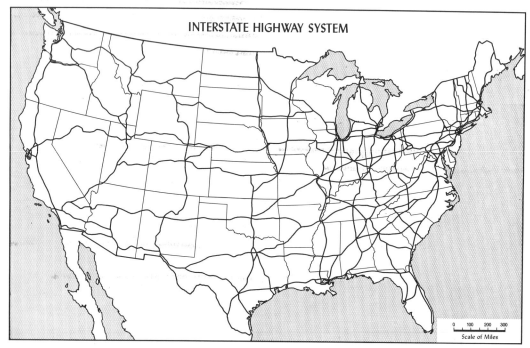

INTERSTATE HIGHWAY SYSTEM

0   100   200   300
Scale of Miles

Means of Transportation

The concept of the Interstate System dates back a number of years prior to implementation in 1956. Previous federal highway policy has resulted in the federal aid primary system of about a quarter of a million miles, the federal aid secondary system (the farm to market system), and certain national parks and forest roads. The result of this previous policy is a relatively fine-scale network linking urban centers of all classes with each other, and linking urban centers with their tributary areas. The Interstate System is more gross in scale—in a sense it lies on top of previous highway systems and it emphasizes linkages within and between major cities.

Perhaps two things may be gleaned from this brief statement. First, the Interstate System may be thought of as a large-city or metropolitan system of highways since it provides links between (and within) metropolitan areas. This represents a marked shift in federal policy because previous highway policy might be characterized as catering to rural areas and small urban centers. Another notion is that the Interstate System may be thought of as a new highway network. In many ways it is more comparable to networks of airline and railroad routes than present highway networks.

How far-reaching will be the location shifts following construction of the Interstate Highway System? The writer is inclined to the view that these changes will be as significant as those induced by other major technological changes in transportation systems—railroad developments or paving of rural roads. . . .

The Interstate Highway System is inducing changes in the relative location of urban centers and, thus, the success of activities within these centers. Locations of cities relative to each other are changing, city tributary areas are shifting, and the relative location of sites within cities is changing.*

Inland Waterways

LOCATION

Two major types of waterway can be distinguished for purposes of regional analysis: the ocean and inland waterways. Most commercial ocean transport involves international trade, which is the main topic in the next chapter. We shall concentrate on inland waterways here. Inland waterways carry tremendous tonnages in four parts of the world.

1. The rather flat plains of Europe and western Russia are laced with numerous rivers and canals, from Britain's Manchester Ship Canal on the west to Russia's Volga River on the east. The densest pattern of waterways in the world is in west central Europe, between the Seine River of France and the Oder River of Germany, a network that includes the world's most heavily trafficked river, the Rhine.

2. The American waterway system consists of two parts: the Great Lakes and the inland waterways. The Great Lakes are unique in

* William Garrison, "Connectivity of the Interstate Highway System," *Papers and Proceedings*, The Regional Science Association, (1960), pages 122-124.

Canals in western Europe carry considerable freight, with hundreds of barges and small vessels (as well as larger vessels on major rivers) moving through northeastern France, western Germany, Belgium, the Netherlands, and Luxembourg. (Courtesy France Actuelle.)

that tremendous vessels, larger than most ocean freighters, are able to navigate deep inside the continent. In 1959 these lakes were opened to large ocean vessels with the completion of new locks and deeper channels in the St. Lawrence River. The inland waterway system consists largely of the Mississippi and its tributaries as well as the intracoastal waterway which is a medley of canals and protected channels skirting the Gulf Coast and Atlantic Coast.

3. Vessels are much smaller but more numerous on the rivers and canals of Asia, particularly in eastern China (the Yangtze River and its canal connections with the North China Plain) and in northeastern India (where the Ganges River carries a heavy load). As for the economic role of these inland waterways, in the United States they carry 15 per cent of all inter-city freight traffic, in Europe, over 30 per cent, and in the Far East, over 50 per cent.

4. Considerable tonnages of freight in the Soviet Union move on the Volga and Don rivers (which were linked in the late 1950's by a canal), and on the Caspian and Black seas.

Elsewhere, as in the great Amazon valley and many valleys of Africa, waterways provide virtually the sole means of getting about. Although in traffic tonnages, they are dwarfed by the systems already mentioned, their relative significance to their regions is probably greater.

CHARACTERISTICS

Depth of channel; lengths of ice-free, high-water, and low-water seasons; and frequency of locks—these are some of the criteria by which we could construct informative maps of the world's waterways. Even more useful would be a map of traffic. Although such maps are not available on a worldwide scale, they are for some countries. To illustrate, Figure 26-11 portrays the movement on inland rivers and canals within the United States. In the whole western half of the country there is no commercial traffic on inland waters excepting the Columbia and Sacramento rivers. And on the East Coast there is only one noteworthy water route to the inte-

Figure 26-11 (*Courtesy Edward L. Ullman and Don Patton, from* American Commodity Flow.)

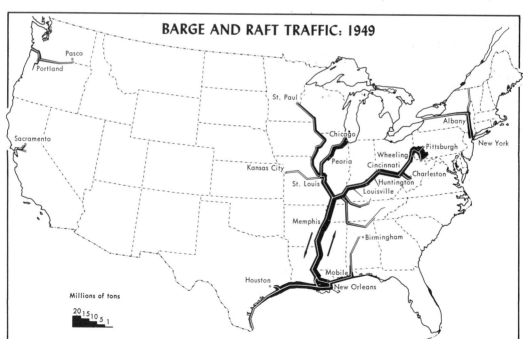

Means of Transportation

rior: the Hudson River-New York State Barge Canal. Clearly, the heart and arteries of the nation's inland water system (apart from the Great Lakes) are the Mississippi River and three major tributary systems: (a) the Ohio River, including *its* tributaries, the Allegheny and Monongahela (nearly 20,000,000 tons of coal a year float down the Monongahela to Pittsburgh—the heaviest inland water traffic, apart from the Great Lake routes, in the Western Hemisphere), (b) the Illinois River-Illinois Barge Canal to Chicago, and (c) the Intra-Coastal Waterway from Texas to Florida. Freight movement on the entire Mississippi system is much greater upstream than downstream since large quantities of petroleum, sulfur, chemicals, timber, and paper are shipped northward and eastward to the economic heartland. The nation's rivers and connecting canals carry 170,000,000 tons of freight annually, a volume only slightly exceeded by that of the Great Lakes.

Traffic on the Great Lakes falls into five main patterns. (1) Iron ore moves from Lake Superior ranges to Chicago, Gary, Detroit, and Lake Erie ports. (2) Coal is shipped from Toledo, Lorain, Ashtabula, and Conneaut (all on Lake Erie) to other lake ports. (3) Petroleum moves from refineries in the Chicago area to numerous lake cities. (4) Limestone is loaded at Calcite, Alpena, and other ports in northern Michigan for shipment to steel mills in cities to the south. (5) Wheat is carried from Duluth-Superior as well as Fort Williams and Port Arthur, to eastern ports. In addition, there is considerable traffic in a diversity of other items such as steel sheets, bars, rails, pipes, beams, and automobiles.

The advantage of inland waterways is cheapness. The disadvantages are that they often flow in the "wrong" direction (for example, the Mississippi and the Ohio), freeze over in winter (Great Lakes shipping is halted for four winter months), and are incapable of moving goods swiftly.

Coastal Shipping Although most ocean shipping is involved in international trade, there is one type that carries domestic traffic. The term *coastal shipping* sometimes is used to identify such movement. United States coastal shipping carries as much tonnage as Great Lakes shipping, with the heaviest traffic, by far, consisting of tanker loads of crude oil and refined products from the Gulf Coast to the Middle Atlantic Coast. Considerable tonnage of domestic traffic moves between the Atlantic and Pacific Coasts via the Panama Canal—a waterway movement termed *intercoastal.*

United States Domestic Waterborne Traffic Of all the tonnage moving in United States domestic water-borne traffic, petroleum and petroleum products are unquestionably the foremost commodity, accounting for 43 per cent of the total; other important items, with their percentages are coal and coke 18 per cent, sand-gravel-stone 13 per cent, iron ore and steel 8 per cent, and logs and timber 4 per cent.

Domestic waterborne traffic constitutes over 70 per cent of all the tonnage moving in and out of United States ports. The leading ports are ranked in Table 26-3, page 482, which reveals that for all Great Lakes ports and all but three of the leading coastal ports (Philadelphia, Baltimore, and Norfolk) domestic traffic exceeds foreign. For the port of New York, domestic traffic is twice that of foreign; for Houston (the nation's second-ranking port) domestic traffic is five times that of foreign. Table 26-3 also indicates the somewhat surprising fact that three of the nation's

Table 26-2 Principal Commodities Carried by Water in United States

Product	Percentage
Total Domestic Water-borne Traffic	100.0
Petroleum and Products	42.6
Coal and Coke	18.0
Sand, Gravel, Stone	12.7
Iron Ore, Iron, Steel	8.0
Logs and Lumber	4.0
Seashells	3.1
Chemicals	2.2
Grains	1.4
All others	8.0

Source: United States Army, Corps of Engineers, *Waterborne Commerce of the United States*, Part 5, National Summaries.

| Port | Total | Foreign | | Domestic |
		Imports	Exports	
UNITED STATES TOTAL	1052.4	213.5	112.1	726.8
Coastal Ports				
New York	154.1	39.1	6.8	108.2
Houston	60.2	3.3	6.8	50.1
New Orleans	50.4	5.2	7.2	38.0
Beaumont-Pt. Arthur	49.2	.3	2.7	46.0
Philadelphia	47.6	23.6	2.1	21.9
Baltimore	40.2	18.9	4.2	17.1
Norfolk	34.9	2.5	15.7	16.7
Los Angeles, Long Beach	26.6	5.7	4.6	16.3
Baton Rouge	25.6	4.0	3.1	18.5
San Francisco Bay ports	22.7	3.3	1.9	17.5
Boston	20.4	5.9	.7	13.8
Great Lakes Ports				
Chicago	39.9	1.9	1.6	36.4
Toledo	33.8	.9	5.4	27.5
Duluth-Superior	31.4	.1	3.3	28.0
Detroit	26.1	2.3	.5	23.3
Indiana Harbor	15.7	.6	.1	15.0
Buffalo	15.2	1.1	.2	13.9
Calcite, Michigan	14.5	—	—	14.5

Source: United States Army, Corps of Engineers, *Waterborne Commerce of the United States,* National Summaries.

four busiest ports are on the Gulf of Mexico. This is because most of our waterborne traffic is domestic, and most of our domestic waterborne tonnage is petroleum and products. In Chapter 15 we saw that the Gulf Coast is one of the world's foremost regions of surplus petroleum, and such ports as Houston, New Orleans, and Beaumont-Pt. Arthur ship tremendous quantities of petroleum to other domestic ports, especially Philadelphia, Baltimore, New York, and Boston. Norfolk is by far the nation's foremost exporter (over twice the outbound tonnage of New York or New Orleans), the product being mainly coal.

Airways

An airway simply extends from one point to another with all the intervening air theoretically available for travel. Actually, of course, airplanes usually follow charted routes marked by beacons and radio beams.

Air routes form a more extensive pattern across the globe than any other transport medium. They penetrate to some of the most remote portions of the world. No longer, in fact, are any extensive regions devoid of air transportation—a generalization that cannot be made for railways, roads, or waterways. Nevertheless, most of the world's air routes serve Anglo-America, Europe, western Russia, and the Far East.

We can map airway traffic according to traditional techniques, as in the preceding maps of traffic flow. But since there are so few points of access to air routes (as compared to roads and railways), it is feasible to plot air traffic in terms of *airport* business. We have adopted this technique in Figure 26-12 which portrays the airway traffic between *leading pairs* of cities. Since it is possible to purchase a ticket (or ship a package between any two commercial airports in the nation, the

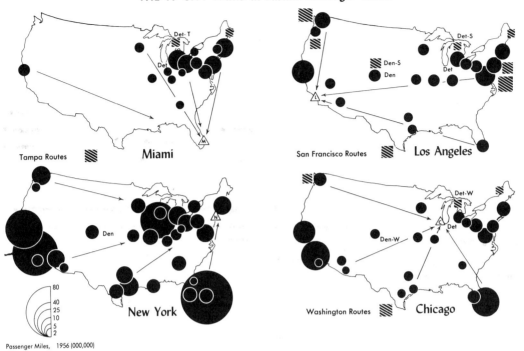

THE 99 CITY PAIRS in Airline Passenger Traffic

Tampa Routes   **Miami**

San Francisco Routes   **Los Angeles**

New York

Washington Routes   **Chicago**

Passenger Miles, 1956 (000,000)

Figure 26-12 (*Source: Edward J. Taaffe, "A Map Analysis of United States Airline Competition,"* The Journal of Air Law and Commerce, *Vol. 25, 1958, pp. 123-124.*)

theoretical number of pairs of stations is tremendous. As it turns out, however, 99 leading pairs of stations account for half of all commercial passenger-mileage. New York and Miami constitute the busiest pair. The next heaviest traffic is between New York and Los Angeles. In third place are New York and San Francisco, slightly ahead of New York and Chicago. Air traffic in the United States converges so intensely on a handful of cities that four of them (New York, Chicago, Los Angeles, and Miami) are involved in 87 of the 99 leading pairs. And the remaining 12 pairs involve either Washington, Tampa, or San Francisco. As Figure 26-12 shows, long-haul traffic is dominant. Most of the symbols stand for trips of at least 500 miles, and the largest ones represent flights exceeding 1000 miles.

Traffic Shadow Concept The number of cities with airports is small enough, and the government publishes enough data on air

passenger travel, so that a scholar can readily analyze certain locational aspects of commercial air passenger traffic. In a study which compared cities in terms of the ratio between the number of airline passenger departures and population, E. J. Taaffe found a *traffic shadow* existing around New York, Boston, Pittsburgh, Cleveland, Detroit, Chicago, San Francisco and a few other large cities. Traffic shadow occurs wherever (a) several cities are located close together, and (b) the largest city in the cluster acts as both the receiving and generating point of air traffic for the entire cluster. Evidence of traffic shadow appears where the ratio for the largest city in the cluster is above normal while the ratios for surrounding cities are below normal. Here are the reasons for traffic shadow: (a) In any cluster of cities the largest city tends to have the most frequent service and the fastest flights to distant terminals, and (b) to travel by air from an outlying member of a cluster to the major airport is likely to involve more time than to drive or take a taxi or bus directly to the airport. New York's traffic shadow extends over most Connecticut airports, over Albany, Scranton, Reading, Newark—and even Philadelphia! Washington's extends over Baltimore, Cleveland's over Akron and Canton, Detroit's over Toledo, and Chicago's over Milwaukee and South Bend.*

Pipelines

Most of the world's pipelines are threaded through three regions: the United States, Europe, and the Middle East. The United States network, which has expanded at a phenomenal rate, now exceeds 430,000 miles, nearly double the mileage of the nation's railways. The American network is actually composed of four entirely different systems: (1) The gas system, which conducts only natural gas, is the most extensive and runs mostly from the gas fields in Texas and adjacent states to the markets in the Northeast (from Nebraska to New England) and to those in California. Although California produces some gas, the state is becoming increasingly dependent on imports from New Mexico, Oklahoma, and Texas. The maximum diameter of these pipes is 42 inches. (2) The petroleum network carries crude oil and the numerous liquids refined from it. Its locational pattern is similar to that of gas pipelines except that the gas network is more extensive and penetrates into more remote places. Canadian petroleum from Alberta is piped across the continent to refineries in Sarnia, Ontario. (3) A third type of cross-country pipeline now moves coal. A 108-mile pipe, 10″ in diameter, was completed in 1947 to move coal from strip mines around Cadiz, Ohio, to a lakeshore thermal-electric power plant on the outskirts of Cleveland. At the Cadiz terminal the coal is powdered and suspended in water; this mixture (called slurry) enters the pipeline. Three pumping stations along the route lift this slurry up and over the rolling Ohio countryside. Delivery time averages 36 hours. At the Eastlake terminal, the slurry is dewatered and the resulting coal dust is blown into furnaces. This pipeline has been so successful that plans are now underway for a 350-mile pipeline to carry 10,000,000 tons of coal a year from West Virginia to Philadelphia and New York. (4) A pipeline and aqueduct system for moving fresh water extends from reservoirs in the Catskill mountains to New York City and from Owens valley to Los Angeles. Technologists are also experimenting with pipeline systems for transporting helium, oxygen, and nitrogen.

European pipelines distribute refined petroleum products from seaport plants to inland markets. Recently, however, the demand for oil derivatives in inland markets of Europe has skyrocketed and stimulated the development of inland refineries. At first these were supplied by crude oil barged up from seaports such as Rotterdam. In 1957 and in 1958 two pipelines were constructed from Wilhelmshaven and from Rotterdam to refineries in the Ruhr. July 1961 saw the beginning of construction of the longest pipeline in Europe, a 475-mile stretch of 34-inch pipe connecting Marseilles with Karlsruhe. This line will serve as a shortcut for Middle Eastern oil which otherwise would have to be shipped around Portugal to North Sea ports.

Pipelines in Russia move crude oil and derivatives from the two great oil fields (the Caucasus and the Volga) to the Industrial Center and the Ukraine and along the Trans-Siberian Railway.

The Middle East network functions primarily as a link between wells in the desert and the refineries and tanker docks located on the Persian Gulf and Mediterranean Sea (Figure 26-15, page 486). Notice how many national boundaries these lines cross. The number of disputes that could and do arise among the nations involved is considerable.

In concluding this discussion of the loca-

* Interesting analyses of traffic shadow and other aspects of air traffic appear in E. J. Taaffe's "Air Transportation and United States Urban Distribution," *Geographical Review*, 1956, pp. 219-38, and "The Urban Hierarchy: An Air Passenger Definition," *Economic Geography*, 1962, pp. 1-14.

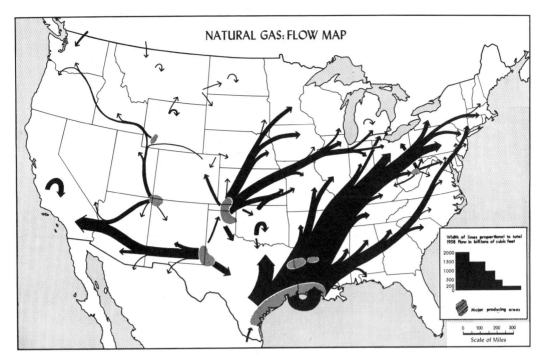

Figure 26-13 (*After James Lindberg.*)

Figure 26-14

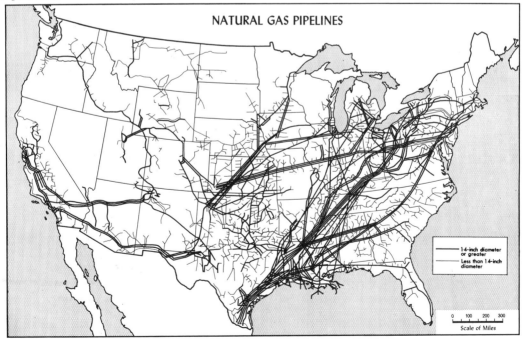

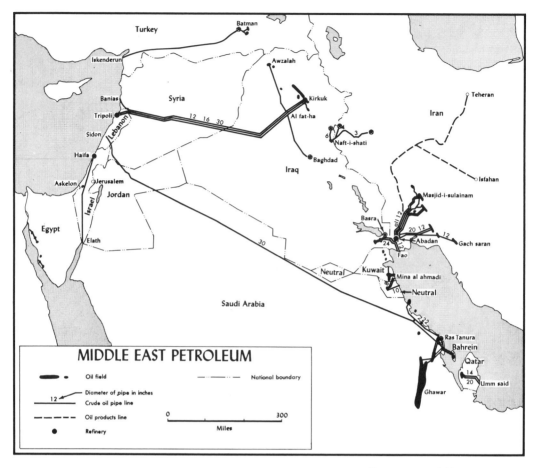

Figure 26-15 (*After* World Oil.)

tion and characteristics of the main means of transport, we must point out that economic geographers need a map of world transportation based on some system of classification by areal associations (or combinations) of transportation media. Such a classification system will enable us to plot world circulation by types of regions comparable to the mixed-farming areas that we touched upon back in Chapter 9.

Relationships between Transportation and Other Phenomena

Numerous forces interact to influence the flow of goods and people from place to place. Conversely, transportation has an influence on many other phenomena. The relationship is reciprocal.

The discussion that follows will mainly concentrate on relationships involved in *economic* transportation; little will be said about *non-economic* transportation, a distinction we made in the opening paragraph of the introduction to Part Seven.

GENERAL FACTORS

In general, six factors (or prerequisites) must be operative if economic transportation is to occur between any two points. We will illustrate these factors with North Dakota and Illinois as examples.

Means of Transportation

1. There must be a *surplus product*, such as wheat in North Dakota.

2. Illinois must *desire* the surplus product. The intensity of desire depends on the culture of the inhabitants of Illinois (that is, their "taste" for wheat flour and its products) and the insufficiency of their own wheat production. Illinois matches up with Dakota since it has millions of citizens who desire bread, pastries, and spaghetti made from wheat flour but who have insufficient grain to satisfy that desire. Where such a relationship exists between two places, they are said to be *complementary.*

3. North Dakota must have a *competitive advantage* in the production of her surplus. No matter how much wheat she produces beyond her own needs, she may fail in her bid for sales of wheat (or flour) to Illinois customers if other wheat growing regions produce wheat at less cost. From our preceding analyses of agriculture, mining, forestry, and other productive activities, we have seen that competitive advantage is the result of a more favorable natural environment, or a more favorable cultural endowment, or both. The advantages of North Dakota in both of these respects for wheat production were spelled out in Chapter 11.

4. Illinois must have the *ability to pay* for Dakota wheat. Ability to pay may take the form either of available currency or of a surplus of some commodity desired by Dakota people (for instance, corn starch, clothing, machinery, and telephones). Such a surplus and a competitive advantage in *its* production depend also on physical environment and cultural traits within Illinois as per 1 and 3.

5. There must be an absence of *intervening opportunity.* Complementariness alone does not bring about trade between two areas; only where there is no nearer complementary source to each will trade be encouraged between Dakota and Illinois.

6. Both ability to pay and absence of intervening opportunity are, in turn, influenced by *transferability*, that is, the *cost* of transportation measured by (a) the time required for the trip, and (b) money, or its equivalent in credit. No matter how perfectly complementary the two areas, no matter how complete the absence of intervening opportunity, there would be no trade in wheat from Dakota to Illinois if transfer costs exceeded the ability and the desire to pay.

The foregoing sextet of factors may operate through complex linkages involving several "third parties"; that is, the wheat need not necessarily go directly from Dakota to Illinois and machinery need not necessarily pass directly from Illinois to Dakota. For example, Dakota wheat might go to Minneapolis millers, the revenue thus received then being spent for shoes and gasoline purchased from Minneapolis distributors. The millers in turn might sell flour to Chicago bakeries, the revenue from such sales being paid out to the flour mills' labor force who use some of it to buy radios made in Chicago.

SELECTED SPECIFIC FACTORS

Several relationships involving railways, highways, waterways, airways, and pipelines apply to the group as a whole and are involved with the operation of the foregoing general factors.

Location of Population There is a moderate locational relationship between transportation and population; that is, the larger the population, the greater the transportation. The two glaring exceptions to this rule are China and India, which have most of the world's people but relatively little of the transportation facilities. Still, the two regions that stand out most boldly in the world patterns of railways, roads, waterways, airways, and pipelines are Europe and Anglo-America, which *are* two thickly peopled continents.

Correlation between population and transportation is closer as the scale becomes finer; that is, within the United States, within Europe, within India, within nearly every nation, the most densely populated areas throb with the greatest amount of transportation.

Other things being equal, an area with large numbers of people tends to have more circulation than one with fewer people. Conversely, transportation has had an influence on location of population. The great migrations of recent times (eastward into Siberia and westward into Anglo-America) have been expedited and even stimulated by transportation facilities. Here then is a reciprocal relationship, a "chicken-and-egg" matter. Which comes first is difficult to say, but it is certain that each influences the other and a chain reaction sets in.

Location of Surplus Production

A still closer correlation exists between production and transportation. Areas that generate a surplus of any commodity in economic demand also foster transportation media, often constructed in the face of stiff impediments, to move that surplus to potential customers. Iron ore lured railways into both Arctic Labrador and tropical Venezuela; coal drew railways up steep gradients of the winding valleys of the Appalachians; forests attracted railways into the Cascade Mountains. And conversely, once the transport arteries begin functioning, the volume of surplus production mounts.

The location of surpluses depends on interaction between the physical environment and cultural forces. An area cannot possibly have a surplus of coal unless nature endowed it with coal resources and unless the inhabitants possess cultural characteristics enabling them to transform the natural resource into an economic surplus. In chapter after chapter we have seen this principle at work—in the discussion of areas characterized by surplus wheat, or lumber, or milk, or machinery.

Location of Markets

As production can determine one end of transportation routes, consumption can fix the other end. Consumption is, in fact, the major cause for the intense development of transportation in Europe and Anglo-America, the world's two main markets. Those large markets, in turn, are due to the presence of large populations and large purchasing power per capita. In turn, a good circulation system has enabled these areas to develop a high standard of living with high purchasing potentials.

Industrialization and Urbanization

These two processes go hand in hand, influencing the spread of economic exchange. Many a railway spur and siding have been built in response to the construction of new factories. Cities invite roads, railways, pipelines, and airways. Whether on a world, nation, state, or county basis, the correlation between transport development and industrial urban development is high, as visual comparisons of the world pattern of manufacturing (page 292) and of major cities (page 520) with atlas maps of world railways, highways, waterways, pipelines, and airways will reveal. Unquestionably cities attract transportation.

Conversely, transportation is a maker of cities. A focus of routes is a favorable location for a city, and cities with the heaviest traffic tend to grow most rapidly. Furthermore, a decline of traffic can cause cities to shrivel. To illustrate: U.S. Highway 20 through New York State runs through many settlements; when the New York State Thruway was constructed, bypassing these settlements, it drained off so much traffic that many business districts suffered, and several gas stations, eating establishments, and other businesses along Route 20 experienced a sharp decline in trade.

A sizable settlement may even disappear from the face of the earth if transportation ceases to nourish it, as illustrated in the case of Grand Detour, which, in the early part of the 19th Century, was one of the major cities in the Rock River Valley of northwestern Illinois.

A grist mill was completed at Grand Detour in 1839, and from 1840 to 1855 it was the largest trade and industrial center in the county and one of the most important in the valley. Its ferry vied with Dixon's.... The great mistake made by the citizens of Grand Detour was to oppose the coming of the railroad under the mistaken idea that its business and manufactures would thereby be dissipated among various upstart towns. So the railroads all passed her by, and left her almost a deserted village.... Even the local post office was eventually discontinued and Grand Detour received its mail by rural delivery from Oregon [Illinois] *

* Way, R.B., *The Rock River Valley* (Chicago) 1926, p. 571.

Means of Transportation

A portion of the Mohawk Valley at Herkimer, New York. Several transportation arteries parallel one another in this part of the valley. From left to right: a local road, the Mohawk River, the New York State Barge Canal, the New York State Thruway, the New York Central Railroad, and the local streets of Herkimer. Railway men cite the above photo as a classic illustration of the subsidized competition they face. (Courtesy New York Central System.)

Culture Occidental culture has had a positive influence on the evolution of transportation. The invention of most of the machines and devices used for transportation today (other than the wheel itself) took place in the Western World. With inventions, the principle holds that improvements in carriers tend to precede improvements in route facilities. Better highways are built only after better vehicles are invented—and usually there is a noticeable time lag separating the two events.

Variation in culture from place to place is most important in explaining the kinds of surpluses that typify areas. North Carolina produces a surplus of tobacco not only because the climate and soils are favorable to this crop but because the men occupying that area have decided to be tobacco specialists.

In nearly every chapter of Parts Three through Six we have seen the importance of the cultural factor in explaining the surpluses of given areas. Were it not for spatial variation in the cultural factor, all areas with similar natural environments would tend to have identical surplus commodities.

Spatial variation in culture also explains certain types of consumption that typify areas. For example, peoples in different countries have developed different tastes; notice that the inhabitants of the United Kingdom and the United States have developed tastes for such nonindigenous beverages as tea and coffee. Every coffee bean and every tea leaf must be imported from distant lands, and considerable transportation is required to meet the demand. But the tastes are different in these two lands: the British are primarily tea drinkers (value of imports of tea into the United Kingdom is 8 times that of coffee—£112,000,000 to £14,000,000) while Americans are mainly coffee drinkers (annual imports of coffee are 21 times those of tea—$1,093,000,000 to $52,000,000). These tastes are associated with a brisk tea trade between the Far East and the United Kingdom and a lively business in coffee between Latin America and the United States.

Vulnerability to Economic Cycles   Improved linkage between regions unquestionably has raised the over-all level of economic development, but it probably has accentuated the variation between depressions and booms. Or, to put it another way, the less dependent an area is on trade with other areas, the less likely that it will be affected by economic fluctuations in those places. Any cyclical variation in the economy of a subsistence realm, for example, will depend solely on factors within its region. But when linkages are interwoven among many areas around the world, economic depression in one is likely to trigger destructive blasts in others.

Government   Government and politics, both national and international, strongly af-

fect the location of transportation. Here are a few examples.

Figure 26-16 presents the pattern of railway lines in an area sharply divided into two sections—not by a mountain range, nor by a deep canyon, but by an arbitrary boundary between Canada and the United States marked off on the flat lands of America's Great Plains.

In the last century the land-grant policy of the United States government was a powerful incentive to railway construction across the western grasslands. Prior to this encouragement there was scarcely any occupancy of these lands except along rivers—the arteries of transportation. But in subhumid lands, navigable waterways are few and far between. Hence, vast areas remained unsettled. Moreover, railway companies did not possess enough risk capital to engage in road building through expansive stretches of unpopulated land. But the federal government believed these lands should be occupied and adopted the policy of donating portions of the public domain to railway companies who would build. For 21 years, beginning in 1850 the government gave away 131,000,000 acres to railway companies, promising a minimum of

Figure 26-16 (*Adapted from August Lösch*, Die Räumliche Ordnung der Wirtschaft, *Jena, 1940, p. 292. Solid lines are railway lines.*)

CANADA-UNITED STATES BORDER AREA

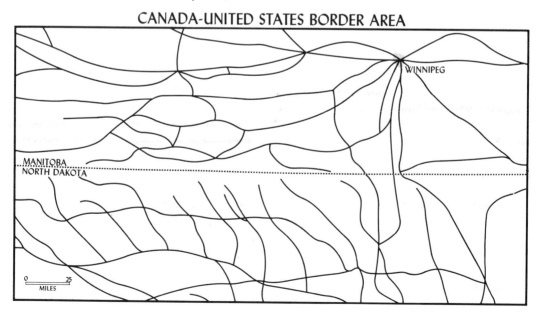

Means of Transportation

one square mile and a maximum of six square miles for every one mile of route laid down. The companies then could sell the land to settlers, thereby realizing earnings to pay for the road building.

Largely because of military as well as economic strategy, the government of Russia built the world's longest railway—the famous Trans-Siberian Railway—from Leningrad through Moscow and Novosibirsk to Vladivostok.

Government policy was also responsible for the construction from 1947 to 1951 of the Arabian railway (from Damman on the Persian Gulf to the capital at Riyadh, 366 miles to the west). Since there was no compelling economic demand for train transportation between these two points, the most plausible conclusion is that Ibn Saud, the Saudi Arabian monarch, had the road built for "status"—since in many underdeveloped parts of the world the presence of a railroad carries a certain amount of prestige.

Whether they are actively involved in the construction of canals and highways or offering inducements to the builders of railways, governments have been positive forces encouraging the growth of transportation. On the other hand, governments can play a role in stopping the circulation of goods. Tariffs and quotas are well-known techniques for this purpose. Less familiar, perhaps, is the type of influence exerted by the government of Iran in nationalizing the oil industry in the early 1950's. During 1950, over 240,000,000 barrels of oil passed through Iranian pipelines to ocean tankers for delivery to foreign markets. But Premier Mossadegh's government expropriated the oil business (whose facilities were largely owned by European and American companies), and the flow trickled down sharply to a mere 9,000,000 barrels in 1953. Traditional customers simply boycotted Iranian oil.

Land Values The relationship between land values and transportation is a fascinating one that apparently varies, depending on the transport medium and the stage of a region's development. Being near to railways tended to raise the value of land during the last century when Land Grant railroads were built. In the early 1850's the federal government had found no takers at $1 per acre for its public domain in the Midwest. But as soon as railways were built a brisk sale developed in land adjacent to the railways at the price of $3 an acre.

In urban areas, however, the relationship between railways and land values is more complex. As one travels out from a major rail center (say, Chicago) along a suburban railroad, he discovers that, as the miles go by, land values gradually rise and fall like giant waves at sea. The crests correspond with outlying settlements possessing a railway station while the troughs correspond with the rural areas between the station settlements. Moreover, the pitch of this imaginary wavy line is downward as one travels outward. Or in different words, as distance from the metropolis increases, the land value for each successive crest decreases. Similarly, each successive trough is slightly lower than the next one nearer the main city.

In addition, there is a relationship between land values and distance from the railroad measured at right angles to the right-of-way. For the first quarter mile, land values are low; beyond that distance they tend to rise and remain high for some distance (which may stretch as much as two miles) before values drop down to the level of those near the railroad. With further distance away from the tracks, values continue to drop. In other words, a suburban railroad can be said to run within a minor valley of land values which reposes within a much broader ridge of land values.*

The relationship between land values and highways indicates a strong tendency for land values (a) to vary directly with nearness to the highway, and (b) with passage of time, to rise more rapidly in proportion to nearness to the highway. Table 26-4 indicates (with data from several cities in diverse parts of

* For further analysis of this relationship see Charles R. Hayes "Suburban Residential Land Values Along the C.B.&Q. Railroad," *Land Economics*, 1957, pp. 177-181.

Table 26-4 *Change in Land Values and Proximity to Highways*

City	Freeway	Period	Change in Land Value		
			In Strip on Either Side of Freeway a Distance of 2 Blocks	In Entire Ward	In Entire Borough
New York	Shore Parkway	1939-1953	+ 76%	+ 19%	+ 14%
New York	Henry Hudson Parkway	1935-1953	+ 102%	− 23%	+ 5%
New York	Grand Central Parkway	1925-1953	+2038%	+501%	+232%
			Group A Contiguous to Freeway	Group B Separated from Freeway by Group A	
Houston	Gulf Freeway	1940-1955	+585%	+242%	
Dallas	Central Expressway	1941-1955	+431%	+100%	
			Industrial Subdivisions		
			Fronting Freeway	Not Fronting Freeway	
Oakland	Eastshore Freeway	1941-1953	+8600%	+5100%	

Source: Garrison, William L. and Marts, Marion E., *Influence of Highway Improvements on Urban Land: A Graphic Summary*, Highway Economic Studies, University of Washington, 1958, pp. 8-19.

the nation) that the value of land near a freeway tends to rise more sharply than that of land farther from the thoroughfare.

A similar relationship tends to exist between land values and pedestrian traffic. In cities where the sidewalk is the artery and the individual human being the "carrier," the greater the number of pedestrians, the higher the land value in dollars per front foot. Figure 26-17 illustrates the correlation between these two variables as measured along a portion of Halsted Street in Chicago.

The Influence of Transportation Media on One Another   On Figure 26-2, railway freight densities are lower in western Europe than in the Soviet Union partly because the numerous canals and rivers in the former region carry so much traffic. For the same reason, West Germany has a lower railway freight density than Poland (Table 26-1). In the United States, passenger travel on railways is so low (Figure 26-4) largely because of competition from highways and airways. Deep within Amazonia, boat traffic on the

Figure 26-17 *These two profiles suggest a close correlation between pedestrian traffic and land values within a city. (Courtesy Brian J. L. Berry from* Comparative Studies of Central Places, *Project Report NONR 2121-18, NR 389-126, February, 1962.)*

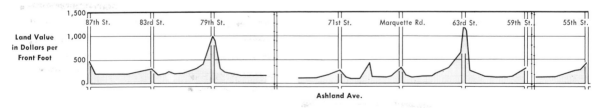

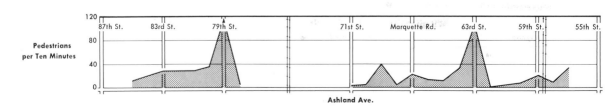

Madeira River (near the Bolivian border) was heavy enough to cause the construction of a 100-mile railway (which is hundreds of miles from any other railway) to function as a bypass around rapids and falls in the Madeira itself. Similarly isolated railways within the Belgian Congo perform the same function as did many routes within the United States during the early days of railroading.

Problem of Integration When transportation develops to the point that the government is involved either in regulating private enterprise or in constructing and operating facilities itself, the complex problem arises of how the railways, highways, waterways, airways, and pipelines can be integrated most efficiently. In the United States this problem is at the root of such questions as these: How free should railways and trucking companies be in setting their rates? Should the government build rights-of-way for trucks, boats, and airplanes but not for railways or pipelines? In the socialistic nations the problem is the same but the question becomes: What share of the national budget should go toward operations of railways, of canals, of roads, and of other transport media?

PHYSICAL FACTORS

Thus far, most of this discussion has dealt with relationships between transportation and cultural matters. Several physical factors are also important. The location of mineral resources such as coal in the Ukraine and iron ore in Quebec have been causal factors influencing railway construction. Forest resources discussed in Chapter 6 have stimulated construction of railways, roads, and flumes. Oases providing water and forage are key points determining the location of caravan routes across deserts. The Oregon Trail, over which thousands of migrants trekked between 1840 and 1870 with their oxen and horses, was located (at least in its stretches from Nebraska to Oregon) mainly according to the availability of three physical elements: water, grass, and firewood (for campsites). The Trail followed a winding rather than a straight course through Wyoming as men chose to go up and down gradients in the wooded foothills of the Laramie Range, the Rattlesnake Range, and the Green Mountains, rather than choosing to take the straighter, flatter route through southern Wyoming's desert. But when engines replaced oxen, the Oregon Trail faded from the scene (indeed, today it can scarcely be identified in much of Wyoming) because railway builders were more interested in straight routes with low gradients; the absence of grass and campfire wood was no hindrance to the railway which was built through southern Wyoming. Water shortage, though, was a handicap; so wells had to be dug at points along the route to supply locomotive tenders.

Topography is probably the physical factor most obviously related to the location of a land transport route. Other things being equal, the builders of transportation routes tend to select the lower gradients, as illustrated by the Hudson-Mohawk route through the Appalachians. Boston and New York probably would be more comparable in size and importance if the Berkshire Mountains were oriented east-west instead of north-south, so as to block off New York instead of Boston from the Mohawk Valley. If the prospects of economic gain are bright enough or the need of the military services strong enough, roads (such as the Burma Road), railroads (for example, several in Switzerland and Peru), airports (Dutch Harbor, Alaska), and pipelines are built in extremely rugged terrain. Men go to great expense in constructing transportation routes through inhospitable environments—if they are sure it will pay to do so.

Alexander, John W., Brown, S. Earl, and Dahlberg, Richard E., "Freight Rates: Selected Aspects of Uniform and Nodal Regions," *Economic Geography*, 1958, pp. 1-18.

Ballert, Albert G., "The Great Lakes Coal Trade: Present and Future," *Economic Geography*, 1953, pp. 48-59.

Bird, James, *The Geography of the Port of London*, London, 1957, 207 pp.

Carter, Richard E., "A Comparative Analysis of the United States Ports and Their Traffic Characteristics," *Economic Geography*, 1962, pp. 162-175.

Chang, Kuei-Sheng, "The Changing Railroad Pattern in Mainland China," *Geographical Review*, 1961, pp. 534-548.

Clark, Colin, "Transport: The Maker and Breaker of Cities," *Town Planning Review*, 1958, p. 239.

Garrison, William L., *The Benefit of Rural Roads to Rural Property*, Washington State Council for Highway Research, Seattle, 1956, 107 pp.

———; Berry, Brian, J. L.; Marble, Duane F.; Nystuen, John D.; and Morrill, Richard L., *Studies of Highway Development and Geographic Change*, Seattle, 1959, 291 pp.

Gould, Peter R., *The Development of the Transportation Pattern in Ghana*, Evanston, 1960, 163 pp.

Green, F. H. W., "Bus Services in the British Isles," *Geographical Review*, 1951, pp. 645-655.

Hance, William A., and Van Dongen, Irene S., "Matadi, Focus of Belgian African Transport," *Annals of the Association of American Geographers*, 1958, pp. 41-72.

Kish, George, "Soviet Air Transport," *Geographical Review*, 1958, pp. 309-320.

Lancaster, Jane, "A Railroad to Great Slave Lake," *The Professional Geographer*, September 1961, pp. 31-35.

Mayer, Harold M., "Prospects and Problems of the Port of Chicago," *Economic Geography*, 1955, pp. 95-125.

Murphey, Rhoads, "China's Transport Problem and Communist Planning," *Economic Geography*, 1956, pp. 17-28.

O'Dell, A. C., *Railways and Geography*, London, 1956, 198 pp.

Pattison, William D., "The Pacific Railroad Rediscovered," *Geographical Review*, 1962, pp. 25-36.

Patton, Donald, "The Traffic Pattern on American Inland Waterways," *Economic Geography*, 1956, pp. 29-37.

Pearcy, G. Etzel, and Alexander, Lewis M., "Pattern of Air Service Availability in the Eastern Hemisphere," *Economic Geography*, pp. 74-78.

——— and ———, "Pattern of Commercial Air Service Availability in the Western Hemisphere," *Economic Geography*, 1951, pp. 316-320.

Pfister, Richard L., "The Commodity Balance of Trade of the Pacific Northwest for Selected Years, 1929-1955," The Regional Science Association *Papers and Proceedings*, 1959, pp. 237-252.

Pounds, Norman J. G., "A Free and Secure Access to the Sea," *Annals of the Association of American Geographers*, 1959, pp. 256-268.

Rodgers, Allan L., "The Port of Genoa: External and Internal Relations," *Annals of the Association of American Geographers*, 1958, pp. 319-351.

Sampson, Henry, editor, *World Railways*, London, 1956, 462 pp.

Sealy, Kenneth R., *The Geography of Air Transport*, London, 1957, 207 pp.

Taaffe, Edward J., "Trends in Airline Passenger Traffic: A Geographic Case Study," *Annals of the Association of American Geographers*, 1959, pp. 393-408.

———, "The Urban Hierarchy: An Air Passenger Definition," *Economic Geography*, 1962, pp. 1-14.

Taaffe, Robert, *Rail Transportation and the Economic Development of Soviet Central Asia*, Chicago, 1960, 186 pp.

———, "Transportation and Regional Specialization: The Example of Soviet Central Asia," *Annals of the Association of American Geographers*, 1962, pp. 80-98.

Tavener, L. E., "The Port of Southampton," *Economic Geography*, 1960, pp. 260-273.

Thoman, Richard S., *Free Ports and Foreign Trade Zones*, Cambridge, Maryland, 1956, 203 pp.

Thomas, Benjamin E., "Railways and Ports in French West Africa," *Economic Geography*, 1957, pp. 1-15.

Thomas, Frank H., *The Denver and Rio Grande Western Railroad, A Geographic Analysis*, Evanston, 1960, 269 pp.

Ullman, Edward L., *American Commodity Flow*, Seattle, 1957, 215 pp.

———, "Rivers as Regional Bonds: The Columbia-Snake Example," *Geographical Review*, 1951, pp. 210-225.

Vance, James E., Jr., "The Oregon Trail and Union Pacific Railroad: A Contrast in Purpose," *Annals of the Association of American Geographers*, 1961, pp. 357-379.

Wallace, William H., "Railroad Traffic Densities and Patterns," *Annals of the Association of American Geographers*, 1958, pp. 352-374.

Weigend, Guido G., "Some Elements in the Study of Port Geography," *Geographical Review*, 1958, pp. 185-200.

Wiens, Herold J., "Riverine and Coastal Junks in China's Commerce," *Economic Geography*, 1955, pp. 248-264.

Wolfe, Roy I., "Transportation and Politics: The Example of Canada," *Annals of the Association of American Geographers*, 1962, pp. 176-190.

———, *An Annotated Bibliography of the Geography of Transportation*, Information Circular No. 29, Department of Highways, Ontario, 1961, 61 pp.

Wrigley, Robert Jr., "Pocatello, Idaho as a Railroad Center," *Economic Geography*, 1943, pp. 325-336.

The Royal Docks of London, downstream from the center of the city.
Land and water carriers make contact at this, one of the world's busiest ports.
(Courtesy British Information Services.)

TWENTY-SEVEN

International trade is of such significance to the world's political and economic life that it is worth being singled out for special consideration.

Approximately 130 countries submit reports on foreign trade to the United Nations, which publishes a valuable and informative *Yearbook of International Trade Statistics*. This source provides data on commodities exported, commodities imported, destinations of exports, sources of imports, and other aspects of trade. The annual value of exports from these nations is approximately $127 billion; the value of imports is $134 billion (Table 27-1). The difference between these figures represents for the most part the value added in transport, for obviously a commodity is worth more at the end of its journey than at the start because of the charges assessed for moving and insuring it. The few countries that do not submit data to the United Nations account for a relatively small volume of exports and imports. United Nations authorities estimate that their Yearbook covers 97 per cent of international trade.

LOCATION AND CHARACTERISTICS

We shall consider the where and what of international trade under the following headings: amount of trade, destination of exports, types of commodities exported, source of imports, types of commodities imported, balance of trade, balance of payments, and major ocean shipping routes.

Amount of Trade Western Europe and Anglo-America account for almost two-thirds

Table **27-1** *International Trade, 1960, in $ Billions*

Place	Imports	Exports
WORLD	134.3	127.5
Western Europe		
United Kingdom	12.3	9.9
West Germany	10.1	11.4
France	6.2	6.8
Netherlands	4.5	4.0
Italy	4.7	3.6
Belgium	3.9	3.7
Sweden	2.8	2.5
Switzerland	2.2	1.8
Denmark	1.8	1.4
Austria	1.4	1.1
Norway	1.4	0.8
Finland	1.0	0.9
Spain	0.7	0.7
Eastern Europe		
East Germany	1.9	1.9
Czechoslovakia	1.8	1.9
Poland	1.4	1.3
Hungary	0.9	0.8
Yugoslavia	0.8	0.5
Romania	0.6	0.7
Bulgaria	0.6	0.5
U.S.S.R.	5.6	5.5
Anglo-America		
United States	14.7	20.3
Canada	5.6	5.5
Latin America		
Venezuela	1.0	2.4
Brazil	1.4	1.2
Argentina	1.2	1.0
Mexico	1.1	0.7
Cuba	—	0.6
Colombia	0.5	0.4
Chile	0.5	0.4
Africa		
Union South Africa	1.5	1.2
Algeria	1.2	0.3
Egypt	0.6	0.5
Rhodesia	0.4	0.5
Nigeria	0.6	0.4
Congo	0.3	0.4
Morocco	0.4	0.3
British E. Africa	0.3	0.3
Ghana	0.3	0.2
Asia		
Japan	4.4	4.0
India	2.2	1.3
Malaya	0.7	0.9
Indonesia	0.5	0.8
Philippines	0.6	0.5
Pakistan	0.6	0.3
Iraq	0.3	0.6
Thailand	0.4	0.4
Israel	0.5	0.2
Burma	0.2	0.2
Syria	0.2	0.1
Lebanon	0.3	0.06
Others		
Australia	2.3	1.9
New Zealand	0.7	0.8

U.N. *Yearbk. of Intl. Trade Stat.*, 1960, Table A.

of the world's international trade. Western European nations together generate $107 billion worth of trade (exports plus imports), 40 per cent of the world total. Of the eleven leading trading nations, seven are western European (Table 27-1). The United Kingdom, West Germany, and France are each involved in the exchange of more goods than any other nation except the United States. The Netherlands, Belgium, and Italy are also high on the list. Anglo-America accounts for almost a fifth of all exports and imports. A $35 billion volume marks the United States as the world's foremost trading country. Canada does about one-third the volume of her southerly neighbor, which places her in fifth position, slightly ahead of the U.S.S.R.

If we think in terms of integrated economic regions, this picture of international trade alters somewhat. Thus, among European nations international trade is to a large extent a matter of traffic with one another. For instance, iron ore shipped from Sweden to Germany figures in the foreign trade of both. In contrast, iron ore shipped from Minnesota to Pennsylvania is counted as domestic trade within the United States. Now, if we take the position that intra-European trade (approximately $60 billion worth) is essentially domestic and therefore subtract it from the $107 billion total, we arrive at the figure of $47 billion for Europe's trade with other regions. Similarly, since Canada and the United States are each other's prime trading partners, if we subtract their mutual traffic from their $46 billion total, we have $29 billion left as the Anglo-America volume of trade with the rest of the world.

The remaining volume of world trade is widely dispersed. Asian countries that submit data to the United Nations (China is the main exception) together account for only slightly more trade than does the United Kingdom. Japan ranks eighth among the world's traders; India has a trade slightly less than Switzerland's; Malaya is roughly equal to that of Denmark or Brazil. The Soviet Union trades $11 billion worth, almost that of Canada. Soviet European satellites, led by East Germany report $16 billion. The

Latin American total is less than that of West Germany. Of the places with appreciable trade figures, Venezuela has a considerable margin over Brazil and Argentina. The sum for all of Africa slightly exceeds that of France. Australia and New Zealand are comparable to the lesser European nations.

Figure 27-1 portrays the locational pattern of international trade by presenting each nation's area in proportion to its share of exports and imports. More strikingly than words, this map illustrates the prominence of Europe and Anglo-America in international commodity exchange.

Destinations of Exports Where do exports go? Of the world's 100 leading trading countries, 64 report the nations of Europe as their top customers; for 29, Britain is the principal buyer; for 11 others, France is. Sixteen nations export primarily to the United States.

The strength of trading bonds can be ex-

pressed by the percentages of total exports from a country to its leading customer. Such proportions range strikingly from highs of 94 per cent (Panama to the United States) and 85 per cent (Somalia to Italy) to lows of 20 per cent (Argentina to the United Kingdom) and 9 per cent (West Germany to the Netherlands). Remember, these percentages stand for sales to each nation's principal market. For selected nations, Table 27-2 shows the strength of trade links in terms of the above percentage. Does this table suggest a correlation between size of this percentage and any other aspect of economic development?

For the world pattern of international trade in terms of destination of exports, see Figure 27-2. A word explaining this map is necessary. Each country's exports were tabulated in terms of individual consignee nations. These latter were grouped in terms of general world area, such as Europe, or Anglo-America. This done, it was possible to see which major world area received the lion's share of any nation's ex-

Figure 27-1 (*Courtesy Andreas and Lois Grotewold and* Economic Geography.)

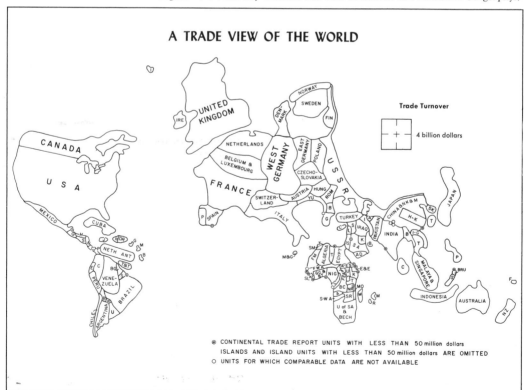

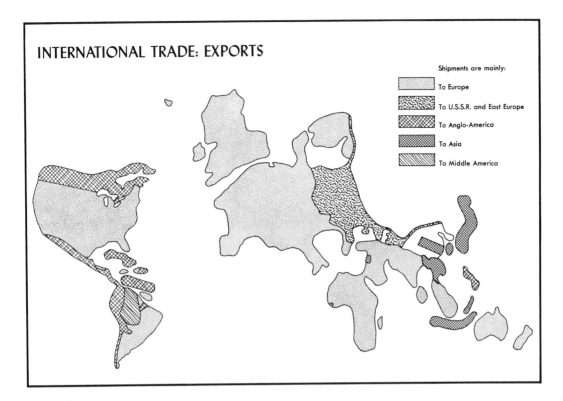

INTERNATIONAL TRADE: EXPORTS

Shipments are mainly:

To Europe
To U.S.S.R. and East Europe
To Anglo-America
To Asia
To Middle America

Figure 27-2

ports. Every nation which shipped more to Europe than to any other area was assigned to the category labeled "export-to-Europe." That realm, it turns out, covers most of the earth, blanketing every single country in Europe, penetrating eastward to India, south-

Table **27-2** *Exports to Leading Customers as a Percentage of Total Exports*

Nation	Percentage of Exports to Its Leading Customer
West Germany	9% to Netherlands
United Kingdom	10% to Australia
France	12% to Algeria
Japan	18% to United States
United States	19% to Canada
U.S.S.R.	20% to East Germany
Union of South Africa	28% to United Kingdom
India	33% to United Kingdom
Australia	37% to United Kingdom
Venezuela	40% to United States
Canada	61% to United States
Algeria	73% to France
Liberia	84% to United States
Panama	94% to United States

Source: Computed from data in United Nations, *Yearbook of International Trade Statistics.*

ward over virtually the entire continent of Africa, westward to the eastern portion of South America, and half way around the globe to Australia and New Zealand.

The "export-to-Anglo-America" realm is restricted to Canada and Latin America (generally the western countries) plus two distant anomalies: Liberia and the Philippines.

The nations in southeast Asia (from Japan on the north, Burma on the west, and Indonesia on the south) export principally to other Asian nations. Only two anomalous countries appear in this region: Malaya, which primarily ships things 8000 miles to Europe, and the Philippines, which sends most of its exports 6000 miles eastward to the United States.

Types of Exports A map of the world in terms of what commodities are exported (Figure 27-3) reveals four regional types.

1. *Manufactures and machinery* are the leading shipments from the United States,

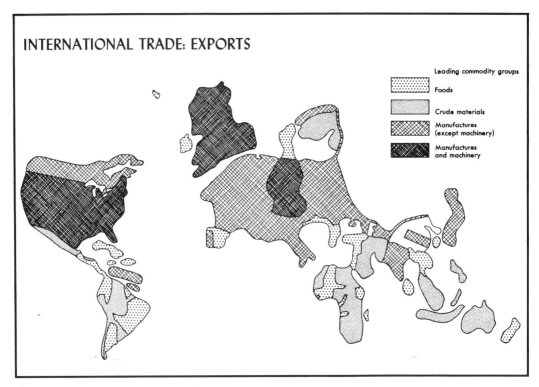

INTERNATIONAL TRADE: EXPORTS

Leading commodity groups

- Foods
- Crude materials
- Manufactures (except machinery)
- Manufactures and machinery

Figure 27-3

West Germany, and Britain; these two classes of commodities account for 73, 86, and 88 per cent respectively of the total exports of these three countries, by value.

2. Near each of these lands are others that export large quantities of *manufactures but not much machinery*; the most prominent (by percentage of manufactures in total exports) are Canada 40, Belgium 72, Austria 57, France 56, Switzerland 52, Italy 51, Norway 41, and the Netherlands 40. Far to the east are two nations whose economy has progressed to this stage: Japan 72 and India 40 (in India, perhaps unexpectedly, shipments of textiles and jute exceed those of tea). These data do not suggest that India is as highly industrialized a nation as the Netherlands; rather they say that whatever the value of India's exports, 40 per cent are represented by manufactured goods.

3. Countries whose leading export is *foods* are more numerous than those in any other category. Moreover, in such lands, foods attain phenomenally high percentages (and usually one or two crops dominate the structure) of total exports. Here are some examples: Mauritius 99 per cent (mostly sugar), Ghana 85 (cacao), Ecuador 93, (cacao and bananas), Colombia 86 (coffee), Costa Rica 98 (coffee and bananas), Dominican Republic 98 (sugar), Iceland 88 (fish), Ceylon 85 (tea), and Burma 84 (rice). Places where the leading export is foods are shown on Figure 27-3; this food group comprises much of Latin America, an outer ring around Europe (from Iceland through Spain to Greece and Turkey), about half of Africa, and a pocket of countries in the southeastern peninsula of Asia.

4. *Crude materials* lead the outbound parade from almost as many countries as foods do. Also, as in food-shipping countries, crude materials, usually one or two, reach very high percentages in the countries' exports: for instance, Pakistan 90 (largely jute and cotton), Brunei 99 (mostly petroleum), Liberia 95 (rubber), Egypt 87 (cotton), Bolivia 97 (tin), Venezuela 95 (petroleum), Surinam 93 (bauxite), and Finland 52

(wood). (This last is the highest European entry in this group.) This fourth category covers much of Africa, the Middle East, and the islands off southeast Asia from the Philippines to Australia.

The variation in exports according to these four categories are given in Table 27-3 for selected nations.

Sources of Imports   From where do imports come? Twenty-nine of the top 100 trading countries report the United Kingdom as the leading source of their imports. Since Great Britain was also the principal consignee for the exports of 29 nations she can claim the position of world's most active trading partner, at least in number of countries involved. Other European nations, France and West Germany in particular, are the main origins of imports for 36 other countries. Thus, two-thirds of the nations of the world import primarily from Europe.

The location of the import-from-Europe realm is shown in Figure 27-4 (constructed by the same method as was Figure 27-2); it blankets every European nation, thrusts its way eastward to India, leapfrogs over southeast Asia to Australia and New Zealand, absorbs every African country except Liberia, and crosses the Atlantic to Latin America. Notice how differently the Western Hemisphere shows up on the import-from-Europe map from what it does on the export-to-Europe map. This has profound implications for Europe's *balance of trade* which will be discussed later.

The import-from-Anglo-America bloc consists of 22 nations which are shown on Figure 27-4. This group includes several nations (primarily Japan and Brazil) that are in the European sphere on Figure 27-2. The main contrasts between Figures 27-2 and 27-4 are these: (a) The European region is larger on the export-to map than on the import-from map, (b) in contrast, the Anglo-American region is larger on the import-from than on the export-to map, and (c) Japan is in the import-from-America group but not the export-

Figure 27-4

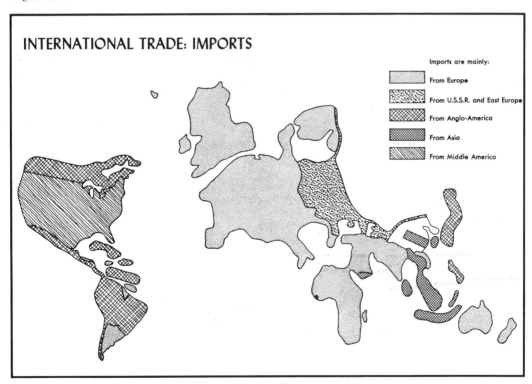

INTERNATIONAL TRADE: IMPORTS

Imports are mainly:

From Europe
From U.S.S.R. and East Europe
From Anglo-America
From Asia
From Middle America

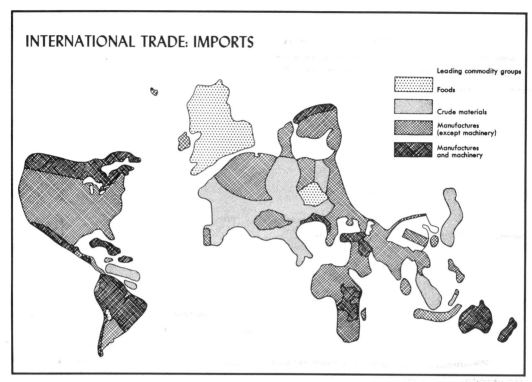

INTERNATIONAL TRADE: IMPORTS

Leading commodity groups

Foods
Crude materials
Manufactures (except machinery)
Manufactures and machinery

Figure 27-5

to-America one. The significance of these observations will be clearer when we get into the matter of balance-of-trade.

Similarity of Trade Linkages   One principle of international trade is this: A nation's leading trading partner tends to be both the leading consignee for its exports and leading source of its imports. This is true whether viewed on a nation-to-nation basis or a nation-to-area basis as a visual comparison of Figures 27-2 and 27-4 indicates.

Type of Imports   We can sort nations into four categories on the basis of imports, too. (1) *Manufactures and machinery* are the leading imports for 21 of the top trading nations, including Canada, Cuba, Mexico, Colombia, Venezuela, Brazil, Peru, Norway, Yugoslavia, Rhodesia, Iran, and Australia. (2) *Manufactures* (other than machinery) dominate the imports of 66 countries, by far the most numerous category. (3) *Foods* and (4) *crude materials* are the foremost imports for only 13 countries, but these include some

of the most vigorous traders: the United Kingdom, West Germany, and France.

Spatial variation by type of imports is mapped on Figure 27-5. The distribution conforms with the well-known principle that countries which export food and crude materials are likely to import manufactures and machinery, and vice-versa. That this principle is not a universal, however, is illustrated by the trading structures of six nations—the United States, Belgium, the Netherlands, Norway, Switzerland, and India—which show manufactures to be the leading import as well as the leading export.

Import structures tend to be far more diversified than export structures. To demonstrate this principle, compare Tables 27-3 and 27-4 (on pages 503 and 504).

Balance of Trade   Some nations have an even or nearly even flow of commodities in and out—for instance, East Germany's exports are valued at $1950 million, her imports at $1963 million. For most countries, however, there is a substantial discrepancy in the value

Table **27-3** *Export Structures of Selected Nations*

Percentages of Total Exports Accounted for
by Four Major Categories *

Place	Foods (Raw and Manufactured)	Crude Materials	Manufactures (Except Foods and Machinery)	Machinery Only
Anglo-America				
Canada	24	29	40 paper	7
United States	12	15	38	35 vehicles
Latin America				
Mexico	23	65 cotton	12	—
Venezuela	1	99 petroleum	—	—
Brazil	74 coffee	25	1	—
Argentina	62 grain	29	9	—
Western Europe				
United Kingdom	6	6	51 textiles	37 vehicles
West Germany	1	13	46 metal items	40
France	15	12	56 textiles	17
Netherlands	34 eggs	9	40	17
Belgium	3	13	72 metal items	12
Italy	24	7	51 textiles	18
Denmark	71 meat	6	9	14
Sweden	5	43 pulp	28	24
Norway	22	30	41 paper	7
Finland	3	52 wood	33 paper	12
Iceland	88 fish	9	3	—
Eastern Europe				
Poland	15	60 coal	20	5
U.S.S.R.	17	40 coal	28	15
Southwest Asia				
Turkey	68 tobacco	30	2	—
Iraq	10	90 petroleum	—	—
Israel	59 oranges	—	41 diamonds	—
Southeast Asia				
Japan	8	6	72 textiles	14
India	30 tea	25	45 textiles	—
Malaya	11	66 rubber	21	2
Indonesia	13	82 rubber	5	—
Pakistan	—	80 jute	20	—
Africa				
Egypt	5	89 cotton	6	—
Rhodesia	21	79 copper	—	—
Liberia	3	95 rubber	2	—
Australia	35	55 wool	9	1

Source: Computed from United Nations, *Yearbook of International Trade Statistics.*
* If any one commodity is pre-eminent it is identified.

of inbound and outbound goods. On the one hand are those countries that buy more than they sell—Japan, for instance, whose purchases abroad exceeded her sales abroad by $436,000,000 in 1960. At the other extreme are such nations as the United States and Venezuela whose exports greatly exceed imports. Countries with an excess of imports over exports are termed *trade debtor nations,* those in the reverse condition are called *trade creditor nations.*

The astonishing fact is that of the largest trading countries, almost 80 per cent are debtors. The size of the negative differentials varies from the $2.413 billion of the United Kingdom to as low as the $5 million of Paraguay. The nations with the largest commodity debt are listed by dollars of difference in

Table 27-4 *Import Structures of Selected Nations*

Percentages of Total Imports Accounted for
by Four Major Categories

Place	Foods (Raw and Manufactured)	Crude Materials	Manufactures (Except Foods and Machinery)	Machinery Only
Canada	11	17	40	32
United States	33	30	34	3
Argentina	10	23	37	30
Brazil	11	7	49	33
United Kingdom	40	40	16	4
West Germany	31	41	23	5
U.S.S.R.	14	35	27	24
Turkey	3	11	50	36
Japan	27	56	9	8
Malaya	29	38	25	8
Australia	7	11	53	29
Egypt	16	13	49	22

Source: Computed from United Nations, *Yearbook of International Trade Statistics.*

Table 27-5, Column A. In such a list, the United Kingdom would seem to be in a desperate position. But the size of the debt by itself may not be too meaningful without reference to total trade. Therefore, it is useful to look at negative differentials from another perspective—*the export/import index.*

If 100 is the index of perfect balance between inbound and outbound shipments, the greater the excess of imports over exports, the lower the index will be. On this basis, the countries with the most severely unbalanced trade are listed in Table 27-5, Column B.

The locational pattern of *trade debtor nations* is portrayed in Figure 27-6. Were it not for West Germany and France, Western Europe would be practically a solid mass of debtor nations. By contrast, the Soviet Union and three of her European satellites report favorable trade balances. African nations resemble those of western Europe in being almost entirely debtors; only Congo, Liberia, and Nigeria are creditors.

On the other side of the balance are the minority of *trade creditor nations*—the 20 per cent of the countries to which the other 80 per cent are obligated. The leading trade creditors are listed by dollars of differential in Table 27-6. The sizes of the positive dif-

ferentials range fantastically from such small surpluses as the $9 million of North Borneo to the $5626 billion of the United States. Other nations with copious credits are Venezuela and West Germany. The size of the surpluses quickly drops after these first three countries, however. Most of the trade creditors have surpluses smaller in value than the deficits of the largest trade debtors, which means,

Table 27-5 *Nations with the Largest NEGATIVE Differentials between Exports and Imports*

(A) Negative Differential in Millions of U.S. Dollars		(B) Export-Import Index	
United Kingdom	$2413	Lebanon	17
Italy	1071	Jordan	18
India	927	Panama	22
Algeria	871	Libya	24
Norway	581	Cambodia	27
Netherlands	503	Vietnam	27
Japan	436	Israel	34
Mexico	426	Cyprus	41
Australia	405	Greece	44
Switzerland	363	Algeria	45
South Africa	317	Mexico	53
Denmark	316	Uruguay	56
Sweden	309	Portugal	57

Source: Computed from United Nations, *Yearbook of Ir Trade Statistics,* 1960, Table A.

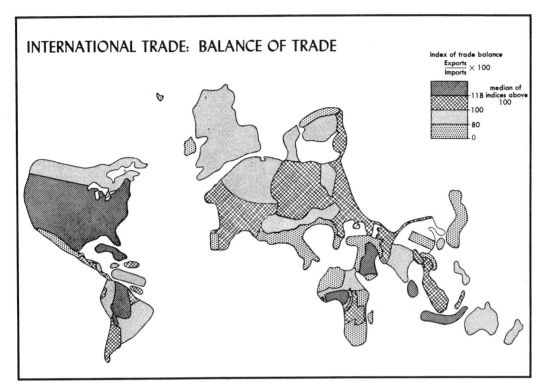

INTERNATIONAL TRADE: BALANCE OF TRADE

Index of trade balance

$\dfrac{\text{Exports}}{\text{Imports}} \times 100$

median of
118 indices above
100

100

80

0

Figure 27-6

of course, that most of the world's trade credit rests in the hands of a very few countries. The distribution of positive differentials (Figure 27-6) shows a heavy concentration in the Western Hemisphere.

The sharp spatial variation in trade differentials is a prominent feature of the geography of international trade; recognition of this condition is fundamental to understanding the economic problems of western Europe,

Japan, the United States, and other nations.

For an illustration of all the foregoing characteristics of international trade in a single nation, see Table 27-7, which identifies the leading exports, imports, consignees, and sources in the foreign trade structure of the United States. Inspection of Part A raises such questions as: What explains the contrast between United States trade with Argentina and that with Brazil? Between that with the Netherlands and that with Norway? Between that with Iran and that with Kuwait? Between that with Malaya and that with Pakistan? How might Israel make up its trade differential with the United States? The sum of United States imports and exports with the Soviet Union is $76,000,000 (roughly comparable to the trade between the United States and Liberia)—is this a surprisingly large amount, a surprisingly small amount—or not surprising? Why? Most of the above questions can be answered at least partially by considering Part B of Table 27-7 and material encountered elsewhere in this book.

Table **27-6**   *Nations with the Largest
POSITIVE Differentials
between Exports and Imports, 1957*

*Positive Differential
in Millions of U.S.
Dollars*   *Export-Import Index*

United States	$5626	Brunei	320
Venezuela	1355	Venezuela	185
West Germany	1312	Liberia	168
France	586	Indonesia	160
Indonesia	266	Dominican Rep.	139
Malaya	253	United States	137

Source: Computed from United Nations, *Yearbook of
Trade Statistics*, 1960, Table A.

Table 27-7 United States: International Trade, 1960 (Value in Millions of Dollars)

Total Imports: $14,652   Total Exports: $20,330

PART A: LEADING TRADING AREAS

Nation	Imports	Exports
Canada	2912	3633
Latin America		
Argentina	99	347
Brazil	563	422
Chile	202	195
Colombia	299	244
Cuba	342	222
Dominican R.	110	41
Ecuador	66	55
Mexico	445	802
Neth. Antilles	269	63
Peru	169	142
Venezuela	942	548
Western Europe		
Austria	50	80
Belg.-Lux.	363	423
Denmark	98	109
France	395	573
Italy	395	649
Netherlands	212	706
Norway	88	89
Sweden	170	299
Switzerland	196	246
W. Germany	895	1052
U. K.	996	1386
Others		
Finland	52	56
Spain	86	203
Poland	39	143
Yugoslavia	40	86
U.S.S.R.	22	54
Middle East		
Iran	53	117
Israel	27	118
Kuwait	124	41
Saudi Arabia	66	43
Turkey	71	125
Asia		
Hong Kong	136	121
India	230	639
Indonesia	216	86
Japan	1127	1325
Malaya	156	17
Pakistan	36	169
Philippines	307	294
Taiwan	20	110
Africa		
Congo	68	26
Egypt	25	151
Ghana	55	17
Liberia	39	36
South Africa	109	277
Australia	144	386
New Zealand	117	75

PART B: COMMODITIES

Imports		Exports	
Food	3390		3149
coffee	1003	wheat and flour	1026
sugar	553	tobacco and cigarettes	476
meat	326	corn	282
fish	304	rice	151
alcoholic beverages	275	dairy products	124
cocoa	166	fruit and nuts	100
tobacco	116		
bananas	80		
Crude materials	4947		5673
crude petroleum	951	cotton	980
petroleum products	596	petroleum products	454
chemicals	451	soybeans and soybean oil	443
wood	350	coal	353
rubber	326	steel scrap	244
iron ore	321	synthetic rubber	200
pulp and waste paper	305		
wool	240		
copper ore	229		
furs	95		
bauxite	78		
Manufactures (except machinery)	4394		4326
paper and board	731	iron and steel	657
textiles	552	textiles	492
iron and steel	483	copper	273
clothing	292	paper	255
precious stones	187	instruments	240
plywood	127	aluminum	149
copper	117		
nickel	116		
aluminum	107		
tin	87		
watches	70		
Machinery	1483		6952
motor vehicles	643	motor vehicles	1244
electrical machinery	319	aircraft	1229
agricultural machinery	89	construction and mining machinery	729
office machinery	69	agricultural machinery	532
		metalworking machinery	354
		radio equipment	335
		office machinery	221
		generators, motors	217
		power generating machinery	181
		air conditioning machinery	132

Source: United Nations, *Yearbook of International Trade Statistics*, 1960.

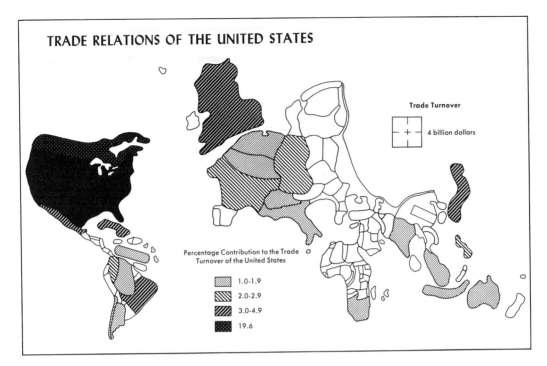

TRADE RELATIONS OF THE UNITED STATES

Trade Turnover

4 billion dollars

Percentage Contribution to the Trade
Turnover of the United States

1.0-1.9
2.0-2.9
3.0-4.9
19.6

Figure 27-7 (*Courtesy Andreas and Lois Grotewold and* Economic Geography.)

Balance of Payments International trade is only one component (albeit the major one) of economic interaction between nations. Nations sell not only goods but also services to one another—such as insurance, capital loans, and transportation services rendered by ocean vessels. Accordingly, economic geographers interested in economic interaction among nations should give attention not only to the flow of commodities (international trade) but also the total flow of money (and credit) between them. When this is done, it is possible to get a view of balance of payments for *all* economic exchange rather than only of balance of trade in commodities. Unfortunately, the geographic method of analysis has not yet been applied by many scholars to the topic of international payments; consequently, there is less material to weave into a textbook on this topic than on international trade.

Even so, information is readily available for some nations. Take the United States, for example: The story of our balance of payments is quite different from that of our balance of trade (Table 27-8). A statement explaining Table 27-8 is in order:

A balance of international payments is a record of a nation's total economic transactions with the rest of the world during a given period of time. It is not a balance sheet since it does not show a nation's total assets abroad or its total liabilities to foreigners, but rather provides a summary of its total receipts from foreign individuals, corporations, governments and international organizations, and its payments to them. It includes transactions related to the supplying of goods and services, the lending and investing of short- and long-term funds and the granting of aid.*

Inspection of Table 27-8 reveals that of all the credit built up in 1961 by this country in its economic activities abroad ($30.1 billion), most of it ($19.9 billion) was the result of sales of our merchandise. Almost all the remainder accrued to us through sales of our services. On the other side of the ledger, of the money and credit that left our hands ($32.6 billion) less than half ($14.6 billion) went to pay for commodities flowing into our ports, and still less ($5.6 billion) went to pay for services purchased from foreigners. The outflow of money for loans and grants came

* Federal Reserve Bank of Chicago, "What Is a Balance of International Payments?" *Business Conditions*, August 1962, p. 14.

to $8.0 billion. Much of this money enabled foreign countries to pay for commodities imported from us—thus "paying for" a substantial portion of our excess of commodity exports over imports ($5.3 billion).

London, Liverpool, Hamburg, Rotterdam, Antwerp, and Le Havre are the leading ports at

Table 27-8 *United States: Balance of International Payments 1961*
(Value in Billions of Dollars)

Type of Payment	Payments Going Out	Payments Coming In		Balance
Trade in commodities	14.6	19.9		+5.3
Exchange of services	5.6	4.3	−1.3	
Military transactions abroad (net)	3.0	0.4	−2.6	
Grants and loans (net)	8.0	3.7	−4.3	
Government	4.1	0.4		
Private Capital	3.9	0.3		
Repayments on U.S. Government loans	—	1.3		+1.3
Foreign loans and investments in United States	—	0.5		+0.5
Remittances and pensions	0.8	—	−0.8	
Unrecorded transactions (net)	0.6	—	−0.6	
Totals			−9.6	+7.1
Over-all Balance	32.6	30.1	−2.5	

Source: United States, Department of Commerce, Office of Business Economics, *Survey of Current Business*, March, 1962, p. 20, Table 1.

All told, our outbound payments exceeded our inbound payments by $2.5 billion in 1961 and have done so every year since 1958. How to overcome this negative balance is a major problem facing the federal government in dealing with the nation's economy.

Similar observations could be made of the balance of payments of other nations; such analysis will be a rewarding field for research.

Ocean Shipping Routes The location of ocean shipping routes (maps of which can be found in almost any economic atlas) * provides an additional perspective on the geography of international trade.

There are two outstanding trunk lines and six other major routes of ocean shipping— and most of them converge on western Europe.

* An excellent wall-map in colors of ocean transportation is the *Wall-Map of World Shipping* published by the Institut für Schiffahrtsforschung, Bremen. It shows sea-borne traffic in terms of both location of route and density of traffic for each of the following: passenger liners, refrigerated cargo shipping, tramp shipping, tanker trade, and ore-carrying shipping.

its eastern terminus, and New York, Philadelphia, Boston, Baltimore, and Montreal do most of the business at the western end. Most of the traffic on this route is of dry goods, particularly machinery, automobiles, clothing, and other manufactured items; wheat is the major foodstuff; there is very little tanker traffic. For most of the length of this route there are no ports of call along the way.

2. Almost as busy is the Mediterranean-Indian Ocean route which runs from west central Europe, around Spain, through the Straits of Gibraltar eastward for 2000 miles to the Suez Canal, and thence an additional 5000 miles to Singapore. Along this route are numerous ports-of-call, principally the oil-shipping ports on the Persian Gulf and on the eastern end of the Mediterranean. At Singapore the route fans out in several directions, primarily northeastward toward Hong Kong and Japan.

3. Linking western Europe to the Caribbean is a heavily-traveled artery over which petroleum, bananas, coffee, and other tropical

A portion of the port of New York as viewed from an altitude of 6500 feet—the Brooklyn shoreline in the foreground, Manhattan in the background, and the Jersey side to the left. The numerous bays and rivers in the New York-New Jersey Port have a frontage of 650 miles of navigable waterways along bulkheads. There are berths for 400 ocean-going ships at 200 deep-water piers. The harbor is ice-free and has a tidal range of 4½ feet; its main entrance channels have a depth of 45 feet. Ten railroads converge on this port, which has the world's largest rail terminal and yard storage capacity—it is capable of accommodating 5000 rail cars. Major highways likewise converge on metropolitan New York, which is served daily by an estimated average of 10,000 long-haul trucks. In 1921 the states of New York and New Jersey signed a compact creating the Port of New York Authority, which is charged with the responsibility of developing and operating terminal and transportation facilities within the Port District—an area with a radius of approximately 25 miles from the Statue of Liberty. The Authority now operates four airports, two tunnels, four bridges, as well as piers, and bus and truck terminals. (Courtesy the Port of New York Authority.)

products move eastward while manufactured goods flow westward.

4. Between Europe and eastern South America, particularly the ports of Rio de Janeiro, Santos, Montevideo, and Buenos Aires, there is heavy traffic.

5. A short but busy artery connects Caribbean America with Anglo-American ports—New Orleans and Galveston—in addition to the ones mentioned under Route 1. Petroleum, iron ore, bauxite, coffee, and bananas are major northbound commodities; automobiles and diverse machinery predominate in the southbound flow.

6. Considerable traffic moves between the West Coast of the United States and the Panama Canal where contact is made with routes mentioned earlier.

7. A noticeable volume of traffic flows between western Europe and southern Africa —and southeastern Australia. Elsewhere, ocean trade routes are dispersed widely over the oceans between latitudes 60° North and 50° South, but none of these routes—not even those crossing the Pacific—carry as much tonnage as the ones identified above.

8. A very dense but comparatively short ocean shipping route connects Tokyo Bay with northern Kyushu. Technically, this is not primarily a route in international trade; but it is mentioned here because it shows up so conspicuously on a map of ocean shipping.

RELATIONSHIPS OF INTERNATIONAL TRADE WITH POPULATION

To understand the location and the characteristics of international trade, we need to recall several relationships that apply to transportation in general, as presented in Chapter 26, and then go on to certain relationships that involve international trade particularly.

The world's total international trade of $261,000,000,000 (the sum of all imports and exports) averages out to around $90 per inhabitant of the earth. But the regional variation in this ratio is striking. The highest ratio prevails in the Netherlands Antilles where concentrated heavy traffic (largely the re-

fining of Venezuelan crude oil for the American and European markets) brings it up to $997 per inhabitant. Other countries with high values of foreign trade per capita are New Zealand $750, Belgium $750, Switzerland $720, Canada $700, Venezuela $690, the Netherlands $670, Sweden $638, Norway $600, Denmark $570, Australia $425, the United Kingdom $405, and Finland $402. The United States is above average, but not so high as these nations; the figure is $205.

At the opposite extreme are countries whose per capita foreign trade is far below the world average: India $9, Pakistan $9, Iran $16, Indonesia $21, Nigeria $23, Burma $26, Thailand $38, U.S.S.R. $41, Romania $43, Egypt $45, Spain $46, Philippines $48, Brazil $49, and Mexico $59.

A world map based on this relationship would show western Europe standing head and shoulders above all other regions (with such isolated exceptions as Venezuela, Netherlands Antilles, Canada, and New Zealand). Eastern Europe and Latin America are at a considerably lower level followed by most of the Asian and African nations. (Interesting questions arise at this point: Is there any correlation between an area's economic health and its per capita foreign trade? Other things being equal (especially level of economic development), does per capita trade tend to shrink with large population?)

TRADE AND POLITICAL ALLIANCES

National governments influence foreign trade in numerous ways, one of the most important being by legislative controls in the form of tariffs, quotas, and embargoes. Most countries also show favoritism to others with which they share some sort of political attachment. We can illustrate this point by six case studies: The Philippines, European colonial empires, the Benelux Customs Union, the Schuman Plan, the European Common Market, and the European Free Trade Association.

The Philippines The Philippines were a United States possession for half a century before they got their independence in 1947.

Although they are only 500 miles from the Asiatic mainland, they still trade principally with their former mistress, 6000 miles away. This situation reflects (a) trading habits established when they were receiving preferential treatment from the United States, and (b) continued preferences. This is the principal explanation of the Philippines' anomalous appearance on Figures 27-2 and 27-4.

European Colonial Empires Empire building led to preferential tariffs and quotas within several families of nations, such as the British Commonwealth, the French Union, and the countries under the rule of the Netherlands, of Belgium, and of Portugal. The influence of these connections is strongly visible in today's geography of foreign trade. For example, the Netherlands Antilles and Indonesia still trade mainly with the Netherlands; Guadeloupe, Algeria, and Vietnam (thousands of miles from one other) trade largely with France. British Honduras, South Africa, India, and Australia (on four widely separated continents) trade principally with Britain. The colonial past and the Commonwealth explain the strong attachment binding Australia to Britain: each is the leading trading partner of the other in spite of their 10,000-mile separation. That 29 nations report Britain as their foremost trading associate largely reflects the large number of nations in the British Commonwealth. Angola exchanges the largest amount of goods with Portugal; the Congo does much more business with Belgium than any other country; and two-thirds of Somalia's business is with Italy.

The power of such political factors cannot be exaggerated. When coupled with the concepts of complementarity and transferability (Chapter 26), they go far to explain why so many countries in Africa, Latin America, and Asia are in the astonishing position of doing ten times as much business with states thousands of miles away than with their neighbors next door. To illustrate, only 5 per cent of the Congo's trade is with African neighbors; Thailand reports scarcely any trade with Burma, China, and its eastern neighbors; British Guiana sells scarcely anything and buys nothing from Venezuela, Brazil, or Surinam; even landlocked Bolivia does only 12 per cent of her business with the countries around her.

Benelux On January 1, 1948, Belgium, the Netherlands, and Luxembourg inaugurated the Benelux Customs Union. The provisions of this agreement were (a) that there should be no tariff barriers on any commodities moving among the three (this meant that shipments of any commodity among them began moving as freely as between New York and Ohio), and (b) that the three should have one common set of tariffs on commodities imported from elsewhere (this meant that the trio functioned as a single region in world economic agreements). Immediately, the Benelux plan proved successful. Foreign trade as well as the over-all economy of the three countries advanced vigorously and stimulated speculation about the feasibility of expanding the idea to adjacent countries.

The Schuman Plan This was a cautious experiment for applying the Benelux scheme to more countries but on fewer commodities. In 1952, six nations (the Benelux trio plus West Germany, France, and Italy) launched a plan for their *steel* industries with these provisions: (a) all tariffs between the six countries were abolished on coal, iron ore, and scrap iron and, (b) on the world market for steel, the six nations were to act as a single competitor. In 1954 refined steel was added to their list of tariff-free goods. Known as the European Coal and Steel Community (ECSC), these six nations enjoyed a pronounced increase in production in all items covered by the Schuman Plan.

European Economic Community So successful was the Schuman Plan that in January, 1958, the six nations launched the *European Economic Community* (known more popularly as the "European Common Market" or EEC) which calls for (a) gradual removal of all barriers to trade among the member countries, (b) the establishment of a common external tariff, (c) the formulation of com-

Hamburg Harbor, one of the focal points of trade in the European Economic Community. In the immediate foreground are storage facilities along a canal. In the left center is a shipyard. Piers and terminals occupy the right center and near background. The city of Hamburg is in the distant background. (Courtesy German Information Center.)

mon policies for agriculture, transportation, and the development of all resources of the six states, and (d) provision for free movement of workers and capital.

A flexible timetable consisting of three stages was set up for achieving these goals. Completion date was planned to be no earlier than 1970 and no later than 1973. The first 10-per-cent reduction in tariffs went into effect in late 1959, the second 10-per-cent cut came in July 1960, the third in January 1961, the fourth in January 1962, and the fifth (the "halfway point") in July 1962—over a year ahead of schedule! At that time it looked as if the goal of complete tariff removal would be reached perhaps as early as 1966. By that time these six countries, from the standpoint of international trade, will constitute a single region which at present contains 180,000,000 people in an area half as large as eastern United States. The gross national product of the Common Market is $150 billion per year, about one-third of that in the United States,

but its annual rate of growth (4.5%) exceeds ours (3.8%). It seems certain that a vigorous new trade competitor has been born, a fact of utmost significance to the Soviet Union and to the United States.

In July 1961, a customs union was established between the EEC and Greece which should pave the way for Greece, at a later date, to become a regular member.

European Free Trade Association
Seven countries (Great Britain, Austria, Denmark, Norway, Portugal, Sweden, and Switzerland) endorsed a plan in July 1959, for a trade association among themselves. In May of 1960 the new organization *European Free Trade Association* (EFTA) officially came into existence. The members covenanted to gradually abolish tariffs among themselves. with 1970 being the deadline for tariff extermination. Each country, however, remained free to decide its own external tariff policies.

The first tariff reduction occurred in July

1960 (less than two months after the EFTA was launched), and was a full 20 per cent. The next cut (10 per cent) came in July 1961 —six months ahead of schedule. The third cut—scheduled for July 1963—was accomplished in March 1962. The fourth cut (leaving tariffs at 50 per cent of their starting level) was voted in June of 1962.

In 1962 steps were taken extending to Finland the privileges of EFTA.

From both camps (EEC and EFTA) the evidence unanimously indicates that as the trade barriers are going down, the economic health is going up.

Thus, as of 1962, Europe was split into several trading zones. The two major associations (originally dubbed "the sixes and sevens") had become the "sevens and eights"; Ireland and Spain remained outside any camp; and the countries of eastern Europe remained rather tightly enmeshed in the Soviet zone.

By the middle of 1962 overtures were being extended, with Great Britain taking the lead, between EFTA and EEC. It would seem highly probable that before long, trade between most countries of Europe will be moving as freely as that between Pennsylvania and Illinois.

OTHER RELATIONSHIPS

Let us mention briefly certain other factors that affect foreign trade.

Investment capital often aligns one country with another. Take Liberia, for example. Liberia is closer to Europe than to the United States, and two dozen of her African neighbors trade largely with Europe. Yet 68 per cent of Liberia's imports and 84 per cent of her exports involve the United States. The principal reason for this state of affairs is that the Liberian economy revolves around rubber plantations that are owned and operated by American rubber companies. Such investment capital often follows political control; hence, the British colonial empire channeled British investments into Commonwealth countries, thereby stimulating the production of items for export to the mother country.

By several stratagems debtor countries aim to overcome their negative differentials in commodity exchanges.

The extremely "unfavorable" balance of commodity trade in Jordan, Lebanon, and Israel can be understood in part when we inspect the map of pipelines in the Middle East (Figure 26-14). Payments received by these governments for granting transit privileges go a long way toward rectifying their trade deficits.

Even religious affiliation can enter into international trade. Israel's gross deficit of exports is counteracted to a large degree by donations of aid funds from Jewish organizations in the United States.

Many nations strive for tourists from creditor nations, notably the United States. In no other nation do foreign countries invest so much money in colorful advertising to lure tourists as in the United States, which, we must remember, is owed most of the debt of nations with "unfavorable" commodity trade balances. The advertising is apparently successful, for each year more than 2,000,000 American tourists travel abroad where they inject over $2 billion into the businesses of their host countries. Nearly 250,000 of them spend $150,000,000 in Britain; over half a million enjoy France to the tune of $170,000,000. Switzerland's income from tourists (Americans plus all others) compensates for her loss through imports.

Many debtor nations carry on trade with the United States because of our foreign aid program. In the decade 1948-1958 we either spent, invested, lent, or donated outright a total of $84 billion, broken down as follows: military spending $36 billion, other government spending $28 billion, government loans $5 billion, private investments $15 billion. American military forces spend $350,000,000 a year in Britain, which practically offsets the deficit piled up by Britain in foreign trade with the United States (Table 27-7).

Nations like Britain, Norway, Japan, and Panama offset some of their trade deficit by earnings received from their merchant fleets, which carry a large share of the world's foreign trade.

Swiss businessmen invest heavily in foreign enterprises; these interest payments almost equal Swiss receipts from tourism.

For a diversity of reasons which relate to differences in both physical endowments and cultural aptitudes, nations of the world engage in a lively exchange of commodities. Certain areas enjoy a much brisker trade than others. The north Atlantic "axis" (United States, Canada, and western Europe) constitutes the heart of the world's international trading pattern.

Even among these nations, man-made barriers still impede, but to a decreasing degree, the circulation of commodities. Nevertheless, vigorous steps are now being taken to remove these restrictions, and it seems likely that within a decade much of the world's trade will encounter greatly curtailed obstacles, provided, of course that the basic stimuli to trade continue to function.

Suggested Reading

Alexander, John W., "International Trade: Selected Types of World Regions," *Economic Geography*, 1960, pp. 95-115.

Bremen World Shipping Year-Book, Institut für Schiffahrtsforschung, Bremen, Germany.

Diebold, William, Jr., *The Schuman Plan: A Study in Economic Cooperation 1950-1959*, New York, 1959, 750 pp.

Grotewold, Andreas, "Some Aspects of the Geography of International Trade," *Economic Geography*, 1961, pp. 309-319.

———, and Grotewold, Lois, "Some Geographic Aspects of International Trade," *Economic Geography*, 1957, pp. 257-266.

Hochwald, Werner, "Dependence of Local Economics Upon Foreign Trade: A Local Impact Study," *Regional Science Association Papers and Proceedings*, 1958, pp. 259-272.

Mayer, Harold M., "Great Lakes-Overseas: An Expanding Trade Route," *Economic Geography*, 1954, pp. 117-143.

Mountjoy, Alan B., "The Suez Canal at Mid-Century," *Economic Geography*, 1958, pp. 155-167.

Smith, Howard R., and Hart, John Fraser, "The American Tariff Map," *Geographical Review*, 1955, pp. 327-346.

Sommers, Lawrence M., "Distribution and Significance of the Foreign Trade Ports of Norway," *Economic Geography*, 1960, pp. 306-312.

Thoman, Richard S., "Foreign Trade Zones in the United States," *Geographical Review*, 1952, pp. 631-645.

Van Valkenburg, S., "Land Use Within the European Common Market," *Economic Geography*, 1959, pp. 1-24.

Warntz, William, "Transatlantic Flights and Pressure Patterns," *Geographical Review*, 1961, pp. 187-212.

PART EIGHT

TERTIARY ECONOMIC ACTIVITY

The five major categories of production we have discussed so far (subsistence economies, commercial gathering, commercial bio-culture, manufacturing, and transportation) employ approximately 95 per cent of the workers of the world. The remaining 5 per cent includes persons in a wide diversity of occupations: retail merchants and clerks, wholesale distributors, government employees, doctors, teachers, lawyers, bankers, insurance salesmen, real estate salesmen, carpenters, plumbers, electricians, telephone operators, radio announcers, garage mechanics, household servants, hotel maids, bellhops, actors, professional athletes, musicians, and many others. The term *tertiary activity* embraces all such economic pursuits, pursuits that do not qualify as primary activities, since they do not involve the harvesting of naturally produced commodities, or as secondary activities, because they do not entail any change in the *form* or the *location* of commodities—pursuits, in short, that involve services.

Each tertiary activity is a spatial variable just as surely as food manufacturing, textile manufacturing, and machinery production are. In truth, we might devote a chapter each to retail trade, wholesale trade, banking, and so on, applying the geographic method of analysis to all. The number of chapters would be large indeed. Fortunately, though there is a relationship among tertiary activities that permits of an alternative approach. *Tertiary activities tend to agglomerate.* That is, retail stores are likely to be in the same places that garages, law offices, dental offices, and other services are. As a result, we do not find a pattern of specialization in large areas—one part of the world in retail trade, another in wholesale trade, another in education, another in medical treatment, and so on. Therefore, because of the high degree of intercorrelation, it is possible to distinguish regions of agglomeration of tertiary activities. And it is through these agglomerations that we shall approach the geography of tertiary activity.

Many geographers prefer the term *trade center* (covering all commercial activity, not just retailing or wholesaling), or *service center*, or *central place*, or *urban place*, for such settlements. These centers vary in size from the characteristically American *roadside*, which may have only one business, say a gasoline station, to the *metropolis*, which consists of thousands of service establishments. In traditional nomenclature, the words *urban* and *city* apply to these clusters after they reach a certain size. Unfortunately, there is no agreement about just how big a settlement must be before it can qualify as a city. Nevertheless, tertiary regions are so distinctive and important economically that we must do our best to analyze them.

One further point needs to be made. Rarely do *tertiary agglomerations* consist *solely* of tertiary activities. At least in the larger settlements a modicum of manufacturing is usually present as well as some commercial transportation. Indeed, there are some settlements where employment in the secondary endeavors (manufacturing and transportation) exceeds that in the tertiary ones. And in some parts of the world there are even settlements where most of the inhabitants earn their living in the commercial primary industries (for instance, mining, fishing, forestry, farming). Still, tertiary activity does tend to occur in agglomerated settlements.

Some textbooks in economic geography do not devote even a chapter to tertiary economic activities or to the service centers in which they chiefly occur. Sometimes the role of cities is recognized in chapters dealing with manufacturing or with transportation, but cities themselves are usually not deemed worthy of a chapter, or one at best. In this book three full chapters are devoted to service centers for the following reasons: They are the nerve centers of the world's commercial economy; the proportion of city dwellers is rapidly expanding throughout the world; and in the United States particularly that proportion is now two-thirds of the nation's people.

In Chapter 28, we will deal with location of tertiary, or service, centers—first on a worldwide basis, afterwards in the United States alone, with considerable attention to the one characteristic of size. Then in Chapter 29 we shall narrow the focus down to consider individual urban areas, observing the characteristics that distinguish one from another, including relationships to other areas. Finally in Chapter 30 we shall apply the geographic method to regions *within* a city.

*Frederikssund, a 500-acre agglomerated settlement 20 miles northwest of Copenhagen.
The market place is in the middle of town. Most buildings are low, three stories at most; older
ones are contiguous, but newer ones, especially one-family houses, are
separated. In the left foreground are new garden plots in a dried-up arm of Roskilde Bay,
around which, years ago, the old town was built in a horseshoe. (Courtesy Danish
Information Office.)*

TWENTY-EIGHT

Where Service Centers Are

THE WORLD PATTERN

Information on the location of service centers is inadequate for constructing a satisfactory world map. The most serious difficulty is that we lack data for the thousands of small centers scattered over the face of the earth. Moreover, scores of fairly good-sized settlements (those containing a few hundred or even a few thousand inhabitants) in some parts of the world are not service centers at all but *farm villages* composed primarily of farm domiciles rather than clusters of commercial establishments.

Yet rather complete figures are available for cities of 100,000 or more inhabitants. Since it is a pretty safe bet that a settlement of this size is too large to be merely a collection of farm dwellings, we can take it for granted that the locational pattern of such cities will shed light on the world pattern of tertiary activity, and on this assumption we have constructed Figure 28-1, page 520. On this map, shaded areas indicate the presence of cities of at least 100,000 inhabitants. All told, there are over 1000 cities in this size category. Rather than plot points for each, however, we have simply drawn a line to enclose all points within 100 miles of a city exceeding 100,000 people. And we have made a further distinction, delimiting areas containing "super," or "millionaire," cities—that is, those with 1,000,000 or more inhabitants. This mapping technique reveals four great urban regions in the world. (Later

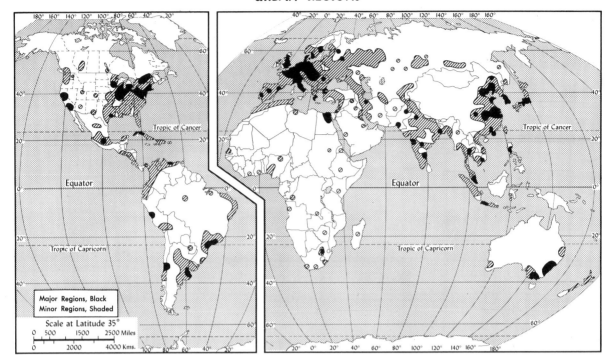

Figure 28-1

(on, we shall make an attempt to define *urban* more accurately.)

1. The foremost area covers almost all of western Europe to the Mediterranean shores, and even includes the Mediterranean fringe of Morocco, Algeria, and Tunis. Eastward prongs extend beyond the Urals and over the Caucasus as far as the Persian Gulf. A southern extension penetrates Turkey and reaches Israel. Within this vast zone are no less than 38 cities of a million or more people. Great Britain alone has seven, Germany has eight, Italy four, Russia three, and the Iberian Peninsula three. In 1935 Europe had 23 of the world's 56 millionaire cities; today it contains 38 of the world's 99.

2. In eastern Asia the zone of urbanism extending from Manchuria to Indonesia contains 22 millionaire settlements. The striking thing about this region is the number of *new* supercities; 13 of them have crossed the million mark since 1935. Five of these are in mainland China, which now claims at least ten cities in the million-plus category. The

tropical portion of this realm is particularly noteworthy in that every one of its supercities assumed millionaire status within the past 25 years.

3. India and Pakistan likewise are experiencing rapid growth in both the population of large cities and the number of supercities. A quarter of a century ago only Bombay and Calcutta were in the one-million-or-more category. Today Madras, Delhi, Hyderabad, Bangalore, Ahmedabad, Karachi, and Lahore have joined the ranks.

4. North America has a cluster of large cities in its eastern portion, from the St. Lawrence Valley on the north to Cuba on the south. There are several detached areas on the West Coast, in Central Mexico, and along the Pacific side of Central America. All told there are 20 millionaire cities in this part of the world.

Elsewhere, urbanism appears in nodes or short belts. The pattern in South America is peripheral, resembling a giant horseshoe (Figure 28-2) with one point in Venezuela and the other in eastern Brazil. Of this continent's six millionaire settlements, three (Lima, Santiago, and Caracas) qualified just recently. Africa has no extensive urban belt except on her western Mediterranean coast; her three super settlements (Alexandria, Cairo, and Johannesburg) are at her antipodes. Spotted around in numerous parts of the continent are a few places that have passed the 100,000 mark. The two metropolises of Australia front on her eastern and southern coasts.

Population Ratio The foregoing discussion has been based on the location of cities exceeding 100,000 inhabitants with little being said about the relative importance of such settlements in the total population picture. Additional light on the relative significance of such settlements will be shed if we ask the question: What proportion of a nation's total population resides in these cities with over 100,000 inhabitants? The answer is expressed as a ratio, or as a percentage, and ranges from maxima of 55 per cent (Australia) and 52 per cent (Great Britain) to a minimum of zero, which applies to nations containing no city this large. Table 28-1 lists selected nations in terms of this ratio.

Figure 28-3 shows the location of urbanism according to this ratio; it presents a markedly different pattern from that in Figure 28-1, which shows the general distribution.

Table **28-1** *Percentage of Total Population in Cities with 100,000 and 20,000 or More Inhabitants*

Nation	Total Population in Millions	Percentage in Cities Exceeding 100,000	Percentage in Cities Exceeding 20,000
Australia	10.0	57	62
England and Wales	45.1	52	71
Japan	92.9	41	65
Argentina	20.4	40	48
Scotland	5.1	37	54
Denmark	4.5	34	43
Netherlands	11.3	33	50
Austria	6.9	33	40
New Zealand	2.3	32	52
Germany	52.7	31	42
Venezuela	6.5	31	—
United States	179.3	28	50
Union of South Africa	15.8	25	13
U.S.S.R.	210.0	24	36
Canada	17.4	23	33
Egypt	26.0	22	37
Mexico	34.0	21	25
Poland	29.7	21	—
Cuba	6.0	20	35
Iran	20.6	18	—
Brazil	64.2	17	30
France	45.0	16	33
Finland	4.3	15	31
Belgium	9.0	11	32
Malaya	6.2	11	21
Thailand	25.0	10	—
Indonesia	90.3	9	—
China	669.0	8	—
India	438.0	8	—
Pakistan	93.8	7	—
Burma	20.2	5	8
Haiti	3.4	4	—
Congo	13.0	3	5
Tanganyika	8.7	2	3
Nepal	8.4	1	2

Source: United Nations, *Demographic Yearbook 1960*, Tables 1 and 8.

Figure 28-2

CITIES

Number of inhabitants
- 15–25,000
- 25–50,000
- 50–100,000
- 100–500,000
- 500,000–1,000,000
- Over 1,000,000

0   1000
        Miles

Service Centers: Location and Size

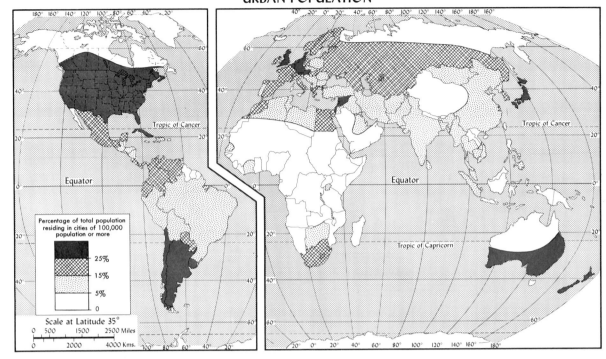

Figure 28-3

THE UNITED STATES PATTERN

Figure 28-4 shows the location of service center regions in the United States. Dark shading covers areas in which no point is more than 30 miles from a city of 50,000 people. Light shading renders areas in which two qualifications are met: (1) There are at least three settlements with over 2500 inhabitants no more than 60 miles apart—thus, one or two small isolated settlements do not count. (2) Boundary lines encompass all points located within 30 miles of one of those settlements meeting requirement 1.

The western half of the country is much less urbanized than the eastern—most of it is blank on Figure 28-4. Cities are few and far between, indeed. Los Angeles and San Francisco stand out sharply not only as foremost cities of the West, but also as the nation's only millionaire agglomerations (except for Houston) outside of the Northeast. Nowhere in the West, however, are cities of 50,000 very far from smaller centers; this is reflected in the map in that there are no circles for 50,000-inhabitant cities surrounded by blank space. Occasionally, however, this situation exists in smaller places. For example, Casper and Sheridan, Wyoming, with 39,000 and 12,000 people respectively, are more than 40 miles from the closest settlement of as many as 2500 inhabitants. Great Falls, Montana, has more than 55,000 people in the same remote situation.

The eastern half of the country unquestionably is more highly urbanized. No point is more than 30 miles from a city, except for rare spots such as the Ozark Hills, Florida's Everglades, and the cut-over region from northern Minnesota to northern Maine.

The foremost urban region of the country is the northeastern parallelogram, bounded by Boston, Washington, St. Louis, and Milwaukee. Within this quadrangle are no fewer than 12 millionaire settlements, most of which define two straight lines, one from Detroit through Cleveland to Pittsburgh, the other through five supercities: Washington, Baltimore, Philadelphia, New York, and Boston.

Besides having most of the nation's large

Service Centers: Location and Size

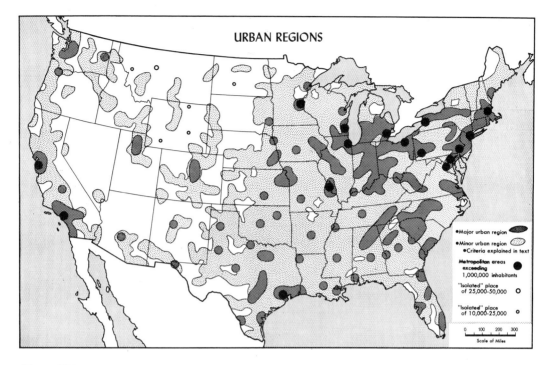

Figure 28-4

cities, the East also contains most of its small service centers. A map of hamlets (Figure 28-5) emphasizes eastern Kentucky, West Virginia, Pennsylvania, and Maryland; in these states, the frequency of hamlets is unusually intense.

Figure 28-5 (*Courtesy Glenn T. Trewartha, from* Annals of Association of American Geographers.)

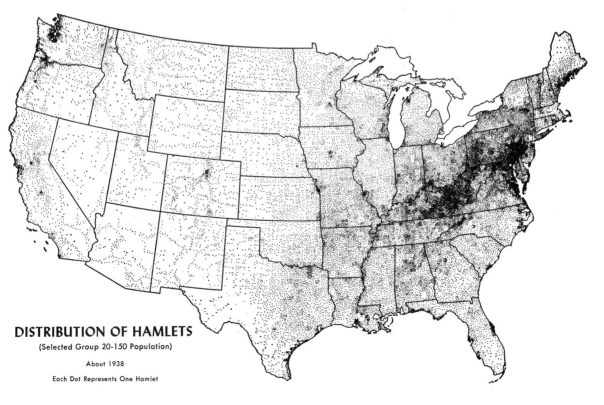

DISTRIBUTION OF HAMLETS
(Selected Group 20-150 Population)

About 1938

Each Dot Represents One Hamlet

Before considering the various size categories of service centers it must be emphasized again that service centers are primarily centers of tertiary functions, Consequently it is possible for a settlement to be quite large and still not be a service center. For example, on the populous plains of the Far East are hundreds of settlements (ranging in size from 100 to 5000 persons) whose main function is residential; in this capacity they serve farmers and their families. Most of the working population are tillers of the soil who commute to their farms in the morning and return to the settlement at night. Such settlements may, on first glance, appear large enough to qualify as service centers, but their role is that of *farm village* because inhabitants produce scarcely any surplus rice, wheat, or poultry to engage in commerce. Regardless of size, a settlement clearly cannot qualify as a service center if most of its residents are engaged in subsistence economies. China, India, Pakistan, and the tropical countries of Asia and Africa have numerous settlements of the farm-village type.

Function varies considerably from one service center to another. Take these samples: London is highly diversified because it serves as the home of the British Parliament, of several universities, and of numerous banking and insurance offices as well as being the center of wholesaling, retailing, and many professional services; Singapore and Hongkong owe their growth mainly to trade; Washington, D.C., and Delhi, India, are essentially government centers. The number of functions in any service center varies with size; that is, the larger the place, the more the types (as well as the volume) of services rendered. This principle will be observed more closely in the next chapter which is devoted largely to spatial variation in economic functions of service centers.

COMMON SIZE CATEGORIES

By size, service centers range from *roadside* to *megalopolis*. A rather complex nomen-clature identifying many different categories has come into existence and merits comment here. Some of the terms are only loosely defined, but some (particularly those adopted by the United States Bureau of the Budget and employed by the Bureau of the Census) are very precise.

Roadside   A roadside is an isolated establishment, such as a lone gasoline station, drive-in eating place, small general store, or motel, situated along a highway. Frequently the operator of such a business resides on the floor above or in a house next door. (On all sides this embryonic settlement is flanked by rural uses of land such as farms, forests, or desert.) Roadsides are restricted almost entirely to the United States, Canada, and Europe—regions of dense highway traffic. Before the automobile age, roadsides were few and far between (except for the "wayside inn" which has been a fixture of the road ever since man ventured to travel more than a day's journey).

Hamlet   A hamlet is larger than a roadside and consists of a few buildings some of which are residential and some commercial.

> ...the unincorporated hamlet represents the first hint of thickening in the settlement plasm. It is neither purely rural nor purely urban, but neuter in gender, a sexless creation midway between the more determinate town and country.

What attributes qualify a settlement for the hamlet category? Glenn Trewartha has proposed the following:

> Defined quantitatively I propose that there must be a minimum of, (1) *four* active residence units, at least two of which are non-farm houses; (2) a total of at least *six* active functional units—residential, business, social or otherwise; and (3) a total of at least *five* buildings actively used by human beings. [In hamlets a building often houses more than one functional unit.] According to the above minimal requirements four farmsteads each located at one corner of a crossroads could not comprise a hamlet even though, as far as residence units are concerned, four are all that is

The hamlet of East Bethel, Vermont, a community consisting of a few homes, a few stores, and a couple of churches. (Courtesy Standard Oil Company of New Jersey.)

required. Counting four or five people to a residence this minimum of four residence units in a hamlet establishes a minimum population of 16 or 20. Spacing of buildings in a hamlet must be such as to give an appearance of compactness exceeding that of ordinary farmstead spacing. In a hamlet composed of the minimum number of buildings, the maximum linear distance between the outermost buildings should not exceed one-quarter mile.

For a number of reasons a population of approximately 150 (not more than 38 residences) was adopted as the maximum for hamlets, and therefore the limit separating them from villages. When settlements reach about that size it was found that there existed a distinct tendency for them to incorporate. Apparently they become conscious of their contrast with the countryside in general, and, as a community, desire more services than the county or township in which they are located is willing to provide. It was found also that in communities with over 150 inhabitants there was a marked tendency for a distinct business core to develop, a feature that is not conspicuous in most hamlets. Teachers and preachers are not so uncommon even in hamlets.

One of the major factors in the birth of hamlets was the presence of small post-offices.

A fairly common center of accretion, having sufficient centripetal power to induce minor coagulation within the open-country settlement plasm, was the fourth-class post office. One of the first requirements in a frontier region of new settlement was some center from which mail could be sent and received. Frontier post offices were established in farm homes, and oc-

casionally in cross-road general stores, blacksmith shops, or similar establishments. From over a wide neighborhood farmers and miners were drawn frequently to a post office center and as a consequence business and service units were attracted to these focal points forming the nuclei of settlement.

In fact, of all the functions represented in hamlets prior to 1900, postal service was the most universal and appears to have been one of the most common reasons for the origin and growth of small cross-roads settlements.*

Village   A village, in turn, is larger and has more functions than a hamlet; we shall adopt population limits of 150-1000 for the village category. To qualify as a village, a settlement should have at least ten business establishments. In addition to those functions found in a hamlet, a village should have such other types as an automobile dealer, a farm implement distributor, a lumber yard, a hardware store, a livestock feed dispensary, and an auto repair shop. Many villages have a graded school and several churches. (NOTE: The use of *village* in geography is not to be confused with its use in political science where it denotes a specific form of government. In that sense a service center could have a population of 50,000 and still be a "village.")

* Glenn T. Trewartha, "The Unincorporated Hamlet," *Annals of the Association of American Geographers*, 1943, pp. 32-40.

Town   A town, in this sequence, loosely ranges in population from around 1000 to 2500 and has additional functions beyond those of a village. Usually there are at least 50 service units, the additional types being a bank, a high school, and a representative of at least one of the professional services (a physician, dentist, veterinarian, or lawyer). Sometimes a weekly newspaper is published. (Like village, *town* means different things to different people. In New England and Wisconsin, for instance, *towns* are governmental subdivisions of counties. In some parts of Europe, *towns* refer to service centers of considerable size.)

City   In this book, we shall apply *city* to service centers that have 2500 or more people, simply and practically because that is the figure chosen by the United States Bureau of the Census to separate *urban* from *rural* settlements, as will be discussed more fully in later paragraphs. Again, a city has a larger number, and greater diversity, of service functions than a town. (On the other hand, some state constitutions declare that a village can incorporate as a *city* if it has only 1000 residents. As with *village* and *town*, the definition given to the word *city* is not everywhere the same.)

The settlement of Kuan, a city of 100,000 population in Szechuan Province, China, is typical of Far Eastern cities. The streets are narrow, the tile-roofed houses small and closely packed. (Eastfoto.)

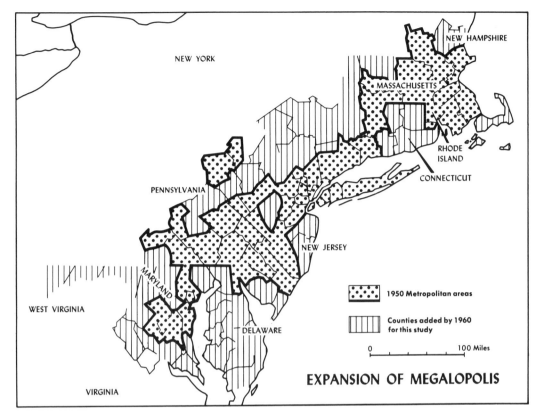

Figure 28-6   (*Courtesy Jean Gottmann, from 20th Century Fund.*)

Conurbation   In this book we shall apply the term *conurbation* to a group of cities that have coalesced, that is, grown together economically while remaining politically independent, as in the Ruhr where Dortmund-Essen-Duisburg and suburbs constitute an urbanized cluster of over 5,000,000 people.

Metropolis   This is a loose term for a large city. Popular usage seems to imply that a metropolis contains at least 500,000 people, although, again, this notion is not at all universal.

The term *millionaire city* is self-evident. There are now 99 urban settlements with over 1,000,000 inhabitants in the world, a phenomenal increase over the 56 in 1935. In 1900 there were only 11.* The world's largest service centers (those with 2,000,000 or more

inhabitants—there are 35) are listed in Table 28-2, page 528.

Megalopolis   This term applies to the most massive concentration of urbanized settlement on the face of the earth—a 600-mile stretch of towns, cities, and supercities, many of which have coalesced (see Figure 28-6). Here is "a phenomenon unique by its size not only in America but in the world. It resulted obviously from the coalescence, recently achieved, of a chain of metropolitan areas, each of which grew around a substantial urban nucleus. The super-metropolitan character of this vast area, the greatest such growth ever observed, called for a special name. We chose the word *megalopolis*." *

The Question of "Urban"   All the terms mentioned thus far, from *roadside* to

---

* For an interesting study of supercities of the world see Audrey Lambert's "Millionaire Cities, 1955," *Economic Geography*, October, 1956, pp. 283-293.

* So writes Jean Gottmann in "Megalopolis: Or the Urbanization of the Northeastern Seaboard," *Economic Geography*, Vol. 33, 1957, pp. 189-200.

Table **28-2** *World's Largest Urban Settlement*

Rank	Urban Agglomeration	Population in Millions
1.	New York	14.1
2.	Tokyo-Yokohama	11.3
3.	London	10.5
4.	Moscow	7.3
5.	Paris	6.7
6.	Osaka-Kobe	6.4
7.	Los Angeles	6.4
8.	Shanghai	6.2
9.	Chicago	5.9
10.	Buenos Aires	5.7
11.	Calcutta	5.7
12.	"The Ruhr"	5.3
13.	Mexico City	4.8
14.	Bombay	4.4
15.	Berlin	4.2
16.	Rio de Janeiro	3.7
17.	Philadelphia	3.6
18.	Leningrad	3.5
19.	Detroit	3.5
20.	São Paulo	3.3
21.	Cairo	2.7
22.	Peking	2.7
23.	Tientsin	2.6
24.	Birmingham (UK)	2.5
25.	Hongkong	2.5
26.	Manchester	2.4
27.	Delhi	2.4
28.	San Francisco	2.4
29.	Boston	2.4
30.	Manila	2.3
31.	Mukden	2.2
32.	Madras	2.2
33.	Milan	2.1
34.	Hamburg	2.1
35.	Saigon	2.0

Source: University of California, International Urban Research, *The World's Metropolitan Areas*, (Berkeley) 1959, pp. 37-63, and United States Bureau of the Census, *Census of Population*, 1960.

megalopolis are still loosely defined and have not been adopted by all scientists. Indeed there is still no general agreement as to what the term *urban* stands for. Consequently it is very difficult to compare urban population from census data of one nation with that of another nation if their opinions differ as to what qualifies as *urban*. Look at the spread among the following: Denmark tabulates as urban every settlement with 250 inhabitants; a 1000 minimum applies in Chile; 1500 is the requirement in Panama. Several countries adhere to a 2000 minimum (Argentina, Austria, Germany, Czechoslovakia, and Portugal

among them). The 2500 basis holds in Mexico and Venezuela as well as the United States. India and Belgium count as urban only those places with 5000 inhabitants, Switzerland and Spain only those with 10,000.

UNITED STATES CENSUS CLASSIFICATIONS

The United States Census publications employ a series of definitions which define rather precisely several categories of urban settlements: *urban place, urbanized area, standard metropolitan statistical area, central city*, and *standard consolidated area*.

Urban Place An urban place is any settlement (whether incorporated or not) with 2500 or more inhabitants. Incorporated urban places can be referred to as *municipalities* (but this term also includes some incorporated places of less than 2500 people).

Any settlement that does not qualify as urban is considered, by the United States Census, to be *rural*. Table 28-3 indicates the structure of United States population, in terms of urban and rural components, by size categories of settlements. All told, the nation contains almost 20,000 service centers, of which 6000 are in the urban category. Their aggregate population is 125,000,000. The nearly 14,000 rural centers have around 10,000,000 people. The remaining 44,000,000 Americans reside on farms or in various types of rural but nonfarm homes.

The population structure by size categories of urban places varies considerably from state to state. Table 28-4, for instance, shows that in California the major size category (over 500,000) accounts for 24 per cent of the state's inhabitants; in Arizona the largest percentage resides in the size category of 100,000 to 500,-000; in Nevada's structure the 50,000-to-100,-000 category is foremost; in Wyoming it is the 25,000-to-50,000 category.

Urbanized Area Many an urban settlement has experienced so great a population expansion (resulting from its own *natural increase*—that is, excess of births over deaths—and also *migration increase*—that is, excess of

Table **28-3** *United States Population in Groups of Places Classified According to Size*

Classification	Population in Millions	Percentage of Total	Number of Settlements
TOTAL	179.3	100.0	19,790
Urban Places (Municipalities)	125.2	69.9	6,041
Places of 1,000,000 or more	17.5	9.8	5
" 500,000 to 1,000,000	11.1	6.2	16
" 250,000 to 500,000	10.8	6.0	30
" 100,000 to 250,000	11.7	6.5	81
" 50,000 to 100,000	13.8	7.7	201
" 25,000 to 50,000	14.9	8.3	432
" 10,000 to 25,000	17.6	9.8	1,134
" 5,000 to 10,000	9.7	5.5	1,394
" under 5,000	8.1	10.1	2,748
Rural	54.1	30.1	13,749
Places of 1,000 to 2,500	6.5	3.6	4,151
" under 1,000	3.9	2.2	9,598
Other rural territory	43.7	24.3	0

Source: United States *Census of Population, 1960*, United States Summary, Table 7.

in-migration over out-migration) that it has spilled over its city limits. In such instances the population of the official *urban place* is actually less than the number of people residing in that particular urban agglomeration. Frequently this kind of growth involves the coalescing of several incorporated suburbs encircling the main municipality. It also includes urban settlement which has crept out into the country, beyond even the corporate limits of

Table **28-4** *United States: Percentage of Population in Groups of Places Classified, by States, According to Size, 1960*

State	Urban Population								Rural Population 1,000 to 2,500
	Total Urban	Over 500,000	100,000 to 500,000	50,000 to 100,000	25,000 to 50,000	10,000 to 25,000	5,000 to 10,000	2,500 to 5,000	
U.S. TOTAL	69	16	13	8	8	10	5	4	4
Vermont	38	0	0	0	9	7	17	5	10
Massachusetts	83	14	11	21	18	8	1	2	2
New York	85	49	6	4	5	8	3	2	2
West Virginia	38	0	0	12	6	7	5	4	7
Iowa	53	0	7	16	8	6	8	6	7
North Dakota	35	0	0	0	22	6	5	1	12
Wyoming	56	0	0	0	25	12	6	13	8
Nevada	70	0	0	40	0	16	4	6	5
North Carolina	39	0	9	6	6	7	4	4	5
Florida	74	0	19	8	9	9	6	5	3
Mississippi	38	0	6	0	12	8	6	5	5
Texas	75	23	15	7	6	9	6	5	4
New Mexico	66	0	21	0	16	12	7	4	4
Arizona	75	0	50	0	3	9	5	4	4
California	86	24	13	12	11	10	3	2	1

Source: United States *Census of Population, 1960*, United States Summary, Table 21.

URBANIZED AREA OF SYRACUSE, NEW YORK

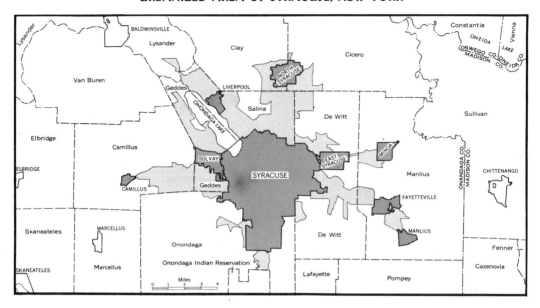

Figure 28-7 *(From U.S. Bureau of the Census. Lined areas are incorporated places; dotted ones are unincorporated.)*

the suburbs. In order to provide a single population figure for this single agglomeration (of diverse areas of government) the term *urbanized area* has been coined. Today, the concept of urbanized area is probably the best for distinguishing between rural and large urban settlements.

As viewed by the United States Census, an urbanized area consists of at least one urban place having 50,000 or more inhabitants (termed *central city*) plus all *contiguous* areas which meet the following criteria: (a) incorporated urban places, (b) other incorporated settlements having at least 100 dwelling units, (c) unincorporated "enumeration districts" with a population density of at least 1000 people per square mile. (An "enumeration district" is an area assigned to a single census enumerator for collection of data. Within unincorporated territory on the fringe of urbanized areas each such district is delimited so as to encompass no more than one square mile of land and no more than 75 housing units.) The map of the Syracuse Urbanized Area (Figure 28-7) illustrates this concept.

Central Cities   There are a few urbanized areas having "twin central cities" neither of which has a population of 50,000 but which are contiguous and have a combined population of at least that amount. Where several contiguous cities each exceed 50,000 the following criteria are adopted to identify the central cities: (a) The largest city within an urbanized area is always a central city, (b) an additional central city may qualify if it has 250,000 inhabitants, or if (c) it has a population of at least one-third that of the largest central city in its urbanized area. Examples of twin central cities are Los Angeles-Long Beach, San Francisco-Oakland, Minneapolis-St. Paul, Providence-Pawtucket, Norfolk-Portsmouth, and Allentown-Bethlehem. Examples of triplet central cities are Springfield-Chicopee-Holyoke in Massachusetts, and Davenport-Rock Island-Moline straddling the Illinois-Iowa border.

Altogether, there are 213 urbanized areas in the United States ranging in size from Tyler, Texas (51,739 inhabitants), to the New York-

Service Centers: Location and Size

Northeastern New Jersey Urbanized Area (14,-114,927 inhabitants). Their aggregate population is 96,000,000 (over half the nation's 1960 total of 179 million). Sixteen urbanized areas have over 1,000,000 people each and a combined total of 52,000,000. These are listed in Table 28-5.

explanation of this condition is that some central cities are tightly ringed by large suburbs and unincorporated fringes; this may result in a large urbanized area population encompassing a relatively small central city.

For the same reason, the ratio between central city population and urbanized area

Table 28-5   Population in Millions of Largest U.S. Urbanized Areas,
             Their Largest Central Cities,
             and Their Standard Metropolitan Statistical Areas

Area	Urbanized Area	Largest Central City	Standard Metropolitan Statistical Area
New York-Northeastern New Jersey	14.1	7.78	10.6
Los Angeles-Long Beach	6.4	2.47	6.7
Chicago-Northwestern Indiana	5.9	3.55	6.2
Philadelphia	3.6	2.00	4.3
Detroit	3.5	1.67	3.7
San Francisco-Oakland	2.4	.74	2.7
Boston	2.4	.69	2.5
Washington	1.8	.76	2.0
Pittsburgh	1.8	.60	2.4
Cleveland	1.7	.87	1.7
St. Louis	1.6	.75	2.0
Baltimore	1.4	.93	1.7
Minneapolis-St. Paul	1.3	.48	1.4
Milwaukee	1.1	.74	1.1
Houston	1.1	.93	1.2
Buffalo	1.0	.53	1.3

Source: United States *Census of Population, 1960,* United States Summary, Tables 23, 29, 36.

Figure 28-8, page 532, shows where the nation's population is, with the larger symbols portraying urbanized area. Note the prominence of the parallelogram mentioned earlier (that is, the area bounded by Boston, Milwaukee, St. Louis, and Washington).

Ratio of Populations of Urban Area and Central City   Inspection of Table 28-5 reveals that there is not a perfect correlation between size of urbanized area and size of the nucleus, that is, the largest central city. For example, the City of Chicago is greater than the City of Los Angeles, but the reverse is true for their urbanized areas. The same can be said for St. Louis and Houston. The

population ranges from a minimum of 27 per cent in Wilkes-Barre, Pennsylvania, to 100 per cent in six places: Amarillo, Laredo, and San Angelo (Texas), Raleigh (North Carolina), Meriden (Connecticut), and Lewiston-Auburn (Maine). Central cities snugly hemmed in by suburbs have low ratios (Boston 29, Providence 31, Pittsburgh 33), while central cities with vigorous annexation policies have maintained ratios of 100 by continually pushing their municipal boundaries out into the countryside ahead of the advancing wave of urban settlement.

Standard Metropolitan Statistical Area   For many types of economic analysis it is

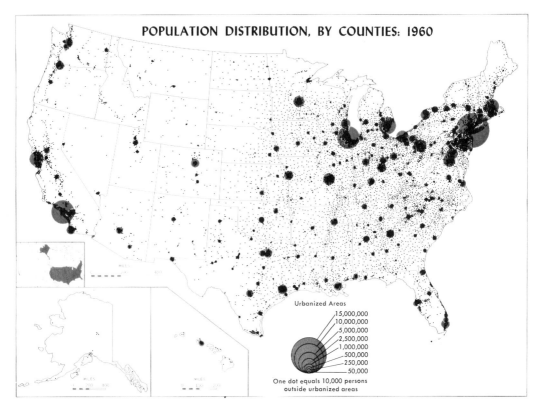

POPULATION DISTRIBUTION, BY COUNTIES: 1960

Urbanized Areas

15,000,000
10,000,000
5,000,000
2,500,000
1,000,000
500,000
250,000
50,000

One dot equals 10,000 persons
outside urbanized areas

Figure 28-8 *(From U. S. Bureau of the Census.)*

necessary to compare data which are collected on a county basis—for example, the labor market areas of the Bureau of Employment Security, the Census of Manufactures, and the Census of Population. To facilitate such comparison the Census publishes urban population figures for certain counties and groups of counties identified as *Standard Metropolitan Statistical Areas* (SMSA's).

An SMSA is a *county* (or a group of contiguous *counties*) containing at least one central city of at least 50,000 inhabitants or twin central cities with an aggregate of 50,000 or more people. In addition to this "core" county (or counties) contiguous counties are included in the SMSA if, according to criteria listed below, they are metropolitan in character and are integrated economically with the central city.

If two or more adjacent counties each have a city meeting specifications for a central city and located within 20 miles of one another (measured between city limits), the counties

are included in the same SMSA unless evidence indicates that the central cities are not economically integrated.

The criteria for measuring the *metropolitan* character of any other contiguous county for possible inclusion in the SMSA are as follows:

1. At least 75 per cent of the labor force working in the county must be in nonagricultural endeavor.

2. The county must also meet at least *one* of the following requirements if it is to qualify as "metropolitan":

a. At least half of its population must reside in contiguous minor civil divisions (in most states these are termed *townships*) with a density of at least 150 persons per square mile, such civil divisions radiating from a central city in the area.

b. The number of nonagricultural workers *employed* in the county must be at least 10 per cent of the number of nonagricultural workers employed in the core county.

c. The number of nonagricultural workers *residing* in the county must be at least 10 per cent of the number of nonagricultural workers residing in the core county.

d. The county must be the place of *employment* for at least 10,000 nonagricultural workers.

e. The county must be the place of *residence* for at least 10,000 nonagricultural workers.

3. The county must meet one of the following requirements if it is to qualify as being "integrated" with the core county:

a. At least 15 per cent of the workers residing in the county must work in the core county (or counties) containing the central city (cities).

b. At least 25 per cent of those working in the outlying county must reside in the core county (or counties) containing the central city (cities).

If data for criteria 3a and 3b are inconclusive, Census authorities then consider such measures of integration as average telephone calls per subscriber per month from the outlying county to the core counties, newspaper circulation reports, and analysis of charge accounts by retail stores in the central cities.*

In total, there are 212 SMSA's in the United States ranging from Meriden, Connecticut (51,850 inhabitants) to New York (10,694,633). Table 28-5 indicates the population for some of the larger SMSA's. Notice that there is not a perfect correlation between population of urbanized area and that of SMSA. Two reasons explain this discrepancy. Counties are not of uniform size; thus, two central cities of equal size in two counties of unequal size would tend to show different SMSA populations. Secondly, a central city whose urbanized area has filled in most of the county would tend to be aug-

* More detailed discussion of these and other criteria employed in delimiting SMSA's appears on pages xxiv-xxv of the United States *Census of Population, 1960,* United States Summary.

Figure 28-9 (*From U. S. Bureau of the Census.*)

STANDARD METROPOLITAN STATISTICAL AREAS
in Northeastern United States, 1960

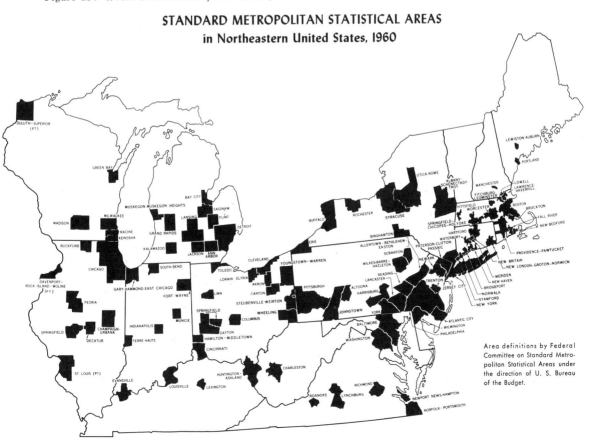

Area definitions by Federal Committee on Standard Metropolitan Statistical Areas under the direction of U. S. Bureau of the Budget.

mented by less in SMSA calculations than would a central city whose urbanized area has filled in much less of a county of the same size.

Most SMSA's contain more people than do their urbanized areas (see Table 28-5). New York is the glaring exception. This monstrous urban mass is now so large that economic integration is no longer able to make it cohere into one SMSA, in terms of Census SMSA criteria. The Newark SMSA and the Paterson-Clifton-Passaic SMSA are contiguous to, but not sufficiently integrated with, the New York SMSA.

Standard Consolidated Areas   Around the nation's two largest *urban places* (New York and Chicago), several contiguous SMSA's and additional counties which do not meet the formal requirements for economic integration but do have considerable interrelationships of other types, have been given a new regional designation: *Standard Consolidated Areas*. The New York-Northeastern New Jersey SCA has a population of 14,759,429 while the Chicago-Northwestern Indiana SCA has 6,794,461.

RANK-SIZE HYPOTHESIS

Some scholars, viewing population structure of major regions by sizes of service centers (such as that for the United States in the last column of Table 28-3) have been impressed with the fact that as the size category increases, the number of settlements per size category decreases. They have formulated the *rank-size hypothesis*. According to this, as a region advances from subsistence into commercial stages, two developments will occur. (1) One service center will tend to outstrip all others in size and become the main city for the entire region. Such a center is termed a *primate city*. (2) Each remaining city will assume a size roughly equal to the population of the primate city divided by that city's rank in the region. This is expressed by the following formula:

$$P_x = \frac{P_l}{R_x}$$

in which P_l is population of the region's largest urban agglomeration, P_x is the population of any other urban agglomeration, and R_x is the rank of that other agglomeration.

To illustrate (referring to data on urbanized areas in Table 28-5): The population of New York is 14.1 million, that of Philadelphia is 3.6 million. Dividing the latter into the former figure gives a quotient of almost 4 which should be the rank of Philadelphia according to this hypothesis. A few moments inspection of Table 28-5 will enable the reader to comment on whether this hypothesis holds more firmly when applied to central cities or to urbanized areas or to SMSA's.

This chapter has dealt with general locational patterns of tertiary settlements and has considered one selected characteristic, that of size. The next chapter continues our train of thought by considering other characteristics and then moving into a discussion of relationships.

Suggested Readings

Amiran, D. H. K., and Shahar, A., "The Towns of Israel: The Principles of Their Urban Geography," *Geographical Review*, 1961, pp. 348-369.

Applebaum, William, "Teaching Marketing Geography by the Case Method," *Economic Geography*, 1961, pp. 48-60.

Davis, Kingsley, editor, *The World's Metropolitan Areas*, Berkeley, 1959, 115 pp.

Dickinson, Robert E., "Rural Settlements in the German Lands," *Annals of the Association of American Geographers*, 1949, pp. 239-263.

———, *The West European City*, London, 1951, 580 pp.

Freeman, T. W., *The Conurbations of Great Britain*, Manchester, 1959, 393 pp.

Fryer, D. W., "The 'Million City' in Southeast Asia," *Geographical Review*, 1953, pp. 474-494.

George, Pierre, *LaVille: Le Fait Urbain a Travers Le Monde*, Paris, 1952, 399 pp.

Gibbs, Jack P., "Growth of Individual Metropolitan Areas: A Global View," *Annals of the Association of American Geographers*, 1961, pp. 380-391.

Gottmann, Jean, "Megalopolis or The Urbanization of the Northeastern Seaboard," *Economic Geography*, 1957, pp. 189-200.

——, *Megalopolis: The Urbanized Northeastern Seaboard of the United States*, N. Y., 1961, 810 pp.

Green, Howard L., "Planning A National Retail Growth Program," *Economic Geography*, 1961, pp. 22-32.

Hamdan, G., "The Growth and Functional Structure of Khartoum," *Geographical Review*, 1960, pp. 21-40.

Harris, Britton, "Urbanization Policy in India," The Regional Science Association *Papers and Proceedings*, 1959, pp. 181-204.

Hoselitz, Bert F., "The Cities of India and Their Problems," *Annals of the Association of American Geographers*, 1959, pp. 223-231.

James, Preston E., "South American Cities," *Annals of the Association of American Geographers*, 1953, pp. 351-352.

Kollmorgen, Walter M., "Settlement Control Beats Flood Control," *Economic Geography*, 1953, pp. 208-215.

Lambert, Audrey M., "Millionaire Cities, 1955," *Economic Geography*, 1956, pp. 283-293.

Mayer, Harold M., and Kohn, Clyde F., editors, *Readings in Urban Geography*, Chicago, 1959, 625 pp.

Mikesell, Marvin W., "Market Centers of Northeastern Spain: A Review," *Geographical Review*, 1960, pp. 247-251.

Murphey, Rhoads, "The City as a Center of Change: Western Europe and China," *Annals of the Association of American Geographers*, 1954, pp. 349-362.

——, *Shanghai: Key to Modern China*, Cambridge, 1953, 232 pp.

Orleans, Leo A., "The Recent Growth of China's Urban Population," *Geographical Review*, 1959, pp. 43-57.

Pickard, Jerome P., *Metropolitanization of the United States*, Washington, 1959.

Proudfoot, Malcolm J., "Public Regulation of Urban Development in the United States," *Geographical Review*, 1954, pp. 415-419.

Ristow, Walter W., *Marketing Maps of the United States—An Annotated List*, Washington, 1951, 52 pp.

Roberts, John M., *et al.*, "The Small Highway Business on U.S. 30 in Nebraska," *Economic Geography*, 1956, pp. 139-152.

Russell, Josiah C., "The Metropolitan City Region of the Middle Ages," *Journal of Regional Science*, Fall, 1960, pp. 55-70.

Shabad, Theodore, "The Population of China's Cities," *Geographical Review*, 1959, pp. 32-42.

Smailes, Arthur E., *The Geography of Towns*, London, 1953, 166 pp.

Smolski, Chester E., "A Study in Sampling: City Size and Population Density," *The Professional Geographer*, March 1962, pp. 8-10.

Spate, O. H. K., and Enayat, Ahmad, "Five Cities of the Gangetic Plain: A Cross Section of Indian Cultural History," *Geographical Review*, 1950, pp. 260-278.

Spelt, J., *The Urban Development in South-Central Ontario*, Assen, 1955, 241 pp.

Stewart, Charles T., Jr., "The Size and Spacing of Cities," *Geographical Review*, 1958, pp. 222-245.

Taaffe, Edward J., "Air Transportation and United States Urban Distribution," *Geographical Review*, 1956, pp. 219-238.

Taylor, Griffith, *Urban Geography*, New York, 1949, 439 pp.

Trewartha, Glenn T., "Chinese Cities: Numbers and Distribution," *Annals of the Association of American Geographers*, 1951, pp. 331-347.

——, "Chinese Cities: Origins and Functions," *Annals of the Association of American Geographers*, 1952, pp. 69-93.

Van Cleef, Eugene, "Some Aspects of Urbanistics," *The Professional Geographer*, May 1957, pp. 2-7.

Wilson, Andrew W., "Urbanization of the Arid Lands," *The Professional Geographer*, November 1960, pp. 4-8.

Wood, Harold A., "The St. Lawrence Seaway and Urban Geography: Cornwall-Cardinal, Ontario," *Geographical Review*, 1955, pp. 509-530.

Woodbury, Coleman, *A Framework for Urban Studies: An Analysis of Urban Metropolitan Development and Research Needs*, Washington, 1959, 29 pp.

*Oskaloosa, Iowa, is now a city of 11,000 inhabitants. In 1937, when
it was analyzed to determine net inflow and outflow of dollars as described on page 559,
it had 10,000 residents. (Courtesy Oskaloosa Chamber of Commerce.)*

TWENTY-NINE

Economic progress from subsistence to commerce has spawned thousands of service centers of various sizes. If all service centers were essentially alike, except for size, the story could end there. But even settlements of equal size can be markedly different in many respects and can be differently related to the regions around them. Because of the really sharp variations, and because cities are playing an ever-increasing role in human life, we should know something about their characteristics and relationships. The present chapter deals with these topics, observing them in one selected area—the United States. The main reason for this selection is that the United States Bureau of the Census collects and publishes the world's most detailed data on economic endeavor in cities of all sizes.

Economic Attributes of Cities

Service centers differ from one another in many ways, some social, some physical, and some economic. It is the latter category of attributes that are of immediate interest to us, particularly volume of business, employment structure, and personal income.

VOLUME OF BUSINESS

The United States Bureau of the Census publishes every few years a very useful *Census of Business*, which gives figures for every state and major city for *retail trade, wholesale trade,* and *selected services*, in terms of number of establishments, value of sales, number of employees, and value of payroll.

Table 29-1   Retail Trade: Leading Standard Statistical Areas in the United States, 1958

Place	Thousands of Establishments	Sales in Million Dollars	Percentage of National Total
UNITED STATES TOTAL	1,788	$199,646	100.0
Twelve Leading SCA's and SMSA's			
1. New York SCA	159	18,489	9.2
2. Los Angeles SMSA	57	9,039	4.5
3. Chicago SCA	59	9,030	4.5
4. Philadelphia	43	4,942	2.5
5. Detroit	30	4,448	2.2
6. San Francisco-Oakland	25	3,579	1.8
7. Boston	24	3,440	1.7
8. Pittsburgh	22	2,638	1.3
9. Washington	11	2,501	1.2
10. St. Louis	19	2,380	1.2
11. Cleveland	15	2,248	1.1
12. Newark	18	2,236	1.1
Five SMSA's with smallest volume of retail trade			
Fitchburg-Leominster, Mass.	.9	95	—
Lewiston-Auburn, Maine	.7	86	—
San Angelo, Texas	.8	81	—
Gadsden, Alabama	.8	80	—
Laredo, Texas	.5	59	—

Source: United States *Census of Business*, Retail Trade, United States Summary, Table 8.

Retail Trade   Illustrative of the kind of information presented in the *Census of Business* is Table 29-1. Note that of the 12 top retailing SCA's (Standard Consolidated Centers) and SMSA's (Standard Metropolitan Statistical Areas), all but Los Angeles and San Francisco are within that familiar northeast quadrant. As we might expect, New York, with its suburbs, constitutes the foremost retail trade market in the nation.

Ratio of Retail Sales per Capita   Another useful indicator of retailing activity is the measure of volume of sales per inhabitant. For example, one would expect New York to rank first in Table 29-1 for the simple reason that it contains the largest number of customers who demand groceries, clothing, furniture, and gasoline. But does New York likewise rank first in terms of the retail sales/inhabitant ratio? The latest published data on this measurement appear in the 1954 Census of Business and indicate that for the nation as a whole this ratio varies sharply among the metropolitan areas, from a maximum of $3,485 in Tucson, Arizona, to only $790 in Wilkes-Barre, Pennsylvania (Table 29-2). For the United States as a whole this ratio is $1,128. Although New York does far more retailing than any other tertiary center, its share of the nation's retail trade is only slightly larger than its share of the population. Consequently, metropolitan New York's per capita average of $1,155 is only $27 above the national figure. That Tucson, Arizona, does the most retail trade per resident reflects in part considerable tourist business. And that Wilkes-Barre has the lowest per capita retail trade among the nation's largest metropolitan areas is a sign that this city is fighting to recover from the slump that has hit the anthracite coal mining industry.

The Census of Business indicates, for each city, not only its *total* amount of retail trade but also the level for individual *types* of business such as grocery stores, meat markets, restaurants, drinking places, and department

Cities: Characteristics and Relationships

Table **29-2** *United States:*
Per Capita Retail Trade

Place	Sales per Inhabitant
UNITED STATES	$1,128
Twelve Leading SMSA's	
1. Tucson, Ariz.	3,485
2. Orlando, Fla.	3,155
3. Sacramento, Calif.	2,562
4. Miami, Fla.	2,488
5. Phoenix, Ariz.	2,445
6. Stockton, Calif.	2,309
7. Fresno, Calif.	2,294
8. Atlanta, Ga.	2,274
9. Charleston, W. Va.	2,248
10. Kalamazoo, Mich.	2,242
11. San Jose, Calif.	2,233
12. Lubbock, Tex.	2,224
Five SMSA's with smallest sales	
Fall River, Mass.	1,031
Gadsden, Ala.	1,030
Wheeling, W. Va.	930
Laredo, Tex.	899
Wilkes-Barre, Penn.	790

Source: United States Bureau of the Census, *Census of Business*, 1954, Retail Trade, U.S. Summary, Table I-N.

Table **29-3** *Retail Trade Activity*
in Cleveland, Ohio, SMSA, 1958

Business	Number of Establish- ments	Total Sales in Thousands of Dollars
TOTAL	15,843	$2,248,822
Grocery stores	2,187	478,030
Automotive dealers	568	323,590
Department stores	31	286,095
Gasoline service stations	1,512	142,618
Clothing, accessory stores	1,138	122,240
Restaurants	1,186	99,942
Drug stores	551	85,124
Furniture stores	574	74,901
Drinking places (alcoholic)	1,576	67,061
Lumber yards	102	66,015
Shoe stores	324	27,870
Hardware stores	410	27,859
Retail bakeries	372	22,349
Jewelry stores	221	14,762
Radio and television stores	132	8,660
Sporting goods stores	71	5.272
Book stores	20	3,332
Antique shops	27	526

Source: United States *Census of Business*, 1958, Retail Trade, United States Summary, Table 8.

stores. Table 29-3 is an example of the kinds of information available and useful not only to professional scholars but also to business firms and young men in the process of selecting a city in which to start a business.

Wholesale Trade The variation among cities in wholesale trade is different from that of retail trade. Table 29-4, page 540, indicates that of the twelve leading wholesaling centers only seven are in the familiar northeast parallelogram. Remember that ten of the twelve leading retailers were here. Clearly, a larger number of wholesaling centers, such as Atlanta, Dallas, Minneapolis-St. Paul, San Francisco, and Los Angeles, achieve national prominence in supplying retailers in their parts of the nation.

Another difference between wholesaling and retailing is that the large metropolitan areas tend to perform relatively more wholesaling than retailing. For example, the New York SCA has 8 per cent of the national population, does 9 per cent of the nation's retailing but accounts for an astonishing 19 per cent of

wholesale merchandising. However, if we compare Tables 29-1 and 29-4 we can observe that with progressively smaller SMSA's the disproportion between wholesaling and retailing tends to shrink until, at last, among the smallest SMSA's, the sales of wholesalers are less than those of retailers. In other words, the economic activity of wholesaling is highly concentrated in a few large tertiary centers dispersed at great distances throughout the country, whereas retailing is less concentrated, appearing in many centers, both large and small.*

Services The Census of Business has a third major section entitled *Selected Services* which contains information on a host of such service enterprises as hotels, laundries, beauty shops, barber shops, photography studios, funeral services, shoe repair shops, advertising offices, credit bureaus, auto repair garages,

* A suggested method for classifying cities in terms of the ratio between wholesale and retail functions appears in William Siddall's "Wholesale-Retail Trade Ratios as Indices of Urban Centrality," *Economic Geography*, 1961, pp. 124-132.

Place	Thousands of Establishments	Sales in Millions of Dollars	Percentage of National Total
UNITED STATES TOTAL	285.0	$284,970	100.0
Twelve Leading SCA's and SMSA's			
1. New York SCA	38.0	54,700	19.1
2. Chicago SCA	12.0	19,738	6.9
3. Los Angeles-Long Beach SMSA	11.3	13,027	4.5
4. Philadelphia	7.1	8,826	3.1
5. Detroit	5.2	8,251	2.9
6. San Francisco-Oakland	5.2	7,458	2.6
7. Boston	5.6	6,898	2.4
8. Minneapolis-St. Paul	2.9	4,941	1.7
9. Cleveland	3.4	4,861	1.7
10. Pittsburgh	3.3	4,513	1.6
11. Dallas	2.7	4,030	1.4
12. Atlanta	2.3	3,998	1.4
Five SMSA's with smallest volume of wholesale trade:	(Actual Count)		
Lorain-Elyria, Ohio	148	47	—
Anderson, Indiana	117	44	—
Pittsfield, Mass.	82	41	—
Laredo, Texas	86	38	—
Gadsden, Ala.	91	31	—

Source: United States *Census of Business*, 1958, Wholesale Trade, United States Summary, Table 1-G.

parking facilities, movie theatres, bowling alleys, and many others.

The Census shows that the service function differs considerably from one place to another. One might think, for example, that ex-penditures for amusement and recreation would vary from city to city in about the same fashion as does population; that is, that New York would do about 8 per cent of the nation's business, somewhat more than twice as much

Table **29-5** *Amusement, Recreation, and Motion Picture Services in the 12 Largest Standard Statistical Areas, 1958*

Place	Number of Establishments	Receipts in Millions of Dollars	Percentage of National Total
UNITED STATES TOTAL	94,241	$5,081.7	100.0
New York SCA	8,696	1,227.9	24.1
Los Angeles SMSA	4,853	548.8	10.8
Chicago SCA	3,375	249.2	4.9
Detroit	2,045	114.6	2.2
San Francisco	1,590	102.5	2.0
Philadelphia	1,776	96.9	1.9
Boston	1,441	83.4	1.6
Washington	883	65.9	1.3
Cleveland	1,185	59.5	1.2
Pittsburgh	1,206	53.1	1.1
Cincinnati	690	51.4	1.0
Baltimore	889	50.6	1.0

Source: United States *Census of Business*, 1958, Selected Services, United States Summary, Table 8.

Cities: Characteristics and Relationship

as Los Angeles, which in turn would slightly exceed Chicago and so on. But as Table 29-5 shows, New York accounts for 24 per cent of the commercial entertainment in the United States, over three times its percentage of the nation's population, and Los Angeles does more than twice as much business of this type than does Chicago. A still different pattern unfolds for specific types of entertainment. For example, receipts from bowling alleys and pool halls are noticeably higher in Chicago than anywhere else in the country, almost half again as much as in New York. Detroit, in third place, is considerably ahead of Los Angeles.

EMPLOYMENT STRUCTURE

The term employment structure, as we have seen, refers to the way the working population of a place is divided up among the various categories of economic activity. The employment structure for the United States urban populace as a whole, given in the first column of Table 29-6, page 542, is a "datum plane," or criterion, against which individual cities can be compared. The employment structures of 15 selected cities are also given in Table 29-6. Notice how they deviate from the national average and from one other.

For cities in general, manufacturing provides the most jobs—29.4 per cent. Retail trade trails in second place with 17.6 per cent of the jobs. Transportation accounts for 6 per cent.

The proportions are strikingly different from city to city, however. In Brawley, California, more people work on farms than in stores. Gloucester, Massachusetts, has a higher percentage in fishing than any other city; nevertheless, its structure is dominated by manufacturing and retailing. In Hibbing, Minnesota, mining provides twice as many jobs as retailing, while in Kannapolis, North Carolina, the textile mills and other factories account for an amazing 70 per cent of all job opportunities. Conneaut, Ohio, is the nation's leading transport city, if we go by its employment structure. No city has as high a percentage in wholesaling as Alisal, Cali-

fornia, nor in retailing as Durant, Oklahoma. Notice the importance of finance in Hartford, of private household jobs in Opelika, Alabama, hotel jobs in Hollywood, Florida, entertainment in Las Vegas, medical employment in Kings Park, New York, education employment in State College (termed "University Park" by some) in Pennsylvania, and government workers in Washington, D.C.

Retail trade is the most universally important economic activity, ranking first in the employment structure of most cities. In those communities where some other line of endeavor ranks first, retailing almost invariably ranks second (except in rare instances such as Conneaut). Figure 29-1, Part A, illustrates how employment structures can be portrayed graphically, using the urban United States, New York, and Hartford as examples.

Classification by Total Employment
In terms of employment structure, cities can be classified in many ways. One system employs letter symbols for the various types of economic activity—M for manufacturing, R retail trade, T transportation, N mining, E education, D medical, and so forth—and lists the three leading categories for each city. According to this system New York would be classified MRT, indicating that manufacturing, retailing, and transportation provide, in that order, the most jobs. Hibbing would be classified NRE since mining, retailing, and education are its leading trio. (Some Swedish geographers have prepared an ingenious map showing, in terms of total employment structures, both the size and function of cities in Europe. Printed in four colors, at a very large scale, with intricate symbols, the map is not amenable to black-and-white reproduction. Yet, this wall map, entitled *Economic Map of Europe*, is so noteworthy an example of the mapping of urban settlements by size and employment structure that every economic geographer should be familiar with it. Compiled and constructed under the direction of William-Olsson, the map is available from Generalstabens Litografiska, Anstalts Förlag, Stockholm, Sweden).

Table **29-6** *Employment Structures: Selected Service Centers*
(with 10,000 or More Inhabitants)

	UNITED STATES URBAN	New York	Brawley, Calif.	Gloucester, Mass.	Hibbing, Minn.	Kannapolis, N. Car.	Conneaut, Ohio	Alisal, Calif.
Employment / Population Ratio (as a Percentage)	40.0	41.5	33.1	34.1	40.7	46.5	40.3	33.3
Percentage employed in: All Activities	100.0	100.0	100.0	100.0	100.0	100.0	100.0	100.0
Agriculture	1.0	0.3	32.8	1.1	0.2	0.5	0.2	3.9
Forestry and fisheries	0.1	—	—	15.0	—	—	1.4	—
Mining	0.9	—	—	—	34.8	—	0.1	0.1
Manufacturing	29.4	30.8	6.8	21.6	4.0	70.2	22.1	12.3
Transportation	6.0	5.9	2.7	3.3	5.4	1.8	40.0	3.5
Wholesale trade	4.3	5.3	6.8	8.3	2.8	0.4	1.1	18.3
Retail trade	17.6	16.0	16.7	16.7	17.1	10.0	13.5	21.1
Finance, insurance	4.4	6.9	1.3	2.6	1.8	1.1	1.9	2.4
Private households	3.2	2.8	2.7	2.9	2.0	2.8	1.2	1.4
Hotels, lodging places	1.1	1.0	1.6	0.6	1.5	0.3	0.4	0.5
Entertainment, recreation	1.2	1.3	1.4	0.8	0.9	0.5	0.7	1.3
Medical	3.5	3.3	1.6	3.1	3.5	0.6	1.9	2.9
Education	3.8	2.7	3.6	2.9	5.9	1.5	2.3	2.3
Public administration	5.2	4.4	3.8	3.8	5.0	0.6	1.5	4.1
Other services	16.7	—	—	—	—	—	—	—

	Durant, Okla.	Hartford, Conn.	Opelika, Ala.	Hollywood, Fla.	Las Vegas, Nev.	Kings Park, N.Y.	State College, Penn.	Washington, D.C.
Employment / Population Ratio (as a Percentage)	32.0	44.4	43.2	38.0	42.0	13.5	29.5	43.7
Percentage employed in: All Activities	100.0	100.0	100.0	100.0	100.0	100.0	100.0	100.0
Agriculture	2.4	0.7	1.4	2.7	0.7	0.9	1.0	0.2
Forestry and fisheries	—	—	—	0.1	—	0.1	0.1	—
Mining	0.5	—	—	—	0.4	—	0.1	—
Manufacturing	8.0	32.9	29.2	5.4	3.9	2.6	2.7	7.4
Transportation	4.3	2.3	2.4	2.3	8.0	1.5	0.7	4.9
Wholesale trade	5.7	3.8	4.2	3.0	2.2	0.2	1.1	2.1
Retail trade	28.4	16.6	17.7	21.8	22.0	7.8	13.4	15.0
Finance, insurance	3.4	12.5	3.0	7.1	2.7	1.1	1.5	4.7
Private households	3.0	2.1	14.7	3.8	3.0	1.2	2.6	4.3
Hotels, lodging places	1.1	0.7	0.8	13.7	10.4	0.6	5.4	1.5
Entertainment, recreation	1.4	0.7	0.8	3.2	15.8	0.5	1.7	0.9
Medical	3.0	4.6	1.8	2.5	2.6	72.0	1.4	3.9
Education	8.9	3.0	3.3	3.3	1.9	2.1	55.1	3.7
Public administration	5.5	4.8	2.9	4.2	5.7	2.0	3.0	31.5
Other services	—	—	—	—	—	—	—	—

Source: Computed from United States Bureau of the Census, *Census of Population*, United States Summary, and each state's volume, *Characteristics of the Population*.

Cities: Characteristics and Relationship

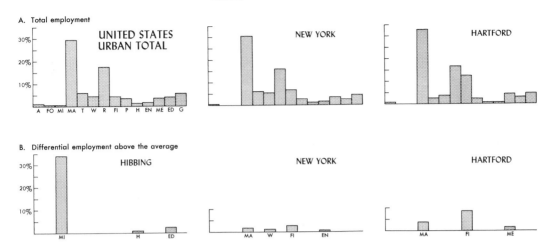

Figure 29-1 (*Symbols: A agriculture, FO forestry and fishing, MI mining, MA manufacturing, T transportation, W wholesale trade, R retail trade, FI finance, P professional services, H households, EN entertainment, ME medical, ED education, G government.*)

Differentials from National Average

But what if we inquire into the activities that are distinctive in a city—that is, the endeavors in which it exceeds the national average by the widest margin? Hollywood, Florida, for example, in the system described above, would be classified RHF, since retail stores, hotels and lodging places, and financial services account for 21.8 per cent, 13.7 per cent, and 7.1 per cent respectively of the jobs in town. Now, when we compare Hollywood's percentages in the several employment categories (Table 29-6) with the national averages, we discover a positive differential of only 4.2 in retail trade (21.8 per cent as against the national average of 17.6 per cent) but a 12.6 differential in hotels and lodging jobs (13.7 per cent minus 1.1 per cent). In this scheme Hollywood stands out far more conspicuously on the national scene in the hotel and lodging business than in retail trade. Therefore, the former is its *most distinctive* economic endeavor. Hollywood would be classified according to the *positive differential system* as HRF, the leading activities, in terms of positive differentials, being the hotel business 12.6, retail trade 4.2, and finance 2.7. On the same basis, Hartford, Connecticut, would be FMD, whereas by the first system it would be MRF.

Part B of Figure 29-1, which uses as examples the employment structures of Hibbing, New York, and Hartford, strikingly reveals the contrast between structures built up in terms of differentials and those founded on total employment.[*]

Standard Deviations

Still another perspective on employment structures is provided by use of the statistical technique of *standard deviation*. Standard deviation is a measure of the average variability of a group of values from the average value, or mean. A detailed explanation of *standard deviation* can be found in any elementary textbook on statistics, but for our purposes here we can say that it is computed by adding up the squares of the *differences* of all values from the mean, dividing that sum by the number of those values, and determining the square root of that quotient. Or, in algebraic symbols,

$$SD = \sqrt{\frac{\Sigma\, d^2}{N}}$$

[*] Further treatment of this method appears in Leigh Pownall's "Functions of New Zealand Towns," *Annals of the Association of American Geographers*, 1953, pp. 332-350.

Cities: Characteristics and Relationships

in which Σ = sum, d = difference between each value and the mean, and N = number of values.

Geographer Howard Nelson, applying this device to employment structures, found, for example, that the standard deviation of employment in retail trade in the United States is 3.63. If a city's percentage of employment in retail trade is equal to the national average plus 3.63, then Nelson classified the city in the R category. If its percentage exceeds the national average by 7.26 (two standard deviations—2 x 3.63) then it is classified R2, if by 10.89 or more (three or more standard deviations), then the city is classified R3. In sum, a single letter symbol indicates an excess of at least one deviation but less than two; the arabic numeral 2 following the letter indicates at least 2 but not 3 deviations; the numeral 3 indicates excess of 3 or more deviations; and more than one letter symbol indicates the city exceeds the average by more than one deviation in more than one category.

Accordingly, Hartford is classified F3 because employment there in the financial category exceeds the national average by more than three standard deviations and because in no other activity does it top the average by as much as one standard deviation. A city that exceeds the national average in no activity by so much as a single deviation is put in the D category—diversified. Selected examples of cities classified by the Nelson system are given in Table 29-7.

Actually, we can construct maps (like Figure 29-2) based on the Nelson classification system. Remember, though, that the appearance of a city on any one map does *not* mean that the indicated activity is the city's *principal* source of jobs. For instance, Trinidad, Colorado, is on the mining map, but mining is *not* its foremost endeavor (actually retail trade is first). Rather, it means, in this case, that Trinidad's percentage of miners exceeds the average by more than one standard deviation.*

* An interesting method for classifying towns in terms of a "functional index" and a "specialization index" has been presented by John Webb in "Basic Concepts In The Analysis of Small Urban Centers of Minnesota," *Annals of the Association of American Geographers,* 1959, pp. 55-72.

Table **29-7** *Economic Classification of Selected American Cities: Nelson System*

New York	F2
Chicago	F
Los Angeles	F
Philadelphia	F
Detroit	Mf
Boston	F
San Francisco, Oakland	F2
Pittsburgh	D
St. Louis	Ps
Cleveland	D
Washington	Pb3, F
Baltimore	D
Minneapolis-St. Paul	F2, W
Milwaukee	D
Cincinnati	D
Buffalo	D
Houston	F
Kansas City	F
New Orleans	T, W, F
Seattle	F2
Alisal, California	W3
Asbury Park, New Jersey	Ps3, R, Pb
Atlanta, Georgia	F2
Brockton, Massachusetts	Mf
Butte, Montana	Mi3
Cheyenne, Wyoming	T3, Pb2
Conneaut, Ohio	T3
Dallas, Texas	F3, W
Denver, Colorado	W,F
Durant, Oklahoma	R2
Hanford, California	R3
Hartford, Connecticut	F3
Hibbing, Minnesota	Mi3
Hollywood, Florida	Ps3, F3
Kannapolis, North Carolina	Mf2
Kearney, Nebraska	R3, Pf2, Ps2, W
Las Vegas, Nevada	Ps3
Madison, Wisconsin	Pf2, Pb, F
Minot, North Dakota	R, T, W
State College, Penn.	Pf3, Ps

D	diversified
F	finance
Mf	manufacturing
Mi	mining
Pb	public administration
Pf	professional services
Ps	personal services
R	retail trade
T	transportation
W	wholesale trade

3—City employment exceeds national urban average by 3 or more standard deviations

2—City employment exceeds national urban average by 2 standard deviations

Absence of numeral indicates the excess is at least 1 standard deviation

Source: Howard Nelson, "A Service Classification of American Cities," *Economic Geography,* 1955, pp. 205-210.

Cities: Characteristics and Relationships

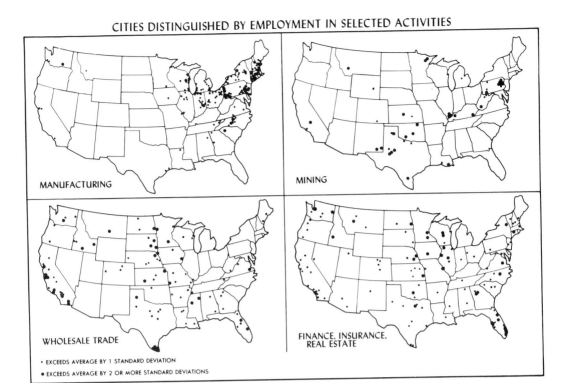

MANUFACTURING

MINING

WHOLESALE TRADE

FINANCE, INSURANCE, REAL ESTATE

• EXCEEDS AVERAGE BY 1 STANDARD DEVIATION
● EXCEEDS AVERAGE BY 2 OR MORE STANDARD DEVIATIONS

Figure 29-2 (*After Howard Nelson.*)

PERSONAL INCOME

Annual personal incomes vary considerably from city to city. In Charleston, South Carolina the median income is $1857, while that in South Bend, Indiana is almost twice as large—$3673. The highest median income in any large American urban area is $3666 in Flint, Michigan. Other high-ranking tertiary centers are Detroit ($3594), Chicago ($3497), and Cleveland ($3446). (Recall Figure 23-3 of hourly earnings as well as the discussion of the automotive and steel industries.) Large cities with low incomes are St. Petersburg, Florida ($1966), Savannah, Georgia ($2065), and Montgomery, Alabama ($2099). As Table 29-9, page 547, shows, manufactural cities tend to have a distinctly higher median income than any other type of city.

Whether the economic character of tertiary centers be appraised in terms of retailing, wholesaling, services, employment structure, or personal income, it is clear that urban settlements vary considerably. But research needs to be done to extract geographic principles from the wealth of data available in United States Census volumes. More on this later under the *economic base concept.*

Associations of Tertiary Activity with Other Phenomena

INTERNAL RELATIONSHIPS

As tertiary endeavor takes root and proliferates in a place, several other phenomena flourish too, and, because of their variation from place to place, add distinctive qualities to service centers.

Six of these phenomena will be discussed in the pages to follow: numbers of inhabitants, changes in numbers of inhabitants, amount of land occupied by the service center, shape of the land occupied, types of usage to which that land is put, and morphology of the settlement.

Numbers of Inhabitants   Generally speaking, there is a strong correlation between job opportunities and population; the larger the number of jobs, the larger the population. It is not surprising therefore to find that the number of jobs in New York (the nation's largest trade center) exceeds the number in Los Angeles, which slightly exceeds that in Chicago. Yet the covariance is not exact. If it were, the labor force of every city would equal 40 per cent of its populace—the national average. The remaining 60 per cent fall in various classes—such as housewives, school pupils, retired persons, or inmates of penal institutions. But this ratio, known as *the E/P ratio* (employment/population), varies from city to city. Computation based on a sampling of larger cities reveals peak ratios of 44.6 in Kannapolis, North Carolina, 44.4 in Hartford, Connecticut, and 43.7 in Washington, D.C., and low rates of 13.5 in Kings Park, New York (where numerous residents spend most of the year in a hospital) and 29.5 in State College, Pennsylvania (where many persons spend most of the year as students in Pennsylvania

State University). New York City's E/P ratio is 41.5.

A minority of Americans are free to choose their place of residence quite apart from the question of job opportunities. Retired pensioners, for example, can often settle anywhere since their income follows them. Many choose communities with amenable climates, such as Santa Cruz, California. One might suppose, then, that these communities would have an extremely low E/P ratio. But what happens is that the pensioners create a demand for grocery stores, clothing stores, barber shops, and other businesses. The E/P ratio of 35.0 for Santa Cruz, for instance, is lower than the average but not as low as might be supposed.

Changes in Numbers of Inhabitants
Tertiary settlements differ in their population changes. For example, in 1960 the three urban places of Wilkes-Barre, Pennsylvania, Alameda, California, and Tuscaloosa, Alabama, each had 63,000 inhabitants. By size alone, they would appear to be three of a kind. But

Figure 29-3

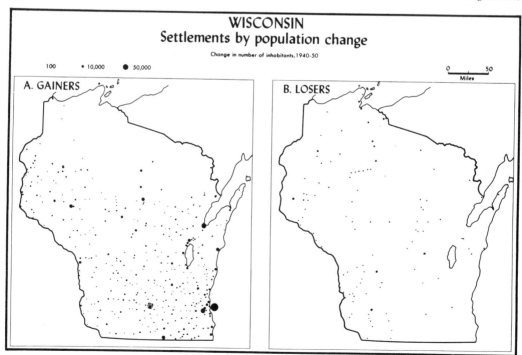

Cities: Characteristics and Relationships

by population *change* they are three entirely different breeds, as shown in Table 29-8.

Table **29-8** *Population Change:*
Selected Urban Places

Place	Number of Inhabitants		
	1960	1950	Change
Wilkes-Barre, Pa.	63,000	76,000	− 7,000
Alameda, Calif.	63,000	64,000	− 1,000
Tuscaloosa, Ala.	63,000	46,000	+17,000

Source: United States Bureau of the Census, *Census of Population, 1960.*

Wilkes-Barre is shrinking, Alameda is holding rather steady, while Tuscaloosa is gaining.

Figure 29-3 illustrates one type of mapping that can be done on the basis of change. Wisconsin had 514 tertiary centers of which 112 lost population between 1940 and 1950 and 402 gained. The gainers are depicted with circles proportional to their increments. Two large gainers stand out: Milwaukee and Madison. The smaller gainers are widely dispersed throughout the state. The 112 losers show an entirely different pattern. Nearly all of them are in the northern and western parts of the state. This pattern is consistent with what we have learned in previous chapters about Wisconsin: the southeastern portion is a region of intense manufacturing, high-value agriculture, high railway traffic density, low freight rates, and a high degree of urbanism; the northwestern section tends to be just the opposite on all these counts.

There is some correlation between rate of population change and the distinctive economic activities of cities. Manufacturing cities are experiencing much smaller growth rates than are cities whose characteristic employment categories are retail trade, finance, and professional and personal services. This is borne out by Table 29-9 in which the vertical columns are identified by symbols in the Nelson system.

Amount of Land   One might suppose that the more people in a service center, the greater its acreage. This correlation tends to hold for urbanized areas since the largest urbanized area (New York with over 14,000,000 people) also covers the most land (1891 square miles). But a study of all urbanized areas reveals that the least population does not correlate with the least land. The former is Tyler, Texas with 51,739 people on 18.6 square miles of land; the latter is Champaign-Urbana, Illinois where 12.4 square miles of land harbor 78,000 residents.

If land and population covaried closely, service centers of the same population should cover the same amount of land, and places the same size should have similar populations.

Table **29-9**   *Averages of Various Criteria by Economic Classification of Cities*

Criteria	All Cities	Mf3 & Mf2	R3 & R2	Pf3 & Pf2	T3 & T2	Mi3 & Mi2	Pb3 & Pb2	Ps3 & Ps2	W3 & W2	F3 & F2
Percentage increase in population, 1940-50	27.9	2.2	39.4	65.0	17.5	31.1	40.0	61.0	30.4	35.6
Percentage 65 years old or older	8.6	7.6	9.0	7.6	9.7	7.4	7.3	9.2	7.7	10.0
Average years of school completed	10.0	8.9	10.5	12.3	10.4	9.7	10.8	11.0	9.9	11.1
Participation in labor force, percentage of males	77.8	82.8	77.1	55.8	78.0	79.2	77.8	73.2	80.0	75.6
Participation in labor force, percentage of females	32.8	35.9	30.3	34.1	29.2	27.1	33.0	33.3	33.0	34.6
Median income	$2643	$3134	$2560	$1674	$2733	$2822	$2658	$2227	$2566	$2780

Source: Howard J. Nelson, "Some Characteristics of the Population of Cities in Similar Service Classifications," *Economic Geography*, (1957), page 97.

Cities: Characteristics and Relationships

Yet the Trenton and Des Moines urbanized areas, each with 240,000 people, cover 75 and 97 square miles respectively; and Greensboro, North Carolina, and Canton, Ohio, each encompass 50 square miles of land, yet their populations are 123,000 and 213,000 respectively.

One way to express this relationship is by the ratios of population per square mile. Put together, all the nation's urbanized areas have 95,848,000 people on 25,544 square miles of land, or a ratio of 3752 people per square mile. At one extreme is York, Pennsylvania, with a density of 9699, at the other is Lewiston-Auburn, Maine, with 680. (New York's density is 7462.)

The question now becomes: Is there any relationship between area and population density? For example, do larger cities tend to be more densely or less densely occupied?

We can portray such covariation in a *scatter diagram* (see page 299 for an explanation of this device), as in Figure 29-4. Each city is represented by a dot, the position of which is determined by the two variables—area in square miles and inhabitants per square mile.

If both population and area increased consistently with size of cities, then the dots in Figure 29-4 would lie in a *straight* line, and that line would be *horizontal* at whatever level prevailed as the urban density per square mile. But this is not the case. If, however, though population and land both increased with city size, but population did so at a faster rate, then the dots on the scatter diagram would conform with a line that trended upward from left to right. That no such line emerges on Figure 29-4 leads to the conclusion that population and amount of land in urbanized areas do not covary spatially at as high a degree as might be supposed.*

Types of Land Usage   Service centers clearly differ markedly in the use of land, though data on this point are scanty. The United States Census, for instance, contains

---

* See Chester Smolski, "A Study in Sampling: City Size and Population Density," *The Professional Geographer*, March 1962, pp. 8-10, for further analysis of this relationship.

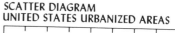

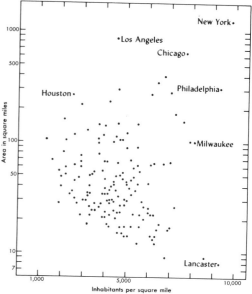

Figure 29-4

very little on land usage. Still, a sample investigation of American cities by Harland Bartholomew and Jack Wood for the Harvard Planning Studies reveals some interesting correlations between this variable and city size (see Table 29-10). Multiple-family dwellings (residences with three or more families) occupy an increasing percentage of land as size of city increases. Other uses that tend to covary positively with population are parks and playgrounds, heavy industry, light industry, and commercial uses. Conversely, some uses shrink relatively as size increases: single family residential areas, public and semipublic uses (such as schools and churches), streets, and vacant land.

Notice the high percentages in streets. Few realize that, in most cities, streets occupy over 20 per cent of the land whereas commercial structures rarely take up more than 4 per cent. On a national average, housing spreads out over approximately two-fifths of a city's territory.

But all these uses vary spatially. As a result of a policy of unusually wide streets in St. Petersburg, Florida, 57 per cent of the city is in streets; at the opposite pole is Bar

Cities: Characteristics and Relationships

Table **29-10** *Mean Percentage of Land Usage in Selected Cities by Size*

	Population of City			
Land Use	Under 50,000	50,000 to 100,000	100,000 to 250,000	Over 250,000
Number of cities studied	28	13	7	5
All land (percentage)	100	100	100	100
Mean Percentage in following uses:				
Residential, one family	34.0	31.0	36.0	28.0
Residential, two families	3.7	4.1	3.6	6.8
Residential, three plus	1.7	2.1	2.2	4.9
Commercial	3.1	2.6	2.9	4.3
Light Industry	2.8	2.1	2.4	3.8
Heavy Industry	2.9	2.7	3.5	4.7
Railways	5.0	4.9	5.4	4.4
Parks, Playgrounds	5.1	6.5	5.7	8.6
Public and Semipublic	13.3	10.9	11.2	9.6
Streets	28.3	33.3	27.6	24.8
Vacant	47.0	38.9	21.9	20.4

Source: Harland Bartholomew and Jack Wood, *Land Uses in American Cities*, Harvard Planning Studies, Vol. XV, 1955, Tables 1, 2, 3, and 4.

Harbor, Maine, with only 16 per cent in streets. Bartholomew and Wood indicate ranges in other uses as follows:

Commercial usage varies from 1.7 per cent in St. Petersburg to 6.5 per cent in West Palm Beach. Residential use covers 64 per cent of Bar Harbor, and only 24 per cent of Utica, New York. Heavy industry spreads over 14 per cent of Newark but is entirely absent in Santa Fe, New Mexico.

The Shape (Outline) of Service Centers

Cities assume a variety of shapes which are related to both physical and cultural factors.

The *strassendorf* (or shoe-string) type is much longer on one axis than the other and usually appears in valleys—numerous towns in Switzerland and West Virginia are examples. Youngstown, Ohio (Figure 29-5, page 550), has a tendency toward linear shape.

Rectangular communities generally occur where the terrain is rather flat *and* where cultural attitudes have decreed that the land be divided into rectangular "blocks," as in Des Moines, Iowa (Figure 29-5).

Circular shapes are often found in old cities that were once surrounded by a wall, or where the main streets all converge on the settlement's center, like spokes on a wheel.

The star shape appears in large cities that are major transport centers; settlement tends to creep out along the transport routes, as in Dayton, Ohio, and Oklahoma City.

Crescent shaped cities sometimes develop around the end of a body of water.

In addition to these simple types there are complex or irregular shapes that indicate responses to a combination of influences. Figure 29-5 shows how different are the shapes of several selected urbanized areas. The particular shape of any specific city is explained by its relationships to both physical features (for instance, the ocean front as at Atlantic City and St. Petersburg, rugged terrain as at Wilkes-Barre and Youngstown, waterways as at Norfolk and Toledo) and cultural features (for example, main line railways and highways as at Dayton, and annexation policies as at Phoenix).

The *morphology* of a city is its "anatomy," the physical form and structure—including street layout, spacing of buildings, size and architectural design of buildings, types and color of building materials, presence or absence of an encircling wall, and so forth. Surely, cities vary enough in these respects from one part of the world to another to enable us to classify them scientifically on

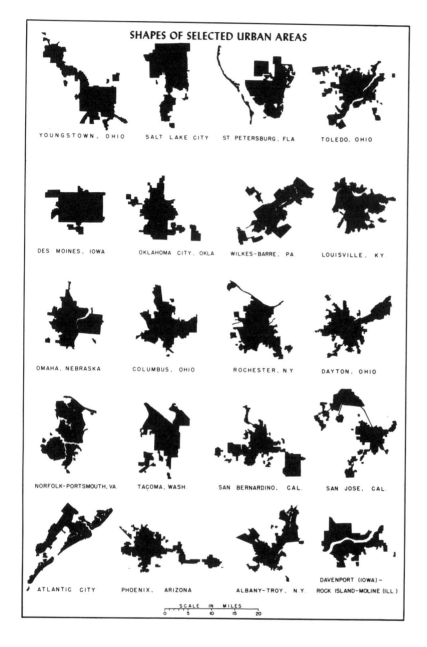

SHAPES OF SELECTED URBAN AREAS

YOUNGSTOWN, OHIO   SALT LAKE CITY   ST PETERSBURG, FLA   TOLEDO, OHIO

DES MOINES, IOWA   OKLAHOMA CITY, OKLA   WILKES-BARRE, PA   LOUISVILLE, KY.

OMAHA, NEBRASKA   COLUMBUS, OHIO   ROCHESTER, N.Y.   DAYTON, OHIO

NORFOLK-PORTSMOUTH, VA.   TACOMA, WASH.   SAN BERNARDINO, CAL.   SAN JOSE, CAL.

ATLANTIC CITY   PHOENIX, ARIZONA   ALBANY-TROY, N.Y.   DAVENPORT (IOWA) – ROCK ISLAND-MOLINE (ILL.)

SCALE IN MILES
0   5   10   15   20

Figure 29-5

the basis of morphology. Such a classification, were it available, might well serve as a basis for delimiting urban regions of the entire world.*

In addition to numbers of people, changes in population, amount of land, uses of land,

---

* Illustrative of what can be done in this direction for one part of the world is Robert Dickinson's book, *The West European City*, Routledge and Kegan Paul, Ltd., London, 1951.

---

shapes of the settlement, and morphology, service centers differ in other ways, such as (a) percentage of population that is foreign-born white (from 20.9 per cent in New Bedford, Massachusetts, to 0.5 per cent in Knoxville, Tennessee), (b) percentage of population that is nonwhite (from 40.5 per cent in Jackson, Mississippi, to 0.2 per cent in Lowell, Massachusetts), and (c) median school years completed by persons 25 years of age and

Cities: Characteristics and Relationships

older (from 12.1 in Lincoln, Nebraska, to 8.0 in Augusta, Georgia).*

All these internal variables need to be investigated before we can understand their relationship to the economic life of a service center. But even that will not be enough. We also need to know how a city is related to other places.

EXTERNAL RELATIONSHIPS

The external relationships of a service center link it to areas of surplus production of some sort. And the link is accomplished by means of transportation arteries over which people travel and surplus goods are shipped. We shall take up these linkages first insofar as they relate to primary production, transportation routes, and topographic features.

Primary Production Cities ultimately depend for their life upon the surplus production of farmers, miners, foresters, and fishermen. But before surpluses of wheat, iron ore, logs, and salmon can be consumed, they must be processed, or manufactured. This need gives birth to service centers whose residents (a) assemble surpluses, (b) change the form of some of the commodities, or (c) ship them on to other service centers, and, in either case, (d) in return distribute tractors, overalls, shoes, flour, and so on to the farmers and other primary producers. Thus, a chain is welded together whereby primary production, transportation, manufacturing, and servicing are all interrelated. If we synthesized the information presented in preceding chapters we would discover a striking correlation between the urban regions on Figure 28-3 and regions of commercial agriculture, mining, forestry, fishing, manufacturing, transportation, and international trade. But the foundation of the whole complex is a solid base of surplus

* Readers interested in such variations will find illuminating analyses in Howard Nelson, "Some Characteristics of the Population of Cities in Similar Service Classifications," *Economic Geography*, Vol. 33, 1957, pp. 95-108, and in Otis D. Duncan and Albert J. Reiss, *Social Characteristics of Urban and Rural Communities*, Wiley and Sons (New York), 1956.

primary production. "Cities do not grow up of themselves. Countrysides set them up to do tasks that must be performed in central places." So wrote Mark Jefferson over thirty years ago. And the people in these countrysides must be generating an excess before they can pay for the services performed for them in tertiary service centers.

A strong correlation also exists between the *mechanization* of primary production and urbanization. The more highly mechanized the agriculture, forestry, and mining of a region, the greater its tendency to urbanize. Not only does mechanization enable the production of a greater surplus, which leads to increase of city services, it also unshackles numerous rural laborers for city jobs. As a result, mechanized primary production stimulates migration from rural to urban places.

Transportation Routes Service centers normally develop at junctions of transportation routes. Typical examples are *road crossings* (as illustrated by thousands of hamlets at rural crossroads), road *junctions* with railways (as in numerous villages and towns), road crossings of nonnavigable streams (as at fords, which so frequently lent their names, —Rockford, Oxford, and Brantford), *river ports* where roads or railways cross navigable streams (Cincinnati, St. Louis, and Duisburg), *railheads* where a railway line ends and roads or water routes converge upon it (as at Faith, South Dakota), *railway junctions* (Kansas City), and *heads of navigation* where waterways make their deepest penetration of a land mass in convergence with roads and railways (London and Chicago). Finally, the world's greatest cities tend to be near the heads of navigation for ocean vessels.

Generally, the greater the convergence of traffic, the larger the service center. Chicago illustrates this point well. Located at the ultimate intrusion by the Great Lakes into the productive interior of America (which had a surplus first of furs and timber and then of agricultural products) Chicago quickly shot out roads and then railroads in all directions from its waterfront. As it happened, the rail-

A village near Fabriano, Italy, a typical Mediterranean town reposing on a hilltop, from which the farmers walk down to their farms. In the foreground is a field which is simultaneously producing a tree crop and grain. The grain is wheat, which is sown in autumn, thrives on winter rains, and is harvested in spring. No grain can survive the arid summers; however, deep-rooted trees (mulberry in this particular field) are sustained through the summer by soil moisture several feet below ground level. Leaves and shoots from these trees are pruned periodically and sold as a cash crop to silkworm nurseries and silk producers in the village. (Courtesy Ernest Vinson.)

roads building eastward from Chicago soon linked up with those heading westward from New York. This is the real explanation of Chicago's position as a railway center, not the widely held fallacy that railroads had to bend around Lake Michigan as they penetrated westward from the East Coast.

In some places, service centers are lined up along the busiest transport routes like beads on a string. Witness, for example, the string of cities from Buffalo to Albany along a route that contains a canal, a railway, a highway, and now, a thruway. A chain of smaller cities stretches in almost a straight line from St. Louis to Indianapolis along the old national turnpike of the 1800's and the present-day main line of the Pennsylvania Railroad as well as U.S. Highway 40.

Topography There is scarcely any correlation between topography and the location of service centers on a world scale. Most city builders have preferred flat sites, so most cities are on plains. Still there are vast plains with no cities, and many hilly areas that do have large settlements. Even the flat-sites principle needs qualification; for centuries, hilltop sites were preferred for protective reasons. After all, assailants could sack a valley town more readily than one built on an impregnable hilltop. Even today in Italy and numerous countries of southern Europe and the Middle East (where urbanism first became extensive) the typical location for villages and many towns is the summit of a hill.

But with the transportation revolution, railways, highways, and canals snaked their way through valleys more readily than across hilltops; and, with improvements in social mores and in law and order, the value of hilltops for protection began to shrink while the value of valley sites for access to transportation rose. Consequently, urban centers that have developed since 1800 have tended to be located in valleys. Urban New York State, Pennsylvania, and California illustrate the tendency of modern cities to attach themselves to valley sites.

The actual movement along transportation routes between a center of tertiary economic activity and other areas is reciprocal with both outbound and inbound phases.

OUTBOUND MOVEMENTS

Commodities   How a city is linked to other places through the outward movement of a particular commodity (say, the circula-

tion, by counties, of a Chicago daily newspaper) is shown in Figure 29-6. Even a casual inspection of this map raises several questions. For example, why the sharp break in circulation at the Missouri border? Why does the *Tribune* penetrate farther into Iowa than into Minnesota? Why the particular pattern in Michigan? Why is the penetration into southwestern Indiana greater than into southeastern Indiana? Since nearly every daily newspaper releases information on its circulation, we can make fascinating maps of the areas tied to a city through this medium.

Figure 29-6

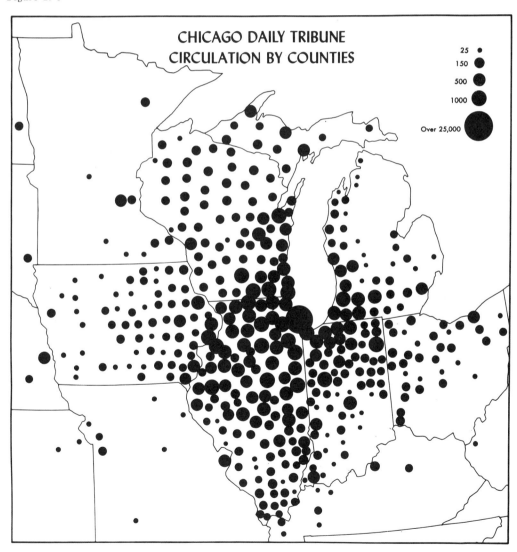

CHICAGO DAILY TRIBUNE
CIRCULATION BY COUNTIES

25
150
500
1000
Over 25,000

Service centers large enough to have post offices can also provide accurate maps showing the exact boundaries of rural delivery. Similarly, we can easily map regions that receive gas, electricity, and telephone service from an urban center.

Concept of Nodal Regions   The circulation of newspapers is a good example to illustrate the concept of nodal regions. *A nodal region is a portion of the earth's surface that is homogeneous in relationship to a node, or central point.* In a sense, Figure 29-6 is the pattern of one nodal region, specifically the one tied by circulation of the *Tribune* to the focal point of Chicago.

Figure 29-7 illustrates how a different criterion—that of *dominance* of newspaper circulation—can be used to delimit nodal regions. Lines are drawn, not around the entire area into which a newspaper circulates, but only around the area in which that paper outsells every other competitor. Accordingly, the Milwaukee nodal region on Figure 29-7 is not the area within which Milwaukee newspapers circulate but rather the area in which they dominate the newspaper market. Thus, even though Chicago papers circulate widely in Wisconsin, the Chicago nodal region on Figure 29-7 is restricted to an extremely small area in the southeast corner of the state tucked in behind the nodal regions of Milwaukee, Racine, Kenosha, and Beloit.

As this map illustrates, most nodal regions contain the city they focus on; however, it is possible for a nodal region to exist without containing its node. Note that one small detached segment of the Milwaukee nodal region is on the tip of Door Peninsula (northeast of the Green Bay Region), and a large detached piece occupies the north-central part of Wisconsin.

Nodes by no means need occur in the center of their regions. Notice how far off-center Madison is in its nodal area, LaCrosse, Chippewa Falls, and Superior in theirs. A principle holds that a city's nodal region will extend farther on the side of weaker competition; for instance, Madison's area extends only 20 miles to the east because of intense competi-

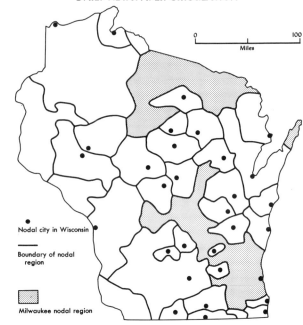

WISCONSIN: NODAL REGIONS OF DAILY NEWSPAPER CIRCULATION

● Nodal city in Wisconsin

— Boundary of nodal region

▨ Milwaukee nodal region

Figure 29-7

tion from Milwaukee papers, but it spreads out 80 miles to the west and northwest where there is much weaker competition. Similarly, the Milwaukee region protrudes much farther to the northwest than to the west (where Madison heads it off) or to the north where several sizable cities (Green Bay, Appleton, Oshkosh, and Fond du Lac) all bid successfully for local readers.

Although the foregoing illustration of nodal regions has been cast in terms of outward movements, the concept could be shown to apply equally well to inbound traffic.

People   Cities, towns, villages, and even hamlets are linked with other places through the travels of their residents: commuters who go elsewhere to work, citizens who go to nearby towns to shop, young folks who go to school in other settlements, traveling salesmen whose work sends them ranging over territories of varying sizes.

For one of these types of movement we have the useful concept of *the employment field,* that is, the area to which the residents

Cities: Characteristics and Relationships

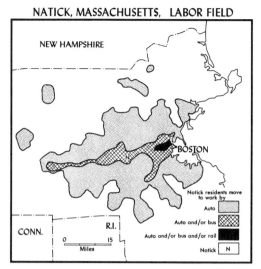

NATICK, MASSACHUSETTS, LABOR FIELD

NEW HAMPSHIRE

BOSTON

Natick residents move to work by

Auto

Auto and/or bus

Auto and/or bus and/or rail

Natick   N

CONN.   R.I.

0   15
Miles

Figure 29-8   (*After James Vance, in* Economic Geography.)

of a settlement commute to work. Illustrative of this concept is Figure 29-8, which shows the location of the Natick, Massachusetts, employment field (or labor field).

Money   Money (including credit) flows out from service centers for numerous reasons. At present it is impossible to measure the total outflow from a city without going directly to every individual and agency within the place to ask them how much money they send out of the city each year, for what purposes, and where they send it. Such a task

Figure 29-9

AN URBAN MILK SHED

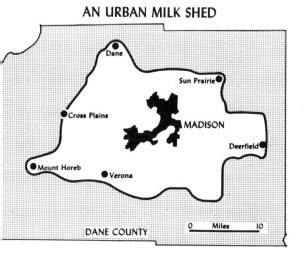

Dane

Sun Prairie

Cross Plains

MADISON

Deerfield

Mount Horeb

Verona

DANE COUNTY   0   Miles   10

is formidable; however, the research staff of *Fortune* magazine did exactly that in Oskaloosa, Iowa, in the late 1930's. They discovered that the 10,000 inhabitants of the town sent out $9,093,000 in one year. Most of this ($8,549,000) was sent out by business firms in payment for the merchandise that stocked their shelves. Only a small amount ($391,000) was spent elsewhere by Oskaloosa customers. A still smaller amount left Oskaloosa through government agencies—for instance, the United States Post Office and several county offices.

INBOUND MOVEMENTS

Commodities   Goods stream into a city, some for local consumption, some for distribution throughout the hinterland, and others for processing in factories before shipment elsewhere. Comparatively little research has been done on such movements; however, some information is available. Figure 29-9 shows the location of the area from which milk moves into Madison, Wisconsin—that is, the "Madison milk shed."

People   Inbound human traffic consists of three major streams: those going *through* the city, those going *to* it in order to work, and those going *to* it to shop. To be sure, there are other categories, but they are mere trickles compared to these three.

Inbound *through* traffic is relatively insignificant for large cities. Even the most hurried tourist tends to stop for at least some purchases in a metropolis. As investigations of highway traffic have revealed, the correlation between the size of a city and the percentage of inbound highway traffic that is just going through is inverse (or negative); the *smaller* the city, the more cars will simply pass on. Through traffic comprises three-fifths of the vehicles entering cities of less than 5,000 inhabitants; for cities in the 5,000-to-10,000 class, the proportion drops to two-fifths. It shrinks to one-fifth for cities in the 25,000-to-50,000 category, and to one-twentieth for cities exceeding 500,000 persons.

Commuters link a city to a surrounding area that may extend outwards for a surprising distance. A survey of the General Motors

Cities: Characteristics and Relationships

Specially-designed double-deck "gallery" passenger coaches handle commuter traffic between Chicago and its suburbs. Each such coach can accommodate nearly 100 people. (Courtesy Chicago, Burlington and Quincy Railroad Company.)

Automotive Division in La Grange, Illinois, reveals that laborers commute from as far away as the city of Dwight, 67 miles to the southwest. (Workers residing in Dwight drive a total of 33,500 miles a year in just travelling to and from work.) A map of automobile commuting to this one factory would show workers driving as far as 60 miles from the north, 45 miles from the northwest, 46 miles from the west, 67 from the southwest, 52 miles from the south, and 35 miles from Indiana to the east. Railway commuters to some service centers travel even further. Residents in Lake Geneva, Wisconsin ride commuter trains 80 miles each way daily to and from Chicago. Railroads radiating out from New York carry thousands of workers, some of whom travel two hours each way by train.

The term *labor shed* is commonly applied to the area from which a city draws commuting labor. So far not much study has been given to this concept, but labor sheds are beginning to receive increasing attention from urban analysts.*

* An excellent example is a study by James E. Vance, Jr., "Labor-Shed, Employment Field, and Dynamic Analysis in Urban Geography," *Economic Geography*, 1960, pp. 189-220.

The concepts of labor shed and employment field are useful in distinguishing, on a *functional basis*, two types of settlements that develop in the countryside surrounding a large city. One type is the *satellite*, which can be defined as a settlement whose labor shed exceeds its employment field. The other type is the *suburb*, in which the relationship is reversed. Notice that these definitions of suburb and satellite are based on their functional relationship to other places and not on their political status or on popular terminology. That is, the general public may consider some specific settlement to be a suburb when in terms of function it is actually a satellite.

The inbound flow of *customers* to a city is sometimes as great as that of commuters and may link a city to an enormous area. In Figure 29-10 we illustrate this relationship by portraying the places with which Madison, Wisconsin, is connected by virtue of patronage of one of its medical institutions.

Money   Customers bring money into a city when they arrive to shop. Additional sums arrive by mail or wire for commodities that are shipped out or for services rendered.

Cities: Characteristics and Relationships

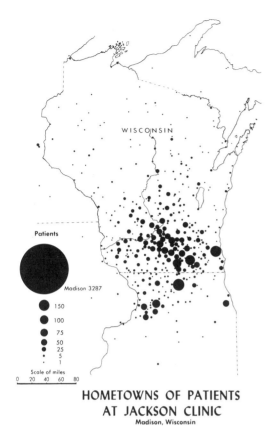

Patients

Madison 3287

● 150
● 100
● 75
● 50
● 25
· 5
· 1

Scale of miles
0 20 40 60 80

**HOMETOWNS OF PATIENTS
AT JACKSON CLINIC**
Madison, Wisconsin

Figure 29-10

In the Oskaloosa project mentioned earlier, the investigators discovered that $9,432,000 poured into Oskaloosa in one year. Of this amount, $8,223,000 resulted from sales outside the town by trade, service, and manufacturing firms; $820,000 was taken in by citizens either through investments elsewhere or through labor on farms or in other service centers; and $389,000 was released locally by government agencies.

Tourism   In recent years, the economy of many service centers has been geared to the intake of money from a new phenomenon —tourism; today many a settlement renders services not so much to people in the immediate hinterland as to travelers from afar. Many communities in Arizona, Nevada, Montana, and northern Wisconsin, and such overseas localities as Lourdes, France, and Positano, Italy, thrive on an increasing number of tourists. Tourism is such a new phenomenon that few scientific studies have been made of it. But the research that has been done turns up some surprises. In Wisconsin, for example, tourism now ranks third (it is surpassed only by manufacturing and agriculture) in bringing money into the state. Each year 1,500,000 fishing licenses are sold to out-of-staters. All told, tourists spend nearly half a billion dollars in Wisconsin, and 95 per cent of them are city-folk from other states; indeed, 55 per cent of them come from Chicago alone. Tourism has been the salvation of unnumbered small service centers (in northern Wisconsin) that came into being as lumbering communities or farm centers and then faced extinction as the timber was cut off and the soil proved too poor for modern competitive farming. But the second-growth forests, although they provide poor timber, offer excellent habitats for wildlife; in addition the tree growth is checking soil erosion so that lakes and streams might be better environments for fish.

Exactly the same story could be told for northern Minnesota, northern Michigan, upper New York, and northern New England where the residents of a host of small service centers earn a living off tourists from Boston, New York, Philadelphia, and other cities to the south.

Trade Area   The region from which a business establishment's customers come or from which it gets money for its goods and services is the *trade area* of that particular business. Rarely do any two types of business in a city have exactly the same trade area. Therefore, there is no such thing, strictly speaking, as *the* trade area of a service center. Rather, a city is surrounded by numerous *trade areas*, one for each service. In popular usage, though, we say a city has *a trade area* from which most of its business comes.

Economic-Base Concept   The money that comes into a city enables us to formulate its *economic base*. Nearly every city depends for its life on the revenue from its trade areas for its services. And yet, some of its business must be formed to meet the needs of its own inhabitants. The former component is termed *basic* economic activity; without revenue from such services the city would probably cease to exist. The component that meets the needs of the city itself is termed *nonbasic*, not because it is unnecessary (for it is most assuredly as necessary for an efficient city as the other) but because it feeds off money that has been brought in already by the basic component.

The *basic* component of a city's economic life consists of such activities as the following: sales by local stores to farmers in the surrounding countryside or to tourists passing through, sales by local wholesalers to retailers in other cities, sales by local factories to buyers located elsewhere, pensions received by local citizens from outside sources, interest received by local residents on capital they have invested in other cities, payments to local government agencies from government offices situated elsewhere. These and other similar endeavors are *basic* to a city's economy.

It is extremely difficult to measure all the money that makes up the basic support of a city's economic life. But we can achieve a partial measurement by means of the employment structure of a city. If a city is not too large, it is possible in a reasonable amount of time to contact every business in town and determine the total number of people employed, and the percentages of the business that meet both local and nonlocal demand. By this system, a store that employs 30 people and does two-thirds of its business with local customers would be credited with 20 nonbasic employees and 10 basic employees. In any city there are some businesses that are mostly *nonbasic*; indeed, neighborhood groceries are entirely so. Some factories on the other hand are strictly *basic*. Most establishments, though, fall somewhere in between these two extremes. In any event, we can make a tally of every business in town, and then determine the size of basic employment. The result can be expressed as a percentage of the city's total employment. This percentage is the *index of basic activity*.

The foregoing method of analysis has been applied to the employment structures of only a few cities but with some interesting results. For instance, the leading economic activity in Madison, Wisconsin, in terms of *total* employment is the general class of *services*, which employ 14,500 persons. But under the method outlined above, it turns out that 10,000 of those service employees belong in the *nonbasic* category, which means that only 4,500 service employees can be classified as basic (Table 29-11). In *basic* employment (Table 29-11 and Figure 29-11), government and manufacturing rank much higher than services. Madison's economy is founded, therefore, on government and industry more than on services. In *nonbasic* employment, however, service and trade outrank manufacturing and governmental employment by a substantial margin. Evidence seems to indicate that for many cities, the structure of *basic* employment is considerably different from that of nonbasic employment, and that each may be obscured in

Table **29-11** *Employment Structures: by Total, Basic, and Nonbasic Categories: Madison, Wisconsin*

Category	Total Employment		Basic Employment		Nonbasic Employment	
	Number	Percentage	Number	Percentage	Number	Percentage
Services	14,500	27	4,500	8	10,000	18
Government	14,300	27	11,300	21	3,000	6
Manufacturing	12,100	23	10,100	19	2,000	4
Trade	10,200	19	3,000	6	7,200	13
Others	2,400	4	300	1	2,100	4
	53,500	100	29,200	55	24,300	45

Source: John W. Alexander, "The Basic-Nonbasic Concept of Urban Economic Functions," *Economic Geography*, (1954), pp. 246-261.

Cities: Characteristics and Relationships

EMPLOYMENT IN MADISON

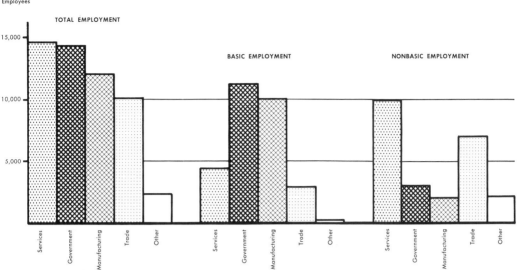

Figure 29-11 (*Courtesy* Economic Geography *and University of Wisconsin Bureau of Business Research.*)

the single composite view of total employment.

Clearly, knowing the total employment structure of a city is not enough. To understand that city's economic functioning we should know what keeps it going, what sustains it. The economic base is one concept for revealing this force. It also gives a criterion by which urban regions could be mapped and by which types of cities could be determined.*

BALANCE OF MOVEMENTS

When we take into account both inbound and outbound movements, we discover some interesting observations. For example, it would seem that every city, to survive, must have a *balance* in the flow of money, a balance between revenues and expenditures. Precisely in

* Further discussion of the concept appears in the author's "The Basic-Nonbasic Concept of Urban Economic Functions" and Hans Blumenfeld, "The Economic Base of Metropolis," *Journal of American Institute of Planners*, September 1955, pp. 114-132. Another publication of unusual interest in this context is the 1955 Annual Report of the Federal Reserve Bank of Chicago which estimates the inbound flow of money attributable to different economic activities in five case-study cities: Decatur, Illinois; Flint, Michigan; Fort Wayne, Indiana; Madison, Wisconsin; and Waterloo, Iowa.

order to investigate this relationship the research staff of *Fortune* magazine conducted their investigation of Oskaloosa, Iowa. They introduced their report with these provocative statements:

A traveler through the American countryside from place to place often comes unexpectedly on a little city spread out on a flat plain or settled in a valley between the hills. He has perhaps never seen it before, and will never see it again: people living there for some reason he cannot explain, a community doing things that are essentially the same things every community does, and yet—by reason of the mere fact that it is where it is—different.

The traveler will very likely ask himself who lives in this town, and why? What keeps it going? What is it there for?

Without pausing to reflect upon the profundity of his question, he will drive on. But his question deserves pause. It is a question that cannot be answered, any more than the meaning of life can be answered. Yet if the traveler were to stop over in the town he could learn some of the answer...

Set down in the middle of a continent, perhaps a thousand miles or more from the sea, it is the prey of vast and distant industrial regions, whose purpose is to draw from it as much money as they possibly can, in exchange for the necessities, near-necessities, luxuries, and adjuncts of civilization. The little city pours out its money year after year to those industrial regions for automobiles, iceboxes, clothes, canned food, and diamond rings, which it very much wants, and thus builds up a huge *negative* factor in what international commerce calls the balance of trade. And this it can very readily do. For small as it is and perhaps almost entirely devoid of manufacturing, the little city itself is an economic beast of prey. To supply itself with money to send to the industrial regions, it sucks money from all the immediately surrounding countryside. There the farmers climb into their automobiles (which they purchased in the little city years ago) and clatter in at comfortable speeds to park slantwise on the main street and buy clothes and tools and diamond rings and legal advice and new sets of teeth. The result of this business with the farmer is what international commerce calls the balance of trade. And if the little city is to live it must see to it that this favorable balance at least equals, if it does not exceed, year after year, the unfavorable balance with the industrial regions.

How the money that the farmers spend in the little city gets back to the farmers to be spent again in the little city, is another story that does not concern us here. The brief and basic fact of that segment of the economic circuit is that the industrial regions must eat, and so they pay the farmers a great part (but never all) of the money that they get from the little city for the products of civilization.*

The Oskaloosa investigation revealed that the inbound money flow slightly exceeded the outbound money flow, thus yielding a small surplus of $339,000 (Table 29-12). This surplus averaged out at around $140 for each of the city's 2700 families that year.

Table **29-12** *Balance of Money Flow, Oskaloosa, Iowa*

	In flow	Out flow	Net
Business	$8,223,000	$8,549,000	−$326,000
Government	389,000	153,000	+ 236,000
Consumers	820,000	391,000	+ 429,000
Total	$9,432,000	$9,093,000	+$339,000

Source: "Oskaloosa Versus the United States," *Fortune,* April, 1938.

Types of Locational Patterns

All these many types of interaction of tertiary settlements with other areas have been influential in determining the locational pattern of hamlets, villages, towns, and cities in the parts of the earth where commercial activity prevails. At least three types of patterns are discernible: dispersed, linear, and clustered.

DISPERSED PATTERN, OR CENTRAL PLACE THEORY

According to a theory advanced by a German geographer, Walter Christaller, there is a tendency for service centers to be dispersed over the countryside in a hexagonal pattern. The strength of this force is best observed in regions where two conditions prevail: (a) the topography is uniform so that no site has any advantage in terms of slope or of physical influences on transport routes, and (b) the economy is such that no site has an advantage in producing such primary products as grain, timber, or coal. Granted these conditions, Christaller postulates that three developments will transpire:

1. Service centers will spring up evenly spaced over the region at a distance equivalent to two hours of nonmechanized travel time. Most service centers predate the automobile era. So since a man could walk or drive a team about three-and-one-half kilometers in one hour (if service centers were so situated that no farmer would be more than one hour from the nearest one), the centers would be about seven kilometers from one another. Theoretically, the trade area around each nucleus, where the rural people who patronize the service center lived, would be a circle with a three-and-one-half-kilometer radius. Because this theory postulates that service centers tend to be located in the center of their area served, it is frequently termed the *central place theory.*

2. But contiguous trade areas circular in shape would, of course, produce either overlaps or voids. Of all geometric shapes, hexagons come the closest to circles, and still neither overlap nor leave voids when packed together. Therefore, Christaller postulated, trade centers would be located in hexagonal patterns and their trade areas would be hexagons instead of circles (see Figure 29-12).

* Quoted by courtesy of *Fortune* from "Oskaloosa Versus the United States," April, 1938.

Cities: Characteristics and Relationships

CHRISTALLER HYPOTHESIS

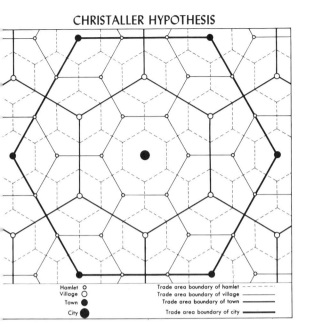

Hamlet ○	Trade area boundary of hamlet	- - - -
Village ○	Trade area boundary of village	——
Town ●	Trade area boundary of town	━━
City ●	Trade area boundary of city	━━━

Figure 29-12

3. A hierarchy of trade centers would develop in this hexagonal framework. The most numerous would be the smallest, mere hamlets, each serving a rural population. The

Figure 29-13 (*After John Brush, in* Geographical Review.)

TRADE CENTERS IN S.W. WISCONSIN

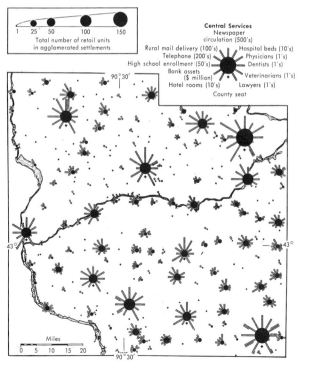

denser the rural population, the *larger* the hamlets would be; but the hamlets would *not* be *closer* together. Hamlets would stay seven miles apart. A second order of settlement would come into existence to render services demanded so infrequently that the trade area of no one hamlet could support them. But if the composite demand from several trade areas could support such a business, it would locate in one of the hamlets. Such a hamlet would begin to grow larger than the others and achieve the status of a village. Accordingly, villages would be larger in size, fewer in number and farther apart then hamlets, and their trade areas would be bounded by six hamlets (Figure 29-12).

By the same process, a third order of service center, towns, would unfold with each town having a hexagonal trade area bounded by six villages. Fourth-order centers would be cities, each of which would service a region whose margins connected six towns.

Unfortunately, the two conditions requisite for this pattern (uniform economy and uniform topography) rarely exist in reality. Two factors in particular (transportation routes and irregular land forms) disrupt the regular hexagons of the Christaller hypothesis. Main transportation routes either nourish hamlets to grow into villages and towns and cities or kill them off. The transportation revolution has left many a fossil hamlet, its former customers having begun to trade in larger settlements now accessible by automobile.

How a few large service centers and many small ones in southwestern Wisconsin have dispersed in fashion somewhat like Christaller's hypothetical pattern is illustrated in Figure 29-13. Notice how the larger centers tend to have more services (that is, more spokes on the hub) and more business in each service (that is, longer spokes).

THE LINEAR PATTERN

This arrangement prevails where service centers, instead of being dispersed, as in the Christaller hypothesis, are strung out along transport routes, often in valleys, or along seacoasts like the resort cities of southern Cal-

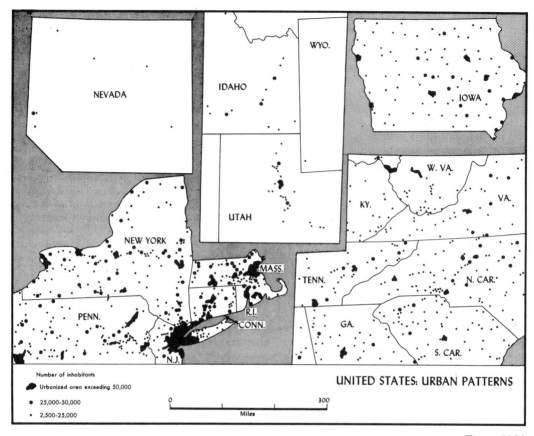

Figure 29-14

ifornia and New Jersey. The line of agglomerated settlements in northeastern Minnesota
correlates with a belt of iron ore mines. Lines
of cities in Utah and Idaho coincide with irrigated farm land at the bases of mountain
ranges (Figure 29-14).

THE CLUSTERED PATTERN

This pattern is usually associated with mining, as in the agglomeration of cities in southern Illinois, where the landforms are not very
rough, and in West Virginia, where local relief
is pronounced (Figure 29-14). One type of
clustered pattern is *the dispersed city*.

The Dispersed City   Under certain conditions, a cluster of cities may actually function as a single *dispersed city*. Oliver Beimfohr
first applied this term to what he observed in
southern Illinois where a total of 14 urban

places are clustered unusually close together
in the four counties of Perry, Franklin, Jackson, and Williamson.

The spacing of these cities is unusual in
that the larger ones do not have several
smaller ones in their hinterlands. Rather, the
larger ones tend to be rather close together.
For example, Carbondale (population 15,000)
is only 7 miles from Murphysboro (population 9,000). Marion (population 11,000) is
only 11 miles from West Frankfort (population 9,000). Nowhere else in Illinois (and
rarely in the nation for that matter) are settlements of such size so close together *except
where they are parts of the same metropolitan
area*, parts of Chicago, say, or St. Louis.

On this basis, some analysts believe that
such a cluster of discrete cities actually function as a single large city—only fragmented
into component parts. From this viewpoint,

Cities: Characteristics and Relationships

the dispersed city in southern Illinois is estimated to have a population of 157,000.*

In terms of function, particularly retail trade, no one of the 14 larger settlements has any clear dominance over the others; that is, the dispersed city has no clear counterpart to a "downtown shopping center." One might suppose that the most populous settlement in this dispersed city would have the largest volume of retail trade; the fact is that the second-, third-, fourth-, and fifth-ranking settlements (in population) all do more business than the largest one. Some of the settlements do appear to have specialized in types of trade; for example, some do a disproportionately large volume of business in furniture, household, and radio goods, while others are disproportionately high in general merchandise—all of which suggests that each settlement is comparable to a specialized business district within an urbanized area.

* Burton, Ian, "Retail Trade in a Dispersed City," *Transactions of the Illinois State Academy of Science*, 1959, pp. 145-150. See also Howard A. Stafford, Jr., "The Dispersed City," *The Professional Geographer*, July, 1962, pp. 8-10.

A random sample taken in West Frankfort revealed that 68 per cent of the inhabitants make habitual purchases of retail goods outside the settlement. Of these individuals, 82 per cent reported the "outside place" to be some other settlement within the dispersed city. The remaining 18 per cent indentified their place of purchase as follows: St. Louis 14 per cent, Chicago 2 per cent, and Evansville 2 per cent.

The foregoing information lends support, in the minds of some scholars, to the hypothesis that the discrete cities of southern Illinois really function as a single metropolitan area—with a few miles of open countryside interspersed between the many fragments that compose it.

Few regions conform perfectly with any one of these basic patterns. But this does not negate the fact that the forces behind these three are at work; rather, each area's pattern results from the interplay of those forces, each of which is stronger in some places and weaker in others.

Suggested Readings

Alexander, John W., "The Basic-Nonbasic Concept of Urban Economic Functions," *Economic Geography*, 1954, pp. 246-261.

Alexandersson, Gunnar, *The Industrial Structure of American Cities*, Lincoln and Stockholm, 1956, 134 pp.

Bartholomew, Harland, and Wood, Jack, *Land Uses in American Cities*, Cambridge, 1955, 196 pp.

Bergsten, Karl Erik, "Variability in Intensity of Urban Fields as Illustrated by Birth-Places," *Lund Studies in Geography*, 1951, No. 3, pp. 25-32.

Berry, Brian J. L., "The Impact of Expanding Metropolitan Communities Upon the Central Place Hierarchy," *Annals of the Association of American Geographers*, 1960, pp. 112-116.

——, and Garrison, William L., "Alternate Explanations of Urban Rank-Size Relationships," *Annals*

of the Association of American Geographers*, 1958, pp. 83-91.

——, and ——, "The Functional Bases of the Central Place Hierarchy," *Economic Geography*, 1958, pp. 145-154.

——, and ——, "A Note on Central Place Theory and the Range of a Good," *Economic Geography*, 1958, pp. 304-311.

Borchert, John R., "The Surface Water Supply of American Municipalities," *Annals of the Association of American Geographers*, 1954, pp. 15-32.

Bracey, H. E., "A Rural Component of Centrality Applied to Six Southern Counties in the United Kingdom," *Economic Geography*, 1956, pp. 38-50.

Brush, John E., "The Hierarchy of Central Places in Southwestern Wisconsin," *Geographical Review*, 1953, pp. 380-402.

——, and Bracey, Howard E., "Rural Service Centers in Southwestern Wisconsin and Soouthern England," *Geographical Review*, 1955, pp. 559-569.

Burghardt, Andrew F., "The Location of River Towns in the Central Lowland of the United States," *Annals of the Association of American Geographers*, 1959, pp. 305-323.

Burton, Ian, "Retail Trade in a Dispersed City," *Transactions of the Illinois State Academy of Science*, 1959, pp. 145-150.

Dacey, Michael F., "The Spacing of River Towns," *Annals of the Association of American Geographers*, 1960, pp. 59-61.

Dickinson, Robert E., "The Geography of Commuting in West Germany," *Annals of the Association of American Geographers*, 1959, pp. 443-456.

Duncan, O. D.; Scott, W. R.; Lieberson, S.; Duncan, B. D.; and Winsborough, H. H., *Metropolis and Region*, Baltimore, 1960.

Eyre, John D., "Sources of Tokyo's Fresh Food Supply," *Geographical Review*, 1959, pp. 455-474.

Gilbert, Edmund W., *The University Town in England and West Germany*, Chicago, 1961, 74 pp.

Godlund, Sven, *The Function and Growth of Bus Traffic Within the Sphere of Urban Influence*, Lund, 1956.

Green, F. H. W., "Community of Interest Areas: Notes on the Hierarchy of Central Places and Their Hinterlands," *Economic Geography*, 1958, pp. 210-216.

Green, Howard L., "Hinterland Boundaries of New York City and Boston in Southern New England," *Economic Geography*, 1955, pp. 283-300.

Gregor, Howard F., "The Local-Supply Agricultural Landscapes," *Annals of the Association of American Geographers*, 1957, pp. 267-276.

Griffin, Paul F., and Chatham, Ronald L., "Urban Impact on Agriculture in Santa Clara County, California," *Annals of the Association of American Geographers*, 1958, pp. 195-208.

Grotewold, Andreas, "Von Thünen in Retrospect," *Economic Geography*, 1959, pp. 346-355.

Hägerstrand, Torsten, "Migration and the Growth of Culture Regions," *Lund Studies in Geography*, 1951, No. 3, pp. 33-36.

Hall, Max, editor, *New York Metropolitan Region Study*, Cambridge, nine volumes, 1959-1961.

Hart, John Fraser, "Functions and Occupational Structures of Cities of the American South," *Annals of the Association of American Geographers*, 1955, pp. 269-286.

Johnson, Hildegard Binder, "A Note on Thünen's Circles," *Annals of the Association of American Geographers*, 1962, pp. 213-220.

Kant, Edgar, "Umland Studies and Sector Analysis," *Lund Studies in Geography*, 1951, No. 3, pp. 5-13.

King, Leslie J., "A Multivariate Analysis of the Spacing of Urban Settlements in the United States," *Annals of the Association of American Geographers*, 1961, pp. 222-233.

Kosinski, Leszek, "On the Functional Structure of Polish Towns," *Przeglad Geograficzny*, 1958, pp. 59-96.

Morrissett, Irving, "The Economic Structure of American Cities," Regional Science Association, *Papers and Proceedings*, 1958, pp. 239-258.

Neft, David, "Some Aspects of Rail Commuting: New York, London and Paris," *Geographical Review*, 1959, pp. 151-163.

Nelson, Howard, "A Service Classification of American Cities," *Economic Geography*, 1955, pp. 189-210.

———, "Some Characteristics of the Population of Cities in Similar Service Classifications," *Economic Geography*, 1957, pp. 95-108.

———, "The Spread of an Artificial Landscape over Southern California," *Annals of the Association of American Geographers*, 1959, pp. 80-99.

Patton, Donald J., "General Cargo Hinterlands of New York, Philadelphia, Baltimore, and New Orleans," *Annals of the Association of American Geographers*, 1958, pp. 436-455.

Pownall, L. L., "The Functions of New Zealand Towns," *Annals of the Association of American Geographers*, 1953, pp. 332-350.

———, "Low-Value Housing in Two New Zealand Cities," *Annals of the Association of American Geographers*, 1960, pp. 439-460.

———, "The Retail Potential of Some Representative New Zealand Towns," *Economic Geography*, 1957, pp. 163-170.

Robinson, G. W. S., "West Berlin: The Geography of an Exclave," *Geographical Review*, 1953, pp. 540-557.

Siddall, William R., "Wholesale-Retail Trade Ratios as Indices of Urban Centrality," *Economic Geography*, 1961, pp. 124-132.

Smith, Robert H. T., "Rigidity of Rail Hinterland Boundaries in Australia," *Annals of the Association of American Geographers*, 1960, pp. 55-57.

Snyder, David E., "Commercial Passenger Linkages and the Metropolitan Nodality of Montevideo," *Economic Geography*, 1962, pp. 95-112.

Solomon, R. J., "Locational Emphasis of the Australian Work Force," *Economic Geography*, 1962, pp. 138-161.

Spelt, Jacob, "Towns and Umlands: A Review Article," *Economic Geography*, 1958, pp. 362-369.

Stafford, Howard A., Jr., "The Dispersed City," *The Professional Geographer*, July 1962, pp. 8-10.

Steigenga, W., "A Comparative Analysis and a Classification of Netherlands Towns," *Tijdschrift voor Economische en Sociale Geografie*, 1955, pp. 105-119.

Studies in Rural-Urban Interaction, Lund Studies in Geography, 1951, No. 3.

Thomas, Edwin N., "Toward An Expanded Central Place Model," *Geographical Review*, 1961, pp. 400-411.

Thompson, John H., "Urban Agriculture in Southern Japan," *Economic Geography*, 1957, pp. 224-237.

Ullman, Edward L., "Trade Centers and Tributary Areas of the Philippines," *Geographical Review*, 1960, pp. 203-218.

Van Burkalow, Anastasia, "The Geography of New York City's Water Supply: A Study of Interactions," *Geographical Review*, 1959, pp. 369-386.

Vance, James E., "Labor-Shed, Employment Field, and Dynamic Analysis in Urban Geography," *Economic Geography*, 1960, pp. 189-220.

Webb, John W., "Basic Concepts in the Analysis of Small Urban Centers of Minnesota," *Annals of the Association of American Geographers*, 1959, pp. 55-72.

Wiegand, Guido, "The Problem of Hinterland and Foreland as Illustrated by the Port of Hamburg," *Economic Geography*, 1956, pp. 1-16.

Wrobel, Andrzej, "Investigations of Passenger Traffic as a Method of Delineating Service Regions," *Przeglad Geograficzny*, 1959, pp. 120-127.

The skyline of Dallas, Texas, a typical large-city profile distinguished
by the central business district. There, demand for land has caused the obliteration of the natural
landscape, which is now replaced by close-packed tall buildings. In the foreground,
on the fringe of the CBD, is the circular Memorial Auditorium with its parking lot.
(Courtesy Dallas Chamber of Commerce.)

THIRTY

Variation from place to place *within* a service center gives rise to distinctive areas; through studying the subdivisions we can better understand the large economic entities. And because in their internal natures service centers differ one from another, analyzing such spatial variation offers a useful geographic approach. Moreover the study has an urgent practical value, for areal variation within a city lies at the root of many a problem bothering today's urbanites. The discussion to follow will be organized around several individual elements whose locational patterns contribute particularly to our understanding of service centers. These are employment, population, types of people, and types of land use. A presentation of theoretical patterns within cities will close the chapter.

Employment

Places of employment are concentrated in comparatively few areas within any city. This principle is illustrated by Figure 30-1 which locates all organizations that employ 100 or more persons in Madison, Wisconsin. The size of each circle is proportionate to the number of employees; the division of each circle is proportionate to the degree to which each organization is *basic* to Madison's economic life. Remember that *basic* endeavor is not a priori more or less important than *nonbasic;* it's a matter of bringing money in. The map shows how highly concentrated employment is in the central and northeastern parts of the city. Except for a few enterprises to the

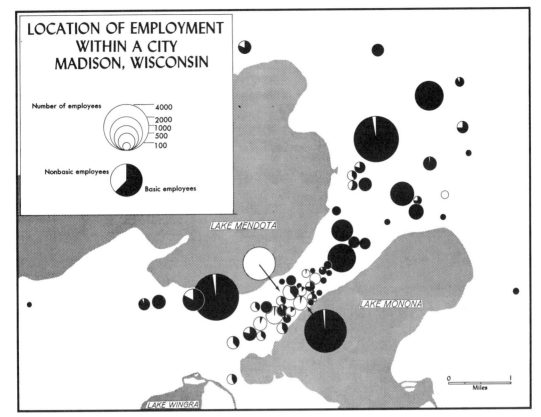

**LOCATION OF EMPLOYMENT
WITHIN A CITY
MADISON, WISCONSIN**

Number of employees

4000
2000
1000
500
100

Nonbasic employees

Basic employees

LAKE MENDOTA

LAKE MONONA

LAKE WINGRA

0   1
Miles

Figure 30-1

south of Lake Mendota, the western part of the city is devoid of large job-makers as is the southern part of the city.

Since places of work are not uniformly spread out, the journey to work for most persons entails considerable movement, all of which converges on those few places where jobs are concentrated. Traffic analysts refer to such areas as *zones of convergence.*

Convergence of traffic would not be so bad were it not for a second matter: nearness to work ranks low on the scale of values by

which the city dweller chooses his residence. Look at Figure 30-2, page 568: If workers tended to live close to their work, the dots would be liberally sprinkled in the vicinity of the Oscar Mayer factory in east Madison; instead, they are widely dispersed, which means that employees are heading for the Oscar Mayer plant from every part of the city. Dozens of them travel clear across town. This situation—which exists in all cities—has a tremendous impact on the problems of urban traffic.

opulation

"Where are the people?" The question has always been pertinent in locating schools and stores, but in recent years it has taken on new significance due to (a) the automobile revolution with its consequent intense traffic congestion, and to (b) the advent of Civil Defense programs. Civil Defense directors must know

where people are if air raid shelters and first aid stations are to be located most efficiently.

In selecting locations for such facilities the civil defense director must be able to read the message carried by at least *two* maps: one of where people *reside* and one of where they *work* and *shop,* or do anything else away from

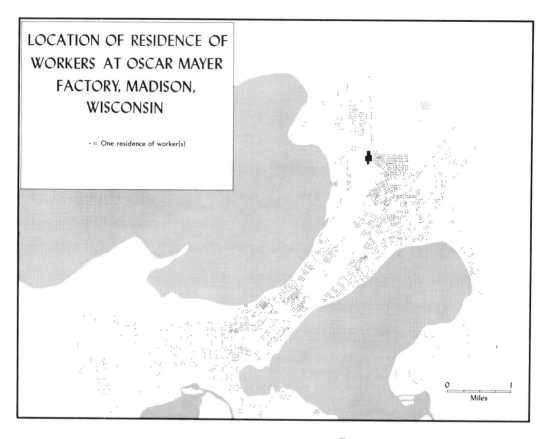

LOCATION OF RESIDENCE OF
WORKERS AT OSCAR MAYER
FACTORY, MADISON,
WISCONSIN

· = One residence of worker(s)

0   Miles   1

Figure 30-2   (*After George P. Stevens.*)

home. The traffic engineers should be familiar with these same patterns if they are to locate thoroughfares effectively.

Unfortunately, research methods have yet to be discovered for feasibly gathering data for such maps of all cities. The only published information is that in the United States *Census of Population*, Vol. III, "Census Tract Statistics." This is a valuable new source of information that tabulates information for small areal units (*census tracts*) within cities; Manhattan Island, for example, is divided into approximately 300 census tracts. This source clearly makes remarkably detailed mapping possible. Yet the Census has certain disadvantages, principally that it presents information for comparatively few cities, and locates people by residence only.

POPULATION PATTERNS

Night-Time Population Pattern   The type of map that *can* be constructed from Cen-

sus information is exemplified by Figure 30-3, which shows the locational pattern of the people of Atlanta, Georgia, *when they are at home*. Certain features stand out clearly that seem to be characteristic of most large service centers. First, there is a hollow core coinciding with the central business district (see p. 575). Not many people reside here, so the center of town is comparatively deserted at night. Immediately surrounding the core is a ring where residential density is high, indeed the highest in town. This juxtaposition can be understood, in part at least, when relationships with land use are considered, as we shall see later in the chapter. Beyond this ring, the density of population tends to taper off gradually until finally, near the edge of the city, densities as low as those in the commercial core are again encountered.

But this pattern is essentially that of the city at night, when it is asleep, rather than when it is awake and performing the functions

Spatial Variation Within a Service Center

that sustain its life. Uunfortunately, the Bureau of the Census does not publish anything on the *daytime* location of a city's people.

Daytime Population Pattern   Even so, field studies of daytime population have been made for a few cities, and they provide some stimulating suggestions. On a typical weekday in Winnipeg, Manitoba, it was found that the "downtown" area (the central business district plus several adjacent blocks containing governmental institutions, several factories and wholesaling establishments, and some residences) contains 102,000 people, which is 27 per cent of the entire population of Winnipeg and its suburbs. Over half (63,000) are employed in the downtown area, 6,000 reside there, and 33,000 are downtown for shopping or other purposes. Within the core of the business district, densities range from 400 to 4,000 per acre. On the fringe of the business district

they vary from 125 to 500 per acre. In the encircling wholesale-industrial zone they range from 400 to 1,500 per acre. In the surrounding residential ring the daytime densities are 30 to 90 per acre. But the nighttime pattern for downtown Winnipeg is entirely different. Density in the commercial core is almost down to zero except for a very few isolated blocks, in every instance hotels, where it rises abruptly to 200-800. The fringe of the business district likewise is nearly deserted except for a few low-class hotels and rescue missions. The wholesale-industrial zone has scarcely any population at night. But surrounding these three parts of the downtown area is the first ring of continual housing where nighttime densities are up 100-200 per acre.*

* Several revealing maps with analytical comment on the Winnipeg study appear in Thomas R. Weir's "Land Use and Population Characteristics of Central Winnipeg," *Geog. Bull.*, 1957, Number 9, pp. 5-21.

Figure 30-3

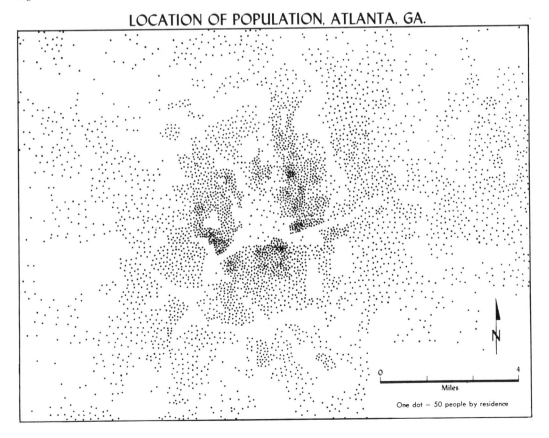

LOCATION OF POPULATION, ATLANTA, GA.

One dot = 50 people by residence

A study of Chicago's central business district (an area 10 blocks long from north to south and 9 blocks wide from east to west, and bounded on the west and north by the Chicago River) showed that between 7:00 A.M. and 7:00 P.M. on a June weekday a total of 950,000 people enter as passengers in some sort of vehicle. Those who come in on foot are difficult to tally, but number somewhere between 150,000 and 200,000. By percentages, passengers arrive by the following means: automobiles 25 per cent, street cars 26, elevated railways 23, buses 9, and railways 17. The peak hour of arrival is from 8:00 to 9:00 A.M. when 192,000 arrive; the slowest hour is from 3:00 to 4:00 A.M. when only 2,342 people enter. The total daytime population (shoppers, workers, sightseers, and so on) in so congested an area as downtown Chicago is extremely difficult to measure; however, employment alone is estimated to account for 373,000 people—several blocks contain 5,000 working persons each, and one has 10,000 employees. The biggest rush for the exits comes between 5:00 and 6:00 P.M., when 197,000 people leave the district.*

Change in Population Pattern The locational pattern of people is in flux in cities that are growing. The changes are most pronounced in the three inner areas: the center, the ring encircling the center, and the territory encircling that second zone. Consider, for example, Table 30-2A, which reveals the spread of the residential void in the center of Frankfurt, Germany where, in the four decades between two field studies made in 1890 and 1933, density dropped from 200 to 121 persons per acre. The adjacent ring also lost people, but the drop was only from 76 to 69 persons per acre. The same principle is illustrated by Chicago and Cleveland (see Table 30-2B). In Chicago the innermost zone lost 23 per cent of its residents during the decade

* For a vast amount of information about Chicago's daytime population and for a thorough description of research methods for tackling such a topic, see Gerald Breese's *Daytime Population of the Central Business District of Chicago*, University of Chicago Press, (Chicago), 1949.

Table **30-1** *Number of Passengers Entering the Central Business District of Chicago, 1926-1946, 7:00 A.M.–7:00 P.M.*

1926	870,000	1939	840,000
1928	893,000	1940	824,000
1929	923,000	1941	823,000
1931	843,000	1942	803,000
1935	755,000	1943	814,000
1936	801,000	1944	796,000
1937	845,000	1945	817,000
1938	812,000	1946	950,000

Source: Gerald Breese, *Daytime Population of The Central Business District of Chicago*, University of Chicago Press, (Chicago), 1949, pp. 114-115.

1910-1920; outer zones had not yet been whittled away by the exodus of residents; indeed, the second zone showed a gain, albeit only one per cent. But in the next decade not only did the inner zone lose an additional 22 per cent but the second zone also succumbed to out-movement and lost 11 per cent. The same story holds for Cleveland although the timing was a bit later. Cleveland's inner zone did not report a loss until 1930, but when loss did set in, it went swiftly (27 per cent) and widely (for both inner zones had been hit by 1930).

A change in the intensity of daytime convergence upon a city's center is revealed by the Chicago study previously cited; the daytime population (arriving by some sort of vehicle) in Chicago's central business district increased from 870,000 in 1926 to 950,000 in 1946. Notice in Table 30-1 how this number did not rise steadily but moved in waves which reflected economic and political events. Thus, with the passage of years it appears that, in some cities at least, the innermost zone is throbbing with increasing numbers of people during the daytime, but is spreading ever outward as a population void at night.

A second area of change is the next outward ring. Instead of being deserted at night, this ring has the densest nighttime population in town and, insofar as it changes, experiences the greatest *absolute* gains of any area within a city. As Table 30-2A shows, this ring in Frankfurt's third zone had an increment of 35 residents per acre. No other zone approached this figure. The Frankfurt study reveals several corollaries of this principle which seem

Spatial Variation Within a Service Cente

Table **30-2** *Changes in Location of People by Residence Within Cities*

Part A. *Absolute Change in Density, Frankfurt, Germany*

Zone	Kilometers from Town Center	Number of People Per Acre		
		1890	1933	Change
1	0-½	200	121	−79
2	½-1	76	69	− 7
3	1-2	33	68	+35
4	2-3	7	25	+18
5	3-4	3	12	+ 9
6	4-5	1	7	+ 6

Part B. *Relative Change in Density, Chicago and Cleveland*

Zone	Miles from Town Center	Chicago		Cleveland	
		1910 to 1920	1920 to 1930	1910 to 1920	1920 to 1930
1	0-2	−23%	− 22%	0%	− 27%
2	2-4	+ 1%	− 11%	+ 29%	− 4%
3	4-6	+40%	+ 13%	+117%	+ 49%
4	6-8	+76%	+ 51%	+290%	+103%
5	8-10	+77%	+112%	+ 69%	+ 95%

Source: Robert E. Dickinson, *City, Region and Regionalism*, Routledge and Kegan Paul, Ltd., (London), 1947, pp. 129 and 135.

to apply in most cities: (a) outward from the ring of greatest increment, every circle grew, (b) the amount of increase diminished with distance from the ring of maximum growth, and (c) all areas that grew were outside of this ring.

The third type-area consists of rings with only modest increments but high percentage gains. Such areas are on the sparsely settled fringe of cities. Thus, the percentage gains in Chicago *rose steadily with increasing outward distance*, from one to 77 per cent (1910-1920) and from 13 to 112 per cent (1920-1930).

These generalized patterns of change result largely from the outward movements of numerous residents. The *outer* fringes, though, are settled by two kinds of "immigrants": those who come from inner portions of the city in a flight to the suburbs and those who move to town from elsewhere and settle on

its margins. The innermost ring of densest residential population is growing for several reasons, the principal one being the influx of outsiders who move to town and are able to afford only cheaper rooms and apartments; thus, this ring is the port of entry to most large cities.

Another criterion for considering changes in location of people is residential mobility. A study of this factor in St. Louis revealed that, in concentric rings increasing in radius by one mile around the city center, residential mobility *decreased* as distance from the center *increased*. An index of mobility designed for the study attained a peak of 45 in the city center and dropped progressively with each zone, through indexes of 43, 39, 31, 29, and 27 to 24 in the seventh zone. In other words, the closer to the center of a city, the higher the rate of turnover in residential occupancy.

Types of People

Not only do numbers of people differ spatially within a city, but types of people

do also. Of course, the criteria for determining types are legion, but among the more frequently considered classifications are race, nativity, education, age, sex, marriage rates, death rates, and median income.

RACE

Granted, the validity of the concept of "race" is suspect in many quarters. Certainly it is emotionally explosive. Still, within the United States, two major racial types are clearly identifiable—Negroes and whites. And the distribution of these groups falls into definite patterns. In some parts of the country, Indians and Orientals form distinct racial enclaves, too. The Negro districts of most large American cities, Chinatown in San Francisco, and the white section of Jackson, Mississippi are examples of this obvious phenomenon. The principle holds almost universally that in the United States nonwhite races tend to locate in pockets within the innermost ring of highest residential density, only gradually spreading out through the ring as well as into the next one. Half of New Orleans is virtually devoid of colored people; but near the center of town they make up from 85 to 100 per cent of the residents in a community one mile wide and two miles long. In Milwaukee the nonwhites account for less than 5 per cent of the residents everywhere except in a small half-mile-square area immediately northwest of the central business district, where the percentage ranges from 65 to 85.

In South African cities, however, the colored peoples reside in areas on the fringe of the city—areas with the highest density.

NATIVITY

The foreign-born also tend to cluster together in regions that stand out conspicuously on city maps. In Figure 30-4 we illustrate this principle with the Puerto Ricans (immigrants and their children) of Manhattan Island. The outstanding concentration is athwart the northeast corner of Central Park. In the blocks within an area roughly half a mile by one mile, Puerto Ricans account for 41 to 76 per cent of the population. Immigrants from Puerto Rico reside in nearly every census tract on Manhattan, although they make up only 2 per cent or less of the residents in

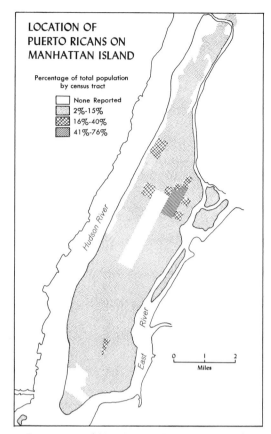

Figure 30-4 (*After Robert Novak, in* Geographical Review.)

half of them. Only in a small zone near the southern tip are they absent.

EDUCATION

Even years of schooling are reflected in residential distribution. For persons 25 years or older, the median number of school years completed is almost always lowest in the center of town; in fact, most large cities have at least one census tract where the median is less than an eighth-grade education.

In Figure 30-5 Los Angeles is divided up into areas determined by the percentage of persons over 25 who have completed at least one year of college. Clearly, the west and north are the better-educated sections of Los Angeles. In Washington, D.C., the lowest educational medians are in the heart of the city (bounded on the southwest by the Potomac, on the southeast by the Anacostia); from there the levels rise in all directions.

Spatial Variation Within a Service Cent

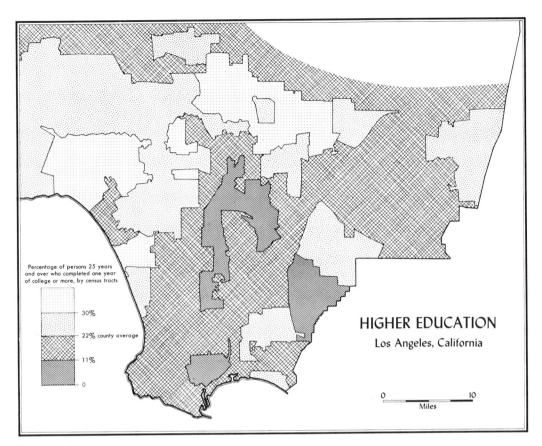

Figure 30-5

AGE

There is a general tendency for the median age of residents to be highest in the center of town and gradually drop toward the fringes. In the center of Los Angeles elderly people (65 or more) make up from 11 to 18 per cent of the population by census tracts. The central tracts of Pasadena range from 13 per cent to 18 per cent in this age group. Near the center of Long Beach the figure reaches 20 per cent (Figure 30-6, page 574). Even if we lower the limit to 21 years, the decline in percentage outward from the center is maintained. In the center of Milwaukee, for instance, 90 per cent of the residents are 21 or over, but on the fringes of the city only 60 per cent of the people are of voting age. This outward decline in median age with distance from city center is explained by several factors: Many families with young children move to the suburbs;

many single adults prefer to live near job opportunities and shopping facilities in the center; many adult couples move back from the suburbs to apartments near the center to be near libraries, theaters, and stores.

Knowing age distributions can be highly practical. Mapping a city on the basis of persons from 5 to 21, for instance, would be valuable to members of the Board of Education and others responsible for allocating funds for school maintenance and construction.

OTHER CRITERIA

Sex Ratios   In most cities the male-female ratio tends to reach a pronounced peak in the center of town and drop off sharply toward the fringes. The top in Milwaukee is 250 in the central business district; the bottom is an unusually low 40 in a zone along the northern lake shore where apartment-dwelling

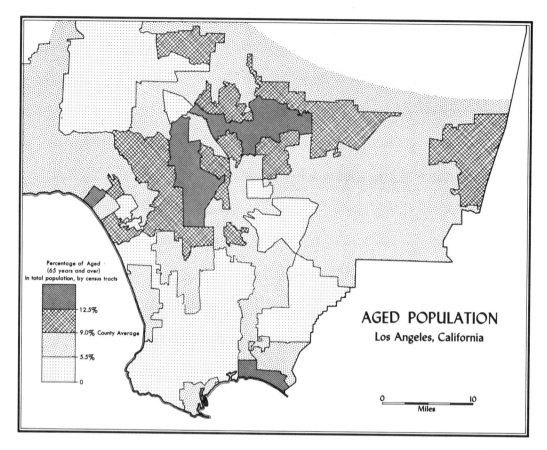

Figure 30-6

widows or office workers live. In the outlying residential districts the figure is around 80. In St. Louis the ratio tapers off from 300 in the center to 90 near the edges.

Marriage Ratios   Married people ordinarily constitute a very low percentage of residents in the central business district, but an ever-increasing percentage toward the edge of town.

Median Income   Income is generally lowest in the center, rising toward the fringe, of a city. The fringe is never a continuous belt of high incomes, however; instead, the wealthy cluster in certain sectors. On a map of Washington, D.C., for instance, the lowest median incomes (less than $2500) all appear in the central part of the city. Along a five-mile perimeter of the Capitol in Washington are striking variations in income level: Due south of the Capitol the median incomes lie between $2500 and $3500; to the southeast they are in the $3500 to $4500 category; straight east is another trough of somewhat low incomes, $2500 to $3500; but to the northeast they exceed $3500; to the north the median is above $4500; in large pockets to the northwest it is greater than $7000; then the median drops again to $3500 along the upper Potomac River.

Death Rates   Death rates are higher in the center of town and grade off slowly toward the fringe from approximately 25 per 1000 among downtown residents to only 8 per 1000 in the outskirts. This of course reflects to a large extent the age pattern mentioned above.

Types of Land Use

Even the most casual observer of large cities knows that men use land for different purposes in different parts of town. Stores, houses, factories, and apartments are not sprinkled ubiquitously throughout the city. Areas tend to be specialized.

This is not so for hamlets, the smallest (except for roadsides) category of service center. As Figure 30-7 shows, hamlets have farmsteads, nonfarm residences, stores, garages, schools, and churches intermixed along the roadway in no particular pattern and often at considerable distances from one another.

As soon as a hamlet begins to grow several things begin to happen, however. A process of separation between the commercial and residential area sets in. And the concentration of business establishments gives rise to a *commercial core*. Within that core, structures are built ever closer together. Then, with continued growth, buildings in the commercial core begin to grow *up*, as businesses begin to

use floors above the ground level. Further growth usually brings the development of distinct industrial zones and certain types of residential areas as well. We can examine each of these three main use categories individually.

COMMERCIAL AREAS

There are at least four principal types of commercial use of land in large cities: centralized commercial areas, commercial strips, dispersed businesses, and shopping centers.

Centralized Commercial Areas: the CBD

Centralized commercial areas are clusters of diverse business establishments usually at intersections of major thoroughfares. The outstanding example of such an area is the Central Business District, termed *CBD* for short.

The central business district is the economic heart of nearly every city. There are exceptions, though, such as factory towns that grew

Figure 30-7 (*Courtesy Glenn T. Trewartha, from* Annals of Association of American Geographers.)

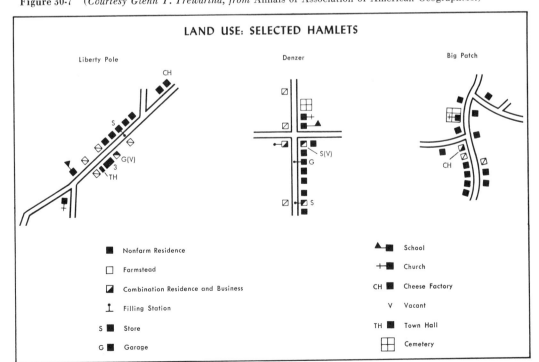

up around a manufacturing plant in the middle of the countryside, such as Kannapolis, North Carolina, which developed around the Cannon textile mills (Chapter 18); or the castle towns in Europe that sprang up around a lord's residence (such as Touraine, France); or cathedral towns (such as Rochester, England, and numerous towns in north-central France) which encircled some religious structure; or garrison towns (such as Aberystwyth, Wales) which began as military posts. But the vast majority of service centers have grown around a retail trading district. The site of origination is called the *point of attachment*, and for most contemporary cities the point of attachment is somewhere within the CBD.

Certain general characteristics of a CBD are well known: the greatest concentration of stores in town (from single proprietorships to huge department stores), the greatest concentration of offices and services (medical, insurance, real estate, banking), the most expensive land and the tallest buildings (to get the most out of such expensive land). Other characteristics are less obvious, however. Vertical zoning, for instance. Ground floors are often given over to retailing, upper levels to offices or manufacturing. In the CBD's of small settlements second floors are often put to residential use. There are also lateral gradations within a CBD, from the *commercial core*, the area of most intense commercial use, to the CBD *fringe*, where commercial use fades out and some other becomes dominant.

The most significant point within the *core* is the *peak land-value intersection* (PLVI), which is the street intersection where land values are higher than at any other in town. This point also has the greatest concentration of pedestrians and, often, the worst automobile congestion. In small cities, land values decrease sharply in all directions as one begins to move away from the PLVI; however, the decrease begins to slacken off toward the edge of the CBD. A curve of land values thus would be concave, in harmony with the the principle that *land values decrease at a decreasing rate with distance from the PLVI*. If the CBD is elongated, the rate of decline is less along the axis than at right angles to it.

However, in the CBD's of large urban agglomerations (such as New York's Manhattan Island) the land values appear to have an undulating profile, dropping with distance from the PLVI and then rising again to secondary peaks as other concentrations of business activity—still within the central part of the metropolis—are encountered.

The edge of the CBD is a transition zone, not a sharp line of demarcation. In most instances it is a peculiar combination of *high land values* and of *low building values*. The land values are high because of the anticipated *invasion* into the still essentially residential area by the expanding CBD. Usually this expansion begins with the conversion of residential properties to business use. Sometimes a new front is constructed to give the appearance, from the street, of a store or office building; but from the alley (or the sides) the structure still looks like a house. The building values remain low, though, mainly because the structures that have not yet been taken over are invariably the oldest buildings in town, the most obsolete in design, and the most deteriorated in condition. Owners of structures so obsolete on land so valuable are understandably reluctant to make improvements on monstrosities that may soon be sold either to be demolished or remodeled. So deterioration sets in; thus the edge of the CBD is, in many cities, a genuine eyesore.

Delimiting the CBD   In spite of the transitional nature of the CBD's margin, city dwellers still need to be able to define it in order to understand their city and handle effectively its many problems. The most scientific system for delimiting the CBD is the Murphy-Vance method. In this system, a block is considered part of the CBD if it fulfills three requirements:

1. A Central Business Height Index of 1. The *Central Business Height Index* (CBHI) of a block is a ratio in which the numerator is the square footage of floor space devoted to typical CBD activities (retail stores and offices; excluded are wholesale outlets, storage warehouses, manufacturing plants other than

Spatial Variation Within a Service Center

| First Floor | | Second Floor | | Upper Floors | | | Block Inventory | |
Use	Space	Use	Space	Use	Space	Adjusted Value	Use	Space
C**	0.350*	C	0.350	C	0.350 x 4	1.400	C	4.935
C	0.385	C	0.315	C	0.315 x 5	1.575	X	2.135
X†	0.665	X	0.665	X	0.665	0.665		
C	0.050							
C	0.050							
C	0.050							
C	0.050							
C	0.050							
C	0.050							
C	0.140							
X	0.070							
X	0.070							
C	0.070						Total	
Total	2.100		1.330			3.640	Space = 7.070	

Source: Raymond E. Murphy and James E. Vance, Jr., "Delimiting the CBD," *Economic Geography*, 1954, p. 207.
  * Measurements are in square inches at a scale of 1 inch to 200 feet on Murphy's and Vance's maps.
  ** C = Floor space used for typical CBD purposes.
  † X = Floor space used for untypical CBD purposes.

those of newspapers, churches, and residences), and the denominator is the *ground area* in square feet.

2. A *Central Business Intensity Index* (CBII) of 50 per cent. This is also a ratio; in this one, the numerator is the same as in the Central Business Height Index, but the denominator is the square footage of all floor space in the block.

Table 30-3 illustrates how these two indexes may be computed. The inventory of land and floor space for a block on the edge of the Tulsa, Oklahoma CBD is itemized. The ground area (identical with first floor space—since this block has no vacant land) is 2100 units of measurement. The total floor space regardless of usage is 7070 units of measurement, but of this there are 2135 units in the non-CBD types, leaving 4935 devoted to CBD purposes. Notice that this block contains fourteen parcels of land, none of which is vacant, eleven of which are only one story tall.

Accordingly, this block merits inclusion within the CBD boundary.

3. A block that meets the above requirements must also be part of a contiguous group of blocks surrounding the PLVI. In addition, a block is included in the CBD even though it fails to meet the first two required indexes if: (a) it is surrounded by blocks that do qualify, or (b) if it is devoted to government buildings and is adjacent to a block that does meet these CBD qualifications.

Changes in the CBD   CBD's are not static; they are dynamic. They are constantly changing in profile, in shape, and in internal composition. Most people assume that if a city grows, its CBD will get larger. This is essentially true, but the statement needs to be qualified. In the first place, CBD's probably grow less rapidly than cities as a whole do— that is, in growing cities, outlying business districts increase at a faster rate than does the

$$\text{Central Business Height Index} \quad = \frac{4935}{2100} = 2.4$$

$$\text{Central Business Intensity Index} = \frac{4935}{7070} = 69.8 \text{ per cent}$$

CBD. In the second place, expanding CBD's do not advance on all fronts. Indeed, activity is distinctly different on two different fronts; on one the CBD is advancing, on another it is receding. The advancing front rolls toward high-quality residential areas. This may seem surprising at first, since the land there is. likely to be more costly than in poor-quality residential zones, but when businessmen choose to invest in CBD structures, they tend to shy away from skid rows and slums. A shift in the CBD usually occurs "at the expense of the better residential areas, areas that have . . . already begun to retrogress as the CBD's advancing shadow of blight falls over them." So write Raymond Murphy and James Vance. The retreating front is usually pulling away from three repelling phenomena: slums, railways, and rivers. As the CBD withdraws, the vacated space adjoining railways and waterfronts tends to be filled up by wholesaling or manufacturing establishments or low-class housing.

The advancing front produces a *zone of assimilation* within the CBD, the receding front a *zone of discard*, each with its own distinctive composition. Assimilation spawns specialty shops, drive-in banks, professional offices, headquarters offices of large corporations, newer hotels, and businesses with a "prestige" factor, such as clothiers with a high reputation for quality merchandise. Discard produces pawn shops, bars, low-grade restaurants, bus stations, cheap movie houses, and businesses with little prestige. Figure 30-8 shows the CBD's analyzed by Murphy and Vance, indicating boundaries, location of zones of assimilation and discard, and also the shift of the PLVI.

The movement of the PLVI can be summed up in two tendencies: It goes in the same direction as the advancing front but lags behind it. As is shown clearly on Figure 30-8, the PLVI stays closer to the receding front. This lag is due principally to the inertia of investment policy. For as the CBD moves, although its traffic pattern will change (the busiest intersection shifting a block or two from the PLVI), financiers and businessmen

are at first reluctant to abandon the investments around that original point. "The pull toward a newer site must build up slowly" (Murphy and Vance). Ultimately, the pull overpowers the inertia, and speculators pour funds into new construction at the new intersection of greatest traffic. As we might expect, then, derelict PLVI's are typical of cities whose *point of attachment* was on a waterfront or railroad.

Problems and Future of the CBD *
Today the chief problems of CBD's are traffic congestion and parking facilities. Some urban observers are convinced that these problems are so severe that the CBD is doomed to extinction, especially when they see business fleeing the CBD for outlying business areas.

CBD's are not really fading away, though. Indeed, their very congestion is a sign of their powerful attraction. In New York City, for example, the last 15 years have seen at least 75 tall buildings thrown up on Manhattan Island, adding 26,000,000 square feet of office space: an *increment* that exceeds the total *existing* office space in any other city of the world except Chicago! And demand in Manhattan, which already had 100,000,000 square feet of office space continues to run ahead of supply, so that rental costs continue to climb (from an average of $4.75 to $5.25 per square foot) and the vacancy rate holds at a mere 1.4 per cent.

Admittedly, the CBD's are losing some businesses. Yet for each firm that leaves, another takes its place, though usually of a different type. Grocery stores, meat markets, and general stores are being replaced by specialty stores and services.

* For further discussion of CBD's see Raymond Murphy and J. E. Vance, "Delimiting the CBD," and "A Comparative Study of Nine Central Business Districts," *Economic Geography*, Vol. 30, 1954, pp. 189-222 and pp. 301-336, and, with Bart Epstein, these authors present the internal nature of CBD's in "Internal Structure of the CBD," *Economic Geography*, Vol. 31, 1955, pp. 21-46. Changes in the amount and type of businesses in a case study area are analyzed in Richard Ratcliff's *The Madison Central Business District*, Wisconsin Commerce Papers, Volume I, Number 5, 1953.

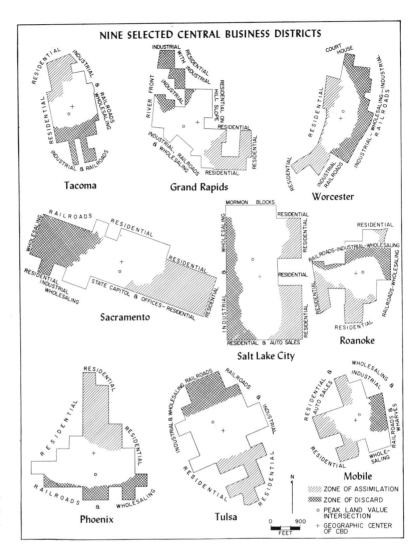

Figure 30-8 (*Courtesy Raymond E. Murphy and James E. Vance, Jr., and Economic Geography.*)

Thus, CBD's are growing, but at a slower rate than outlying business districts; concomitantly, the CBD's are becoming more highly specialized.

Other Centralized Commercial Areas Large cities usually have several secondary clusters of commercial activity that somewhat resemble the CBD but are smaller in size, and less specialized and less diversified in types of business. The larger a metropolis the more and the larger the subsidiary centers. Indeed, many such areas today were, originally, genuine CBD's of separate small cities. Subsequent growth has brought the result that these settlements coalesce with the expanding metropolis.

Commercial Strips Commercial strips, sometimes called *commercial ribbons*, are composed of stores and services strung along main thoroughfares. Usually strips are only one block wide, with residential property (or land given over to some other use) coming right up to the rear of each business tract. In villages and small towns, the CBD itself is often a commercial strip. In length, these strips attain astonishing distances. A mile is common. But in Detroit (Figure 30-9), Los Angeles, Chicago, and New York some are several miles in length. With few exceptions, commercial strips develop along traffic arteries radiating out from the CBD (as the Detroit map clearly shows).

A problem peculiar to every commercial ribbon is the friction between two types of traffic: (a) *through* traffic enroute to and from other parts of the city, often the CBD, and (b) local traffic enroute *to* businesses on the artery. This conflict produces tensions and turmoil; on the one hand there is the demand to prohibit curb parking "to let the traffic through," on the other, the demand from merchants and customers to use the curbs for stowing cars. The general consensus of experts today seems to be that commercial strips are an inefficient use of land, that through traffic and local traffic should be separated into different arteries, and that businesses, rather than being strung out in a ribbon several miles long, should be bunched together so that customers would be able to reach them more easily.*

Dispersed Businesses   Lone grocery shops, or drug stores, perhaps even pairs of stores, sprinkled throughout the older portions of many cities—these are dispersed businesses. Their *raison d'être* is that they are within walking distance for customers. The only kinds of businesses in such minute commercial developments are those that meet the daily needs of people. In the motorized parts of the world, we can easily tell which areas within a city predate the automobile age: Such areas have corner groceries about six blocks apart. But the automobile unshackled citizens from having to walk to the store; now they could drive to stores located much farther than six blocks away; this development, coupled with a public demand for purely residential areas free of commercial zoning, has led to the prohibition of dispersed businesses in new regions within most cities.

Shopping Centers   The new look in urban development calls for both commercial strips and dispersed businesses to give way to shopping centers. Whereas the other types of commercial areas sprang up at random, shopping centers are planned in advance. The objective is to gather businesses in outlying areas in such a way that the advantages of CBD's can be enjoyed without the disadvantages. Accordingly, a large variety of stores are brought close together so that, by one stop, a customer can make many purchases. Such centers are always located so as to be accessible to large numbers of people. Therefore, they occur either near intersections of main arteries, or off to *one* side of a busy thoroughfare, or at a major commuter station (for instance, the station known as "Route 128" on the New Haven Railroad southwest of Boston). The size of such centers is startling. The Cross County Center, seven miles north of Manhattan, covers 70 acres and has 5400 parking slots; Philadelphia's River Park center spreads out over 90 acres and can accommodate 6000 cars at a time. In contrast to CBD's, shopping centers devote land adjoining major thoroughfares—not to store buildings —but to vast parking lots. In their short life to date, shopping centers are doing more business per square foot of floor space than even the central business districts; moreover, land costs and operating costs are generally lower.*

Numerous outlying business districts do not fall clearly into any of the foregoing categories; nevertheless, on closer inspection, they usually turn out to be deviant specimens of either a centralized commercial area, a commercial ribbon, a dispersed establishment, or a shopping center.

INDUSTRIAL AREAS

Industry in most cities includes both wholesaling and manufacturing, and the two

---

* Fascinating discussions of commercial strips are available in Gerard Foster and Howard Nelson, *Ventura Boulevard: A String-Type Shopping Street*, University of California Press, (Los Angeles), 1958 and Brian Berry's "Ribbon Developments in the Urban Business Pattern," *Annals of the Association of American Geographers*, Vol. 49, 1959, pp. 145-155.

* Further reading on the characteristics, relationships and problems of shopping centers is available in Saul Cohen's *Selected Annotated Bibliography on Shopping Centers* published in 1957 by the Kroger Company, Cincinnati, Ohio and *Shopping Centers Re-Studied*, Technical Bulletin No. 30, the Urban Land Institute.

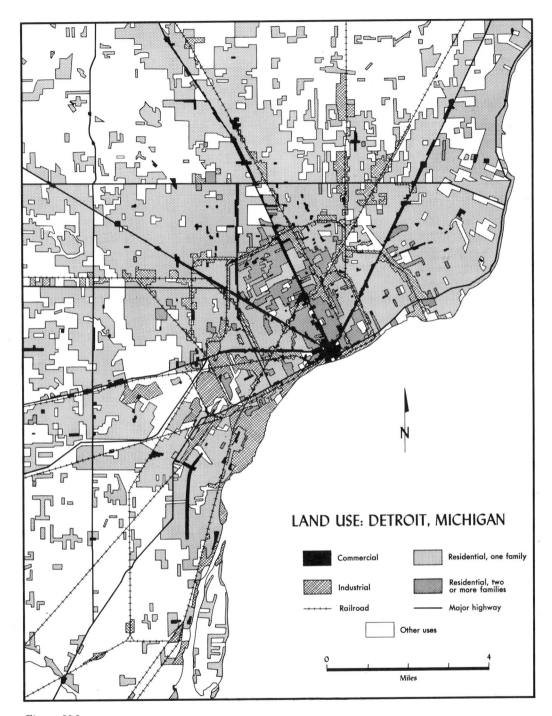

LAND USE: DETROIT, MICHIGAN

	Commercial		Residential, one family
	Industrial		Residential, two or more families
+++++	Railroad	———	Major highway
	Other uses		

0   4

Miles

Figure 30-9

branches gravitate toward specific places within a city.

Within the CBD there often are considerable manufacturing and some wholesaling of light items on the upper floors of commercial buildings. The advantage of the location for industry is proximity to labor, for the very centrality of the CBD, which makes it accessible to customers, simultaneously makes it accessible to large numbers of workers.

Light manufacturing can take advantage of this. Where the first floor serves as a retail outlet, upper floors can be devoted to making the items sold below: For example, hosiery factories in downtown New York. And in towns that sprang up around mill races, factories often remain still on the ground level within the CBD or on its edge.

The margin of CBD's usually contain a city's chief wholesaling district, often threaded through by railway sidings (tracks adjoining buildings for loading purposes), "team tracks" (railway tracks where trucks can load and unload in truck-load lots), freight terminals, and warehouses. A good many truck depots are here, too.

Elsewhere, industrial use is usually related to one or more of the following: (a) access to transportation (canal, railway, or highway) for moving inbound raw materials and outbound products, and (b) relatively cheap land. Notice how the pattern of industrial land in Detroit invariably conforms to the pattern of railways, or highways, or the river front (Figure 30-9). In some cities, swamps or valley bottoms are often filled and devoted to industrial uses (for instance, the Menominee Valley, which splits Milwaukee into a northern and southern half, or the Cuyahoga Valley, which bisects Cleveland, or the Monongahela Valley in Pittsburgh).

Industrialists must ordinarily fight public opinion in selecting a site on which to build. Many cities in the United States have zoning laws that prohibit them from much of the city's acreage. In a sense, then, they get what is left after commercial and residential interests have had their pick. But two new concepts are changing this: (a) planned industrial tracts, and (b) zoning tolerance for light industries.

Planned Industrial Tract   This is to industry what a planned shopping center is to retailing. A large piece of land is set aside for industry and all other uses are zoned out. Streets are laid out, water mains and sewers installed, power lines designed, railway spurs and roads are positioned—all from the standpoint of the needs of factories and warehouses.

The industrial heart of Lawrence, Massachusetts, looking downstream over the Merrimack River, which has been dammed (lower right). From above the dam, water is channeled off in two long mill-races, flanking the river, one on each side and separated from the main channel. Factories line the river banks. (Courtesy Lawrence Eagle-Tribune and Chamber of Commerce.)

Rotterdam, the Netherlands. Acres of multistoried row houses typify the older residential sections of many European cities. Apartment houses of recent design (distant background) have more open space between them. Barges in the immediate foreground give witness to Rotterdam's port function. (Courtesy Standard Oil Company of New Jersey, The Lamp.)

Five miles east of the CBD of Dallas, Texas, is an example of just such a scheme: "Brook Hollow," a 1200-acre stretch of former farm land, has been developed solely for industry. With attractive factories so positioned as to reduce traffic congestion and with enough land devoted to parking to accommodate the cars of everyone who drives, the tract is turning out to be an appealing place for people to work.

Zoning Tolerance The premise here is that certain light industries, small in size, should not be banned from residential neighborhoods but should actually be welcomed. Workers can then go home for lunch. This is no small factor in a culture where so many mothers of school-age children work in industry. Cross-town travelling can thereby be reduced, thus easing the city's traffic pains.

We can usually discern two broad residential regions on a land-use map of a city (see Figure 30-9). *Multiple-family housing* (structures with two or more families) tend to cluster in the center of town. Occasionally they appear within the CBD itself or within the industrial ring that sometimes encircles the CBD. Usually, though, they crop up in the next outer ring, immediately beyond the warehouses and factories. Multiple-family structures correlate closely with the zone of maximum population density (in the nighttime pattern). Most of these residences were built originally as apartment houses; but many a house at the edge of the CBD has either been converted into a rooming house (recall the dwelling pattern of single persons within a city) or subdivided into two or more apartments. The unit rents here are rather low, but the number of apartments is often so high that the rental income per house is great. Landlords have tradionally met the continuing demand from the poor for housing by further subdividing these houses into an ever-increasing number of ever-smaller dwelling units. The result is the cheapest housing *and* the most severe overcrowding. Thus, slums are born. It is in just such areas that *planned housing tracts* have recently been launched. Applying the basic concept behind the shopping center and the industrial tract, proponents of the housing-tract philosophy try to design large chunks of land for the optimum residential use.

Some of these schemes resort to remedial surgery, whereby slum buildings are razed and replaced by modern apartments—for instance, Stuyvesant Town on the Lower East Side of Manhattan and Lake Meadows on the near South Side of Chicago.

Multiple-housing tracts are becoming common now in outlying areas, too. La Brea Heights in Los Angeles is an imposing array of towers six miles west of the Los Angeles central business district. And no longer is it surprising to find apartments being built on the urban fringe where city meets country.

Anyone building a *single-family* house tends to avoid the CBD, the industrial areas, and the multiple-housing area. In most cities, single-family residences cover more acres than any other type of structure, generally in the city's outer reaches. Most American city-dwellers today place high values on such land use and strongly resist invasions by any other type.

Other types of land use concern geographers, too, of course. Are there any principles that operate in the location of schools, churches, parks, playgrounds, cemeteries, airports, and golf courses? Such questions are of great moment to economic geographers. And what about the location of freeways, of one-way streets, of streets where parking is banned, of parking lots, of bus routes, and of subways? These are problems of practical and theoretical concern to city planners. And they can be attacked by the same techniques of geographic analysis we have adopted here.

Urban Pattern

Analysis of the several locational patterns we have just observed supports the conclusion that there are three basic types of designs, or patterns, which seem to be woven into the fabric of any given city: the concentric-ring pattern; the sector, or wedge, pattern; and the multiple-nuclei pattern.

In the *concentric-ring pattern*, the CBD is in the center surrounded by at least four concentric rings. The first is a zone of *transi-tion* where old residential structures are being taken over by business and light manufacturing, and where slum conditions are frequent. The next ring is residential, with multiple-family structures predominant. The third ring is also residential, but given over to single-family houses; in this zone, lots are wider than in the inner rings. The final ring is also dominated by single family residences on still wider lots; usually, a city's highest-class homes are in this ring. The idea of concentric rings is often termed the *Burgess hypothesis* after its author, the noted sociologist E. W. Burgess.

The *sector, or wedge, pattern* pertains when different types of land use and different population densities are located within areas that either taper toward the CBD like pieces of pie (as does the triangular zone of single-family residences pointing toward the center of Detroit from the west) or taper outward like the points of a star (as do the prongs of some CBD's or the high-class residential areas of some cities). Sometimes the idea of sector or wedges is called the *Hurd-Hoyt hypothesis* after R. M. Hurd and Homer Hoyt.

In the *multiple-nuclei pattern,* besides the CBD, several points within the city draw traffic and stimulate development around them nearly as much as does the CBD. Examples of such nuclei are big-scale industrial installations (such as Chicago's stockyards), large public institutions (universities or hospitals), government office centers, or major military establishments. Occasionally this idea is termed the *Harris-Ullman hypothesis* after the two geographers who first formulated it, Chauncy Harris and Edward Ullman.*

THE COLBY HYPOTHESIS

The foregoing are useful *descriptive* theories. The *Colby hypothesis* offers a *dynamic* explanation of urban development. According to this theory (formulated by Charles Colby) the pattern of any city at any given moment is the result of two great forces at work: centripetal and centrifugal. *Centripetal* forces are of two types: (1) Residents and businesses are lured into a city from elsewhere by the amenities and economic advantages of being in town. (2) Within the city itself, both people and businesses on the fringe are drawn towards the CBD because the central point provides the

best access to either customers or labor or simply its characteristic institutions, such as stores, theatres, or libraries. Some parents who have reared their children in the suburbs, for instance, are beginning to respond to this pull by moving back into town. *Centrifugal* forces, on the other hand, drive people and businesses out of the CBD into outlying areas and out of the city into the suburbs; in some instances the power is strong enough to drive them clear out of the service center. Flight from congestion and a yearning for open space are the major motives.

Urban Fringe   As a result of these two opposing forces, there develops at the fringe of a city a zone of transition which in some respects resembles the one encircling the CBD. The *urban fringe* is a stretch of land that is in the process of changing from rural to urban use. Typically, population density becomes too high for rural classification but too sparse for urban, as the vanguard of the urban army of settlement proceeds outward, often ahead of surfaced streets, and of city services such as water and sewerage. Many an urban fringe, indeed, is dotted by hand pumps and septic tanks. With too many children for country schools yet too few to warrant a city school, and with a location far from existing city schools, the fringe areas are a problem to education authorities. Strange juxtapositions develop as the wave of new residences (usually one-floor houses but sometimes multistory apartments) sweeps up to and encircles an old farm house and barn. The latter are sometimes converted into retail outlets—for instance a furniture store—or some other urban use. Occasionally, too, a farm will resist the invasion and stand islanded by the urban wave.*

---

* More thorough discussion of these three patterns appears in Chauncy Harris and Edward Ullman, "The Nature of Cities," *Annals of the American Academy of Political and Social Science,* 1945, pp. 7-17.

* For further information on this unique zone of transition see George Wehrwein, "The Rural-Urban Fringe," *Economic Geography,* Vol. 28, 1942, pp. 217-228 and Peter Fielding, "Dairying in Cities Designed to Keep People Out," *The Professional Geographer,* January, 1962, pp. 12-17.

Applebaum, William, "A Technique for Constructing a Population and Urban Land Use Map," *Economic Geography*, 1952, pp. 240-243.

———, and Cohen, Saul B., "The Dynamics of Store Trading Areas and Market Equilibrium," *Annals of the Association of American Geographers*, 1961, pp. 73-101.

Berry, Brian J. L., "Ribbon Developments in the Urban Business Pattern," *Annals of the Association of American Geographers*, 1959, pp. 145-155.

Borchert, John R., "The Twin Cities Urbanized Area: Past, Present, Future," *Geographical Review*, 1961, pp. 47-70.

Brookfield, H. C., and Tatham, M. A., "The Distribution of Racial Groups in Durban," *Geographical Review*, 1957, pp. 44-65.

Carol, Hans, "Hierarchy of Central Functions Within the City," *Annals of the Association of American Geographers*, 1960, pp. 419-438.

Cohen, Saul B., and Applebaum, William, "Evaluating Store Sites and Determining Store Rents," *Economic Geography*, 1960, pp. 1-35.

Davies, D. Hywel, "Boundary Study as a Tool in CBD Analysis: An Interpretation of Certain Aspects of the Boundary of Cape Town's Central Business District," *Economic Georgraphy*, 1959, pp. 322-345.

———, "The Hard Core of Cape Town's Central Business District: An Attempt at Delimitation," *Economic Geography*, 1960, pp. 53-69.

Epstein, Bart J., "Evaluation of an Established Planned Shopping Center," *Economic Geography*, 1961, pp. 12-21.

Fellmann, Jerome D., "Pre-Building Growth Patterns in Chicago," *Annals of the Association of American Geographers*, 1957, pp. 59-82.

Fielding, Gordon J., "Dairying in Cities Designed to Keep People Out," *The Professional Geographer*, January, 1962, pp. 12-17.

Foster, Gerard J., and Nelson, Howard J., *Ventura Boulevard: A String-Type Shopping Street*, Los Angeles, 1958, 63 pp.

Fuchs, Roland J., "Intraurban Variation of Residential Quality," *Economic Geography*, 1960, pp. 313-325.

Higbee, Edward, *The Squeeze: Cities Without Space*, New York, 1960, 348 pp.

Horwood, Edgar M., and Boyce, Ronald R., *Studies of the Central Business District and Urban Freeway Development*, Seattle, 1959, 184 pp.

Maboqunje, Akin, "The Growth of Residential Districts in Ibadan," *Gegraphical Review*, 1962, pp. 56-77.

Mayer, Harold M., "Review of Chicago Area Transportation, Final Report," *Economic Geography*, 1961, pp. 373-374.

Megee, Mary, "The American Bottoms: The Vacant Land and the Areal Image," *The Professional Geographer*, November, 1961, pp. 5-9.

Murphy, Raymond E., and Vance, J. E., Jr., "A Comparative Study of Nine Central Business Districts," *Economic Geography*, 1954, pp. 301-336.

———, and ———, "Delimiting the CBD," *Economic Geography*, 1954, pp. 189-222.

———, and ———, and Epstein, Bart J., "International Structure of the CBD," *Economic Geography*, 1955, pp. 21-46.

Nelson, Howard J., "The Vernon Area, California," *Annals of the Association of American Geographers*, 1952, pp. 177-191.

Pattison, William D., "The Cemeteries of Chicago: A Phase of Land Utilization," *Annals of the Association of American Geographers*, 1955, pp. 245-257.

Peters, W. S., "A Method of Deriving Geographic Patterns of Associated Demographic Characteristics within Urban Areas," *Social Forces*, 1956, p. 62.

Proudfoot, Malcolm J., "Chicago's Fragmented Political Structure," *Geographical Review*, 1957, pp. 106-117.

Reinemann, Martin W., "The Pattern and Distribution of Manufacturing in the Chicago Area," *Economic Geography*, 1960, pp. 139-144.

Scott, Peter, "The Australian CBD," *Economic Geography*, 1959, pp. 290-314.

Thomas, Edwin N., "Areal Associations Between Population Growth and Selected Factors in the Chicago Urbanized Area," *Economic Geography*, 1960, pp. 158-170.

Viet, Jean, *New Towns*, A Selected Annotated Bibliography. UNESCO, 1960, 84 pp.

PART NINE

MEASUREMENT, THEORY, AND PLANNING

In Parts One through Eight of this book we have dealt with population and specific types of economic endeavor, attempting to show their general locational pattern, their distinguishing characteristics, and some of the relationships pertinent to them. The strategy has been to proceed from the less complex to the more complex categories of economic pursuits; accordingly, we began first with *primitive* gathering then moved "upward" through *subsistence* grazing, subsistence cultivation, *commercial primary* production (fishing, forestry, bioculture, and mining), commercial *secondary* production (manufacturing and transportation), and finally into commercial *tertiary* endeavors.

Now we turn attention to some ideas that are pertinent to the entire array of economic activities. In Chapter 31 we tackle the problem of measurement, specifically, the measurement of a single economic endeavor (for example: How much manufacturing is there in Sweden?) and then the measurement of association between an endeavor and some other phenomenon (for instance, how strong is the correlation, or association, between the location of cash-grain farming and the location of flat land?).

In Chapter 32 we deal with location theory—attempts to formulate statements that express principles governing the location of economic activity. Some theories endeavor to state cause-and-effect relationships; other theories express relationships that are more matters of "associations" than of causal or consequential connections.

In the final chapter, 33, we shall essay a few summarizing comments about the current levels of areal development, first on a world scale and then on a national scale. We shall direct our attention toward a few problems that demand solution, problems with which spatial analysts (whether they be beginning students in geography, advanced geographic researchers, or professional regional planners) should be concerned. In the process, we shall make mention of specific efforts that have been made to improve the economic health of areas, some on a large scale and some on a small scale.

Does cash-grain farming tend to be located on flat land? Is it possible to measure the correlation between the two? This is the sort of scientific inquiry that engages geographers today. For a study of this particular question, see page 606.

THIRTY-ONE

Knowledge of the amount and kind of economic endeavor in any given place, understanding of the comparison of places in amount and type of economic activity, and comprehension of the way an economic activity is related to some other phenomenon—all these goals of scientific investigation require accurate *measurement* of economic activity.

We shall be concerned here with two types of measurement. One is the measurement of a single economic activity, the second the measurement of the association between two phenomena: an economic activity and another variable—for example, manufacturing and population. In a sense, the former provides answers to the first two questions (on location and characteristics) of the geographic method we have been following, while the latter serves the third question (on relationships).

Measuring a Single Economic Activity

How much manufacturing is there in India? What is the leading manufactural industry in France? What is the leading industrial nation in Europe? How much agriculture is there in the U.S.S.R.? What is the leading type of agriculture in Guatemala? Where are the major agricultural areas of China? What is the most important mining activity in the United States? What nations lead the world in harvesting forest products? How important is fishing in the economic life of Japan? How important is wholesale trade in the economy of Winnipeg?

Answering such questions of where and what requires quantification of individual economic activities. Such quantification is necessary in order to study those endeavors by themselves or in relation to one another.

CHOOSING CRITERIA

All very well to know that we must measure, but how do we select the relevant elements for measurement? At the outset of any scientific investigation, we must formulate our objectives as clearly as possible. This done, we must make a choice of the criteria that will be the most useful measuring-sticks in working toward those objectives. If we are analyzing the geography of cotton production, for instance, should we measure that activity in terms of the number of cotton-growing farms, the number of acres devoted to cotton production, the number of bales of cotton produced, the value of cotton crops, or something else?

Or again, suppose we are analyzing the locational pattern of agriculture to determine the "leading" state in the United States. In terms of *acres of land in farms*, Texas, with 168,000,000 acres, is the nation's leading agricultural state. But when we adopt *value of farm products sold* as our criterion, then California, with $2.8 billion, ranks far ahead of any other state. If *average value of farms* be the criterion, Arizona is the front runner, since the average farm value there is $178,818. If average value of farm land *per acre* is the standard, then New Jersey, where an acre of farm land runs $538.76, is the foremost state. Examples could be cited not only from agriculture, but also from all other classes of economic endeavor to illustrate the fact that different locational patterns of an activity may be revealed by different criteria. Clearly, we must be careful to select the right criterion in tracing the aspect we want to study.

Figure 31-1 portrays an example of a pattern produced when a "leading" (or "first-

Figure 31-1   (*After John Weaver, from* Economic Geography.)

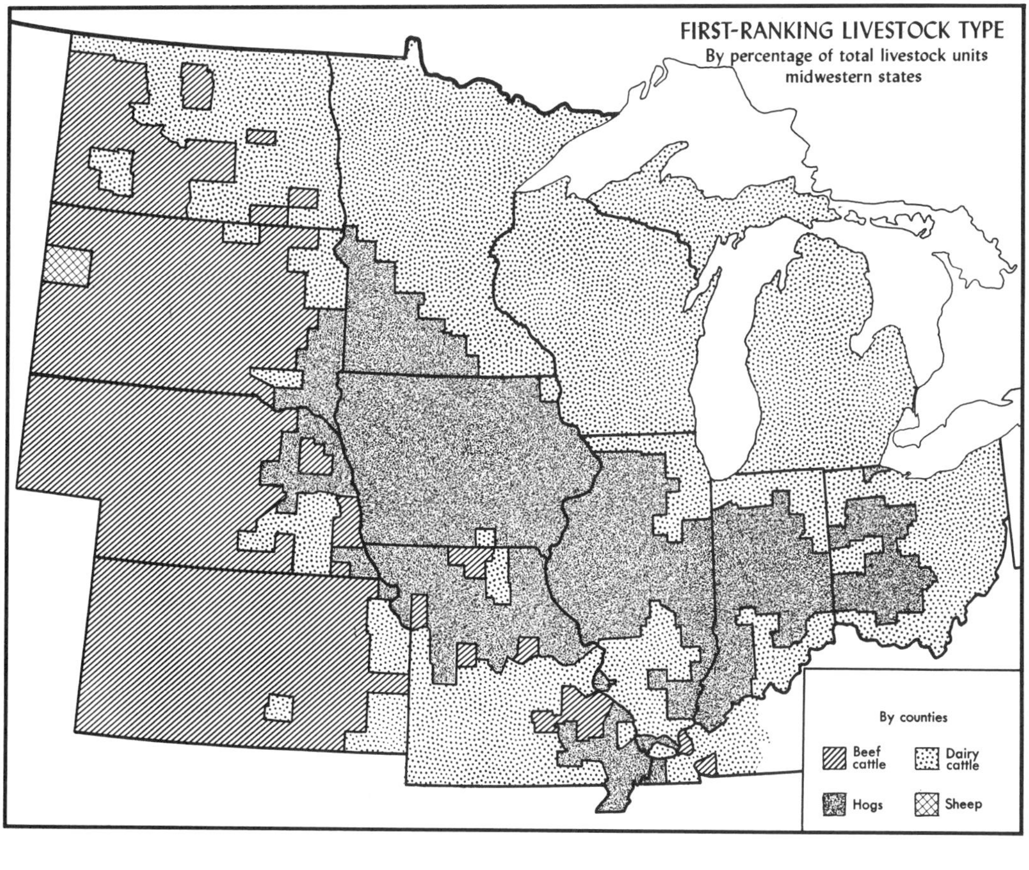

ranking") element is taken as the mapping unit. In this map of 12 contiguous midwestern states, counties are the areal units of measurement, and the "first-ranking" type of livestock on farms is the criterion for measurement. This map reveals the location of several agricultural regions, particularly those specializing in dairy farming and in mixed farming.

Clearly, then, regardless of the economic activity being investigated, the choice of criteria is a fundamental problem every analyst must face.

Measuring Geographic Association

In Chapter 1 we pointed out that relationships between geographic phenomena can be approached from four different perspectives: from the standpoint of physical and cultural conditions, or of intraregional and extraregional relationships, or of cause and effect, or of covariation. Advocates of this last approach, which is comparatively new and has been applied in only a few geographic studies, emphasize the importance of the *geographical association* of phenomena as they vary from place to place. The term has a precise meaning: That is, if two phenomena reach high values in the same places and low values in similar other places, they are said to have a close geographical association.

The question naturally arises: How does one determine whether two phenomena are geographically associated? There are numerous possibilities for determining such association, nine of which will concern us here. These are: the visual comparison of maps, the ratio map, the location quotient, the coefficient of geographic association, index of concentration, analysis of rank, scatter diagrams, the coefficient of correlation, and the mapping of residuals from regressions.

VISUAL COMPARISON OF MAPS

Suppose we were interested in understanding the geographic relationship between labor force (measured in terms of total number of people employed) and manufacturing (measured in terms of number of manufactural employees) in the state of Ohio. Now, first we might select *counties* as our areal unit of measurement and proceed to construct two maps, one based on *number of employees in manufacturing*, the other on the total *number of employed people*. For the first, in each county we would plot the number of manufactural employees. Then we would apply in each county a visual symbol (say, a circle), the size of which would be proportionate to the number of employees (Figure 31-2). Similarly, for the labor force, county by county, for the second map. The next task would be to compare the two maps. If each portrayed the *same pattern*, we could conclude that the two phenomena have a close geographic association.

The difficulties of the visual inspection method are two-fold. First, an enormous amount of time would be required to construct a series of such maps for any large region. For the United States, which contains more than 2000 counties, data would have to be plotted in each county, the size of symbols would have to be computed mathematically, and the symbols would have to be put on the maps. The second difficulty is more serious: Even when the maps are done, visual comparison is subject to human differences. Various scholars inspecting the results might arrive at different conclusions. One analyst might conclude that the two maps revealed essentially *the same* pattern, another that the two patterns were *almost* the same ("rather similar"), and a third, impressed with the differences between the two maps, might conclude that in his opinion, their patterns should not even be termed "similar." In other words, *visual inspection alone permits little scientific quantification of the similarity in locational patterns portrayed by different maps.*

In a scientific analysis of the visual comparison method, Harold McCarty and Neil Salisbury of the State University of Iowa ran several experiments with geography scholars to determine the reliability of this method in appraising the degree of association between isopleth maps.* Here are some of their findings and conclusions.

It is easier for the eye to measure the degree of association between two maps if their correlation is highly positive (see Chapter One and later in this chapter) than if it is weakly positive. Appraisal of correlation by this method becomes highly erratic where the correlation is negative.

In brief, the findings do not support the contention that visual comparisons of isopleth maps provide an effective means of determining or demonstrating the degree of association that exists between sets of spatially distributed phenomena. Only in cases in which the degree of association is very high does the process produce results which approach the standards of accuracy generally demanded in present-day research and teaching. In situations involving lesser degrees of association, the visual-comparison procedure must be viewed as an inadequate substitute for measurement where a determination of the extent of such an association is required.

On the other hand, visual methods produce generally satisfactory results, even among untrained stu-

* An isopleth is a line on a map and connects points of equal value. On one side of the line is an area of higher values; on the other side of the line is an area of lower values. For an example of isopleths, see Figure 31-5, page 606.

dents, when the sole object is to select pairs of maps whose distributions are most highly correlated when several alternative choices are available....

If the degree of association is very high, and if the direction of that association is positive, map comparison may be expected to produce reasonably good results, provided the maps are comparable with respect to colors and intervals. In cases involving lesser degrees of association, however, there is no assurance that the desired effect will be created.*

THE RATIO MAP

In drawing a ratio map, a geographer endeavors to show the degrees of relationship between two variables as they differ from place to place. The method for constructing a ratio map is to show in each areal unit, not the value of each of the two elements separately, but rather the *ratio* between the two. For example, the varying relationship from county to county between the number of manufacturing employees and number of persons in the labor force can be expressed in terms of *the percentage of employed persons in manufacturing.*

* Harold H. McCarty and Neil E. Salisbury, *Visual Comparison of Isopleth Maps as a Means of Determining Correlations Between Spatially Distributed Phenomena,* (Iowa City), 1961, 81 pp.

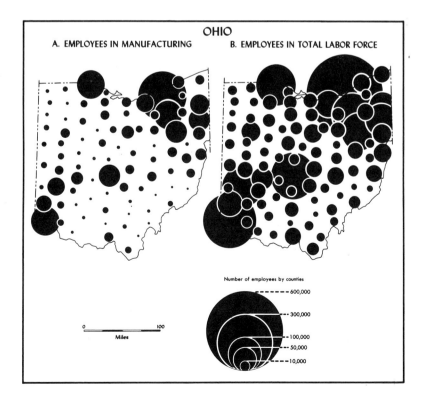

Figure 31-2

If two phenomena vary *similarly* from county to county, the ratio between them will tend to be *constant*, in which a close geographic association exists. But if they vary dissimilarly from place to place, so will the ratio. And the greater its variation, the weaker the geographic association between the two elements.

In the state of Ohio, the ratio between number of manufactural employees and total number of workers varies from a maximum of 53.9 per cent in Trumbull County to 5.4 per cent in Gallia County. For the state as a whole the figure is 36.6 per cent. From such variation relative to the state percentage, we can discern four categories of counties. Of Ohio's 88 counties, 20 are above the state percentage, leaving 68 below. The median percentage for the 20 above-average counties is 42.0 per cent. Median refers to the mid-point, and so splits any group into two halves. Of these 20 counties, 10 are *above* 42 per cent, 10 are *below* 42 per cent—but still above the 36.6 state percentage. The median for the 68 below-average counties is 25 per cent, 34 counties below, 34, above—yet all below the state average percentage. Our first category, then, consists of 10 counties that are above not only the state percentage but also the median of above-average counties, the second category of 10 counties above the state's ratio but less than the above-average median, the third of 34 counties whose ratios are between 25 and 36.6 per cent, and the fourth, likewise of 34 counties, those with ratios of less than 25 per cent. The last step, then, is to present the four categories on the map by distinctive shading.

Spatial variation in the relationship between manufactural employment and total employment in Ohio on a county basis is shown in Figure 31-3, where each county is shaded with a symbol indicating to which of the four categories it belongs.

Ratio maps are useful in showing how closely any two variables—whether they be manufactural employment and total employment, or wheat yields and rainfall, or value of retail trade sales and number of inhabitants—are associated as they differ from place to place.

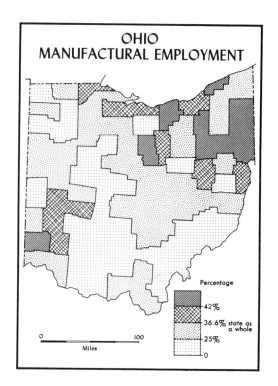

Figure 31-3

LOCATION QUOTIENT

The *location quotient* concept was introduced in Chapter 23 where we described its computation in a manufacturing example, but it can be used for any other economic endeavor. In brief, the location quotient is a ratio of ratios. To illustrate: The ratio of *employment in agriculture* to *population* for the United States as a whole is:

$$\frac{\text{employment in agriculture}}{\text{population}} = \frac{7,384,000}{179,323,000} = 4.1\%$$

The ratios of these two variables for selected Midwestern states are as follows:

North Dakota $\quad \dfrac{94,000}{632,000} = 14.8\%$

South Dakota $\quad \dfrac{94,000}{680,000} = 13.8\%$

Nebraska $\quad \dfrac{158,000}{1,411,000} = 11.2\%$

Kansas $\quad \dfrac{165,000}{2,178,000} = 7.5\%$

Minnesota $\quad \dfrac{267,000}{3,413,000} = 8.1\%$

Iowa	$\dfrac{293{,}000}{2{,}757{,}000} = 10.6\%$
Missouri	$\dfrac{280{,}000}{4{,}319{,}000} = 6.5\%$
Wisconsin	$\dfrac{299{,}000}{3{,}951{,}000} = 7.5\%$
Illinois	$\dfrac{256{,}000}{10{,}081{,}000} = 2.5\%$

The location quotient of agricultural employment for each state is determined by dividing its percentage by the national percentage of 4.1. If a state has a location quotient exceeding 1.00 it has "more than its share" of the nation's agricultural employees; a quotient of under 1.00 (the quotient can never be less than zero) indicates "less than its share."

In brief, the formula for the location quotient in this illustration is as follows:

$$\frac{\dfrac{\text{state's employment in agriculture}}{\text{state's employment in all activities}}}{\dfrac{\text{United States employment in agriculture}}{\text{United States employment in all activities}}}$$

Accordingly the location quotients for these nine states in terms of their population and agricultural employment are as follows:

North Dakota	$\dfrac{14.8}{4.1} = 3.6$
South Dakota	$\dfrac{13.8}{4.1} = 3.3$
Nebraska	$\dfrac{11.2}{4.1} = 2.7$
Kansas	$\dfrac{7.5}{4.1} = 1.8$
Minnesota	$\dfrac{8.1}{4.1} = 1.9$
Iowa	$\dfrac{10.6}{4.1} = 2.6$
Missouri	$\dfrac{6.5}{4.1} = 1.6$
Wisconsin	$\dfrac{7.5}{4.1} = 1.8$
Illinois	$\dfrac{2.5}{4.1} = 0.6$

The foregoing methods have proved highly useful for many purposes of geographic analysis. However, some geographers believe that more fruitful results can be obtained from methods that are mathematically more sophisticated. We shall now examine six such methods. All endeavor to apply the techniques of mathematics to the problem of measuring the association between two phenomena as they vary from place to place. Each of them, in its own way, can shed some light on the degree to which the two locational patterns are alike, in terms of *geographic association*.

COEFFICIENT OF GEOGRAPHIC ASSOCIATION

We shall illustrate the computation of the *coefficient of geographic association* in terms of three categories of employment: (1) manufacturing, (2) food manufacturing, and (3) electrical machinery manufacturing. Our areal units will be the 48 contiguous states.

First construct a table of values as in Table 31-1. List each areal unit in the left-hand column; in columns to the right (2 and 4 in Table 31-1), enter each areal unit's *percentage* of the national total of whatever phenomena are under investigation. Obviously, to establish these values, other numerical data are previously required. To illustrate: Iowa has 1.2 per cent of the nation's total manufacturing, 3.1 per cent of the nation's food manufacturing, and 0.9 per cent of the nation's electrical machinery manufacturing, all measured in terms of employment.

The next step is to compute for each state the *difference* between its percentage in each industry and its percentage in total manufactural employment. For Iowa the difference for the food industry would be determined as follows: food industry percentage (3.1) minus total manufactured employment percentage (1.2) yields a *difference* of +1.9. If a state's percentage in any particular manufacturing is *less than* its percentage in all manufacturing, then its difference is a negative figure; Iowa's differential for the electrical machinery industry is −0.3.

Now compute the *sum* of *either* the positive differences *or* the negative differences. (It makes no difference which is chosen since their totals will be exactly the same.) Divide that figure by 100 and subtract it from unity (1.000). The result is the coefficient of geographic association for the industry in question.

Table **31-1**   *Table of Values for Computing Coefficient of Geographic Association in Selected Industries*

	Employment by Percentages of United States Totals				
Areal Unit	*(1) All Manufacturing*	*(2) Food Industry*	*(3) Difference (Column 2 minus Column 1)*	*(4) Electrical Industry Machinery*	*(5) Difference (Column 4 minus Column 1)*
UNITED STATES	100	100		100	
Maine	0.7	0.7		—	−0.7
New Hampshire	0.5	0.2	−0.3	0.7	+0.2
Vermont	0.2	0.1	−0.1	—	−0.2
Massachusetts	4.4	2.9	−1.5	7.9	+3.5
Rhode Island	0.8	0.4	−0.4	0.4	−0.4
Connecticut	2.6	0.8	−1.8	3.5	+0.9
New York	12.3	9.5	−2.8	13.0	+0.7
New Jersey	5.1	3.7	−1.4	10.8	+5.7
Pennsylvania	9.3	7.0	−2.3	10.9	+1.6
Ohio	8.2	5.2	−3.0	9.4	+1.2
Indiana	3.7	2.9	−0.8	7.1	+3.4
Illinois	7.6	8.6	+1.0	14.3	+6.7
Michigan	6.5	3.8	−2.7	2.2	−4.3
Wisconsin	2.7	3.8	+1.1	3.8	+1.1
Minnesota	1.3	3.0	+1.7	0.7	−0.6
Iowa	1.2	3.1	+1.9	0.9	−0.3
Missouri	2.4	3.3	+0.9	2.2	−0.2
North Dakota	—	0.2	+0.2	—	
South Dakota	—	0.5	+0.5	—	
Nebraska	0.3	1.7	+1.4	0.2	−0.1
Kansas	0.8	1.4	+0.6	—	−0.8
Delaware	0.2	0.3	+0.1	—	−0.2
Maryland	1.6	2.3	+0.7	1.3	−0.3
Virginia	1.5	1.7	+0.2	—	−1.5
West Virginia	0.8	0.5	−0.3	0.4	−0.4
North Carolina	2.7	1.5	−1.2	1.1	−1.6
South Carolina	1.4	0.5	−0.9	—	−1.4
Georgia	1.9	2.1	+0.2	0.2	−1.7
Florida	0.8	1.8	+1.0	0.1	−0.7
Kentucky	0.9	1.6	+0.7	0.9	
Tennessee	1.6	1.7	+0.1	0.4	−1.2
Alabama	1.4	1.0	−0.4	0.2	−1.2
Mississippi	0.6	0.7	+0.1	0.1	−0.5
Arkansas	0.5	0.8	+0.3	0.2	−0.3
Louisiana	0.9	1.9	+1.0	—	−0.9
Oklahoma	0.5	0.9	+0.4	0.1	−0.4
Texas	2.6	4.1	+1.5	0.5	−2.1
Montana	0.1	0.2	+0.1	—	−0.1
Idaho	0.1	0.4	+0.3	—	−0.1
Wyoming	—	—		—	
Colorado	0.2	0.6	+0.4	—	−0.2
New Mexico	—	0.1	+0.1	—	
Arizona	0.2	0.3	+0.1	—	−0.2
Utah	0.2	0.5	+0.3	—	−0.2
Nevada	—	—		—	
Washington	1.2	1.6	+0.4	0.1	−1.1
Oregon	0.9	1.1	+0.2	1.0	+0.1
California	6.6	9.0	+2.4	5.4	−1.2
TOTALS	100.0	100.0	19.9 19.9	100.0	25.1 25.1

Source: Computed from United States *Census of Manufactures*.

Now for the food industry in our example, the sum of the positive (or negative) differences is 19.9 (column 3). Divide that by 100, which gives .199. Subtract that figure from 1.000 to find the coefficient, in this case, .801.

For employment in electrical machinery manufacturing, add up the differences recorded in column 5 of Table 31-1. Since the sum is 25.1, the coefficient is .749 (25.1 ÷ 100 = .251; 1.000 − .251 = .749).

The higher the figure, of course, the closer the correlation. Accordingly, we can conclude that within the United States, the food-processing varies from place to place in closer association with all manufacturing than does the electrical machinery industry.

The coefficient of geographic association may reach 1.00, if two phenomena are perfectly associated geographically, varying from place to place in exactly the same manner and degree. At the other extreme the coefficient may reach 0.000 if two activities are located so dissimilarly that *all* the persons engaged in such activity are in locales containing *no* one engaged in the other. In this instance, the sum of the differences would be 100.

Sometimes the coefficient of geographic association is called the *coefficient of linkage* or the *coefficient of similarity*. Although illustrated above with manufacturing, this device, whatever the name, can be used for measuring the association of any pair of phenomena.

INDEX OF CONCENTRATION

The index of concentration is a measure of the degree to which an activity is concentrated regionally. It is based on a comparison between the distribution of two phenomena—in the illustration to follow we shall use employment in the transport machinery industry and number of inhabitants. The index of concentration is computed as follows:

1. Determine the total population of the United States and the total employment in transport machinery factories.

United States population (1960 census)	179,323,175
Employment in transport machinery factories	1,557,759

2. Take one-half the employment figure in the industry (the significance of the *half* will be apparent later).

Transport machinery
employment: 1,557,759 ÷ 2 = 778,879

3. For each state compute the employment/population ratio in terms of the number of transport machinery workers per 1000 persons. For example, the ratio for Michigan is as follows:

Population in thousands:	7,823
Employees in transport machinery:	252,370
Ratio: transport machinery employees per 1000 population:	32.2

4. List the states in descending order according to the above ratio (see Table 31-2, columns A and B).

5. For each state in the array, indicate the number of employees in the transport machinery industry (Table 31-2, column C) and in thousands, the population, (column D).

6. Beginning with the state that has the highest *ratio* (for the transport machinery industry, this state is Michigan), add up the *number of employees* by state until a cumulative figure equal to *half* the national total is reached. (The last state listed may bring the cumulative sum to more than one-half, therefore it must be pro-rated.) The states that contribute to this cumulative figure constitute the *areas of concentration* of the industry being measured. As Table 31-2 reveals, for the transport machinery industry, the areas of concentration are Michigan, Connecticut, Washington, Kansas, Indiana, and most of California.

7. Compute the percentage of employment in this industry in California required to bring the cumulative employment to 778,879 (half the national total in this industry).

California:	(a)	total employment in transport machinery:	264,550
	(b)	required for cumulative total:	261,514
		Percentage b/a	98.7%

8. Apply this percentage to California's population. $15,717,000 \times 98.7\% = 15,512,000$

9. Enter 15,512 (98.7% of California's population in thousands) in column D of Table 31-2.

10. Add up the entries in column D. The total is 35,563.

11. Convert this figure (35,563) to a percentage of the nation's total population.

(a) United States
    population: 179,323,000
(b) Population total in
    column D: 35,563,000

Percentage b/a: 19.8%

This step reveals that one-half of the nation's transport machinery workers are concentrated in an area that contains only 19.8 per cent of the nation's people. (This is obviously a highly concentrated industry since half its employment is packed into just six states.)

12. Subtract the percentage figure just computed (19.8) from 100. The result, 80.2, is the *index of concentration* for the transport machinery industry. In 1954 the index was 82.8; the difference today indicates that this industry has become less concentrated.

The higher this index, the greater the geographic concentration of the industry, the lower the index, the more widespread or scattered the industry. A truly ubiquitous industry would have an index of 50, if by *ubiquitous* we mean that the industry is located in direct proportion to the population, that the two are perfectly *associated geographically* with each other. The index could never reach 100, for that would mean that all of the employment in an industry exists in an area containing no people. Neither could the index drop below 50. (If a person did arrive at an index of 40, for example, it would indicate an error in calculation—probably that he failed to array the states properly and entered in his table in steps 3 and 4 some states which did not belong so high in the ranking.)

In Table 31-2 we also show computations

Table **31-2** *Computation of Index of Concentration*

TRANSPORT MACHINERY INDUSTRY

United States population: 179,323,175

United States employment in manufacture of transport machinery: 1,557,759

Half of the total employment in the industry is: 778,879

Column A	Column B	Column C	Column D
States	Number of Transport Machinery Employees per 1,000 Population	Employees in Transport Machinery Industry	Population in Thousands
Michigan	32.2	252,370	7,823
Connecticut	27.8	70,612	2,535
Washington	24.2	69,744	2,853
Kansas	20.6	44,890	2,178
Indiana	17.1	79,749	4,662

Cumulative total of above five states: 517,365 ⎫
                                                 ⎬ Total:
Additional number of employees required to equal   778,879
  half the national total: 261,514 ⎭ ⎱
                                                    ⎰ 98.7% 15,512 (98.7% of
California   16.8   264,550 ⎰   California's
                                                               population of
                                                               15,717,000)

                                                               35,563, which
                                                               is 19.8% of
                                                               total United
                                                               States population

Index of Concentration (100 minus 19.8) is 81.2.

for determining the index of concentration for the bread and related products industry. That this is a far more ubiquitous business than the transport machinery industry is revealed by the following characteristics: (a) Twelve states are required to make the cumulative half of the national total employment, (b) there is little difference in *ratio* (column B) among these twelve states, and (c) the index of concentration is only 61.4. In 1954 the index was 62.5; the bread industry is getting closer to a ubiquitous pattern.

Several major industries in the United States are listed in Table 31-3, page 600, by their *indexes of concentration*. High indexes indicate that various combined relationships give competitive advantages to only a few locations; low indexes indicate that interacting relationships favor numerous places, none of which has a markedly superior competitive advantage.

Although the foregoing discussion of the *index of concentration* was based on data for individual states and for manufacturing,

the concept can be applied to counties, cities, or any other areal unit one chooses and to any type of economic activity.

ANALYSIS OF RANK

Another method for quantifying relationships is *correlation of rank*. By this technique, which can be applied to any criteria or any areal units, places are first simply arrayed according to their rankings in terms of whatever phenomena are under study. Suppose, for example, that we are interested in observing the relationships among population, employment in the baking industry, and employment in meat-packing plants as they vary from state to state in the United States. Our first step would be to construct three lists, each ranking the states in descending order in terms of one of the criteria. How such a list would be constructed is shown in Table 31-4, which gives the ten leading states in each category.

If we compare the three columns we find that the rankings are not exactly the same in any two lists. Even so, the first two columns

Table **31-2** *Computation of Index of Concentration* (*Continued*)

BREAD AND RELATED PRODUCTS INDUSTRY

United States employment in manufacture of bread and related products: 256,963

Half of the total employment in the industry is: 128,481

Column A	Column B	Column C	Column D
Rhode Island	2.45	2,110	859
Maine	2.09	2,032	969
Pennsylvania	2.06	23,490	11,319
Massachusetts	2.01	10,457	5,148
New York	1.98	33,156	16,782
Missouri	1.88	8,144	4,319
Ohio	1.83	17,884	9,706
Nebraska	1.66	2,331	1,411
Wisconsin	1.58	6,259	3,951
Illinois	1.56	15,744	10,081
Connecticut	1.48	3,733	2,535

Cumulative total of the above eleven states: 125,340 ⎫
Additional number of employees required to equal half the national total: 3,141 ⎬ Total: 128,481

Michigan   1.39   10,877 ⎭ 29.0% ⎰ 2,260 (29.0% of Michigan's population of 7,823,000)

69,340 which is 38.6% of total United States population

Index of Concentration (100 minus 38.6) is 61.4.

Table 31-3 Index of Concentration for Selected Industries
in the United States

| Industry | Index of Concentration | Number of States in Area of Concentration | State with Highest Employment-Population Ratio | |
			Name	Employees per 1,000 Population
Motor Vehicles	95.3	2	Michigan	54.3
Textile	92.3	6	South Carolina	60.9
Tractors	92.2	2	Illinois	6.3
Footwear	92.1	5	New Hampshire	32.4
Metal-Working Machinery	89.0	5	Vermont	14.9
Leather	88.6	7	New Hampshire	39.4
Petroleum	88.4	6	Wyoming	9.0
Rubber Tires	87.9	2	Ohio	39.2
Office Machinery	87.9	3	Connecticut	7.7
Blast Furnaces	87.6	3	Pennsylvania	16.4
Engines	87.6	4	Wisconsin	4.0
Tin Cans	86.4	4	Maryland	1.9
Aircraft	85.8	5	Connecticut	27.5
Hardware	85.7	5	Connecticut	9.8
Instruments	85.0	4	Connecticut	7.8
Lumber	84.3	13	Oregon	49.2
Construction Machinery	84.3	6	Wisconsin	3.4
Canning	81.6	8	Delaware	6.6
Transport Machinery	81.2	6	Michigan	32.2
Apparel	80.8	3	New York	25.6
Pulp	80.3	13	Maine	17.4
Meat Packing	78.8	13	Iowa	10.6
Machinery	76.0	8	Connecticut	36.4
Fabricated Metals	74.8	7	Connecticut	22.1
Printing	72.5	7	New York	11.3
Service Machinery	71.9	9	Indiana	4.0
Chemicals	71.5	12	Delaware	18.8
Electrical Machinery	71.2	8	New Jersey	21.3
Furniture	70.8	11	North Carolina	8.1
Bakery Products	61.4	12	Rhode Island	2.4

Source: Computed from data in United States *Census of Manufactures.*

Table 31-4 Ranks of Ten Leading States in Terms of Selected Criteria

Rank	(1) Population	(2) Employment in Bakery Products	(3) Employment in Meat Packing
1	New York	New York	Iowa
2	California	Pennsylvania	Illinois
3	Pennsylvania	California	Minnesota
4	Illinois	Ohio	Ohio
5	Ohio	Illinois	Nebraska
6	Texas	Michigan	Texas
7	Michigan	Texas	Pennsylvania
8	New Jersey	Massachusetts	Indiana
9	Massachusetts	New Jersey	California
10	Florida	Missouri	Wisconsin

Source: United States, *Census of Manufactures, 1958,* Bakery Products, Table 2 and Meat Products, Table 2 and *Census of Population, 1960,* United States Summary.

Measurement of Location and Association

are considerably more alike than are columns 1 and 3 or columns 2 and 3. Therefore, we can conclude that there is a closer relationship between *population* and *employment in the bakery industry* than between any other pair of variables appearing in this table. The more similar the rankings, the closer the relationship as revealed by the rank-analysis method.

The rank-analysis method presents some severe difficulties, however. One is the matter of *differences between rank values*. Ten states (as in Table 31-4) might conceivably have exactly the same rankings in two listings, but their relative values in the two might be vastly different from one another. Measuring them by rank alone would not reveal such differences. Another difficulty is the question of *ties:* If four states have exactly the same value, what ranking is ascribed to each?

To help overcome this difficulty, statisticians have developed formulae for computing *rank correlations* which are mathematical measurements of the similarity between two lists of rankings. However, the degree of mathematical sophistication involved is such that the author believes these are beyond the scope of this volume and are best reserved for advanced courses in economic geography.

SCATTER DIAGRAM

A relatively simple yet very helpful device for portraying visually the relationship between different phenomena is the *scatter diagram*, a graph on which one plots dots, each one representing an areal unit (say, a state, a county, or a city). This technique has already been touched upon in Chapter 17. In the paragraphs to follow, we shall illustrate the scatter-diagram technique in terms of number of inhabitants, employment in retail trade, and agricultural employment expressed as a percentage of total population. For convenience, we have arbitrarily selected nine contiguous midwestern states as our areal units. And in demonstrating the steps in the construction of a scatter diagram we shall use the data given in Table 31-5 for the nine states.

Now, a scatter diagram portrays the relationship between any *two* phenomena, so we can deal with only two of these elements at a time. Therefore, Figure 31-4, Part A, relates to *population* and *employment in retail trade*, Part B to *population* and *percentage of population employed in agriculture* (page 602).

The vertical axis of a scatter diagram is scaled for plotting one variable, the horizontal axis for plotting a second. The scales need not be the same. Thus, each areal unit can be represented by means of a single dot, whose position is fixed by that place's value on each of the two scales. For example, on Figure 31-4, Part A, Minnesota is represented by a dot opposite 3.4 on the vertical scale (because her population is 3,413,864) and opposite 1.4 on the horizontal scale (because 145,954 of her inhabitants are employed in trade).

Table **31-5**   *Selected Data for Nine Contiguous Midwestern States*

State	Population 1960	Employees in Retail Trade	Employment in Agriculture as a Percentage of Total Employment, 1959
Illinois	10,081,158	463,808	2.5
Wisconsin	3,951,777	164,030	7.5
Missouri	4,319,813	192,596	6.5
Iowa	2,757,537	118,429	10.6
Minnesota	3,413,864	145,954	8.1
Kansas	2,178,611	92,480	7.5
Nebraska	1,411,330	64,723	11.2
South Dakota	680,514	26,374	13.8
North Dakota	632,446	25,053	14.8

Source: United States Bureau of the Census, *Census of Population, 1960,* Volume II, and *Census of Business, 1958, Retail Trade,* and United States Department of Agriculture, *Agricultural Statistics,* 1960.

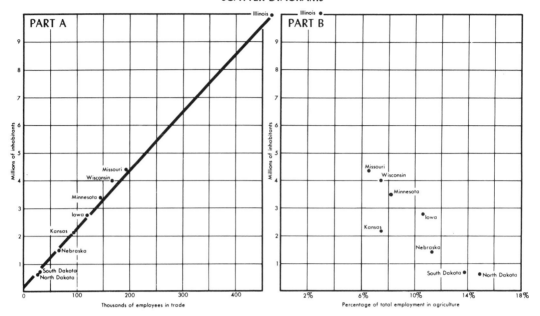

SCATTER DIAGRAMS

PART A

Millions of inhabitants

Illinois ●

Missouri ●
Wisconsin ●

Minnesota ●

Iowa ●

Kansas ●

● Nebraska

● South Dakota
North Dakota

Thousands of employees in trade

PART B

Millions of inhabitants

Illinois ●

Missouri ●
Wisconsin ●

Minnesota ●

● Iowa

Kansas ●

Nebraska ●

South Dakota ●   ● North Dakota

Percentage of total employment in agriculture

Figure 31-4

After we have plotted all the dots on a scatter diagram, we can answer the following:

First, do the dots tend to align? If they do *not*, there is little correlation between the two variables. Dispersion of dots suggests scarcely any covariation of the variables in the areas being plotted. If the dots *do* tend to align, then correlation exists (unless the line is exactly horizontal or exactly vertical, either of which indicates that one of the two measurements is a spatial constant, and does not vary from place to place). And the nearer the dots lie to a line, the closer the relationship between the two.

Second, *if the dots do align, in what direction is the line oriented?* If the line slants *upward*, from left to right, it indicates positive (or direct) correlation. That is, as one variable *increases*, the other variable *increases* also, as illustrated by Part A of Figure 31-4. If the line slants *downward* from left to right it indicates *negative* (or inverse) correlation. That is, as one variable *increases*, the other variable *decreases*, as illustrated by Part B of Figure 31-4. The name given to this hypothetical line is *regression line*.

We can discern quite a bit about the correlation of two variables by inspecting a scat-

ter diagram. But we can be far more precise if we go on to compute the regression line mathematically. We shall examine this operation in connection with Figure 31-4, Part A.

Regression Line   Three major steps are involved in computing a regression line: construction of a Table of Values, computation of the *a* value of the regression line, and computation of the *b* value of the regression line.

1. Construction of a Table of Values: A Table of Values contains data for the two relevant phenomena (in our example, population and employment in trade) in five columns (see Table 31-6). Column 1 lists values in each areal unit for one of the phenomena being studied, the one plotted on the horizontal axis or the scatter diagram; column 2 contains the *squares* of the values in column 1; column 3 shows values for the second phenomenon being studied, the one plotted on the vertical axis; column 4 has the *squares* of those in column 3; the entries in column 5 are *products* of the values in column 1 and those in column 3. Each areal unit being studied has one entry in each of the five columns.

Table **31-6** *Table of Values: Selected Criteria for Nine Midwestern States* *

State	Column 1 (Value Graphed on Horizontal Axis of Scatter Diagram) Employment in Trade (000's)	Column 2 Square of Value in Column 1	Column 3 (Value Graphed on Vertical Axis of Scatter Diagram) Population (in millions)	Column 4 Square of Value in Column 3	Column 5 Product of Values in Columns 1 and 3
Illinois	463	214,369	10.0	100.00	4630.0
Wisconsin	164	26,896	3.9	15.21	639.6
Missouri	192	36,864	4.3	18.49	825.6
Iowa	118	13,924	2.7	7.29	318.6
Minnesota	145	21,025	3.4	11.56	493.0
Kansas	92	8,464	2.1	4.41	193.2
Nebraska	64	4,096	1.4	1.96	89.6
South Dakota	26	676	.6	.36	15.6
North Dakota	25	625	.6	.36	15.0
TOTALS	1,289	326,939	29.0	159.64	7220.2
Statistical symbols for items in above columns:	x	x^2	y	y^2	xy
Symbols for Totals	Σx	Σx^2	Σy	Σy^2	Σxy

* Values are based on data in Table 31-5.

Statisticians have adopted certain symbols for each of the various components of Table 31-6: Thus, x for the phenomenon quantified in column 1, y for that in column 3, and Σ for the total of any column.

2. Computation of the a value of the regression line: The a value is the point of origin of the regression line on the vertical axis, that is, it is the point from which the line moves from left to right across the scatter diagram.

The value of a is computed by determining a ratio, both the numerator and denominator of which are built up from the totals appearing at the bottom of columns in the Table of Values, as shown below. (The reader should not attempt to memorize this formula but rather read through it endeavoring to see how each part of it relates to the Table of Values.)

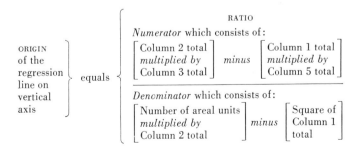

The above equation can be expressed tersely, in the language of statistical symbols, thus:

$$a = \frac{(\Sigma x^2 \cdot \Sigma y) - (\Sigma x \cdot \Sigma xy)}{(N \cdot \Sigma x^2) - (\Sigma x)^2}$$

The solution to the equation for one example is accomplished by substituting in the proper places the entries from Table 31-6:

$$a = \frac{(326{,}939 \cdot 29.0) - (1{,}289 \cdot 7{,}220.2)}{(9 \cdot 326{,}939) - (1{,}289)^2}$$

$$a = \frac{9{,}481{,}231.0 - 9{,}306{,}837.8}{2{,}942{,}451 - 1{,}661{,}521}$$

$$a = \frac{174{,}393.2}{1{,}280{,}930.0}$$

$$a = 0.13$$

The figure just reached must be read in millions, since that is the unit of measurement used in calibrating the vertical axis on Figure 31-4A. Thus, the regression line on Figure 31-4, Part A, intersects the vertical axis at the value of 0.13 million.

3. Computation of the b value of regression line: The b value is the average change in y with a given change in x. That is, for every one unit of measurement marked off on the horizontal axis, the regression line moves *vertically* the number of units indicated by the b value. The b value is computed by solving this equation:

$$b = \frac{(N \cdot \Sigma xy) - (\Sigma x \cdot \Sigma y)}{(N \cdot \Sigma x^2) - (\Sigma x)^2}$$

When the appropriate entries from the Table of Values are inserted in the above equation, it reads as follows:

$$b = \frac{(9 \cdot 7{,}220.2) - (1{,}289 \cdot 29.0)}{(9 \cdot 326{,}939) - (1{,}289)^2}$$

$$b = \frac{64{,}981.8 - 37{,}381.0}{2{,}942{,}451 - 1{,}661{,}521}$$

$$b = \frac{27{,}600.8}{1{,}280{,}930.0}$$

$$b = 0.021$$

This figure must be read in millions of population per thousand of trade employees, since these are the units in which the vertical and horizontal axes of Figure 31-4A are calibrated. The regression line then, moves *upward* at the

rate of 0.021 million vertical units for each horizontal unit; for every 100,000 employees in retail trade (horizontal axis) the regression line will rise 2.1 millions on the population scale (vertical axis). The regression line on Part A of Figure 31-4 does this.

The regression line on Figure 31-4 Part B has not been constructed—in hopes that the reader might want to try his hand at constructing it himself. (NOTE: The a value will be positive, the b value will be negative.)

What do the two scatter diagrams in Figure 31-4 tell us? Part A (on the relationship between *population* and *employment in trade*) shows a positive correlation—as population increases, there is a tendency for employment in trade to increase.

Part B (on the relationship between *population* and the *agricultural percentage of total employment*) shows a negative correlation—as population increases from state to state (at least for these nine states), there is a tendency for the relative importance of agriculture in the employment structure to decline.

We can discern something about the relationship between two spatial variables if we construct a scatter diagram to show their variation through different areas. We can learn more about their relationship by plotting their regression line, and still more if we compute their *coefficient of correlation*.

COEFFICIENT OF CORRELATION

One of the best-known and most frequently used methods for measuring the relationship between two phenomena is the *Pearson Product Moment Coefficient of Correlation*.

If two phenomena vary similarly from place to place (that is, if both tend to reach their high values in the same places and their low values in other, similar, places), under the Pearson formula they have a coefficient that is a *positive* number.

If such covariation is perfect, their correlation is said to be complete, and by the Pearson formula the coefficient would be +1.00. (This would occur, for instance, if the dots on a scatter diagram conformed to a straight line slanting upward.)

On the other hand, if two criteria vary

oppositely (that is, if one reaches a high value in those places where the other is low, and vice versa) the coefficient is a *negative number*, which indicates a *negative* (or *inverse*) *correlation*. The more unlike the two patterns, the closer their coefficient approaches −1.00, a figure that indicates complete inverse variation. (This would occur if the dots on a scatter diagram conformed to a straight line slanting downward.)

If two things vary from place to place with absolutely no relationship between them (neither *positive* or *negative*) the coefficient is 0.00. (This would occur if the dots on a scatter diagram were uniformly dispersed.)

Plainly, then, the closer to + 1.00 the coefficient of correlation between two spatial variables, the stronger their positive geographic association; the closer to −1.00, the stronger their negative geographic association.

The formula for computing the coefficient of correlation between two variables is a scientific device that is a useful aid to understanding of relationships in physical science and in social science. Unfortunately, the first encounter with this formula is apt to be dismaying, partly because its symbols may be new and partly because the process requires slow and careful study. The basic steps in its application are as follows:

1. Construct a Table of Values in exactly the same fashion as in computing the *a* and *b* values of the regression line.

2. Compute the value of the coefficient of correlation by solving the equation at the bottom of this page—a ratio in which both the numerator and denominator are built up from the totals of columns in the Table of Values.

This equation is expressed as follows in statistical symbols (*r* stands for *coefficient of correlation*):

$$r = \frac{(N \cdot \Sigma xy) - (\Sigma x \cdot \Sigma y)}{\sqrt{(N \cdot \Sigma x^2) - (\Sigma x)^2} \cdot \sqrt{(N \cdot \Sigma y^2) - (\Sigma y)^2}}$$

We can figure the coefficient of correlation between population and employment in trade as they vary through the nine midwestern states listed in Table 31-5 by transposing to the above formula the appropriate totals from the Table of Values (Table 31-6):

$$r = \frac{(9 \cdot 7{,}220.2) - (1{,}289 \cdot 29.0)}{\sqrt{(9 \cdot 326{,}939) - (1{,}289)^2} \cdot \sqrt{(9 \cdot 159.64) - (29.0)^2}}$$

$$r = \frac{64{,}981.8 - 37{,}381.0}{\sqrt{2{,}942{,}451 - 1{,}661{,}521} \cdot \sqrt{1{,}436.76 - 841.0}}$$

$$r = \frac{27{,}600.8}{\sqrt{1{,}280{,}930} \cdot \sqrt{595.76}}$$

$$r = \frac{27{,}600.8}{1{,}134 \cdot 24.4} = \frac{27{,}600.8}{27{,}669.6}$$

$$r = 0.99$$

A coefficient of 0.99 is extremely high and indicates that there is an uncommonly close geographic association between population and employment in retail trade in these nine

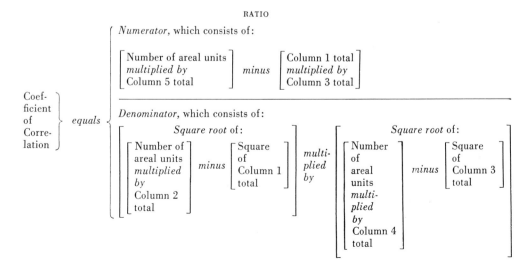

midwestern states. (The coefficient of correlation for Figure 31-4B is not presented here—in hopes that the reader may want to work it out for himself. NOTE: It will be a negative number and will be somewhere between —60 and — 90.)

As yet, very few geographic researchers have employed coefficient analysis—for two reasons. One is that geographers have thought in terms of this concept only very recently; the other reason is that computing coefficients of correlations consumes a vast amount of time. The recent development of punch-card processing equipment, however, is overcoming this second obstacle; time and experience should overcome the first.

A few attempts to apply the coefficient of correlation method to the measurement of geographic association of economic activities have been made.* Two studies will be cited here, one on the relationship between *cash-grain farming* and *flat land*, one on several correlations involving the *machinery* industry.

Correlation between Cash-Grain Farming and Flat Land   The objective in one research project conducted by John Hidore at the State University of Iowa was to see whether there was any correlation between cash-grain farming and flat land in the midwestern United States. The definitions adopted for the two

* For example, see John K. Rose, "Corn Yield and Climate in the Corn Belt," *Geographical Review,* (1936), pp. 88-102, and John C. Weaver, "Climatic Relations of American Barley Production," *Geographical Review,* (1943), pp. 569-588.

phenomena are as follows: A cash-grain farm is one on which at least 50 per cent of the value of all farm products sold comes from the sale of grains. *Flat land* is land with slopes of less than three degrees.

Hidore first constructed two maps to show the locational pattern of these two phenomena in eight contiguous states—North Dakota, South Dakota, Nebraska, Kansas, Minnesota, Iowa, Missouri, and Illinois: Figure 31-5 (left) shows the pattern of cash-grain farming, and Figure 31-5 (right) shows that of flat land, both maps being on a county basis.

Visual comparison of these two maps (as in the method mentioned earlier in this chapter) suggests that there is some association between these two variables. Both attain their highest values in three regions (northeastern Illinois, the spring wheat region of the Dakotas, and the winter wheat region of Kansas). Furthermore, they both attain their lowest values in similar regions (northern Nebraska, southern Missouri, and a belt along the Mississippi from Minnesota to Illinois).

Still, the visual inspection method, useful as it is, provides no method for measuring the degree of similarity between the two patterns. But since both maps were constructed on the same areal unit basis, it was possible to compute coefficients of correlation between these two phenomena as they varied among the 730 counties in the case study area. The resulting coefficient is +.652, a figure that, being much closer to +1.00 than to 0.00, indicates a positive geographic association.

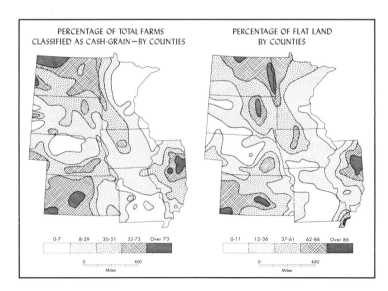

PERCENTAGE OF TOTAL FARMS CLASSIFIED AS CASH-GRAIN—BY COUNTIES

PERCENTAGE OF FLAT LAND BY COUNTIES

0-7 8-29 30-51 52-73 Over 73

0-11 12-36 37-61 62-86 Over 86

0   400
Miles

0   400
Miles

Figure 31-5 (*After John Hidore.*)

When coefficients were run for counties in separate states, it was found that the association between these two variables is strongest in the counties in Illinois and Kansas, and weakest through the counties of Missouri and South Dakota (see Table 31-7). In other words, the states in which cash-grain farming is most important tend to be the states in which this type of agriculture is most closely associated with flat land.

It must be emphasized that such high correlations do *not* suggest that flat land *determines* the degree to which cash-grain farming develops. Two hundred years ago the land in this region was essentially as flat as it is now—but it supported no cash-grain farming. In short, high correlations do not prove cause-and-effect relationship. But they *are* a quantitative *measurement of association*. Further research can build upon such measurement, however, and subsequently *may* prove that flat land is one of several factors that *influence* the location of cash-grain farming—after cultural forces have given birth to the type.

Correlations Involving the Machinery Industry

If we should compare a map of the machinery industry with that of blast furnaces and steel mills, or with that of petroleum and coal products, or of food manufactures, or of any other industry, we could—by the method of visual inspection—arrive at some general statement about whether there seemed to be any similarity (or *association*) between any pair of patterns.

But the computation of coefficients of correlation for employment in such industries

(as they vary from state to state among all states in the United States) reveals that the machinery industry is far more nearly associated geographically with certain industries than with others, as in Table 31-8, page 608. Specifically, it is most closely related, spatially, with nonferrous foundries, but shares virtually no relationship, spatially, with the lumber and wood products industries.

In a research project (conducted by Harold McCarty, John Hook, and Duane Knos) at the State University of Iowa, the coefficient of correlation method was applied in testing three hypotheses on the machinery industry.

The first hypothesis was that the number of workers in the machinery industry will vary directly with the percentage of manufacturing workers in the total employment structure. For each state in the United States, the researchers computed the percentage of the total labor force accounted for by manufacturing. Coefficients were then calculated, showing the correlation between this percentage and employment in the machinery industry. The resulting coefficient of +.564 indicates a definite positive association.

The second hypothesis was that the machinery industry was more market-oriented than raw-material-oriented. This was tested by computing correlations between the machinery industry and (a) "earlier-stages" industries (that is, industries that process metal before it is shipped to other factories), and (b) "later-stages" industries (those that process metal goods in a stage that may be sold to the general consumer public, to nonmanufacturing business users, or to other factories). If the hypothesis is sound, then the coefficients measuring the correlation of machinery with earlier-stages industries should be lower than those for later-stages industries. Part A of Table 31-8 shows that this is the case.

The third hypothesis was that the machinery industry is more closely associated with metal-consuming industries than with non-metal-consuming industries. This was tested by computing coefficients between numbers of workers in the machinery industry and those in the industries listed in Part B of Table 31-8. If the hypothesis is valid, then the coefficients

Table **31-7** *Coefficients of Correlation between Percentage of Flat Land and Percentage of Cash-Grain Farms in Selected States on a County Basis*

State	"r"	State	"r"
Illinois	+.690	Minnesota	+.581
Kansas	+.671	North Dakota	+.552
Nebraska	+.652	Missouri	+.398
Iowa	+.644	South Dakota	+.303

Source: John J. Hidore, *The Relationship Between Cash-Grain Farming and Flat Land in the Western Midwest*, unpublished Master's thesis, Department of Geography, State University of Iowa, (1958), p. 32.

PART A		PART B	
Other Metal-Consuming Industries	*r*	*Non-Metal-Consuming Industries*	*r*
(Earlier-stages Industries)		Paper and Allied Products	+.778
Blast Furnaces, Steel Mills, etc.	.657	Food Products	+.775
Primary Nonferrous Metals	.145	Furniture and Fixtures	+.753
(Later-stages Industries)		Printing and Publishing	+.749
Iron and Steel Foundries	.879	Rubber Products	+.707
Nonferrous Foundries	.959	Chemical Industries	+.662
Other Primary Metals Industries	.927	Leather Products	+.512
Hardware, Cutlery, Hand Tools	.741	Apparel Manufactures	+.471
Heating and Plumbing Equipment	.896	Petroleum and Coal Products	+.467
Metal Stamping and Coating	.954	Textile Products	+.176
Fabricated Wire Products	.842	Lumber and Wood Products	−.009
Electrical Machinery	.876		
Motor Vehicles and Equipment	.514		

Source: Harold H. McCarty, John C. Hook, and Duane S. Knos, *The Measurement of Association in Industrial Geography*, Department of Geography, State University of Iowa, (Iowa City, 1956), pp. 82 and 123.

in Part B should be lower than those in Part A. This is seen to be true; indeed, the highest coefficient in Part B, +.778, is exceeded by no fewer than seven of the entries that appear in Part A.

MAPPING OF RESIDUALS FROM REGRESSION

One of the better systems for portraying the spatial relationships of two (or more) variables is the mapping of residuals from regression. This system will be illustrated by an example involving nine hypothetical counties which are listed in Table 31-9 in terms of their values for two variables: percentage of population that is urban and average family income. Note that Jackson County tops the list in income and that Gray leads the array in urban percentage.

Comparison of the county rankings in the two parts of Table 31-9 reveals that the sequences are somewhat similar. Thus, we conclude that there is at least a weak positive correlation. But let's look at the locational pattern of these two variables.

Figure 31-6, Part 1 shows the location of the nine counties. Map 2 of that series shows the location of average family income among the nine counties and reveals that the higher incomes are in the northern portion of the map. Notice that the three middle-value counties (Dunkirk, Essex, and Florence) are shaded alike as are the three highest-value counties

(Gray, Howe, and Jackson) and the three lowest-value counties (Adams, Ballert, and Calhoun).

When percentage of the population that is urban is considered, counties Essex, Howe, and Florence have the middle values and are shaded alike on Map 31-6 Part 3; counties Ballert, Calhoun, and Adams have the lowest values and are shaded alike as are the three highest values in counties Dunkirk, Jackson, and Gray.

Map 3 in the series indicates that the lowest

Table **31-9** *Nine Hypothetical Counties*

County	Average Family Income
Jackson	$6000
Howe	5500
Gray	5000
Florence	4500
Essex	4000
Dunkirk	3500
Calhoun	3000
Ballert	2500
Adams	2000

County	*Urban Population as a Percentage of Total Population*
Gray	80
Jackson	75
Dunkirk	70
Florence	65
Howe	60
Essex	55
Adams	50
Calhoun	45
Ballert	40

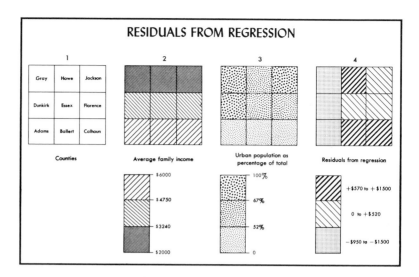

RESIDUALS FROM REGRESSION

Figure 31-6

urban percentages appear in the south so that the locational pattern is somewhat similar to the pattern in Map 2, but the patterns are not precisely the same. The scatter diagram in Figure 31-7 indicates that there is a definite positive correlation between these two variables—as visual inspection of Maps 2 and 3 suggests.

The regression line clearly slopes upward from left to right—revealing the average areal relationship between these two variables. The question now is this: Is there any way to measure the degree to which counties are "above average"—relative to this regression line and which counties are "below average." And if so, is it possible to map counties in terms of their departures or differentials from

Figure 31-7

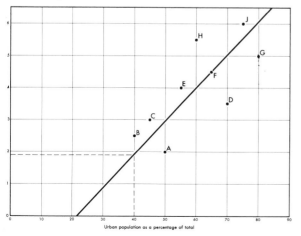

that regression line, that is, from the average relationship?

Residuals provide the answer, and these can be mapped.

Suppose we decide to map the nine counties (a) in terms of *dollars of family income* greater than would be the case if there were a perfect relation between the two variables—as defined by the regression line, that is, the average relationship, or (b) in terms of *dollars of family income* less than the average relationship. Take county B (Ballert) for example. In Table 31-9 it appears as one of the *lowest*-ranking counties in terms of income. But its income *relative to its percentage of urban population* is rather high as indicated by its dot on the scatter diagram being above the regression line. For a county with 40 per cent urban population it would be expected (insofar as relationships among the nine counties are concerned) to have an average family income of $1900 (that is, the 40 per cent population value intercepts the regression line opposite 1900 on the vertical axis).

The next step is to determine the difference between the *actual income* ($2500) and the *computed income* ($1900) which would obtain if the county's dot (with 40 per cent urban population) were on the regression line. This difference is the residual value—$600 in this instance. In formula form:

Residual = Actual Value minus Computed Value.

If the actual value is greater than the computed value, the residual is a *positive* value; if the actual value is less than the computed value, the residual is a *negative* value.

The residuals for the nine counties are shown in Table 31-10.

In Table 31-9 Jackson ranks first on income; but in terms of residuals from regression with urban percentage, Table 31-10 shows that Howe ranks first—and that three other counties outrank Jackson. Map 4 in the series of Map 31-5 shows each county in terms of its residual family income.

A residual from regression is defined as that part of the magnitude which a phenomenon reaches within a given unit area which is independent of the areal association between the given phenomenon and the other factors included in the investigation.*

In this chapter we have dealt with several methods for analyzing the relationship, or

* Edwin N. Thomas, *Maps of Residuals from Regression: Their Characteristics and Uses in Geographic Research*, (Iowa City), 1960, p. 12.

Table **31-10** *Residuals for Nine Hypothetical Counties*

County	Actual Average Family Income	Computed Average Family Income on the Regression Line	Residuals from Regression
Howe	$5500	$4000	+$1500
Ballert	2500	1900	+ 600
Calhoun	3000	2430	+ 570
Essex	4000	3480	+ 520
Jackson	6000	5550	+ 450
Florence	4500	4500	0
Adams	2000	2950	− 950
Gray	5000	6200	− 1200
Dunkirk	3500	5000	− 1500

association, between phenomena as they differ spatially. Although most of our examples were drawn from manufacturing and agriculture, the methods are nevertheless equally valid for measuring the geographic associations of any economic endeavors.

Suggested Readings

Alexander, John W., and Lindberg, James B., "Measurements of Manufacturing: Coefficients of Correlation," *Journal of Regional Science*, Summer 1961, pp. 71-81.

Berry, Brian J. L., "An Inductive Approach to the Regionalization of Economic Development," in Norton Ginsburg, editor, *Essays on Geography and Economic Development*, Chicago, 1960, pp. 78-107.

Coppock, J. T., and Johnson, J. H., "Measurement in Human Geography," *Economic Geography*, 1962, pp. 130-137.

Duncan, Otis D. *et al*, *Statistical Geography: Problems in Analyzing Areal Data*, Glencoe, 1961, 191 pp.

Hagood, M. J., "Statistical Methods for Delineation of Regions Applied to Data on Agriculture and Population," *Social Forces*, 1943, pp. 287-97.

Hart, John Fraser, "Central Tendency in Areal Distributions," *Economic Geography*, 1954, pp. 48-59.

Mackay, J. Ross, "A New Projection for Cubic Symbols on Economic Maps," *Economic Geography*, 1953, pp. 60-62.

McCarty, Harold H.; Hook, John C.; and Knos, Duane S., *The Measurement of Association in Industrial Geography*, Iowa City, 1956, 143 pp.

McCarty, Harold H., and Salisbury, Neil E., *Visual Comparison of Isopleth Maps as a Means of Determining Correlations Between Spatially Distributed Phenomena*, Iowa City, 1961, 81 pp.

Prior, Roger A., and Dessel, Murray D., *Diversification of Manufacturing Employment for States and Metropolitan Areas: A Research Tool*, Washington, 1960, 21 pp.

Robinson, Arthur H., "On Perks and Pokes," *Economic Geography*, 1961, pp. 181-183.

———, "The Necessity of Weighting Values in Correlation Analysis of Areal Data," *Annals of the Association of American Geographers*, 1956, pp. 233-236.

———, and Bryson, Reid A., "A Method for Describing Quantitatively the Correspondence of Geographical Distributions," *Annals of the Association of American Geographers*, 1957, pp. 379-391.

———; Lindberg, J. H.; and Brinkman, L., "A Correlation and Regression Analysis Applied to Rural Farm Population Densities in the Great Plains," *Annals of the Association of American Geographers*, 1961, pp. 211-222.

Spate, O. H. K., "Quantity and Quality in Geography," *Annals of the Association of American Geographers*, 1960, pp. 377-394.

Thomas, Edwin N., *Maps of Residuals from Regression: Their Characteristics and Uses in Geographic Research*, Iowa City, 1960, 60 pp.

Thompson, John H., "A New Method for Measuring Manufacturing," *Annals of the Association of American Geographers*, 1955, pp. 416-436.

Wright, J. K., "Some Measures of Distributions," *Annals of the Association of American Geographers*, 1937, pp. 177-211.

The Ford Motor Company plant in Detroit is a large integrated economic activity consisting of blast furnaces (coal, ore, and limestone piles are in foreground,) steel mills, a body factory, and an automotive assembly line. What theories of location can be formulated to explain the development of economic activities in specific places such as this? (Courtesy Ford Motor Co. Archives.)

THIRTY-TWO

With the amazing growth in population in the last 300 years has come an associated increase in economic interaction as the peoples of different areas exchange their surpluses. This orderly exchange of commodities and services between places, some of which are thousands of miles apart, has produced a worldwide pattern of *geographic organization.* Through his economic and political decisions, man has organized a series of interrelated areas, each with its own distinctive role in the world's economy. To be sure, some parts of the world have remained virtually untouched by changes in human society, but most of the world today is dominated by societies that, at an ever accelerating rate, are coming into closer and closer association with one another. Areas specialize in producing distinctive products, and many areas now consume an ever greater variety of products coming from an ever larger number of source areas. Economically, the world is constantly becoming more complex. Faced with this complexity, the student of economic geography naturally aspires toward a set of principles by which he can understand the *areal organization of economic activity*—the manner in which the diverse areas of the earth are interrelated.

A *location theory,* as we shall use the term herein, is an endeavor to account in a consistent, logical way for the locational pattern of economic activity and for the manner in which economic areas are interrelated. A theory need not be all-encompassing, of course, but may cover only one aspect of economic activity.

If we are to accept the idea that economic geography is becoming the branch of human knowledge whose function is to account for the location of economic activities on the various portions of the earth's surface, it seems reasonable to expect the discipline to develop a body of theory to facilitate the performance of this task.

At the outset it seems desirable to inquire into the most probable and desirable characteristics of such a body of theory, if one were to come into existence. Certainly it would consist, in essence, of a large number of interrelated and noncontradictory principles each of which would account for the location of some type of economic activity. With such a group of principles the geographer would be able to provide satisfactory explanations of the location of the world's agricultural regions, manufacturing industries, and all other types of economic occupance. These principles would be essentially similar to those developed by other physical and social sciences, except that they would be concerned with locations rather than with those physical and social processes which are the main concern of the systematic sciences.*

With all the material presented in preceding chapters to drawn on, we could mention many location theories that have been proposed; however, we shall discuss only eight of them, eight which have been comparatively well conceived: (1) the von Thünen theory, (2) a weight-loss and transportation-cost theory, (3) a labor-differential and transportation-cost theory, (4) the Weber theory, (5) the Fetter theory, (6) the interaction theory, (7) the theory of intervening opportunity, and (8) the nested-hierarchy theory. There is one other theory that would deserve discussion in association with this other group—the Christaller, or *central-place* theory. But since we presented it in Chapter 29, we shall not elaborate further on it here except to say that it was one of the first theories dealing with the results of the influences of transportation, interaction, and intervening opportunity on the location of cities, and other trading centers, and that it was formulated by Walter Christaller, German economist and economic geographer born in 1893. It has been one of the most widely discussed theories on economic location.

Most theories consist of two main components: premises and propositions (or postulations). A *premise* (as the term is used in this context) is a statement that, for the purposes of the theory, is accepted as being true. Now, a premise may be either a statement of proven fact, or it may be an assumption or presupposition. In any case, all theories are built upon one or more such premises. A *proposition* (or *postulation*) is a statement that is likely to be true in the light of the premises. In phrasing a theory, one can usually introduce *premises* by the words "since" or "if," *postulates* by the word "then."

"*If* a factory has a weight-loss ratio of 90 per cent, and *if* all other factors are equal, *then* the factory will tend to locate near its raw material."

"*If* a factory has a weight-loss ratio of zero, and *since* freight rates on finished products usually exceed those on raw materials, and *if* all other factors are equal, *then* the factory will tend to locate in its market area."

The Von Thünen Theory

Apparently, the very first attempt to devise a scientific theory explaining the location of an economic activity can be credited to Johann Heinrich von Thünen, who lived in Germany from 1783 to 1850. Both a scholar and a farm operator, von Thünen formulated his famous theory on the basis of 40-years' experience in managing an agricultural estate near the city of Rostock in Mecklenburg.

The von Thünen theory tries to account for the types of agriculture that will prosper around an urban market. It rests upon several premises.

PREMISES

Von Thünen theorized that *if* a "laboratory" could be constructed according to seven conditions, *then* agriculture would tend to locate in a specific determinable pattern. These are the conditions proposed:

1. There is an isolated area consisting of

* H. H. McCarty, "An Approach to a Theory of Economic Geography," *Economic Geography*, (1954), p. 95.

just one city and its agricultural hinterland. Such an area could be called "an isolated state," for example, feudal states in the Middle Ages.

2. The city is the market for surplus products from the hinterland and receives products from no other area.

3. The hinterland ships its surpluses to no other market except its city.

4. The hinterland has a homogeneous physical environment favorable to the production of mid-latitude plants and animals.

5. The hinterland is inhabited by farmers *desiring* to maximize their profits and *capable* of adjusting their type of farming to the demands of the market.

6. The hinterland is traversed by only one means of land transportation. (In von Thünen's day this was the horse and wagon, not counting, of course, pedestrians.)

7. Transportation costs are directly proportional to distance and are borne entirely by the farmers who ship all food "fresh."

POSTULATES

Given this controlled laboratory system, then different types of agriculture would develop around the city in discrete concentric rings.

The greatest distance from the city at which any given type of farming *could* be conducted depended on selling price at the market, production cost on the farm, and transport cost between the two. Any profit a farmer realized depended on the relationship of these three variables, as expressed in the following formula: $P = V - (E + T)$. This means that profit (P) equals the value of commodities sold (V) minus both total production expenses (E) such as labor, equipment and supplies, and transportation costs (T) in getting the commodities from farm to market.

In the light of this formula, look at Table 32-1. In this table the data are based on von Thünen's observations that the costs expended and prices received *per acre* (or per any other *unit of land area*) vary with commodity. Take wood and grain. The product from an acre of wood commands a higher market price than does that from an acre of grain; but the greater volume of wood requires more trips to market, hence it costs more to move to market the wood harvest of an acre than the grain harvest.

The three factors of market price, production cost, and transfer cost, are given hypothetical values in columns 1, 2, and 3 of Table 32-1 to demonstrate how a farmer's profit

Table **32-1** *Von Thünen Theory: Prices, Costs, and Profits per Acre for Selected Commodities by Distance from Market*

Rings: Units of Distance from Market	WOOD				GRAIN			
	(1) Market Price (MP)	(2) Production Costs (PC)	(3) Transport Costs (TC)	(4) Profit (P)	(1) MP	(2) PC	(3) TC	(4) P
½	200	140	10	50	80	50	3	27
1	200	140	20	40	80	50	6	24
1½	200	140	30	30	80	50	9	21
2	200	140	40	20	80	50	12	18
2½	200	140	50	10	80	50	15	15
3	200	140	60	0	80	50	18	12
3½	200	140	70	0	80	50	21	9
4	200	140	80	0	80	50	24	6
4½	200	140	90	0	80	50	27	3
5	200	140	100	0	80	50	30	0

Source: Adapted from Andreas Grotewold, "Von Thünen in Retrospect," *Economic Geography*, (1959), pp. 346-355.

(column 4) decreases with increasing distance from the market.

The farthest distance at which farmers could profitably cultivate wood would be within 3 units of distance from the town. Beyond that distance, transport costs would be so great as to eat up all profit. Grain, however, as Table 32-1 shows also, *could* be produced at a profit as far out as 4½ distance units. In other words, the farmers close to the city would have a wide range of selections in deciding which commodities to produce for sale. The distant farmers had fewer choices. One principal theme in the von Thünen theory is that *the number of profitable options decreases with distance from the city market.*

At the other extreme, there is no least distance within which a farmer *could not* make a profit on any given commodity. Yet there is a minimum distance within which he *would not* choose to produce a given commodity because some other commodity yielded a greater profit.

Figure 32-1 (*After Andreas Grotewold, in* Economic Geography.)

THE LOCATION OF AGRICULTURAL PRODUCTION AFTER VON THÜNEN

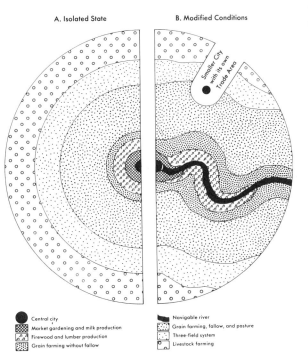

From these two principles—that an outer distance for each type of farming would be determined by declining profits depending principally on transport costs and that an inner distance would be determined by more lucrative alternatives—von Thünen postulated that six concentric zones of agriculture would develop around the market city.

Zone #1   The land nearest the market would be used to produce *perishable* items, principally milk and vegetables (that is, market gardening) as in Figure 32-1, Part A. These activities would be concentrated in the inner zone because of the slowness of transportation and the absence of food-preserving techniques, such as refrigeration or canning. Zone #1 would extend outward in proportion to the city's need; the greater the demand for milk and vegetables, the greater the radius of Zone #1. Moreover, since city dwellers would insist on a certain volume of milk and vegetables, they would pay prices high enough to make it more profitable for farmers in Zone #1 to produce these items than wood, grain, or other commodities.

Zone #2   The inhabitants of the second concentric zone would specialize in producing *wood*, with firewood in much greater demand than lumber. (In von Thünen's day, firewood was the main type of fuel, and the heating of houses provided the main market for fuel.) Von Thünen demonstrated, from accurate accounts kept on his Mecklenburg estate, that forestry yielded greater returns to the farmer near the city than did any other type of production except fluid milk and vegetables. The outer limit of Zone #2 would depend on the amount of wood demanded by the market.

As to the advantage of growing wood or grain, however, Table 32-1 indicates that farmers as far out as 2 distance units would prefer to grow wood instead of grain.

Zones #3, #4, and #5   These areas would tend to be devoted mainly to grains and other crops. The distinctions among these zones need not be spelled out here, except to note that with distance from the city the intensity of cultivation would decrease. This is indicated by the proportion of fallow land— zero in Zone #3, 14 per cent in Zone #4, and 33 per cent in Zone #5.

Although wood commanded (in von Thünen's day) a higher market price than grain, it would be grown only for subsistence needs beyond Zone #2. For there was a critical distance (2½ units of distance in Table 32-1) beyond which a farmer realized greater profits in grain. Indeed, beyond 3 units of distance his profits in commercial wood production would be zero. Conversely, farmers in the second ring would grow grain for subsistence purposes, and although they *could* realize a profit on commercial grain sale (indeed a greater profit on grain sales than the grain farmers in Zone #3), they would choose to specialize in sales of wood.

Zone #6 This would be the region of livestock farming. Marketed products would be of two types: livestock, which could be driven to market, hence cutting transport costs almost to zero; and cheese, which is not highly perishable, and which is valuable enough to be able to stand rather high transport costs.

How the von Thünen theory would be modified by the presence of a navigable river and a smaller market city, is illustrated in Part B of Figure 32-1. The river would provide cheaper transportation, hence its effect would be to lengthen out the zones along its course. The smaller city would serve zones around itself on a smaller scale than those around the larger city and extending farther on the side away from the main city.

Although the basic forces von Thünen tried to explain in his theory are still operative, it is difficult to find examples today, and for several reasons. Numerous new forms of transport (truck, barge, railway) are cheaper than horses and wagons. Moreover, transportation costs are neither directly proportional to distance nor do they increase similarly in all directions. Perishable goods can be moved long distances under refrigeration, in air-tight cans, or by other means of preservation. Finally, firewood is no longer the major domestic fuel. Even so, the von Thünen theory was a pioneering step in developing a theory of location of certain economic activities.[*]

A Theory of Weight Loss and Transport Costs

A theory that expresses the relationship between weight-loss and transport costs is pertinent to understanding the location of manufacturing.

The first four cases cited illustrate how this theory can be applied in an attempt to understand the location of manufacturing. We shall cast the illustrations in terms of a single factory that processes raw materials (R) from a single source area (SR) into a single finished product (P) for sale at a single market (MP) which is in a different location from that of the source of raw materials. The weight-loss-transport-cost theory is useful in answering the question: "Where will the factory tend to locate?"

In the four illustrations to follow, the two variables are *weight-loss ratio* and *transportation costs*. All other factors are considered invariable. Obviously, in reality other things are *not* equal, but to observe the interaction of any two variables, all other elements must be held constant. The transport costs cited in the illustrations conform to the well-known principle that freight rates are usually higher per ton of finished product than per ton of raw material from which the product is made (Table 32-2).

In Case A of Table 32-2, the factory would tend to locate at the market because the burden of transport costs would be less than if the factory located at the source of raw materials. In Case B the factory would again tend to locate at the market. But in Cases C and D, the factory would tend to locate at the source of raw material. In Case D, transport costs are listed as different than in Cases A, B and C. Were transport costs for D the same as the

* See A. Grotewold, "Von Thünen in Retrospect," *Econ. Geog.*, 1959, pp. 346-355, and H. B. Johnson, "A Note on Thünen's Circles," *Annals of the Assoc. of Amer. Geog.*, 1962, pp. 213-220.

Table 32-2 *Weight Loss and Transport Costs in Four Hypothetical Cases*

		Transport Costs	
Illustrative Cases	*Weight-Loss Ratio*	*If Factory Locates at Source of Raw Materials:*	*If Factory Locates at Market:*
Case A. 1000 tons of *R* are processed into 1000 tons of *P*	0%	1000 tons of *P* must be shipped to *MP* $20 per ton is the transport cost on *P* from *SR* to *MP* Transport cost: $20,000	1000 tons of *R* must be shipped from *SR* $10 per ton is the transport cost on *R* from *SR* to *MP* Total transport cost: $10,000
Case B. 1000 tons of *R* are processed into 600 tons of *P*	40%	600 tons of *P* must be shipped to *MP* $20 per ton Transport cost: $12,000	Transport costs are the same as in Case A: $10,000
Case C. 1000 tons of *R* are processed into 400 tons of *P*	60%	400 tons of *P* must be shipped to *MP* $20 per ton Transport cost: $8,000	Transport costs are the same as in Case A: $10,000
Case D. 1000 tons of *R* are processed into 500 tons of *P*	50%	500 tons of *P* must be shipped to *MP* $17 per ton is the transport cost on *P* from *SR* to *MP* Transport cost: $8,500	1000 tons of *R* must be shipped from *SR* $9 per ton is the transport cost on *R* from *SR* to *MP* Transport cost: $9,000

previous trio, then the answer would be inconclusive—and the factory's location would be determined entirely by other relationships.

Here is the theory that synthesizes the relationships between weight-loss ratio and transportation costs shown in these cases: The greater the percentage of weight loss in a manufacturing process, the stronger the tendency for a factory to locate at a source of raw material. All other things being equal, though, a market location may be preferable, depending on the transport charges on raw material and on finished product relative to the weight-loss ratio; the greater the spread between the total charges (*not* the per-unit rate, which will inevitably be lower on raw material), the stronger the pull of the market on factory location.

Numerous industries discussed in Part Six

illustrate the applicability of the foregoing theory; for instance, copper concentrating, copper refining, farm machinery manufacturing, automobile assembly, and baking.

What about intermediate locations between market and raw material? For example, in Case B where the weight-loss ratio is 40 per cent, why wouldn't the factory tend to locate at a point two-fifths of the distance from market to raw material? Suppose the weight-loss ratio were 50 per cent. Wouldn't the factory entrepreneurs do well to choose a site midway between their customers and their source of raw materials?

The answer is to be found in the *tapering principle* of freight-rate structures. As we saw in Chapter 26, freight charges, generally speaking, do not increase directly with distance; rather they increase *at a decreasing rate*

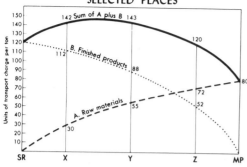

AGGREGATE TRANSPORT CHARGES AT FIVE SELECTED PLACES

Figure 32-2 (*After E. M. Hoover.*)

Figure 32-3 (*After E. M. Hoover.*)

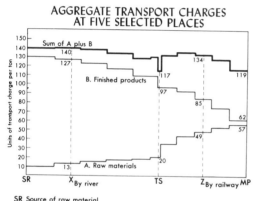

AGGREGATE TRANSPORT CHARGES AT FIVE SELECTED PLACES

SR Source of raw material

TS Transshipment point

MP Market for finished product

with distance. That is, the charge for hauling a commodity 500 miles is usually less than 5 times that for hauling it 100 miles. Figure 32-2 illustrates this principle; the dashed line shows the rate on a ton of raw material moving from SR. The rate on a ton of raw material from *SR* to *MP* is $80, whereas the rate from *SR* to *Y* is $55 even though the distance from *SR* to *Y* is only one-half the distance from *SR* to *MP*. If the factory builders chose to locate at *X*, they would pay transport charges

of $30 per ton of raw material, while a location at *Z* would necessitate payments of $72 on such shipments.

The gradient of transport charges on finished products is shown by the dotted line. Accordingly, if a factory located at SR the transport charges per ton of finished product moving to *MP* would be $120. If the factory located at *Y*, charges would be $88.

The significance of these two gradients is to be seen in the pattern of the solid curve which connects the summation values of the raw material curve and the finished product curve. Thus, in Case A from Table 32-2, where the weight-loss ratio is zero, if the factory is located at *Y*, the freight charges will be $55 per ton of raw material received and $88 per ton of product shipped, for a total of $143.

Because of the tendency of freight rates to taper off with distance, intermediate locations are at a competitive disadvantage with points of origin or destination. This principle holds true regardless of the weight-loss ratio and regardless of relative freight rates.

Still, intermediate locations *can* enjoy a favorable position under certain conditions: (a) if in-transit rate privileges are granted (Chapter 26), or (b) if trans-shipment (such as transfer from water carrier to rail carrier) is necessitated at the intermediate point, or (c) if there is some other departure in freight-rate structures from the curve shown in Figure 32-3. In Figure 32-3, we see how a trans-shipment point would be a favorable location for a factory in a region where freight-rate structures were of the stair-step rather than the gradient type. A factory that processed raw materials from *SR* for sale in *MP* would (given a weight loss of zero) face a total transport burden of $138 per ton if it located at *SR*, $140 if it located along the river at *X*, $117 if it located at the point of trans-shipment (*TS*), and $139 if it located at *MP*.

A Theory of Labor Differentials and Transport Costs

One enormous influence on the location of any economic activity is the cost of labor. This is a matter not only of hourly wages but also of hourly production. Other things

being constant, worker A at $2.50 per hour is actually cheaper labor than worker B at $2.40 if A produces 50 units in an hour to B's 40. In the case of A, the cost of labor per unit of output is $2.50 ÷ 50 = 5¢ whereas the cost for B is $2.40 ÷ 40 = 6¢. The principle can be drawn that *all other things being equal, a factory will tend to locate in an area where unit labor costs are lowest, irrespective of hourly wage rates.*

Immediately this question arises: Can factories in an area with low unit labor costs compete successfully if that area is far from both markets and raw materials? Would not a competing factory located at either the market or at the raw material be better off? For example, Chicago has both steel mills and factories that require machinery. Accordingly, a lathe manufacturer located in Chicago would be in the same metropolitan area with his main source of raw material and with many customers. Could a lathe manufacturer in Rockford, Illinois, 90 miles to the west, dependent for steel on those Chicago mills, compete successfully for sales to those Chicago customers? At first thought one might reply negatively, since the Rockford plant would have to bear transport charges on a 90-mile shipment of steel and a 90-mile backhaul of lathes, both of which would be unnecessary for the Chicago factory.

But the problem merits further consideration. Let's examine two cases, in one of which (Case A) the two cities have similar labor productivity but different wage rates, and in the other of which (Case B) the variables are reversed, as follows:

Hourly Wage Rates

	Chicago	Rockford
Case A:	$2.20	$2.10
Case B:	$2.30	$2.30

Man-Hours of Labor to Produce a Lathe

	Chicago	Rockford
Case A:	1000	1000
Case B:	1000	960

Assuming that all other costs are equal, we can solve the above case problems by means of the work-sheet (Table 32-3), in which we list the figures for the various conditions.

In both instances, a Rockford lathe-maker could compete successfully with a Chicago competitor despite the drawbacks in his location.

We can sum up this location theory as follows:

All other things being equal, the greater

Table **32-3** *Work-Sheet of Comparative Production Costs*

Components	Case A		Case B	
	Chicago Lathe Factory	Rockford Lathe Factory	Chicago Lathe Factory	Rockford Lathe Factory
Transport charges on steel from Chicago steel mill	$15	$40	$15	$40
Number of man-hours required to make identical lathes	(1000)	(1000)	(1000)	(960)
Hourly wage per hour	($2.20)	($2.10)	($2.30)	($2.30)
Total labor cost per lathe	$2200	$2100	$2300	$2208
Transport charges on lathe to Chicago customer	$35	$100	$35	$100
All other costs are assumed to be equal	——	——	——	——
	$2250	$2240	$2350	$2348

an area's savings in labor costs (attributable to either low hourly wage rate or high productivity per hour, or both) the greater the distance handicap that can be overcome in processing materials from far-away sources for sale to far-away markets.*

The Weber Theory

The first person to work up a comprehensive theory accounting for the location of manufacturing was Alfred Weber. Weber was a German economist who taught at the University of Prague from 1904-1907 and the University of Heidelberg from 1907-1933. In 1909 he published his famous *Theory of the Location of Industries* incorporating several ideas that had been partially formulated by Wilhelm Launhardt in the 1880's.

PREMISES AND POSTULATES

Weber began with several *premises*:
1. The unit of analysis is a single, isolated country that is homogeneous in terms of climate, topography, race of people, technical skills of the population, and is under one political authority.
2. Some natural resources (for instance, water and sand) are ubiquitous whereas others (such as coal and iron ore) occur only in "fixed" locales.
3. Available workers are not ubiquitous; rather, they are "fixed" in specific places.
4. Transportation costs are a function of *weight* and *distance*, increasing in direct proportion to length of shipment and weight of cargo.

Weber *postulated* that, given the controlled laboratory just described, manufacturing plants would be located in response to three forces: relative transport costs, labor costs, and something he called "agglomeration," which will be defined in a moment.

ROLE OF TRANSPORT COSTS

Weber theorized that the transport costs would operate in distinctively different ways in different cases. We shall examine a couple of situations to see how.

Case A: One Market and One Raw Material
If just one locale demands the product, and if only one raw material is involved in the process, then there are three possible locations for manufacturing.

1. If the raw material is *ubiquitous*, then the factory will locate at the market, since at this point the lowest transport costs would prevail on both material and product.
2. If the raw material is *fixed* (that is, localized in a specific place) and if it is *pure* (that is, its weight-loss is zero), then the factory can locate in either the market or at the source of materials.
3. If the raw material is *fixed* and *gross* (by *gross*, Weber meant that weight was lost in the manufacturing process), then the industry would locate at the source of material. Remember that it was one of his premises that transport charges were directly proportional to weight of cargo, whether it was raw material or finished product.

Case B: One Market and Two Raw Materials
If customers for a product are in only one place and the product is manufactured from two raw materials (R_1 and R_2), then manufacturing will tend to locate in one of the following several ways:

1. If both R_1 and R_2 are ubiquitous, then manufacturing will be at the market for the same reason as in Case A-1.
2. If R_1 is ubiquitous and R_2 is *fixed* elsewhere than at the market, and if both are *pure*, then manufacturing will be at the market. Transport charges will have to be paid on only R_2. Were the factory at the source of

---

* The preceding pair of theories dealing with weight-loss ratios, labor differentials, and transportation costs are discussed at length and at a much higher level of sophistication in several publications such as those by Edgar M. Hoover and Walter Isard which are cited at the end of this chapter.

R_2, transport charges would have to be paid on the finished product, which, since both materials are pure, would equal their combined weights.

3. If both raw materials are *fixed* and *pure*, the factory will be at the market. Both components would be sent directly to the consumption area for processing since this would give the lowest aggregate transportation cost (Figure 32-4). Otherwise, if the factory located at either the source of R_1 or the source of R_2, additional transport charges would have to be paid on that leg of the journey on which the product moved to market (M). Any manufacturing using pure materials from two sources will always locate at the place where finished products are consumed. The only exception would be if one of the raw materials, in being shipped to the market area, passed through the place where the other raw material was produced. This locale would be equally attractive as the factory site.

4. If both raw materials are *fixed* and *gross*, the solution is complex. To solve it, Weber introduced his famous *locational triangle*. One point is the market (M), another is the source of R_1 (SR_1), and the third is the source of R_2 (SR_2); Figure 32-4 (Case B-4) shows how the locational triangle is constructed.

To illustrate: Suppose that both R_1 and R_2 lose 50 per cent of their weight in the manufacturing process, and that 2000 tons of each are required a year. If the factory were located at M, the total transport cost for a year would be (a) 2000 tons × 100 miles = 200,000 ton-miles on R_1 from SR_1 to M, plus (b) 200,000 ton-miles on R_2 from SR_2 to M, or 400,000 ton-miles in all. If the factory were located at SR_1 the burden would be (a) 2000 tons × 100 miles = 200,000 ton-miles on R_2 from SR_2 to SR_1, plus (b) 2000 tons × 100 miles = 200,000 ton-miles on the finished product from SR_1 to M, also 400,000 ton-miles. However, if the factory were located at point X, midway between SR_1 and SR_2, the transport burden would be as follows: (a) 2000 tons × 50 miles = 100,000 ton-miles on R_1 from SR_1 to X, plus (b) another 100,000 ton-miles on R_2 from SR_2 to X, plus (c) 2000

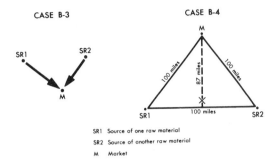

Figure 32-4

tons × 87 miles = 174,000 ton-miles on finished product from X to M, or a total of 374,000 ton-miles. This is less than the burden facing an enterprise located at either M or SR_1 or SR_2.

If the two raw materials do not have the same weight-loss ratio, and if different amounts are required, the factory would tend to locate nearer one of the raw material sources so as to lessen the burden of transportation costs.

We could analyze many other cases, such as two markets and two raw material sources, or three of one and two of the other, and so on, applying Weber's locational triangle, or variations of it (such as a *locational quadrilateral*) to any situation.

Critics have assailed Weber's locational triangle concept on two major counts: Freight rates are not directly proportional to distance, and they are not, ton for ton, the same on finished products as on raw materials. But in spite of these criticisms, Weber's locational figure can be adjusted to realistic transport charges, and it surely was a major step forward in the advancement of location theory. He laid bare the fact that transportation costs are theoretically the most fundamental element determining the location of manufacturing.

ROLE OF LABOR COSTS

Weber went on to recognize that labor costs too vary spatially and therefore could wield an influence on the location of a factory. Conceivably, a locality handicapped by high transport costs might be able to offset that disadvantage through savings in wages. Hence, this dual question as an entrepreneur decides on location for a factory: In any given place, how much would a firm have to pay in transport costs and how much would it have to pay in labor costs?

To help answer the question, Weber introduced the concept of the *isodapane*. This is a line connecting the locus of points of equal total costs. Since this statement calls for some elaboration and illustration, let us examine Figure 32-5 in detail. It represents a very simple problem involving a single market, *M*, and a single raw material source, *SR*. Behind the construction of Figure 32-5 are certain assumptions: (1) Transport costs are the same per ton-mile for raw materials and finished products. The concentric circles around *M* portray transport charges from all points to *M*; those around *SR* portray transport charges to all points from *SR*. Both sets of circles are spaced to represent one unit of transport cost *per ton*. (2) The raw material is gross and loses 50 per cent of its weight, which means that two tons of material enter the factory for every ton of product that leaves it.

Now, if the factory were located at *SR*, every ton of product shipped from *SR* to *M* would bear 10 units of transport cost. If the factory were located at *M*, the amount would be 20 units of transport cost, since two tons of material would have to move the ten distance units from *SR* to *M* for every ton of product made at the factory.

Suppose the factory were at *X*. The aggregate transport cost would consist of eight units on raw materials (two tons to the fourth concentric circle around *SR*), plus ten units on product (one ton to *M* from the tenth concentric circle around *M*), or 18 units in all. The heavy solid line in the Figure is an isodapane connecting all points at which transport cost would total only 18 units. Point *Y*, for instance, would bear 13 transport cost units on two tons of raw material moving six and

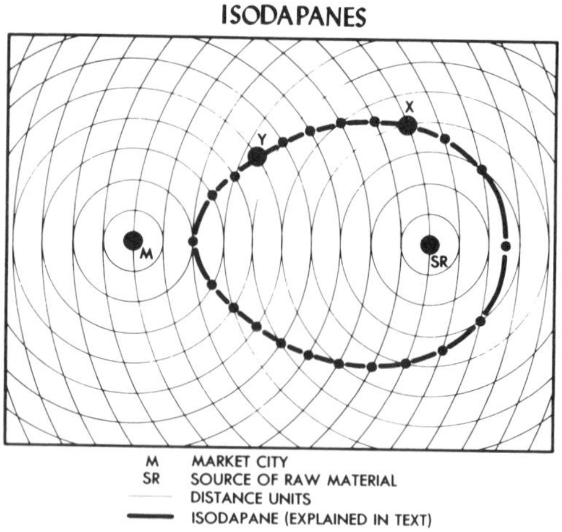

ISODAPANES

M	MARKET CITY
SR	SOURCE OF RAW MATERIAL
	DISTANCE UNITS
—	ISODAPANE (EXPLAINED IN TEXT)

Figure 32-5

one-half units of distance plus five cost units on one ton of product.

This type of isodapane has very little value if transport costs are the sole determinant in the location of industry. But as soon as any other variable is introduced, it may well be that some place other than *SR* or *M* would have a great advantage. Isodapanes reveal how great the advantage in that other place would have to be in order to offset its disadvantage in terms of transport costs, thereby luring industry to that location.

As Figure 32-5 shows, all points on the isodapane bear a transport cost burden of 18, a handicap of eight cost units compared to *SR*. Accordingly, all points on that line would have to possess an advantage of at least eight units in labor cost (per ton of finished product) in order to lure a factory in this enterprise. Weber's contribution of isodapanes provided a technique for the systematic introduction of a new variable (such as labor) into a theoretical scheme.*

* More detailed discussion of the Weber theory, particularly his suggestion regarding *agglomeration* (the advantages inherent in factories locating near to each other) is presented in Stuart Daggett, *Principles of Inland Transportation*, New York, 1941, pp. 467-475; C. J. Friedrich, *Alfred Weber's Theory of the Location of Industries*, Chicago, 1928, 256 pp., and Walter Isard, *Location and Space Economy*, New York, 1956, pp. 176-182.

Location Theory

The Fetter Theory

Another theory deals with the location of the boundary between trade areas around two trade centers and derives its name from one of the first scholars to give it expression, F.A. Fetter. We shall see how the theory applies by considering three cases involving two trade centers, X and Y. It will become evident that the theory is applicable whether X and Y are two factories competing for sales to the hinterland or whether they are two wholesalers or two retailers or two competitors in any other kind of business who are concerned with both transport costs and production costs.

SAMPLE CASES

Case A   Assume that X and Y are similar in terms of both production costs and transport costs, the latter being exactly the same per ton-mile in all directions from each place, and increasing with distance at the same rate. Each circle and arc on Figure 32-6 represents a given distance from its own center. Points D, E, and F mark the boundary line separating the trade area of X from that of Y since they bear the same transport-cost burden to both places. Notice that the values of the places on a boundary line need not be identical, only that they are equal in each case with respect to the trade centers.

Accordingly, all other things being equal, if production costs and transport costs surrounding two centers are identical, the boundary between their trade areas will be a straight line that is at right angles to a line connecting the two centers. This is shown by line 2 on Figure 32-6.

Case B   If transport-cost structures around two centers are similar, but if production costs are dissimilar, the trade-area boundary will be a curved line that is *closer to* and *bends around* the center with the higher production costs. This is shown on Figure 32-6 by line 1, which connects all points with equal total costs (production plus transport) in relation to X and Y.

To illustrate: Suppose that both X and Y

are wholesaling centers for a product that is manufactured far to the right of Y. Suppose also that through transportation routes are so laid out that consignments from the factory destined for the wholesaler at X must pass through city Y first; and that wholesale prices in X are therefore higher per commodity unit than those in Y (say, $50 in Y and $54 in X). Assume that transport charges on shipments from X and from Y are $1 per distance unit as stepped off by the concentric circles. Under these conditions, point G is on the trade-area boundary line, because the aggregate costs there are $61 from Y ($50 plus $11 of shipping charges) and $61 from X ($54 plus $7). Point H is also on the boundary line since its aggregate costs are $59 from both Y ($50 plus $9) and X ($54 plus $5).

Case C   If the conditions in the foregoing case are reversed, so that production costs are constant but transport costs vary, the trade-area boundary will be a curved line that is *closer to* and *bends around* the center with the higher transport costs. This is shown on Figure 32-6 by line 3, which connects all points of equal aggregate costs (production plus transport) for both X and Y.

To illustrate: Assume that production costs per unit of commodity are $50 in both X and

Figure 32-6

FETTER'S THEORY

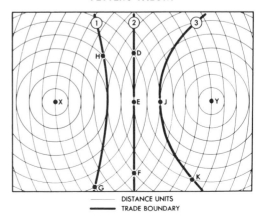

DISTANCE UNITS
TRADE BOUNDARY

Y but that transport charges around Y increase at the rate of $2 per distance unit while those around X increase at the rate of $1. Point J lies on the trade-area boundary line since its combined costs in trading with X and Y are $58. Point K also lies on the line since its costs relative to both X and Y are $62.

Another theory that deals specifically with the location of trade-area boundaries is Reilly's Law of Retail Gravitation. We shall take it up below under the general topic of the interaction theory.

The Interaction Theory

The interaction theory is that the strength of the economic connections between two places varies positively according to their size and negatively according to the intervening distance. The larger the populations of the two places, the greater their economic interaction, but the greater the distance between them, the less the interaction. For example, suppose there are three cities, X (with 20,000 people), Y (with 10,000), and Z (with 30,000), located as in Figure 32-7, with Y in the middle, 50 miles from X and 100 miles from Z. How would the amount of business contacts between Y and X compare to that between Y and Z? The interaction theory suggests an answer; namely, that the amount of business will vary *directly* with the *product* of the two populations and *inversely* with the distance between them.

The theory is expressed in the following formula:

$$i = \frac{P_1 P_2}{d}$$

In this equation, i = interaction, P_1 = population of one of the places, P_2 = population of the other place, and d = distance between them. Accordingly, the index of business between X and Y would be computed as follows:

$$\frac{10,000 \cdot 20,000}{50} = \frac{200,000,000}{50} = 4,000,000$$

The index number between Y and Z as follows:

$$\frac{10,000 \cdot 30,000}{100} = \frac{300,000,000}{100} = 3,000,000$$

Thus, the interaction between Y and Z would tend (other things being equal) to be only three-fourths as strong as that between X and Y.

Other evidence in support of this theory shows that the interaction theory holds for number of telephone messages, for number of bus passengers, for weight of railway express shipments, and for other types of interaction that generally occur between numerous pairs of cities.*

Sometimes the *interaction* concept is called the *gravity* or *potential* concept because of similarity with Newton's law of gravitation which postulates that the potential power of attraction between two bodies increases with the product of their masses and decreases with distance between them. The formula cited above is the simplest, most elementary expression of the interaction theory. Some economic endeavors appear to have spatial relationships that truly conform to this formula. But the interaction of other phenomena seems to correlate more closely with some modification of the formula, such as $ixy = (Px\,Py)/d^2$ in which ixy = interaction between place X and place Y, P = population, and d = distance. Such interaction varies positively with

* See G.K. Zipf, *Human Behavior and the Principle of Least Effort*, Cambridge, Mass., 1949.

Figure 32-7

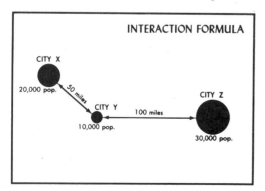

INTERACTION FORMULA

CITY X
20,000 pop.
50 miles
CITY Y
10,000 pop.
100 miles
CITY Z
30,000 pop.

product of populations but negatively with the *square* of the distance.* In a word, the *interaction* theory and its derivatives declare that the strength of economic linkage between two places varies *positively* with some exponent of the product of their populations and *negatively* with some exponent of their intervening distance. This will be apparent in two variations of gravity theory: the breaking-point theory and the law of retail gravitation. Let us look at each of these.

THE BREAKING-POINT THEORY

The first modification of the interaction theory is the *breaking-point theory*, which is an endeavor to provide a way to predict the location of the boundary line separating trade areas around two cities unequal in size. Referring to Figure 32-7 again, where would the boundary line run separating the trade area of City Y from that of City Z? Would it be halfway between the two cities, or closer to one of them? And if the latter, how close would it be?

The breaking-point theory endeavors to predict the location of this line by means of the following formula:

RATIO

$$\left.\begin{array}{l}\text{Distance of breaking}\\\text{point from the}\\\text{smaller trade center}\end{array}\right\}\text{ equals }\left\{\begin{array}{l}\textit{Numerator: } \text{distance between the}\\\qquad\qquad\text{two trade centers}\\\hline\textit{Denominator:}\\\text{1 plus the square root of}\left\{\begin{array}{l}\text{Population of larger city}\\\qquad\textit{divided by}\\\text{Population of smaller city}\end{array}\right\}\end{array}\right.$$

In symbols, the ratio is:

$$\frac{d}{1 + \sqrt{Pop\ Z/\ Pop\ Y}}$$

From Figure 32-7 the appropriate values can be inserted in the formula as follows:

$$\text{Distance from } Y = \frac{100}{1 + \sqrt{\dfrac{30,000}{10,000}}} =$$

$$\frac{100}{1 + \sqrt{3}} = \frac{100}{1 + 1.73} = \frac{100}{2.73} = 36.6 \text{ miles}$$

* For an illustrative study of this modification see Edward J. Taaffe, "The Urban Hierarchy: An Air Passenger Definition," *Economic Geography*, 1962, pp. 1-14.

In reality, of course, the position of a trade area boundary is influenced not only by the forces of *distance* and *size* of trade centers (as considered in the interaction theories just cited) but also by the forces explained by Fetter's Law as well as by variations in landforms, by location and nature of transportation routes, by political boundaries, and so on. But when these are equalized, interaction theories tend to hold for retail trade.

LAW OF RETAIL TRADE GRAVITATION

A second modification of interaction theory is W. J. Reilly's *Law of Retail Trade Gravitation*, an attempt to provide a way to predict the volume of retail trade patronage that a city's residents will give to other cities. For example, in Figure 32-7, what are the relative volumes of patronage that inhabitants of City Y will give to businesses in City X and to those in City Z?

Reilly's theory can be stated as follows:

$$\frac{\text{Volume of Y's patronage to X}}{\text{Volume of Y's patronage to Z}} =$$

$$\frac{\text{Population of X}}{\text{Population of Z}} \cdot \left(\frac{\text{Distance Y-Z}}{\text{Distance Y-X}}\right)^2$$

From Figure 32-7, we can insert values in the above formula, thus:

$$\frac{\text{Volume of Y's patronage to X}}{\text{Volume of Y's patronage to Z}} = \frac{20,000}{30,000} \cdot \left(\frac{100}{50}\right)^2$$

$$= \frac{2}{3} \cdot (2)^2 = \frac{2}{3} \cdot 4 = \frac{8}{3}$$

Thus, for every three dollars of goods that Y's inhabitants purchase in Z, they will tend to purchase eight dollars' worth in X. The principle can be summed up this way:

The degree to which the residents of a city patronize another city is directly proportional to the other city's population and inversely proportional to the square of the distance between them.

For a final example of the interaction theory at work, consider the following remarks on the *fertility rings* in the agricultural hinterlands around Chinese cities.

An important tie between countryside and city is the fertilizer in the form of night soil which the latter provides. Since the amount of night soil is most abundant in the vicinity of cities and large towns it is the land closest to the urban centers which is most heavily fertilized and yields the largest returns. Thorp writes: "Every large city and town which I have observed in China is surrounded by a more or less irregular ring of very fertile soils which usually extends at least as far as a man may walk and return in one day." The fertility rings around cities are most concentrated just outside the city walls where market gardens occupy much of the land. Here the soils are as black and rich as typical chernozems. On the North China Plain one can often tell when he is approaching a city by the improved appearance of the crops. Thorp suggests, as a rule of thumb, that for the first few kilometers around each city the fertility of the soil roughly varies inversely with the distance, or perhaps the square of the distance from the city.†

A Theory of Intervening Opportunities

The movement of people and goods from place to place has long been an interesting topic of investigation by social scientists. Why do people go *where* they go—to work, to play, to shop, to worship—why don't they select some alternative place that can likewise meet their needs? One endeavor to describe at least one "law" governing such movements is the *theory of intervening opportunities*, formulated by sociologist Samuel Stouffer thus: "The number of persons going a given distance is directly proportional to the number of opportunities at that distance and inversely proportional to the number of intervening opportunities."

The theory was tested in a case study of residential mobility in Cleveland, Ohio. Moves by Cleveland families during a three-year period were tabulated and classified in terms of (a) the linear distance between the old home and the new, and (b) the number of intervening opportunities. To qualify as an *intervening opportunity*, a dwelling had to meet four requirements: (1) It had to be vacant so that it was available to receive a family. (2) Its price had to be comparable to that of the dwelling into which the family actually moved. (3) It had to be located in a neighborhood free of racial or ethnic barriers that would bar the family from selecting it. (4) It had to be located closer to the original dwelling than was the place actually chosen. Stouffer found that there was a definite tendency for the number of family moves of a given distance to be directly proportional to the number of opportunities at that distance and inversely proportional to the number of intervening vacant homes in the same price range and available for occupancy.**

The Nested-Hierarchy Theory

To understand this theory, we must define certain terms.*

Human occupance encompasses all human activities that are conducted in any type of establishment. Examples of *units of occupance* are farm fields, domiciles, farms, mines, stores, and factories. It is out of these units that the pattern of human occupance of the earth has been woven. This pattern, whatever its design, is not haphazard; it has been formed by the application of creative choice and by the application of energy to the processes of meeting man's economic needs. As a result, man's various occupance units become *interconnected*.

The nested-hierarchy theory is built around three major postulates. The first is that some of these interconnections are between *uniform* areas, which are homogeneous in terms of

---

* See Allen K. Philbrick's "Principles of Areal Functional Organization in Regional Human Geography," *Economic Geography*, (1957), pp. 299-336.

† Glenn T. Trewartha, "Chinese Cities: Origins and Functions," *Annals of the Association of American Geographers*, (1952), p. 86.

** For a full explanation of this theory see Samuel Stouffer, "Intervening Opportunities: A Theory Relating Mobility to Distances," *American Sociological Review*, (1940), pp. 845-867.

occupance. Examples of small *uniform* areas are an oat field, or a corn field. A larger example of a uniform area would be a farming region containing hundreds of occupance units, individual farms in this case.

The second postulate is that other interconnections between occupance units give rise to *nodal* areas. A *nodal* area consists of several different uniform areas that are connected to a focal point. An example of a small nodal area is a single farm that consists of several unlike fields (each of them a uniform area) which are organized around the farmstead, which functions as the node. A large nodal area would be the trade area of a village, which consists of diverse uniform areas (farms, residential areas, commercial areas) all tied to the village as a trading center.

Thus, according to the second postulate, human occupance is focal in character. That is, the activity of any occupance unit focuses on some nodal place. This is true of an oat field on a farm, a farm in a village trading area, a village in the trading area of a larger city, and a large city in the trading area of a metropolis. Sometimes this concept is termed the principle of *focality*.

A nodal area, regardless of magnitude, has three distinct components: a node, an internal area, and an external area. We can stay with the example of a village trade area to illustrate these three components. The village itself is the *node*; the *internal area* consists of the hinterland from which rural occupants come to patronize establishments in the village; the *external area* consists of all the interconnections that link the village to larger cities from which village retailers get their supplies and to which the villages' forward surplus farm produce from the farms in the internal area.

The third postulate in this particular theory is that occupance units are arranged in a nested hierarchy of functional areas, the hierarchy being characterized by alternate shifts from uniform relationship to nodal organization as the size and complexity of the units of occupance progress from smaller to larger portions of the earth's surface. In other words, as we shift our attention from small areas to large areas, we encounter *successive alterna-tion* in type of areal organization: from uniform to nodal to uniform to nodal, and so on. A farm, for example, contains homogeneous fields, each of which is a uniform area; but the farm unit as a whole is a nodal region containing several unlike fields organized around the farmstead. This plus neighboring farms forms a higher-order uniform region.

Accordingly, man's occupance of the earth can be classified in terms of seven orders of magnitude, each of which contains two types of areas: uniform and nodal. Thus:

Order Number	Area Type	Example
7	nodal	Primate city (for instance, New York). Different seventh-order uniform areas focus on the primate city.
7	uniform	A group of contiguous sixth-order nodal areas.
6	nodal	Major metropolis and its trade area (for example, Chicago). Different sixth-order uniform areas focus on a great metropolis.
6	uniform	A group of contiguous fifth-order nodal areas.
5	nodal	Metropolis and its trade area (say, St. Louis, Missouri). Different fifth-order uniform areas focus on a metropolis.
5	uniform	A group of contiguous fourth-order nodal areas.
4	nodal	Large city and its trade area (South Bend, Indiana). Different fourth-order uniform areas focus on a large city.
4	uniform	A group of contiguous third-order nodal areas.
3	nodal	City and its trade area (Kankakee, Illinois). Different village trade areas focus on a city.
3	uniform	A group of contiguous village trade areas.
2	nodal	Village and its trade area (Boswell, Indiana). Different second-order uniform areas focus on a village.
2	uniform	A group of contiguous farms.
1	nodal	Farm. Different fields focus on a farmstead.
1	uniform	Individual field on a farm.

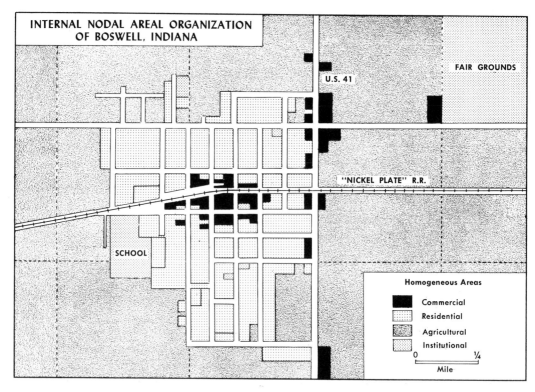

Figure 32-8 (*Courtesy Allen K. Philbrick and* Economic Geography.)

We have already shown how a farm and its fields are examples of *first-order* nodal and *first-order* uniform areas respectively.

An area of *contiguous* first-order nodal areas constitutes a uniform area of the *second order*. A group of contiguous farms, a group of contiguous residences, and a group of contiguous stores compose, respectively, agricultural, residential, and commercial uniform areas of the second order.

A group of second-order homogeneous areas that differ from one another but in which life is organized around a focal point constitute a second-order nodal area. Homogeneous areas of residences, of farms, of stores, of institutions (each area homogeneous within itself) make up a quartet of different yet uniform areas which focus upon Boswell, Indiana, as illustrated in Figure 32-8. That figure shows the location of the *node* and some of the *in-*ternal portion of the Boswell nodal area; Figure 32-9 shows the rest of that *internal* portion, and Figure 32-10 shows *external* components of the Boswell nodal area.

Overlap begins to set in with second-order nodal areas; that is, the periphery of Boswell's internal area overlaps with those of neighboring second-order nodal centers.

Third order and all succeeding orders proceed upward, each encompassing an increasingly larger number of interconnections with other places.

Each unit of occupance regardless of size— provided it is involved in commercial life— functions as a component of two types of areas *simultaneously:* a uniform area that consists of other components similar to it, and a nodal area in which these similar components plus several dissimilar components focus on a node.

Location Theory

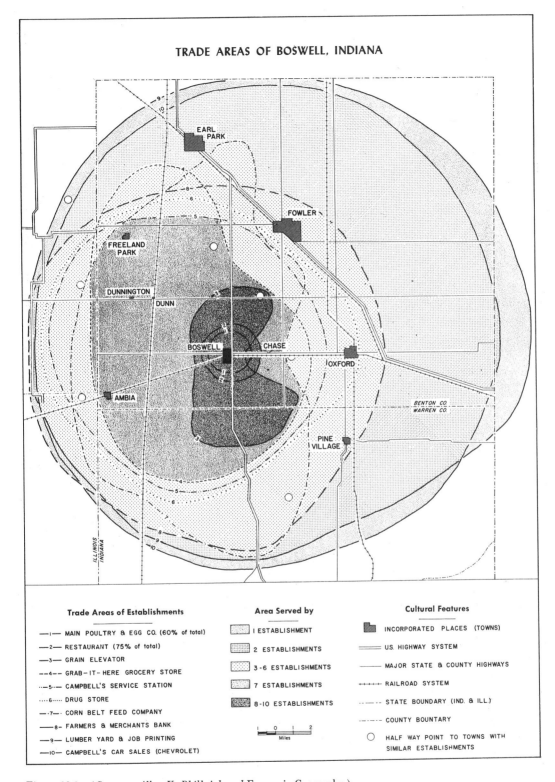

TRADE AREAS OF BOSWELL, INDIANA

Trade Areas of Establishments

— 1 — MAIN POULTRY & EGG CO. (60% of total)
— 2 — RESTAURANT (75% of total)
— 3 — GRAIN ELEVATOR
— 4 — GRAB-IT-HERE GROCERY STORE
···5··· CAMPBELL'S SERVICE STATION
····6···· DRUG STORE
— 7 — CORN BELT FEED COMPANY
— 8 — FARMERS & MERCHANTS BANK
— 9 — LUMBER YARD & JOB PRINTING
— 10 — CAMPBELL'S CAR SALES (CHEVROLET)

Area Served by

☐ 1 ESTABLISHMENT
☐ 2 ESTABLISHMENTS
☐ 3-6 ESTABLISHMENTS
☐ 7 ESTABLISHMENTS
☐ 8-10 ESTABLISHMENTS

1 0 1 2
Miles

Cultural Features

▨ INCORPORATED PLACES (TOWNS)
═══ U.S. HIGHWAY SYSTEM
─── MAJOR STATE & COUNTY HIGHWAYS
+++++ RAILROAD SYSTEM
·─·─· STATE BOUNDARY (IND. & ILL.)
·──·── COUNTY BOUNTARY
○ HALF WAY POINT TO TOWNS WITH SIMILAR ESTABLISHMENTS

Figure 32-9 (*Courtesy Allen K. Philbrick and* Economic Geography.)

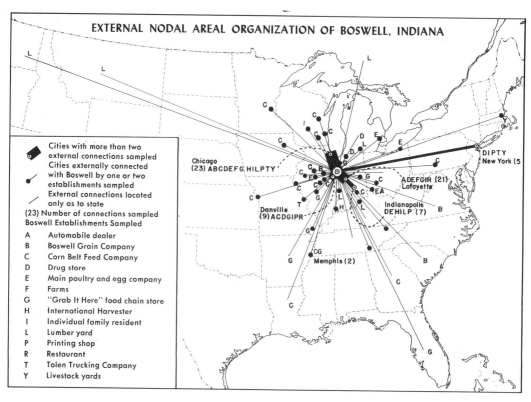

EXTERNAL NODAL AREAL ORGANIZATION OF BOSWELL, INDIANA

Cities with more than two external connections sampled

Cities externally connected with Boswell by one or two establishments sampled

External connections located only as to state

(23) Number of connections sampled

Boswell Establishments Sampled

A   Automobile dealer
B   Boswell Grain Company
C   Corn Belt Feed Company
D   Drug store
E   Main poultry and egg company
F   Farms
G   "Grab It Here" food chain store
H   International Harvester
I   Individual family resident
L   Lumber yard
P   Printing shop
R   Restaurant
T   Tolen Trucking Company
Y   Livestock yards

Chicago (23) ABCDEFG HILPTY

Danville (9) ACDGIPR

Memphis (2)

DIPTY New York (5

ADEFGIR (21) Lafayette

Indianapolis DEHILP (7)

Figure 32-10   (*Courtesy Allen K. Philbrick and* Economic Geography.)

Suggested Readings

Berry, Brian J. L., "Recent Studies Concerning the Role of Transportation in the Space Economy," *Annals of the Association of American Geographers*, 1959, pp. 328-342.

Fulton, Maurice, and Hoch, J. Clinton, "Transportation Factors Affecting Locational Decisions," *Economic Geography*, 1959, pp. 51-59.

Garrison, William L., "Spatial Structure of the Economy: I, II, III," *Annals of the Association of American Geographers*, 1959, pp. 232-239; pp. 471-482; 1960, pp. 357-373.

Greenhut, Melvin L., *Plant Location in Theory and Practice*, Chapel Hill, 1956, 338 pp.

——, "Space and Economic Theory," Regional Science Association, *Papers and Proceedings*, 1959, pp. 267-280.

Hoover, Edgar M., *The Location of Economic Activity*, New York, 1948, 310 pp.

Isard, Walter, *Location and Space-Economy*, New York, 1956, 350 pp.

Lewis, W. Arthur, *The Theory of Economic Growth*, London, 1955, 453 pp.

Lösch, August, *The Economics of Location*, New Haven, 1954, 520 pp.

Lukermann, Fred, "The Role of Theory in Geographical Inquiry," *The Professional Geographer*, March 1961, pp. 1-6.

——, and Porter, P. W., "Gravity and Potential Models in Economic Geography," *Annals of the Association of American Geographers*, 1960, pp. 493-504.

McCarty, H. H., "An Approach to a Theory of Economic Geography," *Economic Geography*, 1954, pp. 95-101.

Orr, Earle W., "A Synthesis of Theories of Location, of Transportation Rates, and of Spatial Price Equilibrium," Regional Science As-

sociation, *Papers and Proceedings*, 1957, pp. 61-73.

Philbrick, Allen K., "Principles of Areal Functional Organization in Regional Human Geography," *Economic Geography*, 1957, pp. 299-336.

Stouffer, Samuel, "Intervening Opportunities: A Theory Relating Mobility to Distances," *American Sociological Review*, 1940, pp. 845-867.

Ullman, Edward L., "Regional Development and the Geography of Concentration," Regional Science Association, *Papers and Proceedings*, 1958, pp. 179-198.

Warntz, William, "Geography of Prices and Spatial Interaction," Regional Science Association, *Papers and Proceedings*, 1957, pp. 118-129.

——, "Transportation, Social Physics, and the Law of Refraction," *The Professional Geographer*, July 1957, pp. 2-7.

Vällingby, one of Stockholm's 25 new suburbs built since World War II. The subway railroad to Stockholm runs diagonally across the picture. The central business district has been built over the tracks; it is encircled by high-rise apartments. Beyond these are groups of lower, smaller multiple-housing units and, further out, single-family structures. (Courtesy Gunnar Alexandersson; photo by Oscar Bladh, Stockholm.)

THIRTY-THREE

Throughout this book our goal has been to understand spatial variation in economic activity around the world. As a means to that end, we have used the regional (or areal) method of analysis as a framework around which to organize knowledge of spatial differentiation. Beginning with a view of the world's population pattern we have gone on to consider the individual activities by which people meet their economic needs. With all this as background, we can now survey the totality of economic activity and make some concluding observations about the delimitation of regions, about general world regions of economic development and areal (or regional) planning.

Delimitation of Regions

Throughout this book our attention has been drawn to numerous maps showing boundary lines around regions. Frequently the area inside the line has been solid black while that outside the line has remained untouched. Sometimes the area inside has been shaded, or lined, or dotted—but in such instances the boundary line is a conspicuous feature.

Such a device is helpful in presenting an initial view of spatial variation—but it has one pitfall. It gives the impression that the difference is abrupt from one side of the boundary to the other. Rarely is such abruptness found in reality. Rather, spatial variation of most phenomena is gradual; consequently the most important part of a region is not its boundary but its core, or heart. A region in reality is rarely a homogeneous area separated from a different region by a *boundary line,* but rather a homogeneous area surrounded by a *transition zone* in which characteristics of one *core area* blend with those of the next. This is a very important principle of geography to keep in mind whenever one studies a map of regions of economic activities.

General World Areas of Economic Development

We can attempt to sum up what we know about world economic activity from two standpoints: *level* of economic development, and *interregional connections.*

LEVEL OF ECONOMIC DEVELOPMENT

In Figure 33-1 we see the locational pattern of five major types of economic regions as determined by progress up the ladder of economic advancement. Areas of Type 1 have a predominantly exchange (or commercial) economy with a relatively high level of productivity. Areas of Type 2 are also mainly exchange economies but still contain large sectors of subsistence economy and have only a moderate level of productivity. Areas of Type 3 are distinguished, for the most part, by subsistence economies, though they do contain some elements of exchange economy; in general, activity in this type is at a relatively low level of productivity. Type 4 consists of areas that are almost entirely subsistence in nature and have a low productivity level. Type 5 areas contain few people and are largely undeveloped. If we compare Figure 33-1 with the front endpaper (world population) and with the back endpaper (world areas of diet deficit) we can bring out several important truths that are basic to many of the world's economic and political problems. For example, most of the world's people are located in areas where the level of economic development is exceedingly low; on the other hand, the regions where the level of development is high are small in extent and they support a minority of the world's inhabitants. Clearly, the stage is set for reaction on the part of the masses in areas 3 and 4 as information trickles through to them about the differential between their level of living and that in areas 1 and 2. These

Figure 33-1 (*Courtesy Richard Hartshorne and University of Chicago Department of Geography, Essays on Economic Geography. Symbols explained in text.*)

KINDS AND LEVELS OF ECONOMIC DEVELOPMENT

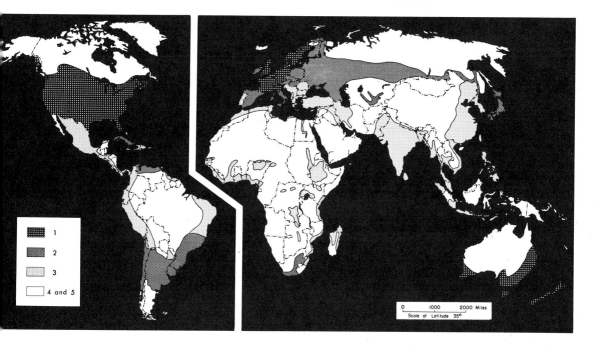

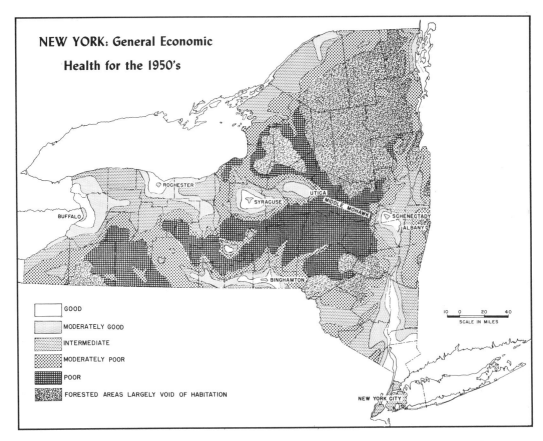

NEW YORK: General Economic Health for the 1950's

GOOD

MODERATELY GOOD

INTERMEDIATE

MODERATELY POOR

POOR

FORESTED AREAS LARGELY VOID OF HABITATION

SCALE IN MILES
10   0   20   40

ROCHESTER   SYRACUSE   UTICA   MIDDLE MOHAWK   SCHENECTADY   ALBANY
BUFFALO   BINGHAMTON
NEW YORK CITY

Figure 33-2 *This map is one example of how spatial variation in level of economic attainment can be portrayed by a composite of patterns of several variables: per capita income, 1958; increase in per capita income, 1950-1957; average unemployment, 1949-1958; percentage of growth of total employment, 1947-1956; percentage of population in the 20- to 59-year age group in 1950; percentage of population growth, 1950-1956; percentage increase in value added by manufacturing, 1947-1954; increase in annual average weekly wage and salary earnings, 1950-1958; percentage of growth in retail sales, 1948-1958. (Map courtesy John H. Thompson and Annals of Assn. of American Geogs.)*

three maps are probably the most important to keep in mind in trying to understand the significance of current events involving the political aims and stratagems of nations.

In recent years, increasing attention has been directed by an increasing number of scholars in all the social sciences toward problems of *underdeveloped* and *stranded* areas.

Underdeveloped Areas   Here is a concise statement of some of the problems facing underdeveloped areas:

Economic progress is measured by a rising standard of consumption of goods and services, which involves

changes in the character and also the location of production. Different regions do not advance at the same rate, and serious locational problems are raised by these differences.

In a primitive region, the high costs of transport prevent the development of much specialization of production and require that each locality produce nearly the whole range of commodities it consumes. Local self-sufficiency is the rule, and the only known ways to live on this basis are by hunting, fishing, grazing, or cultivation of the soil. Products not essential to existence have little place in such primitive economies.

An advance to higher living standards requires more trade. Such trade permits each locality to share, to some extent, the production advantages of other localities and to attain a better consumption standard by concentrating on the lines of production in which it has the greatest relative advantage. The essentials for increasing trade are reduction of transfer (i.e. transport) costs and increased specialization of production, involving shifts of resources to new uses.

To secure a continually larger income from the same area, there must be continually increasing intensity of land use. Gradations of intensity in agriculture run from range grazing through cereals and other extensive crops through fruit and dairy farming to poultry keeping and truck gardening. A few fortunately situated agricultural countries like Denmark have kept increasing populations well abreast of advancing world standards of living by following this sequence of increasingly intensive forms of agriculture.

Much more generally, however ... economic progress depends eventually on industrialization, i.e., the development of manufacturing. This is a commonly accepted generalization, though the reasons behind it are not well understood.*

The analysis of underdeveloped areas is a study in itself and the subject of an increasing body of literature, some items of which are identified in the bibliography of this chapter. One of the questions receiving frequent attention is this: What are the criteria by which an underdeveloped area is identified? Is comparative standard of living a valid criterion? That is, is an area underdeveloped if that standard is lower than the one prevailing in a so-called "developed area," say Germany, or Britain, or the United States? If such comparison is not valid, is comparison with some abstract standard more meaningful? For instance, are Germany, Britain, and the United States underdeveloped because they are all in process of raising their living standards to

* Edgar M. Hoover, *The Location of Economic Activity*, McGraw-Hill, 1948, pp. 187-188.

some higher level? In a word, how does one determine whether an area is developed or underdeveloped? The answer is still being worked out.

Stranded Areas   A stranded area is a comparatively small region that at one time kept abreast of contiguous areas in economic development but then suffered a curtailment of opportunity. Consequently, as the surrounding territories moved ahead, they left the stranded area as an island of relatively lower production and income. In size, stranded areas are rather small, even as small as a single city. Domestic examples of stranded areas are the southern Appalachian coal mining area from West Virginia to Tennessee, the anthracite-mining area of northeastern Pennsylvania, the old Cotton Belt from South Carolina to Alabama, the cut-over area of upper New England and of northern Michigan, Wisconsin, and Minnesota, several copper mining settlements in upper Michigan, and several gold mining towns in the western United States.

The causes for becoming stranded are diverse. One common factor is the depletion of natural resources. Mineral deposits (such as gold, copper, oil, and gas) may be used up. Forests may be cut over, fish stocks depleted, or soil seriously damaged—as when wheat farming invaded the grazing lands of America's subhumid Great Plains.

A second powerful influence involves changes in relationships with other places that may leave an area stranded even when its natural resources are still in good supply. Such changes are expressed as a drop in de-

Ghost towns are widely scattered over the western United States, over 300 in Colorado alone. Eureka (near Silverton) at one time had a population of 3000. Its economic life was based on the Sunnyside mine and mill, which began operations in 1873 and at peak employed over 500 people. (Colorado Department of Public Relations.)

mand for the stranded area's products. A drop in demand may be attributable to declining incomes in the markets the stranded area supplies, or to obsolescence of product, or to increasing competition from other areas, or to new trade restrictions.

Some areas become stranded because of the interplay of both factors, as happened to the copper mining industry in upper Michigan— not only did the copper reserves diminish but stiff competition was offered by newer, richer and more productive copper mining ventures in the western United States and central Africa. The problem of unemployment bedeviling Scranton, Wilkes-Barre, and a few other cities in eastern Pennsylvania stems not only from a reduction in easily mined anthracite but also from the sudden shift in public preference from anthracite to fuel oil for heating homes and business structures.*

AREA REDEVELOPMENT ADMINISTRATION

In early 1961 the United States Congress passed, and on May 1 the President signed into law, the Area Redevelopment Act (ARA) designed to help underdeveloped areas recoup their economic strength. The background for this Act is described as follows.

One of the anomalies of our modern society is the continuing existence, even during periods of national prosperity, of geographic pockets in which chronic unemployment and underemployment are excessively high.

These areas regardless of the national rhythm of recession and recovery have been unable to develop local economic strength. These are the areas that, in a manner of speaking, never really recovered from the Great Depression of the 30's.

The victims of changing times and changing technologies, these areas pockmark our nation. And as long as they exist, they constitute a drag on the national, state, and local economies.

Aside from considerations of the suffering sustained by the individuals in these areas, they are a drag, first of all, because they fail to produce at the same rate as the rest of the nation. . . . They are a drag, too, because the unemployed and the underemployed are transformed from taxpayers into tax users. They not

only are unable to contribute to the support of their communities, their States and their Federal Government, they simultaneously turn to tax-supported programs—unemployment compensation and public assistance, chiefly—to sustain themselves.†

The first step in this program is the designation of areas that qualify for federal assistance under the redevelopment act. Areas are generally designated on a county basis. Different criteria are employed for urban and for nonurban counties.

Urban counties qualify if (a) they have a high current rate of unemployment (in excess of 6 per cent), and (b) they have had it over "a long period of time." A sliding scale is used for this latter attribute: The area's jobless rate must have been at least 50 per cent above the national average for three of the last four years, or 75 per cent above for two of the last three years, or 100 per cent above for one of the last two years.

Nonurban counties qualify under any one of four types, the two most explicit being, (a) counties having a median *family* (not *per capita*) income of $1560 a year or less, and (b) counties having a median *farm* income of $1170 or less; this figure is lower than that in (a) because a farm family can produce a good share of its food.

Nonurban counties also qualify if they are carry-overs from the Department of Agriculture Rural Areas Development Program or if 60 per cent of their farms are designated as "Class VI Farms"—the least remunerative commercial farms in the nation.

As of mid-1962 there were 873 designated areas plus 50 Indian Reservations in 47 contiguous states (only Vermont was free of one), Puerto Rico, the Virgin Islands, Guam, and Samoa. These areas had an aggregate population of 35,000,000 and a labor force exceeding 13,000,000, of whom over 1,000,000 were unemployed—a rate of 8 per cent (national average was 5.5 per cent). In some areas the jobless rate had reached 30 per cent.

The most prominent regions of designations

---

* A stimulating and provocative series of essays on problems of underdeveloped and stranded areas appears in a volume edited by Norton Ginsburg, cited in the bibliography at the close of this chapter.

† Victor Roterus, Remarks at Annual Conference of the Association of American Geographers, Miami Beach, Florida, April 24, 1962.

Levels of Areal Development; Regional Planning

were (a) the coal problem areas (the Appalachian, Eastern Interior, and eastern Oklahoma-Texas fields), (b) the cut-over region from northern Minnesota to northern New York, (c) the lumbering areas of the Pacific Northwest (from Montana to Washington to northern California), (d) the textile centers of New England, and (e) labor surplus areas in the Southeast—a broad belt from North Carolina to eastern Texas.

Provisions of the Act for these areas are as follows:

1. Loans to help new businesses to get started and old ones to expand—but not to relocate.

2. Loans to help finance new public facilities (such as sewers and roads) which a community must provide in order to aid businesses creating new jobs—but not relocation of jobs.

3. Programs to train jobless workers.

4. Technical assistance to help an area plan and execute its own program of economic development. This program, known as the Over-all Economic Development Program (OEDP) is the area's own blueprint for progress.

After an area is officially designated it must formulate its OEDP before ARA assistance is given, in accord with the principle that "economic development must percolate up from the community, not trickle down from a central source." Accordingly, each area must provide its own initiative, do its own planning, and generate risk capital. "Self-help" is the underlying philosophy, as the ARA offers only training, counsel, and "seed money" to help the local economies grow.

Within a year of the Act's passage, 515

areas and 20 reservations had submitted their OEDP's—well over half the designated units.

As Figure 33-3, page 638, shows, the pattern of economic areas can be broken down first into two great families, subsistence and exchange; the latter can be further classified into two subtypes, nodal and uniform. The message of the map is twofold: (a) The *subsistence* world is confined largely to the tropics and to the very high latitudes, and (b) the *exchange* world is basically a single far-flung area functioning around one great *node*, or *core*, that straddles the North Atlantic ocean. This focal zone in the world's economy extends from east-central Anglo-America through west-central Europe. Most of this nodal area is situated in the Northern Hemisphere, but outliers have sprung up (in Latin America, Africa, and Australia) whose economies mesh closely with that of the core. Sometimes the term "integrated commercial world" is applied to this vast exchange area. The nested-hierarchy theory receives good supportive evidence on this map in that diverse uniform regions, each of which is homogeneous, (for instance, major cropland regions, major ranch land regions, major forest regions, and major mining areas) are all functionally integrated with the economic life of the great industrial core flanking the North Atlantic. Consequently, the world's major sea lanes converge on this supernode, linking it with distant places.

(We might make a case for transferring the category "plantation agriculture" from the subsistence world to the exchange world. At least the concepts of plantation farming as we presented them in Chapter 12 would make such a change defensible.)

Regional Planning

Having inspected the world pattern of production, exchange, and consumption of economic wealth, we cannot help but anticipate the future and ask normative questions. What kind of a pattern is most desirable? How does the ideal pattern differ, if at all, from the present pattern? Is it possible to change the

pattern, so as to conform with the ideal? If so, how can this be done?

On an enormous scale, the process of answering these questions is similar to the planning a family does in determining the best possible use of the house and the property it occupies. Many scientists now believe that

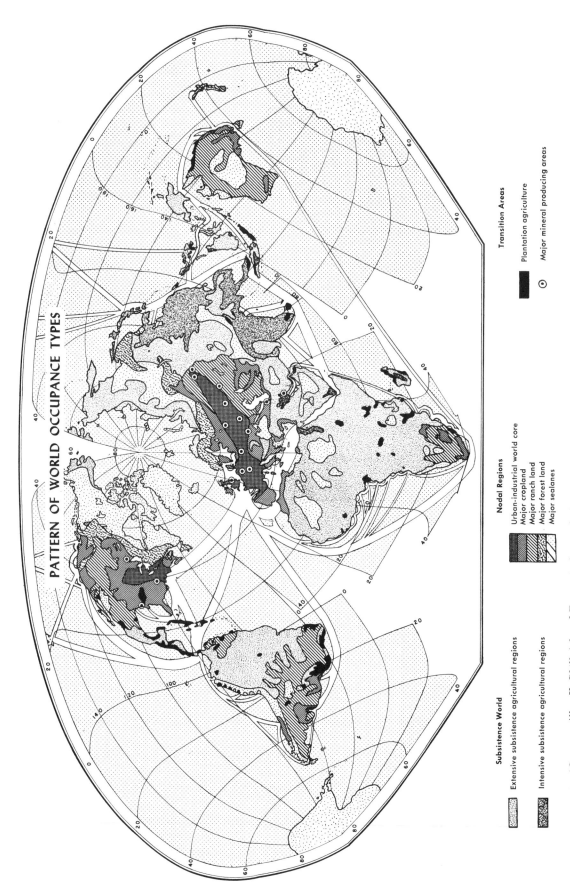

PATTERN OF WORLD OCCUPANCE TYPES

Subsistence World

Extensive subsistence agricultural regions

Intensive subsistence agricultural regions

Nodal Regions

Urban-industrial world core

Major cropland

Major ranch land

Major forest land

Major sealanes

Transition Areas

Plantation agriculture

⊙ Major mineral producing areas

Figure 33-3 *(Courtesy Allen K. Philbrick and* Economic Geography.*)*

large groups of people occupying large areas can also cooperate in following orderly plans for increasing the returns from their lands and properties without sacrificing the values of freedom. As a result of this conviction, more and more areal planning is being done in the United States and elsewhere on at least three distinct levels: *city planning, state planning,* and *regional planning.*

CITY PLANNING

City planning, in which the regional method of analysis is applied to individual cities, is rooted in the conviction that the problems of cities—traffic congestion, parking congestion, residential blight, dead subdivisions, need for conveniently located parks, and so on—can be solved by research and foresight.

Improving a city clearly calls for organized schemes and efforts. Cities do not grow spontaneously into efficient areas of human habitation. In fact, a city is like a house. One can build a house by the hit-and-miss method, a room here, a room there, and continue to tack on rooms and additions from time to time as needs arise. But no part of such a house is related, by forethought, to any other part: They just "happen" to be built against one another. The result is a monstrosity that is badly designed, awkward, inefficient, and costly to maintain. The tragic fact is that most cities have grown just this way—without forethought of plan or pattern. The settled areas have continually expanded and spilled over haphazardly into the hinterland. From time to time new sections are tacked on to the community, and the result is often a monstrosity with fantastic street patterns, awkward traffic snarls, areas of blight—all of which makes for a less efficient community, one that is increasingly expensive to service and maintain.

In contrast, a house may be carefully designed by an architect, so that its parts fit together. In such a house there is an orderly arrangement of rooms and passages. It is efficient. It is pleasing to look at and live in and economical to maintain. Likewise, a community may grow according to an orderly arrangement. This is where city planning has

a role to play. City planners are the architects who design the city. Two main jobs confront them: designing new areas and redesigning older areas.

Design of New Areas   Expansion of a city into the countryside calls for a blueprint for the transformation of farmland and other rural land into efficient accretions to the urban totality. As the planner gazes out over the rural-urban fringe he must face such questions as: Where should schools be located? How much land should be set aside for each school? Where should major thoroughfares be located? How should interstitial areas between thoroughfares be laid out—with winding street patterns, or grids, or some other design? What areas should be zoned for apartments, for large-lot single-family dwellings, for small-lot single-family structures? Should land be set aside for shopping centers? If so, how much and where should it be located? Will there be a need for land for industrial uses? (If so, it should be demarcated in large parcels—at least a few hundred acres—zoned to keep other users out and situated near railways, main highways, and on land which is not too valuable.) The general thinking by planners now is that at least 5 per cent of a city's land should be set aside for recreational purposes. Hence, the need for deciding what parts of the farm land to be annexed should be devoted to parks, golf courses, wildlife refuges, or other types of recreational uses. Additional questions deal with matters like positioning storm sewers in such a manner that heavy rains and melting snow can run off with no flooding. Rural land adjoining a city usually is not faced with a serious problem at this point (unless it is in a valley bottom) since most of the earth's surface is covered with soil into which much of the water seeps. Water which isn't absorbed by the soil often is retarded in its run off by pasture grasses or other ground cover. But when such land is transformed into city, it is almost entirely resurfaced—and water-proofed! Roofs, streets, driveways, and sidewalks absorb no water—neither do they impede its run-off. Heavy rains and melting snow produce volumes of water which must be quickly conducted away to prevent flooding.

But the city planner's design for the urban fringe cannot be executed if the land is outside the city's jurisdiction. Hence, the urgency by many cities to annex the fringe while it is still in a rural state—before urban types of buildings are constructed beyond the city limits.

Annexation   The question of annexation is a complex one with several pros and cons. From the standpoint of the city, the main advantage to annexing rural land is that the city can be sure that the land is laid out in a manner which fits in with the over-all city plan. Furthermore, as the fringe is built up, property taxes paid by its occupants will flow into the city coffers—thereby expanding the municipal tax base. The main disadvantage is that, for the first few years after annexation, the city is likely to spend more to service the fringe (with fire protection, police protection, schools, street maintenance, snow-removal, and so forth) than it receives in tax revenues from the fringe. This is the main reason why some citizens of the city resist vigorous annexation policies, preferring to wait until the fringe is occupied sufficiently so that its property taxes at least come close to equalling the cost of services the city will render it. A factory or commercial establishment in the fringe is often looked upon as a juicy plum, and is coveted for annexation, since the principle is almost universal that such properties are taxed at a higher rate than the services they receive are worth.

The other side of the annexation coin is the attitude of the fringe dwellers. From their viewpoint there are also both advantages and disadvantages. By annexing to the city they generally stand to benefit by receiving better fire protection (therefore lower fire insurance premiums), storm sewers, better schools, and other services. On the other hand, the cost of such services is likely to raise their taxes above the level formerly paid to their rural governing unit. Moreover, there may be a loss of certain freedoms, often things which on the surface seem trivial but which mean a great deal to some fringe dwellers. For example, some cities have ordinances governing parking in residential areas and prohibit a resident from leaving a car anywhere except on his own property.

Regulations by which cities can annex land are carefully proscribed by state governments in the United States and by national governments in most other countries. These laws differ somewhat but one such set of controls stipulates that for any parcel of fringe land to be annexed the following conditions must be met. (1) A petition must be circulated describing accurately the boundaries of the fringe parcel which is proposed for annexation. (2) The parcel must be contiguous to the city. (3) At least 50 per cent of the land

Los Angeles, looking east on Wilshire Boulevard in 1922. San Vicente Boulevard runs southeast from the lower left corner of the picture. At the left in the middle background is a small oil field, to the right of which are the La Brea tarpits, a noted fossil site. (Courtesy Howard Nelson; photo by Spence Air Photos.)

owners in the fringe must sign the petition favoring annexation. (4) Such signers must own at least 50 per cent of the acreage in the land to be annexed. (5) The city council must vote to annex the parcel.

Under such rules, confused gerrymandering of city limits can result, since petitions can be drawn up to annex highly irregular shapes of land areas—in order to include favorable voters and exclude those resisting annexation.

Redesign of Old Areas City planners also face the problems of built-up areas within the city. In some instances these areas are chaotic in design and obsolete in construction, necessitating a complete overhaul. In others the problems are less severe and require less stringent measures. The treatment of these older problem areas can be divided into three categories: urban conservation, urban renewal, and urban redevelopment.

Urban conservation involves no change in land use. Rather, by neighborhood clean-up campaigns, by enforcing building codes and sanitation ordinances, it aims to encourage the upkeep and maintenance of houses, stores, and other buildings, thereby resisting the incidence of blight.

Urban renewal, which is more involved is applied to areas already blighted. Generally it entails no major change in land use but may call for the demolition of obsolete struc-tures and the replacement by new structures performing the same function—for example, replacing slums with new apartments.

Urban redevelopment is the most ambitious form of redesign and calls for the bulldozing of large areas of land and building up an entirely different layout with new street designs and functions. The construction of Cobo Hall along downtown Detroit's riverfront, Stuyvesant Town in New York, Lake Meadows in Chicago, and the Civic Center in Los Angeles are examples of such remedial surgery.

Today the concepts of city planning can be used to weave present and future developments into a logical pattern. In many cities, planners have actually revamped portions of the old pattern—by widening old streets, providing open spaces with parks and boulevards—but at high cost. Yet the cost may be even higher if cities are allowed to deteriorate at the present rate. It would seem evident that every citizen should be familiar with city planning and should be encouraged to do what he can in the years ahead to encourage wise planning by the city in which he settles.

The Planned Town Some cities were well planned in advance and laid out in great detail prior to settlement. Around 3000 B.C. the city of Kahun, Egypt was laid out in rectangular form, housing slaves and artisans

The same area of Los Angeles in 1956. Urban expansion has completely filled in the urban-rural fringe here. San Vicente Boulevard is now a divided, multilane thoroughfare; on Wilshire is the famous "Miracle Mile" (in middle background), one of the nation's most luxurious commercial ribbons. The tarpits area is now a public park. Derricks and wells have been replaced by high apartments. (Courtesy Howard Nelson; photo by Spence Air Photos.)

Shoppers Mall in Kalamazoo, Michigan. Three blocks in the heart of the central business district were ripped up and replaced with a landscaped mall for pedestrians only. The first two blocks were opened in 1959, the third in 1960—the first permanent such conversion in the U. S. Kalamazoo has 82,000 people. The nearest comparable service center is Battle Creek (with 45,000), 25 miles east. (Kalamazoo County Chamber of Commerce; photo by Kalamazoo Gazette.)

working on the nearby Illahun pyramid. In approximately the same period the cities of Mohenjo-Daro and Harrapa (in the Indus Valley) were laid out in a regular grid pattern. Beginning around 400 B.C. several Greek towns (such as Olynthus, Priene, and Miletus) were designed and laid out on a grid pattern with an extra large "block" in the center devoted to the *agora*—the market place which served as the center of business and political life. There appears to have been comparatively little planning of cities during Roman times although occasional military towns apparently were laid out on a grid basis.

In the eighteenth century a new type of city plan, *the Baroque*, was adopted in designing several European cities which functioned as political or religious centers. This plan featured radials—major thoroughfares which focused on the royal palace or a great cathedral like spokes on the hub of a wheel. Lateral streets were sometimes circular, conforming to the shape of the city wall. Karlsruhe and Mannheim in Germany and Versailles, France, are examples of Baroque cities.*

In the Western Hemisphere, Philadelphia (planned in 1682 by William Penn) and

* For an interesting discussion of the types of cities which developed in past ages see Arthur Gallion's *The Urban Pattern*, (New York), 1950.

Savannah, Georgia, are early examples of planned cities. In 1791 George Washington hired a French planner, Charles L'Enfant, to design this nation's new capital city. Early in the 1800's planners laid out a radial street pattern around Detroit's business center and a grid pattern for most of Manhattan.

But throughout most of the history of urbanism, city planning has lain dormant, and most cities grew on a hit-or-miss basis, becoming increasingly crowded and congested and, in the opinion of some people, ugly environs in which to live.

A renaissance in city planning has developed within the past 40 years. Nearly every American city of 100,000 has a city planning department, which, in large cities such as New York, Los Angeles, and Chicago, is staffed by scores of employees. And in Europe increasing attention to planning is being paid by both local organizations and branches of the national government. In some countries, principally Britain and Sweden such planning has given birth to several "New Towns."

The "New Towns"   In the last several years there has been a rebirth of the "New Town Concept"—the building of a new city according to a predetermined plan. These have become increasingly numerous since World

War II and appear in diverse parts of the world. Examples are Brasilia and Volta Redonda, Brazil, and Pyskowice, Nowe Tychy, and Nowa Huta in Poland. Examples in the United States are Levittown, New York, and Levittown, Pennsylvania, which were ventures by private planners, and Oak Ridge, Tennessee, and Richland, Washington, which were planned by the Federal Government around atomic energy research plants. But the most spectacular examples of New Town planning in recent years have occurred in Sweden and Great Britain.

In Sweden, most of the new towns have been built in the countryside encircling major cities, for example, Kortedala outside Göteborg. There are 25 new towns around Stockholm of which Vällingby, Farsta, Högdalen, and Bjorkhagen are examples. In the postwar period most of Stockholm's expansion has been channelled to a series of new suburbs west and south of the central city, located along a subway system. Each of these suburbs, usually built on forest land owned by the city, has a shopping center adjacent to a subway station. Around the center are apartment houses of varying sizes and forms and on the periphery one-family dwellings, or row-houses. Each new town has from 5,000 to 25,000 inhabitants, 80 per cent of whom live in apartments within walking distance of the center with its supermarkets, banks, and other business facilities. Some shopping centers are larger than the rest, and their department stores serve several suburbs for less frequent shopping. Vällingby, located eight miles west of downtown Stockholm, is one of the largest centers. Its shops were opened in November, 1954. About 20,000 people live within walking distance (0.6 miles) and 80,000 within a radius of 2.5 miles. The woods between the suburbs are as a rule left intact for recreation. All new town suburbs have been planned by the city planning agency, but they have been built by private contractors, and most property is owned by cooperatives and private firms.

Sweden's latest new town is Brëdang, construction of which was scheduled to begin in September, 1962, with occupancy by the first families in the autumn of 1963. Brëdang,

located on the highway between Stockholm and Södertälje, is being designed for a population of 17,000, and will contain 36 apartment buildings (each of which will be eight stories high and contain 70 dwelling units) situated around the city center which contains business facilities and the subway station. Farther out will be areas of two- and three-story houses, none of which will be more than 500 meters from the subway station.

Britain likewise has a considerable number of new towns, constructed, for the most part, after passage by Parliament of the New Towns Act of 1946. Objectives of this legislation were partly to decentralize population from overcrowded and poorly housed areas within the great cities, partly to disperse industry, and partly to rehabilitate depressed areas. Authority to carry out this legislation was given the Ministry of Town and Country Planning (now known as Housing and Local Government). The designated powers were three-fold: (a) designation of the site of a new town after consultation with local authorities, (b) establishment of a Development Corporation responsible for planning and building the new town, and (c) provision of loan funds to the Development Corporation, repayable to the Treasury. After a town is occupied and has established its own local government, the Development Corporation is dissolved.

There are 15 new towns in Britain, eight of them located in a ring around London at a distance ranging from 25 to 30 miles from the center of the metropolis. The other seven are scattered in different parts of the country, but usually near a metropolitan area. As for functions of the new towns, three types are discernible.

The new towns in the London Ring (Table 33-1) were designed to absorb around 550,000 people from the British capital. Most of them were built on sites where there already existed a small settlement with established water supply, electricity, and communications.

A second type of new town is that positioned in depressed areas, usually old mining zones, where unemployment is high, housing poor, and the need for economic and social rehabilitation great. Examples are Cwmbran

Table **33-1**   *Progress of New Towns*

Name	Corporation Appointed	Designated Area (Acres)	Population Proposed	Population Dec. 1961	Manufacturing Before Designation	Employment Dec. 1961
London Ring						
Basildon	1949	7,818	106,000	56,000	not known	9,540
Bracknell	1949	2,950	54,000	21,563	179	5,656
Crawley	1947	6,047	70,000	55,000	1,300	13,778
Harlow	1947	6,395	80,000	56,700	333	12,000
Hatfield	1948	2,340	25,000	21,500	1,500	654
Hemel Hempstead	1947	5,910	80,000	56,500	6,200	14,102
Stevenage	1946	6,156	80,000	44,000	2,600	11,900
Welwyn Garden City	1948	4,317	50,000	36,000	8,000	5.255
Total: London Ring		41,933	545,000	347,263	20,000	72,885
Others in England and Wales						
Corby	1950	2,696	55,000	37,500	none	1,900
Cwmbran	1949	3,160	55,000	31,000	17,000	90
Newton Aycliffe	1947	865	20,000	12,800	none	none
Peterlee	1948	2,350	30,000	12,935	none	1,000
Scotland						
East Kilbride	1947	10,250	70,000	32,500	380	7,520
Glenrothes	1948	5,730	50,000	13,500	1,683	1,917
Cumbernauld	1956	4,150	70,000	6,400	71	1,510
Total: Great Britain		71,134	895,000	493,898	40,000	86,822

Source: Town and Country Planning Association, "The New Towns in 1961," *Town and Country Planning,* Vol. 30, No. 1, January 1962, pp. 27-29.

(near the eastern margin of the South Wales coalfield), and Newton Aycliffe and Peterlee in the Durham coal area. This trio of settlements is not concerned with metropolitan spillover but with the regrouping of existing population for better living conditions.

The third type of new town is designed around a major industry which is new to the site. A new mine on the Fifeshire coalfield (about 50 miles northeast of Glasgow, Scotland) will employ 2500 men; for them and their families and employees in services, the new town of Glenrothes was designed. Somewhat similar is the town of Corby, about 60 miles north of London, which actually began in 1934 as a new town built around a new steel mill. The steel company itself designed a town and built 2300 houses. But with postwar development, the need for expansion convinced the Town and Country Planning Board that growth should be provided for under the New Town Act.

Thus, British New Towns came into existence to perform quite different roles.*

STATE AND REGIONAL PLANNING

State planning applies to a whole state the concepts just discussed. As yet, very few states in the United States have instituted planning departments. This does not mean that planning is absent. States do plan for the building of roads and purchase of land for state parks or forests, but generally such planning is done by the state highway department

* For further information on British New Towns see the following:

Kenneth C. Edwards, "The New Towns of Britain," *Problems of Applied Geography*, Polish Academy of Sciences, Institute of Geography, Geographical Studies No. 25, (Warsaw), 1959, pp. 141-146; see also *The New Towns of Britain*, Central Office of Information Reference Pamphlet, (London), 1961, 20 pp.; "The New Towns in 1961," *Town and Country Planning*, Town and Country Planning Association, Vol. 30, No. 1, January, 1962.

or state forestry department rather than by a state planning department. State planning is much less developed than city planning.

Regional planning is the name given to the design for large areas, such as groups of counties, or river basins—areas that often cross over political boundaries. Soil conservation districts, drainage districts, watershed areas are all specialized applications of the regional planning principle.

The agency for such regional planning may be a private organization such as the Wisconsin Valley Improvement Association, an organization of businessmen, public officials, and other citizens concerned about solving problems facing the economy of the upper Wisconsin River Valley. Their best-known slogan, "One Less River To Boss," epitomizes the spirit of the project.

But most regional planning is carried on by government agencies. In the United States the Tennessee Valley Authority was the first large-scale effort, and probably is the most familiar and most notable example. The Missouri Valley Authority covers a larger territory. In Britain, the Town and Country Planning Ministry has performed exhaustive research in analyzing land use and many other phenomena as a basis for planning decisions. The Netherlands, Sweden, and numerous other countries are actively engaged in regional planning.

Inevitably this topic leads to political debate, since regional planning is a type of activity which on the one extreme may be carried out entirely by groups of citizens apart from the central government or, on the other extreme, may be carried out entirely by the state—as in the Soviet Union. In between is a broad transition zone from which men must choose the degree of authority for planning they desire to vest in government.

Figure 33-4   (*Courtesy Tennessee Valley Authority.*)

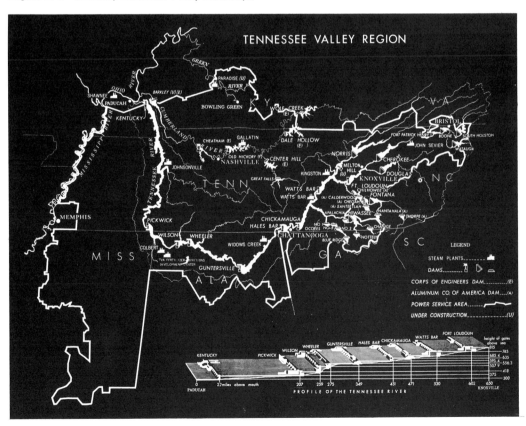

In conclusion, it must be admitted that it is impossible in a text of this type to deal at length with the concept of regional planning.* But the field has become an area of study in itself. And as interest in this problem has grown, many colleges have begun to offer degrees in City and Regional Planning and the number of professional planners is growing.

Retrospect and Prospect

This book was written in the conviction that a person can better understand the world if he knows something about the spatial variation and areal relationships of economic activities. Accordingly the author had two goals in mind as he wrote: (a) to give the reader information about spatial variation in economic endeavor (knowledge of areas of economic activity), and (b) to encourage him to develop his ability to apply the geographic method of analysis.

Throughout the book, ideas and facts have been organized directly or indirectly around three basic questions that, the author believes, constitute the distinctive geographic method of analysis. Since it is the method that is the hallmark of geography as a science, the author hopes that the reader will remember the basic questions long after he has forgotten the facts that constitute the content of these chapters.

Two of the major problems confronting the science of economic geography involve the third basic question of the geographic method as employed in this textbook. The chances are that the next few years will find economic geographers giving considerable attention to the identification of those relationships which are the most significant. Theoretically, the spatial arrangement of economic endeavor might be found to be related to a host of other variables. Which of these relationships are the most significant ones? Investigation of this problem inevitably leads to the problem of the measurement of relationships. What are the most meaningful methods for measuring the relationship between economic endeavor and other variables? It seems likely that the initial steps in mathematical quantification of associa-

tion touched upon in Chapter 31 will be followed in the future by increasing attention in this direction. In the words of Charles Colby, in a presidential address to the Association of American Geographers, "Geographic thought in the coming decades, I predict, will call for much greater accuracy and much deeper penetration than has been true in the past. The application of statistical methods, I believe, will introduce new types of measurement, will clarify present methods of analysis, and will give us results which are quantitatively exact as well as qualitatively true."

As it sheds increasing light on the spatial arrangement of economic production, exchange, and consumption, the science of economic geography will help us all better understand the world in which we live. It will contribute to our understanding of newspaper, television, and other reports of the problems and actions of nations. It will be of help to businessmen facing questions of where to locate factories, wholesale distribution facilities, retail outlets, or other service establishments. It can be of assistance to city planners and national government authorities facing decisions of how to make the best use of the available resources—both physical and cultural.

This swings our attention around to what many people feel to be the single most important function of college education: to develop skill in handling questions—both formulating and answering them—skill, in fact, in making decisions. But this immediately raises another question: How does one know when he is making the *right* decision? Economic geography—or any science—can answer the question "What is?" But science alone cannot answer the question "What ought?" It can only provide information and insight that the individual and society can manipulate in accordance with those value systems which

---

* Interested students will be stimulated by reading Robert Dickinson's *City, Region and Regionalism*, (London), 1947, in which he traces the historical background of regional planning and the regional method of analysis.

they have chosen on the basis of their life philosophy. May college education be a healthy stimulus to student and teacher alike in choosing those value systems (and the means to those ends) that will help realize the best in life for the world's population.

Suggested Readings

Ackerman, Edward A., *Geography as a Fundamental Research Discipline*, Chicago, 1958, 37 pp.

Belshaw, Horace, *Population Growth and Levels of Consumption—with Special Reference to Countries of Asia*, New York, 1956, 223 pp.

Bowsher, Norman N.; Daane, J. Dewey; and Einzig, Robert, "The Flows of Funds Between Regions of the United States," Regional Science Association, *Papers and Proceedings*, 1957, pp. 139-159.

Calef, Wesley, "Land Management Policy: The Organization Problem," *Annals of the Association of American Geographers*, 1952, pp. 327-331.

Chapin, F. Stuart, Jr., *Urban Land Use Planning*, New York, 1957, 397 pp.

Colby, Charles C., *Pilot Study of Southern Illinois*, Carbondale, 1956, 94 pp.

Cressey, George B., "Changing the Map of the Soviet Union," *Economic Geography*, 1953, pp. 198-207.

Dozier, Craig L., "Northern Parana, Brazil: An Example of Organized Regional Development," *Geographical Review*, 1956, pp. 318-333.

Duncan, Craig, "Resource Utilization and the Conservation Concept," *Economic Geography*, 1962, pp. 113-121.

Federal Reserve Bank of Chicago; "Depressed Areas—Some Lessons from the Past," *Business Conditions*, June 1961, pp. 5-12.

Friedmann, John, "Regional Planning: A Problem in Spatial Integration," The Regional Science Association, *Papers and Proceedings*, 1959, pp. 167-180.

Fryer, D. W., "World Income and Types of Economies: The Pattern of World Economic Development," *Economic Geography*, 1958, pp. 283-303.

Hance, William A., *African Economic Development*, New York, 1958, 307 pp.

————, "The Gezira: An Example in Development," *Geographical Review*, 1954, pp. 253-270.

Inskeep, Edward L., "The Geographer in Planning," *The Professional Geographer*, March 1962, pp. 22-24.

Keller, Frank Leuer, "Institutional Barriers to Economic Development—Some Examples from Bolivia," *Economic Geography*, 1955, pp. 351-363.

Manners, Gerald, "Regional Protection: A Factor in Economic Geography," *Economic Geography*, 1962, pp. 122-129.

Miernyk, William H., "Labor Mobility and Regional Growth," *Economic Geography*, 1955, pp. 321-330.

Page, John L., and Mather, Eugene, "The Geography of Crab Orchard: A Submarginal Area in Southern Illinois," *Economic Geography*, 1943, pp. 362-371.

Shabad, Theodore, "The Soviet Concept of Economic Regionalization," *Geographical Review*, 1953, 214-222.

Shimkin, Dimitri B., "Economic Regionalization in the Soviet Union," *Geographical Review*, 1952, pp. 591-614.

Taskin, George A., "The Soviet Northwest: Economic Regionalization," *Geographical Review*, 1961, pp. 213-235.

Thoman, Richard S., "Economic Geography and Economic Underdevelopment," *Economic Geography*, 1962, p. 188.

Thomas, Frank H., "Economically Distressed Areas and the Role of the Academic Geographer," *The Professional Geographer*, March 1962, pp. 12-16.

Thomas, Morgan D., "Imports, Industrialization, and the Economic Growth of Lesser Developed Countries," *The Professional Geographer*, September 1961, pp. 13-16.

Ullman, Edward L., "Amenities as a Factor in Regional Growth," *Geographical Review*, 1954, pp. 119-132.

————, "Human Geography and Area Research," *Annals of the Association of American Geographers*, 1953, pp. 54-66.

INDEX

215-217; and soil, 218-219; types, *diagram*, 210; in U.S., 210-215

Biotic pyramid, 75-77

Bituminous coal, 226-232 (*See also* Coal *and* Mining)

Bjornevatn (or Kirkenes) field, 236

Blast furnace, 354-356 (*diagram*, 354)

Blumenfeld, Hans, 559

Boswell, Indiana, nodal area, 628 (*maps*, 628, 629, 630)

Boundary line of region, 633

Breaking-point theory, 625

Breese, Gerald, 570

Brewing, commercial, 308-309 (*U.S. map*, 308)

Bridge industries, *defined*, 302

Buffalo, New York, flour mills, 302

Building-material minerals, 244

Bulk-break point transportation centers, 304-305

Burges, E. W., 584

Burton, Ian, 563

Bushmen of Australia, 33

Butte, Montana, copper district, 240

Butter, 132

b value of regression line, 604

C

CBD (central business district) 575-585; changes, 577-578; delimiting, 576-577; and industry, 580-583; patterns, 584-585; problems, 578-580; and residence, 584; subsidiary centers, 579-580

Cacao, 89, 189: international trade, *table*, 188

Calcium, 242

Caliche, 242

Calves (*See also* Livestock ranching *and* Meat packing): slaughter by cities, *table*, 301

Camayura tribe, 33

Campos, grass varieties, 112

Canada: dairying, 129-130; iron, 233-234, 236-238; manufacturing, 425-427 (*map*, 425; *photos*, 403, 426); oil, 265

Canals, 479-481: and mining, 280

Canning and freezing, 294-296 (*U.S. map*, 295)

Capital, risk (*See* Risk capital)

Carp, 51, 204

Carrying capacity of habitat, 110

Cash-grain: corn, 169; correlation with flat land, 606-607; in mixed farming, 140

Catalan forge, 280

Cattle ranching, 109-120 (*for dairy cattle, see* Dairy farming): carrying capacity, 110-111; contrast with nomadic herding, 111; drive, *photo*, 112; and farming, 117-119; history in U.S., 119-121 (*map*, 120); natural requirements, 111-114; and population, 114-115; roundup, *photo*, 113; slaughter, by cities, *table*, 301; trade, 116-117; traffic flow, Colorado, *map*, 117; U.S. sales, *map*, 143; world pattern, 109-119 (*map*, 143)

Caucasus oil field, 255

Cause and effect, 13-14

Census, U.S. (*See also* Population): of Business, 537-540; classification of urban settlements, 528-534; districts, *map*, 423; of Manufacturers, 324; of Mineral Industries, 274; tracts (small areal units), 568

Central twin city, 530-531

Central place, 516: theory of, 560, 613

Centrifugal forces, in Colby hypothesis, 585

Centripetal forces, in Colby hypothesis, 585

Cerro Bolivar mining district, 234

Characteristics of economic activity, as basic question, 10

Charante tribe, 33

Cheese, 132-134

Chernozem soils, 146-147, 173-175

Chicago: industrial structure, 417-418; population pattern, 570-571 (*tables*); *Tribune* circulation area, *map*, 553

Chickens (*see* Poultry)

Chile, nitrates, 242

China (*See also* Intensive subsistence farming): coal, 229; industry, 460-461 (*photo*, 461); Kuan, *photo*, 526

Christaller, Walter, 560, 613

Chromium, 238-239

Circulation system of world, 467 (*See also* Transportation)

Cities (*See* Service centers)

Citrus fruit, 163-164 (*map*, 164; *photo*, 163)

City planning, 639: annexation, 640-641; Los Angeles, *photos*, 640-641; of new areas, 639-640; of old areas, 641; planned towns, 641-644

Civil defense, 567-570

Class rates, railways, 474

Cleveland: manufacturing area, 416; population pattern, 570-571 (*table*, 571); trade, *table*, 539

Cleveland (England) iron ore field, 232

Clustered pattern of cities, 562-563

Coal, 226-232: anthracite, 226; bituminous, 226; drift mining, 276; Europe, 226-228 (*map*, 228); international trade, *table*, 231; lignite, 226; and manufacturing, 231; mining in Ruhr, *photo*, 224; open-pit and underground mining, 276; production regions, 226-229 (*table*, 227); reserves, 230-231 (*tables*, 229, 230); seams, *diagram*, 277; trade, 231-232; U.S. 229 (*table*, *map*, 230); U.S.S.R., 229 (*map*, 228)

Coastal shipping, 481-482

Cobalt, 238

Coefficient of correlation, 604-608: for copper industry, *table*, 337; for machinery industry, *table*, 608; for manufacturing, 289-290 (*table*, 290); of geographic association, 595-597

Coefficient of linkage, 597

Coefficient of similarity, 597

Coffee, 190: drying in Brazil, *photo*, 190; international trade, *table*, 188

Cohen, Saul, 580

Coir, 89

Coke, 355, 357

Coker, J. A., 285

Colby, Charles, 585, 646

Collecting, forest, 88-89, 90

Commercial areas, 574-580: CBD, 575-579; commercial strips, 579-580; dispersed businesses, 580; shopping centers, 580

Commercial core, 575

Commercial bioculture (*See breakdowns under individual types*): animal farming, 201-209; dairy farming, 124-137; fishing, 71-86; food manufacturing, 294-310; forest gathering, 88-104; grain farming, 167-183; Mediterranean agriculture, 154-165; mid-latitude crop farming, 191-200; tropical crop farming, 184-190

Commercial economy, *defined*, 29, 66-67

Commercial farm types, 212

Commercial manufacturing (*See also individual industries*): four periods, 395

K

Kahun, Egypt, 642
Kalamazoo, *photo*, 642
Kapok, 89
Karaganda coal mines, 229
Karlsruhe, circular streets, 642
Katanga copper mines, 240
Kerr, Donald, 427
Kiruna iron mines, 233, 276
Kitimat alumina mill, 343, *map*, 344
Knos, Duane S., 13
Kollmorgen, Walter M., 176
Kosher market, 302
Krasnoyarsk, 87
Krivoi Rog, 234
Kuan, China, *photo*, 526
Kuriyan, George, 62-64
Kuwait, 263, 267-268 (*photo*, 268)
Kuzbass (*See* Kuznetsk Basin)
Kuznetsk Basin, 229, 344, 455-456 (*map*, 455)

L

Labor cost differentials, 618-620
Labor field (*See* Employment: field)
Labor shed, *defined*, 556
Labrador iron ore, 236-237
Lake Maracaibo, 259
Lake Michigan fishing, 84-86
Lambert, Audrey, 527
Lamprey, 84-86
Land, 10: amount in urban settlement, 547-549; area by countries, *tables*, 18, 216; percentage in farms, by countries, *table*, 216; use, types in cities, 548-549, 575; values and highways, 491-493; values and pedestrian traffic, *diagram*, 492; values and transportation, 491
Landes sand dunes, 103
Lapland, 37, 39-40
Lapps, 40
Law of retail trade gravitation, 625
Lawrence, Massachusetts, *photo*, 582
Leaching, 43
Lead, smelter production, *table*, 352
Leading region, determination of, 391-393
Leather industry, 320-322: manufacture, U.S. *map*, 321; shoes, *map*, 323
Lemon grove, *photo*, 163
Lena coal fields, 230
Leningrad, 452

Levels of economic development, 632-637
Lianas, 93
Light industry, in opposition to heavy, 407
Lignite, 226-231
Lincoln iron field, 232
Lindberg, James B., 290, 485
Linear pattern of cities, 561-563
Livestock raising, 160-161 (*See also* Ranching): grazing, 160 (*photo*); open-range, 119; organized ranch, 119-121; ranching, 108-122; in U.S., 119-123; in world, *map*, 110
Llanos, 112 (*See also* Savanna)
Lloyd, Trevor, 236
Local relief, *defined*, 453-454
Location: as basic geographic question, 9-10; factors, 288; initial, 351; quotient, 406-407, 594-595; survival, 351-352; theory (*See* Location theory)
Location theory, 612-613: breaking-point theory, 625; fertility rings, 626; Fetter theory, 623-624; interaction theory, 624-626; intervening opportunities, 626; law of retail trade gravitation, 625; nested-hierarchy theory, 626-630; theory of labor differentials and transport costs, 618-620; theory of weight loss and transport costs, 616-618; Von Thünen theory, 613-616; Weber theory, 620-622
Locational inertia, 322
Locational triangle, 621
Lofoten Islands fishing, *photo*, 75
Loft industries, 319
Log floats, *photo*, 87, 94
London: manufacturing, 429-432; port, *photo*, 495; as service center, *photo*, 7
Lorraine-Saar Region, 232, 440-441
Los Angeles: aged people, 574 (*map*); aircraft industry, 370-371; education of populace, 573 (*map*); growth, *photos*, 640-641
Luleå, 235-236
Lumber: camps, 100; products, 323-325; in U.S., *map*, 324
Lumbering: *defined*, 88; mid-latitude gathering, 90-91; tropical gathering, 90

M

Machine-tools, 394-395, *photo*, 386
Machinery manufacture, 367-402:

aircraft, 369-373; construction and mining, 399; electrical, 387-390 (*U.S. map*, 388); employment in, 392; farm, 396-399; international trade, *table*, 402; leasing, 322; location, 390-391 (*map*, 391); metal-working, 393-395; motor vehicles and equipment, 373-381; nonelectrical, 390-402; office, 395; rail vehicles, 384-385; service, 395-396; shipbuilding, 383-384
Madison: employment location, 566-567 (*maps*, 567-568); employment structure, 558-559 (*graph*, 559, *table*, 558); milk shed, 555 (*map*); patrons of clinic, 556 (*map*, 557)
Magna, Utah, 334
Maize (*See* Corn)
Manchuria, 229
Manganese, 238-239
Manhattan, 319-320: garment center, *photo*, 320; Puerto Ricans, *map*, 572
Manila hemp, 89
Man/land ratio, 22-23: in grain farming, 175; in intensive subsistence farming, 55-56; in primitive cultivation, 44; in primitive herding, 38
Mannheim, 642
Manufacturing, 288-462 (*See also* *individual industries and areas*): consumer goods, 239; criteria for measuring, 289-290; *defined*, 288; employment, world *table*, 291; leading states and metropolises, *table*, 406; location factors in, 288-291; primary, 292; producer goods, 239; secondary, 292; wages, *map*, 417; Weber theory, 620-622; world, *map*, 292
Manure, 56-57 (*See also* Fertilizer): cycle, 57; in mixed farming, 144-145 (*map*)
Maps: mapping residuals from regression, 606-610; ratio, 593-594; use in geography, 3, 9-10; visual comparison of, 592-593
Maracaibo, Lake, *photo*, 261
Market milk, 126-127
Marketing associations, *defined*, 165
Marshall, Anthony, 40
Marts, Marion E., 492
Mass production, 375
Massachusetts textile labor, 315
Mather, Eugene C., 57, 111, 145-146
Mau Mau movement, 45